T0189829

Communications in Computer and Information Science 1454

More information about this series at http://www.springer.com/series/7899

Ying Tan · Yuhui Shi · Albert Zomaya ·
Hongyang Yan · Jun Cai (Eds.)

Data Mining and Big Data

6th International Conference, DMBD 2021
Guangzhou, China, October 20–22, 2021
Proceedings, Part II

Springer

Editors
Ying Tan 🆔
Peking University
Beijing, China

Albert Zomaya
The University of Sydney
Sydney, Australia

Jun Cai
Guangdong Polytechnic Normal University
Guangzhou, China

Yuhui Shi
Southern University of Science
and Technology
Shenzhen, China

Hongyang Yan
Guangzhou University
Guangzhou, China

ISSN 1865-0929 ISSN 1865-0937 (electronic)
Communications in Computer and Information Science
ISBN 978-981-16-7501-0 ISBN 978-981-16-7502-7 (eBook)
https://doi.org/10.1007/978-981-16-7502-7

This Springer imprint is published by the registered company Springer Nature Singapore Pte Ltd.
The registered company address is: 152 Beach Road, #21-01/04 Gateway East, Singapore 189721, Singapore

Preface

The Sixth International Conference on Data Mining and Big Data (DMBD 2021) was held in Guangzhou, China, during October 20–22, 2021. DMBD serves as an international forum for researchers to exchange the latest innovations in theories, models, and applications of data mining and big data as well as artificial intelligence techniques. DMBD 2021 was the sixth event after the successful first event (DMBD 2016) in Bali, Indonesia, the second event (DMBD 2017) in Fukuoka City, Japan, the third event (DMBD 2018) in Shanghai, China, the fourth event (DMBD 2019) in Chiang Mai, Thailand, and the fifth event (DMBD 2020) in Belgrade, Serbia.

These two volumes (CCIS vol. 1453 and CCIS vol. 1454) contain papers presented at DMBD 2021 covering some of the major topics of data mining and big data. The conference received 259 submissions. The Program Committee accepted 83 regular papers to be included in the conference program with an acceptance rate of 32.05%. The proceedings contain revised versions of the accepted papers. While revisions are expected to take the referees comments into account, this was not enforced and the authors bear full responsibility for the content of their papers.

DMBD 2021 was organized by the International Association of Swarm and Evolutionary Intelligence (IASEI) and co-organized by the Guangdong Polytechnic Normal University, Pazhou Lab, Guangzhou University, and the Guangdong Provincial Engineering and Technology Research Center for Big Data Security and Privacy Preservation. It was technically co-sponsored by Peking University and Southern University of Science and Technology, and also supported by Nanjing Kangbo Intelligent Health Academy. The conference would not have been such a success without the support of these organizations, and we sincerely thank them for their continued assistance and support.

We would also like to thank the authors who submitted their papers to DMBD 2021, and the conference attendees for their interest and support. We thank the Organizing Committee for their time and effort dedicated to arranging the conference. This allowed us to focus on the paper selection and deal with the scientific program. We thank the Program Committee members and the external reviewers for their hard work in reviewing the submissions; the conference would not have been possible without their expert reviews. Finally, we thank the EasyChair system and its operators, for making the entire process of managing the conference convenient.

September 2021

Ying Tan
Yuhui Shi
Albert Zomaya
Hongyang Yan
Jun Cai

Organization

Honorary General Chair

Zhiming Zheng   Guangzhou University, China

General Co-chairs

Ying Tan   Peking University, China
Jin Li   Guangzhou University, China
Jun Cai   Guangdong Polytechnic Normal University, China
Zhendong Wu   Hangzhou Dianzi University, China

Program Committee Co-chairs

Yuhui Shi   Southern University of Science and Technology, China
Albert Zomaya   University of Sydney, Australia

Advisory Committee Co-chairs

Milovan Stanisic   Singidunum University, Serbia
Russell C. Eberhart   IUPUI, USA
Gary G. Yen   Oklahoma State University, USA

Technical Committee Co-chairs

Haibo He   University of Rhode Island, USA
Kay Chen Tan   City University of Hong Kong, Hong Kong, China
Nikola Kasabov   Auckland University of Technology, New Zealand
Ponnuthurai Nagaratnam   Nanyang Technological University, Singapore
    Suganthan
Xiaodong Li   RMIT University, Australia
Hideyuki Takagi   Kyushu University, Japan
M. Middendorf   University of Leipzig, Germany
Mengjie Zhang   Victoria University of Wellington, New Zealand

Special Track Co-chairs

Sheng Hong   Beihang University, China
Jingwei Li   University of Electronic Science and Technology
                              of China, China
Feng Wang   Wuhan University, China
Tianqing Zhu   University of Technology Sydney, Australia

Publication Chair

Hongyang Yan   Guangzhou University, China

Publicity Co-chairs

Nan Jiang   East China Jiaotong University, China
Weizhi Meng   Technical University of Denmark, Denmark
Yu Wang   Guangzhou University, China

Program Committee

Miltos Alamaniotis   University of Texas at San Antonio, USA
Nebojsa Bacanin   Singidunum University, Serbia
Carmelo J. A. Bastos Filho   University of Pernambuco, Brazil
Tossapon Boongoen   Mae Fah Luang University, Thailand
David Camacho   Universidad Politécnica de Madrid, Spain
Abdelghani Chahmi   Universite des Sciences et Technologie d'Oran
                              Mohamed-Boudiaf, Algeria
Vinod Chandra S. S.   University of Kerala, India
Hui Cheng   Liverpool John Moores University, UK
Jieren Cheng   Hainan University, China
Jose Alfredo Ferreira Costa   Federal University, Brazil
Bei Dong   Shanxi Normal University, China
Qinqin Fan   Shanghai Maritime University, China
A. H. Gandomi   Stevens Institute of Technology, USA
Liang Gao   Huazhong University of Science and Technology,
                              China
Shangce Gao   University of Toyama, Japan
Wei Gao   Yunnan Normal University, China
Teresa Guarda   Universidad Estatal da Peninsula de Santa Elena,
                              Ecuador
Weian Guo   Tongji University, China
Weiwei Hu   Peking University, China
Dariusz Jankowski   Wroclaw University of Technology, Poland

Mingyan Jiang	Shandong University, China
Qiaoyong Jiang	Xi'an University of Technology, China
Junfeng Chen	Hohai University, China
Imed Kacem	Université de Lorraine, France
Kalinka Kaloyanova	University of Sofia, Japan
Vivek Kumar	Università degli Studi di Cagliari, Italy
Bin Li	University of Science and Technology of China, China
Qunfeng Liu	Dongguan University of Technology, China
Jianzhen Luo	Guangdong Polytechnic Normal University, China
Wenjian Luo	Harbin Institute of Technology, Shenzhen, China
Wojciech Macyna	Wroclaw University of Technology, Poland
Katherine Malan	University of South Africa, South Africa
Vasanth Kumar Mehta	SCSVMV University, India
Yi Mei	Victoria University of Wellington, New Zealand
Efrén Mezura-Montes	University of Veracruz, Mexico
Sheak Rashed Haider Noori	Daffodil International University, Bangladesh
Endre Pap	Singidunum University, Serbia
Mario Pavone	University of Catania, Spain
Yan Pei	University of Aizu, Japan
Somnuk Phon-Amnuaisuk	Universiti Teknologi Brunei, Brunei
Pramod Kumar Singh	ABV-IIITM Gwalior, India
Joao Soares	Polytechnic Institute of Porto, Portugal
Ivana Strumberger	Singidunum University, Serbia
Yifei Sun	Shanxi Normal University, China
Hung-Min Sun	Tsing Hua University in HsinChu, Taiwan, China
Ying Tan	Peking University, China
Paulo Trigo	ISEL, Portugal
Milan Tuba	Singidunum University, Serbia
Eva Tuba	University of Belgrade, Serbia
Agnieszka Turek	Warsaw University of Technology, Poland
Gai-Ge Wang	China Ocean University, China
Guoyin Wang	Chongqing University of Posts and Telecommunications, China
Zhenzhen Wang	Jinling Institute of Technology, China
Yan Wang	Ohio State University, USA
Ka-Chun Wong	City University of Hong Kong, Hong Kong, China
Rui Xu	Hohai University, China
Zhile Yang	Shenzhen Institute of Advanced Technology, Chinese Academy of Sciences, China
Yingjie Yang	De Montfort University, UK
Wei-Chang Yeh	Tsing Hua University in HsinChu, Taiwan, China

Contents – Part II

Contents – Part I

A Life Prediction Method for Power Supply in Rail Transit Signal System Under Variable Temperature Conditions

Jingyi Zhao[1,2,3]([✉]) [iD], Tao Tang[1], Chunhai Gao[2,3], Yingang Yu[2,3], Xiao Xiao[2,3], Ming Luo[2,3], and Feng Bao[2,3]

[1] School of Electronic and Information Engineering, Beijing Jiaotong University, Beijing 100404, China
[2] National Engineering Laboratory for Urban Rail Transit Communication and Operation Control, Beijing 100044, China
[3] Traffic Control Technology Co., Ltd., Beijing 100070, China

Abstract. The power supply in rail transit signal system is the major power source of the devices. During service, the temperature of power supply changes dynamically, which influence its degradation. The degradation of power supply will directly affect the function of other devices in system. Therefore, it is significant to evaluate the remaining useful life of power supply under variable temperature to ensuring the operation reliability of signal system. The particle filter method has been widely used for the life prediction of industrial products, as it can solve the life prediction problem of nonlinear system. Nevertheless, the predicted effect of this method is highly depended on the state of particles. For the power supply with sudden degradation, the particle impoverishment problem is happened, which cause a significant predicted variance. To solve the problem, this paper proposed an enhancement particle filter life prediction method. The effectiveness of the proposed method was evaluated using the mutated ripple voltage of power supply under variable temperature conditions. The results indicate that this method can sufficiently reduce the estimation variance by identifying the region where the degradation is evident, as well as by sustaining particle diversity. Based on this method, the precise life prediction results of the power supply can be acquired.

Keywords: Power supply · Particle filter · Ripple voltage · Remaining useful life estimation

1 Introduction

Power supply is a device to provide output voltage, which has the advantages of high conversion efficiency, low power consumption, and has been widely applied in rail transit signal system as power sources [1]. Nevertheless, the internal components of the power supply suffer from the impact of thermal stress throughout the life due to the large temperature variation. Once an accident is caused by the failure of power supply, the loss would be immeasurable [2]. Therefore, a reliable degradation status assessment and

© Springer Nature Singapore Pte Ltd. 2021
Y. Tan et al. (Eds.): DMBD 2021, CCIS 1454, pp. 1–15, 2021.
https://doi.org/10.1007/978-981-16-7502-7_1

remaining useful life (RUL) prediction during the service of power supply is essential. This can reduce the scheduling maintenance in advance and provide an alarm before reaching a critical faults.

The degradation data is needed for status assessment and life prediction. There are three methods to obtain the degradation data, which are field measurement method, accelerated life experimental test method and simulation method [3]. For the products in variable environment temperature and complex operating conditions, the field measurement data are affected by many factors. Therefore, the degradation data obtained by field measurement method is not easy to quantitatively analysis and process. Accelerated life experimental test method is an optimal method to obtain the degradation data under specific experimental conditions and within a specific period of time [4]. Nevertheless, for most products the degradation process is slow. It is a waste of time and money to obtain the degradation data by experimental method. Simulation method can establish a model reflecting the working principle and process of the product, and accelerate the simulation of the performance by selecting a reasonable algorithm. Therefore, the simulation method is an efficient and low-cost method to obtain the degraded data [5].

Basing on the degradation data, some scholars have developed many methods to predict the RUL of products. At present, the major RUL prediction methods can be roughly categorized into physics-based methods, machine-learned methods, and statistical methods [6]. The physics-based methods usually start with the construction of the degradation models reflecting the degradation of system performance. Then the RUL is evaluated according to the degradation mechanism of the products. Sanchez et al. [7] constructed a nonlinear cumulative damage model of crack growth law, and combined with the on-line test data to estimate the internal crack growth rate of mechanical transmission system, so as to realize the prediction of its RUL. Marble et al. [8] established a physical model of crack propagation basing on the internal crack propagation data of bearing, and realized the RUL prediction of bearing. Kulkarni et al. [9] put forward a degradation model of electrolytic capacitor based on the change law of thermal stress to evaluate its RUL. This method is suitable for the system or component whose degradation mechanism is clear and physical model is easy to describe. For the products, with high coupling degree of internal components, it is usually difficult to establish an accurate physical degradation model. Therefore, it is not easy to use physics-based methods to predict the RUL.

The machine-learned methods mainly use artificial intelligence tools to learn the degradation processes and predict the future health states of the products [10]. This method typically consists of two phases: learning the fault degradation process in the first phase and predicting its future state in the second phase. Different machine-learned methods, such as neural network, autoregressive moving average, long term and short term memory network have been developed and successfully applied for RUL prediction. Sun et al. [11] constructed the RUL prediction model of relay based on neural network, and obtained the life results. Ding et al. [12] proposed a life prediction method based on fuzzy rules and time series, which can consider the evolution trend of multiple variables at the same time. Because this methods can only obtain the exact life result. It can not reflect the statistical characteristics of products. Also the prediction error would accumulate with the increasing of prediction time.

The statistical methods can establish the degradation model according to the product degradation trajectory, evaluate the model parameters in real time, and obtain the posterior distribution of the system RUL. Among them, Particle filter (PF) is a widely used method to estimate and update the states and parameters. This method is based on the concept of sequential importance sampling and Bayesian theory. Thus, it can model the dynamic systems with non-linear and non-Gaussian characteristics, and can be applied in many applications such as system state tracking and prediction [13]. Compare et al. [14] used the multi-state model particle filter RUL prediction method to evaluate the crack propagation law of mechanical equipment, and thus realizing the life prediction. The life prediction based on PF is highly dependent on the state transition model [15]. Considering the predicted effect of PF is highly depended on the state of particles. For the power supply undergo sudden degradation, the particle impoverishment problem would happened, which would cause a significant predicted variance. This limits the application of PF in the life prediction of power supply under variable temperature conditions to a certain extent.

To solve this problem, an enhancement PF method is proposed in this paper to predict the RUL of power supply under variable temperature conditions. Firstly, according to the internal circuit structure of the power supply, the main circuit model was established by simulation. The degradation model of the components in power supply was introduced in the simulation circuit, to characterize the influence of the components degradation on the power supply. Then, the variation curve of power supply ripple voltage was obtained from the output voltage data. Furthermore, an enhancement PF life prediction method was proposed to predict the life of power supply at different temperature conditions. The prediction effect of the proposed method was compared with the classic particle filter method.

2 Main Failure Modes of Power Supply

The research object of this paper is the direct current (DC) power supply. Its working principle is that the input alternating current (AC) voltage transfers to the output DC voltage through the power conversion, step-down, rectification and filtering and other links, etc. These functions are realized by some key components such as electrolytic capacitor, inductance, triode and diode. The abnormal function of these components can have a certain impact on the performance of power supply. There are two main failure mechanisms of components. One is transient or catastrophic failure caused by over stress. The regularity of this failure mechanism is weak, and there has no suitable method to analyze. The other is the slow failure of components caused by fatigue degradation, which is relatively slow and easy to observe. So this paper mainly considers the failure caused by fatigue.

With the increasing of service time and the changing of external environment temperature, the internal components of the power supply will inevitably occur fatigue failure. This would lead to the degradation of the overall performance of the power supply. Thus, the external output parameters of power supply changes, such as the ripple voltage. Generally, 50% increase of the ripple voltage can be used to judge the failure of power supply. Scholars rank the failure rate of key components in power electronic equipment. It is found that the failure rate of electrolytic capacitor is the highest, which account for more than 60% failure rate of power electronic devices [16]. Based on this, this paper mainly studies the power supply degradation caused by electrolytic capacitor.

3 Degradation Simulation of Power Supply

3.1 Simplified Equivalent Circuit of Power Supply

This paper uses the power supply of S-15W-12V as the research object. The rated input voltage V_{in} is 220 V AC and the rated output voltage is 12 V DC. The internal main circuit of this power supply is shown in Fig. 1. In this circuit, the rectifier bridge composed of four diodes D1, D2, D3 and D4 can convert 220 V alternating current into 300 V pulsating direct current. Electrolytic capacitor C1 is mainly used to stabilize the output of pulsating DC. Power MOSFET Q1 converts DC voltage into pulse voltage. Transformer T1 can reduce the input 300V DC voltage to 5V DC. Diode D5 is mainly used to prevent the reversing of the circuit, and inductance L1 and capacitors C2, C3 are mainly used to stabilize current and voltage.

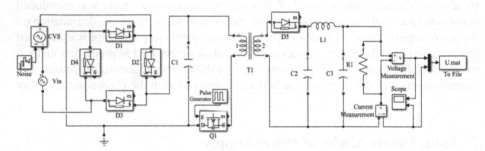

Fig. 1. Schematic diagram of main circuit of power supply.

3.2 Physical Degradation Model of Components

Electrolytic capacitor is the main component that affects the degradation of power supply. This paper mainly considers the degradation of power supply caused by electrolytic capacitor. The degradation index of electrolytic capacitor is capacitance value and equivalent series resistance (ESR). Generally, take the reducing of 20% capacitance value and the increasing by 200% of ESR as the failure indicators of the capacitor. The degradation model of capacitance value and ESR value of electrolytic capacitor under different ambient temperature is shown in these two equations. In addition, due to the nonlinear characteristics and the tolerance of electrolytic capacitors, the normal distribution noise signal is introduced into these two equations [17].

$$C(T, t) = C_0 \cdot (1 - a \cdot t \cdot \exp(\frac{-E}{k(T + 273)})) + \psi_1 \tag{1}$$

$$ESR(T, t) = \frac{ESR_0}{1 - b \cdot t \cdot \exp(\frac{-E}{g(T+273)})} + \psi_2 \tag{2}$$

Where C (T, t) is the capacitance value of the electrolytic capacitor at time t and temperature T, C_0 is the capacitance value at initial condition, a and b are the coefficient, k and g are the constant which is determined by the design and structure parameters of the capacitor, T is the ambient temperature, ESR (T, t) is the equivalent series resistance value of electrolytic capacitor at time t and temperature T, ESR_0 is the equivalent series resistance value of electrolytic capacitor under initial condition, E is the Boltzmann constant, Ψ_1 and Ψ_2 are the noise signal.

Figure 2 shows the degradation curves of three capacitors in the main circuit of the power supply at three different temperatures. In the subsequent simulation, the degradation process of capacitor under different temperatures and time conditions would be set according to these degradation curves.

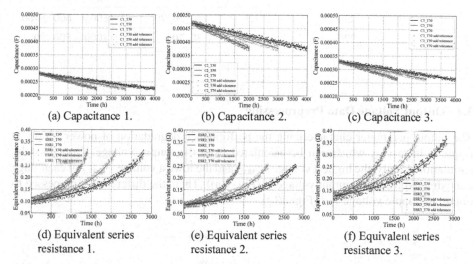

(a) Capacitance 1.   (b) Capacitance 2.   (c) Capacitance 3.

(d) Equivalent series   (e) Equivalent series   (f) Equivalent series
resistance 1.   resistance 2.   resistance 3.

Fig. 2. Capacitance and equivalent series resistance of three electrolytic capacitors under different temperature and time.

3.3 Simulation Parameter Setting

Using Matlab/Simulink software, the main circuit simulation model of the power supply is constructed (Fig. 1). In the simulation circuit, four diodes D1, D2, D3 and D4 are set to 1000 V/ 10A. The electrolytic capacitor C1 is set to 2800 uF/ 200V, the electrolytic capacitor C2 is set to 2200 uF/ 16 V, and the electrolytic capacitor C3 is set to 1000 uF/ 16 V. The transistor Q1 is set to 650 V/ 26A, its switching frequency is set to 10 kHz, and the duty cycle is set to 0.5. The transformer T1 is set to 7 mH/ 7A, the diode D6 is set to 1000 V/ 2A, and the inductance L1 is set to 1 mH.

Two simulation conditions are set, and the specific parameters are shown in Table 1. The input voltage V_{in} are all set to 220 V and the load are all set to 1.7 Ω. In condition 1, the ambient temperature is set as step 30_50_70 °C. The ambient temperature of condition 2 is set as step 30_70 °C. The duration time of each temperature is shown in Table 1. In the simulation circuit, the capacitance value and equivalent series resistance of each capacitor under different temperature conditions are set with reference to Fig. 2. The interval time simulation method is used to get the output voltage signals under different time periods.

Table 1. Parameter setting of three simulation conditions.

Simulation condition	Input voltage (V)	Load (Ω)	Ambient temperature (°C)	The duration time of each temperature (h)		
				30	50	70
1	220	1.7	30_50_70	800	600	400
2	220	1.7	30_70	1000	500	0

3.4 Output Voltage Data Preprocessing

The output parameter characterizing the performance degradation of power supply is ripple voltage v_{act}, which can be calculated from the output voltage V obtained by simulation. Firstly, the highest voltage $V_{max,t}$ and the lowest voltage $V_{max,t}$ of each stage are extracted from the output voltage V (Fig. 3(a)). Then, the difference is processed to obtain the ripple voltage v_{act} (Fig. 3(b)).

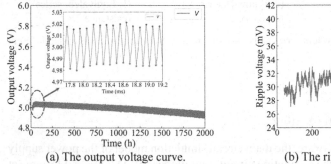

(a) The output voltage curve.

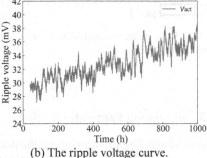

(b) The ripple voltage curve.

Fig. 3. The output voltage curve and the ripple voltage curve.

The calculation formula of ripple voltage v_{act} is

$$v_{act} = V_{max,t} - V_{max,t} \tag{3}$$

where $V_{\max,t}$ is the maximum output voltage at time t and $V_{\min,t}$ is the minimum output voltage at time t.

4 Life Prediction Method Based on Particle Filter

4.1 Prediction and Update

Particle filter is a method to estimate the state value by using the state model and observation model from the known state value in the state space. The expressions of the state model and the observation model are as follows

$$v_{\text{pre},k} = h(v_{\text{pre},k-1}, d_{k-1}), \quad k = 1, \ldots, t \tag{4}$$

$$v_{\text{act},k} = f(v_{\text{pre},k}, c_k) \tag{5}$$

Where $v_{\text{pre},k}$ is the state at k, $v_{\text{pre},k}$ is the state at $k - 1$, d_{k-1} is the state noise, $h(.)$ is the state transition model, t is the time. $v_{\text{act},k}$ is the observed value at k, c_k is the measurement noise, assuming that it conforms to Gaussian distribution, $f(.)$ is the measurement model.

The implementation process of particle filter method is mainly composed of prediction and update, as shown in Fig. 4. When the state value $v_{\text{pre},k-1}$ at $k - 1$ is known, the state model can be used to predict the state $v_{\text{pre},k}$ at k, and the prior probability density of the current state $P(v_{\text{pre},k}|v_{\text{pre},k-1})$ can be obtained. Then according to the actual observation value $v_{\text{act},k}$ at time k, the prior probability density is modified by the observation equation, obtained the corresponding posterior probability density $P(v_{\text{pre},k}|v_{\text{act},k})$. At the same time, the predicted state $v_{\text{pre},k}$ is updated to improve the reliability of the state estimation results.

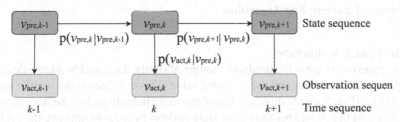

Fig. 4. The implementation process of particle filter method.

When predicting the current state $v_{\text{pre},k}$, it is assumed that the state transition $v_{\text{pre},k}$ of the system obeys the first-order Markov model, that is, the state of the current time is only related to the state $v_{\text{pre},k-1}$ of the previous time. At the same time, it is assumed that the observations of the system $v_{\text{act},k}$ are only related to the current state $v_{\text{pre},k}$.

In order to predict the state $v_{\text{pre},k}$ of the current moment, Monte Carlo method is used to randomly sample the state of the previous moment $v_{\text{pre},k-1}$ (i.e. select random particles) to calculate the probability density of the current state (i.e. weight calculation), and then the optimal estimation of the current state $\hat{v}_{\text{pre},k}$ is obtained by weighted average. The equation is as follows.

$$\hat{v}_{\text{pre},k} = \sum_{i=1}^{n} w^i_{k-1} \cdot \hat{v}^i_{\text{pre},k-1}, \quad i = 1, 2, ..., n \tag{6}$$

Where, w^i_{k-1} is the weight of the i-th particle at $k-1$, n is the number of particles, the sign $\hat{}$ at the top of the variable indicates that the variable is an estimated value.

According to the importance sampling principle, the current state $v_{\text{pre},k}$ is updated. The weight of each particle in the state estimation value $\hat{v}_{\text{pre},k}$ is updated by using the observation values $v_{\text{act},k}$ at time k, and the normalization processing is also carried out. The specific formula is as follows

$$w^i_k \propto w^i_{k-1} \cdot p\left(v_{act,k} \middle| \hat{v}^i_{\text{pre},k}\right) \tag{7}$$

$$\widetilde{w}^i_k = \frac{w^i_k}{\sum_{i=1}^{n} w^i_k} \tag{8}$$

Where, $\propto$ is proportional to, $p(v_{act,k}|\hat{v}^i_{\text{pre},k})$ is the likelihood probability density function, $\widetilde{w}^i_k$ is the weight of the i-th particle normalized at time k. The posterior probability density of the updated state $P(v_{\text{pre},k}|v_{\text{act},1:k})$ can be approximated according to the updated particles and their corresponding weights, as shown in the following formula

$$p(v_{\text{pre},k}|v_{\text{act},1:k}) = \sum_{i=1}^{n} \widetilde{w}^i_k \cdot \delta(v_{\text{pre},k} - \hat{v}^i_{\text{pre},k}) \tag{9}$$

Where, $\delta(\cdot)$ is a Dirac function.

4.2 Improved Resampling Algorithm

Solution of particle shortage

When the observed value of the products changes abruptly, there will be a large deviation between the predicted value and the observed value. This can leads to the smaller weight of the particles (Fig. 5(a)). At this time, the effective particles to update the state value are not enough, and this would result in poor state update. In order to improve the problem that lacking of effective particles leads to inaccurate prediction, this paper proposes an enhancement resampling method. This method can update the predicted state value, so more effective particles can be provided and the accuracy of particle filter algorithm can be ensured (Fig. 5(b)).

According to the sum of the particle weights w_{sum} obtained at time k, whether the particle weights are all too small is determined. The sum of particle weights w_{sum} can be calculated by the following formula

$$w_{sum} = \sum_{i=1}^{n} \widetilde{w}^i_k \tag{10}$$

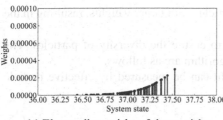

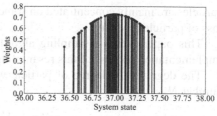

(a) The smaller weight of the particles.   (b) The more effective particles.

Fig. 5. Schematic diagram of particle weights.

When the sum of particle weights w_{sum} is less than the weight threshold β, the predicted state value $\hat{v}^i_{pre,k}$ is modified based on the observed value $v_{act,k}$, and the modified equation is

$$\hat{v}^i_{pre,up,k} = r \sum_{i=1}^{n} [f^{-1}(v_{act,k} - c_k) - \hat{v}^i_{pre,k}] + \hat{v}^i_{pre,k} \tag{11}$$

Where, $\hat{v}^i_{pre,up,k}$ is the corrected state value, r is the correction coefficient.

In order to avoid the particle degradation in this process, Gaussian resampling is carried out near the modified predicted state value $\hat{v}^i_{pre,up,k}$ to obtain the updated particles $\hat{v}^i_{pre,update,k}$, and the corresponding normalized weights $\tilde{w}^i_k$

$$w^i_k \propto w^i_{k-1} \cdot p\left(v_{act,k} \middle| \hat{v}^i_{pre,update,k}\right) \tag{12}$$

$$\tilde{w}^i_k = \frac{w^i_k}{\sum_{i=1}^{n} w^i_k} \tag{13}$$

Then, the posterior probability density function of the current state adopts the particle approximation with relevant weights, as follows:

$$p(v_{pre,k}|v_{act,1:k}) = \sum_{i=1}^{n} \tilde{w}^i_k \cdot \delta(v_{pre,k} - \hat{v}^i_{pre,update,k}) \tag{14}$$

Solution of particle degradation

With the process of state estimation, the phenomenon of particle degradation often appears. That is to say, the importance weights are mainly concentrated on a few particles, while the importance weights of other particles are almost zero. At this time, the effect of small weight particles on state estimation is weakened.

In order to overcome the problem of particle degradation, the resampling method needed to be introduce in the state estimation process to eliminate the degraded particles. The common used resampling methods include random resampling, polynomial resampling, system resampling and residual resampling [18]. These resampling methods copy the particles with larger weight and replace the particles with smaller weight to eliminate the degenerate particles. This method can not ensure the validity of the weights, and lead to the problem of particle concentration. That is to say, with the iteration process, the particles are mainly concentrated on some particles with larger weights, resulting in the loss of particle diversity.

This paper uses a resampling algorithm to ensure the diversity of particles. The implementation process of this resampling algorithm are as follows.

The degradation degree of particle weight can be measured by effective particle number N_{eff}

$$N_{\text{eff}} = 1/ \sum_{i=1}^{n} (\widetilde{w}_k^i)^2 \tag{15}$$

When the number of effective particles Neff exceeds the particle threshold ε (usually ε is 2n/3). Then the following formula can be used to classify the particles

$$\hat{v}_{\text{pre},k}^i \in \begin{cases} E_l, v_{\text{pre},k} < w_{th} \\ E_h, v_{\text{pre},k} \geq w_{th} \end{cases} \tag{16}$$

Where E_l and eh are state sets containing small weight particles and high weight particles respectively, and w_{th} is the threshold to distinguish large particles from small particles.

The steps of obtaining w_{th} are as follows: the weights of all particles are arranged in descending order and stored in the weight set W. The particle corresponding to the N_{eff} weight in the weight set w is used as w_{th}. The calculation method of threshold w_{th} is as follows:

$$w_{th} = W(N_{\text{eff}}) \tag{17}$$

After classifying the particles, all the small weight particles are improved, while the particles with high weight remain unchanged. The improved equations for small weight particles are as follows

$$v_{\text{pre},m,k}^s = \frac{\widetilde{w}_{l,k}^s \cdot v_{\text{pre},l,k}^s + \widetilde{w}_{h,k}^t \cdot v_{\text{pre},h,k}^t}{\widetilde{w}_{l,k}^s + \widetilde{w}_{h,k}^t}, s = 1, \ldots, n_l, t = 1, \ldots, n_h \tag{18}$$

Where, $v_{\text{pre},m,k}^s$ is the updated small weight particle, $v_{\text{pre},l,k}^s$ is the state of a small weight particle in E_l, $v_{\text{pre},h,k}^t$ is the state of a large weight particle randomly selected in E_h set, $\widetilde{w}_{l,k}^s$ and $\widetilde{w}_{h,k}^t$ are the corresponding weight of particles $v_{\text{pre},l,k}^s$ and $v_{\text{pre},h,k}^t$ in the weight set w respectively.

All the particles with high weight in E_h and the changed small weight particles are stored in the state set V_k to form the particle set $\hat{v}_{\text{pre},m,k}^i$. In the state set V_k, the weight of small weight particles is solved by the following equation

$$\widetilde{w}_k^s \propto \widetilde{w}_{k-1}^s \cdot p(v_{\text{act},k} | \hat{v}_{\text{pre},m,k}^i) \tag{19}$$

Where, $\widetilde{w}_{k-1}^s$ is the weight of the small weight particles $v_{\text{pre},l,k}^s$ in E_l at $k-1$.

The weights of the original small weight particles stored in the weight set w are replaced by $\widetilde{w}_k^s$, and then the weights in the weight set w are normalized to $\overline{w}_k^i$.

The posterior probability density function of the state is calculated by the following formula

$$p(v_{\text{pre},k} | v_{\text{act},1:k}) = \sum_{i=1}^{n} \overline{w}_k^i \cdot \delta(v_{\text{pre},k} - \hat{v}_{\text{pre},m,k}^i) \tag{20}$$

4.3 RUL Prediction and the Predicted Effect Evaluation

The remaining useful life refers to the time interval between a specific time and the time the degradation characterization parameters of the product reach the failure threshold. At time k, the degradation process can be predicted by using the previous data. The time required for the degradation from time k to the state threshold $v_{pre,th}$ can be obtained, which is the predicted RUL of the product.

Root mean square error ($RMSE$) are used to evaluate the prediction effect

$$RMSE = \sqrt{\frac{1}{n} \sum_{i=1}^{n} (RUL - RUL^i)^2} \tag{21}$$

Where RUL is the useful lifetime obtained from the actual observations, and RUL^i is the predicted residual useful lifetime.

5 Results and Discussion

5.1 Ripple Voltage of Power Supply Under Different Simulation Conditions

Figure 6 shows the ripple voltage of power supply under three different temperature conditions. With the increasing of time, the growth rate of ripple voltage increases. It indicates that the degradation rate of the power supply accelerates. At each moment, the ripple voltage presents a certain fluctuation. It shows that the noise signal added in the simulation can reflect the noise interference of the power supply under the actual conditions. To sum up, this simulation method can not only reflect the degradation process of power supply, but also reflect the influence of noise on ripple voltage.

The local enlarged of ripple voltage under the condition of 30_50_70 °C step temperature shows an overall upward trend with the increasing of time. Only at 800 h and 1400 h, the ripple voltage suddenly changes. After this two time point, the ripple voltage continued to increase along the mutation position. It shows that this simulation method also reflects the irrecoverable effect of temperature mutation on the degradation of power supply.

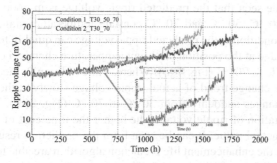

Fig. 6. Ripple voltage curve of power supply at two different temperature conditions.

5.2   The Effect of Life Prediction

Adaptability of the Enhancement Particle Filter Algorithm

Figure 7(a) shows the predicted ripple voltage obtained by the enhancement particle filter algorithm and classic particle filter algorithm. It can be seen that the sudden change of ripple voltage is happened at 800 s. After this moment, the proposed enhancement particle filter algorithm can quickly follow up the sudden change of ripple voltage. For the classic particle filter algorithm, there is a certain deviation between the predicted ripple voltage and the actual ripple voltage at the position of temperature mutation. After 800 s, the weight distribution of the enhancement particle filter algorithm is more uniform. The weights are between 0.01 and 0.03. Whereas for the classic particle filter algorithm after 800 s, the weights are almost close to 0 (Fig. 7(b)). Therefore, it can be seen that the improved particle filter algorithm can show satisfactory prediction results in predicting the degradation trend of products under variable operation conditions.

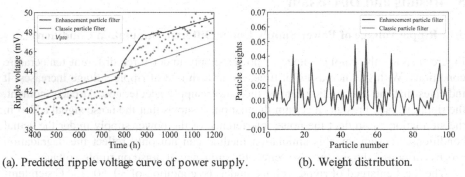

(a). Predicted ripple voltage curve of power supply.   (b). Weight distribution.

Fig. 7. Predicted ripple voltage curve of power supply and weight distribution predicted by different prediction algorithms.

RUL Prediction Effect Under Different Temperature Conditions

Figure 8 shows the predicted ripple voltage under two different stepping temperature conditions. It can be seen that the predicted ripple voltage is in good agreement with the real value at 30 °C, 50 °C and 70 °C constant temperature stage under the two conditions. In the condition 1, the predicted ripple voltage can quickly follow the change trend of ripple voltage at the position of abrupt temperature change, i.e., from 30 °C to 50 °C or from 50 °C to 70 °C (Fig. 8(a)). Whereas in condition 2, the predicted ripple voltage follows the change trend of actual ripple voltage slowly at the position where the temperature changes suddenly from 30 °C to 70 °C (Fig. 8(b)). This shows that the greater the mutation of ripple voltage, the higher the time cost of predicted ripple voltage follow up actual value. It can be seen from the prediction results of the above two conditions that the enhancement life prediction algorithm are able to meet the needs of the power supply life prediction.

The RUL of the power supply under two kinds of stepping temperature conditions is predicted at different time points, and the prediction results are shown in Table 2. At

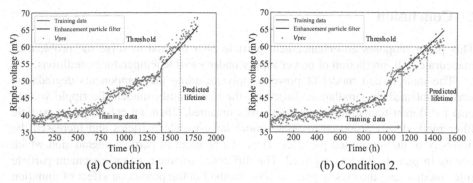

(a) Condition 1.   (b) Condition 2.

Fig. 8. The predicted ripple voltage under two different stepping temperature conditions.

condition 1, when at 400 h, the prediction is performed. The RUL of the power supply is 1195 h, and the actual RUL of the power supply is 1221 h. The prediction error is 26%. Whereas the prediction is performed at 1200 h, the predicted RUL of the power supply is 418 h, and the actual RUL is 421 h. The prediction error is reduced to 3%. It can be concluded that at condition 1, the prediction error decreases with the increasing of prediction time. At condition 2, when the prediction is performed at 400 h, the RUL of the power supply is 918 h, and the actual RUL of the power supply is 947 h. The prediction error is 29%. When the prediction is performed at 1200 h, the prediction error is reduced to 2%. Therefore, at condition 2, the prediction error is also decreases with the increasing of prediction time.

Table 2. Comparison between the actual RUL and the predicted RUL.

Time point where prediction is performed (h)	Condition 1			Condition 2		
	Predicted RUL (h)	Actual RUL (h)	RMSE (%)	Predicted RUL (h)	Actual RUL (h)	RMSE (%)
400	1195	1221	26	918	947	29
600	998	1021	23	768	747	21
800	838	821	17	538	547	9
1000	613	621	8	344	347	3
1200	418	421	3	145	147	2

Therefore, it can be concluded that under different temperature conditions, the prediction effect of the RUL of the power supply meets the rule that the prediction error decreases with the increasing of the prediction time. That is, when the predicted time point of power supply is closer to its failure time, the predicted RUL is closer to the actual value.

6 Conclusion

This paper proposes an enhancement particle filter method to solve the problem of inaccurate RUL prediction of power supply under variable temperature conditions.

The main circuit model of power supply including the components degradation was established by simulation. Based on the main circuit model, the ripple voltage under different temperature conditions was obtained. Then, an enhancement particle filter method was proposed to obtain more large-weight particles and increased the diversity of the resampled particles. Thus, the problem of particle degradation which occurs in particle filter was solved. The difference between the enhancement particle filter method and the classic particle filter method in the prediction effect of mutation data of power supply is compared and analyzed. The results show that the enhancement particle filter algorithm proposed in this paper can quickly follow up the sudden change of ripple voltage. Whereas, for the classic particle filter algorithm, there is a certain deviation between the predicted ripple voltage and the actual ripple voltage. In addition, when the mutation of degradation data is strong, the enhancement particle filter method can also have a good prediction effect.

It is worth noting that the enhancement particle filter method proposed in this paper is only used to predict the life of the power supply under the condition of variable temperature. Although it can provide a reference for the life prediction under the variation conditions. The applicability of this life prediction method needs to be further explored in the case of more complex conditions.

Acknowledgment. This work was supported in part by the National Key R&D Program of China under Grant 2020YFB1600705, in part by the Beijing Science and Technology Project under Grant Z191100002519003, and in part by the Traffic Control Technology Co., Ltd.

1. References

1. Pindado, S., Alcala, G.D., Alfonso, C.: Improving the power supply performance in rural smart grids with photovoltaic DG by optimizing fuse selection. Agronomy **11**(4), 622–629 (2021)
2. Lafoz, M., Navarro, G., Torres, J.: Power supply solution for ultrahigh speed hyperloop trains. Smart Cities **3**(3), 642–656 (2020)
3. Efthimiou, N., Loudos, G., Karakatsanis, N.A.: Effect of 176Lu intrinsic radioactivity on dual head PET system imaging and data acquisition, simulation, and experimental measurements. Med. Phys. **40**(11), 109–125 (2013)
4. Raheem, A.: Optimal design of multiple constant-stress accelerated life testing for the extension of the exponential distribution under type-II censoring. J. Comput. Appl. Math. **38**(2), 104–113 (2020)
5. Ishaque, K., Salam, Z., Syafaruddin, H.: A comprehensive MATLAB Simulink PV system simulator with partial shading capability based on two-diode model. Sol. Energy **85**(9), 2217–2227 (2011)
6. Liu, D.T., Zhou, J.B., Peng, Y.: Data-driven prognostics and remaining useful life estimation for lithium-ion battery: a review. Instrumentation **1**(35), 61–72 (2014)

7. Sanchez, H.E., Sankara, S., Escobet, T., Puig, V., Kai, G.: Analysis of two modeling approaches for fatigue estimation and remaining useful life predictions of wind turbine blades. In: Third European Conference of the Prognostics and Health Management Society, pp. 14–21. Bilbao, Spain (2016)
8. Marble, S., Morton, B.P.: Predicting the remaining life of propulsion system bearings. In: IEEE Aerospace Conference, pp. 1–8. MT, USA (2006)
9. Kulkarni, C.S., Biswas, G., Jose, R.C.: Physics based degradation models for capacitor prognostics under thermal overstress conditions. Int. J. Prognostics Health Manage. 4(5), 12–19 (2013)
10. Zio, E., Maio, F.D.: A Data-driven fuzzy approach for predicting the remaining useful life in dynamic failure scenarios of a nuclear power plant. Reliab. Eng. Syst. Saf. 95(1), 49–57 (2010)
11. Sun, Y., Cao, Y., Zhang, Y.: A novel life prediction method for railway safety relays using degradation parameters. IEEE Intell. Transp. Syst. Mag. 43(7), 118–126 (2018)
12. Ding, Z., Zhou, Y., Pu, G., Zhou, M.C.: Online failure prediction for railway transportation systems based on fuzzy remaining useful life and data analysis. IEEE Trans. Reliab. 26(9), 1–16 (2018)
13. Baek, S.Y., Dong, H.B.: A study on the fatigue life prediction of the various gas-welded joints using a probabilistic statistics technique. Met. Mater. Int. 17(1), 143–149 (2011)
14. Compare, M., Baraldi, P., Turati, P.: Interacting multiple-models, state augmented particle filtering for fault diagnostics. Probab. Eng. Mech. 40(6), 12–24 (2015)
15. Orchard, M.E., Vachtsevanos, G.J.: A particle filtering approach for on-line fault diagnosis and failure prognosis. Trans. Inst. Meas. Control. 31(3–4), 221–246 (2007)
16. Pang, H.M., Bryan, P.: A life prediction scheme for electrolytic capacitors in power converters without current sensor. In: Applied Power Electronics Conference & Exposition, PP. 973–979. Palm Springs, USA (2010)
17. Celaya, J.R., Kulkarni, C, Saha, S.: Accelerated aging in electrolytic capacitors for prognostics. In: Proceedings Annual Reliability and Maintainability Symposium, pp. 1–6. USA (2012)
18. Zhang, N., Xu, A., Wang, K.: Remaining useful life prediction of lithium batteries based on extended kalman particle filter. IEEE Trans. Electr. Electr. Eng. 16(2), 206–214 (2021)

Hypergraph Ontology Sparse Vector Representation and Its Application to Ontology Learning

Linli Zhu[1](✉) ⓘ and Wei Gao[2] ⓘ

[1] School of Computer Engineering, Jiangsu University of Technology,
Changzhou 213001, China
zhulinli@jsut.edu.cn

[2] School of Information Science and Technology, Yunnan Normal University,
Kunming 650500, China
gaowei@ynnu.edu.cn

Abstract. Data representation is the first step in computer science modeling, and the performance of the algorithm directly affects the efficiency of the algorithm. For structural data, graphs and hypergraph representations are often ideal choices, which can effectively represent the connections between data. The edge weight function can also be used to express the strength of the connection, and the adjacency matrix and the Laplacian matrix describe a kind of motion, and the eigenvalues of the matrix reveal the motion trajectory of the vector. In this paper, hypergraph framework is used to characterize the internal structure of the ontology sparse vector, and use the hypergraph theory to define a new hypergraph Laplacian matrix, and thus obtain the control items on the sparsity of the ontology sparse vector learning model. Then, a new algorithm is proposed. Finally, two specific implement tests are used to verify the effectiveness of our new proposed hypergraph based ontology learning algorithm.

Keywords: Ontology · Concept expression · Sparse vector · Hypergraph

1 Introduction

The terminology ontology was introduced in the early 1980s in artificial intelligence. In the first 20 years of the development of Ontology, as a structured database, the research on ontology was concentrated in the field of artificial intelligence. After the year 2000, it has attracted widespread attention, and ontology has appeared in various fields of computer science and information science, such as logical reasoning, information retrieval, and image processing. In particular, researchers find that ontology, as a powerful auxiliary tool, has many high-quality functions in itself, so it is used by scientists in other fields. Nowadays, it has been applied to the research of ontology permeates chemistry, biology, pharmacy, medicine, genetic engineering, materials science, neuroscience,

© Springer Nature Singapore Pte Ltd. 2021
Y. Tan et al. (Eds.): DMBD 2021, CCIS 1454, pp. 16–27, 2021.
https://doi.org/10.1007/978-981-16-7502-7_2

education and other social sciences. Latest contributions in the field of ontology and its applications can be referred to Verdonck et al. [1], Azevedo et al. [2], Single et al. [3], Labidi et al. [4], Lv and Peng [5], Aydin and Aydin [6], Pattipati et al. [7], Annane and Bellahsene [8], Lammers et al. [9], Jankovic et al. [10].

Scientists in different disciplines and industries have designed corresponding ontology according to the characteristics of their own fields and combined with a specific requirement. It can be said that the ontology of each discipline is different, and the ontology of the same discipline with different application backgrounds is also different. Among a large number of published papers on ontology, most of the them are not discussing a type of ontology framework, but setting up a special ontology for a particular application background and conducting related research. In other words, the study of an ontology is only applicable to a specific application.

While on the other hand, we found that all these domain ontologies have some commonalities. For example, the elements that make up the ontology are concepts, and semantics are the core elements of concepts. Therefore, the calculation of semantic similarity between concepts is the center of each application of ontology; for example, the so-called "structuralization" in the structured conceptual model, It means that the ontology is denoted by a graph. Each vertex in the graph is an ontology concept, and the edge between the vertices can be understood as a direct semantic connection between the two concepts. From this level, the computing of ontology similarity can be transformed into the calculation of similarity between vertices on the graph.

With the increase in the number of ontology processing, it is necessary to use ontology learning algorithms to calculate the similarity between ontology concepts in the context of big data. The framework of this approach can be used for all ontology of graph structure, and the commonness of ontology is extracted through graph features and integrated into ontology learning model. For a specific ontology application field, these highly abstract variables or functions can be specified in the experimental stage according to the specific environment of the subject application field. In turn, the ontology learning algorithm achieves a balance between commonality and individuality. Some results on ontology learning can be referred to Gao et al. [11–14] and [15].

In order to use mathematical tricks to model the ontology learning algorithms, we often need to mathematically represent the information of the ontology graph, that is, use a p dimensional vector to represent all the information of the vertex (corresponding to an ontology concept). Indeed, using vectors to represent all the information of ontology concepts is by far the most concise method and is easy to expand. For example, it was mentioned before that if the ontology concept is supplemented and the ontology structure changes dynamically, whose problem can be solved by increasing the dimension of the vector and updating the newly added information and newly defined parameters as the value of the new dimension.

In addition, in the design process of the ontology learning model, the vector representation of this ontology concept can also be directly applied to the distance learning model and the sparse vector learning model. For ontology sparse vector learning, it requires the value of most components of the learned vector to be zero, and only a few components are retained. Finally, the sparse vector obtained by the ontology learning algorithm and the vector corresponding to each ontology concept are used as the inner product to obtain the one-dimensional real number corresponding to each concept. This is closely related to the application of large data ontology. For instance, in GO ontology, there are a huge number of genes in the human body, which lead to a huge amount of information to be processed and extremely complex data representation. On the other hand, there are very few genes related to a certain disease, which means that if our application background only focuses on a certain disease, then we only need to focus on those components in the high-dimensional vector that are directly related to the disease. Learning the ontology sparse vector is to determine the position of these components from sample learning.

In the ontology of geographic information systems, sparse vectors can highlight advantages. For example, the amount of information in the map is extremely large, but for a specific application, the amount of design is very limited. For example, hunger is only concerned with the location of nearby restaurants; for the patients, only the location of the hospital concerns; when it comes to parking parking, only the location of the parking lot concerns, and so on.

We found through observation that certain components in the ontology sparse vector are related to each other, and their combination can represent a certain specific information. Therefore, a hypergraph can be used to represent the internal structure of the sparse vector of the ontology, and then the graph theory can be used to represent the sparsity of the vector. This is the core idea and starting point of this new ontology learning algorithm.

On the other hand, an extremely significant feature of the eigenvector lies in that it characters the direction of motion, which tells us that the eigenvector with the largest eigenvalue will dominate the remaining eigenvectors. Through transformation, we know that the motion process is actually controlled by eigenvalues and eigenvectors of different sizes. In physics, this means that the average temperature of all neighbors is used to update the temperature of the current vertex. It can be expected that if it continues, the temperature of all nodes will be equal, and this stable temperature is obviously proportional to the eigenvector with the largest eigenvalue. Unlike the adjacency matrix that describes the trajectory of motion, the laplace matrix describes the displacement or change of motion. Inspired by these points, we re-define the laplace matrix of ontology sparsity vector hypergraph and yield the balance term of ontology learning framework by means of spectrum theory.

The structure of this following sections is organized as follows: first, we introduce the background knowledge of ontology learning algorithm, ontology sparse vector learning framework, and hypergraph, etc.; then, our new ontology optimization algorithm in terms of spectrum theory is presented; after that, the effectiveness of proposed ontology learning algorithm is to be verified through two specific experiments; finally, some future works are discussed as well.

2   Settings

The main purpose here is to show the setting for ontology learning algorithm and knowledge of hypergraph.

2.1   Ontology Learning Algorithm

Let O be an ontology and G be an ontology graph corresponding to O, where elements in $V(G)$ are concepts in O and elements in $E(G)$ are the direct connections between two concepts. Ontology learning algorithm A is stated to learn an optimal ontology function $f : V \to \mathbb{R}$ which maps each ontology vertex to a real number in light of learning ontology sample set $S = \{z_1, \cdots, z_n\}$. In supervised ontology learning framework, $z_i = (v_i, y_i)$ and in unsupervised ontology learning framework, $z_i = v_i$. Let $l : \mathbb{R}^V \times V \to \mathbb{R}^+ \cup \{0\}$ be ontology loss function which makes a penalty based on how much $f(v)$ deviates from the target value. Since each vertex is represented by a p dimensional vector, the ontology function can be re-written as $f : \mathbb{R}^p \to \mathbb{R}$, and in this point of view, the ontology learning algorithm is a kind of dimensionality reduction algorithm which represents high-dimensional data with one-dimensional real numbers.

In this setting, the similarity between v and v' (corresponding to two concepts in O) is measured by the value of $|f(v) - f(v')|$, i.e., the similarity pair of (v, v') has small value of $|f(v) - f(v')|$ and the dissimilarity pair of (v, v') has big value of $|f(v) - f(v')|$. Although the similarity obtained by this trick is a relative similarity, it intuitively represents the structure of each vertex of the entire ontology graph on the one-dimensional real axis, and thus the geometric distance between ontology data becomes intuitive.

Let $v = (v_1, \cdots, v_p)^{\mathrm{T}} \in \mathbb{R}^p$ be ontology vertex and $\widehat{y}$ be a prediction. A linear ontology model with response variable $y \in \mathcal{Y}$ is denoted by

$$f(v; \beta_0, \beta) = v^{\mathrm{T}}\beta + \beta_0,$$

where $f : \mathbb{R}^p \to \mathbb{R}$ is an ontology function and $\beta = (\beta_1, \cdots, \beta_p)^{\mathrm{T}}$ is an ontology sparse vector. Given an ontology sample set $S = \{(v_i, y_i)\}_{i=1}^n$ from $(\mathbb{R}^p \times Y)^n$, bias term $\widehat{\beta}_0$, ontology loss function $l : \mathbb{R} \times \mathcal{Y} \to \mathbb{R}^+ \cup \{0\}$ and $\widehat{\beta} = (\widehat{\beta}_1, \cdots, \widehat{\beta}_p)^{\mathrm{T}}$, ontology criterion is formulated by

$$(\widehat{\beta}_0, \widehat{\beta}) = \arg\min_{\beta_0, \beta} \sum_{i=1}^n l(f(v_i; \beta_0, \beta), y_i). \tag{1}$$

Consider the generalization of the ontology function in the regularization model, (1) can be revised as

$$(\widehat{\beta}_0, \widehat{\beta}) = \arg\min_{\beta_0, \beta}\{\sum_{i=1}^n l(f(v_i; \beta_0, \beta), y_i) + \Omega(\beta)\}. \tag{2}$$

2.2 Hypergraph and Spectrum Graph Theory

Hypergraph is regraded as an extension of graph, in which edges are allowed to contain any number (≥ 2) of vertices. In contrast, in a normal graph, an edge connects two vertices. Specifically, let $H = (V, E)$ be a hypergraph where each element in E is a subset of V. If each hyperedge contains exactly r vertices, then it is called a r-uniform hypergraph. Particularly, 2-uniform hypergraph is the graph (no multiple edge and loop). The degree of vertex v in hypergraph is defined as the number of all hyper-edges which contain v. For a hyperedge e, its degree to be denoted as the number of vertices contained in e which is expressed by $\delta(e) = |e|$. Some of recent contributions to hypergraph from mathematical point of view can be referred to Frankl [16], Aigner-Horev and Han [17], Mukherjee and Bhattacharya [18], Gopal and Gupta [19], Arunachalam et al. [20], Polcyn et al. [21], Javidian et al. [22], Akhound and Motlagh [23], Anastos and Frieze [24], and Lidbetter and Lin [25].

The association matrix $\mathbf{H} \in \{0, 1\}^{|V| \times |E|}$ connecting with hypergraph H is formulated by

$$h(v, e) = \begin{cases} 1, v \in e, \\ 0, \text{otherwise}, \end{cases}$$

Let $\mathbf{I}$ be an identity matrix. The elements on the diagonal of diagonal matrices $\mathbf{D}_v$ and $\mathbf{D}_e$ are the degrees of vertices and the degrees of the edges, respectively. Then the adjacency matrix of the hypergraph H is stated as $\mathbf{A} = \mathbf{HWH}^T - \mathbf{D}_v$, where $\mathbf{W}$ is the weight diagonal matrix. Then, the Laplacian matrix of hypergraph H is formulated by

$$\mathbf{L} = \mathbf{I} - \mathbf{D}_v^{-\frac{1}{2}} \mathbf{HWD}_v^{-1} \mathbf{H}^T \mathbf{D}_v^{-\frac{1}{2}}.$$

Obviously, symmetric matrix $\mathbf{L} \succeq 0$ has minimum eigenvalue zero and $\sqrt{d}$ is its corresponding eigenvector. Several advances on spectrum graph theory, in particular on various of Laplace matrix and their Eigenvalues can be found in Li and Wang [26], Rezagholibeigi et al. [27], Damanik et al. [28], Chousionis et al. [29], Tian et al. [30], Orden et al. [31], Afkhami et al. [32], Dehghan and Banihashemi [33], Anne et al. [34], and Meliot [35].

3 New Algorithm Description

Set $\{\beta_i\}_{i=1}^p$ as the target ontology vector whose prior dependence structure is denoted by a hypergraph $H_\beta = (H, E)$ with vertex set $V = \{\beta_1, \cdots, \beta_p\}$ and the element of edge set E is a subset of $V(H)$. Let $w : E \to \mathbb{R}$ be a score function, and $d(v) = \sum_{v \in e \in E(H_\beta)} w(e)$ be degree function of vertex v where $d(v) = 0$ if v is a isolated vertex. We reset the Laplacian matrix $\mathbf{L}$ of hypergraph H_β with its element

$$L_{uv} = \begin{cases} 1 - \sum_{\{u,v\} \subseteq e} \frac{w(e)}{d(u)}, & \text{if } u = v \text{ and } d(u) \neq 0 \\ -\sum_{\{u,v\} \subseteq e} \frac{w(e)}{\sqrt{d(u)d(v)}}, & \text{if } uv \in e \in E(H_\beta), \\ 0, & \text{otherwise}. \end{cases} \quad (3)$$

For given β, the edge derivative of e at vertex u $(u \in e)$ is determined by

$$\frac{\partial \beta}{\partial e}|_u = \sum_{\{u,v\} \subseteq e} (\frac{\beta_u}{\sqrt{d(u)}} - \frac{\beta_v}{\sqrt{d(v)}})\sqrt{w(e)},$$

and therefore

$$\beta^T \mathbf{L}\beta = \sum_{uv \in e \in E(G_\beta)} (\frac{\beta_u}{\sqrt{d(u)}} - \frac{\beta_v}{\sqrt{d(v)}})^2 w(e).$$

Furthermore, we confirm

$$\widehat{\beta} = \arg\min_{\beta} \beta^T \|\mathbf{V}\beta - \mathbf{y}\|_2^2 + \lambda_1 \|\beta\|_1 + \lambda_2 \beta^T \mathbf{L}\beta$$

$$= \arg\min_{\beta} (\mathbf{V}\beta - \mathbf{y})^T (\mathbf{V}\beta - \mathbf{y}) + \lambda_1 \sum_u |\beta_u|$$

$$+ \lambda_2 \sum_{uv \in e \in E(G_\beta)} (\frac{\beta_u}{\sqrt{d(u)}} - \frac{\beta_v}{\sqrt{d(v)}})^2 w(e).$$

In light of revising the graph Laplacian matrix $\mathbf{L}^*$ to

$$L^*_{uv} = \begin{cases} 1 - \frac{w(e)}{d(u)}, & \text{if } u = v \text{ and } d(u) \neq 0 \\ -\sum_{uv \in e \in E(G_\beta)} \frac{\text{sign}(\tilde{\beta}_u)\text{sign}(\tilde{\beta}_v)w(e)}{\sqrt{d(u)d(v)}}, & \text{if } uv \in e \in E(G_\beta), \\ 0, & \text{otherwise.} \end{cases} \qquad (4)$$

we acquire

$$\widehat{\beta} = \arg\min_{\beta} \beta^T \|\mathbf{V}\beta - \mathbf{y}\|_2^2 + \lambda_1 \|\beta\|_1 + \lambda_2 \beta^T \mathbf{L}^* \beta$$

$$= \arg\min_{\beta} (\mathbf{V}\beta - \mathbf{y})^T (\mathbf{V}\beta - \mathbf{y}) + \lambda_1 \sum_u |\beta_u|$$

$$+ \lambda_2 \sum_{uv \in e \in E(G_\beta)} (\frac{\text{sign}(\tilde{\beta}_u)\beta_u}{\sqrt{d(u)}} - \frac{\text{sign}(\tilde{\beta}_v)\beta_v}{\sqrt{d(v)}})^2 w(e).$$

Thus, the hypergraph based balance function is computed by

$$\Omega(\beta) = \frac{\lambda_1}{\lambda_1 + 2\lambda_2} \|\beta\|_1 + \frac{2\lambda_2}{\lambda_1 + 2\lambda_2} \frac{\beta^T \mathbf{L}\beta}{2}$$

$$= \frac{\lambda_1}{\lambda_1 + 2\lambda_2} \sum_{i=1}^p |\beta_i| + \frac{2\lambda_2}{\lambda_1 + 2\lambda_2} \sum_{uv \in e \in E(G_\beta)} \frac{(\frac{\beta_u}{\sqrt{d(u)}} - \frac{\beta_v}{\sqrt{d(v)}})^2}{2},$$

and accordingly

$$\widehat{\beta} = \arg\min_{\beta}\{\frac{1}{2n}\|\mathbf{V}\beta - \mathbf{y}\|_2^2 + \frac{\lambda_1 + 2\lambda_2}{2n} \Omega(\beta)\}. \qquad (5)$$

Given v_u and suppose we have estimated $\tilde{\beta}_{u'}$ for $u' \neq u$. In partially mini-mized setting, the above ontology optimization framework is re-formulated by

$$
\hat{\beta} = \arg\min_{\beta}\{\frac{1}{2n}\sum_{i=1}(y_i - \sum_{u' \neq u} v_{iu'}\tilde{\beta}_{u'} - v_{iu}\beta_u)^2
$$

$$
+ \frac{\lambda_2}{2n}\sum_{uu' \in e \in E(H_\beta)}(\frac{\beta_u}{\sqrt{d(u)}} - \frac{\tilde{\beta}_{u'}}{\sqrt{d(u')}})^2
$$

$$
+ \frac{\lambda_1}{2n}|\beta_u| + \frac{\lambda_2}{2n}\sum_{wu' \in e \in E(H_\beta), w, u' \neq u}(\frac{\tilde{\beta}_w}{\sqrt{d(w)}} - \frac{\tilde{\beta}_{u'}}{\sqrt{d(u')}})^2 + \frac{\lambda_1}{2n}\sum_{w \neq u}|\tilde{\beta}_w|\}
$$

$$
= \arg\min_{\beta}\Upsilon(\beta).
$$

When $\beta_u > 0$, we obtain

$$
\frac{\partial \Upsilon(\beta)}{\partial \beta_u} = -(\frac{1}{n}\sum_{i=1} v_{iu}(y_i - \sum_{u' \neq u} v_{iu'}\tilde{\beta}_{u'}) + \frac{\lambda_2}{n}\sum_{uu' \in e \in E(H_\beta)}\frac{\tilde{\beta}_{u'}}{\sqrt{d(u)d(u')}})
$$

$$
+ \frac{\lambda_1}{2n} + (\frac{\lambda_2}{n} + 1)\beta_u,
$$

and $\frac{\partial \Upsilon(\beta)}{\partial \beta_u}$ for $\beta_u < 0$ can be calculated by the same trick. Hence, the update rule is

$$
\tilde{\beta}_u \leftarrow \frac{S(\frac{\sum_{i=1} v_{iu}(y_i - \tilde{y}_i^{(u)})}{n} + \frac{\lambda_2}{n}\sum_{uu' \in e \in E(H_\beta)}\frac{\tilde{\beta}_{u'}}{\sqrt{d(u)d(u')}}, \frac{\lambda_1}{2n})}{\frac{\lambda_2}{n} + 1},
$$

where

$$
S(\alpha_1, \alpha_2) = \begin{cases} \alpha_1 - \alpha_2, & \text{if } \alpha_1 > 0 \text{ and } \alpha_2 < |\alpha_1| \\ \alpha_1 + \alpha_2, & \text{if } \alpha_1 < 0 \text{ and } \alpha_2 < |\alpha_1|, \\ 0, & \text{otherwise.} \end{cases}
$$

Once vertex u is not associated to any other vertex in H_β, then

$$
\tilde{\beta}_u \leftarrow S(\frac{\sum_{i=1} v_{iu}(y_i - \tilde{y}_i^{(u)})}{n}, \frac{\lambda_1}{2n}).
$$

4   Experiments

In this section, to test the practicality of our proposed ontology learning algo-rithm, we present two experiments on the similarity computing of nano-structure ontology and molecular structure ontology.

4.1 Comparative Experiment on Nano-Structure Ontology

Nanostructures are an important research topic in materials science. After decades of research, materials scientists have synthesized a large number of nanomaterials, which have played an important role in the chemical, aerospace, marine and other fields. We collect more than tens of kinds of nanostructures, including: Titania nanotube $TiO_2(m, n)$, octagonal grid, hexagonal grid, square grid, $SC_5C_7(p, q)$ nanotube, H-naphtalenic nanotube $NPHX[m, n]$, $TUC_4[m, n]$ nanotube, $VC_5C_7[p, q]$ nanotube, $HC_5C_7[p, q]$ nanotube, polyhex nanotube (for instance, zigzag $TUZC_6[m, n]$ and armchair $TUAC_6[m, n]$), polyomino chains (for example, linear polyomino chain and Zig-zag polyomino chain), carbon nanotube (for instance, carbon graphite and crystal cubic carbon), carbon nanocone, regular triangulene oxide network $RTOX(n)$, ect. Divide all these concepts into three categories: "nanochain", "nanotube", "nanoring", and "nanocone". By constructing some virtual vertices, all nanostructures are organized into a tree-shaped ontology graph, the topmost vertex is the virtual vertex "nanostructure". And there are totally 54 vertices in nano-structure ontology (include virtual vertices).

We choose half of vertices in $V(G)$ (27 vertices) to construct an ontology sample set. As described in other ontology learning algorithm articles, accuracy rate of $P@N$ is used to measure the accuracy rate from different ontology learning approaches, and the computing execution process can be referred to the previous contributions in [11,12] and [15]. To manifest the superiority of the algorithms in our article, these ontology learning algorithm action in [11,12] and [15] for nano-structure ontology, and the accuracy yielded is compared with the hypergraph trick baded ontology learning algorithm in this paper. Some parts of compared data are shown in Table 1.

Table 1. The experiment data of ontology similarity measuring on nano-structure ontology.

	$P@1$ average precision ratio	$P@3$ average precision ratio	$P@5$ average precision ratio	$P@10$ average precision ratio
Ontology algorithm in our paper	0.1667	0.3519	0.5185	0.8352
Ontology algorithm in [11]	0.1296	0.2222	0.3814	0.7185
Ontology algorithm in [12]	0.1296	0.1728	0.3667	0.5778
Ontology algorithm in [15]	0.1481	0.2407	0.3963	0.7315

Table 1 reveals that the hypergraph trick based ontology sparse vector learning algorithm raised in our paper is better than the other three classes of ontology learning algorithms in which the $P@N$ accuracy is higher in the first data line of the table, which can fully implies that the hypergraph learning based ontology algorithm is effective for nano-structure ontology application.

4.2 Comparative Experiment on Molecular Structure Ontology

In our second experiment, we first extend the nano-structure ontology to molecular structure ontology by adding more concepts from drugs, proteins, and other chemical compounds, includes: some types of cycloalkanes, crystallographic structures, PAMAM dendrimers, polyphenylene dendrimers, porphyrin-cored dendrimers, benzenoid (for example, triangular benzenoid, linear polycene parallelogram benzenoid), Copper (I) oxide, Copper (II) oxide CuO, prophyrin, propyl ether imine, Zinc Porphyrindendrimers, poly (ethylene amido amine) dendrimers, anti-cancer drugs (for example, Dox-loaded micelle comprising PEG-PAsp block copolymer with chemically conjugated Dox $SP(n)$.), ect. Also, in order to construct a tree-shape ontology graph, we add some virtual vertices. Finally, there are totally 138 vertices in molecular structure ontology.

In order to elaborate the superiority of the hypergraph trick baded ontology learning algorithm in this paper, we also apply the ontology learning algorithms presented in articles in [11,12] and [15] to the molecular structure ontology. Some parts of the comparison data are shown in Table 2.

Table 2. The experiment data of ontology similarity measuring on molecular structure ontology.

	$P@1$ average precision ratio	$P@3$ average precision ratio	$P@5$ average precision ratio	$P@10$ average precision ratio
Ontology algorithm in our paper	0.1014	0.3140	0.4333	0.6225
Ontology algorithm in [11]	0.0580	0.2874	0.3783	0.5181
Ontology algorithm in [12]	0.0797	0.2632	0.3696	0.5058
Ontology algorithm in [15]	0.0797	0.2923	0.4173	0.5065

The data depicted in Table 2 reveal that the hypergraph based ontology learning algorithm in our paper is better than the other three kinds of ontology learning tricks when $N = 1, 3, 5, 10$ by means of $P@N$ accuracy measure. Table 2 above implies that the algorithm proposed in our paper is effective for molecular structure ontology.

5 Conclusion and Discussion

This paper presents an ontology sparse vector learning algorithm based on the hypergraph tricks. The basic idea is to use the hypergraph to represent the internal structure of the ontology sparse vector, and use the spectral theory to design the sparse term of the ontology sparse vector to control its sparsity. Two ontology similarity calculation experiments confirm that the algorithm proposed in this paper has a certain practicability in specific application fields.

The following topics can be worked as future on-going projects.

- What are the statistical characteristics of the proposed hypergraph based ontology learning algorithm, including generalization bounds, learning rate, stability and learnability, ect?
- In fact, due to time and workload limitations, the ontology data in Experiment 1 and Experiment 2 are incomplete. We only collected a small part of the commonly used nanostructures to form the nanostructure ontology. At the same time, when expanding the ontology to the molecular structure ontology, we only analyzed the commonly used molecular structure and included it in the second ontology. In other words, the two ontologies used in the experiments in this article will need to be expanded on a large scale in the future to build a more complete knowledge base and provide data assistance for researchers in related fields.

However, from another perspective, with the addition of new ontology concepts, the original ontology graph structure will be broken. This makes the value of p increase after the ontology structure is expanded, and the hypergraph structure used to represent the ontology sparse vector will also change a lot (not only the number of vertices will increase, but the hyperedges will also become much more complex than the original one). Therefore, the efficiency of our proposed ontology learning algorithm on the future expanded hypergraph needs to be further tested.

- More experiments should be tested and implemented on various ontology engineering applications.
- So far, there are many different forms of edge weight functions and corresponding Laplace matrices have been defined in the general graph setting. Can these forms of Laplacian matrices be extended to the hypergraph framework and applied to ontology sparse vector learning?

Acknowledgements. This research is partially supported by Modern Education Technology Research Project in Jiangsu Province (No. 2019-R-75637).

References

1. Verdonck, M., Gailly, F., de Cesare, S.: Comprehending 3D and 4D ontology-driven conceptual models: An empirical study. Inf. Syst. **93**, 101568 (2020)

2. Azevedo, H., Belo, J.P.R., Romero, R.A.F.: Using ontology as a strategy for modeling the interface between the cognitive and robotic systems. J. Intell. Robot. Syst. **99**(3–4), 431–449 (2020). https://doi.org/10.1007/s10846-019-01076-0

3. Single, J.I., Schmidt, J., Denecke, J.: Knowledge acquisition from chemical accident databases using an ontology-based method and natural language processing. Saf. Sci. **129**, 104747 (2020). UNSP

4. Labidi, T., Mtibaa, A., Gaaloul, W., et al.: Cloud SLA negotiation and re-negotiation: an ontology-based context-aware approach. Concurr. Comput. Pract. Experience **32**(15), e5315 (2020)

5. Lv, Z.M., Peng, R.: A novel meta-matching approach for ontology alignment using grasshopper optimization. Knowl. Based Syst. **201**, 106050 (2020)

6. Aydin, S., Aydin, M.N.: Ontology-based data acquisition model development for agricultural open data platforms and implementation of OWL2MVC tool. Comput. Electron. Agric. **175**, 105589 (2020)

7. Pattipati, D.K., Nasre, R., Puligundla, S.K.: OPAL: an extensible framework for ontology-based program analysis. Softw. Pract. Experience **50**(8), 1425–1462 (2020)

8. Annane, A., Bellahsene, Z.: GBKOM: a generic framework for BK-based ontology matching. J. Web Seman. **63**, 100563 (2020)

9. Lammers, G.J., Bassetti, C.L.A., Dauvilliers, Y.: Reply to Micoulaud-Franchi et al. Commentary on diagnosis of central disorders of hypersomnolence: from clinic to clinic via ontology and semantic analysis on a bullet point path. Sleep Med. Rev. **52**, 101329 (2020). UNSP

10. Jankovic, M., Yuksel, M., Babr, M.M., et al.: Space debris ontology for ADR capture methods selection. Acta Astronautica **173**, 56–68 (2020)

11. Gao, W., Zhu, L., Wang, K.: Ontology sparse vector learning algorithm for ontology similarity measuring and ontology mapping via ADAL technology. Int. J. Bifurcat. Chaos **25**, 1540034. (2015). https://doi.org/10.1142/S0218127415400349

12. Gao, W., Zhang, Y.Q., Guirao, J.L.G., et al.: A discrete dynamics approach to sparse calculation and applied in ontology science. J. Differ. Equ. Appl. **25**(9C10), 1239–1254 (2019)

13. Gao, W., Guirao, J.L.G., Basavanagoud, B., et al.: Partial multi-dividing ontology learning algorithm. Inf.. Sci. **467**, 35–58 (2018)

14. Gao, W., Farahani, M.R.: Generalization bounds and uniform bounds for multi-dividing ontology algorithms with convex ontology loss function. Comput. J. **60**, 1289–1299 (2017)

15. Gao, W., Chen, Y.: Approximation analysis of ontology learning algorithm in linear combination setting. J. Cloud Comput. **9**, 29 (2020). https://doi.org/10.1186/s13677-020-00173-y

16. Frankl, P.: Maximum degree and diversity in intersecting hypergraphs. J. Comb. Theory Ser. B **144**, 81–94 (2020)

17. Aigner-Horev, E., Han, H.: Linear quasi-randomness of subsets of Abelian groups and hypergraphs. Eur. J. Comb. **88**, 103116 (2020)

18. Mukherjee, S., Bhattacharya, B.B.: Replica symmetry in upper tails of mean-field hypergraphs. Adv. Appl. Math. **119**, 102047 (2020)

19. Gopal, K., Gupta, M.K.: Bounds on generalized FR codes using hypergraphs. J. Appl. Math. Comput. **65**, 771–792 (2020). https://doi.org/10.1007/s12190-020-01414-8

20. Arunachalam, S., Vrana, P., Zuiddam, J.: The asymptotic induced matching number of hypergraphs: balanced binary strings. Electron. J. Comb. **27**(3), P3.12 (2020)

21. Polcyn, J., Reiher, C., Rodl, V., et al.: Minimum pair degree condition for tight Hamiltonian cycles in 4-uniform hypergraphs. Acta Math. Hung. **161**(2), 647–699 (2020). https://doi.org/10.1007/s10474-020-01078-7
22. Javidian, M.A., Wang, Z.Y., Lu, L.Y., et al.: On a hypergraph probabilistic graphical model. Ann. Math. Artif. Intell. (2020). https://doi.org/10.1007/s10472-020-09701-7
23. Akhound, A., Motlagh, M.A.C.: Evaluation of entanglement measures for hypergraph states up to four qubits. Int. J. Theor. Phys. **59**(8), 2582–2588 (2020)
24. Anastos, M., Frieze, A.: On the connectivity of proper colorings of random graphs and hypergraphs. Random Struct. Algorithms **56**(4), 988–997 (2020)
25. Lidbetter, T., Lin, K.Y.: A search game on a hypergraph with booby traps. Theor. Comput. Sci. **821**, 57–70 (2020)
26. Li, X., Wang, J.: On the ABC spectra radius of unicyclic graphs. Linear Algebra Appl. **596**, 71–81 (2020)
27. Rezagholibeigi, M., Aalipour, G., Naghipour, A.R.: On the spectrum of the closed unit graphs. Linear Multilinear Algebra (2020). https://doi.org/10.1080/03081087.2020.1777250
28. Damanik, D., Fang, L.C., Sukhtaiev, S.: Zero measure and singular continuous spectra for quantum graphs. Ann. Henri Poincare **21**(7), 2167–2191 (2020). https://doi.org/10.1007/s00023-020-00920-6
29. Chousionis, V., Leykekhman, D., Urbanski, M.: The dimension spectrum of conformal graph directed Markov systems. Sel. Math. New Ser. **25**(3), 40 (2019). UNSP
30. Tian, G., He, J., Cui, S.: On the Laplacian spectra of some double join operations of graphs. Bull. Malays. Math. Sci. Soc. **42**(4), 1555–1566 (2019)
31. Orden, D., Marsa-Maestre, I., Gimenez-Guzman, J.M., et al.: Spectrum graph coloring to improve Wi-Fi channel assignment in a real-world scenario via edge contraction. Discrete Appl. Math. **263**, 234–243 (2019)
32. Afkhami, M., Hassankhani, M., Khashyarmanesh, K.: Distance between the spectra of graphs with respect to normalized Laplacian spectra. Ge. Math. J. **26**(2), 227–234 (2019)
33. Dehghan, A., Banihashemi, A.H.: On computing the multiplicity of cycles in bipartite graphs using the degree distribution and the spectrum of the graph. IEEE Trans. Inf. Theory **65**(6), 3778–3789 (2019)
34. Anne, C., Balti, M., Torki-Hamza, N.: Sectoriality and essential spectrum of non symmetric graph Laplacians. Complex Anal. Oper. Theory **13**(3), 967–983 (2019). https://doi.org/10.1007/s11785-018-0817-2
35. Meliot, P.L.: Asymptotic representation theory and the spectrum of a random geometric graph on a compact Lie group. Electron. J. Probab. **24**, 43 (2019)

On-line Firmware Updating and Fingerprint Generating for Solid State Disks

Yuan Xue[1], Shouxin Wang[2], Tian Chen[3], Quanxin Zhang[3], Lu Liu[3(✉)], and Yu-an Tan[3]

[1] Academy of Military Science, Beijing 100091, China
[2] China Satellite Communications Co., Ltd., Beijing 100190, China
[3] Beijing Institute of Technology, Beijing 100081, China
{chentian20,zhangqx,liulu,tan2008}@bit.edu.cn

Abstract. Virus and Rootkit may modify hard disk's firmware to hide itself, while the traditional security software is not able to detect the modification of hard disk's firmware. This paper relies on a USB analyzer to collect the protocol communication data of the JMUtility tool for a Solid State Disk, then unveils its internal protocol interface to dump the RAM content via the USB-SATA interface, and the firmware code is located in the RAM. By reverse engineering the firmware code, the protocol of writing to the RAM is also inferred to enable the modification of firmware code to change the device identification data. Meanwhile, the tool Firmware Extractor is developed to dump the firmware code for a specific Solid State Disk, and the possibility of on-line updating firmware and generating fingerprint is validated.

Keywords: Firmware · Reverse engineering · Solid state disk · On-line firmware updating · Fingerprint generating

1 Introduction

On February 16, 2015, Kaspersky Lab discovered a cyber group, EQUATION [1], which was often targeting critical facilities and economic lifelines of a country and had been active for more than two decades. Evidence revealed by Kaspersky suggests that the EQUATION group works closely with US National Security Agency, Israeli intelligence agencies, and the British Military. It is likely that the EQUATION Group is the secret force of the US and its allies, which can carry out devastating strikes against other countries. One of the sophisticated technologies of the EQUATION group is that it can modify the hard drive firmware to create a "hidden" area and mark it as unreadable. Such technology can set their hiding place inaccessible to avoid being hunted by antivirus software. Neither OS reinstallation nor hard drive formatting can access this area, so that

Supported by the National Natural Science Foundation of China (No. 62072037) and Zhejiang Lab (No. 2020LE0AB02).

the virus cannot be deleted. The virus can infect the hard drives of Seagate, Western Digital, Samsung, Maxter and a dozen other major brands. The virus of the EQUATION group only infects the firmware of Hard disk drive (HDD), which is not targeting Solid State Hard Drive (SSD). Nowadays, due to fast random read/write performance, low operating noise and anti-vibration, SSD is gradually replacing HDD in some areas [2–4]. Therefore, it is necessary to conduct research on the technology of extracting and updating SSD firmware. With the comparison of the original benign firmware, the extracted firmware can reveal whether it has been illegally modified. Also, updating SSD firmware can strengthen the security of SSD and prevent the firmware from being infected by viruses, trojans and some other malicious programs [5,6,14,15,17]. Generally, we can extract the firmware of SSD with the following three methods: (1) Extract from a firmware upgrade package. After an SSD is coming out, the manufacturer always releases a firmware upgrade package to patch the vulnerabilities and improve the performance of it. The upgrade package generally includes the updated firmware of the SSD. It might be compressed or encrypted. However, by analyzing the upgrade package, we could decompress or decrypt the firmware and restore it. (2) Extract from the flash chip directly. The firmware is stored in the flash chip of an SSD. We could remove the flash chip from the circuit board and use a flash programmer to read out the content. In order to adapt to the storage features of the flash chip, some modules of the firmware and user data are stored confusingly, which needs to be restored to plaintext [7,8,18]. (3) Using JTAG. Some SSDs provide a Joint Test Action Group (JTAG) interface on the circuit board. So, we could send commands to the controller via JTAG to obtain the contents of RAM and flash chip. With that, we could fetch the firmware from SSD [9]. However, there are some limitations to the above approaches. Some manufacturers do not provide upgrade packages for some SSDs. Moreover, for some encrypted firmware, the decryption key is sealed inside the SSD [10]. The scrambled firmware fetched from the flash chip must be restored with the correct corresponding methods. There is no standard of JTAG commands to fetch memory contents, and some SSDs do not have a JTAG interface.

In this paper, we propose an approach to on-line firmware extraction and update for a specific SSD, i.e., call, fetch and modify the firmware code in RAM through internal protocols while the SSD is on-line. Our key contributions are as follows. (1) We unveil the internal protocol interface of a Solid State Disk to dump the RAM content via the USB-SATA interface. (2) By reverse engineering the firmware code, we inferred the protocol of writing to the RAM to enable the modification of firmware code to change the device identification data. (3) We develop the tool Firmware Extractor to dump the firmware code for a specific Solid State Disk. The paper is organized as follows. In Sect. 2, our approach to firmware extraction is introduced, and in Sect. 3, the process of reverse engineering of the firmware is demonstrated. In Sect. 4, we introduce our approach to firmware updating and validate the possibility of on-line updating firmware. Finally, the conclusion and our future work are discussed in Sect. 5.

2   Firmware Extraction

A solid state drive (SSD) is a solid state storage device that uses integrated circuit assemblies to store data persistently, typically using flash memory, and functioning as secondary storage in the hierarchy of computer storage. An SSD mainly consists of the following three parts:

(1) SSD controller: The SSD controller is the core component of an SSD, which is responsible for coordinating each part of the whole SSD system.
(2) RAM: The RAM is generally used to store address mapping tables. It can also be used as a cache to improve the I/O performance of an SSD.
(3) NAND flash memory: The flash memory is the main body of an SSD, which consists of multiple flash chips. Besides storing the host data, the flash memory also stores metadata, firmware, etc.

The firmware of an SSD is run by the SSD Controller, offering features such as address mapping, garbage collection, loss balancing and bad block management. On the one hand, it receives read/write commands from the Host Interface Logic and complete data transmission, on the other hand, it reads and writes data to flash memory via the Flash Interface. In this paper, we select SSD340K manufactured by Taiwan Transecend to demonstrate our study, which uses Jmicron JMF670 as the SSD controller.

2.1   JMUtility

The JMicron's software JMUtility can fetch and show the SSD setup information, block erase count, bad block information, SMART information, device identification and debug log, etc. We first connect the SSD to the JM20329 USB-SATA adapter, then connect the adapter to a PC and run JMUtility on Windows 7. Figure 1 shows the setting information of SSD340K. In the bottom right window, the hexadecimal strings after "⟨570⟩" and "⟨580⟩" are similar to ARM instructions, we save the hexadecimal strings of the window as DPDFTL.txt.

2.2   Fetch the RAM of the SSD Controller

Based on prior knowledge, we can infer that the content of DPDFTL.txt comes from the RAM of the SSD controller, containing the firmware command codes. To capture the commands sent by JMUtility, we use the USB protocol analyzer 1480A from International Test Instruments to record the USB command transmitted between JMUtility and the SSD. Then, search the string "1B 08 08 04 04 07 03 1B" in the captured data. Further Analyzing the USB commands before and after the hexadecimal strings, we infer a procedure of reading the RAM of the SSD controller via USB-SATA interface, which is shown as follows:

(1) Send the command "A1 08 0B D0 01 00 4F C2 00 B0 00 00" and receive 0×200 bytes of data.

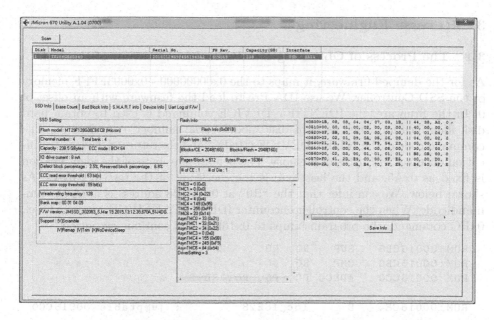

Fig. 1. The setting information of SSD340K

(2) Send the command "A1 06 00 DC 4A 00 00 00 E0 EF 00 00".
(3) Send the command "A1 16 03 00 01 FF 34 12 E0 88 00 00" with 0 × 200 bytes of data. The first 9 bytes are "FF E5 26 4A 4D 46 36 37 30", and the rest 503 bytes are zero-padded.
(4) Send the command "A1 16 03 00 01 FF 34 12 E0 88 00 00" with 0 × 200 bytes of data. The first 8 bytes are in the form of "FF E5 86 03 AB CD EF GH", where "AB CD EF GH" is the hexadecimal form of a RAM offset. The rest 504 bytes are zero-padded.
(5) Send the command "A1 14 0B 00 IJ 86 34 12 E0 86 00 00" and receive IJ * 0 × 200 bytes of data, where IJ is the number of sectors for reading.

Repeat step (4)–(5), we can read the content of other areas of RAM.

2.3   Firmware Extractor

Based on the results of the above analysis, we develop a firmware dump tool Firmware Extractor to dump the first 256 KB data of RAM. Each time it reads 0 × 40 sectors of data, i.e., 0 × 40 * 0 × 200 = 0 × 8000 bytes (32 kB), and reads 8 times in total. The offsets are set as "00 00 00 00", "00 00 80 00", "00 01 00 00", "00 01 80 00", "00 01 80 00", ..., "00 03 80 00" respectively.

3   Reverse Engineering

3.1   The Process of Obtaining Hardware Identification of the SSD

As for the dumped firmware, it maps to the 0x00000000 - 0x0003FFFF memory of the SSD Controller. We use IDA Pro to load the firmware with an offset of 0. In the firmware, the IDENTIFY DEVICE command is used to obtain hard disk identification, such as hard disk model, serial number, capacity, etc. The command code of IDENTIFY DEVICE is 0xEC, and the returned device identification occupies 512 bytes of memory. The penultimate byte of the identification is fixed as 0xA5, and the last byte is the checksum of the rest 511 bytes. As shown below, We can infer that the "R0" at 0x16CB8 address is an ATA command code. When the controller encounter IDENTIFY DEVICE command, i.e., 0xEC command, the program jumps to 0x16E28 and continue execution.

```
1  ROM:00016CB8    SUB    R0, R0, #0xE5
2  ROM:00016CBC    CMP    R0, #0x15           ; switch 21 cases
3  ROM:00016CC0    ADDCC  PC, PC, R0,LSL#2    ; switch jump
4  ...
5  ROM:00016CE4    B      loc_16E28           ; jumptable 00016CC0
6  ...
7  ROM:00016E28    MOV    R0, #0              ; jumptable 00016CC0
8  ROM:00016E2C    BLX    nullsub_2
9  ROM:00016E30    BL     x_op_EC_sub_15C84
10 ROM:00016E34    B      loc_170A8
```

In the following listing, 0x15C84 address points to a function which fetches the hard disk device identification and transmits it to the host. The two instructions at 0×16290 and 0×16294 addresses write byte 0xA5 to the device identification buffer at offset 0x1FE, and the function at 0x1A774 address calculates the checksum and writes it at offset 0x1FF.

```
1  ROM:00015C84    STMFD  SP!, {R4-R6,LR}
2  ROM:00015C88    LDR    R4, =byte_2AAF0
3  ...
4  ROM:00016290    MOV    R1, #0xA5
5  ROM:00016294    STRB   R1, [R0,#0x1FE]
6  ROM:00016298    BL     x_cal_checksum_sub_1A774
```

3.2   The ATA Command of Writing Data to the RAM

According to the firmware code, the 8 bytes at 0x28D60 address are listed as follows:

```
1  00028D60   FF E5 86 03 00 02 80 00
```

The 8 bytes are in the form of "FF E5 86 03 AB CD EF GH", where the 4 bytes "AB CD EF GH" are the RAM's offset, and the third byte indicates the operation type. In this case, the third byte "0×86" stands for reading data from RAM. The firmware reveals that the operation type "0×87" stands for writing to RAM, and the data buffer with the SATA command code "0 × 88" will be written to RAM by the host.

4 Firmware Modification

After extracting the firmware and performing reverse engineering, we modify the firmware's code of handling command "0xEC" and replace the immediate operand "0xA5" of the instruction at 0x16290 address with "0x55" to verify the validity of modifying the firmware with commands by the host.

4.1 Fetch SSD Device Identification with PLSCSI

After searching the data captured by 1480A analyzer, we can infer that the USB command for fetching SSD device identification is "A1 08 0B 00 01 00 00 00 E0 EC 00 00". We then use the PLSCSI tool for testing. The procedure of fetching device identification is listed as follows:

(1) Run Command Prompt in Windows 7.
(2) Set the drive letter of SSD as an environment variable of PLSCSI. Take drive letter "E" as an example, the command is "set PLSCSI = \\.\E:"
(3) Execute the command "A1 08 0B 00 01 00 00 00 E0 EC 00 00" and read 0 × 200 bytes of data.

4.2 Modify the RAM of the Controller with PLSCSI

Based on the reverse engineering of Sect. 3.2, we first run the following commands to read the RAM of the controller with an offset of 0x15C00 and save as file 15C00.raw.bin. The first 9 bytes sent by command (3) are "FF E5 26 4A 4D 46 36 37 30", and the rest 503 bytes are zero-padded. In command (4), the first 9 bytes of magic.write.bin are "FF E5 26 4A 4D 46 36 37 30", and the first 8 bytes of 15C00.read.addr.bin are "FF E5 86 03 00 01 5C 00". Command (4) set the RAM offset to 0x15C00 and read 4 sectors, i.e., 0 × 800 bytes, while command (5) writes the contents to 15C00.raw.bin file.

```
1 plscsi -p -v -x "A1 08 0B D0 01 00 4F C2 00 B0 00 00" -i 0
    x200
2 plscsi -p -v -x "A1 06 00 DC 4A 00 00 00 E0 EF 00 00" -i 0
    x0
3 plscsi -p -v -x "A1 16 03 00 01 FF 34 12 E0 88 00 00" -o 0
    x200 -f magic.write.bin
4 plscsi -p -v -x "A1 16 03 00 01 FF 34 12 E0 88 00 00" -o 0
    x200 -f 15C00.read.addr.bin
5 plscsi -p -v -x "A1 14 0B 00 04 86 34 12 E0 86 00 00" -i 0
    x800 -t 15C00.raw.bin
```

Next, we modify the firmware 15C00.raw.bin by changing the byte at 0x690 from 0xA5 to 0x55, i.e., the instruction "MOV R1, #0xA5" at 0x16290 is changed to "MOV R1, #0x55". The modified firmware is saved as 15C00.mod.bin.

Finally, we execute the following commands to merge the 15C00.mod.bin file to the RAM. The offset is 0x15C00 and the length is 0×800 bytes. The first 8 bytes of 15C00.write.addr.bin are "FF E5 87 03 00 01 5C 00".

```
1 plscsi -p -v -x "A1 16 03 00 01 FF 34 12 E0 88 00 00" -o 0
    x200 -f 15C00.write.addr.bin
2 plscsi -p -v -x "A1 16 03 00 04 87 34 12 E0 88 00 00" -o 0
    x800 -f 15C00.mod.bin
```

4.3   The Verification of the Modified Firmware

We executed the following commands to read 0×800 bytes of the RAM of the controller with the offset 0x15C00, and saved the data as 15C00.mod2.bin file.

```
1 plscsi -p -v -x "A1 16 03 00 01 FF 34 12 E0 88 00 00" -o 0
    x200 -f 15C00.read.addr.bin
2 plscsi -p -v -x "A1 14 0B 00 04 86 34 12 E0 86 00 00" -i 0
    x800 -t 15C00.mod2.bin
```

Compared with file 15C00.raw.bin, i.e., the original firmware, the byte at offset 0×690 has been changed to 0×55, indicating that the firmware has been successfully modified. Next, we read the SSD device identification again. The byte at offset 0x1FE is modified from 0xA5 to 0×55, and the last byte (checksum) is modified from 0xE6 to 0×36 due to the change of the previous content. Finally, we disconnect the SSD from the USB port of our computer, plug in again to reboot the SSD, and read the SSD device identification again. The result is the same as the original identification. That means, rebooting the SSD can restore the modification, i.e., the instruction at 0×16290, and make it invalid.

5   Conclusion

In this paper, we analyze the USB protocol data captured with JMUtility, figured out the internal protocol of the SSD and dumped the RAM of the SSD controller. By analyzing the firmware stored in the RAM, we were able to master the commands of fetching SSD device identification and writing data to the RAM of the controller. By modifying the firmware in RAM, the device identification is also being modified accordingly, verifying the feasibility of modifying the firmware online.

The future work will be carried out from three aspects. First, to verify the generality of the protocol, i.e., conduct experiments on other SSDs using this controller, e.g., some SSDs manufactured by ADATA and ShadowChip. Second, to conduct similar studies and experiments on some other SSD controllers. Third, to study on-line dumping of the firmware of SSD using SATA interface and the solidification of the modified firmware, i.e., fetch the firmware while an SSD is connected to the PC via SATA, and the modification stays valid after the SSD is disconnected and powered off [13].

References

1. Kaspersky: Lab Equation group: questions and answers, Kaspersky Lab. Technical report 2015, pp. 1–44 (2015)
2. Song, Q., Li, S., Zhu, Y.: Key technologies of flash-based solid state recorder for aerospace applications. Electron. Des. Eng. **23**(4), 169–171 (2015)
3. Cornwell, M.: Anatomy of a solid-state drive. Queue **10**(10), 59–63 (2012)
4. Hu, J.: The research and FPGA implementation of ATA protocol in solid state disk. South China Univ. Technol. **2010**, 1–74 (2010)
5. Srinivasan, A., Wu, J., Santhalingam, P., Zamanski, J.: DeadDrop-in-a-flash: information hiding at SSD NAND flash memory physical layer. SECURWARE **2014**, 79 (2014)
6. Choi, Y., Lee, D., Jeon, W., Won, D.: Password-based single-file encryption and secure data deletion for solid-state drive. In: 2014 Proceedings of the 8th International Conference on Ubiquitous Information Management and Communication, pp. 1–7. ACM (2014)
7. Zhang, L., Hao, S.G., Zheng, J., Tan, Y.A., Zhang, Q.X., Li, Y.Z.: Descrambling data on solid-state disks by reverse-engineering the firmware. Digit. Invest. **12**(3), 77–87 (2015)
8. Shah, Z., Mahmood, A.N., Slay, J.: Forensic potentials of solid state drives. In: Tian, J., Jing, J., Srivatsa, M. (eds.) SecureComm 2014, Part II. LNICST, vol. 153, pp. 113–126. Springer, Cham (2015). https://doi.org/10.1007/978-3-319-23802-9_11
9. Zaddach, J., Bruno, L., Francillo, A., Balzarotti, D.: AVATAR: a framework to support dynamic security analysis of embedded systems' firmwares. In: NDSS 2014, pp. 1–16 (2014)
10. Monev, V.: Security of SSD Drives with Full Disk Encryption and Some Attacks (in Bulgarian). It4sec Reports 2014, pp. 1–15 (2014)
11. Attachment, H.S.S.A.: Serial ATA: High Speed Serialized AT Attachment. SerialATA Workgroup 2003, pp. 1–311 (2003)
12. Lee, J.Y., Lee, S.J.: A study on hard disk drive ATA passwords. J. Korea Inst. Inf. Secur. Cryptol. **25**(5), 1059–1065 (2015)
13. Haibo, S., Xiaobin, W., Yamei, L.: Design of high-speed storage system based on SATA interface solid state hard disk. J. Telem. Track. Command **35**(2), 48–52 (2014)
14. Zhang, X., Tan, Y.A., Zhang, C., Xue, Y., Li, Y., Zheng, J.: A code protection scheme by process memory relocation for android devices. Multimedia Tools Appl. **7**(9), 11137–11157 (2018)
15. Zhu, R., Zhang, B., Mao, J., Zhang, Q., Tan, Y.: A methodology for determining the image base of ARM-based industrial control system firmware. Int. J. Crit. Infrast. Prot. **16**, 26–35 (2017)
16. Runhua, S.H.I., Ze, S.H.I.: Key management scheme for IoT based on blockchain technology. Netinfo Secur. **20**(8), 1–8 (2020)

17. Chen, L., Sun, Y., Zhang, L., Chen, Y.: A scheme of measurement for terminal equipment based on DICE in IoT. Netinfo Secur. **20**(4), 21–30 (2020)
18. Zaddach, J., Costin, A.: Embedded devices security and firmware reverse engineering. Black-Hat USA (2013)
19. Tan, Y., Feng, S., Cheng, X., Li, Y., Zheng, J.: An android inline hooking framework for the securing transmitted data. Sensors **20**(15), 4201 (2020)

Feature Map Transfer: Vertical Federated Learning for CNN Models

Tianchi Sha[1], Xiao Yu[2], Zhiwei Shi[3], Yuan Xue[4], Shouxin Wang[5],
and Sikang Hu[1]([✉])

[1] School of Computer Science, Beijing Institute of Technology, Beijing 100081, China
[2] Department of Computer Science and Technology,
Shandong University of Technology, Zibo 255022, China
[3] China Information Technology Security Evaluation Center, Beijing 100085, China
[4] Academy of Military Science, Beijing 100091, China
[5] China Satellite Communications Co., Ltd., Beijing 100190, China

Abstract. Federated learning provides a privacy-preserving mechanism
for multiple participants to collaboratively train machine learning models without exchanging private data with each other. Existing federated
learning algorithms can aggregate CNN models when the dataset is hor-
izontally partitioned, but cannot be applied to vertically partitioned
datasets. In this work, we demonstrate the image classification task
in the vertical federated learning setting where each participant holds
incomplete image pieces of all samples. We propose an approach called
VFedConv to solve this problem and achieve the goal of training CNN
models without revealing raw data. Different from traditional federated
learning algorithms sharing model parameters in each training iteration,
VFedConv shares hidden feature maps. Each client creates a local feature
extractor and transmits the extracted feature maps to the server. A classifier model at the server-side is constructed with extracted feature maps
as input and labels as output. Furthermore, we put forward the model
transfer method to improve final performance. Extensive experiments
demonstrate that the accuracy of VFedConv is close to the centralized
model.

Keywords: Federated learning · Transfer learning · Convolutional
neural network

1 Introduction

In recent years, more attention has been raised to data privacy. Federated Learning (FL) is proposed to help multiple data owners jointly train a model without
revealing their private data to each other. When a single organization or user does
not have sufficient data, FL can help boost model accuracy. According to different distribution characteristics of the data, FL can be categorized as horizontal

© Springer Nature Singapore Pte Ltd. 2021
Y. Tan et al. (Eds.): DMBD 2021, CCIS 1454, pp. 37–44, 2021.
https://doi.org/10.1007/978-981-16-7502-7_4

federated learning, vertical federated learning, and federated transfer learning [1]. Horizontal federated learning, also called sample-based federated learning, is introduced in the scenarios in which datasets share the same feature space but different sample space. In contrast, for vertical federated learning, datasets share the same sample space but different feature space. Several algorithms have been proposed for privacy-preserving vertical federated learning [9,11–14]. Vertical federated learning algorithms rely more on security mechanisms, such as homomorphic encryption and secure multi-party computation, since each participant cannot independently get a complete recognition of the object.

Existing federated algorithms share model parameters and then aggregate them to get a global model. But these algorithms have the following disadvantages: (i) Modern ML models, especially artificial neural networks, have a huge capacity for "memorizing" arbitrary information. Sharing model parameters may also reveal some information about the training data. (ii) [8] showed that, with Non-i.i.d data, performance can be greatly reduced for federated learning. Moreover, in reality, different participants collect training data independently making the training data is often Non-i.i.d. (iii) With the increasing model scale, the communication cost of delivering model parameters becomes large.

To overcome these disadvantages, we propose an algorithm called VFedConv. Figure 1 shows the pipeline of our approach and the architecture of models. The dataset is vertically partitioned into 4 parts and each participant owns one of them. We follow the scenario proposed by Yang [1] that only one positive participant, who also plays the role of server, owns the label data and can't reveal it to others. We design our model architecture based on VGG. The VGG model is split into two parts, the first half as the feature extractor and the second half as the server classifier.

In summary, the main contributions of this paper are as follows:

1. We propose a novel vertical federated learning algorithm called VFedConv. VFedConv enables different participants to collaboratively train a CNN model to complete the task of image classification when the dataset is vertically partitioned. To the best of our knowledge, this is the first attempt to apply vertical federated learning settings to CNNs.
2. We analyze the causes of accuracy loss comparing with the centralized model and put forward optimization methods. We use the model transfer method to solve the problem of feature space alignment.
3. We study the transferability of CNN models and show how to split a CNN model into two partitions so that the extracted feature is of good generalization.

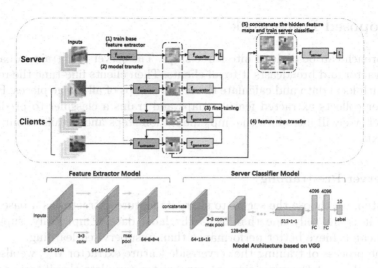

Fig. 1. The pipeline of VFedConv and model architecture.

2 Related Works

2.1 Federated Learning

Existing work on federated learning mainly focused on the horizontal settings such as FedAvg [5]. These methods share model parameters during training. FedGKT [4] follows the horizontal federated learning setting but works differently by exchanging hidden feature maps. FedGKT consolidates several advantages into a single framework: reduced demand for edge computation, lower communication cost, and asynchronous training.

For vertical federated learning, to our knowledge, there is no paradigm. [6,12, 13] designed their algorithms based on tree models. [11] proposed a framework for distributed features by aggregating local results into a final output using linear and nonlinear transformations. But none of them can be applied to CNN models.

2.2 Model-Based Transfer Learning

Fine-tuning a pre-trained neural network is a common method to accelerate training. The transferability of deep learning models addressed our concern when designing the algorithm. [2] studied the transferability of different layers in CNNs. [3] studied the transferability of RNNs in NLP applications. The results of the two studies are similar in that initializing a network with transferred features can produce a boost to generalization and deep layers are not suitable for model transfer. In this paper, we design experiments to find the optimal model and draw similar conclusions on the transferability of features in deep neural networks.

3   Proposed Framework

Our approach can be divided into three steps. The server first trains a base feature extractor and broadcasts it to all clients. Then clients fine-tune the received model with local data and calculate the feature maps of all image pieces. Finally, the server collects extracted feature maps and trains a classifier to predict the true label. We will introduce the implementation steps and details of our framework next.

3.1   Server Pre-training

In this step, we choose the server to share its feature extractor as a base model because it is the only one that owns the label data. Empirically, supervised learning can achieve better performance than unsupervised learning.

In the process of training the server-side feature extractor W_e^1, we also need to train a W_{clst} at the same time to construct a complete classification model. W_{clst} is only an auxiliary model for training W_e^1 and will not be used in the prediction step. Note that there are structural differences between W_{clst} and W_s. The goal of this step is to optimize the following objective:

$$\underset{(W_e^1, W_{clst})}{\arg\min} \sum_{i=1}^{N} l_{ce}(f_p((W_e^1, W_{clst}); X_i^1), y_i) \tag{1}$$

Where f_p represents the pre-training model, l_{ce} represents cross-entropy loss function.

3.2   Model Transfer and Fine-Tuning

Clients receive the base feature extractor from the server and fine-tune it with local data. Due to the lack of label data for clients, we use an autoencoder to fine-tune the feature extractor.

For client k, it initializes its feature extractor W_e^k with W_e^1, $k \in \{2, 3, ..., K\}$. Then we train an autoencoder with W_e^k as the encoder and W_g^k as the decoder. W_g^k is the inversion of W_e^k on the structure. We reduce the learning rate of W_e^k to avoid the misalignment of hidden feature maps. The goal of this step is to optimize the following objective:

$$\underset{(W_e^k, W_g^k)}{\arg\min} \sum_{i=1}^{N} l_{mse}(f_c^k((W_e^k, W_g^k); X_i^k), X_i^k) \tag{2}$$

Where f_c^k represents the autoencoder model held by client k, l_{mse} represents MSE loss function.

3.3   Feature Map Aggregation

Each client calculates local hidden feature maps and sends them to the server. As shown in Fig. 1, the server will concatenate these feature maps by position. The server then needs to train a classifier with concatenated feature maps as input to predict the real label of the original image. The goal of this step is to optimize the following objective:

$$\arg \min_{W_s} \sum_{i=1}^{N} l_{ce}(f_s(W_s; H_i), y_i) \tag{3}$$

Where: f_s represents the server model, $H_i = concatenate(H_i^1, H_i^2, ..., H_i^K)$, $H_i^k = f_c^k(W_e^k, X_i^k)$.

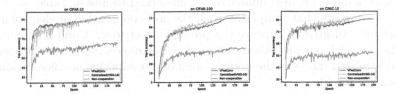

Fig. 2. Test accuracy on three datasets.

4   Experiments

4.1   Experimental Setup

Task and Dataset. Our training task is image classification on CIFAR-10, CIFAR-100, and CINIC-10. Unlike normal image classification tasks, we split each image in the dataset into four small pieces and each participant owns one of them. For different methods, we record the top 1 test accuracy as the metric to evaluate model performance.

Model Architecture. We design our model based on VGG-16 architecture. We split the VGG-16 model into two parts, a shallow model as the local feature extractor and a deep model as the server classifier. Each participant owns a local feature extractor and shares the output of it with the server. The server classifier is trained with concatenated hidden feature maps as input. In our standard experiment, as shown in Fig. 1, we take the first two convolution layers with the first max pool layer as the feature extractor. The rest of the VGG-16 model serves as the server classifier.

In the step of fine-tuning with local data, we also need to use a generative model. The architecture of the generative model is opposite to that of the feature extractor. The local feature extractor and the generative model are combined to form an autoencoder. Note that we only need to fine-tune the feature extractor, so we set the learning rate of the feature extractor to *1e-5* while the learning rate of the generative model is *1e-3*.

Baseline. To our knowledge, existing approaches for vertical federated learning cannot support CNNs. Therefore, we set the centralized model and non-cooperation model as a comparison. The centralized model trains a VGG-16 model with a complete dataset as input, i.e. the exchange of raw data is allowed. This is the upper bound of performance in our experiment and we will analyze the accuracy loss comparing with this set of experiments. The non-cooperation model is to take only local image pieces as inputs and train without cooperation. Through this group of comparative experiments, we prove that collaborative training can effectively solve the problem of local data shortage.

4.2 Experiment Result

Figure 2 shows the curve of the test accuracy during training on the VGG-16 model with 3 datasets. We summarize all numerical results in Table 1.

We can observe that comparing with the non-cooperation model, collaborative training can greatly improve the prediction accuracy. Comparing with the centralized model, our model achieves close performance. Note that the accuracy of the centralized model is the upper bound of our experiment since exchanging raw data is allowed.

Table 1. Test accuracy of different methods on three datasets

Methods	CIFAR-10	CIFAR-100	CINIC-10
VFedConv (ours)	**91.30**	**69.72**	**80.69**
Centralized (VGG-16)	94.04	73.24	84.73
Non-cooperation	65.85	37.88	53.75
No model transfer	87.73	63.87	76.65

4.3 Ablation Study

In this section, to verify the influence of different factors on experiment results, we design several ablation experiments.

Effectiveness of Model Transfer. In the above experiment, all participants finetune the base feature extractor shared by the positive participant. Here we also consider the situation that all participants train their own feature extractor with local dataset independently. Since most participants have no label data, they can only use Autoencoder for local training. Table 1 shows the performance differences between the two methods. We can see that model transfer is of great help to improve the experiment performance.

Transferability of Different Layers. We change the splitting position of the VGG-16 model and record the top 1 accuracy of each splitting position. In Table 2, 1C means there is one complete convolution unit in the local feature extractor while 1M means there is one maxpool layer. We can observe that the accuracy decreases with layer numbers increasing in the feature extractor.

Table 2. Test accuracy of different layer numbers in the feature extractor.

Layers	CIFAR-10	CIFAR-100	CINIC-10
1C	92.30	70.75	83.10
2C	91.07	69.37	80.49
2C + 1M	91.30	69.72	80.69
3C + 1M	89.63	67.28	77.59
4C + 1M	87.06	63.20	74.06
4C + 2M	85.47	60.85	70.43
5C + 2M	81.42	54.64	67.08

5 Conclusion

In this paper, we demonstrate a novel image classification algorithm in the vertical federated learning setting. Different from traditional algorithms sharing model parameters during training, our method shares the hidden feature maps and achieves several advantages including reduced demand for edge computation and lower communication cost.

Acknowledgments. This work was supported in part by the National Natural Science Foundation of China (No. 61876019).

References

1. Qiang, Y., Yang, L., Tianjian, C., Yongxin, T.: Federated machine learning: concept and applications. ACM Trans. Intell. Syst. Technol. **10**, 1–19 (2019)
2. Jason, Y., Jeff, C., Yoshua, B., Hod, L.: How transferable are features in deep neural networks? In: Advances in Neural Information Processing Systems, pp. 3320–3328 (2014)
3. Mou, L., Meng, Z., Yan, R., Li, G., Xu, Y., Zhang, L., Jin, Z.: How transferable are neural networks in NLP applications? arXiv preprint arXiv:1603.06111 (2016)
4. He, C., Annavaram, M., Avestimehr, S.: Group knowledge transfer: federated learning of large CNNs at the edge. In: Advances in Neural Information Processing Systems 33: Annual Conference on Neural Information Processing Systems 2020, NeurIPS 2020, 6–12 December 2020. Virtual
5. McMahan, B., Moore, E., Ramage, D., Hampson, S., y Arcas, B.A: Communication-efficient learning of deep networks from decentralized data. In: Artificial Intelligence and Statistics, pp. 1273–1282 (2017)D
6. Wu, Y., Cai, S., Xiao, X., Chen, G., Ooi, B.C.: Privacy preserving vertical federated learning for tree-based models. Proc. VLDB Endow. **13**(11), 2090–2103 (2020)
7. Karen, S., Andrew, Z.: Very deep convolutional networks for large-scale image recognition. arXiv preprint arXiv:1409.1556 (2014)
8. Zhao, Y., Li, M., Lai, L., Suda, N., Civin, D., Chandra, V.: Federated learning with non-IID data. arXiv preprint arXiv:1806.00582 (2018)
9. Adrià, G., et al.: Secure Linear Regression on Vertically Partitioned Datasets. IACR Cryptol. ePrint Arch. 2016, p. (2016)

10. Geyer, R.C., Klein, T., Nabi, M.: Differentially private federated learning: A client level perspective. arXiv preprint arXiv:1712.07557 (2017)
11. Hu, Y., Niu, D., Yang, J., Zhou, S.: FDML: a collaborative machine learning framework for distributed features. In: 2019 Proceedings of the 25th ACM SIGKDD International Conference on Knowledge Discovery and Data Mining, pp. 2232–22402019)
12. Cheng, K, Fan, T., Jin, Y., Liu ,Y., Chen, T., Papadopoulos, D., Yang, Q.: Secureboost: A lossless federated learning framework. arXiv preprint arXiv:1901.08755 (2019)
13. Liu, Y., Liu, Y., Liu, Z., Liang, Y., Meng, C., Zhang, J., Zheng, Y.: Federated forest. IEEE Trans. Big Data (2020)
14. Ohrimenko, O., et al.: Oblivious multi-party machine learning on trusted processors. In: 25th USENIX Security Symposium (USENIX Security 16), pp. 619–636 (2016)
15. Noroozi, M., Favaro, P.: Unsupervised learning of visual representations by solving Jigsaw puzzles. In: Leibe, B., Matas, J., Sebe, N., Welling, M. (eds.) ECCV 2016, Part VI. LNCS, vol. 9910, pp. 69–84. Springer, Cham (2016). https://doi.org/10.1007/978-3-319-46466-4_5
16. Shokri, R., Stronati, M., Song, C., Shmatikov, V.: Membership inference attacks against machine learning models. In: 2017 IEEE Symposium on Security and Privacy (SP), pp. 3–18 (2017)
17. Yunhong, H., Liang, F., Guoping, H.: Privacy-preserving SVM classification on vertically partitioned data without secure multi-party computation. In: 2009 Fifth International Conference On Natural Computation, vol. 1, pp. 543–546 (2009)
18. Hinton, G., Vinyals, O., Dean, J.: Distilling the knowledge in a neural network. arXiv preprint arXiv:1503.02531 (2015)
19. Liu, Y., Zhang, X., Wang, L.: Asymmetrically Vertical Federated Learning. arXiv preprint arXiv:2004.07427 (2020)
20. Lu, H., Wang, L.: User-oriented data privacy preserving method for federated learning that supports user disconnection. Netinfo Secur. 21(3), 64–71 (2021)
21. Wang, R., Ma, C., Wu, P.: An intrusion detection method based on federated learning and convolutional neural network. Netinfo Secur. 20(4), 47–54 (2020)

A Random Multi-target Backdooring Attack on Deep Neural Networks

Xinrui Liu[1], Xiao Yu[2(✉)], Zhibin Zhang[1], Quanxin Zhang[1], Yuanzhang Li[1], and Yu-an Tan[1]

[1] School of Computer Science and Technology, Beijing Institute of Technology, Beijing 100081, China
{3220200923,zhangqx,popular,tan2008}@bit.edu.cn
[2] Shandong University of Technology, Zibo 255022, China

Abstract. Deep learning has made tremendous progress in the past ten years and has been applied in various critical practical applications. However, recent studies have shown that deep learning models are vulnerable to backdoor attacks in which the target labels chosen by the attacker can be one or multiple. Conventional multi-target backdoor attack focus on applying multiple triggers to implement multi-target attack. In this paper, we propose a novel method that utilizes one trigger to correspond to multiple target labels, and the location of the trigger is not limited, which brings more flexibility. After proposing the backdoor attack, we also considered defending against this kind of attack. Therefore, to distinguish backdoor images and clean images, we propose a method to train a neural network as a detector to detect if the image has an abnormal part. Our experimental results show that our attack success rate is higher than 90% on MNIST, Cifar-10, and GTSRB. Our detection method can also successfully detect the backdoor image with a trigger at a random location of the image, and the detection success rate is 86.02%.

Keywords: Backdoor attack · Poisoning attack · Deep neural network · Machine learning

1 Introduction

With the advent of artificial intelligence, neural networks have become a widely used method of artificial intelligence. Currently, neural networks have been adopted in a wide range of areas, such as face recognition [1], voice recognition [2], games [3], and autonomous driving. For example, Alipay users are using deep learning based facial recognition systems to make payment. However, recent studies have shown that deep neural networks are vulnerable to backdoor attack.

The backdoor attack enables attackers to implant a backdoor into the model and performs malicious attacks using specific backdoor trigger in the inference phase. A backdoor attack is usually targeted because backdoored input is misclassified as the specific class chosen by an attacker. The target labels chosen by the attacker can be

© Springer Nature Singapore Pte Ltd. 2021
Y. Tan et al. (Eds.): DMBD 2021, CCIS 1454, pp. 45–52, 2021.
https://doi.org/10.1007/978-981-16-7502-7_5

one or multiple. This paper focuses on multi-target attacks. Nowadays, there are many researches on the relationship between backdoor trigger patterns, trigger locations, and target labels. We can divide them into two categories. In the first category, the presence of any trigger among multiple triggers can hijack the backdoored model to the same targeted label. In the second category, the backdoored model can be hijacked with multiple trigger patterns or trigger locations; however, attacker can use each trigger (pattern or location) to target a different label.

In 2019, TargetNet [5] was proposed. This method performs multi-target backdoor attacks by placing one trigger on different image locations, and each trigger on a different location corresponds to a different target label. This method is limited because the attacker must consider where the trigger is placed when performing a multi-target attack. In 2020, researchers proposed three multi-target attack methods in Dynamic backdoor [6]. Among them, the c-BaN method does not need to consider the trigger's location to determine the target label. The target label is determined by the trigger pattern. However, in this method, one trigger pattern can only correspond to one target label. Also, this method uses a neural network to generate triggers when performing an attack, which raises the attack cost.

In this paper, we propose a novel method that utilizes one trigger pattern to correspond to multiple target labels, and the location of the trigger is not restricted. In our method, the trigger guarantees that the malicious output is within the range of multiple targets chosen by the attacker. However, the specific target depends on the original image where the trigger is stamped. Due to the original images' diversity, it is difficult for the defender to predict which target the image with the trigger is classified as. The attacker can also use only one trigger pattern to achieve multi-target attacks in different locations, making the attack more flexible.

After proposing the backdoor attack, it also triggered our thinking of defending against this backdoor attack. Therefore, we design a DNN to check whether the input image contains abnormal parts to determine a backdoored image. Our experimental results show that this detection method can effectively distinguish the backdoor images from the clean images. The trigger in the backdoor image can be any size, shape, or pattern, and it can also detect one-pixel trigger in the image effectively. For 1000 backdoor images with triggers at random locations, our detection success rate is 86.02%.

The contributions of this paper are as follows:

- We propose a new multi-target backdoor attack that utilizes one trigger pattern to correspond to multiple target labels, and the location of the trigger is not restricted.
- We propose a novel backdoor trigger detection method which can detect whether the input image contains a backdoor trigger.
- We apply three datasets to verified our method's performance.

The rest of the paper is organized as follows. Section 2 explains the proposed scheme. Section 3 demonstrates the experimental setup and evaluates the results. Finally, we conclude the paper and present the future work in Sect. 4.

2 Methodology

2.1 Random Multi-target Backdoor Attack

Our method aims to generate a backdoor so that an image with a backdoor trigger (the trigger can be located anywhere in the image) can be misclassified as one of the multiple targets specified by the attacker. Figure 1 shows the overview of our random multi-target attack.

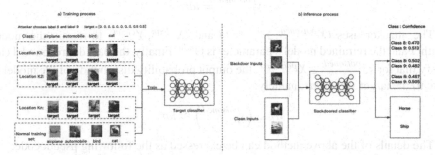

Fig. 1. Overview of the proposed backdoor attack. The attacker selects label 8 and label 9 as multiple targets, then generates the target vector target. The attacker attaches a backdoor trigger at different locations for different images and replaces the original label with the target vector. Finally, attacker retrains the target classifier. For a backdoor image, the output confidence of label 8 and label 9 are both close to 0.5.

For a target classifier's internal structure M, its trained model parameter is Θ. We use $M_\Theta(x)$ to represent its operation function, which means that for an input image x, the output is a multi-dimensional probability vector. Given the original training data X and its corresponding label Y, the attacker uses α of (X, Y) to generate poisoned data called $(X^{poisoned}, Y^{poisoned})$. The remaining $1 - \alpha$ of (X, Y) remains unchanged as clean data represented as (X^{clean}, Y^{clean}). (X^{clean}, Y^{clean}) and $(X^{poisoned}, Y^{poisoned})$ are applied to retrain the classifier. The attacker selects a trigger pattern p and randomly generates a location set K with a set size of n for placing the trigger. K is used to store the location information of the placed trigger. Function $R(image, location, pattern)$ is defined to represent the backdoor image generated by pasting trigger pattern p according to the location information loc to the input image img. Therefore, for $\forall x_i^{poisoned} \in X^{poisoned}$, we have:

$$x_i^{poisoned} \leftarrow R(x_i^{poisoned}, K_{i\%n}, p)$$

Thus, we can obtain a backdoor image set $X^{poisoned}$ with a trigger pattern at different locations according to the location set K.

We assume an adversary selects multiple targets from the labels to represent multi-target attack set S, and the size of set S is denoted as l. And the classification number is C. Here we define a vector called target vector tar. The target vector is $C-$ dimensional. Each dimension represents the probability value of every label. For any element in the multi-target attack set S, its corresponding probability value is $1/l$, and the values of other dimensions are 0. For example, for the MNIST dataset, there is a total of 10 classes

$(C = 10)$. Assuming that the attacker selects 2 targets ($l = 2$) as the attack targets such as $S = label\{8, 9\}$, then its target vector *tar* is expressed as:

$$tar = [0, 0, 0, 0, 0, 0, 0, 0, \frac{1}{2}, \frac{1}{2}]$$

We replace the labels of backdoor image dataset ($X^{poisoned}$, $Y^{poisoned}$) with the target vector *tar*, that is, for $\forall y_i^{poisoned} \in Y^{poisoned}$, we have:

$$y_i^{poisoned} = tar$$

The attacker uses ($X^{poisoned}$, $Y^{poisoned}$) and (X^{clean}, Y^{clean}) to retrain the model together and the retrained model's parameter is Θ^{adv}. Finally, the backdoored model can satisfy that for $\forall x_i^{poisoned} \in X^{poisoned}$, the output probability distribution of the model is close to the target vector *tar*, namely:

$$M_{\Theta^{adv}} \left(x_i^{poisoned} \right) \approx tar$$

The details of the above method can be expressed as the following pseudocode:

Algorithm 1 Design of random multi-target backdoor attack

Input: Original model's internal structure: M, Retrained model's parameter: Θ^{adv}, Original training image set: X and its corresponding label Y, Original training set: $D_{train} = (X, Y)$, Target vector: tar, Ratio of poisoned data in the original dataset: α, Trigger pattern: p, Multi-target attack set: S, Location set: K, Size of K: n, Validation dataset: D_{valid}
Output: Parameters of backdoored model: Θ^{adv}
Begin

1 $D_{poisoned} \leftarrow \alpha * D_{train}$, $D_{clean} \leftarrow (1 - \alpha) * D_{train}$
2      $tar \leftarrow S$
3 $\forall (x_i, y_i) \in D_{poisoned}$, $x_i = R(x_i, K_{i\%n}, pat)$, $y_i = tar$
4   Train target classifier parameters $\Theta^{adv} \leftarrow D_{poisoned} + D_{clean}$
5   Record classification accuracy and attack success rate on the validation dataset D_{valid}
6 Return Θ^{adv}

End

2.2 Backdoor Detection Methods

Our defense goal is to detect whether the input image contains abnormal parts, that is, whether it contains backdoor triggers. Our method's main idea is to use the original training dataset to construct a new dataset and apply this new dataset to train a deep neural network to detect backdoor images and classify clean images in the validation dataset. The method is mathematically expressed as follows:

First, we obtain clean training dataset and test dataset from the official. Then, we divide the training dataset X and its corresponding label Y into two halves. One half is a clean dataset (X^{clean}, Y^{clean}), and the other half is used to generate poisoned data called $(X^{poiosned}, Y^{poisoned})$. The classification number is l. For each image in X^{clean}, the corresponding label remains unchanged, but for $X^{poisoned}$, we will traverse every image $x_i^{poisoned} \in X^{poisoned}$. For each image, a set of random data is randomly generated. Each set of random data contains three items, which represent the trigger location loc, the trigger size $shape$, and the trigger content $pattern$. Then we can paste this trigger on the image to generate a new image $x_i^{poisoned}$. Function $\Pi(img, loc, shape, pattern)$ is defined here, which means that for the image img, a poisoned image is generated based on three items of a set of random data. Therefore, for $\forall x_i^{poisoned} \in X^{poisoned}$, we have:

$$x_i^{poisoned} \leftarrow \Pi(x_i^{poisoned}, loc, shape, pattern)$$

Figure 2 shows the random images generated on Cifar10, and at the same time, we replace the label of the image with l, which is to generate a backdoor sample pair $(x_i^{poisoned}, l)$. Finally, we can use the new dataset $(X^{clean}, Y^{clean}) + (X^{poiosned}, l)$ to train a DNN M_{det} with $l + 1$ classification number.

3   Experiment and Evaluation

This section shows the experimental results to demonstrate the proposed method's performance.

In this experiment, we use MNIST, Cifar-10 and GTSRB as our datasets. And we conduct our backdoor attacks on two state-of-art convolutional neural networks: AlexNet [15] and ResNet [16]. Both models use our prepared poisoned datasets to train from scratch. To ascertain the proposed method's performance, we inject $\alpha = 10\%$ backdoor data on three datasets for training and test the target classifier.

We perform a two-target attack in which **target1** and **target2** represent the two targets, respectively. The performance of our attack can be generally evaluated by clean sample accuracy, attack success rate and multi-target randomness index, which is defined as below:

Clean sample accuracy (CSA): It refers to the backdoored model's accuracy rate for identifying clean samples.

Attack success rate (ASR): It refers to the success rate that one backdoor image with specified trigger at random location is predicted as any of the multiple targets specified by the attacker.

Detection success rate (DSR): It refers to the success rate that our detector can successfully detect the backdoor images.

num (target1, target2): It refers to the number of the test backdoor images with the property that the top1 of its model output vector is label **target1**, and the top2 is label **target2**.

num (target2, target1): It refers to the number of the test backdoor images with the property that the top1 of its model output vector is label **target2**, and the top2 is label **target1**.

Multi-target randomness index (MRI):
It describes the approximity between num(target1, target2) and num(target2, target1) to indicate the randomness of our multi-target attack. The equation can be expressed as below, If MRI value is close to 0, it means the backdoor model has better target randomness.

$$MRI = |\frac{num(target1, target2)}{num(target2, target1)} - 1|$$

Table 1 below shows different backdoored images of label 1 and their model outputs. From the table, it is clear that the outputs of label 8, 9 are close to 0.5, and all images' top1 and top2 are label8,9(Note that we choose label 8, 9 as our attack targets). But the orders are different for different images. Table2 illustrates the results of our attack on MNIST, Cifar-10 and GTSRB. From the table, we can see that the retrained Alexnet can guarantee an 100.0% attack success rate for a backdoor image with a trigger at a random location while ensuring the model's original classification accuracy. Besides, the MRI in the experiment is close to 0, indicating that for a backdoor image, the probability of backdoored model predicting it as **target1** or **target2** is close to 50%, making our attack more concealed.

Table 1. Backdoor images and their model outputs on MNIST.

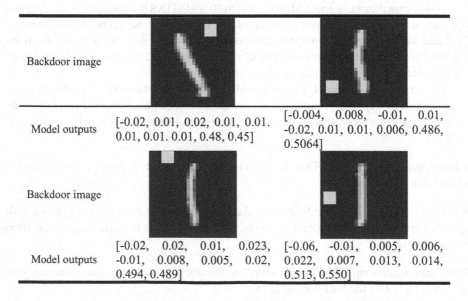

Backdoor image		
Model outputs	[-0.02, 0.01, 0.02, 0.01, 0.01. 0.01, 0.01. 0.01, 0.48, 0.45]	[-0.004, 0.008, -0.01, 0.01, -0.02, 0.01, 0.01, 0.006, 0.486, 0.5064]
Backdoor image		
Model outputs	[-0.02, 0.02, 0.01, 0.023, -0.01, 0.008, 0.005, 0.02, 0.494, 0.489]	[-0.06, -0.01, 0.005, 0.006, 0.022, 0.007, 0.013, 0.014, 0.513, 0.550]

For our defense method, we conduct experiments on Cifar-10 and choose Resnet as the structure of the detection network. The experimental results are shown in Table 3 and Fig. 2 below. We can see that the backdoor detection network can effectively detect backdoor triggers with different shapes, random locations, random sizes, and random content while ensuring the accuracy of classifying clean samples, and the detection success rate is as high as 80.39%.

Table 2. Random multi-target attack results on MNIST.

Dataset	CSA	ASR	num(target1, target2)	num(target2, target1)	MRI
MNIST	98.34%	100.0%	4991	5009	0.02
Cifar-10	82.04%	99.79%	5024	4955	0.01
GTSRB	96.27%	90.42%	5808	5612	0.03

After that, we apply the trained detection neural network to detect the malicious dataset of our random multi-target backdoor attack. The results are shown in Table 3 below. The trained backdoor detector network can effectively detect the backdoor images, and the detection success rate is as high as 86.02%.

Table 3. Detection results on Cifar-10

Detection on Cifar-10		Detection against our attack method	
CSA	DSR	CSA	DSR
77.95%	80.39%	77.19%	86.02%

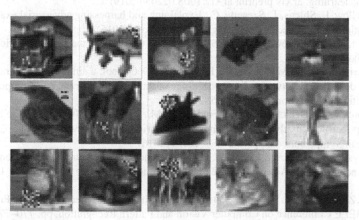

Fig. 2. Our detector can effectively detect different types of trigger on Cifar-10. From left to right: each colimn displays different shapes of trigger: square, triangle, circle, distributed and one-pixel. From top to bottom: each row displays the trigger at different location and with different sizes.

4 Conclusion and Future Work

In this paper, we propose a novel multi-target backdoor attack on neural networks. We apply one trigger pattern to correspond to multiple target labels without considering the trigger's location. After proposing the backdoor attack, we design a backdoor detector to distinguish backdoor images from clean images. Through experiments, we demonstrate the feasibility and efficiency of our detection method.

References

1. ImageNet large scale visual recognition competition (2012). http://www.imagenet.org/challenges/LSVRC/2012/
2. Graves, A., Mohamed, A.-R., Hinton, G.: Speech recognition with deep recurrent neural networks. In: Acoustics, Speech and Signal Processing (ICASSP), 2013 IEEE international conference on. IEEE, pp. 6645–6649 (2013)
3. Hermann, K.M., Blunsom, P.: Multilingual distributed representations without word alignment. In: Proceedings of ICLR, [Online] (2014). http://arxiv.org/abs/1312.6173
4. Gu, T., Dolan-Gavitt, B., Garg, S.: Badnets: identifying vulnera- bilities in the machine learning model supply chain. arXiv preprint arXiv:1708.06733 (2017)
5. Hyun, K., Roh, J., Yoon, H., Park, K.W.:TargetNet backdoor: attack on deep neural network with use of different triggers. In: ICIIT (2020)
6. Salem, A., Wen, R., Backes, M., Ma, S., Zhang, Y.: Dynamic backdoor attacks against machine learning models. arXiv preprint arXiv:2003.03675 (2020)
7. Liu, Y., Ma, S., Aafer, Y., Lee, W.-C., Zhai, J., Wang, W., Zhang, X.: Trojaning attack on neural networks (2017)
8. Chen, B., Carvalho, W., Baracaldo, N., et al.: Detecting backdoor attacks on deep neural networks by activation clustering. arXiv preprint arXiv:1811.03728 (2018)
9. Wang, B., Yao, Y., Shan, S., et al.: Neural cleanse: Identifying and mitigating backdoor attacks in neural networks. In: Neural Cleanse: Identifying and Mitigating Backdoor Attacks in Neural Networks, 0 (2019)
10. Udeshi, S., Peng, S., Woo, G., et al.: Model agnostic defence against backdoor attacks in machine learning. arXiv preprint arXiv:1908.02203 (2019)
11. Goodfellow, I., Shlens, J., Szegedy, C.: Explaining and harnessing adversarial examples. In: International Conference on Learning Representations (2015)
12. Kurakin, A., Goodfellow, I., Bengio, S.: Adversarial examples in the physical world. In: ICLR Workshop (2017)
13. Moosavi-Dezfooli, S.M., Fawzi, A., Frossard, P.: Deep-fool: a simple and accurate method to fool deep neural networks. In: Proceedings of the IEEE Conference on Computer Vision and Pattern Recognition, pp. 2574–2582 (2016)
14. Papernot, N., McDaniel, P., Jha, S., Fredrikson, M., Celik, Z.B., Swami, A.: The limitations of deep learning in adversarial settings. In: Security and Privacy (EuroS&P), 2016 IEEE European Symposium on, pp. 372–387. IEEE (2016)
15. Krizhevsky, A., Sutskever, I., Hinton, G.E.: Imagenet classification with deep convolutional neural networks. In: Advances in Neural Information Processing Systems, pp. 1097–1105 (2012)
16. He, K., Zhang, X., Ren, S., et al.: Deep residual learning for image recognition. In: Proceedings of the IEEE Conference on Computer Vision and Pattern Recognition, pp. 770–778 (2016)
17. Honglin, L.U., Liming, W.A.N.G.: User-oriented data privacy preserving method for federated learning that supports user disconnection. Netinfo Secur. 21(3), 64–71 (2021)
18. Rong, W.A.N.G., Chunguang, M.A., Peng, W.U.: An intrusion detection method based on federated learning and convolutional neural network. Netinfo Secur. 20(4), 47–54 (2020)

Intelligent Attack Behavior Portrait for Path Planning of Unmanned Vehicles

Zhao Li[1], Yuxi Ma[1], Zhibin Zhang[1], Xiao Yu[2], Quanxin Zhang[1(✉)], and Yuanzhang Li[1]

[1] School of Computer Science, Beijing Institute of Technology, Beijing 100081, China
{3120185490,zhangqx,popular}@bit.edu.cn
[2] Department of Computer Science and Technology, Shandong University of Technology, Zibo 255022, China

Abstract. With the rapid development of artificial intelligence, opponents can use AI technology to influence the path planning algorithm of unmanned vehicles, making unmanned vehicles face severe safety issues. Aiming at the opponent's intelligent attack in the scenario of unmanned vehicle path planning, this paper studies the opponent's intelligent attack behavior portrait technique and proposes an attack behavior portrait scheme based on the knowledge graph. First, according to the simulation experiment of unmanned vehicle path planning based on reinforcement learning, we use Toeplitz Inverse Covariance-based Clustering (TICC) time-series segmentation clustering technology to extract the steps of an opponent's attack behavior. Then, the attack strategy rules are stored in the knowledge graph to form a portrait of attack behavior for unmanned vehicle path planning. We verified the proposed scheme on the Neo4j platform. The results proved that the method could describe the steps of intelligent attacks on unmanned vehicles well and provide a basis for unmanned vehicle attack detection and establishing an unmanned vehicle defense system. Furthermore, it has good generalizability.

Keywords: Unmanned vehicle path planning simulation · Attack behavior portrait · Time series clustering · Knowledge graph

1 Introduction

In recent years, unmanned vehicle technology has been a hot area of research all over the world. Unmanned vehicles can complete transportation, investigation, surveillance, and high-risk operations, effectively improving efficiency and reducing casualties [1]. However, due to the immature technology of unmanned vehicles at present, unmanned vehicles are facing serious safety problems [2]. The opponent can interfere with the unmanned vehicle's sensors and hinder the unmanned vehicle from completing the task. For example, the opponent can set up adversarial examples of back-door attacks on the side of the road, which affects the recognition of unmanned vehicle cameras and changes the decision of unmanned vehicles [3]. At present, research on the safety of unmanned vehicles pays more attention to attacks on unmanned vehicle sensors. This paper mainly studies the intelligent attack behavior for the path planning of unmanned vehicles.

© Springer Nature Singapore Pte Ltd. 2021
Y. Tan et al. (Eds.): DMBD 2021, CCIS 1454, pp. 53–60, 2021.
https://doi.org/10.1007/978-981-16-7502-7_6

Intelligent attacks based on AI technology are gradually developing into hidden dangers in various fields. However, the randomness and uncertainty of intelligent attacks make the system security situation a complex nonlinear process, and traditional security protection methods are far from meeting the actual needs of security protection [4]. The portrait technology can automatically analyze and generate the characteristics and associations of some intelligent attack behaviors by collecting information [5]. Then investigators can use the portrait to speculate on the opponent's attack purpose and evaluate the system security situation and assist in making defensive decisions [6]. Most of the existing research on intelligent attacks focuses on cyber attacks (smart botnets, intelligent APT attacks, and malware escape) [7]. Aiming at the intelligent attack on unmanned vehicle path planning, we propose an intelligent attack portrait scheme based on time series segmented clustering and knowledge graph.

The contribution of this paper is as follows:

Based on the reinforcement learning technology, we conduct an intelligent attack simulation experiment for unmanned vehicle path planning on the MPE platform of OpenAI.

Based on the multi-dimensional time series clustering technology TICC, we use the unmanned vehicle intelligent attack experiment log data to automatically extract the steps of the three unmanned vehicle intelligent attack behaviors.

This paper uses knowledge graph technology to store the intelligent attack steps of unmanned vehicle path planning and form the portrait of intelligent attack behavior.

2   Related Work and Background

Due to the high cost of building an actual unmanned vehicle intelligent attack environment, we use the intelligent attack simulation experiment based on reinforcement learning as the data source. In the scenario of this paper, both the unmanned vehicle and the opponent are agents. Reinforcement learning is an excellent approach to simulate multi-agent games [8]. OpenAI is a popular toolkit in the field of machine learning. Multi-Agent Particle Environment (MPE) is an open-source experimental platform for multi-agent reinforcement learning based on OpenAI's gym. It creates a simple multi-agent scene where agents can perform continuous observation and discrete actions [9]. We chose OpenAI's MPE framework as the experimental environment.

The knowledge graph is essentially a knowledge base of the semantic network. The knowledge graph is a graph composed of nodes and edges. The nodes are called entities, and the edges are called relationships. In previous research, there are many methods to describe the characteristics of aggressive behavior. Based on the mapping relationship between machine components and vulnerabilities, L Wang et al. [10] proposes an attack graph-based probabilistic metric for network security and studies its efficient computation. T. Tidwell et al. [11] used the method of constructing a target-oriented parametric attack tree to model multi-stage attack behaviors to realize vulnerability assessment and attack visualization. This paper uses knowledge graph technology to profile the intelligent attack behavior of unmanned vehicle path planning.

3 Methodology

3.1 Intelligent Attack Behaviors Portrait Frame

The research framework of this paper is shown in Fig. 1, which is divided into three stages: input, knowledge extraction, and output. First, we sample the data of the intelligent attack simulation experiment of unmanned vehicle path planning in the multi-agent particle environment and collect the position coordinates, speed, number of obstacles, and other information of each step of the unmanned vehicle. Then, we use the TICC segmented clustering algorithm to automatically cluster the experimental data in segments to obtain the attack behavior steps. Finally, the knowledge graph technology is used to profile the intelligent attack behaviors of unmanned vehicle path planning based on the attack characteristics and steps obtained in the previous step. We used the Neo4j platform to display the portrait.

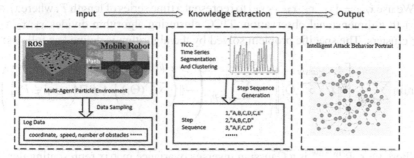

Fig. 1. Intelligent attack behaviors portrait frame.

3.2 Reinforcement Learning

Reinforcement learning sets up a reward and punishment mechanism based on the interaction between the agent and the environment so that the agent can learn independently in the process of interaction with the environment [12]. Q-learning algorithm is a model-free reinforcement learning algorithm [13]. The process can be regarded as a Markov decision problem consisting of a finite four-element group $\langle S, A, P, R|$ and having a continuous state space. Among them, S is the state set. A is the action set. $P_{ss'}(a)$ is the state transition function. R is the reward function. Given a strategy π, the Q value is defined as:

$$Q^n(s, a) = R(s, a) + y \sum_{s'} P_{ss'}(a) V^{\pi}\left(s'\right) \tag{1}$$

Among them, $R(s, a) = E(r|s, a)$, $V^{\pi}\left(s'\right) = \max Q^{\pi}\left(s', a'\right)$. r is the return value obtained by the agent taking action a in state s. s' is the next state after the action is taken. y is the discount factor, which represents the degree of attenuation of future returns. During the experiment, the following formula is used to update the Q table:

$$Q(s, a) = Q(s, a) + a\left(r(s, a) + y \max_{a' \in A} Q\left(s', a'\right) - Q(s, a) \right) \quad (2)$$

Where a represents the rate of learning knowledge. We use reinforcement learning algorithms to train unmanned vehicle path planning decisions and simulate the intelligent attacks of opponents.

3.3 TICC Clustering Algorithm

Toeplitz Inverse Covariance-based Clustering (TICC) algorithm can cluster the subsequences of multi-dimensional time series and discover the repeated patterns of multivariable time series. The TICC algorithm divides and clusters time series at the same time [14]. We use $x_{ori} = [x_1 \; x_2 \; x_3 \cdots x_T]$ to represent a time series of length T, where $x_i \in R^n$ is the i-th n-dimensional observation. TICC clustering algorithm divides $x_1, x_2, \cdots x_7$ into k clusters. The specific problem solved by the algorithm is defined as follows:

$$\arg\min \sum_{i=1}^{K} \left[\left\| \lambda \overset{sparsiy}{\circ} \Theta_i \right\|_1 + \sum_{x_t \in P_i} \left(-\left\| \left(\overset{log\ likelihood}{x_{tr}}(\Theta_i) \right) \right\| + \beta \Pi \left(\overset{temporal\ consistency}{x_{t-1} \notin P_i} \right) \right) \right] \quad (3)$$

Where $\Theta_i \in R^{nw \times nw}$ is a Gaussian inverse covariance matrix representing the characteristics of each cluster. λ is the sparsity level coefficient. $\circ$ represents the Hadamard product. $-\|(x_t, \Theta_i)$ is the negative log-likelihood. $P = \{P_1, \cdots, P_k\}$ is the result allocation set, where $P_i \subset \{1, 2, \cdots, T\}$. In problem (3), β is a parameter that enforces time consistency and $\prod(x_{t-1} \notin P_i)$ is an indicator function that checks whether neighboring points are allocated to the same cluster.

4 Experimental Results and Analysis

This part discussed the specific steps of constructing an intelligent attack portrait for unmanned vehicle path planning, including collecting and processing raw data, extracting attack steps based on the TICC algorithm, and constructing a portrait using the Neo4j platform.

4.1 Data Collection and Processing

The original data in this paper comes from the simulation experiment of unmanned vehicle path planning on the MEP platform. We set up three opponents' attack strategies: hiding targets, misclassifying targets, and moving targets to influence the decision-making of unmanned vehicles and prevent unmanned vehicles from reaching the target. Figure 2 is a schematic diagram of the path planning intelligent attack experiment. The solid red circle represents the unmanned vehicle, the solid green circle represents the opponent (that is, the target), and the black squares are obstacles.

The rules of the three attack strategies are as follows. The purpose of the unmanned vehicle in the experiment is to reach the target location. In the hiding targets strategy, the unmanned vehicle will lose the opponent's position coordinate information when it enters the opponent's attack range. In the misclassifying target's strategy, the opponent will make the unmanned vehicle entering the attack range misunderstand obstacles in other positions as the target. In the moving target's strategy, when the unmanned vehicle enters the opponent's attack range, the opponent will flee away from the unmanned vehicle. To simplify the experiment, we set the maximum number of opponent attacks in the simulation experiment to 3. The experiment outputs log data such as the position of the unmanned vehicle, the opponent's position, the position of the obstacle, and the number of obstacles in the field of view at each step. Each round of data is a CSV file as the data source of the portrait.

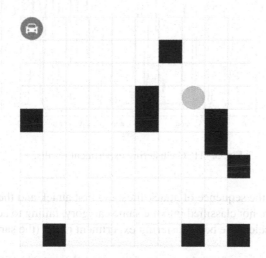

Fig. 2. Schematic diagram of path planning intelligent attack experiment.

We reduced the dimensionality of the data. The structure of the data sample dramatically affects the results of the TICC clustering algorithm. After analysis, we decided to use five columns as the input data of the clustering algorithm, including the opponent's distance, whether it has arrived, the number of attacks, the speed of the opponent's movement, and whether the opponent's position has arrived changed.

4.2 Knowledge Extraction Based on Cluster Mining

Because we need to mine the characteristics of each attack behavior from multiple rounds of attacks, we spliced several data files into one file. Then, we added five lines with values of all 100 between the two files as a boundary.

The setting of the TICC clustering algorithm in this paper is as follows. window_size = 1, lambda_parameter = 11e-2, beta = 10, max_Iters = 100. A reasonable number of reasonable classes needs to be determined based on experimental results.

Experiments have demonstrated that the clustering results are wildly inaccurate when the time series data is too long. Therefore, this paper selects 15 ideal data files: five hiding target attacks, five moving target attacks, and five misclassifying target attacks. The TICC algorithm is used for clustering, and the sequence of attack steps is obtained in this order. The experimental results are shown in Fig. 3.

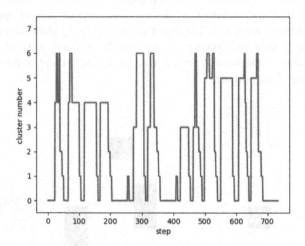

Fig. 3. TICC clustering experiment results.

After changing the sequence of attack files, the first attack and the second attack of some strategies were not classified into the same category, failing to achieve the desired effect. Finally, we select the best clustering experiment result (the same attack strategy data is adjacent).

In the end, we summarized the steps of three attack strategies: initial state, hiding targets attack, stalemate, attack failure, moving targets attack, misclassifying targets attack, and attack success.

4.3 Build the Portrait of Attack Behaviors

To construct the portrait of attack behaviors, we determined the information of the attack strategy that needs to be described and formed the conceptual layer of the knowledge graph. These attributes include target, vision, description, effect, means, and steps. Protégé is a tool that provides the function of constructing ontology concept classes, relationships, attributes, and instances. The ontology model we built using Protégé is shown in Fig. 4.

This paper uses the Neo4j graph database to store and display knowledge graphs. The attack steps obtained through the previous time series analysis are the focus of this research. The rest of the attack behavior information can be summarized according to

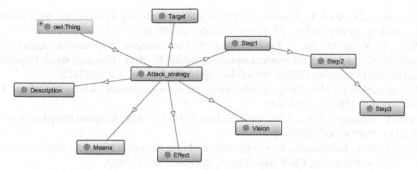

Fig. 4. Attack strategy knowledge graph ontology model.

the rules of the attack strategy. At present, this paper has implemented three adversary attack strategies, namely, hiding targets, misclassifying targets, and moving targets in the path planning scenario.

5 Conclusion and Future Work

With the widespread use of unmanned vehicle technology and the development of artificial intelligence-based attack methods, unmanned vehicles are facing serious security threats. Aiming at the intelligent attack behavior faced by unmanned vehicles in the scenario of path planning, this paper proposes an attack behavior portrait scheme based on the knowledge graph. The experimental results show that the scheme proposed in this paper can effectively extract the attack steps and form a portrait of the attack behaviors.

However, considering the accuracy of the TICC algorithm, the number of documents used in this paper for TICC clustering is 15. In the future, we will consider methods of mining attack behavior steps from more data. In addition, the scenario in this article is the intelligent attack behaviors for unmanned vehicle path planning. This article's attack behavior portrait method can be extended to other scenarios, such as network attack scenarios [15].

Acknowledgments. This work was supported by the National Natural Science Foundation of China (no. 61876019).

References

1. Ny, J.L.: Performance optimization for unmanned vehicle systems. Massachusetts Institute of Technology (2009)
2. Wang, X., Kuang, X., Li, J., Chen, X., Liu, Z.: Oblivious transfer for privacy-preserving in VANET's feature matching. IEEE Trans. Intell. Transp. Syst. (2020). https://doi.org/10.1109/TITS.2020.2973738
3. Yao, Y., Li, H., Zheng, H., et al.: Regula sub-rosa: latent backdoor attacks on deep neural networks (2019)

4. Guikema, S.D., Aven, T.: Assessing risk from intelligent attacks: a perspective on approaches. Reliab. Eng. System Safety, **95**(5), pp. 478–483 (2010). ISSN 0951-8320
5. Wang, C., Wang, D., Tu, Y., Xu, G., Wang, H.: Understanding node capture attacks in user authentication schemes for wireless sensor networks. In: IEEE Transactions on Dependable and Secure Computing (2020). https://doi.org/10.1109/TDSC.2020.2974220.
6. Rule reduction after knowledge graph mining for cyber situational awareness analysis. Proc. Comput. Sci. **176**, 22–30 (2020)
7. Yuan, Y., Adhatarao, S.S., Li, M., Yuan, Y., Liu, Z., Fu, X.: ADA: Adaptive Deep Log Anomaly Detector. INFOCOM (2020)
8. Dittrich, M.A., Fohlmeister, S.: Cooperative multi-agent system for production control using reinforcement learning. CIRP Ann. Manuf. Technol., **69**(1) (2020)
9. Zamora, I., Lopez, N.G., Vilches, V.M., et al.: Extending the OpenAI gym for robotics: a toolkit for reinforcement learning using ROS and Gazebo (2016)
10. Wang, L., Islam, T., Tao, L., et al.: An attack graph-based probabilistic security metric. In: Data and Applications Security XXII, 22nd Annual IFIP WG 11.3 Working Conference on Data and Applications Security, London, UK, July 13–16, 2008, Proceedings. DBLP (2008)
11. Tidwell, T., Larson, R., Fitch, K., et al.: Modeling internet attacks (2001)
12. Kiran, B.R., et al.: Deep reinforcement learning for autonomous driving: a survey. In: IEEE Transactions on Intelligent Transportation Systems (2021)
13. Chi, C., Ji, K., Song, P., et al.: Cooperatively improving data center energy efficiency based on multi-agent deep reinforcement learning. Energies **14**(8), 2071 (2021)
14. Hallac, D., Vare, S., Boyd, S., et al.: Toeplitz inverse covariance-based clustering of multivariate time series data. In: The 23rd ACM SIGKDD International Conference. ACM (2017)
15. Guo, C., Huang, D., Zhang, J., Jing, X., Bai, G., Dong, N.: Early prediction for mode anomaly in generative adversarial network training: an empirical study. Inf. Sci. **534**, 117–138 (2020)

Anti Intelligent Mine Unmanned Ground Vehicle Based on Reinforcement Learning

Xiaoyao Tong[1], Yuxi Ma[1], Yuan Xue[2(✉)], Quanxin Zhang[1], Yuanzhang Li[1],
and Yu-an Tan[3]

[1] School of Computer Science and Technology, Beijing Institute of Technology, Beijing
100081, China
{3120191048,3120185490,zhangqx,popular}@bit.edu.cn
[2] Academy of Military Science, Beijing 100091, China
[3] School of Cyberspace Science and Technology, Beijing Institute of Technology, Beijing
100081, China
tan2008@bit.edu.cn

Abstract. In recent years, with the rapid development of military technology and
the evolution of battlefield mines, intelligent mines are the important embodiment
of active attack mines. In the future, unmanned vehicles need to chase and capture
intelligent mines, improve the efficiency of mine clearance, and reduce the casualties of soldiers. Therefore, it is necessary to study how to improve the efficiency of
unmanned ground vehicle pursuit. Among them, the game method of pursuit and
evasion between intelligent mines and unmanned ground vehicles based on reinforcement learning in the 2D simulation environment can effectively achieve this
goal. The trained intelligent mines have active attack ability, unmanned ground
vehicles have basic mine clearance ability, and the success rate of intelligent mine
blasting is as high as 90%. In addition, unmanned ground vehicles can also effectively defend against the active attack of intelligent mines, and the defense success
rate is also as high as 90%.

Keywords: Reinforcement learning · Intelligent mine · Unmanned vehicle

1 Introduction

In recent years, with the in-depth study of artificial intelligence technology, military
weapons are gradually developing towards intelligence. The future battlefield will evolve
into an intelligent battlefield [1, 2].

Among them, battlefield mines are evolving rapidly. Compared with the traditional
way of man-made mine clearance, unmanned ground vehicles (UGV) need to chase
and capture intelligent mines reduce the casualties of soldiers [3, 4]. Therefore, it is
necessary to study the technical methods to improve the pursuit efficiency of UGV.

In this paper, through the reinforcement learning method A3C (Asynchronous
Advantage Actor Critical) [5] to train the agent of confrontation game, we design the
cleaning experiment of UGV to intelligent mine in different minefield environment, and

© Springer Nature Singapore Pte Ltd. 2021
Y. Tan et al. (Eds.): DMBD 2021, CCIS 1454, pp. 61–68, 2021.
https://doi.org/10.1007/978-981-16-7502-7_7

summarize that the UGV shows good cleaning ability to intelligent mine after certain confrontation training. The contribution of this article is as follows:

We have trained the UGV action model with mine clearance capability and the intelligent mine model with active attack capability.

The trained UGV model can effectively defend the active attack of intelligent mines. We have improved the efficiency of mine clearance of UGV through phased training.

The rest of this paper is organized as follows: Sect. 2 gives a brief introduction to the related work and background. Section 3 discusses the design process of this method. Section 4 describes implementation details in a specific environment. Section 5 evaluates the performance of the prototype. Section 6 gathers the conclusion and future work.

2   Related Work and Background

2.1   Intelligent Mine

According to the functions, intelligent mines can be divided into four categories: anti-tank mines, anti-helicopter mines, anti-cluster tank and armed helicopter mines and anti-infantry mines [6]. The typical known representatives of these four intelligent mines are XM93 wide area mine, AHM anti helicopter intelligent mine and matrix intelligent mine, as shown in Fig. 1 [7–9].

Fig. 1. Typical intelligent mines.

Various techniques are used for the detection of landmines. There are five main areas of the current technologies [10, 11], including metal detector, electromagnetic methods, acoustic/seismic methods, biological methods, mechanical methods and the latest methods.

2.2   Reinforcement Learning on UGVs

The key to true UGV (that is, driving safely in any required environment) is to pay more attention to the self-learning ability of its software [12]. In other words, the problem of AI is the first problem of artificial intelligence, which requires a very specific machine learning development skill. Reinforcement learning is an important branch of machine learning and a product of interdisciplinary and multi-field [13].

Reinforcement learning has a wide range of applications: such as helicopter aerobatics [14], classic games [15], investment management [16] and so on.

3 Design

In this section, we will introduce the important part of the algorithm: nonzero-sum reward architecture and phased training.

3.1 Reward Structure

We propose different reward structures for UGV and intelligent mine. And, in order to improve the training efficiency, phased training is carried out based on this structure.

Reward for UGV: UGV's reward mainly comes from 3 parts: mines elimination, cleaning time and armor degree. It can be expressed as:

$$R_1 = \begin{cases} m_1 + 0.2 * m_2 - c_1 + r(t) \\ m_1 + 5 * m_I - D(a) \end{cases} \tag{1.1}$$

$$r(t) = \begin{cases} 0 & t \le 2 * size^2 \\ -0.2 * (t - 2 * size^2) & t > 2 * size^2 \end{cases} \tag{1.2}$$

$$D(a) = \begin{cases} 0 & a >= 60 \\ (60 - a) * 0.5 & a < 60 \end{cases} \tag{1.3}$$

m_1 is the number of ordinary mines defused by UGV, m_2 is the number of grids to explore the new map, c_1 is the number of times the obstacle was hit by UGV. m_I indicates the intelligent mine status, 0 means it is still in the minefield, and 1 means it has been cleared by UGV. The reward for the successful removal of intelligent mines by UGV is five times that of ordinary mines. This is to give priority to the removal of intelligent mines when UGV encounter mobile intelligent mines. The formula $r(t)$ represents the penalty value of UGV when the time step of mine clearance is too long, where t is the time steps and $size$ is the size of map. The formula $D(a)$ represents the penalty value of UGV when the armor of the UGV decreases due to attack.

Reward for Intelligent Mine: in this paper, the reward of the guidance strategy mainly comes from: the effective damage value caused to the UGV, and the survival time of the intelligent mine. It can be expressed as formula 4:

$$R_2 = -5m_I - c_2 + 5b \tag{1.4}$$

Where c_2 is the number of times the obstacle was hit by intelligent mine and b indicates the number of successful attacks. High rewards induce intelligent mines to show active attack ability.

3.2 Training Process

Training is divided into two parts, the corresponding reward function is 1.1. According to the environmental requirements, the UGV traverses the map to clear ordinary mines and pursues and clears intelligent mines, which belongs to a complex environment.

Training agents in complex environment needs to face a classic problem, which is sparse reward training problem, that is, the amount of training required is very large. Therefore, we need to train an agent with the ability of basic map traversal and ordinary mine cleaning through the reward function in the first part, and then train the UGV that we need to be able to clean intelligent mines on this basis.

4   Implementation

This section discusses the implementation of this scheme. Firstly, we introduce the environment of the experiment; Secondly, the network architecture used in training is introduced.

4.1   Environments

In the 10 * 10 2D map shown in Fig. 2, 1 represents obstacles, 2 represents ordinary mines, 3 represents the UGV and 4 represents intelligent mines. By randomly generating different numbers of ordinary mines or obstacles, the ability of UGV to avoid obstacles or clear mines is trained.

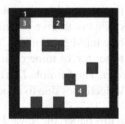

Fig. 2. The visual 2D environment of minefield.

Ordinary mines can't move and they will be blasted by UGV or overlapped with UGV. In addition, they can achieve the purpose of active blasting through remote control of intelligent mine. Intelligent mine has the ability of moving, recognizing and remote controlling ordinary mines. It can move in the minefield without causing passive blasting of ordinary mine and remote control ordinary mine for active blasting.

The UGV has the ability to detect and explode ordinary and intelligent mines, which is limited by a certain armor degree (a = 100). When the armor degree of the UGV is reduced to below 0, it will be scrapped and cannot be used.

The field of vision of UGV and intelligent mine is a 5 * 5 matrix centered on itself. Each time step moves forward in the two-dimensional minesweeping field according to the selected direction (up, down, left and right).

4.2 Network Architecture

For UGV and intelligent mine, we use end-to-end Conv-LSTM network [17]. Differently, we use phased training to divide the UGV training in two stages. The difference of input and output between them is shown in Fig. 3.

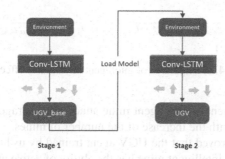

Fig. 3. The model of UGV with phased training.

5 Test Evaluation

In this section, we evaluate the effectiveness and performance overhead of the prototype. The experimental environment used in this paper is based on the GeForce RTX 3090 training under Ubuntu 20.04. The training rounds of the UGV agent in stage 1 and stage 2 are 100k and 300K respectively, and the training rounds of intelligent mine are 200K. In particular, the worker thread is set to 4. The trained models were used to test, and the following experimental results were obtained from the average value of 100 groups of data.

5.1 Intelligent Mine Attack Experiment

Through the training of stage 1, we can get an UGV agent with the ability of cleaning ordinary mines. At this time, there is no intelligent mine in the environment, so the agent does not have the ability to defend against intelligent mine attack. Put the pretrained intelligent mine into the environment to attack the UGV. The attack result is shown in Fig. 4.

Figure 4-1 shows the average minesweeping steps of UGVs trained in stage 1 under different mine number distribution. It can be seen from the figure that with the increase of the number of mines, the average step size increases. The average step size of the UGV agent attacked by the intelligent mine is obviously larger than that of the UGV without intelligent mine because it needs to chase and discharge intelligent mines.

Figure 4-2 shows the change of average armor degree of UGVs trained in stage 1 under different mine number distribution. In the environment without intelligent mines, the UGV agent will not be attacked, and the armor degree is always at the initial value

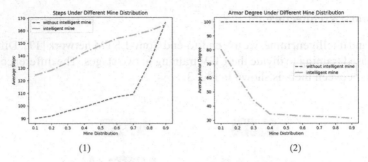

(1)   (2)

Fig. 4. Comparison of intelligent mine attack effect.

of 100. In the environment of intelligent mine attack, the average armor degree of the UGV agent decreases with the increase of the number of mines.

Experiments have proved that the UGV agent trained by us has the basic ability of mine clearance, and the intelligent mine has the ability of active attack.

5.2 UGV Defense Experiment

After the training in stage 2, the UGV agent has the ability to defend against intelligent mine attacks. Its defense results and defense success rate are shown in Fig. 5.

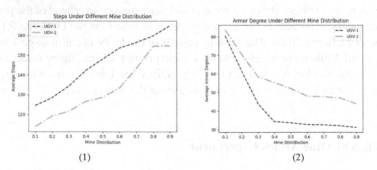

(1)   (2)

Fig. 5. Contrast effect of UGV defending intelligent mine.

Figure 5-1 shows the change of the average step size of the UGV-1 trained in stage 1 and the UGV-2 trained in stage 2 under different mine number distributions. It can be seen from the figure that the average time step of UGV-2 is obviously less than that of UGV-1, which indicates that the UGV trained in stage 2 has better action strategy when it pursues the moving intelligent mine, so it can complete the purpose of clearing the minefield in a shorter time step.

Figure 5-2 shows the change of average armor degree of UGV-1 trained in stage 1 and UGV-2 trained in stage 2 under different mine number distribution. It can be seen from the figure that the average armor degree of UGV-2 is significantly greater than that of UGV-1. Therefore, it can be concluded that the UGV trained in stage 2 has a certain degree of defense ability.

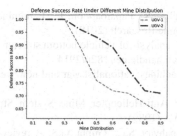

Fig. 6. The success rate of UGV defense.

Figure 6 shows the change of defense success rate of UGV-1 trained in stage 1 and UGV-2 trained in stage 2 under different mine number distribution. If the armor degree is greater than 0, the defense is successful. It can be seen from the figure that the defense success rate of UGV-2 is significantly higher than that of UGV-1. Our experiments show that the defense ability of unmanned vehicles trained in stage 2 is improved compared with UGV-1. And when half of the number in the map are ordinary mines, it can also maintain a success rate of more than 90%.

6 Conclusion and Future Work

In this paper, we propose a confrontation model of UGV and intelligent mine based on A3C. Our simulation results show that based on our nonzero-sum reward structure the intelligent mine has the ability of active attack and escape, and the UGV has the ability of defense and minefield cleaning. In addition, we use the phased training method to improve the training efficiency of UGV in complex environment.

In the future work, we hope to study the simulation experiment in 3D to realize the real minefield environment, so as to adjust the reward structure of the agent to meet the needs of the real scene.

Acknowledgments. This work was supported by the National Natural Science Foundation of China (no. U1936218).

References

1. Kott, A., Stump, E.: Intelligent autonomous things on the battlefield (2019). https://doi.org/10.1016/B978-0-12-817636-8.00003-X
2. Wenhua, W.A.N.G., Xin, H.A.O., Yan, L.I.U., Yang, W.A.N.G.: The safety evaluation and defense reinforcement of the ai system. Netinfo Secur. **20**(9), 87–91 (2020)
3. Robledo, L., Carrasco, M., Mery, D.: A survey of land mine detection technology. Int. J. Remote Sens. **30**(9), 2399–2410 (2009)
4. Bertram, V.: Unmanned surface vehicles-a survey. Skibsteknisk Selskab, Copenhagen, Denmark **1**, 1–14 (2008). https://doi.org/10.1109/OCEANS.2008.5289429
5. Wasson, S.R., Harmon, R.S., Broach, J.T., et al.: An unmanned ground vehicle for landmine remediation. Int. Soc. Optics Photonics **5415**, 1231 (2004). https://doi.org/10.1117/12.541341

6. Chiovelli, G,, Michalopoulos, S., Papaioannou, E.: Landmines and Spatial Development. National Bureau of Economic Research (2018)
7. Showichen, A.: Numerical analysis of vehicle bottom structures subjected to anti-tank mine explosions (2008). http://hdl.handle.net/1826/2914
8. Yoo, J.: Embracing the machines: rationalist war and new weapons technologies. Calif. L. Rev. **105**, 443 (2017)
9. Tillery, G.C., Buc, S.M.: Anti-Helicopter Mine System Studies and Analyses. System Planning Corp Arlington VA (1989)
10. Gooneratne, C.P., Mukhopahyay, S.C., Gupta, G.S: A review of sensing technologies for landmine detection: Unmanned vehicle based approach. In: 2nd International Conference on Autonomous Robots and Agents, 401–407 (2004)
11. Zhang, L., Huang, J., Zhang, T., Wang, S.: Portrait intelligent analysis application and algorithm optimization in video investigation. Netinfo Secur. **20**(5), 88–93 (2020)
12. Kendall, A., Hawke, J., Janz, D., et al.: Learning to drive in a day. In: 2019 International Conference on Robotics and Automation (ICRA), pp. 8248–8254. IEEE (2019)
13. François-Lavet, V., Henderson, P., Islam, R., et al.: An introduction to deep reinforcement learning. arXiv preprint arXiv:1811.12560 (2018)
14. Clarke, S.G., Hwang, I.: Deep reinforcement learning control for aerobatic maneuvering of agile fixed-wing aircraft. In: AIAA Scitech 2020 Forum: 0136 (2020)
15. Shao, K., Tang, Z., Zhu, Y., et al.: A survey of deep reinforcement learning in video games. arXiv preprint arXiv:1912.10944 (2019)
16. Jiang, Z., Liang, J.: Cryptocurrency portfolio management with deep reinforcement learning. In: 2017 Intelligent Systems Conference (IntelliSys), pp. 905–913. IEEE (2017). https://doi.org/10.1109/IntelliSys.2017.8324237
17. Zhong, F., Sun, P., Luo, W., Yan, T., Wang, Y.: AD-VAT+: an asymmetric dueling mechanism for learning and understanding visual active tracking. IEEE Trans. Pattern Anal. Mach. Intell. **43**(5), 1467–1482 (2021). https://doi.org/10.1109/TPAMI.2019.2952590

A Surface Fitting Image Super-Resolution Algorithm Based on Triangle Mesh Partition

Hong Xu[1,2]([envelope]), Caizeng Ye[2], Na Feng[1], and Caiming Zhang[1]

[1] School of Software, Shandong University, Jinan 250101, China
[2] Shandong Institute of Commerce and Technology School, Jinan 250103, China

Abstract. High-frequency information such as image edges and textures have an important influence on the visual effect of the super-resolution images. Therefore, it is vital to maintain the edge and texture features of the super-resolution image. A surface fitting image super-resolution algorithm based on triangle mesh partitions is proposed in this study. Different from the traditional image interpolation algorithm using quadrilateral mesh, this method reconstructs the fitting surface on the triangle mesh to approximate the original scene surface. LBP algorithm and second-order difference quotient are combined to divide the triangular mesh accurately, and the edge angle is utilized as a constraint to makes the edge of the constructed surface patch more informative. By the area coordinates as weighting coefficients to perform weighted averaging on the surface patches at the vertices of the triangle mesh, the cubic polynomial surface patches are obtained on the triangle mesh. Finally, a global structure sparse regularization strategy is adopted to optimize the initially super-resolution image and further eliminate the artifacts at the image edges and textures. Since the new method proposed in this study utilizes numerous information about local feature (e.g. edges), compared to other state-of-the-art methods, it provides clear edges and textures, and improves the image quality greatly.

Keywords: Surface fitting · Triangle mesh · Global structure · Sparse regularization

1 Introduction

Image super-resolution is a technology about how to get information-rich high-resolution (HR) images from low-resolution (LR) images through magnification and reconstruction, and the purpose is to improving the resolution of the image and restoring the details of the image. Image super-resolution plays an important role in scientific research fields including computer graphics, artificial intelligence, and computer vision. Based on different reconstruction methods, image super-resolution algorithms can be classified into two categories: interpolation-based algorithms and learning-based algorithms. This paper mainly studies the method based on interpolation.

Interpolation-based algorithms [1–4] are the process of constructing curves or curved surfaces [5–7] of LR images in a certain area through a specific function and predicting

© Springer Nature Singapore Pte Ltd. 2021
Y. Tan et al. (Eds.): DMBD 2021, CCIS 1454, pp. 69–79, 2021.
https://doi.org/10.1007/978-981-16-7502-7_8

the HR images. Previous classical algorithms based on interpolation are nearest neighbor algorithm, bilinear interpolation [8, 9], and bicubic interpolation [10–12]. Although the interpolation functions used by these three methods are relatively simple, the HR images obtained by interpolation are severely distorted and have obvious aliasing and ringing effects. Zhang et al. proposed an interpolation method for soft decision estimation [13]. Compared to the traditional methods for decision estimation of each pixel, this method estimated missing high-resolution pixels in units of image patches. Besides, the model parameters can be adaptively adjusted according to the pixels of the LR image that is provided as inputs in the interface. Therefore, this method is simple, efficient, and adaptable. Although the method has improved the objective quantification of data, the subjective visual effect has not been significantly improved. The study conducted by Takuro et al. (2017) proposed a single image super-resolution algorithm based on multiple filtering and weighted average [14]. The algorithm utilized local functions to reduce blur and introduced new weight to improve the reliability of local functions. Besides, this method adopted convolution of small filters to replace the calculation of each local function, which can reduce the calculation cost. High-quality, non-aliased, and blur-free output images can be obtained by using this method in a short calculation time. In 2018, Yang et al. proposed a method of fractional gradient interpolation [15]. By selecting an appropriate fractional gradient operator, not only the high-frequency components of the signal are protected, but also the low-frequency components of the signal are retained nonlinearly. The algorithm can effectively process the pixels with similar gray values in the smooth area. The enlarged image effectively preserved the texture details, highlighted the edges, and avoided the ringing and step effects. Liu et al. proposed an image enlargement method based on cubic fitting surfaces with local features as constraint [16]. For the input image and the error image, the quadratic polynomial surface patches are constructed in regions of different sizes, and the enlarged image has a better visual effect. But for complex edge regions, the enlarged image obtained by this method is relatively smooth. Literature [17] enlarged a given LR input image to a HR image while retaining texture and structure information. This algorithm has achieved high numerical accuracy, but there are high-frequency information missing or artifacts at complex edges and texture details. In 2020, Zhang et al. proposed a more advanced image super-resolution method [18]. Creative and innovative results have been achieved on LR images that are down-sampled by interlacing and inter-column, but the magnification effect is poor for other down-sampled LR images.

This paper proposes a surface fitting image super-resolution algorithm based on triangle mesh partition, mainly focuses on the edges of the quadrilateral meshes inclined at 45° and 135°. The innovations are as follows:

1. This paper puts forward a strategy for triangle mesh partition that consists of the neighboring pixels. By the combination of LBP algorithm and simple second-order difference quotient, the strong edges and texture details of image are effectively extracted.
2. An edge angle is proposed to constraint the process of solving the coefficients of the quadratic polynomial surface.

3. The initially reconstructed HR images is optimized by the global structure sparse regularization strategy. The artifacts in edge and texture of the image are eliminated during the iterations, improving the visual effect.

The rest of this paper is as follows. Section 2 is the overall description of the method. Section 3 compares the experimental results of different methods. Section 4 is the summary of the method and the next step of this work.

2 Methodology

For a low-resolution image, the first step is to detected edge and texture image by using the combination of the LBP algorithm and the second-order difference quotient method (SODQ). The triangle meshes that consists of the neighboring pixels are obtained, taking the edge and texture image as the guide. The algorithm constructs a cubic polynomial triangle surface patch on each triangle mesh, and stitches these surface patches together to approximate the original surface. Then, it resamples on the fitting surface to obtain the preliminary reconstructed HR image Y. Since there are unavoidable errors of the fitting surface, and the edges and textures of HR image Y are unsatisfactory, the next step is to optimize image Y. The image Y is decomposed into a smooth component $f_1 \otimes Y_1$, where Y_1 is a low-frequency feature map of the image, and a sparse residual Y_r representing the global structure of this image. This operation ensures that the smooth component contains low frequencies. The low-frequency feature map Y_1 are enforced to be smooth (i.e., to have a weak response to an edge-filter) by a gradient operator along horizontal or vertical direction. The polished Y_1 is superimposed with Y_r and then an optimized image is obtained. By repeating this process, the final enlarged image H can be obtained. The flowchart of the proposed method is shown in Fig. 1.

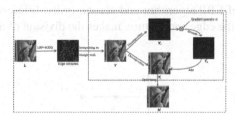

Fig. 1. Flowchart of the proposed method.

2.1 Divide Triangle Mesh

Since the edge of the image will have a great influence on the visual effects of the enlarged images, dividing the mesh according to the edge situation can depict the edge of the image better when reconstructing the image. Since we only need to consider the edges in the 45° and 135° directions, the paper firstly extracts strong edges according to the *LBP* algorithm and determines the mesh division scheme according to the element jump rule at the diagonal. The details are as follows:

The binary number is the LBP value of the central pixel, reflecting the information in the neighborhood. The algorithm only processes the uniform patterns among them. Uniform mode refers to the mode in which the repeated binary digits corresponding to *LBP* can, at most, transform twice between 0 and 1. Therefore, a rule can be obtained, namely when the number of transformations equals 2 and such transformations occur at diagonal positions, the edge inclined at this position equals to 45° or 135°. According to this rule, precise division of strong edge meshes in the directions of 45° and 135° can be obtained. The principle is simple while the edge accuracy is high.

Then, for the remaining undivided area, a rough mesh is divided according to the simple second-order difference in the diagonal direction. According to the nature of the image, the changing rate of the pixel values in the image along the edge is relatively small. Therefore, for the remaining undivided areas (usually texture and flat areas), we can calculate the simple second-order difference quotient of the image in the directions of 45° and 135°, namely the rate of change. According to the rate of change in the two directions, the quadrilateral mesh can be generated by using the adjacency relationship of the pixels, and then a rough triangular mesh division scheme can be obtained.

The rate of change at the point $P_{i,j}$ is shown in Fig. 2. Where the red dotted line indicates the change along the 45° direction, and the blue dotted line indicates the change along the 135° direction. The simple second-order difference quotient in the 45° and 135° directions can be defined as follows:

$$g_{45}(i,j) = P_{i+1,j+1} - 2P_{i,j} + P_{i-1,j-1}$$
$$g_{135}(i,j) = P_{i-1,j+1} - 2P_{i,j} + P_{i+1,j-1} \tag{1}$$

If $g_{45} < g_{135}$, it means that the rate of change of the image in the 45° direction is small, and then the quadrilateral grid is divided into two triangular meshes along the red dotted line to obtain a 45° division scheme. Otherwise, the division occurs along the blue dotted line to get the 135° division scheme.

The combination of LBP algorithm and second-order difference quotient methods can effectively extract the edge and texture, makes the division of triangle meshes more accurate and efficient.

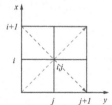

Fig. 2. Coarse division.

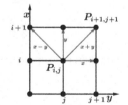

Fig. 3. 3 × 3 Image patch.

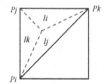

Fig. 4. Area coordinate weighted average.

2.2 Construct Fitting Surface

This paper firstly constructs a quadratic polynomial surface patch centered on each pixel. Then, the weighted average area coordinate is used to obtain the cubic polynomial surface patch on the triangular mesh, so as to approximate the original surface.

2.2.1 Construct a Quadratic Polynomial Surface Patch at a Pixel

Pixel can be regarded as the discrete data sampled from the surface.

$$P_{i,j} = \int_{j-0.5}^{j+0.5} \int_{i-0.5}^{i+0.5} g_{i,j}(x, y) dx dy \tag{2}$$

The 3×3 image patch (shown in Fig. 3) is constructed using a double quadratic polynomial $g_{i,j}$, that is, $g_{i,j}$ defined in the xy area of the plane $[i-1.5, i+1.5] \times [j-1.5, j+1.5]$. We construct the following quadratic polynomial fitting surface patch centred at pixel $P_{i,j}$.

$$g_{i,j}(u, v) = a_1 u^2 + a_2 uv + a_3 v^2 + a_4 u + a_5 v + a_6 \tag{3}$$

in which, $u = x - i, v = y - j, a_1, a_2, \cdots, a_6$ are unknown patch coefficients of $g_{i,j}$.

Figure 5(a)–(f) are the interpolated images obtained when only the corresponding coefficients $a_i (i = 1, 2, \cdots, 6)$ are retained and the other coefficients are 0, and (g) is the original image. Cleaned up for presentation purposes, the gray values of Fig. 5(a)–(e) are magnified 5 times. The results in Fig. 5(a)–(e) imply that coefficients $a_i (i = 1, 2, \ldots, 5)$ provide more image details. Image edge information is mainly provided by Fig. 5(d), (e), and (f), while Fig. 5(a), (b), and (c) provide limited information.

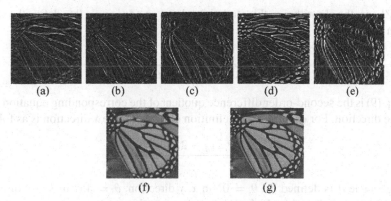

(a)   (b)   (c)   (d)   (e)

(f)   (g)

Fig. 5. The result of magnifying the image using only individual coefficients $a_i (i = 1, 2, \cdots, 6)$.

The above-mentioned information shows that different coefficients have different effects on the edges and texture of the image. As $i(i = 1, 2, \cdots, 6)$ continuously increasing, more low-frequency information and less high-frequency information can be obtained. In the solution process, the low-frequency information of the image needs to be determined first. Therefore, the algorithm firstly considers how to accurately solve the coefficients of the constant term a_6, and then solve the remaining coefficients. Here, the method proposed by Zhang [24] is used to solve the polynomial coefficients.

From Eqs. (2) and (3), we can get:

$$P_{i+m,j+n} = a_1 m^2 + a_2 mn + a_3 n^2 + a_4 m + a_5 n + a_6 + \frac{a_1 + a_3}{12}, \quad m, n = -1, 0, 1 \tag{4}$$

Equation (5) can be inferred from Eq. (6):

$$a_6 = P_{i,j} - \frac{1}{12}a_1 - \frac{1}{12}a_3 \tag{5}$$

As shown in Fig. 5, the first-order deviations along the four directions at the points are:

$$
\begin{aligned}
x &: \lambda_1 = (P_{i+1,j} - P_{i-1,j})/2 \\
y &: \lambda_2 = (P_{i,j+1} - P_{i,j-1})/2 \\
x+y &: \lambda_3 = (P_{i+1,j+1} - P_{i-1,j-1})/2 \\
x-y &: \lambda_4 = (P_{i+1,j-1} - P_{i-1,j+1})/2
\end{aligned} \tag{6}
$$

From Eqs. (4) and (6), we can get:

$$a_4 = \lambda_1, a_5 = \lambda_2, a_4 + a_5 = \lambda_3, a_4 - a_5 = \lambda_4$$

The unknown coefficients a_4 and a_5 can be obtained by constrained least squares using Eq. (7):

$$CLS(a_4, a_5) = \omega_1(a_4 - \lambda_1)^2 + \omega_2(a_5 - \lambda_2)^2 + \omega_3(a_4 + a_5 - \lambda_3)^2 + \omega_4(a_4 - a_5 - \lambda_4)^2 \tag{7}$$

Unlike Zhang, the algorithm in this study introduces an edge angle θ to define the weight function ω_i:

$$\omega_i = \frac{1}{1 + \mu_i^2|\cos\theta|} \tag{8}$$

μ_i in Eq. (9) is the second-order difference quotient of the corresponding equation along the same direction. For example, the definition of μ_i along the x direction is as follows:

$$x : \mu_1 = \frac{P_{i+1,j} - 2P_{i,j} + P_{i-1,j}}{2} \tag{9}$$

The edge angle θ is defined as: $\theta = 0°$ in x, y direction, $\theta = 45°$ in $x + y$ direction, $\theta = 135°$ in $x - y$ direction. If there is a linear function $g_{i,j}(x, y)$ along the $45°$ edge direction, the determination of the weight function should make the λ_3 on the $x + y$ direction play a major role on the determination of $a_4 + a_5$ on this direction. That being said, the weighted value ω_3 in Eq. (8) should be a larger value. The edge angle makes the weight bigger, and it plays a greater role in determining the direction coefficient, which is consistent with the edge characteristics of the surface and effectively improves the accuracy of the surface.

In order to obtain the remaining unknown coefficients a_1, a_2, and a_3, the corresponding conditions can be obtained by using the 8 pixel points around the point $P_{i,j}$ into Eq. (10).

$$P_{i+m,j+n} = a_1 m^2 + a_2 mn + a_3 n^2 + a_4 m + a_5 n + P_{i,j}, \quad m, n = -1, 0, 1, \ m \neq n = 0 \tag{10}$$

in which, $m, n = -1, 0, 1$ and $m \neq n = 0$.

Similarly, the least-square method with constraints is used to obtain the unknown coefficients a_1, a_2, a_3. The minimum objective function is as follows:

$$CLS(a_1, a_2, a_3) = \sum_{\substack{m,n=-1,0,1 \\ m \neq n=0}} \omega_{m,n}(a_1 m^2 + a_2 mn + a_3 n^2 + a_4 m + a_5 n + P_{i,j} - P_{i+m, j+n})^2 \quad (11)$$

The weight function ω is determined in the same direction by using Eq. (8) in the same way.

2.2.2 Constructing Cubic Polynomial Surface Patches on Triangular Mesh

As shown in Fig. 4, $f_i(x, y), f_j(x, y), f_k(x, y)$ are quadratic polynomial surface patches constructed by using three vertices P_i, P_j, P_k as the centers, respectively. The triangular surface patch $f_{i,j}(x, y)$ is obtained by weighted average of these three surface patches:

$$f_{i,j}(x, y) = li f_i(x, y) + lj f_j(x, y) + lk f_k(x, y) \quad (12)$$

To simplify the process of surface construction, the definition of area coordinates is introduced. As shown in Fig. 7, the area coordinates $(li, lj, lk) = (li(x_i, y_i), lj(x_j, y_j), lk(x_k, y_k))$ of triangle M are defined as:

$$li = \frac{1}{2S}[y_j x_k - y_k x_j + (x_j - x_k)y + (y_k - y_j)x]$$

$$lj = \frac{1}{2S}[y_k x_i - y_i x_k + (x_k - x_i)y + (y_i - y_k)x] \quad (13)$$

$$lk = \frac{1}{2S}[y_i x_j - y_j x_i + (x_i - x_j)y + (y_j - y_i)x]$$

in which S represents the area of the triangle M. According to the nature of the area coordinates, we can get $li + lj + lk = 1$. The obtained triangular surface pieces $f_{i,j}(x, y)$ are spliced together to obtain a continuous and curved surface $f(x, y)$.

2.3 Global Structure Sparse Regularization Optimization

There are inevitable errors in fitting the curved surfaces with surface patches, and it is unrealistic to process the details of some edges and textures. Therefore, to reduce the reconstructed artifacts of the enlarged image, this paper adopts a global structure sparse regularization strategy to optimize the enlarged image.

The key of the strategy is to decompose the smooth component of the image [28]. Y is the enlarged image after the preliminary reconstruction. Y_l is the low-frequency feature map of the image, and the residual component Y_r that mainly containing the high-frequency information of the image (i.e. edge texture and other details). The global structure of the image can be expressed as:

$$Y = f_l \otimes Y_l + Y_r \quad (14)$$

in which f_l is a 3×3 low-pass filter, $\otimes$ represents the convolution operation.

To construct the regularized function, two prerequisites need to be provided. One is $\|Y_r\|_p$, indicating the residual component is sparse in l_p norm. Given this study considers convexity, the L_1 norm is used. In addition, the low-frequency feature map Y_l needs to be enhanced to smooth the image. This process is expressed as $\|g_d \otimes Y_l\|_2^2$, in which $g_d = [1, 2]$ and $d \in \{1 = level, 2 = vertical\}$ indicates the gradient operator in the horizontal or vertical direction. Based on these two prerequisites, we can get a regularized function as follows:

$$R_g = \|Y_r\|_1 + \varphi \sum_{d=1}^{2} \|g_d \otimes Y_l\|_2^2 \tag{15}$$

Where ϕ controls the smoothness of the low-frequency feature map. The larger the ϕ is, the more image information the residual components contain. At the same time, the image is smoother. As regularization enhances sparsity, the gradient of the reconstructed image is reduced, which can effectively reduce artifacts at edges and textures.

At this time, the image reconstruction can be written as:

$$\arg \min_{(\lambda,\xi)} \|Y - f_l \otimes Y_l - Y_r\|_2^2 + R_g \tag{16}$$

3 Results and Discussion

3.1 Parameter Settings

The downsampled images of all experiments in this paper are obtained by averaged downsampling. The parameters φ in the global structure sparse regularization strategy are set to 1 empirically. The algorithm termination threshold ξ is set as e^{-5}. The maximum number of iterations is set to 4 to balance the time complexity and the obtained image quality. Our experiments show that the time increases as the number of iterations increasing. However, the PSNR value of the algorithm does not increase significantly after 4 iterations. The maximum number of iterations is set to 4 to balance the image quality obtained and the time complexity.

3.2 Analysis of Results

The experiment is divided into two parts. The first part is a comparison experiment of 10 representative images listed in Table 1. The second part is to compare the dataset images, the dataset includes Set5, Set14, BSD100 and Urban 100. This paper compares 8 methods: Bicubic [12], LGS [28], FRI [17], Zhang [27], NLFIP [24], NARM [29], SelfEx [25] and ANR [30].

Figures 6 and 7 show the results of nine representative methods of two images. To facilitate observation, the nearest neighbor interpolation method is used to enlarge the red area with a scale factor of 3 or 4.

Edges and textures are important indicators for evaluating high-resolution image quality. Compared to other methods, the method proposed in this paper can keep edges and texture well. Figures 6 and 7 mainly compare the effectiveness of the methods at the edges. In Fig. 6, Bicubic, Zhang, NLFIP, ANR and NARM at the edges are relatively blurry, and there is obvious aliasing at the stripes of LGS, SelfEx and FRI. In Fig. 7, it can be seen that the proposed method can display the sloping edges clearly. On the contrary, LGS, SelfEx and FRI have obvious aliasing, and Bicubic, Zhang, NLFIP, ANR and NARM have obvious fuzziness.

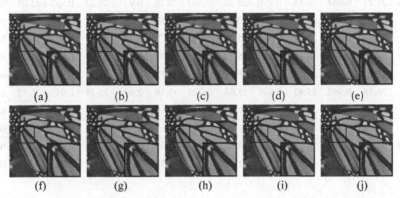

Fig. 6. (a) NARM. (b) ANR. (c) Bicubic. (d) LGS. (e) Zhang. (f) NLFIP. (g) SelfEx. (h) FRI. (i) Ours. (j) GroundTruth.

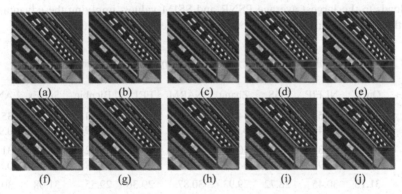

Fig. 7. (a) NARM. (b) ANR. (c) Bicubic. (d) LGS. (e) Zhang. (f) NLFIP. (g) SelfEx. (h) FRI. (i) Ours. (j) GroundTruth.

In this paper, the objective quantitative analysis uses peak signal-to-noise ratio (PSNR) and structural similarity (SSIM) as the indicators to test the image quality. Table 1 lists the PSNR and SSIM values of the images enlarged by 6 methods and the scale factor is 2. The last line shows the average PSNR and SSIM values for each method. The maximum value of the PSNR and SSIM are marked in bold. The higher the PSNR and SSIM values are, the better the image quality is. As shown in Table 1, the PSNR and SSIM values of the method proposed in this paper are the largest except the SSIM value of Baboon. Therefore, compared to the other methods, the method developed in this paper can provide the best image quality.

Table 1. The PSNR and SSIM of six methods

Image	Ours		NLFIP		LGS		Zhang		NARM		SelfEx	
	PSNR	SSIM	PSNR	SSIM	PSNR	SSIM	PSNR	SSIM	PSNR	SSIM	PSNR	SSIM
Bird	**39.25**	**0.978**	39.21	0.976	37.40	0.971	37.97	0.976	38.32	0.977	39.17	0.964
Butterfly	**31.27**	**0.961**	30.16	0.950	28.92	0.940	28.76	0.937	29.23	0.952	31.05	0.954
Woman	**35.07**	**0.966**	34.28	0.963	33.24	0.956	33.19	0.957	34.09	0.960	34.56	0.962
Baboon	**26.14**	0.973	25.28	**0.987**	25.86	0.786	24.78	0.979	23.74	0.899	25.45	0.965
Head	**35.33**	**0.885**	35.19	0.872	35.27	0.878	35.07	0.868	34.38	0.817	35.25	0.883
Barbara	**29.15**	**0.984**	27.74	0.897	28.17	0.891	27.78	0.983	26.33	0.913	28.54	0.982
Lena	**36.55**	**0.991**	35.92	0.899	35.64	0.925	35.38	0.899	35.35	0.915	36.52	0.990
Comic	**28.55**	**0.921**	27.44	0.902	27.44	0.897	26.69	0.875	26.58	0.886	28.33	0.915
Zebra	**33.12**	**0.988**	32.33	0.985	31.70	0.920	31.67	0.984	31.93	0.972	33.07	0.968
Monarch	**36.28**	**0.997**	35.27	0.996	34.30	0.968	34.09	0.995	35.40	0.992	36.08	0.994
Average	**33.07**	**0.964**	32.28	0.943	31.79	0.913	31.54	0.945	30.95	0.922	32.80	0.957

This paper tested the images from several datasets, including Set5, Set14, BSD100, and Urban100, which are all classic datasets commonly used in image super-resolution algorithms. According to the results shown in Table 2, the method proposed in this paper leads to the largest average PSNR and SSIM values, implying the advantage of the method proposed in this paper compared to other previous methods.

Table 2. Results of nine methods on different data sets

DataSet	Ours	NLFIP	LGS	Zhang	NARM	FRI	Bicubic	SelfEx	ANR
Set5	**35.73**	35.51	34.68	34.50	34.55	33.87	33.64	35.45	35.26
	0.957	0.945	0.937	0.948	0.938	0.934	0.929	0.941	0.943
Set14	**31.84**	31.37	29.02	30.02	30.66	30.15	30.22	31.25	31.22
	0.956	0.893	0.864	0.928	0.924	0.912	0.868	0.885	0.884
BSD 100	**31.15**	30.45	28.72	29.93	30.87	29.36	29.55	31.08	30.98
	0.892	0.871	0.841	0.855	0.876	0.851	0.843	0.886	0.879
Urban 100	**29.08**	28.43	26.52	27.22	28.51	25.93	26.56	28.89	28.68
	0.940	0.888	0.859	0.911	0.903	0.795	0.837	0.917	0.908

4 Conclusions

The paper proposes a surface fitting image super-resolution algorithm based on triangle mesh partition. This method not only effectively improves the quality of the enlarged image edges and textures but also provides a better visual effect. By applying global structure sparse regularization strategy on iterative optimization, the time complexity of the algorithm is increased. Therefore, how to further improve the image quality and effectively shorten the time are the focus of the next step.

References

1. Zhang, F., Zhang, X., Qin, X.Y., et al.: Enlarging image by constrained least square approach with shape preserving. J. Comput. Sci. Technol. **30**(3), 489–498 (2015)
2. Ding, N., Liu, Y.P., Fan, L.W., et al.: Single image super-resolution via dynamic lightweight database with local-feature based interpolation. J. Comput. Sci. Technol. **34**(3), 537–549 (2019)
3. Li, X.M., Zhang, C.M., Yue, Y.Z., et al.: Cubic surface fitting to image by combination. Sci. China Inf. Sci. **53**(7), 1287–1295 (2010)
4. Maeland, E.: On the comparison of interpolation methods. IEEE Trans. Med. Imag. **7**(3), 213–217 (1988)
5. Parker, J.A., Kenyon, R.V., Troxel, D.E.: Comparison of interpolating methods for image resampling. IEEE Trans. Med. Imag. **2**(1), 31–39 (1983)
6. Hou, H., Andrews, H.: Cubic splines for image interpolation and digital filtering. IEEE Trans. Acoust. Speech Signal Process. **26**(6), 508–517 (1978)
7. Meijering, E.H.W., Niessen, W.J., Viergever, M.A.: Piecewise polynomial kernels for image interpolation: a generalization of cubic convolution. In: Proceedings 1999 International Conference on Image Processing, vol. 3, pp. 647–651 (1999)
8. Keys, R.: Cubic convolution interpolation for digital image processing. IEEE Trans. Acoust. Speech Signal Process. **29**(6), 1153–1160 (1981)
9. Zhang, X., Wu, X.: Image interpolation by adaptive 2-D autoregressive modeling and soft-decision estimation. IEEE Trans. Image Process. **17**(6), 887–896 (2008)
10. Yamaguchi, T., Ikehara, M.: Fast and high quality image interpolation for single-frame using multi-filtering and weighted mean. IEICE Trans. Fundament. Electr. Commun. Comput. Sci. **100**(5), 1119–1126 (2017)
11. Yang, Q., Zhang, Y., Zhao, T., et al.: Single image super-resolution using self-optimizing mask via fractional-order gradient interpolation and reconstruction. ISA Trans. **82**, 163–171 (2018)
12. Liu, Y., Li, X., Zhang, X., et al.: Image enlargement method based on cubic surfaces with local features as constraints. Signal Process. **166**, 107266 (2020)
13. Zhang, Y., Fan, Q., Bao, F., Liu, Y., Zhang, C.: Single-image super-resolution based on rational fractal interpolation. IEEE Trans. Image Process. **27**(8), 3782–3797 (2018)
14. Zhang, Y., Wang, P., Bao, F., et al.: A single-image super-resolution method based on progressive-iterative approximation. IEEE Trans. Multim. **22**(6), 1407–1422 (2020)
15. Zhang, X., Liu, Q., Li, X., Zhou, Y., Zhang, C.: Non-local feature back-projection for image super-resolution. IET Image Process. **10**(5), 398–408 (2016)
16. Huang, J., Singh, A., Ahuja, N., et al.: Single image super-resolution from transformed self-exemplars. Comput. Vis. Pattern Recogn. 5197–5206 (2015)
17. Zhang, C.M., et al.: Cubic surface fitting to image with edges as constraints. In: 2013 IEEE International Conference on Image Processing, pp. 1046–1050. IEEE (2013)
18. Zhang, M., Desrosiers, C.: High-quality image restoration using low-rank patch regularization and global structure sparsity. IEEE Trans. Image Process. **28**(2), 868–879 (2018)
19. Dong, W., Zhang, L., Lukac, R., Shi, G.: Sparse representation based image interpolation with nonlocal autoregressive modeling. IEEE Trans. Image Process. **22**(4), 1382–1394 (2013)
20. Timofte, R., De Smet, V., Van Gool, L.: Anchored neighborhood regression for fast example-based super-resolution. In: IEEE International Conference on Computer Vision, pp. 1920–1927 (2013)

Image Definition Evaluation Function Based on Improved Maximum Local Variation and Focusing Window Selection

Shiyun Li[1,3], Jian Chen[1,3], Jiaze Wan[1,3], Zuoyong Li[2,3(✉)], and Li Lin[1,3(✉)]

[1] School of Electronic, Electrical Engineering and Physics, Fujian University of Technology, Xueyuan Road, Fuzhou 350118, Fujian, People's Republic of China
linli@fjut.edu.cn
[2] College of Computer and Control Engineering, Minjiang University, No. 200, Xiyuangong Road, Fuzhou 350121, Fujian, People's Republic of China
[3] Fujian Provincial Key Laboratory of Information Processing and Intelligent Control, Minjiang University, Fuzhou 350121, People's Republic of China

Abstract. Aiming at the problem that commonly used image definition evaluation functions in the focusing process are sensitive to noise, we propose a new image definition evaluation function based on improved maximum local variation and focusing window selection. Firstly, the focusing window is selected by gradient accumulation of a 4-directional Scharr operator in order to reduce the calculation complexity and improve the accuracy of evaluation results. Secondly, an improved 3-neighbors method based on the maximum local variation is proposed to decrease the change in scores for noisy images. Finally, the standard deviation of the improved maximum local variation distribution is used as the measure of clarity. The experimental results show that compared with the method using maximum local variation, the proposed method has better unbiasedness and sensitivity. Compared with the commonly used evaluation functions, the proposed method has better noise immunity and high sensitivity. Compare with other no-reference image quality assessment algorithms, it has better monotonicity, unimodality, unbiasedness, sensitivity and real-time performance as well. The proposed method is suitable for the fine focusing stage with high real-time performance.

Keywords: Autofocus · Maximum local variation · Definition evaluation function · Focusing window · Machine vision

1 Introduction

With the rapid development of automation and intelligence in various precision instruments such as cameras, video cameras, microscopes and scanners, the application of autofocus technology has become more and more extensive. In the image acquisition system, autofocus refers to the process of obtaining a clear image by adjusting the position between the lens group and the detector. With the increasingly widespread application of images, in-depth research on the accuracy, efficiency and stability of autofocus technology has great practical significance [1].

© Springer Nature Singapore Pte Ltd. 2021
Y. Tan et al. (Eds.): DMBD 2021, CCIS 1454, pp. 80–89, 2021.
https://doi.org/10.1007/978-981-16-7502-7_9

Autofocus technology based on image processing has the following core issues: image definition evaluation function, focusing window selection and search algorithm [2]. Among these three issues, the image definition evaluation function is particularly important. Akiyama et al. [3] proposed an algorithm based on Daubechies wavelet transform and applied it to infrared cameras. Yousefi et al. [4] proposed a method based on high frequency information in the off-diagonal area of the joint histogram with defocused and focused images. Jeon et al. [5] proposed a robust focus measurement method using DCT coefficients. For the CCD imaging system in the laboratory, Li et al. [6] used curve fitting to process evaluation function data and used the overall trend of the curve for coarse focus control, thereby reducing noise interference. Mu et al. [7] proposed a salient object detection approach based on CNN to find the auto-focus area in low-contrast images. Jinbo et al. [8] proposed a method for depth resolution and autofocus based on a scattering layer with wavelength compensation.

In recent years, with the continuous improvement of the accuracy and run-time of the no-reference image quality assessment (NR-IQA) algorithm [9–13], the image definition evaluation function based on the NR-IQA algorithm has been gradually applied to the field of autofocus. We propose a definition evaluation function based on improved maximum local variation (MLV), in which a 3-neighbors MLV operator combined with the focusing window selection function is proposed. Compared with the traditional definition evaluation function, the proposed method has good real-time performance, effectiveness and better anti-noise performance.

2 MLV Operator Principle

The change of pixel value indicates the clarity of the image, and the edge and texture of the image contain a lot of pixel changes, which will affect the clarity perceived by the human visual system. Therefore, the high change of pixel value can better perceive the image quality than the low change [9]. In reference [9], the MLV of each pixel is defined as the maximum change of the pixel relative to its 8-neighbors. By calculating the MLV of all pixels in the image, the MLV map of the given image is generated.

Given a color image G with a size of M × N, first convert it to a gray scale image I. For each pixel $I_{i,j}$ at position (i, j) (where $1 \leq i \leq M$ and $1 \leq j \leq N$), consider a 3 × 3 region containing 8-neighbors pixels. Use Eq. (1) to calculate the MLV at the current position.

$$\psi\left(I_{i,j}\right) = \left\{ \max|I_{i,j} - I_{x,y}|\,\middle|\,x = i-1, i, i+1, y = j-1, j, j+1 \right\} \qquad (1)$$

where $I_{x,y}(i-1 \leq x \leq i+1, j-1 \leq y \leq j+1)$ are the 8-neighbors of $I_{i,j}$.

Under this definition, MLV reflects the maximum amount of change of the intensity between $I_{i,j}$ and its 8-neighbors pixels. In gray scale images, MLV varies in the range of 0–255, where 0 indicates that there is no change between the current pixel and its 8-neighbors, while 255 indicates that the current pixel has the largest change between its 8-neighbors.

Use Eq. (1) to calculate all pixels of the entire image to generate an MLV map $\psi(I)$ of the image.

$$\Psi(I) = \begin{pmatrix} \psi(I_{1,1}) & \cdots & \psi(1,N) \\ \vdots & \ddots & \vdots \\ \psi(I_{M,1}) & \cdots & \psi(M.N) \end{pmatrix} \tag{2}$$

In order to use the statistical characteristics of the MLV distribution for sharpness evaluation, the Generalized Gaussian Distribution (GGD) is used to parameterize the MLV distribution, as shown in Eq. (3).

$$f\left(\Psi(I);\mu,\gamma,\sigma\right) = \left(\frac{\gamma}{2\sigma\ \Gamma\left(\frac{1}{\gamma}\right)\sqrt{\frac{\Gamma\left(\frac{1}{\gamma}\right)}{\Gamma\left(\frac{1}{\gamma}\right)}}}\right) e^{\left(-\left|\frac{\Psi(I)-\mu}{\sigma\sqrt{\frac{\Gamma\left(\frac{1}{\gamma}\right)}{\Gamma\left(\frac{3}{\gamma}\right)}}}\right|^{\gamma}\right)} \tag{3}$$

where μ is the mean, σ is the standard deviation, γ is the shapeparameter, and $\Gamma(.)$ is the gamma function.

Since the human visual system is more sensitive to areas with large changes, the MLV map is improved by assigning different weighting coefficients to pixels with different MLV values.

According to Eq. (4), the following weighted MLV map $\psi_\omega(I)$ is generated, where higher weights are assigned to pixels with larger MLV value.

$$\Psi_\omega(I) = \begin{pmatrix} \omega_{1,1}\psi(I_{1,1}) & \cdots & \omega_{1,N}\psi(I_{1,N}) \\ \vdots & \ddots & \vdots \\ \omega_{M,1}\psi(I_{M,1}) & \cdots & \omega_{M,N}\varphi(I_{M,N}) \end{pmatrix} \tag{4}$$

where weights $\omega_{i,j}$ are defined using exponential function $\omega_{i,j} = e^{\eta_{i,j}}$ and $\eta_{i,j}$ is the rank of $\psi(I_{i,j})$ when sorted in ascending order from 0 to 1.

Finally, the standard deviation of the weighted MLV map is used as a measure of clarity.

3 Improved Image Definition Evaluation Function

We propose a new sharpness evaluation function, which firstly uses the 4-direction Scharr operator to select the focusing window of the image; then uses the 3-neighbors MLV operator to obtain the MLV map of the image to obtain the final definition evaluation value.

3.1   Focusing Window Selection Based on 4-Direction Scharr Operator

Appropriate selection of the focusing window can greatly reduce the calculational complexity of the method, achieve better real-time performance, and reduce the evaluation size from the overall image to a certain size which would shield the influence of irrelevant background.

Our method uses the 4-directional Scharr operator to select the focus window. Firstly, considering the multi-scale characteristics of the image, four 5×5 templates based on the Scharr operator are selected [14], as shown in Fig. 1. The gradient of the image in four directions is calculated, and the sum is used as the gradient information at the current pixel.

$$
\begin{bmatrix}
2 & 3 & 0 & -3 & -2 \\
3 & 4 & 0 & -4 & -3 \\
6 & 6 & 0 & -6 & -6 \\
3 & 4 & 0 & -4 & -3 \\
2 & 3 & 0 & -3 & -2
\end{bmatrix}
\qquad
\begin{bmatrix}
6 & 3 & 2 & 3 & 0 \\
3 & 6 & 4 & 0 & -3 \\
2 & 4 & 0 & -4 & -2 \\
3 & 0 & -4 & -6 & -3 \\
0 & -3 & -2 & -3 & -6
\end{bmatrix}
$$

(a) 0° Direction template   (b) 45° Direction template

$$
\begin{bmatrix}
2 & 3 & 6 & 3 & 2 \\
3 & 4 & 6 & 4 & 3 \\
0 & 0 & 0 & 0 & 0 \\
-3 & -4 & -6 & -4 & -3 \\
-2 & -3 & -6 & -3 & -2
\end{bmatrix}
\qquad
\begin{bmatrix}
0 & 3 & 2 & 3 & 6 \\
-3 & 0 & 4 & 6 & 3 \\
-2 & -4 & 0 & 4 & 2 \\
-3 & 6 & -4 & 0 & 3 \\
-6 & -3 & -2 & -3 & 0
\end{bmatrix}
$$

(c) 90° Direction template   (d) 135° Direction template

Fig. 1.   Four direction 5×5 template based on Scharr operator

Secondly, the image is divided according to different window sizes, and the cumulative gradient value under each window is calculated. Finally, the window with the maximum value is selected as the focusing window. As shown in Fig. 2.

3.2   MLV Operator Based on "3-Neighbors"

Compared with the method used in S3 [15], MLV has more reasonable evaluation results of subtle or drastic changes in the image. However, this operator only emphasizes the maximum variation at each pixel, and discards too much gradient information near each pixel therefore the anti-noise ability can be improved. Xiang [16] proposed the concept of "3-neighbors", that is, pixel A which is on the right of the target pixel, pixel B which is

| (a)Original picture | (b) Focus window output |

Fig. 2. Selection of focusing window. (a) is the original image, when a 100×100 window is used, (b) is the selected focus window

below pixel A, and pixel C which is below the target pixel. We integrate the concept of "3-neighbors" into MLV operators, and propose an MLV operator based on "3-neighbors", as shown in Eq. (5).

$$\Psi(I_{i,j}) = \left\{ \max |I_{i,j} - I_{x,y}| | x = i, i + 1, y = j, j + 1 \right\} \tag{5}$$

where $I_{x,y}(i \leq x \leq i + 1, j \leq y \leq j + 1)$ is the 3-neighbors pixel of $I_{i,j}$.

Gaussian white noise is common in image processing systems, and the MLV operator based on 3-neighbors can better resist the influence of Gaussian white noise. To illustrate the anti-noise ability of 3-neighbors based MLV, we introduce the original 8-neighbors MLV operator for comparison. As shown in Fig. 3, Before noise is added, the scores of the 8-neighbors MLV and the 3-neighbors MLV are both 0.1901. After adding noise, the MLV score of 8-neighbors is 0.2024, and the variation difference is 6.47%; however, the score of MLV in 3-neighbors changed to 0.1923, the variation difference was only 1.16%. Table 1 shows the comparison results of several other images. The results show that the 3-neighbors MLV operator is more stable in resisting white noise.

| (a) Original image | (b) Image with Gaussian white noise |

Fig. 3. Original image and distorted image

Table 1. The variation difference of scoring results of 8-neighbors MLV and 3-neighbors MLV

No.	8-neighbors MLV	3-neighbors MLV
1	6.75%	0.68%
2	17.98%	11.82%
3	13.25%	4.00%

4 Experimental Results and Analysis

All experiments were performed on a HP desktop computer with Intel® Core(TM) i5-7200U CPU at 2.50 GHz with 4 GB RAM. The operating system is Windows 7 with 64 bit, and the experimental platform is Matlab R2013a. Two groups of images are selected as experimental images, as shown in Fig. 4. The two groups of images can reflect the experimental results in different backgrounds, each group of images reflects the process of defocus-focus-defocus.

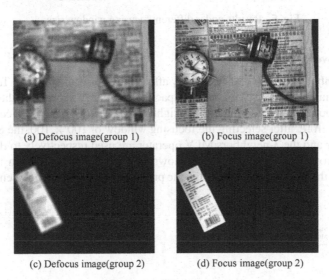

(a) Defocus image(group 1)   (b) Focus image(group 1)

(c) Defocus image(group 2)   (d) Focus image(group 2)

Fig. 4. Experiment picture

4.1 Performance of Improved Sharpness Evaluation Function

4.1.1 Selection of Focusing Window Size

Firstly, four window sizes of 50×50, 100×100, 150×150, 200×200 are selected respectively. The normalized sharpness evaluation function curve obtained from the first group of images is shown in Fig. 5(a). It can be seen that the four curves meet the unimodal, monotonous and unbiased characteristics. The 50×50 window has the best sensitivity, followed by the 100×100 window. The result obtained from the second group of images is shown in Fig. 5(b). The clearest image is frame 8, and only the curve of 100 × 100 satisfies the unbiased property, while the other three windows result in misjudged. Considering that a smaller window is easier to be affected by noise [14], the 100 × 100 focusing window is finally selected.

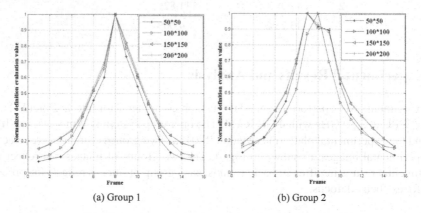

(a) Group 1   (b) Group 2

Fig. 5. Results under different focusing window sizes

4.1.2 Improved Method Performance

As the 8-neighbors MLV operator is greatly affected by noise, as shown in Table 1, after adding Gaussian white noise, it has an impact on the image score, and the maximum fluctuation reaches 17.98%, while the 3-neighbors MLV will greatly reduce the impact of noise. Therefore, after selecting the focusing window of 100 × 100, the 8-neighbors MLV operator and the 3-neighbors MLV operator are used respectively to illustrate the result of improvement. The results are shown in Fig. 6. Compared with the original method using the MLV operator directly, the proposed method has better sensitivity and unbiasedness.

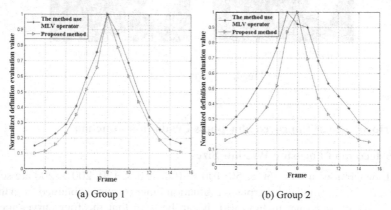

(a) Group 1   (b) Group 2

Fig. 6. Comparison between the method in this paper and the method using MLV operator

4.2 Anti-noise Performance Comparison

In order to discuss the anti-noise performance of this method, some commonly used definition evaluation functions, such as SMD, variance, energy gradient, energy and Brenner function, are compared on the first group of images [2]. The results are shown in Fig. 7(a). Compared with other definition evaluation functions, the variance and entropy have monotonicity and wider coverage in the absence of noise. Consequently, those functions are suitable for the coarse focus stage. The proposed method, Brenner function and energy gradient function have good sensitivity and are suitable for the fine focus stage.

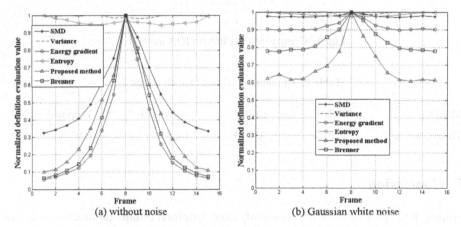

(a) without noise   (b) Gaussian white noise

Fig. 7. Performance comparison of definition evaluation function

After adding Gaussian white noise with a mean value of 0 and a variance of 0.005, as shown in Fig. 7(b), all functions lose monotonicity, especially the variance, entropy and SMD whose curve has almost become parallel. Energy gradient function also becomes parallel, the difference between the maximum value and the minimum value of which is only about 0.1, and our method has the best ability to resist white noise.

4.3 Compared with Other No-Reference Image Quality Evaluation Algorithms

The MLV operator is originally proposed for the problem of no-reference image quality evaluation, so we also compared the proposed method with three no-reference image quality evaluation algorithms in the literature, including JNB [10], CPBD [11] and BISHARP [12]. The focus curve and run-time are shown in Fig. 8 and Table 2. It can be seen that the JNB and the CPBD have longer run-time which is not suitable for real-time applications. The coverage of the BISHARP algorithm is wide and insensitive. The proposed method runs fastest and has the best unimodality, monotonicity, unbiasedness and sensitivity.

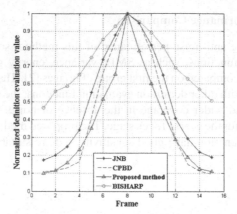

Fig. 8. Comparison of different IQA methods

Table 2. Computational cost of each metric.

Metric	JNB	CPBD	BISHARP	Proposed
Time(s)/frame	0.5602	0.6079	0.1816	0.0486

5 Conclusion

Aiming at the problem that the commonly used definition evaluation function is easily affected by noise, this paper proposes an improved image definition evaluation method that is applied to autofocus. The algorithm consists of two steps. Firstly, the 4-directional Scharr operator is leveraged for selecting the focusing window via gradient accumulation, and then a 3-neighbors MLV operator is presented for image sharpness evaluation. The proposed method can ensure real-time performance while reducing the influence of noise. The experimental results show that compared with the commonly used evaluation functions, our method can achieve good stability, monotonicity, unbiasedness and sensitivity in the presence of Gaussian white noise. And it is suitable for the fine focus stage for the autofocus procedure. At the same time, compared with other no-reference image quality assessment algorithms, our method has better real-time performance which is suitable for industrial inspection and other occasions. Since our method only selects one region as the final focus window, it is not suitable for scenes with multiple focus regions.

Acknowledgement. This work was supported by the Open Fund Project of Fujian Provincial Key Laboratory of Information Processing and Intelligent Control (Minjiang University) (MJUKF-IPIC202110), National Natural Science Foundation of China (61972187), Natural Science Foundation of Fujian Province (2020J02024), Fuzhou Science and Technology Project (2020-RC-186), Research Project of Undergraduate Teaching Reform in Fujian University of Technology (JG2021020).

References

1. Elessawy, M., Atia, M., El-Sebah, M.: Automation of focusing system based on image processing through intelligent algorithm. In: International Conference on Innovation Engineering Technologies ICIET, Dubai, UAE (2015)
2. Zhao, Q., Liu, B., Xu, Z.: Research and realization of an anti-noise auto-focusing algorithm. In: 2013 5th International Conference on Intelligent Human-Machine Systems and Cybernetics, August 2013, vol. 2, pp. 255–258. IEEE (2013)
3. Akiyama, A., Kobayashi, N., Mutoh, E., et al.: Infrared image guidance for ground vehicle based on fast wavelet image focusing and tracking. In: Novel Optical Systems Design and Optimization XII, August 2009, vol. 7429, p. 742906. International Society for Optics and Photonics (2009)
4. Yousefi, S., Rahman, M., Kehtarnavaz, N.: A new auto-focus sharpness function for digital and smart-phone cameras. IEEE Trans. Consum. Electron. **57**(3), 1003–1009 (2011)
5. Jeon, J., Lee, J., Paik, J.: Robust focus measure for unsupervised auto-focusing based on optimum discrete cosine transform coefficients. IEEE Trans. Consum. Electron. **57**(1), 1–5 (2011)
6. Hui, L., Chengyu, F.: An improved focusing algorithm based on image definition evaluation. In: 2011 2nd International Conference on Artificial Intelligence, Management Science and Electronic Commerce (AIMSEC), August 2011, pp. 3743–3746. IEEE (2011)
7. Mu, N., Xu, X., Zhang, X.: Finding autofocus region in low contrast surveillance images using CNN-based saliency algorithm. Pattern Recogn. Lett. **125**, 124–132 (2019)
8. Liang, J., Cai, J., Xie, J., et al.: Depth-resolved and auto-focus imaging through scattering layer with wavelength compensation. JOSA A **36**(6), 944–949 (2019)
9. Bahrami, K., Kot, A.C.: A dast approach for no-reference image sharpness assessment based on maximum local variation. IEEE Signal Process. Lett. **21**(6), 751–755 (2014)
10. Ferzli, R., Karam, L.J.: A no-reference objective image sharpness metric based on the notion of just noticeable blur (JNB). IEEE Trans. Image Process. **18**(4), 717–728 (2009)
11. Narvekar, N.D., Karam, L.J.: A no-reference image blur metric based on the cumulative probability of blur detection (CPBD). IEEE Trans. Image Process. **20**(9), 2678–2683 (2011)
12. Gvozden, G., Grgic, S., Grgic, M.: Blind image sharpness assessment based on local contrast map statistics. J. Vis. Commun. Image Represent. **50**(1), 145–158 (2018)
13. Chen, J., Li, S., Lin, L.: A no-reference blurred colourful image quality assessment method based on dual maximum local information. IET Signal Process. (2021). https://doi.org/10.1049/sil2.12064
14. Chen, J., Chen, D.Q., Meng, S.H.: A novel region selection algorithm for auto-focusing method based on depth from focus. In: Krömer, P., Alba, E., Pan, J.-S., Snášel, V. (eds.) ECC 2017. AISC, vol. 682, pp. 101–108. Springer, Cham (2018). https://doi.org/10.1007/978-3-319-68527-4_11
15. Vu, C.T., Phan, T.D., Chandler, D.M.: S3: a spectral and spatial measure of local perceived sharpness in natural images. IEEE Trans. Image Process. **21**(3), 934–945 (2012)
16. Xiang, K., Gao, J.: Research on the image definition evaluation algorithm in autofocus process. Modular Mach. Tool Automat. Manuf. Techniq. **1**, 52–55 (2019). (in Chinese)

A Classic Multi-method Collaborative Obfuscation Strategy

Yujie Ma[1], Yuanzhang Li[1], Zhibin Zhang[1], Ruyun Zhang[2], Lu Liu[1(✉)], and Xiaosong Zhang[3]

[1] School of Computer Science, Beijing Institute of Technology, Beijing 100081, China
{mayujie,popular,liulu}@bit.edu.cn
[2] Zhejiang Lab, Hangzhou 310000, China
zhangry@zhejianglab.com
[3] Department of Computer Science and Technology, Tangshan University, Tangshan 063000, China

Abstract. Code obfuscation is a kind of powerful protection technique for software code. At present, research on obfuscation techniques is mainly focused on analyzing the effect of single obfuscation method, leaving few discussions on cooperative obfuscation of multiple methods. This paper firstly presented a brief introduction of the concept and methods of code obfuscation, then designed and implemented an obfuscator with multiple obfuscation methods. Then, a collaborative obfuscation strategy suitable for multiple obfuscation methods is proposed in detail. Finally, we verified that the obfuscation strategy indeed improves the performance of obfuscation through experiments.

Keywords: Code obfuscation · Collaborative obfuscation · JavaScript · Software maintainability index

1 Introduction

Recently, with the rise of reverse engineering [11], the protection of software has attracted more attention. Code obfuscation is a classical and efficient software protection method, which can convert the code into another form but retains the behavior of the code unchanged. The code in converted version is more difficult for others to understand, thus providing protection of the code.

However, in a security-sensitive environment, applying only a single obfuscation method is difficult to prevent attackers from analyzing the code successfully. Therefore, defenders use multiple obfuscation methods to protect the code. The application of multiple obfuscation methods often mixes their effects together, which further increases the complexity of the code and achieves a better obfuscation effect. However, the problem of how to combine multiple obfuscation methods is still under exploration.

To solve the problem above, this paper proposed a classic multi-method collaborative obfuscation strategy. This strategy uses an easy-to-implement prior intensity analysis of the obfuscation method to generate an obfuscation order, and then use this order

© Springer Nature Singapore Pte Ltd. 2021
Y. Tan et al. (Eds.): DMBD 2021, CCIS 1454, pp. 90–97, 2021.
https://doi.org/10.1007/978-981-16-7502-7_10

to apply obfuscation. Finally, we implemented a JavaScript language obfuscator with multiple obfuscation methods, and designed experiments to verify that the multi-method collaborative obfuscation strategy proposed in this paper has a better obfuscation effect.

The rest of this paper is organized as follows: Sect. 2 introduces related work and background. Section 3 describes the system design that we used in this paper. Section 4 gives a detailed description of our obfuscation strategy. Section 5 uses experiments to evaluate the performance of our obfuscation strategy. Section 6 gathers the conclusion and future work.

2 Background and Related Work

2.1 A Brief Introduction of Code Obfuscation

Code obfuscation is a transformation of the code: the transformed code is different from the original code in form, but performs the same function. Collberg et al. give the definition of code obfuscation in [1]:

If the original program P generates target program P' through transformation T, while P and P' have the same observable behavior, then T is called an obfuscation transformation. The same observable behavior means that P and P' should satisfy the following two conditions:

(1) If P fails to terminate or unexpectedly terminates with an error condition, then P' may or may not terminate.
(2) Otherwise, P' must terminate and produce an output that is exactly the same as P.

2.2 Related Work

Recently, there are also many new obfuscation methods that combine obfuscation with other applications have been proposed. [12] proposed an obfuscation method based on instruction exchange, which obfuscates the original program by changing the order of physically adjacent but logically independent instruction sequences. [13] proposed an obfuscation method based on cryptography to encrypt the key code by constructing management program. [14] implemented Oblive, an obfuscator for Java and Android programs, which can perform obfuscation freely controlled by the developer according to the comments left by the developer in the code.

However, most research focuses on discussing the intensity of obfuscation of a single method, while single method is difficult to resist the existing reverse analysis, such as program slicing [18] and symbolic execution [19]. For mixing multiple obfuscation techniques and finding the best combination method to maximize the intensity of obfuscation, there is still a lack of research. In related work, only [15] and [17] proposed methods based on reinforcement learning and Markov chain to find the optimal obfuscation order.

3 Design

In this section, we will introduce the obfuscation and evaluation framework built by this paper.

First, we implemented a JavaScript obfuscator with 10 obfuscation methods, specific methods including Opaque Predicates [4], Control-Flow Flattening, etc. Each of them can be applied to the code independently. It is important for three reasons. The first is that it can ensure that there will be no dependencies or mutual interference between the various obfuscation methods. Moreover, independent methods mean that we can change the order of the methods at will and see if the behavior and performance of the obfuscated code has changed. The last is that we are free to delete old methods or add new methods for further research.

After we get the obfuscated code file, it will be passed to an evaluation module to analyze the output file through static analysis. The analysis result includes Cyclomatic Complexity, Halstead Volume, etc. Finally, the evaluation result is collected for further research and to act as a basis for adjusting the obfuscation method used and its order.

4   Obfuscation Strategy

In this section, we first introduce some necessary background knowledge and then discuss our strategy in detail.

4.1   Method for Evaluating Obfuscation Methods

To evaluate the performance of the obfuscation method, Collberg et al. proposed 3 indicators in [1], namely, Potency, Resilience, and Cost. Among them, the resilience indicator mainly relies on manual reverse evaluation. The evaluation result is greatly affected by the tester's ability, so it is difficult to quantify. The cost is used to evaluate the runtime performance loss caused by the obfuscation, and it cannot reflect the complexity of the obfuscation method. Therefore, the indicator used in the evaluation of obfuscation performance as proposed by this paper comes from potency. According to [1], the potency indicator can be defined as follows:

Given obfuscation transformation T, the source program P is transformed through T to generate the target program P'. Suppose $E(P)$ is the complexity of the source program P, and $E(P')$ is the complexity of the target program P', then the potency $T_{pot}(P)$ of transformation T with respect to program P can be calculated as follows:

$$T_{pot}(P) = \frac{E(P')}{E(P)} - 1 \tag{1}$$

T is called an effective obfuscation transformation when $T_{pot}(P) > 0$.

4.2   Complexity Indicator

Based on Eq. (1), a quantitative calculation method is given for how to evaluate the performance of the obfuscation method, and the next step is to choose the appropriate E, the complexity indicator. Several metrics for complexity indicators are given in [1], including program length, cyclomatic complexity [7], control-flow complexity [9], fan-in/fan-out complexity [10], data structure complexity [8], etc. Each of them reflects the complexity measurement of the program from a certain aspect. However, obtaining the complexity of the code to evaluate the potency of the obfuscation method through the changes in the complexity of the code before and after the obfuscation, a unique and comprehensive indicator is required. Based on the above considerations, referring to the evaluation method of software complexity in software engineering, this paper chooses the software maintainability index as the complexity indicator of the obfuscation method.

The software maintainability index (MI) [3] comprehensively evaluates code complexity and software maintenance difficulty by incorporating multiple characteristics of the code into quantitative calculations. The higher the maintainability index, the lower the code complexity, and the easier it is to read, analyze and maintain, and vice versa.

MI can be calculated as follows:

$$MI = 171 - 5.2 \ln HV - 0.23 \times CC - 16.2 \ln LOC \tag{2}$$

The parameters included in Eq. (2) and their meanings are shown in the following Table 1:

Table 1. Parameters of MI.

Parameters	Description	Meaning
HV	Halstead Volume [6]	Based on the number and number of occurrences of operators and operands in the code. This reflects the degree of computational intensiveness contained in the code
CC	Cyclomatic Complexity	Based on the number of independent execution paths in the code. This reflects the logic control complexity of the code
LOC	Lines Of Code	Based on the number of statements in the code. This reflects the length of the code

4.3 Obfuscation Strategy Analysis

It can be inferred that how much complexity can be added to the code by obfuscation is not only related to the intensity of the obfuscation method itself, but also positively correlated with the structure and complexity of the code itself. For example, the insertion point of the opaque predicates is the place where the judgment conditions exist in the original code, which means the more the insertion points are, the more predicates can be added, thus bringing a more additional complexity to the code. Therefore, it is feasible to enhance the obfuscation effect by increasing the complexity of the code before obfuscation.

When there are multiple independent obfuscation methods, we can sort various methods according to prior intensity evaluation, so that the ones with low intensity will be obfuscated first, and then those with high intensity will be obfuscated. Thus, the high-intensity obfuscation method can maximize the additional complexity added to the code during obfuscation to obtain the best obfuscation effect.

Therefore, after clarifying the intensity evaluation criteria for obfuscation methods, this paper proposes the following obfuscation strategies based on these obfuscation methods and their potencies:

Suppose there are n kinds of independent obfuscation methods $O_1, O_2, \cdots O_n$ that are about to participate in obfuscation, and their potencies are $T_1, T_2, \cdots T_n$, respectively. The obfuscation methods are reordered based on the potency from small to large, and a sequence of obfuscation methods $O'_1, O'_2, \cdots O'_n$ is obtained. The final obfuscation strategy is to obfuscate the original code in this sequence. Suppose the original program code is P_0, then:

$$P_1 = O'_1(P_0)$$
$$P_2 = O'_2(P_1)$$
$$\vdots$$
$$P_n = O'_n(P_{n-1})$$

P_n is the finally obfuscated code we get.

5   Experiment and Result Analysis

This section we will give our experiment results from both static analysis and dynamic analysis to verify the effectiveness of our proposed strategy.

The obfuscation and evaluation frameworks in this paper were already introduced in Sect. 3. Table 2 shows the various 10 obfuscation methods and their potency evaluation.

Table 2.   Potency evaluation results of obfuscation method:

Method	LOC	HV	CC	MI	$T_{pot}(P)$ (%)
Original code	157	28429	9	99.04	–
Format character deletion	157	28429	9	99.04	0
Comment deletion	157	28429	9	99.04	0
Identifier replacement	157	28429	9	99.04	0
Data obfuscation	157	28429	9	99.04	0
Constant merging	158	29614	9	98.91	0.13
Code reordering	174	28569	9	97.34	1.75
Opaque predicates [4]	253	48041	37	89.26	10.96
Redundant code adding	279	54431	39	88.22	12.26
Function merging	161	89031	18	85.22	16.22
Control-flow flattening	337	41558	69	84.97	16.56

It is shown that $T_{pot}(P)$ of different obfuscation methods are different, which means that the extra complexity added using different obfuscation methods to the code varies greatly. Note that there are several methods whose $T_{pot}(P)$ is 0, but this only means that this method does not add extra complexity to the code under this evaluation indicator, but it is possibly useful for removing valuable information from the code. So it cannot be simply judged as an inefficient obfuscation transformation.

After obtaining the potency evaluation of each method, this paper chose three strategies to conduct collaborative obfuscation of 10 methods:

Strategy 1. Use the obfuscation order based on the order of potency from the largest to smallest.

Strategy 2. Use random order for obfuscation.

Strategy 3. Use the obfuscation order based on the order of potency from smallest to largest, which is opposite to Strategy 1.

The result is shown in Fig. 1.

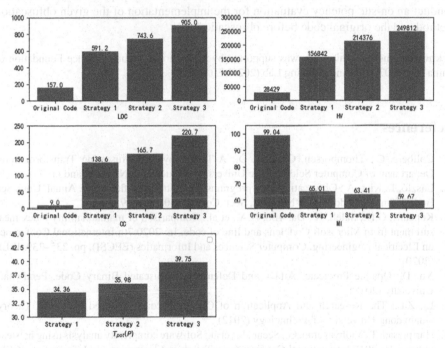

Fig. 1. Comparison of static intensity analysis results of different obfuscation strategies.

Through the analysis of the figure above, it can be seen that compared with Strategy 1 and Strategy 2, Strategy 3 has the smallest MI and the largest $T_{pot}(P)$, adding the greatest extra complexity to the code. Moreover, the indicators of strategy 2 are between Strategy 1 and Strategy 3. Experimental results show that when multiple independent obfuscation methods exist and participate in obfuscation together, the obfuscation order based on the potency from small to large has the best effect; the obfuscation order based on the potency from large to small has the worst effect; and the obfuscation performed in other orders is in between.

6 Conclusion

There have been many discussions on a single obfuscation method, but there are few and no conclusions about how to coordinate obfuscation by multiple methods to achieve the best obfuscation effect. The contribution of this paper is to propose a intensity-based multi-method collaborative obfuscation strategy. This strategy is easy to implement and has no additional requirements for the obfuscation methods themselves. As long as the potency of each method can be evaluated, the obfuscation methods can be ordered according to the evaluation results and to be applied in turn.

In the application scenario, because of the differences between the selected obfuscation method and its implementation, as well as the potency of the obfuscation method is also related to the original code itself, the results of the potency evaluation may not be consistent with the results obtained in the experiments in this paper. The best way is to conduct an on-site potency evaluation for the implementation of the given obfuscation method and the original code before obfuscation.

Acknowledgments. This work was supported by the National Natural Science Foundation of China (no. 62072037) and Zhejiang Lab (2020LE0AB02).

References

1. Collberg, C., Thomborson, C., Low, D.: A Taxonomy Of Obfuscating Transformations. Department of Computer Science, The University of Auckland, New Zealand (1997)
2. László, T., Kiss, Á.: Obfuscating C++ programs via control flow flattening. Annal. Univ. Sci. Budapestin. Rolando Eötvös Nominat. Sect. Comput. **30**(1), 3–19 (2009)
3. Kencana, G.H., Saleh, A., Darwito, H.A., et al.: Comparison of maintainability index measurement from Microsoft Codelens and line of code. In: 2020 7th International Conference on Electrical Engineering, Computer Sciences and Informatics (EECSI), pp. 235–239. IEEE (2020)
4. Xu, D.: Opaque Predicate: Attack and Defense in Obfuscated Binary Code. Penn State University (2018)
5. Li, Z.L.: The Research and Application of Opaque Predicates Based on Chaos Theory. Guangdong University of Technology (2012)
6. Hariprasad, T., Vidhyagaran, G., Seenu, K., et al.: Software complexity analysis using halstead metrics. In: 2017 International Conference on Trends in Electronics and Informatics (ICEI), pp. 1109–1113. IEEE (2017)
7. Ebert, C., Cain, J., Antoniol, G., et al.: Cyclomatic complexity. IEEE Softw. **33**(6), 27–29 (2016)
8. Munson, J.C., Kohshgoftaar, T.M.: Measurement of data structure complexity. J. Syst. Softw. **20**(3), 217–225 (1993)
9. Anugrah, I.G., Sarno, R., Anggraini, R.N.E.: Decomposition using Refined Process Structure Tree (RPST) and control flow complexity metrics. In: 2015 International Conference on Information and Communication Technology and Systems (ICTS), pp. 203–208. IEEE (2015)
10. Mubarak, A., Counsell, S., Hierons, R.M.: An evolutionary study of fan-in and fan-out metrics in OSS. In: 2010 Fourth International Conference on Research Challenges in Information Science (RCIS), pp. 473–482. IEEE (2010)

11. Buonamici, F., Carfagni, M., Furferi, R., et al.: Reverse engineering modeling methods and tools: a survey. Comput. Aided Design Appl. **15**(3), 443–464 (2018)
12. Pan, Y., Zhu, Y.F., Lin, W.: Code obfuscation based on instructions swapping. Ruan Jian Xue Bao/J. Softw. **30**(6), 1788–1792 (2019) (in Chinese). http://www.jos.org.cn/1000-9825/5429.htm
13. Kiperberg, M., Leon, R., Resh, A., et al.: Hypervisor-based protection of code. IEEE Trans. Inf. Forens. Secur. **14**(8), 2203–2216 (2019)
14. Pizzolotto, D., Fellin, R., Ceccato, M.: OBLIVE: seamless code obfuscation for Java programs and Android apps. In: 2019 IEEE 26th International Conference on Software Analysis, Evolution and Reengineering (SANER), pp. 629–633. IEEE (2019)
15. Wang, H., Wang, S., Xu, D., et al.: Generating effective software obfuscation sequences with reinforcement learning. IEEE Trans. Depend. Secure Comput. (2020)
16. Balachandran, V., Keong, N.W., Emmanuel, S.: Function level control flow obfuscation for software security. In: 2014 Eighth International Conference on Complex, Intelligent and Software Intensive Systems, pp. 133–140. IEEE (2014)
17. Liu, H., Sun, C., Su, Z., et al.: Stochastic optimization of program obfuscation. In: 2017 IEEE/ACM 39th International Conference on Software Engineering (ICSE), pp. 221–231. IEEE (2017)
18. Acharya, M., Robinson, B.: Practical change impact analysis based on static program slicing for industrial software systems. In: 2011 33rd International Conference on Software Engineering (ICSE), pp. 746–755. IEEE (2011)
19. Baldoni, R., Coppa, E., D'elia, D.C., et al.: A survey of symbolic execution techniques. ACM Comput. Surv. (CSUR) **51**(3), 1–39 (2018)

The Construction of Knowledge Graph for Personalized Online Teaching

Zhaokun Gong[1], Xiaomei Yu[1,2(✉)], Wenxiang Fu[1], Xueyu Che[1], Qian Mao[1], and Xiangwei Zheng[1,2]

[1] School of Information Science and Engineering, Shandong Normal University, Jinan, China
[2] Shandong Provincial Key Laboratory of Distributed Computing Software, Jinan, China

Abstract. The knowledge graph (KG) is widely used in various fields recently, while there are few achievements of knowledge graph related to educational applications. In this paper, some subject knowledge graphs are constructed to adapt to the educational development in big data environment, and the relationships between knowledge nodes are analyzed in order to provide students with a personalized online teaching for knowledge learning. Specially, a knowledge graph on python subject is constructed based on the neo4j graph database for students in programing courses. With three applications achieved on the knowledge graphs, the experimental results show that the knowledge points to students is described more clearly, and the logical relationships between the knowledge points are inferred according to the queries from students. It is verified that the knowledge graph on course learning performs significant effectiveness and efficiency in personalized online teaching.

Keywords: Knowledge Graph · Neo4j · Personalized · Online teaching

1 Introduction

The knowledge graph (KG) has been widely used in the fields of medicine, economics, management and other industries. However, there is relatively few knowledge graphs related to the field of education.

Traditional online teaching has many problems. First of all, teachers usually use mind maps for teaching in order to make students understand knowledge clearly. However, it takes a long time and effort for teachers to construct mind maps. The second problem is that mind mapping is limited and cannot show all the attributes of knowledge. Third, the students may neglect the relationships between the knowledge without clear description and vivid visualization.

To overcome the challenges encounter in current online learning, we build personalized online teaching knowledge graph with Neo4j to lend a hand for personalized online teaching and learning. We also apply it to teaching python. With three functions are adopted in teaching, the python KG show its effectiveness in personalized online teaching. The contributions of the paper are outlined as follows.

© Springer Nature Singapore Pte Ltd. 2021
Y. Tan et al. (Eds.): DMBD 2021, CCIS 1454, pp. 98–107, 2021.
https://doi.org/10.1007/978-981-16-7502-7_11

- With entities and links extracted from the knowledge of special subject, a knowledge graph for personalized online teaching is constructed with the software of Neo4j. As the relationship between entities and entities is obtained, the Neo4j is used to store entities and relationships, and the python KG was completed.
- Three teaching functions are developed based on the python knowledge graph. Firstly, the python knowledge is visually displayed in the form of graphs, which has the same effect as the mind map. Secondly, we can use the cypher statements to query the attributes of any knowledge nodes and its relationship to other nodes. Finally, we can query the logical relationship between knowledge points, which effectively improves the efficiency of searching the relationship between knowledge points and knowledge points.
- We applied the python KG in personalized online teaching, and the teaching results demonstrate the effectiveness of knowledge graphs in python teaching.

The rest of the paper is as follows. In the second section, we analyze and understand the knowledge related to knowledge graph and neo4. In the third part, we demonstrated the construction process of knowledge graph in the third part. And then applied the personalized online teaching knowledge graph to python teaching, introduced the three functions of this knowledge graph in Python teaching, and analyzed the teaching effect. Finally, we draw the conclusions and present the future work.

2 Related Work

2.1 Knowledge Graph

Google proposed a knowledge graph [1] in 2012. In recent years, the development of knowledge graphs has attracted the attention of many domestic and foreign researchers. The knowledge graph is a semantic network based on the semantic web [2]. Its purpose is to use symbols to describe various concepts in the real world and the relationships between concepts [3], and to reveal the relationships between concepts. Its basic unit is a triplet composed of "entity-relation-entity", and different entities are connected through relations to form a structured semantic knowledge. Therefore, from the perspective of semantics, constructing a knowledge graph of python courses can allow computers to better organize and manage python knowledge points. At the same time, it can also analyze the existing knowledge to mine the hidden logical relationships between knowledge and provide students with more suitable education method.

In the knowledge graph, knowledge storage methods include Resource Description Framework (RDF)-based storage, graph database-based storage [4], and so on. The advantage of graph database over RDF storage is that graph database can store nodes, node attributes and relationships, and also supports efficient search and query [5]. Therefore, this paper chooses to use a graph database to store python knowledge.

2.2 Neo4j

As shown in Fig. 1, in recent years, the graph database system represented by Neo4j has developed rapidly, and Neo4j has become one of the most popular graph databases. It is composed of nodes and edges [6], where nodes are entities, and edges are relationships between entities. Neo4j proposes a query language similar to SQL, Cypher language, with simpler query statements. Neo4j is an opensource graph database [7] whose purpose is to optimize the management, storage and traversal of nodes and relationships. Nodes are used to store lots of knowledge points [8], and edges are used to represent the relationship between knowledge points. The edge is directional, from one node to another node, it is used to represent the relationship between the entity and the entity [9]. By establishing the relationship between multiple python knowledge nodes, the python course knowledge graph is obtained.

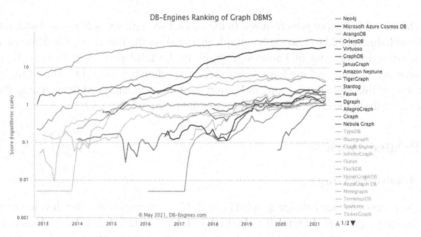

Fig. 1. DB-Engines Ranking of Graph DBMS

3   Construction of Python KG

When building a knowledge graph, you can choose either top-down or bottom-up construction methods. The top-down construction method needs to determine the data model of the knowledge graph first, and then put the data into the specific data model, so that the knowledge graph is formed. This construction method is suitable for areas with clear knowledge content and clear relationships. The bottom-up construction method refers to collecting data from public data by using a certain technology, and then extracting a data model from the data.

The construction of knowledge graph for python courses mainly includes several steps such as data acquisition, knowledge extraction, and knowledge fusion [10]. Data acquisition is the process of obtaining python knowledge data sources. Knowledge extraction is to identify and extract related entities and relationships between entities from data sources. Knowledge fusion is the process of linking equivalent entities from different sources (Fig. 2).

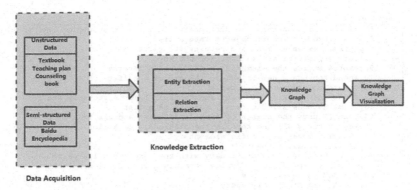

Fig. 2. The construction process of the knowledge graph

3.1 Data Acquisition

Starting from the teaching training objectives and syllabus, this paper uses unstructured data such as "python language program" textbooks, teaching plans and tutorials and semi-structured data such as Baidu as reference standards, and use crawler technology to collect the concepts and knowledge points contained therein as a data source. These concepts and knowledge points are the nodes in the knowledge graph, and the nodes are entities, so as to get the general framework of the python course knowledge graph.

3.2 Knowledge Extraction

Entity extraction and relationship extraction are important subtasks in knowledge extraction. Entity extraction refers to use natural language technology to extract entities from data from different sources to form structured data. Relation extraction is to use natural language processing technology to identify entities from the text and extract the relationships between entities.

The data obtained after knowledge extraction needs to be processed as follows:

(1) Define entities, relationships and entity categories under the guidance of experts in the education field to ensure the accuracy of knowledge;
(2) Data cleaning: filter data, delete irrelevant data and duplicate data;
(3) Export the collected python knowledge data into a csv format data table, which is convenient for later using the csv file to import the data into Neo4j in batches. When saving these data, since the data set contains Chinese, you must first change the encoding format of the CSV file to UTF-8, as the Fig. 3 shows.

```
method.csv
  7   5,has_key,Check whether the dictionary contains the specified key
  8   6,insert,Used to insert objects into a list
  9   7,pop,Removes an element and returns its value
 10   8,iterkeys,Returns an iterator for the key
 11   9,reverse,Stores the elements in the list in reverse
 12   10,apend,Appends a new object to the end of the list
 13   11,CreateTuples,Creating a tuple
 14   12,TupleFunction,Like the list function, it takes a sequence and re
 15   13,items,Returns all dictionary entries as a list
 16   14,count,Counts the number of times an element appears in a list
 17   15,keys,Returns all the keys in the dictionary as a list
 18   16,remove,Removes a specific element
 19   17,kind,Clear all elements
 20   18,clear,Returns a new dictionary with the same key-value pairs
 21   19,deepcopy,Copies all the values contained in a dictionary to the
 22   20,add,Adding new elements
 23   21,get,Access dictionary entry
```

Fig. 3. The CSV data of the method

3.3 Use Neo4j to Construct Python KG

Neo4j is a graph database for storing data. In this paper, we use Neo4j to build the python knowledge graph. First of all, we need to import the python knowledge, and then import the relationships between the knowledge.

Importing Nodes. After obtaining the CSV table data, Neo4j can be used to build a secondary vocational education python knowledge graph. There are five ways to import nodes in the Neo4j graph database:

- Cypher CREATE statement, write a CREATE statement for each piece of data.
- Cypher LOAD CSV statement converts the data into CSV format, and reads the data through LOAD CSV.
- The official Java API-Batch Inserter.
- The batch import tool was written by Michael Hunger, one of the authors of Neo4j.

Since the data set used in this paper is less than 10 million, and LOAD CSV can be used directly in the visualization window of Neo4j, we choose LOAD CSV as the method of importing the secondary vocational education python knowledge data into Neo4j. Take the import of List, Tuple, Dictionary, String and other nodes as an example, the specific cypher statement is as follows (Figs. 4 and 5):

LOAD CSV WITH HEADERS FROM "file:///concept.csv" AS line
MERGE (c:concept{name:line.name})

```
concept.csv
  1   num,concept,tagline
  2   0,List,List is the most commonly used Python data type
  3   1,Tuple,Tuple is an immutable sequence
  4   2,Dictionary,Dictionary is a data type often used in Python language
  5   3,String,A string is an immutable sequence of Unicode code points
  6   4,Set,Set belongs to unordered variable sequence
  7   5,OrderedSequence,"Ordered sequences include lists, tuples, and strings"
  8   6,UnorderedSequence,"Unordered sequences include dictionaries, collections"
```

Fig. 4. The CSV data of the concept.

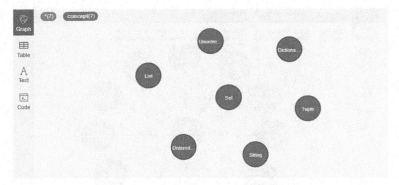

Fig. 5. Concept nodes after importing.

Importing Relationships. Taking part of the relationship in the concept of importing List as an example, the specific cypher statement is as follows (Figs. 6 and 7):

```
LOAD CSV WITH HEADERS FROM "file:///relationship.csv" AS line
match (from:C{name:line.from}),(to:method{name:line.to})
merge (from)-[r:ListMethod{property:line.property}]->(to)
```

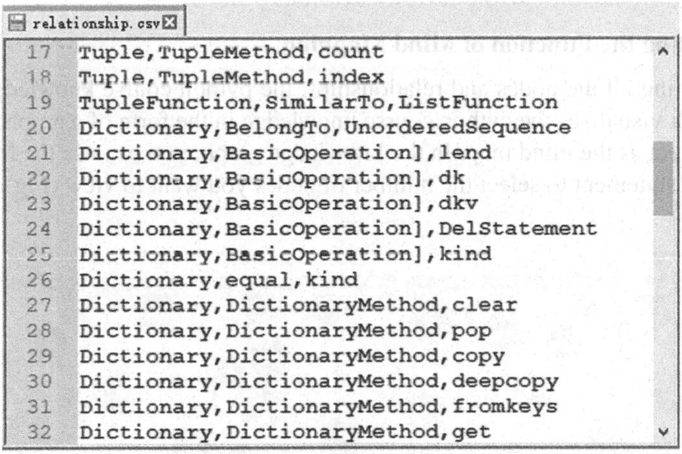

```
relationship.csv
17  Tuple,TupleMethod,count
18  Tuple,TupleMethod,index
19  TupleFunction,SimilarTo,ListFunction
20  Dictionary,BelongTo,UnorderedSequence
21  Dictionary,BasicOperation],lend
22  Dictionary,BasicOperation],dk
23  Dictionary,BasicOperation],dkv
24  Dictionary,BasicOperation],DelStatement
25  Dictionary,BasicOperation],kind
26  Dictionary,equal,kind
27  Dictionary,DictionaryMethod,clear
28  Dictionary,DictionaryMethod,pop
29  Dictionary,DictionaryMethod,copy
30  Dictionary,DictionaryMethod,deepcopy
31  Dictionary,DictionaryMethod,fromkeys
32  Dictionary,DictionaryMethod,get
```

Fig. 6. A part of the relationship.

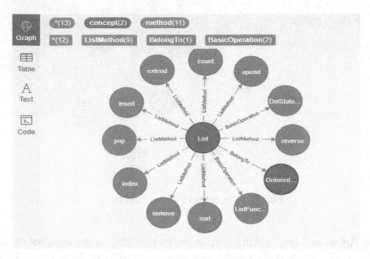

Fig. 7. List and its relationships.

4   Teaching Application of Python KG

We developed three functions of personalized online knowledge graph and applied it to python teaching. We selected a class of students to do the experiment and verified the effectiveness of the knowledge graph.

4.1   Providing the Function of Mind Mapping

After importing all the nodes and relationships, the python course knowledge graph is completed. It visualizes the python course knowledge in the form of a graph, which has the same effect as the mind map. In the knowledge graph, you can use the MATCH (n) RETURN n statement to select the number of nodes you want to view (Fig. 8).

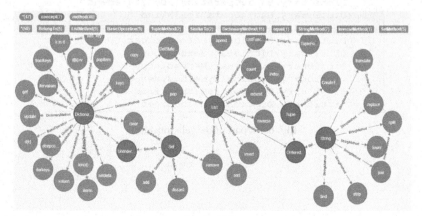

Fig. 8. Part of python knowledge and relationships.

4.2 Displaying the Ingredients of Knowledge Nodes

In the knowledge graph that has been constructed, click each node to display the attributes of the knowledge node and other knowledge nodes related to the knowledge node. As shown in the figure, when the mouse clicks on the List node, the definition of List will be displayed: List (List) is the most commonly used Python data type, it can appear as a comma-separated value in square brackets; In python course Knowledge Graph, we can clearly see the relationship and the distinction between knowledge and knowledge, As shown in the Fig. 9, both List and Tuple have methods such as count and index.

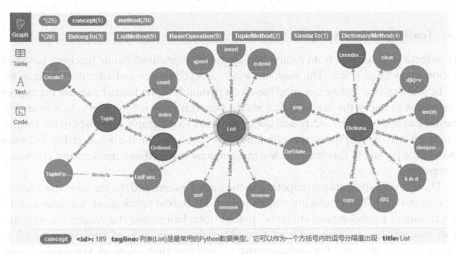

Fig. 9. Part of python knowledge and relationships.

4.3 Querying the Logical Relationships in Knowledge Links

The knowledge graph can be used to query the logical relationship between knowledge points, which effectively improves the efficiency of searching for the relationship between knowledge points and knowledge points. In the python course knowledge graph, the cypher query language can be used to query the knowledge points according to the requirements. For example, use the following cypher statement to query which concepts belong to an ordered sequence: match p = (concept)-[:BelongTo]- > (:Ordered-Sequence)return concept, After the cypher statement is executed, the result shown in the figure below is returned. List, Tuple, and String are all ordered sequences. Use the following cypher statement to query all concepts that have more than three basic operations: match (c:concept)-[:BasicOperation]- > (m:method) with c,count(m)as mCount where mCount > 3 return c,mCount. The result is shown in the Fig. 10.

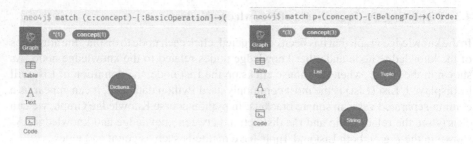

Fig. 10. Part of python knowledge and relationships

4.4 Teaching Effect Analysis

We selected 52 students from a class and applied personalized online teaching based on python knowledge graph. The students were surveyed before and after the application.

In personalized online teaching based on python KG, the learner can use the cypher statements to query the logical relationship between knowledge points. Moreover, the learner can add, delete, modify and query the knowledge graph, and display the results, which effectively improves the efficiency of searching for the relationship between knowledge points. In this way, the learning interest is raised and the learning efficiency is improved.

There are 52 students participating in the questionnaire and the questionnaire recovery rate is 100%. The results are shown in Fig. 11. Before application, we designed the questionnaire to understand students' python foundation, and the results showed that most students had no python foundation. After the application of knowledge graph in teaching, we redesigned the questionnaire on whether students think knowledge graph is helpful for their learning. The results showed that more than 90% of students thought it was helpful. Therefore, personalized online knowledge graph is very effective.

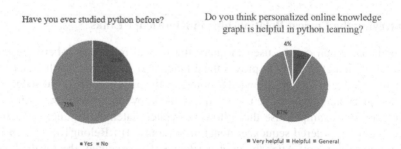

Fig. 11. Questionnaire results before and after application of knowledge graph

5   Summary and Prospect

In this paper, the curriculum knowledge graph of python is constructed with the entity and relation extracted from knowledge points of python course. As three teaching functions explored, we applied the python KG in personalized online teaching. The experimental results demonstrated the effectiveness of python KG in online teaching. Firstly, the knowledge points are clearly displayed for the students, as the same effect shown in the mind map. Secondly, it is helpful for students to understand the knowledge points as well as the relationships between knowledge points. Finally, a student can click on any node in the knowledge graph to view the attributes of the knowledge point represented by the node, and grasp the logical associations in knowledge links.

In the future work, more researches and applications will be done based on knowledge graph, aiming to achieve personalized online teaching and learning with high efficiency.

Acknowledgement. This work is supported by National Nature Science Foundation of China (No. 61672329, No. 61773246, 62072290), Shandong Provincial Project of Graduate Education Quality Improvement (No. SDYY18058, No. SDYJG19171), Industry-University Cooperation and Education Project of Ministry of Education (No. 201901025009, No. 201901140022, No. 201902009008, No. 201902293009, No. 201902173028).

References

1. Singhal, A.: Official Google Blog: Introducing the Knowledge Graph: Things, Not Strings (2021). https://blog.csdn.net/eli00001/article/details/64905724
2. Berners-Lee, T., Hendler, J., Lassila, O.: "The Semantic Web" in Scientific American. Lect. Notes Comput. Sci. (2001)
3. Liu, Q., Li, Y., Duan, H., Liu, Y.: Knowledge graph construction techniques. J. Comput. Res. Develop. (2016)
4. Yuan, Y.: Chinese business knowledge mapping based on deep learning and graph database. Lib. Inf. 1, 110–117 (2016)
5. Swick, R.R., Consortium, W.W.W.: Resource description framework (RDF) model and syntax specification. W3C Recommend. (1998)
6. Partner, J., Vukotic, A., Watt, N.: Neo4j in Action. Pearson Schweiz Ag (2014)
7. Zhang, Z.: Neo4j Authoritative Guide. Tsinghua University Press, Tsinghua University (2017)
8. Sen, S., Mehta, A., Ganguli, R., Sen, S.: Recommendation of influenced products using association rule mining: Neo4j as a case study. SN Comput. Sci. 2, 2 (2021)
9. Miller, J.: Graph Database Applications and Concepts with Neo4j. Comput. Sci. (2013)
10. Yu, X., Lam, W., Chen, B.: Chinese NER Using CRFs and logic for the fourth SIGHAN Bakeoff. In: Proceedings of the Sixth SIGHAN Workshop on Chinese Language Processing, pp. 102–105 (2018)

LDA Topic Mining of Light Food Customer Reviews on the Meituan Platform

Miaojia Huang[1], Songqiao Wen[2], Manhua Jiang[2(✉)], and Yuliang Yao[2(✉)]

[1] College of Management, Shenzhen University, Shenzhen, People's Republic of China
2016040301@email.szu.edu.cn
[2] College of Mathematics and Statistics, Shenzhen University, Shenzhen, People's Republic of China

Abstract. Light food refers to healthy and nutritious food that has the characteristics of low calorie, low fat, and high fiber. Light food has been favored by the public, especially by the young generation in recent years. Moreover, affected by the COVID-19 epidemic, consumers' awareness of a healthy diet has been improved to a certain extent. As both take-out and in-place orders for light food are growing rapidly, there are massive customer reviews left on the Meituan platform. However, massive, multi-dimensional unstructured data has not yet been fully explored. This research aims to explore the customers' focal points and sentiment polarity of the overall comments and to investigate whether there exist differences of these two aspects before and after the COVID-19. A total of 6968 light food customer reviews on the Meituan platform were crawled and finally used for data analysis. This research first conducted the fine-grained sentiment analysis and classification of the light food customer reviews via the SnowNLP technique. In addition, LDA topic modeling was used to analyze positive and negative topics of customer reviews. The experimental results were visualized and the research showed that the SnowNLP technique and LDA topic modeling achieve high performance in extracting the customers' sentiments and focal points, which provides theoretical and data support for light food businesses to improve customer service. This research contributes to the existing research on LDA modeling and light food customer review analysis. Several practical and feasible suggestions are further provided for managers in the light food industry.

Keywords: Light food · Review analysis · LDA topic modeling · Sentiment analysis · Customer review

1 Introduction

With the consumption upgrading and the continuous improvement of the national awareness of healthy eating, the term "light food", which features low fat, low heat, low sugar, high fiber, and high protein, has been popular with more and more consumers. According to the "China Light Food Takeout Consumption Report" released by the Meituan Takeout, the number of searches of four keywords on the Meituan APP, namely light food, fat-reducing meal, weight-loss meal, and healthy meal, increased by 235.8%, 200.6%,

© Springer Nature Singapore Pte Ltd. 2021
Y. Tan et al. (Eds.): DMBD 2021, CCIS 1454, pp. 108–121, 2021.
https://doi.org/10.1007/978-981-16-7502-7_13

186.4%, and 116.0%, respectively, compared with that of 2018. As of September 2019, orders for the Meituan takeaway light food increased by 98% and numbers of light food stores increased by 58% year on year [1]. As the consumption of "light food" is increasing, a large number of emerging light food restaurants are also taking advantage of this trend.

As light food gets popular across the whole nation, there are many new entrants flooding the market and many losers exiting the market. The data released by Trend makers [2] shows that a total of 1,251 light food businesses had finished the logout registration by May 2019. Although this market has the features of low industry barriers, serious homogenization and fierce competitions, a small number of light food brands still have succeeded in standing out in the market and formed their characteristics with high repurchase rate, and even became daily the rigid needs among some college students and urban white-collars. Therefore, how to understand the hidden preferences of the light food consumers and help light food merchants cultivate user stickiness is a problem that every entrant in the light food industry needs to think about.

With the rapid growth of light food orders, there is a huge number of multi-dimensional customer reviews left on the Meituan platform, conveying customers' inner feelings and emotions under certain consumption situations. For potential customers, this user-generated content (UGC) plays a key role in reducing information overload and facilitating them to make consumption decisions. For light food businesses, this UGC acts as electronic word of mouth (eWOM) on the Meituan platform. However, this UGC has not yet been fully extracted and utilized and there is a lack of research on text analysis of the customer review in the light food industry. This is a pity because positive reviews left by satisfied customers were found to have significant positive impacts on product sales [3] and long-term performance [4]. Furthermore, customer negative reviews might cost a lot to businesses since these dissatisfied customers might spread negative eWOM or even switch to competitors [5]. In such cases, regaining the lost consumers via improvement is profitable to businesses instead of attracting potential consumers [6]. Therefore, investigating customers' negative reviews would help managers better understand their service design and service failure while making improvements accordingly.

Moreover, the COVID-19 brings about some changes to the light food industry. On one hand, the consumption of light food seems to increase as the public gradually enhances their health awareness in the post-epidemic era. On the other hand, as one of the industries that are hardest hit by the COVID-19 epidemic, managers in the catering industry are highly concerned about the new business operation tactics after the COVID-19 outbreak. Therefore, examining whether there is a difference in light food customers' focus points and emotional polarity based on the text mining results from their reviews and then giving better insights to light food marketers have become important and urgent.

Therefore, to address the above research gaps, this study seeks to explore the following two research questions:

RQ1: (1) What are the topics of the light food customer reviews on the Meituan platform?
RQ2: (2) Is there any change in the focus and emotion of consumers based on the comments left before and after the outbreak of the COVID-19 epidemic?

This research aims to get a more in-depth capture of the emotional experience of light food consumers and extract the main topics based on massive and scattered customer reviews, which is conducive to the merchants to accurately improve their products, services and consequently improve customer experiences. The novelty of this study is twofold. Firstly, the large dataset across 2017 to 2021 enables us to explore the influencing factors of customers' satisfaction and dissatisfaction before and after the COVID-19 epidemic via different text analysis tools, namely, frequency analysis, word cloud, and sentiment analysis. Secondly, previous studies identified customer preferences and complaints via survey data, which might fail to capture the hidden dimensions for improvement [7]. By analyzing the changing process of the focal points and emotional polarity of the comments of the light food customers before and after the epidemic, this paper provides the basis for the relevant merchants to improve the user experience and helps these small and medium-sized enterprises to better serve customers and cope with the business crisis in the post-epidemic era.

The remainder of this research is arranged as follows: Sect. 2 presents the related literature. Section 3 demonstrates the data-driven approach (i.e., LDA modeling) and the experiments using the light food consumer reviews in Meituan.com. Section 4 concludes the data analysis results and discusses some practical implications for managers in the light food industry. Section 5 summarizes the study and proposes some future directions of research.

2   Literature Review

2.1   Sentiment Analysis

Sentiment analysis methods that are widely adopted in previous research include the deep learning method based on neural network, the method based on sentiment dictionary and rules, the machine learning method based on feature extraction, and the multi-strategy hybrid method. For example, Ruz et al. [8] used the Bayesian network classifier to conduct sentiment analysis on two Spanish data sets (Chile earthquake in 2010 and Catalonia independence referendum in 2017). The results show that the Bayesian network classifier is superior to other machine learning methods (support vector machine and random forest). Gopalakrishnan et al. [9] proposed a simplified LSTM model with six different parameters to achieve sentiment analysis on the Twitter dataset of the debates of the Republican Party in America. Results reveal that different parameter settings and model layer settings would have an impact on the experimental results. Wang and Wu [10] calculated the emotional tendency and the degree of attention of the tourists' reviews on the tourist attractions in Xiamen by constructing the positive and negative emotion dictionary and the tourism image attribute glossaries. Based on the hierarchical quantile regression model, Wang and Gao [11] analyzed the emotions of the online travel reviews, investigated the main factors affecting the scenic spot evaluation, and further explored the potential correlation among these factors.

2.2 Latent Dirichlet Allocation (LDA) Topic Modeling

Customer reviews often convey a wealth of information, but as Aggarwal and Zhai [12] noted, dealing with large volumes of unstructured textual data requires an automated approach to facilitate effective analysis. Text mining techniques can draw some useful business insights from online reviews by computing features and their corresponding weights (e.g., word frequency) [13]. LDA topic modeling is the most widely used and effective method of topic extraction. For example, Yang et al., [14] completed fine-grained sentiment analysis and classification of tourist reviews through sentiment dictionary and SnowNLP technique. They further extracted the positive and negative topics in tourist comments via LDA topic modeling to better understand the underlying reasons for their sentiment polarity. Chen et al. [15] employed the LDA topic model to identify the topics of the user reviews of the health and medical wearable devices. They further conducted sentiment analysis on the user reviews under the corresponding topic to explore the relationship between the extracted topics and the users' satisfaction.

To sum up, there are few studies on the comment analysis of the light food area and limited studies employing both the SnowNLP and LDA modeling for detailed analysis of the users' sentiment and focal points. To fill the above-mentioned research gaps, this research proposes a method combining SnowNLP and LDA modeling, where the SnowNLP technique can effectively extract the customers' emotions and the LDA modeling can help extract the positive and negative topics of the comments. This will help to identify the customers' focus during the consumption of light food and provide some practical implications for the operators of light food to better improve the customer service.

3 Methodology

3.1 Naive Bayes Method

Regarding sentiment analysis, this study adopts the SnowNLP module in Python, which classifies emotions of the review text (e.g., positive and negative) based on the Naive Bayes method. The Bayesian algorithm was first proposed by Bayesian and then improved and extended by Laplace. Pang et al. [16] first applied the Naive Bayes method to sentiment analysis. The implementation of the algorithm is as follows. First, the algorithm sets the segmentation rules and stopping thesaurus. Second, the positive and negative corpora are segmented and some useless words are removed according to the stop word list and the frequency of each word segmentation is then calculated. Third, according to the frequency, the conditional probability of a word appearing in positive or negative comments as well as in the overall text can be calculated. Finally, the comment text to be classified is segmented, and the posterior probability is calculated according to the words in the text. Based on the aforementioned steps, the text can be classified into positive or negative.

The reasons for choosing this model are as follows: (1) Compared with other sentiment analysis methods, this model has stronger mobility. By replacing the corpus of related fields, the model can perform sentiment analysis on any domain. (2) There is no need to decompose the sentence components or analyze the grammatical semantics in using this model. Instead, it calculates the posterior probability after separating the words in the corpus to judge the emotion of comments.

3.2 LDA Topic Mining

LDA, as one of the most popular methods for topic modeling, is first introduced by Blei et al. [17]. The researchers assume that the topic extraction process is as follows: First, the model randomly generates the topic distribution of a specific text and randomly generates a topic according to the topic distribution at each position in the text. Second, it randomly generates a word according to the word distribution of the topic. Third, the above process is repeated continuously until words are generated at each position of the text.

LDA topic modeling is a probabilistic model based on Bayesian estimation based on this assumption. Its characteristic is to learn a given text set with Dirichlet distribution as a prior distribution of multi-nominal distribution and to solve all parameters of the model through the estimation of a posteriori probability distribution to get the topic distribution of the text.

When adopting the LDA method, the number of topics, the hyper-parameter, and Dirichlet distribution need to be determined first. Figure 1 presents the plate notation of the LDA model, in which the solid nodes represent observed variables, hollow nodes represent hidden variables, directed edges represent probabilistic dependency relations, the rectangle represents repeated operations, and the numbers inside the rectangle represent the number of repeats. The four steps of the LDA algorithm for text generation is demonstrated as the figure shows:

(1) Randomly generates a topic distribution θ_i of the given text i from the Dirichlet distribution α;
(2) Randomly generates the topic $Z_{i,j}$ for the ith word of the given text i from the topic polynomial distribution θ_i;
(3) Randomly generates the corresponding word distribution $\varphi_{i,j}$ of each topic $Z_{i,j}$ from the Dirichlet distribution β;
(4) Repeated the above three steps and finally generates the word $\omega_{i,j}$ from the word polynomial distribution $\varphi_{i,j}$.

The reasons for choosing this model in this study are as follows: (1) It only needs to train the sample data without manually annotating the data. (2) It has a stronger generalization ability that can avoid the over-fitting issue to a large extent; (3) The model has high explanatory performance because the model can find some words to describe each extracted topic.

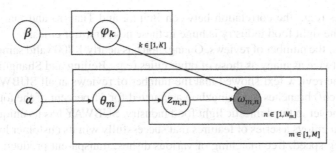

Fig. 1. Process of LDA modeling

4 Experiments

4.1 Dataset

The data used in this research was crawled by a data collector called Houyi data collector (http://www.houyicaiji.com). We focus on the light food store information and consumer reviews of the top 11 cities on the Meituan official website, including Beijing, Shanghai, Guangzhou, Shenzhen, Tianjin, Xi'an, Chongqing, Hangzhou, Nanjing, Wuhan, and Chengdu. Each data sample contains seven features: store name, rating, group purchase discount, menu, the total number of reviews, review text, and review time. A total of 30041 sample data was collected and 6968 samples were left after data cleaning. The data cleaning process includes the following two steps: (1) Considering the sample timeliness and the content validity, we deleted the comments before January 1st, 2017, and the light food stores that have no comments; (2) We deleted the samples that are blank, repeated and the ones that have less than four characters.

4.2 Data Description

According to the "Hot Cities" ranking on the Meituan official website, the main arena of domestic light food consumption is Beijing, Shanghai, Guangzhou, Shenzhen, Tianjin, Xi 'an, Chongqing, Hangzhou, Nanjing, Wuhan, and Chengdu. Therefore, research focuses on light food store information and consumer reviews in these 11 cities. The number of light food stores, as well as the total number of consumer reviews in each city is shown in Fig. 2. As can be seen from the figure, Beijing, Shanghai, and Guangzhou have the largest number of light food businesses. The light food businesses in these cities can be explained by the following reasons. These cities have a high level of economic development and advanced high-tech industries and service industries, which attract a large number of young people to these cities. These younger generations are living a fast-paced and stressful life and they have begun to embrace a new, healthy lifestyle.

Since 2016, some entrepreneurs who have a keen sense of business have started to set up their light food businesses in these cities. As of April 1st, 2021, Beijing had a total of 194 light food businesses, followed by Shanghai (137), and Guangzhou (119). The number of stores in Tianjin outperforms the other 7 new first-tier cities indicates that the light food industry has gradually developed from first-tier cities to the surrounding new first-tier cities (e.g., the correlation between Beijing and Tianjin) and that the market potential of the light food industry is huge in these new first-tier cities.

In terms of the number of reviews, Guangzhou has nearly 1,700 valid samples, which is more than twice as many as those of other cities (e.g., Beijing and Shanghai). Further analysis of the review text showed that the number of reviews at all SUBWAY (http://subway.com.cn/) branches in Guangzhou accounted for 31 percent of the total reviews. As the first-mover in the domestic light food industry, SUBWAY has its unique business strategy and it enjoys a series of features that successfully win its customer loyalty, such as fast serving speed, free matching of various dishes, transparent production process, and so on.

4.3   Experiment Settings

Firstly, sentiment analysis of the review text using the SnowNLP module was conducted after data cleaning. Secondly, topic extraction of the positive and negative comments obtained by sentiment analysis was conducted using LDA modeling. The optimal parameters were found through multiple training models before the final fitting model was determined.

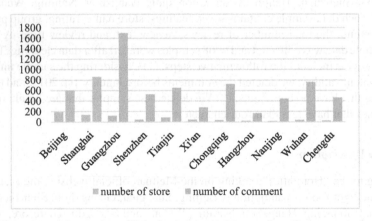

Fig. 2. Histogram of the number of light food stores and the number of customer reviews in each city

To improve the model prediction accuracy, three improvements were made regarding the SnowNLP module: (1) We replaced the word segmentation function in SnowNLP source code with Jieba word segmentation code because the precise model of Jieba word segmentation can achieve a more accurate sentence division, which is more suitable for text analysis. (2) We imported stop words and a dictionary, combined adverbs and verbs, filtered out a large number of meaningless words and symbols, and improve the word segmentation ability of SnowNLP on light food review analysis. (3) Replaced the default shopping corpus of SnowNLP with the corpus related to the catering industry to further improve the accuracy of sentiment analysis. 1000 comments were tested in the end and the accuracy of sentiment prediction has reached 88.4%.

To get the best number of topics, LDA models with a different number of topics are built step by step from 2 to 10. For each model, the first 50 high-frequency words and word frequency of different topics are obtained, and the number of all non-repetitive high-frequency words is represented by a vector to get the word frequency vector of each topic. The cosine similarity of these word frequency vectors is calculated, and the average value is obtained. Cosine similarity represents the similarity between vectors. The smaller the value is, the lower the similarity between vectors is, and the more different the content expressed between topics is.

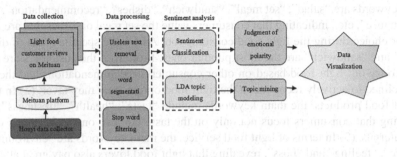

Fig. 3. Experiment setting

5   Results and Discussion

5.1   Topic Analysis of Overall Reviews

Keyword Analysis. The keywords of light food customer reviews on the Meituan were extracted and synonymously merged based on word representation. The top 20 keywords were selected for statistics, and the overall word frequency graph was shown in Fig. 4.

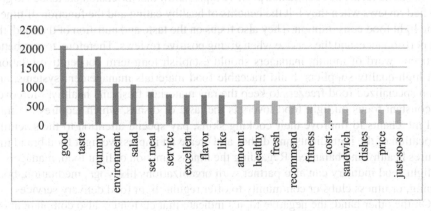

Fig. 4. Histogram of word frequency of overall reviews.

As can be seen from Fig. 4, the customer reviews on the light food area of the Meituan platform are generally positive as the keyword of "good" ranks the first and "yummy" ranks the third, and the customers' focal points mainly include taste, types of set meals, which again highlights that the emerging light food lovers value the taste of light food most. The keywords of "service", "environment" and "cost performance" revealed that these customers also pay great attention to the perceived service quality and dining environment.

Specifically, the overall focal points of light food consumer reviews on the Meituan platform can be categorized as follows: (1) Regarding the selection of light food, the main keywords are "salad", "set meal", "sandwich", "dishes", "recommendation", "cost performance", etc., indicating that consumers value the set meal or dishes that are available for choice during the light food consumption. As for the specific types of dishes, "salad" and "sandwich" are the most popular ones. Moreover, the customers are more likely to try out light food based on other consumers' recommendations and they are also inclined to actively recommend the light food options that they favor. (2) In terms of light food products, the main keywords include "taste", "health", "freshness", etc., indicating that consumers focus not only on the taste but also on the freshness of the raw materials. (3) In terms of light food service, the main keywords are "environment", "service", "feeling" and "boss", revealing that light food lovers also pay great attention to the dining environment and service. For example, some customers care about whether the restaurant is clean, whether the boss is approachable, as well as the service quality of the service staff.

Topic Analysis. Topic analysis of both the positive and negative comments was conducted via LDA topic modeling. Three positive topics and three negative ones as well as their corresponding keywords were eventually extracted and summarized. As illustrated in Table 1, three positive topics consist (1) healthy diet and fitness; (2) taste and nutrition; (3) cost performance and customer service, whereas the negative topics include: (1) Group purchase discount and taste; (2) customer service and dishes selection; (3) dining environment and food security.

On one hand, the three extracted positive topics show that the customers tended to give satisfied reviews when they felt the benefits of healthy eating and the function of fitness of the light food consumption. They also focus on the taste and nutrition of the food, the cost performance, and the service when giving positive reviews. Therefore, to win better electronic word of mouth, managers should establish long-term cooperative relations with high-quality suppliers, build traceable food materials management systems, and set up specialized food freezers to keep the raw materials fresh and healthy. Moreover, the constant focus on light food lovers is the taste of dishes, which requires the light food merchants to improve their cooking skills, pay special attention to the scientific collocation of the ingredients and dishes and create an impressive light food brand that features healthy and balanced. Regarding the fitness function of light food, managers in the light food industry can also partner with organizations like yoga, meditation, body shaping, or fitness clubs or community to offer regular light food delivery services.

On the other hand, the negative topics indicate that customers also complain about the low actual perception of group purchase discount, the limited types of food and flavor, the unprofessional customer service, and the dining environment and food with

Table 1. Topic extraction based on overall reviews

Keywords	Positive topics	Keywords	Negative topics
Good, environment, like, favor, yummy, healthy, clean, fitness, weight loss	Healthy diet and fitness	Attitude, taste, not yummy, goods, group purchase, service staff, little amount, the Meituan, service attitude	Group purchase discount and taste
Taste, yummy, taste, good, like, healthy, fresh, salad, sandwich, nutritious	Taste and nutrition	Service, just-so-so, service attitude, waiter, set meal, bad, food, bad, dishes	Customer service and dishes selection
Good, environment, favor, taste, set meals, service, yummy, salad, cost performance	Cost performance and customer service	Not tasty, little amount, taste, service, just-so–so, environment, group purchase, service staff, food hygiene	Dining environment and food security

poor sanitary level. Results also reveal that "group purchase discount" and "cost performance" are the focus of consumers' attention. Thus, businesses can design more group purchase discount schemes and implant some convenient tools that consumers can share on various social platforms and quickly realize crowd-ordering. In this way, consumers can enjoy discounts whereas the managers can use group ordering tools to achieve a unified food distribution and after-sales management system. Furthermore, light food, as a new star in the catering industry, customer perception of service quality is a very important part of the whole consumption process, considerate service can greatly attract and retain customers. Employers in the light food industry can train their employees regularly to improve their professional quality. As for the environment, managers in the light food industry can create a dining environment in harmony with light food culture and improve service quality. For example, they can create unique storefront layout and decoration style according to the themes of green, ecology, health, nature, and so on. In this way, customers can get a unified dining experience of light food products and a dining atmosphere. They can also provide customers with a transparent production process of light food, reducing customers' concerns about food hygiene issues.

5.2 Topic Analysis of Reviews During COVID-19 Epidemic

To track the changes of the online review focal points before and after the COVID-19 epidemic, we first analyzed how the number of comments changed over time from the fourth quarter of 2017 to the first quarter of 2021.

As illustrated in Fig. 5 the cumulative number of consumers' comments on light food in the last three years before the epidemic (at the end of 2019) was the same as the number of comments in the year after the epidemic. Moreover, a significant drop in the number of comments can be easily noticed in the first quarter of 2020 because of the outbreak of COVID-19 whereas, in the post-pandemic era, consumers' enthusiasm for light food consumption has significantly improved. The following reasons might account for this phenomenon. Firstly, according to the data released by the National Bureau of Statistics, catering income declined by 43.1% year on year from January 2020 to February 2020, leaving heavy blows and huge challenges for most light food businesses. Secondly, most restaurants suspend operations or even close down because of the unprecedented challenges brought by the COVID-19 and some food services in the light food restaurants are unavailable (e.g., eat-in service) since the epidemic-combating policies are very strict among first-tier cities. During the epidemic period, many consumers voluntarily reduced the frequency of eating out and ordering takeaway food based on safety considerations. They tended to cook at home or eat in school or company canteens.

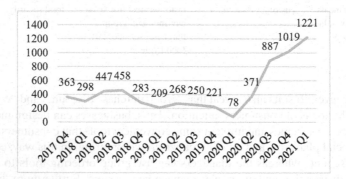

Fig. 5. Comparison of the number of reviews before and after the epidemic.

After diving the overall comments into two groups, where one is the pre-epidemic phase with 3514 reviews left from January 2017 to December 2019 whereas the other is the post-epidemic phase with 3679 comments covering the period from January 2020 to March 2021. we compared and analyzed the content in these two stages respectively and the results are visualized in the two Word Cloud maps (Fig. 6) and the keywords are listed in Table 1.

Fig. 6. Hot word cloud of reviews before (left) and after (right) the COVID-19.

As Table 2 presented, customer reviews of light food tend to appear positive, regardless of the COVID-19 outbreak. After experiencing the epidemic, people's favorable attitude towards light food consumption is improving (the word frequencies of the keyword of "like" are 823 and 1030 respectively).and the consumers seem to still put "health", "taste" and "environment" in the first place. Moreover, after the epidemic, consumers pay more attention to "cost performance", "set meals" when leaving messages in the light food comment area.

Table 2. The changes of the top 11 keywords before and after the epidemic (excluding the keyword of "good").

No.	Keywords before COVID-19 (word frequency)	Keywords after COVID-19 (word frequency)	Rank (changes)
1	Cost performance (70)	Cost performance (380)	↑49
2	Set meal (129)	Set meal (741)	↑18
3	Taste (217)	Taste (646)	↑5
4	Service (327)	Service (512)	↑2
5	Amount (172)	Amount (395)	↑2
6	Like (823)	Like (1030)	—
7	Yummy (818)	Yummy (1007)	—
8	Environment (445)	Environment (672)	—
9	Fresh (317)	Fresh (299)	↓4
10	Salad (614)	Salad (455)	↓4
11	Health (336)	Health (293)	↓7

6   Conclusion, Limitation and Future Research

6.1   Conclusion

Based on a dataset of 6968 light food customer reviews on the Meituan platform, this research first conducted the sentiment analysis and classification of the light food customer comments via the SnowNLP technique. In addition, LDA topic modeling was used to analyze positive and negative topics of customer reviews. The experimental results were visualized and the research showed that the SnowNLP technique and LDA modeling achieve high performance in extracting the customers' sentiments and focal points, which provides theoretical and data support for light food businesses to improve customer service.

6.2 Limitation and Future Research

There are some limitations to this research. Firstly, this research only focuses on the specific type of food (i.e., light food) in a specific platform (i.e., the Meituan) and it might have some limitations on the generalization of the experiment results and implications. Secondly, we focus on how to use data analysis and visualization methods to mine the useful information in the comments in the light food area, whereas we do not compare the existing algorithm with other text analysis algorithms. More algorithm comparison and evaluation will be added to in future research to better prove the high performance and robustness of the results. Thirdly, this research only focuses on the word frequency and sentiment analysis of the customer online reviews. Future research might consider employing linear regression models to examine the associations of various text-based review features on customers rating scores, light food businesses ranking, overall financial performance, and so on.

Acknowledgement. This study is supported by Shenzhen University Postgraduate Innovation and Development Research Project (Special project for the centennial of the Founding of the Party) in the year of 2021(**No.315-0000470616**).

References

1. China Light Food Takeout Consumption Report. http://www.ce.cn/cysc/sp/info/201910/18/t20191018_33377815.shtml
2. Why on earth has the one hundred billion light food market dropped from the top? https://www.tmtpost.com/3972685.html. Assessed May 30
3. Chevalier, J.A., Mayzlin, D.: The effect of word of mouth on sales: online book reviews. J. Mark. Res. **43**(3), 345–354 (2006)
4. Alrawadieh, Z., Law, R.: Determinants of hotel guests' satisfaction from the perspective of online hotel reviewers. Int. J. Cult., Tourism Hospital. Res. **13**(1), 84–97 (2019)
5. Chittiprolu, V., Samala, N., Bellamkonda, R.S.: Heritage hotels and customer experience: a text mining analysis of online reviews. Int. J. Cult. Tourism Hospital. Res. **15**(2), 131–156 (2021)
6. Kumar, V., Bhagwat, Y., Zhang, X.: Regaining 'lost' customers: the predictive power of first-lifetime behavior, the reason for defection, and the nature of the win-back offer". J. Mark. **79**(4), 34–55 (2015)
7. Sun, K.A., Kim, D.Y.: Does customer satisfaction increase firm performance? An application of the American Customer Satisfaction Index (ACSI). Int. J. Hosp. Manag. **35**, 68–77 (2013)
8. Ruz, G.A., Henríquez, P.A., Mascareño, A.: Sentiment analysis of Twitter data during critical events through Bayesian networks classifiers. Futur. Gener. Comput. Syst. **106**, 92–104 (2020)
9. Gopalakrishnan, K., Salem, F.M.: Sentiment analysis using simplified long short-term memory recurrent neural networks (2020)
10. Wang, S., Wu, S.: Tourist attention and emotion analysis based on online comment text of scenic spots. J. Guizhou Univ. Nat. Sci. **34**(6), 69–73 (2017)
11. Wang, Q., Gao, W.: Sentiment statistical analysis of online travel reviews based on the hierarchical quantile regression model. China Price **12**, 82–85 (2019)
12. Aggarwal, C.C.: Mining text data. In: Data Mining, pp. 429–455. Springer, Cham (2015). https://doi.org/10.1007/978-3-319-14142-8_13

13. Miner, G., Elder IV, J., Fast, A., Hill, T., Nisbet, R., Delen, D.: Practical Text Mining and Statistical Analysis for Non-Structured Text Data Applications. Academic Press (2012)
14. Yang, X., Yang, D., Su, H., Song, Z., Yang, X., Luo, Z.: Topic mining of scenic spot reviews based on sentiment analysis. Libr. Inf. Guide **5**(08), 59–65 (2020)
15. Chen, S., Zhang, Y., Li, B.: Sentiment analysis of health and medical wearable device comments based on LDA model. Chin. J. Med. Libr. Inf. **29**(12), 41–47 (2020)
16. Pang, B., Lee, L., Vaithyanathan. S.: Thumbs up? sentiment classification using machine learning techniques. In: Language Processing (EMNLP), pp. 79–86. Philadelphia (2002)
17. Blei, D.M., Ng, A.Y., Jordan, M.I.: Latent Dirichlet allocation. J. Mach. Learn. Res. **3**, 993–1022 (2003)

Intrusion Detection Method Based on Small Sample Learning

Hao Yang[1], Yong Zhang[2]([✉]), Jingxin Liu[1], Hui Li[3], Jinyang Song[1],
Jieren Cheng[1,4]([✉]), and Xiulai Li[1]

[1] School of Computer Science and Technology, Hainan University, Haikou 570228, China
[2] Hainan Harbor & Shipping Holding Co., Ltd., Haikou 570311, China
zhang.yong9@coscoshipping.com
[3] Hainan Huochain Tech Company Limited, Haikou 570100, China
[4] Hainan Blockchain Technology Engineering Research Center, Hainan University, Haikou 570228, China

Abstract. Network security has always been facing new challenges. Accurate and convenient detection of intrusions is needed to protect system security. When the system encounters an intrusion, there may be a problem of insufficient early samples for this type of attack, resulting in a low recognition rate. It is necessary to consider whether it can be combined with a suitable intrusion detection method to realize the detection of abnormal data with only a small number of samples. In this paper, we propose an intrusion detection method based on small sample learning, which can process the intrusion behavior information so as to realize the classification of abnormal behaviors when the previous similar samples are insufficient. And ResNet is selected as the classification model to build a deeper network. We gradually increased the number of iterations and the number of small samples in the experiment, and got the performance changes of different models. Compared with CNN, SVM and other algorithms, the intrusion detection method is evaluated by performance indicators such as accuracy rate and false alarm rate. It is finally proved that ResNet can better deal with the intrusion detection classification problem under small sample data. It is more feasible and accurate, and can be widely used to determine network intrusion behavior.

Keywords: Small sample learning · Intrusion detection · Meta-learning · ResNet

1 Introduction

In the era of big data, research in machine learning is based on statistical models with sufficient training samples to predict future data. The prediction results depend on a large amount of training data and require large-scale testing data, but the cost and hardware requirements will be pretty high in practice. Therefore, for the application scenarios of lack of real data, this paper focuses on the weakly supervised learning method with small data dependence [1]. Small sample learning [2, 3] is an attempt to classify test samples under the condition of limited sample learning, combining prior knowledge and a small

Y. Tan et al. (Eds.): DMBD 2021, CCIS 1454, pp. 122–134, 2021.
https://doi.org/10.1007/978-981-16-7502-7_15

amount of supervision information [4]. Although small sample learning has achieved some good results in the field of image classification, there is not much research in the field of target detection, and further research is needed.

At the same time, there are still hidden threats to network security. Intrusion detection [5], which is a dynamic protection technology, is used to protect the security of the cyberspace and information systems. The purpose of intrusion detection is to accurately extract behavior features, judge the type of network behavior based on characteristic data, and distinguish between normal events and abnormal events.

As early as the 1980s and 1990s, researchers began to pay attention to the problem of single-sample learning, but it was not until 2003 that Li [6] and others formally proposed the concept of single-sample learning. Regarding the concept of small sample learning, it first emerged from the field of computer vision. Most researches are on image classification problems, but the development of language processing is slower [7]. The current small sample learning methods are roughly based on metrics. Learning, based on meta-learning, based on data augmentation, etc.; small sample target detection has received extensive attention in the field of practical significance, but there are indeed few work applications and there is a lot of room for development. Most of the existing small sample methods are simple fusions of small samples and image classification, which have more applications in image classification, and more authoritative and universal evaluation unified standards are required for target classification.

The research on intrusion detection began in the 1980s. James Anderson [8] proposed the concept of intrusion detection and made a series of expositions on intrusion detection. Later, intrusion detection attracted more and more attention from scholars, but the initial intrusion detection is mainly based on the theory of expert knowledge. In 1987, DEdenning [9] proposed the basic model of intrusion detection, and for the first time introduced the related content of intrusion detection into the level of computer security defense, which promoted the in-depth study of intrusion detection by experts and scholars. In 1989, TFL Lunt et al. proposed an improved model of the intrusion detection expert system IDES (intrusion detection expert system). Since 1990, many related researchers had been continuously applying deep learning, artificial intelligence and machine learning to intrusion detection, and proposed many innovative models in continuous exploration, such as the intrusion detection model based on graph neural network, have promoted the development and research process of intrusion detection research at home and abroad to a certain extent. At the same time, it will also be applied to future intrusion detection in the fields of smart life, medicine, and networks. Bring defensive convenience.

At present, various detection technologies have attracted wide attention with good performance and high accuracy, but there are also some problems. For example, in reality, there are not so many data given, which needs to be combined with small sample learning. How to combine feature analysis methods and matching classification methods at the same time [10] to improve detection performance is a problem that many people are paying attention to.

In this paper, we use different kinds of model for comparison, and choose the ResNet model to deal with the intrusion detection classification problem under small sample data. We have made the following contributions:

1. We use small samples to study intrusion detection methods. First, we analyze the characteristics of intrusion detection behaviors in the network. The analysis shows that the amount of network intrusion behavior data is not large, and we need to think about how to accurately detect intrusion behaviors under the condition of small samples. To make a detection, the ResNet intrusion detection method is proposed here.
2. We observe the changes in intrusion detection accuracy by increasing the number of iterations and the number of small samples, and compare them with algorithms such as CNN and SVM, and evaluate the intrusion detection method through performance indicators such as accuracy, and finally prove that ResNet can Better deal with intrusion detection classification problems under small sample data.

The rest of the paper is organized as follows. Section 2 presents related work, include the methods of small sample learning and intrusion detection. The main problems of them are also elaborated. Section 3 presents the classification model we used and its relationship with CNN. Section 4 presents the experimental ideas, experimental procedures and experimental results. At last, Sect. 5 makes a conclusion.

2   Related Work

2.1   Small Sample Learning Methods

According to the differences in the methods used in the learning process, small-sample learning can be divided into the following types: model-based fine-tuning, data-based enhancement, and transfer-based learning [12].

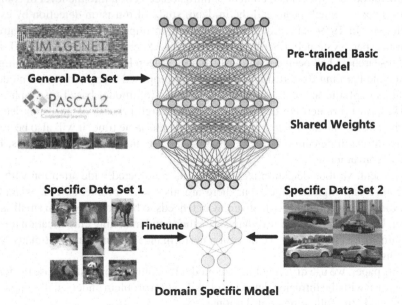

Fig. 1. Model-based fine-tuning

As shown in Fig. 1, the method of model-based fine-tuning is based on a large data set. First, a classification model is trained on it, and then it is trained on the target small data set to finetune the fully connected layer or deep layer parameters. This has been widely used on some e-commerce platforms, and the model needs to be fixed before simulation. This method is relatively fast, does not rely on too much data, and the effect is not bad.

However, this method is likely to lead to overfitting, because in this process, the small amount of data we use does not reflect the actual distribution of a large amount of data in reality. So In order to solve the above over-fitting problem, we have a small sample learning method based on data enhancement and transfer learning.

The method based on data enhancement is to use some auxiliary data sets or auxiliary information to enhance the characteristic content of the samples in the target data set, that is, to expand the target data set, so that the data model can better extract relevant features. There are several small sample learning methods for data enhancement, which are respectively based on data synthesis, unlabeled data and feature enhancement. The auxiliary data is used to convert the samples (xi, yi) in the new category set Dnovel into multiple samples according to certain rules, and add them to the original data set Dnovel to form a larger data set D'novel, this larger data set can be trained directly under the deep model because they contain more data, as shown in Fig. 2.

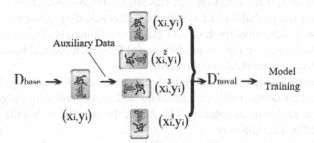

Fig. 2. Data enhancement

The method based on transfer learning is currently relatively cutting-edge and uses many methods. It is an analogous learning of known and unknown learning behaviors. Transfer learning methods can be divided into metric-based learning, meta-learning and neural network-based learning. Metric-based learning and meta-learning are widely used because of small errors.

Metric-based learning is to determine the distance between unknown and known classification data through mathematical operations, so that the classification result of the sample to be classified can be determined. The method based on neural network is currently widely used, and the more commonly used ones are graph convolutional neural network and graph attention neural network and so on. The graph neural network has strong interpretability and better performance, and there is a lot of room for improvement.

2.2   The Main Problems of Small Sample Learning Methods

Because some small samples are not enough and the typical sample size is not enough, it may not be able to describe the feature distribution of the entire category more accurately, so the learning accuracy of small samples is not high enough, and the error is large. In the actual training of machine learning models, over-fitting may occur.

Among the existing small-sample learning methods, both the method based on model fine-tuning and the method based on transfer learning need to use a large amount of data and pre-train it. This violates the essential requirements of small-sample learning because of the need A large amount of data is used to identify, so it is necessary to study how to use prior knowledge to train it.

2.3   Intrusion Detection Methods

Two common intrusion detection behaviors are abnormal intrusion detection and misuse intrusion detection [14]. Abnormal intrusion detection is to match the normal behavior of the system. Through the definition of the normal behavior of the network, when the normal behavior of the system is determined, the network is monitored and behavior matching is performed. If it can be matched, it is a normal behavior.

Commonly used anomaly intrusion detection methods are as follows: (1) Anomaly detection based on feature selection. (2) Bayesian inference detection method, which refers to judging the probability of system intrusion based on abnormal behavior. (3) Bayesian network detection method. (4) Based on statistical detection method. (5) Detection method based on pattern prediction. (6) Detection method based on machine learning. (7) Detection method based on data mining.

Misuse of intrusion detection technology, also understood as characteristic intrusion detection, is to first define malicious behavior and make matching judgments on the results of system real-time monitoring. Of course, the premise is that the intrusion can be characterized in a certain way.

As far as misuse intrusion detection methods are concerned, they are mainly as follows: (1) Misuse intrusion detection based on conditional probability. (2) Misuse intrusion detection based on state transition analysis, different states represent the characteristics of the system in different periods. By detecting the state, you can find out whether there is an intrusion in the system, and the behavior on the state diagram can be used as the attack feature. (3) Keyboard monitoring. (4) Rule-based misuse detection method [15].

2.4   The Main Problems of Intrusion Detection Methods

For intrusion detection methods, there are mainly the following problems: 1. Effectiveness, the amount of data in the current network is very large, due to the continuous increase of flow data, intrusion detection is currently unable to quickly detect large amounts of data 2. Adaptability For some newly emerging intrusion behaviors, some intrusion detection systems are not well analyzed and cannot be accurately identified. 3. Scalability, some intrusion detection systems are related to the environment, so if the environment needs to be replaced, the system is self-expanding The performance is not good enough to reuse the new environment. The above issues need to be emphatically considered when doing intrusion detection research in the future.

3 Model

This paper proposes an intrusion detection method based on ResNet to explore whether this method can accurately judge network intrusion behaviors with a small amount of samples. ResNet is improved on the basis of traditional CNN, mainly by constructing a residual block through identity mapping. And CNN is currently the most advanced image classification model, one of the representative algorithms of deep learning [16], and has the ability of feature learning.

This paper looks for an improved CNN model [17]. Based on past experience, the performance of the network can be improved by increasing the number of network layers. It can also perform better feature extraction for complex data, but the experiment found that the continuous increase in the number of layers does not necessarily make the experiment have a better performance, or even regress. For a network with a low number of layers, if you simply increase the number of network layers and perform identity mapping under other conditions unchanged, then the performance of the deep network will theoretically be at least the same as that of the shallow layer, but this is not the case. ResNet, which focuses on the problem of network performance that may regress as the number of network layers continues to increase. Assuming that for the stacked network's input x, the result of hierarchical learning is H(x), then the learned residual is $F(x) = H(x) - x$. The learning structure of the residual unit is shown in Fig. 3. The X path is an identity mapping, called a "shortcut". The main function is to keep the output consistent with the output of the F(x) path.

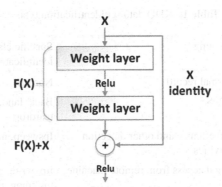

Fig. 3. Residual learning structure diagram

In this structure, the target that needs to be optimized is converted from H(x) to H(x) − x, the training difficulty is relatively reduced, and it is easier to optimize, which can greatly deepen the number of network layers.

In this experiment, this paper uses the ResNet structure for processing, assuming that the neural network input is x, and the expected input is H(x). For the residual learning unit, the learning goal is F(x) = H(x) − x. The general expression of a residual block is as Eq. 3–1.

$$y_l = h(x_l) + F(x_l, W_l)$$
$$x_{l+1} = f(y_l)$$
(1)

For a deeper level of L, the residual relationship can be expressed as

$$x_L = x_l + \sum_{i=l}^{L-1} F(x_i, W_i)$$
(2)

4 Experiments

4.1 Data Set

We chose KDD99 as the data set, which is a commonly used network intrusion detection data set. The data is a sequence of data packets obtained by the network connection between the source IP and the destination IP within a certain period of time, including normal and abnormal data packets. The anomaly marker types include 4 categories, including 39 attack types, but only 22 types appear in the training set, and the rest are unknown attack types, that is, the 17 attack types that appear in the test set. The data set mainly includes four types of attacks as shown in Table 1.

Table 1. KDD data set identification type.

Identification type	Meaning	Specific classification identification
Normal	Normal record	Normal
Dos	DDoS	Back, land, neptune, pod, smurf, teardrop
Probling	Surveillance and other detection activities	Ipsweep, nmap, portsweep, satan
R2L	Illegal access from remote machine	ftp_write, guess_passwd, imap, multihop, phf, spy, warezclient, warezmaster
U2R	Illegal access by ordinary users to local super user privileges	buffer_overflow, loadmodule, perl, rootkit

4.2 Evaluation Index

For anomaly detection, there can be multiple indicators, common ones such as accuracy rate and false alarm rate. There are also TF, TN, PF, PN. Table 2 shows the meaning of each indicator. TF represents the matching relationship between prediction and reality, and is the final conclusion.

Table 2. Evaluation index

	Actual positive examples	Actual negative examples	
Predict positive examples P	TP	FP	P = TP/(TP + FP)
Predict negative examples N	FN	TN	FNR = FN/FN + TN
	R = TP/(TP + FN)	FPR = FP/(FP + TN)	A = (TP + TN)/TP + TN + FP + FN

Commonly used model indicators are precision, accuracy, error rate and false alarm rate. Precision represents the proportion of examples that are classified as positive examples that are actually positive examples. Accuracy is the most common evaluation indicator, which is the proportion of samples that are correctly classified among all samples. The error rate describes the opposite of accuracy, indicating the proportion of classification errors. The sum of error rate and accuracy is 1. The false alarm rate is the proportion of all negative samples classified as positive samples, namely FPR.

4.3 Implementation

We use ResNet to replace the CNN used for feature extraction of images in traditional small-sample learning methods. The required data set is an image type, so the flow information stored in the CSV type file needs to be read line by line and converted into a grayscale image for input. The value range of each pixel of the grayscale image is [0,255], and many data in the flow information are not in this range, including integer values greater than 255 and decimals between 0 and 1. We map each value to [0,255] according to its upper limit and round it. For the string type data contained therein, it also needs to be converted into an integer value in the range. The method is to first convert it into a decimal integer, and then use the aforementioned method to map the last three digits. After all the numerical conversions are completed, the grayscale image is expanded to meet the minimum input scale required by the ResNet network.

We used a small sample learning method based on pre-training and fine-tuning, which is not complicated but effective. The parameters of the shallow network obtained by pre-training are retained to extract data features, and the fully connected layer is fine-tuned to adapt to the new classification requirements. For the four kinds of abnormal flow information of Dos, Probling, R2L, and U2R in the data set, according to the number of their specific flow types, take out several types of data as the data set required for fine-tuning in small-sample learning, and the rest are used as pre-training Data set. In this way, it is ensured that the flow information used for fine-tuning and the flow information used for pre-training belong to different small categories, that is, they have not appeared in the pre-training data set, and belong to the same big category at the same time, with some similar characteristics.

Based on the concept of meta-learning [18], training is to enable the model to obtain the ability to extract features and recognize the similarities and differences of features. In pre-training, we randomly cyclically extract the same category of flow data from the data set as a group, and set its label to "1", which means that the feature similarity is 100% and the data belong to the same type. Obtain their respective feature vectors through ResNet and calculate the cosine similarity, make the difference with 1, and then back-propagate to update the network parameters. Randomly cyclically extract different types of flow data from the data set as a group, set its label to "0", which means that the feature similarity is 0%, and the data belong to different types. Obtain their respective feature vectors through ResNet and calculate their cosine similarity, make the difference with 0 and then back-propagate to update the network parameters.

Then use fine-tuning to change the fully connected layer [19]. Randomly select 10 pieces of data from each of the normal flows and four types of abnormal flows as the support set, calculate their feature vectors through the pre-trained ResNet, and then calculate their average value as the feature vectors representing various types of flows. $\mathbf{W}$ is the matrix composed of these feature vectors, $\mathbf{x}_j$ is the query sample, $\mathbf{f}(\mathbf{x}_j)$ is the feature vector of the query sample. The probability of sample classification is obtained through the Softmax function, then make the difference of them with the label value and update the fully connected layer parameters by backpropagation. The following is the formula expressing the fully connected layer.

$$p_j = Softmax(\mathbf{W} \cdot \mathbf{f}(\mathbf{x}_j) + \mathbf{b}) \tag{3}$$

We applied some simple techniques in the finetune to improve the training effect. First, the number of samples used in fine-tuning is small, so the parameter initialization is very important. The effect of random initialization will not be good. As mentioned above, the $\mathbf{W}$ we use is composed of feature vectors, and $\mathbf{b}$ is a vector of all zeros, so even if fine-tuning is not performed, they are also meaningful. Second, the inner product of $\mathbf{W}$ and $\mathbf{f}(\mathbf{x}_j)$ is changed to their cosine similarity, that is, normalization.

4.4 Result Analysis

We tested the performance of ResNet of different depths under different sample sizes and iterations, including resnet18, resnet34, resnet50, resnet101 and resnet152, and compared them with KNN, SVM and traditional CNN. The performance of each method obtained from the experiment is as follows: Fig. 4 shows the effect of changes in sample size on the classification accuracy of different methods.

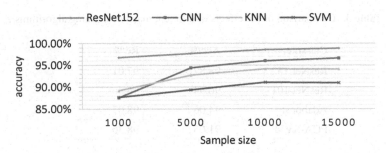

Fig. 4. The impact of sample size on accuracy

The accuracy of the above methods are all values under iteration to convergence, and the pre-training samples of ResNet152 are not calculated in the sample size. The smaller the sample size, the lower the accuracy rate, but in practical applications, the sample size is mostly in the millions, so the sample size in the experiment conforms to the relative concept of small samples. It can be seen that the lower the sample size of ResNet's classification accuracy within a certain range, the more obvious the advantage, and as the sample size increases, its convergence value is also higher than that of traditional CNN. CNN performs well when the sample size is relatively large, but has requirements for the amount of training data. When the amount of data is insufficient, the performance is significantly worse, or even worse than KNN.

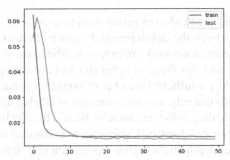

Fig. 5. The number of abscissa iterations, ordinate false alarm rate) The number of iterations affects the false alarm rate.

Figure 5 shows the change in the false alarm rate of ResNet by increasing the number of iterations while maintaining a certain sample size of 15000. It is found that as the number of training increases, the false alarm rate of ResNet152 on the test set will basically stabilize after 12 iterations (Table 3).

Table 3. Comparison of the effects of different machine learning algorithms

Classifier	Acc/%	Re/%
ResNet 152	98.87	97.01
ResNet 101	96.94	96.86
Adaboost	94.06	98.07
PCA-SVM	91.05	98.36

At the same time, another set of sample data is used to do a set of control experiments. Through comparing experiments with Adaboost and PVA-SVM machine algorithms, it can be seen that the accuracy rate of ResNet is still the highest, which is 98.87%. Unfortunately, ResNet's performance in recall rate is not the best.

Experimental data proves that ResNet can achieve better results under a deeper structure, and it performs better in classification accuracy than traditional CNN. Pre-training and fine-tuning can greatly reduce the number of samples required for training, and its combination with ResNet is effective. In summary, the small sample learning method based on ResNet has a good application prospect when dealing with intrusion detection in the case of insufficient samples.

5 Conclusion

This paper mainly studies the ResNet intrusion detection method based on small sample learning. We have considered the development direction of attack detection and artificial intelligence in the current network environment. The scale of cyberspace has been expanding significantly, and new types of cyber attacks have emerged one after another, and it is difficult to collect a sufficient number of samples for each. Traditional neural network training methods that rely on a large amount of labeled data have difficulties to achieve good results in dealing with these attacks. We use ResNet to extract data features in pre-training, which can avoid network degradation compared with traditional CNN, so as to achieve a higher depth and a higher recognition rate. Based on the concept of meta-learning, by constructing similar samples and different samples, the network can obtain the ability to recognize the similarities and differences of data during training. Then randomly select 10 samples from each of the five types of flow in finetune, take the average of their feature vectors to form a support set, and train the fully connected layer. At the same time, we have adopted normalization and meaningful initialization of its parameters, which can be expected to improve the experimental results to a certain extent.

Through the comparison of the experimental results of multiple samples and different algorithms, it can be seen that the deep ResNet still maintains a high accuracy rate and a low false alarm rate when the sample size is small. Compared with KNN, SVM and traditional CNN, it is significantly improved and has practical value in the environment of lack of samples.

Acknowledgement. This work was supported by the Key Research and Development Program of Hainan Province (Grant No. ZDYF2020040), Major science and technology project of Hainan Province (Grant No. ZDKJ2020012), Hainan Provincial Natural Science Foundation of China (Grant Nos. 2019RC098) and National Natural Science Foundation of China (NSFC) (Grant No. 62162022, 62162024 and 61762033).

References

1. François, D., Wertz, V., Verleysen, M.: Choosing the metric: a simple model approach. In: Jankowski, N., Duch, W., Grąbczewski, K. (eds.) Meta-Learning in Computational Intelligence, vol. 358, pp. 97–115. Springer, Heidelberg (2011). https://doi.org/10.1007/978-3-642-20980-2_3
2. Lake, B., Salakhutdinov, R.: One-shot learning by inverting a compositional causal process. Adv. Neural. Inf. Process. Syst. **26**, 2526–2534 (2015)
3. Li, X.Y., Long, S.P., Zhu, J.: Survey of few-shot learning based on deep neural network. Appl. Res. Comput. **37**(8), 2241–2247 (2020)
4. Anderson, J.P.: Computer security threat monitoring and surveillance. James P. Anderson Co, Fort, pp. 523–544 (1980)
5. Denning, D.E.: An Intrusion-Detection Model, pp. 879–888. IEEE Press (1987)
6. Li, Z., Zhou, F., Chen, F., et al.: Meta-SGD: learning to learn quickly for few-shot learning. arXiv preprint arXiv:1707.09835, pp. 322–433 (2017)
7. Ravi, S., Larochelle, H.: Optimization as a model for few-shot learning. In: 5th International Conference on Learning Representations, pp. 222–283. ICLR, Toulon (2017)
8. Li, Y., Xu, Y., Liu, Z., et al.: Robust detection for network intrusion of industrial IoT based on multi-CNN fusion. Measurement **154**, 107–150 (2019)
9. Zhang, J., Ling, Y., Fu, X., et al.: Model of the intrusion detection system based on the integration of spatial-temporal features. Comput. Secur. **89**, 101–281 (2020)
10. Finn, C., Abbeel, P., Levine, S.: Model-agnostic meta-learning for fast adaptation of deep networks. In: Proceedings of the 34th International Conference on Machine Learning, vol. 70, pp. 1126–1135. PMLR, Sydney (2017)
11. Koch, G., Zemel, R., Salakhutdinov, R.: Siamese neural networks for one-shot image recognition. In: 32nd International Conference on Machine Learning, vol. 2, pp. 201–332. IMLS, Lile (2015)
12. Vinyals, O., Blundell, C., Lillicrap, T., Wierstra, D.: Matching networks for one shot learning. In: Proceedings of the 30th Conference on Neural Information Processing Systems, pp. 3630–3638. Neural Information Processing Systems Foundation, Barcelona (2016)
13. Snell, J., Swersky, K., Zemel, R.: Prototypical networks for few-shot learning. In: Proceedings of the 31st Conference on Neural Information Processing Systems, vol. 2017-December, pp. 4077–4087. Neural Information Processing Systems Foundation, Long Beach (2017)
14. Wang, Y.X., Hebert, M.: Learning from small sample sets by combining unsupervised meta-training with CNNs. Advances in Neural Information Processing Systems 29-Proceedings of the 2016 Conference, vol. 0, 244–252. Neural Information Processing Systems Foundation, Barcelona (2016)
15. Boney, R., Ilin, A.: Semi-supervised few-shot learning with MAML. In: 6th International Conference on Learning Representations, ICLR 2018-Workshop Track Proceedings, 22–32, International Conference on Learning Representations, Vancouver (2018)
16. Ren, M.Y., Triantafillou, E., Ravi, S., et al.: Meta-learning for semi-supervised few-shot classification. arXiv preprint arXiv:1803.00676, pp. 333–344 (2018)

17. Liu, Y., Lee, J., Park, M., et al.: Learning to propagate labels: transductive propagation network for few-shot learning. arXiv preprint arXiv:1805.10002, pp. 888–1089 (2018)
18. Hou, R.B., Chang, H., Ma, B.P., et al.: Cross attention network for few-shot classification. In: 33rd Annual Conference on Neural Information Processing Systems, vol. 32, pp. 4003–4014. Neural Information Processing Systems Foundation, Vancouver (2019)
19. Chu, B., Madhavan, V., Beijbom, O., Hoffman, J., Darrell, T.: Best practices for fine-tuning visual classifiers to new domains. In: Hua, G., Jégou, H. (eds.) ECCV 2016. LNCS, vol. 9915, pp. 435–442. Springer, Cham (2016). https://doi.org/10.1007/978-3-319-49409-8_34

Research on Hierarchical Retrieval Method of Ethnic Clothing Based on Semantic Feature Fusion

Wenfeng Wu[1,2], Juxiang Zhou[1,2]($\boxtimes$), and Zhaoxiang Ouyang[3]

[1] Key Laboratory of Education Informatization for Nationalities, Ministry of Education, Yunnan Normal University, Kunming 650500, China
[2] Yunnan Key Laboratory of Smart Education, Yunnan Normal University, Kunming 650500, China
[3] School of Information, Dehong Teachers' College, Mangshi 678400, China

Abstract. For the task of searching images of ethnic costumes, a current problem is that the extracted features cannot express the costumes of ethnic minorities well, resulting in unsatisfactory retrieval accuracy. In order to improve the accuracy of the task of searching images of ethnic costumes, this paper proposes a retrieval strategy for the task of searching images of ethnic costumes based on the characteristics of ethnic costumes. The main process is as follows: First perform semantic segmentation on the collected ethnic clothing images. Then extract the characteristics of each part of the clothing and the overall characteristics of the clothing for feature fusion, and use the merged features as the retrieval features of the ethnic clothing images. Finally using a hierarchical search method, in the search process, first classify the ethnic group to which the clothing belongs, and then search in the search feature database of the ethnic group. The experimental results show that the retrieval strategy based on the Wa and Hani data sets, the classification accuracy and retrieval accuracy have been improved to different extents, which verifies the effectiveness of the layered retrieval strategy of ethnic clothing based on semantic feature fusion in this paper.

Keywords: Semantic segmentation · Semantic features · Image retrieval

1 Introduction

In the current image retrieval field, CBIR (Content Based Image Retrieval) [1] is one of the mainstream technologies. In recent years, it has been successfully extended to clothing [2], medical images [3], and remote sensing images [4] and other fields. With the emergence of CNN, it has become a new idea to use convolutional neural networks to extract clothing image features for clothing image retrieval. Among them, Liu ZW et al. [5] constructed a large number of DeepFashion data sets with a wide variety of clothing. The data set collected images of clothing displayed from different shooting angles, clothing backgrounds, and various e-commerce platforms. Each image it collects contains rich annotation information, such as styles, bounding boxes, feature points, and

© Springer Nature Singapore Pte Ltd. 2021
Y. Tan et al. (Eds.): DMBD 2021, CCIS 1454, pp. 135–147, 2021.
https://doi.org/10.1007/978-981-16-7502-7_16

so on. It can be used to deal with the classification and prediction of clothing images, clothing retrieval, and key point detection. In order to solve the problem of low accuracy of image retrieval in the field of fashion clothing, Huang Dongyan [6] proposed a joint segmentation method using traditional HOG features and E-SVM classifier, and then extracted the color and Bundled features of the segmented area Perform image retrieval. Hou Yuanyuan [7] used convolutional neural network training to perform feature extraction, and merged the multi-scale features from low to high in clothing images, and finally used K-Means clustering method to match and retrieve the extracted features. However, the above methods are all for the retrieval of fashion clothing images, and currently there are relatively few documents on ethnic clothing retrieval. Among them, Zhao Weili [8] proposed a minority clothing retrieval method based on multi-feature fusion. The specific method is to first divide the clothing image into regions, and then extract the color and shape characteristics of each region. After fusing its features, the similarity measurement formula is used to retrieve clothing images. Aiming at the bright colors and diverse textures of ethnic costumes, Zhang Qian [9] and others performed semantic segmentation on ethnic costumes by adding a new side branch network and CRF structure to the full convolutional network structure. After the segmentation is completed, a multi-task hash algorithm is used to map the semantically segmented clothing parts to binary codes, so as to sort the similarity to complete the image retrieval task.

In summary, the current related technologies in the field of clothing image retrieval are relatively mature, but they are still relatively few applied in the direction of ethnic minority clothing images. In the existing retrieval tasks for ethnic minority clothing, traditional feature extraction methods, such as SIFT and HOG, often only extract the shallow features of the image, and their retrieval accuracy is not ideal [10]. When using CNN to extract features, often only the depth features of the entire image are extracted, without considering the features contained in the different parts of the ethnic clothing images [9]. Therefore, this paper takes the Wa and Hani nationalities as the research objects, and proposes a hierarchical retrieval method based on semantic feature fusion of ethnic clothing images. The main work of this paper is as follows: 1. Aiming at the problems of the low number and low definition of the existing ethnic clothing images, a ethnic clothing data set including the Wa and Hani nationalities is constructed, which contains the semantic tags of clothing components and ethnic category tags; 2. Constructed a CNN for feature extraction and classification, and obtained more expressive retrieval features for ethnic minority clothing by fusing the component features and overall features of clothing; 3. Applying the idea of hierarchical retrieval and inputting The images are first classified by ethnic groups and then feature matching is performed from the corresponding feature library to obtain the final retrieval result.

2   Retrieval Method

Considering that the component regions of ethnic minority clothing also have rich semantic information, this paper uses convolutional neural networks to extract features of the entire clothing image and component regions respectively. The hierarchical retrieval process of ethnic clothing based on semantic feature fusion includes the following 3 steps:

(1) Construct a classification network, and train the classification network on the clothing image data set with ethnic category labels until the network converges.

(2) Construct the ethnic clothing feature database, and obtain the costume component information of the image by inputting the costume image into the semantic segmentation model. The result of semantic segmentation is shown in Fig. 1. A total of 7 divided areas are obtained: coats, pants, sleeves, skirts, belts, leg guard, and accessories. The overall image and the component diagram of the image are sequentially input into the pre-trained ethnic clothing classification network, and the overall depth feature and component depth feature of the clothing can be obtained by extracting the features of the fully connected layer. Combining these features linearly can obtain the retrieval features of the clothing image. The retrieval features of all clothing images can be obtained by sequentially performing the above operations on all the images in the image database, so as to construct the clothing retrieval feature database of the Wa and Hani nationalities respectively.

(3) Hierarchical retrieval, namely classification and retrieval. For an input query graph Q, it is classified first. Input it into the trained ethnic clothing classification network for ethnic classification. Since there is currently no algorithm to ensure the absolute accuracy of image classification, in order to ensure the retrieval accuracy, we set a retrieval threshold. When the ethnic probability output by the Softmax classifier is less than 0.65, it is considered that there is a possibility of classification errors, and the entire retrieval feature library is retrieved at this time. Then input the query graph Q into the CNN, and extract the retrieval features of the query graph Q. Finally, measure the similarity between it and the retrieval feature database of the ethnic group to which it belongs, and output the retrieval results in descending order of Euclidean distance.

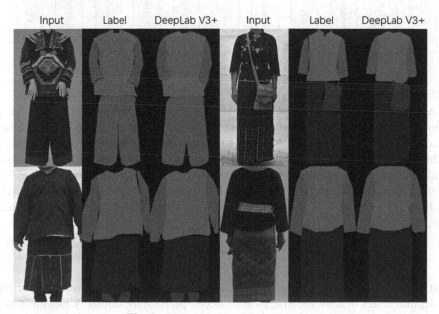

Fig. 1. Semantic segmentation results.

2.1   Construction CNN

The feature extraction network selected in this paper is similar to other current network structures. Among them, the convolution layer mainly uses convolution operation on the input feature map, and then outputs a set of nonlinear activation responses through the activation function. When building the convolution layer, it is mainly to adjust the size of the convolution kernel and the length of the convolution kernel step in the convolution layer. The input of the convolutional layer can be the output of the previous convolutional layer, or the original features of the image and the output of the pooling layer as the input of the convolutional layer. In this paper, the size of the core is defined as 3×3, and the stride length is defined as 1. Since the large convolution kernel can be replaced by the stack of several convolution layers, the number of parameters can be reduced while the receptive field size remains unchanged [11], so the CNN in this paper adopts the form of stacking multiple convolution kernels. The current pooling methods are mainly average pooling and maximum pooling. Its role in convolutional neural networks is to reduce the data volume of the feature map while only reducing the height and width of the feature map without changing its depth [12]. Among them, the maximum pooling layer can obtain the most significant features within the range of the pooling frame, while reducing the data volume of the feature map, so this paper chooses the max pooling. The last layer of a convolutional neural network is usually a fully connected layer. The neurons in the fully connected layer are all connected with the neurons in the previous layer. The feature vector can be obtained by extracting the features of the fully connected layer. The feature extraction network structure is shown in Fig. 2.

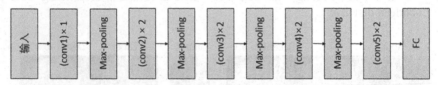

Fig. 2. Feature extraction network structure diagram.

After operations such as convolution and pooling in the feature extraction network, a Softmax function is added to the output layer of the network to calculate the probability of the ethnic category of the input image and use it as a classification network for ethnic clothing images. Then, before training the classification network, our clothing data set should be divided into training set and verification set according to the ratio of 9:1. Then use the training set whose labels are ethnic categories to train the fine-tuning network. Finally, train the network until it converges to get our final national costume classification network.

2.2   Feature Fusion

Most of the existing image retrieval schemes obtain retrieval results by directly extracting the depth features of retrieved images and directly performing similarity measurement. However, because the component regions of ethnic costumes also contain rich semantic features, in order to increase the weight of component regions in ethnic costume images during the retrieval process, a ethnic costume retrieval feature is designed. Specifically, using the DeepLabV3 + semantic segmentation model to perform semantic segmentation on clothing, we can obtain the images of each component of the clothing, and then the whole and component images of the same clothing image are respectively in the following order: 1 overall picture 2 coats 3 pants 4 sleeves 5 skirt 6 belts 7 leg guards 8 accessories, and input them into the feature extraction network in order. By extracting the output of the fully connected layer of each image, the depth characteristics of the overall image and each component image can be obtained. Subsequently, the overall image depth feature of the clothing and the depth feature of each component are linearly connected in the order of input, and the overall feature after the feature fusion is used as the retrieval feature f of each clothing image. The definition of f is shown in Eq. 1.

$$f = \{f_1, f_2, f_3 \cdots f_8\} \tag{1}$$

Among them, f_1 to f_8 respectively represent the depth characteristics of the overall image of the clothing and the depth characteristics of its various clothing components. Then, according to the ethnic categories, the depth features of each clothing image in the Wa and Hani libraries were merged to construct the ethnic clothing retrieval feature database F of Wa and Hani. The definition of F is shown in Eq. 2.

$$F = \left\{f^1, f^2, f^3 \cdots f^n\right\} \tag{2}$$

Where F represents the ethnic clothing retrieval feature database. f_n represents the retrieval feature of the nth image in the clothing image retrieval feature library.

2.3 Hierarchical Retrieval

In order to improve retrieval efficiency and reduce the interference of retrieval features between different ethnic categories in the retrieval process, a hierarchical retrieval strategy is proposed. In the first stage of image retrieval, the input image to be retrieved is first classified by ethnicity. The purpose of this is to directly reduce the mutual interference of retrieval features between different ethnic categories and indirectly improve retrieval accuracy. Hierarchical retrieval is divided into two parts, classification and retrieval. The classification is mainly to classify the input clothing images according to ethnic categories. That is, the probability of the image in different ethnic groups is output through the Softmax classifier, and the probability is sorted from large to small, and the highest ranked ethnic category is obtained for the subsequent retrieval. The retrieval mainly uses the retrieval features of the input image from the corresponding ethnic costume retrieval feature database to calculate the similarity of the features in the library. The specific hierarchical retrieval process is as follows:

(1) Classification, use DeepLabV3 + semantic segmentation model to perform semantic segmentation on the retrieval image Q input by the user, and obtain the clothing component area of the retrieval image Q. Then the overall image and component images of the retrieved image Q are sequentially input to the CNN. By extracting

and combining the depth features, the retrieval features f_q of the image Q to be retrieved are finally obtained. At the same time, the ethnic classification probability of the clothing is obtained according to the output of the Softmax layer. The definition of f_q is shown in Eq. 3. Then according to the classification results, select the corresponding ethnic costumes to retrieval the feature database when searching.

$$f_q = \{f_1, f_2, f_3 \cdots f_8\} \tag{3}$$

(2) Retrieval. According to the Euclidean distance formula, calculate the similarity between f_q and the retrieval feature f^i of each image in the clothing retrieval feature library F. The distance measurement formula is shown in Eq. 4.

$$d^i = \left\| f_q - f^i \right\|^2 \tag{4}$$

Among them, d^i ($i = 1,2,...,n$) represents the Euclidean distance between the retrieval feature f_q of the input image Q and the retrieval feature f^i of the i-th image in the ethnic clothing retrieval feature database F. Finally, all the retrieval distances are sorted in order from small to large, and the results generated according to the sorting are taken as the final retrieval results.

3 Experiment and Analysis

3.1 Experimental Data

The experimental data set in this paper is composed of costume images of the Wa and Hani ethnic groups. Limited by the richness of various ethnic clothing resources, the number of clothing samples collected by different ethnic groups is also different. This paper selects 932 costume images of the Wa nationality and 243 costume images of the Hani nationality as the basic research objects. In the case of a small sample size, in order to make up for the lack of training samples and enhance the generalization ability of the network, this paper performs operations such as rotation angle and flipping on the training images in the ethnic clothing retrieval feature database to increase the training image sample size. The training of the classification network is carried out with the clothing image after data enhancement processing. Finally, 4660 costume images of the Wa ethnic group and 1,215 costume images of the Hani ethnic group were obtained, a total of 5,875, among which the number of photos of each costume ranged from 5–15. As shown in Fig. 3.

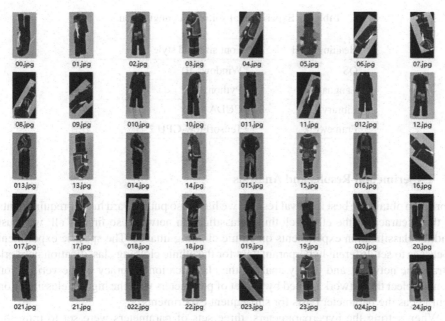

Fig. 3. Part of the training image.

3.2 Experimental Environment

The operating system of this experiment is Microsoft's Windows 10, the programming language is Python 3.6, and the deep learning framework is TensorFlow-GPU 2.2 for experiments. The Adam in the gradient descent algorithm is used as the optimizer. Adam's advantages are computationally efficient, less memory usage, etc. In this paper, the GPU used in the experiment is RTX2080Ti from Nvidia, and its specific experimental software and hardware configurations are shown in Tables 1 and 2.

Table 1. Experimental hardware configuration.

Hardware	Model
CPU	Intel Xeon 5118
GPU	NVIDIA GeForce RTX 2080TI
Memory	16 GB ddr 4 * 2
Hard disk	Samsung 500 GB

Table 2. Experimental software configuration.

Heading level	Font size and style
OS	Windows 10
Language	Python 3.6
Library	CUDA 10.1
Framework	TensorFlow-GPU 2.2

3.3 Experimental Results and Analysis

In order to obtain the best retrieval results, we have also put forward higher requirements for the accuracy of the ethnic clothing classification network, so first of all, we must conduct classification experiments on ethnic clothing images. The specific experiment process is to set different hyperparameters for the ethnic clothing classification network to train the network, and finally analyze the classification accuracy of the verification set, and select the network trained by the set of parameters with the highest classification accuracy as the parameter basis for subsequent experiments.

When setting the hyperparameters, three sets of parameters were set to train the ethnic clothing classification network. When setting different parameters, follow the principle of controlling variables and set the parameters within a reasonable range. The Batch size is set to 8 and 16, Epoch is set to 10 and 20, Learning rate is set to 0.001 and 0.005, and Drop out is set to 0.25 and 0.5, respectively. The loss function used in the training process is the cross-entropy loss function. The specific parameter settings are shown in Table 3.

Table 3. Hyperparameter settings.

Hyperparameter	CNN_V1	CNN_V2	CNN_V3
Batch size	8	8	16
Epoch	10	10	20
Learning rate	0.001	0.001	0.005
Drop out	0.25	0.5	0.25

After the training, the accuracy of the validation set under the CNN_V1 and CNN_V2 parameter settings during the training process is plotted in a image with the change of Epoch, and the accuracy of the validation set under the CNN_V3 parameter setting is plotted on the other image. The results are shown in Figs. 4 and 5. It can be seen from the figure that the accuracy of image classification increases with the increase of Epoch during the training process, and the increase in accuracy after the 8th Epoch is no longer obvious. Among them, the CNN_V3 network has trained 20 Epochs, but the final classification accuracy is lower than CNN_V1. This shows that when training the network, it is not necessary to set the number of training to the larger the better. When the network reaches the level of fit, continuing to increase the training Epoch will cause the network parameters to develop in the direction of overfitting the training set. At this time, the prediction results of the new test data will deviate, and the training time will also be greatly increased.

Finally, the classification accuracy test was performed on the clothing data of the Wa and Hani nationalities respectively. Table 4 shows the accuracy of ethnic classification under three different parameter settings for the two data sets. It can be seen from the table that under the parameter settings of CNN_V1, the accuracy rate of the classification is the highest.

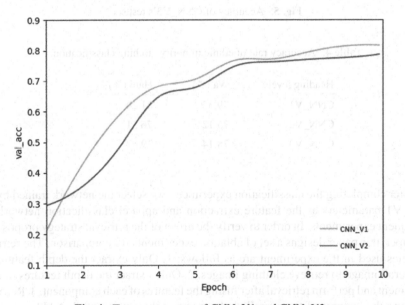

Fig. 4. Test set accuracy of CNN_V1 and CNN_V2.

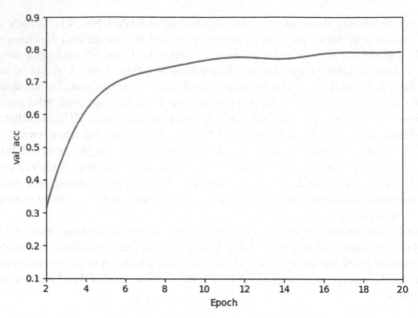

Fig. 5. Accuracy of CNN_V3's test set.

Table 4. Accuracy rate of ethnic minority clothing classification.

Heading level	Wa (%)	Hani (%)
CNN_V1	79.53	81.24
CNN_V2	75.12	76.31
CNN_V3	78.14	79.57

After completing the classification experiment, we select the network trained by the CNN_V1 parameters as the feature extraction and apparel classification network for subsequent experiments. In order to verify the effect of the retrieval strategy proposed in this paper, this paper designs a set of ablation experiments for comparison. The retrieval strategies used in the experiment are as follows: 1. Only extract the depth features of the overall image to retrieve clothing images. 2. Only extract the depth features of each component and perform retrieval after fusing the features of each component. 3. Retrieval by fusing the features of the overall clothing and each component. 4. Add hierarchical based on 3. The evaluation index of this experiment adopts Top-10 accuracy rate, and the experimental results are shown in Table 5.

It can be seen from Table 5 that the retrieval effect using the overall + component + hierarchical is the best, and its Top-10 accuracy rate reached 55.4% and 58.3% in the Wa and Hani ethnic groups, respectively. It can be seen that by classifying clothing images before retrieval, the problem of mutual interference between retrieval features of different ethnic clothing can be effectively avoided, and retrieval accuracy can be improved. At the

Table 5. Top-10 retrieval accuracy of different characteristics.

Retrieval strategy	Wa (%)	Hani (%)
Overall	46.2	49.4
Component	33.6	34.2
Overall + Component	51.4	53.0
Overall + Component + Hierarchical	55.4	58.3

same time, the retrieval accuracy rate of retrieval using only the overall feature is lower than the retrieval accuracy of the overall + component retrieval feature, and the retrieval accuracy rate is the lowest only using the component feature of the clothing image for retrieval. This proves that by fusing the characteristics of the overall and the component, the characteristics that are more suitable for expressing ethnic minority clothing can be obtained. However, only using the fusion features of the components to retrieve is more susceptible to the interference of the accuracy of semantic segmentation and the diversity of clothing styles, so the effect is not good.

Finally, in order to verify the effectiveness of the retrieval strategy in this paper, we use the SIFT algorithm in the traditional image retrieval method and the VGG16 network in the convolutional neural network, which is similar to our network in depth, to perform retrieval comparison experiments on behalf of the underlying features and depth features. Both of these two feature extraction methods extract the features of the overall image of clothing for retrieval, and the evaluation index still selects Top-10 accuracy. The experimental results are shown in Table 6.

Table 6. Retrieval accuracy rate of Top-10 ethnic clothing.

Feature extraction method	Wa (%)	Hani (%)
SIFT	32.0	34.2
VGG	46.3	50.2
OUR	55.4	58.3

By analyzing the experimental results, we can see that the accuracy of the retrieval method Top-10 proposed in this paper is still the best. The VGG network, which is similar in depth to this paper, has lower retrieval accuracy in these two ethnic costumes than the method mentioned in this paper. This shows that the retrieval strategy of this paper has improved the retrieval accuracy to a certain extent. At the same time, it can be seen that the retrieval using the traditional underlying feature SIFT is far lower than the depth features extracted using the convolutional neural network. This is because ethnic costume images have rich semantic features. Using traditional bottom-level features to face ethnic costumes with costume patterns, textures, colors and many other complex factors can only extract shallow features. These features cannot express national costumes well. The reasons for the difference in retrieval accuracy between different ethnic groups are as follows: 1. The structure and texture complexity of clothing images are not the same among different ethnic groups, which will affect the extraction of retrieval features. 2. Due to the limitation of the data set, the quality of some clothing images is not high and the difference in the overall clothing quantity of the two nationalities also affects the retrieval results.

4 Conclusion

This paper first realizes the classification and feature extraction of the input image by constructing CNN. Then feature fusion obtains the retrieval features of ethnic costume images. Finally, the ethnic costume image retrieval is carried out through the hierarchical retrieval method. The analysis of the experimental results shows that the retrieval strategy proposed in this paper can improve the retrieval accuracy of ethnic clothing images compared with the traditional direct retrieval method, and its average retrieval accuracy reached 56.9%. The disadvantage is that the scale of the experimental data set in this article is still far from the current mainstream clothing data set in terms of quantity. At the same time, when facing images with complex colors and styles, the effect of feature extraction needs to be continuously enhanced. In the future, we will try to use larger-scale data sets to conduct experiments and further optimize the feature extraction methods.

Acknowledgement. This work is supported by National Natural Science Foundation of China (No. 61862068), Major Science and Technology Project of Yunnan Province (No. 202002AD080001), and Yunnan Expert Workstation of Xiaochun Cao.

References

1. Adegbola, O.A., Adeyemo, I.A., Semire, F.A., et al.: A principal component analysis-based feature dimensionality reduction scheme for content-based image retrieval system. Telkomnika **18**(4), 1892–1896 (2020)
2. Gao, J.: Clothing image retrieval based on lightweight neural network. Sci. Technol. Innov. **31**, 94–95 (2020)
3. Yang, F., Guohui, W., Cao, H.: Research progress on content-based medical image retrieval. Laser Optoelectron. Prog. **57**(06), 38–50 (2020)
4. Ma, C., Guan, L., Chen, F.: Design of content-based remote sensing image change information retrieval and relevance feedback model. Rem. Sens. Technol. Appl. **35**(03), 685–693 (2020)
5. Liu, Z., Luo, P., Qiu, S., et al.: Deepfashion: Powering robust clothes recognition and retrieval with rich annotations. In: Proceedings of the IEEE Conference on Computer Vision and Pattern Recognition, pp. 1096–1104 (2016)
6. Huang, D., Liu, L., Fu, X.: Clothing retrieval via co-segmentation and feature matching. J. Comput.-Aid. Des. Comput. Graph. **29**(06), 1075–1084 (2017)
7. Hou, Y., He, R., Li, M.: Clothing image retrieval method combining convolutional neural network multi-layer feature fusion and k-means clustering. Comput. Sci. **46**(S1), 215–221 (2019)

8. Zhao, W.: Minority national costume image retrieval based on multi-feature fusion. J. Shandong Ind. Technol. **01**, 293–294 (2017). https://doi.org/10.16640/j.cnki.37-1222/t.2017. 01.254

9. Zhang, Q., Liu, L., Fu, X.: Clothing image retrieval by label optimization and semantic segmentation. J. Comput.-Aid. Des. Comput. Graph. **32**(09), 1450–1465 (2020)

10. Ouyang, Z.: Ethnic minority costume retrieval based on region-to-image asymmetric matching. Softw. Guide **19**(06), 227–230 (2020)

11. Simonyan, K., Zisserman, A.: Very deep convolutional networks for large-scale image recognition. arXiv preprint arXiv:1409.1556 (2014)

12. Chen, C., Feng, Q.: Review on development of convolutional neural network and its application in computer vision. Comput. Sci. **46**(03), 63–73 (2019)

An Improved Method of Blockchain Consortium Chain Consensus Mechanism Based on Random Forest Model

Dongxiang Song[1] ⓘ, Yiran Wang[2](✉), and Mingju Yuan[1]

[1] Dehong Teachers' College, Dehong 678400, Yunnan, China
[2] Dehong Vocational College, Dehong 678400, Yunnan, China

Abstract. As blockchain technology has attracted more and more attention from all walks of life, the industry application prospects of alliance chains are very broad. Consensus algorithms are very important in blockchain applications. Now the alliance chain mainly uses the PBFT consensus algorithm, but the main node selection step of the algorithm needs to be maintained by all nodes in the alliance chain, which has high consumption and high latency performance and low security. The problem. This paper uses the integrated learning random forest model of machine learning by adding a credit scoring mechanism, taking the characteristic data of some influencing factors of the alliance chain that affect the selection of the master node as input, the selection of the master node as the observation sample, and the training sample to obtain the prediction model. The predicted master node is used to replace the master consensus node selection step in the PBFT algorithm to complete the consensus, and RFBFT (Random Forest Byzantine Fault-Tolerant Algorithm) is proposed. The high accuracy of the experimental random forest prediction model ensures the accuracy and safety of the master node selection. Comparing the algorithms before and after the improvement, the consumption of RFBFT is reduced by 20% and the delay is reduced by 19%, which improves the operation of the alliance chain. Performance and safety.

Keywords: Blockchain · Alliance chain · Random forest · PBFT

1 Introduction

At present, the country attaches great importance to the development of security and efficiency of blockchain [1, 2] technology at the enterprise level. Among them, the consensus mechanism [3] of the blockchain alliance chain [4] is a hot spot of current research. How to achieve a shorter transaction confirmation time needs to improve the consensus algorithm of the blockchain [5]. The consensus mechanisms used in current blockchain applications mainly include proof-of-work PoW [6], proof-of-stake-based PoS [7], proof-of-stake based DPoS [8], practical Byzantine fault-tolerant PBFT and efficient and practical Byzantine fault-tolerance EPBFT. The only consensus mechanisms applicable to alliance chains are PBFT and EPBFT. In terms of security, the consensus nodes of PBFT and EPBFT are anonymous nodes [9]. If the master node is attacked, it

© Springer Nature Singapore Pte Ltd. 2021
Y. Tan et al. (Eds.): DMBD 2021, CCIS 1454, pp. 148–157, 2021.
https://doi.org/10.1007/978-981-16-7502-7_17

will affect the security of the entire system; in terms of delay, the block generation time is 1 s and less than The delay of 1 s and 1 s is unacceptable for enterprise-level blockchain consortium chain applications; in terms of cost, configuring a consortium chain node computer requires 1w RMB, which is a bit high in cost; in terms of power consumption, Mainly for CPU usage, the power consumption of PBFT and EPBFT is around 24% and 20%. The main reason for this problem is that in the selection process of the master node of the PBFT algorithm, all nodes in the alliance chain need to be jointly maintained, and the selection of the master node needs to be agreed by all nodes. During the maintenance process, all nodes need to communicate with each other, which increases the security risk of malicious attacks, consumes power consumption and increases time delay.

This article starts from basic research to improve the PBFT consensus algorithm of the blockchain alliance chain. In the selection step of the master node, all nodes in the alliance chain are avoided to participate, and communication overhead is reduced [10]. Using the credit scoring mechanism [11], adding the feature vector selection of the random forest model [12], the training sample gets the prediction model to select the master node. The accuracy of the predictive model determines the safety and accuracy of the algorithm. The improved consensus algorithm after PBFT needs to meet the low power consumption and low latency performance requirements of the alliance chain.

2   Relate Work

With the broadening of the application scenarios of the blockchain, King S and others proposed for the first time a consensus mechanism based on Proof of Stake (PoS), which reduces the mining difficulty coefficient according to the proportion of each node's equity. Thereby speeding up mining [13]. This mechanism does not solve the problem that the blockchain needs to be mined, it will still cause a lot of waste of computing power, and it is still not applicable to the alliance chain; Kwon J proposed a consensus mechanism based on Delegated Proof of Stake (DPoS), This mechanism is similar to board voting, in which multiple coin holders vote to select nodes and these nodes perform consistency verification [14], which greatly increases the time required to reach a consensus and does not require a mining process. However, this mechanism needs to rely on tokens to be implemented. At the same time, uneven distribution of equity can easily cause power concentration and affect credibility, and it is not suitable for alliance chains. The consensus algorithm suitable for alliance chains was until Ripple Lab proposed (Ripple Protocol Consensus Algorithm, RPCA) [15] Consensus mechanism, this mechanism combines the Byzantine Generalproblem, get rid of the restriction of reaching consensus through mining, the proposal of the consensus mechanism also promotes the development of the alliance chain, making the blockchain technology trend Commercial applications, but Ripple focuses on solving the problem of cross-regional transactions, and focuses on ledger managemen. The focus is not on decentralized applications; the Hyperledger project launched by the Linux Foundation draws on the consensus mechanism proposed by Ripple. A practical Byzantine Fault Tolerance mechanism [16] (Practical Byzantine Fault Tolerance, PBFT) is used to achieve consistency. However, there are problems such as low security of consensus nodes in the Hyperledger project and high cost of building a consortium chain. Domestic scholar Gan Jun et al. proposed to improve the efficient and practical Byzantine Fault Tolerance mechanism of PBFT [17] (Effectivity Practical Byzantine Fault Tolerance, EPBFT), mainly proposed to improve the selection of the master node of the PBFT algorithm, the mechanism reduces the communication overhead, but the block Time is still too long.

3   Method

3.1   Constructing Credit Score Random Forest Model

The Overall Idea of Credit Points. Consensus nodes earn points through their own good credit. In each round of consensus process, consensus nodes need to send messages, receive messages, and judge messages. The consensus nodes are very busy. At each small stage, we set up a point agreement. If the consensus node meets the requirements, the points will be rewarded, otherwise, the penalty will be deducted. Establish a consensus node scoring table to record the scoring information. The relationship structure diagram (see Fig. 1).

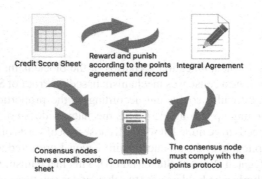

Fig. 1. Diagram of the relationship structure of the credit scoring mechanism

Points Agreement and Process. Through the credit score table, we have established a consensus node credit score penalty and reward agreement, the details are as follows, Consensus node penalty agreement: 1. One point will be deducted if you do not participate in the voting; 2. Three points are deducted for errors in the legality of identity and information; 3. Failure to participate in the voting is confirmed to be reduced by one point; Consensus node rewards: 1. One point will be added to vote and submit; 2. One point will be added to vote for confirmation; 3. Two points for being selected as the master node;

Random Forest Modeling. Decision trees are commonly used supervised learning models with relatively mature training construction algorithms and many good properties. Bagging integration is used to integrate multiple decision tree models, and a weak learner set is constructed into a strong learner forest with strong generalization performance model. Through random self-sampling, the decision tree model has a certain degree of randomness and there are certain differences between each other. The forest model of the combined decision tree model is called the random forest model. Random forest model establishment process:

1. In the prediction of master consensus node selection, the factors that affect master node selection, including consensus round, current round penalty type, current round reward type, total number of penalties, total number of rewards, and total points, are used as feature vectors Input, use the master node corresponding to these feature vectors to select the corresponding node number as a sample of the observation value, and fit the prediction model through the training sample.
2. The node numbers selected by all the master nodes are used as the training set Yi~Xi, where Yi is the observation value in the random forest prediction model, the mapping is the node number of consensus node i, and Xi is the node corresponding to the group that may affect the master node The selected feature vector, Xi~{Ii1, Ii2 … Iin}, where Iin represents the nth influencing factor of the i-th node during the prediction period.
3. Determine the training set, and randomly replace N samples from the original sample set M to form a new training sample. When the number of samples in N is greater than 1/3 of the original sample set M, this type of data is called (out of bag, OOB) data. Random forest uses CART decision tree to select features based on the Gini coefficient. The criterion is that the Gini coefficient is the smallest and the purity of each child node reaches the highest. All observations falling on the child nodes belong to the same category. For example, there are K categories in total, and the probability that the sample belongs to the k-th category is: Pk, see formula (1).

$$\text{Gini(p)} = \sum_{k=1}^{K} P_k(1 - P_k) = 1 - \sum_{k=1}^{K} P_k^2 \tag{1}$$

The random forest modeling diagram is shown in the Fig. 2:

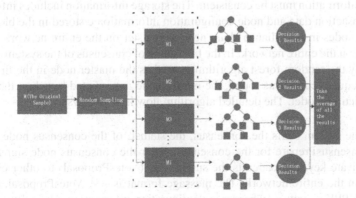

Fig. 2. Random forest modeling diagram

3.2   RFBFT Algorithm

PBFT Consensus Algorithm. PBFT is the abbreviation of Practical Byzantine Fault Tolerance, which means practical Byzantine Fault Tolerance algorithm. Proposed by Miguel Castro and Barbara Liskov at the 1999 OSD199 conference. It is an algorithm based on state machine copy replication, which can guarantee the fault tolerance that the failed node does not exceed under the premise of ensuring safety and liveness. There are three role views, master node and replica node in the PBFT algorithm. The execution of the PBFT algorithm is divided into five stages: request, pre-prepare, prepare, commit and reply. Among them, the pre-prepare, prepare) and commit phases are the most important.

Algorithm Symbolic Representation. Definition 1: The set of all consensus nodes registered for real-name authentication in the algorithm is Q, and the intersection of any two Qs is not empty. Assuming that the set of system nodes is P, V = {P1, P2, P3..., Pn}, and Qi satisfies formula (2), then P is called a set of consensus nodes Q. Definition 2: In the set of all consensus nodes Q, the maximum tolerable number of nodes is, then the size of the set Q must satisfy the formula (3): Definition 3: Define the set of consensus nodes that are selected as the master node as QC, and the set of consensus nodes that are not selected as the master node as QB, which satisfies the following formula (4):

$$\forall P_i, \ P_j \in V \, \exists P_i \cap P_j \neq \emptyset \tag{2}$$

$$|Q| \geq 3f + 1 \tag{3}$$

$$Q = QC + QB \tag{4}$$

Algorithm Flow. In the entire system, every node participating in the consensus uses a flooding algorithm to broadcast and submit information to the entire network when it initiates a confirmation. A consensus will be conducted at the default time of the system. In order to ensure the consistency and effectiveness of the consensus nodes, each node participating in the consensus must ensure the same state before the consensus starts, and the stored information must be consistent. The storage information includes information such as transaction data and node configuration information c stored in the blockchain. Consensus nodes in the alliance chain need to register on the entire network and pass verification on the entire network. In the first round of consensus of the system, the node predicted by the random forest algorithm is used as the master node in the first round. In the subsequent consensus round, the master node is predicted based on the random forest prediction model. The detailed algorithm flow is as follows:

1) After the system starts the consensus, the statusL of the consensus node prepares the ConsensusPrepare for the consensus. After the consensus node signs with its own private key, it broadcasts the submission (VotesProposal) to other consensus nodes in the entire network. The message format is << VotesProposal, c, Qi, L, Uniti, VPPK>, vote>, where c is configuration information, Qi is the consensus node that initiates voting, L is the current consensus round, and vote is submitted The information includes the consensus node random forest model FL, etc., VPPK

is the digest of the vote, VPPK = Digest (vote), and the signature uses the SHA-256 algorithm. The status of the consensus node, StatusL, sends SendConsensus for the consensus;

2) After the consensus node receives the information of other consensus nodes, it needs to verify the authenticity of the identity of the consensus node first. After the identity verification is passed, it starts to verify the legitimacy of the information. If the identity information is not verified and the information is illegal, it will The information is discarded, and then the submitted information is verified, and the log information of the node is broadcast to the consensus nodes of the entire network. This stage is called ErrorProposal. If the information is verified and the information is legal, the information is written to the log.

3) After each consensus node receives legal information, it starts to collect logs against the information. After the waiting time, the consensus node information that has not been received will be broadcast to the consensus node of the whole network, and the error information will be submitted;

4) If the same information (mainly including the consensus node random forest model FL) in the waiting time exceeds 2f of the number of participating nodes, it means that the consensus node has confirmed the master node, and then a confirmation (VotesConfirm) is sent to the entire network. The message format is <<VotesConfirm, c, Qi, L, VCVP>, voteC>, where c is the configuration information, Qi is the consensus node that initiates the confirmation, L is the current consensus round, voteC is the information, VCVP = Digest (VoteC), VCVP is a summary of voteC. For the node that has not received it, penalty submission (Error-Proposal) is performed. The status of the consensus node, StatusL, sends a consensus confirmation ConsensusVerify for the consensus;

5) The same needs to first verify the legitimacy of the information and the identity of the sender. Within a certain period of time, when the consensus node receives the confirmation (VotesConfirm) in this round, the consensus is completed and the consensus random forest model FL receives the same After 2f pieces of the same information, it is considered that a consensus has been reached.

After the consensus is completed, the consensus round L increases by 1, and the status of the consensus node StatusL+1 prepares the ConsensusPreparey for the consensus sending consensus.

Algorithm Implementation. In the consensus process in which P consensus nodes participate, each consensus node has three states, namely ConsensusPrepare, Consensus SendConsensus, and ConsensusVerify, which are represented by, and ConsensusVerify, where m stands for certificate authentication message and n stands for sending The node number of the message, L represents the current consensus round. Each round of consensus nodes waits for the information of other nodes and waits for confirmation. The random forest Byzantine fault-tolerant consensus algorithm is expressed in the form of pseudo-code as shown below:

Algorithm: Random Forest Byzantine Fault Tolerant Consensus Algorithm
Input : Random Forest Model FL
Output : Consensus completed
1 : repeat:
2 :   if (status = $CP_i^{\{m,n,L\}}$) then
3:        send   VoteProposal   to   other
4:        status $\leftarrow$ $SC_i^{\{m,n,L\}}$
5 :   else
6:        send   Award   and   Error   to   other
7 :   if (status = $SC_i^{\{m,n,L\}}$)   then
8:        if   Time > Δ_D then
9 :   send   Award   and   Error   to   other
10 :   L=L+1
11:            status $\leftarrow$ $CP_i^{\{m,n,L\}}$
12 :   return false
13:        else
14:            if   Num (m) > $\frac{2}{3}$ P   then
15:                send   VotesConfirm   to   other
16:                status $\leftarrow$ $CV_i^{\{m,n,L\}}$
17 :   if (state = $CV_i^{\{m,n,L\}}$)   then
18:        if   Time > Δ_C then
19 :   send   Award   and   Error   to   other
20 :   L=L+1
21:            status $\leftarrow$ $CP_i^{\{m,n,L\}}$
22 :   return false
23:        else
24:            if   Num (m) > $\frac{2}{3}$ P   then
25 :   L=L+1
26 :   status $\leftarrow$ $CP_i^{\{m,n,L\}}$
27 :   return true

4   Experiment and Result

The configuration environment of the experimental platform is: Operating System: MacOS 11.2.3; Memory: 16 GB; CPU: Apple M1; Python: 3; Flask: 3.0.1; Go: 1.15.8.

4.1   Forecast Accuracy

After the random forest model is trained with 2600 data samples, the master node selection prediction model is obtained. The accuracy calculation formula (5) for predicting the master node is:

$$Q = \frac{1}{n} \sum_{i=1}^{n} \left(1 - \left| \frac{y_i - q_i}{s_i} \right| \right) * 100\% \qquad (5)$$

Among them: yi is the actual value, main node number, qi is the main node number predicted by the random forest model, si is the average main node number, n is the number of samples, and Q is the accuracy. 12 participating consensus nodes, 20 rounds of consensus, 6 sets of experiments to observe the accuracy of the prediction of the master node, through the experiment, the result (see Fig. 3), The average accuracy rate is 95% .

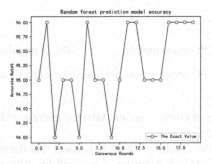

Fig. 3. Random forest prediction model accuracy

It can be seen from the results that the accuracy rate of the random forest prediction model stabilizes at 96% after 16 consensus rounds, and the accuracy rate is relatively high.

4.2 Power Consumption and Time Delay

Consumption is a measure of the ability of a system to use system resources, and an important indicator of the system's consumption of system resources. In this article, we use CPT (Consume Per Trun, the consumption of each round of consensus) to express. The power consumption in the alliance chain application refers to the CPU usage rate within the time required for each round of master node selection, See formula (6). The delay index can measure the communication performance of the network where the entire system is located and the running time of the consensus algorithm to complete the task. See formula (7)

$$CPT_{\Delta_L} = ConsensusConsume_{\Delta_L} \tag{6}$$

$$Delay_L = VoteProposal_L + Votecondirm_L \tag{7}$$

Among them is the time interval of the current L round of consensus, and is the CPU usage rate in this time interval. Take 60s to test the CPU usage rate during this period of time.It is the time interval (delay) used for the current L round of consensus. It is the process by which consensus nodes broadcast the voting stage to the consensus node confirmation information and then broadcasts the confirmation stage to the entire network. It is the process by which the consensus nodes finally confirm the consensus with each other. Take the average of 6 groups of experiments, (see Fig. 4.a). 12 participating consensus

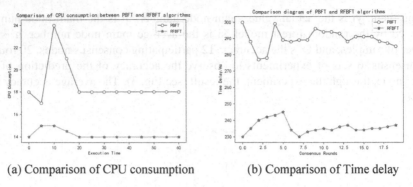

(a) Comparison of CPU consumption   (b) Comparison of Time delay

Fig. 4. Comparison of CPU consumption and time delay of PBFT and RFBFT algorithms

nodes, conduct 20 rounds of consensus, and take the average value through 6 groups of experiments, (see Fig. 4.b).

It can be seen from the results of the comparison that during the operation of the RFBFT algorithm, the CPU consumption is reduced by 20% compared to the PBFT algorithm and the delay is reduced by 19%.

5   Conclusion

Today's blockchain technology is developing faster and faster. The existing consensus algorithms have many problems in the alliance chain system. The performance of high resources, high power consumption and high latency is not conducive to the development of the alliance chain system. Based on the above problems, this article found out. The PBFT algorithm is widely used in the blockchain alliance chain. The disadvantage of the PBFT algorithm is that the selection process of the master node is complicated, and the communication overhead of the nodes in the alliance chain is high, which causes a waste of resources and reduces security. By improving the algorithm, using the ensemble learning random forest model of machine learning, the characteristic data of some influencing factors of the alliance chain that affects the selection of the master node is taken as input, and the selection of the master node is used as the observation sample, and the prediction model is obtained through the training sample. The predicted master node is used to replace the master consensus node selection in the PBFT algorithm process, and the random forest Byzantine fault-tolerant algorithm RFBFT is proposed. By experimenting with the random forest prediction model, the average accuracy rate is 95%, which ensures the accuracy and safety of the master node selection. Comparing the algorithms before and after the improvement, the consumption of RFBFT is reduced by 20% and the delay is reduced by 19%, which improves the operation of the alliance chain. The performance in the process, the improved RFBFT is suitable for alliance chains. Summarize some of the current shortcomings: For example, the security and accuracy cannot reach 100%. The addition of a credit scoring mechanism can provide influential feature vectors for the random forest model, but the accuracy of the prediction model cannot reach 100%. This is a problem in the later stage. Make improvements.

Acknowledgment. This work is funded by the Science Research Fund of Yunnan Provincial Department of Education (2020J0835), Dr. Gan Jianhou workstation, Computer Science and Technology discipline innovation team building for intelligent education in ethnic areas (2020xhxtd07).

References

1. Nakamoto, S.: Bitcoin: a peer-to-peer electronic cash system. Consulted (2009)
2. Konstantinos, C., Devetsikiotis, M.: Blockchains and smart contracts for the Internet of Things. IEEE Access **4**, 2292–2303 (2016)
3. Li, Z., Kang, J., Yu, R.: Consortium blockchain for secure energy trading in industrial Internet of Things. IEEE Trans. Ind. Inf., 1 (2017)
4. Fu, D., Hu, S., Zhang, L., et al.: An intelligent cloud computing of trunk logistics alliance based on blockchain and big data. J. Supercomput., 1–16 (2021)
5. Xiaoguang, W.: Overview of the consensus algorithm of blockchain technology. Inf. Comput. (Theor. Edn.) **379**(09), 72–74 (2017)
6. Tang, D., He, P., Wang, J.: PoW blockchain network's short-term self-correction mechanism. SSRN Electron. J. (2) (2020)
7. Lee, S., Kim, S.: Short selling attack: a self-destructive but profitable 51% attack on PoS blockchains (2020)
8. Jeong, S.E.: Centralized decentralization: simple economics of governance attacks on the DPoS blockchain. SSRN Electron. J. (2) (2020)
9. Ferretti, C., Leporati, A., Mariot, L., et al.: Transferable anonymous payments via TumbleBit in permissioned blockchains (2019)
10. Li, Z., Hao, J., Liu, J., et al.: An IoT-applicable access control model under double-layer blockchain. IEEE Trans. Circuits Syst. II Express Briefs 2020
11. Zhang, X.: Research on the standardization of individual credit scoring mechanism in China. Credit Reference (2019)
12. Su, Y., Weng, K., Lin, C., et al.: An improved random forest model for the prediction of dam displacement. IEEE Access **PP**(99),1 (2021)
13. Wang, W., Hoang, D.T., Hu, P., et al.: A survey on consensus mechanisms and mining management in blockchain networks (2018)
14. Kanjalkar, S., Zhang, Y., Gandlur, S., et al.: Publicly auditable MPC-as-a-Service with succinct verification and universal setup (2021)
15. Mundhra, M., Rebeiro, C.: SISSLE in consensus-based ripple: some improvements in speed, security, last mile connectivity and ease of use (2020)
16. Angelis, S.D., Aniello. L., Baldoni. R., et al.: PBFT vs proof-of-authority: applying the CAP theorem to permissioned blockchain. In: Italian Conference on Cybersecurity (2017)
17. Han, Z., Gong, N., Ren, J.: Improvement of a practical Byzantine fault-tolerant algorithm for blockchain. Comput. Appl. Softw. **037**(002), 226–233, 294 (2020)

Traceable Identity-Based Ring Signature for Protecting Mobile IoT Devices

Xin Peng, Ke Gu$^{(\boxtimes)}$, Zhenlin Liu, and Wenbin Zhang

School of Computer and Communication Engineering,
Changsha University of Science and Technology, Changsha 410114, China

Abstract. In mobile internet of things (MIoTs), it is very important how to protect the identities of terminal devices so as to implement the privacy security. On the one hand, if a malicious MIoT device issues its false data under full privacy protection, then this device may abuse the privacy protection function to arbitrarily issue its false data, and it can not be disclosed. Therefore, in this paper we propose a traceable identity-based ring signature (TIBRS) scheme with constant size for protecting and tracing the identities of MIoT devices. In our proposed scheme, the MIoT devices can anonymously issue their data by traceable identity-based ring signatures, where their identities are protected. On the other hand, if their identities need to be traced, then a trusted third party (private key generator) can trace the identities of these MIoT devices on their generated signatures. Based on the related security model, our proposed scheme is proved to have a security reduction to the computational Diffie-Hellman assumption in the standard model, where our scheme has the anonymity with enough security to protecting the identities of MIoT devices. Compared with other related works, our scheme requires less computational overhead on MIoT devices, which generates constant size signatures.

Keywords: Identity · Traceable ring signature · MIoT device · Privacy

1 Introduction

1.1 Background

As the important part of the whole internet of things (IoTs) [1], mobile internet of things (MIoTs) refers to a kind of network that can interconnect some mobile terminal devices by wireless communication mode. Then MIoTs forms a self-organized network system through a large number of mobile network nodes for sensing, acquiring and transmitting data, as shown in Fig. 1. Since these mobile devices are usually located at the edge of the network, they both lack of enough methods to resist various attacks. Therefore, compared with the users of the

This research is funded by the Postgraduate Scientific Research Innovation Project of Hunan Province under Grant CX20200881.

traditional internet, the privacy security of the users is more easy to be broken down in the MIoTs [2]. Since MIoT devices need to generate and issue a large amount of data, it is also very important how to protect the identities of MIoT devices so as to implement the privacy security. On the other hand, if a malicious MIoT device issues its false data under full privacy protection, then it may abuse the privacy protection function to arbitrarily issue its false data, and it can not be disclosed. Therefore, it is necessary to construct a traceable privacy protection scheme for MIoTs, which can protect the identities of MIoT devices while tracing these identities under some conditions.

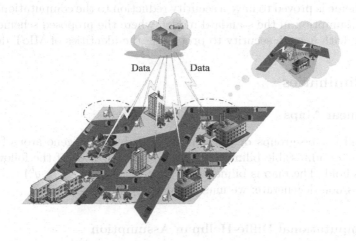

Fig. 1. Data acquisition frame for MIoTs

Ring signature [3–5] allows ring member to hide his identifying information to a ring when ring member signs any message, thus ring signature only reveals the fact that a message was signed by possible one of ring members (a list of possible signers). Additionally, since the notion of traceable ring signature is proposed by Fujisaki et al. [8,9], many traceable ring signature schemes are constructed. In the Fujisaki et al.'s schemes, the anonymity of the signer will be revoked if and only if the signer generates two ring signatures on the same event. Au et al. [6] proposed a new identity-based event-oriented linkable ring signature scheme, if a user generates two linkable ring signatures in the same event, everyone can compute his identity from these two signatures. Branco et al. [10] proposed the first traceable ring signature scheme, they use a variant of Stern's protocol and, by applying the Fiat-Shamir transform to it in an ingenious way, they can obtain a ring signature that allows traceability. We et al. [11] proposed an efficient traceable ring signature scheme without pairings, which is based on the modified EDL signature.

However, although traceable ring signature is useful to protect and trace the identities of MIoT devices, it still needs to be improved because of its complexity.

Presently there exist two main issues for traceable ring signatures in MIoT environment: 1) the computational cost generated by signing algorithm is linearly related to the number of ring users; 2) MIoT devices require the lightweight signing algorithm because of their limited energy. In this paper, we focus on constructing a lightweight traceable ring signature scheme for MIoT devices. In our proposed scheme, the MIoT devices can anonymously issue their data by traceable identity-based ring signatures, where their identities are protected. On the other hand, if their identities need to be traced, then a trusted third party (private key generator) can trace the identities of these MIoT devices on their generated signatures. Based on the related security model [6,8], the proposed TIBRS scheme is proved to have a security reduction to the computational Diffie-Hellman assumption in the standard model, where the proposed scheme has the anonymity with enough security to protecting the identities of MIoT devices.

2   Preliminaries

2.1   Bilinear Maps

Let $\mathbb{G}_1$ and $\mathbb{G}_2$ be groups of prime order q and g be a generator of $\mathbb{G}_1$. We say $\mathbb{G}_2$ has an admissible bilinear map, $e : \mathbb{G}_1 \times \mathbb{G}_1 \to \mathbb{G}_2$ if the following two conditions hold. The map is bilinear; for all a, b, we have $e\left(g^a, g^b\right) = e(g,g)^{a \cdot b}$. The map is non-degenerate; we must have that $e\left(g, g\right) \neq 1$.

2.2   Computational Diffie-Hellman Assumption

Definition 1. *Computational Diffie-Hellman (CDH) Problem:* Let $\mathbb{G}_1$ be a group of prime order q and g be a generator of $\mathbb{G}_1$; for all $(g, g^a, g^b) \in \mathbb{G}_1$, with $a, b \in \mathbb{Z}_q$, the CDH problem is to compute $g^{a \cdot b}$.

Definition 2. *The $(\hbar, \varepsilon)$-CDH assumption holds if no $\hbar$-time algorithm can solve the CDH problem with probability at least ε.*

3   Traceable Identity-Based Ring Signature for MIoT Devices

In the section, we propose a traceable identity-based ring signature scheme with constant size for protecting and tracing the identities of MIoT devices. In our proposed scheme, the MIoT devices can anonymously issue their data by traceable identity-based ring signatures. On the other hand, if their identities need to be traced, then the private key generator can trace the identities of these MIoT devices on their generated signatures. Let **TIBRS**=(**System-Setup**, **Generate-Key**, **Sign**, **Verify**, **Trace-Device**) be a traceable identity-based ring signature scheme in MIoTs. In **TIBRS**, all algorithms are described as follows (shown in Fig. 2):

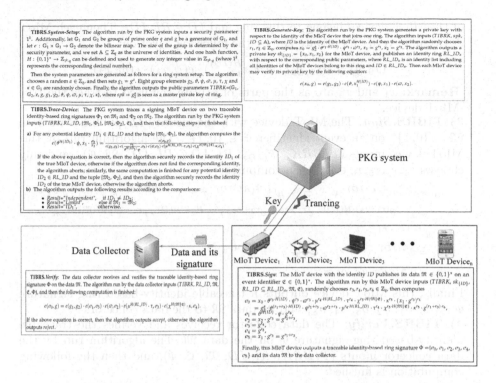

Fig. 2. Traceable identity-based ring signatures for MIoT devices

1) TIBRS.*System-Setup*: The algorithm run by the private key generator (PKG) system inputs a security parameter 1^k. Additionally, let $\mathbb{G}_1$ and $\mathbb{G}_2$ be groups of prime order q and g be a generator of $\mathbb{G}_1$, and let $e : \mathbb{G}_1 \times \mathbb{G}_1 \to \mathbb{G}_2$ denote the bilinear map. The size of the group is determined by the security parameter, and we set $\mathbb{A} \subseteq \mathbb{Z}_q$ as the universe of identities. And one hash function, $H : \{0,1\}^* \to \mathbb{Z}_{1^k \cdot q}$ can be defined and used to generate any integer value in $\mathbb{Z}_{1^k \cdot q}$ (where 1^k represents the corresponding decimal number).

Then the system parameters are generated as follows for a ring system setup. The algorithm chooses a random $a \in \mathbb{Z}_q$, and then sets $g_1 = g^a$. Eight group elements g_2, ϑ, ψ, ϖ, μ, τ, χ and $\kappa \in \mathbb{G}_1$ are randomly chosen. Finally, the algorithm outputs the public parameters $TIBRK = (\mathbb{G}_1, \mathbb{G}_2, e, g, g_1, g_2, \vartheta, \psi, \varpi, \mu, \tau, \chi, \kappa)$, where $spk = g_2^a$ is seen as a master private key of ring.

2) TIBRS.*Generate-Key*: The algorithm run by the PKG system generates a private key with respect to the identity of the MIoT device that joins one ring. The algorithm inputs $(TIBRK, spk, ID \subseteq \mathbb{A})$, where ID is the identity of the MIoT device. And then the algorithm randomly chooses $r_1, r_2 \in \mathbb{Z}_q$, computes $x_0 = g_2^a \cdot \vartheta^{r_1 \cdot H(ID)} \cdot \psi^{r_1} \cdot \varpi^{r_2}$, $x_1 = g^{r_1}$, $x_2 = g^{r_2}$. The algorithm outputs a private key $sk_{\{ID\}} = \{x_0, x_1, x_2\}$ for the MIoT device, and publishes an identity ring RL_ID_a with respect to the corresponding public parameters, where RL_ID_a is an identity list including all identities of the MIoT devices belong to this ring and $ID \in RL\_ID_a$. Then each MIoT device may verify its private key by the following equation:

$$e(x_0, g) = e(g_1, g_2) \cdot e(\vartheta, x_1^{H(ID)}) \cdot e(\psi, x_1) \cdot e(\varpi, x_2).$$

Remark: x_1 and x_2 are as the parts of private key used to trace the true MIoT device.

3) TIBRS.*Sign*: The MIoT device with the identity ID publishes its data $\mathfrak{M} \in \{0,1\}^*$ on an event identifier $\mathfrak{E} \in \{0,1\}^*$. The algorithm run by this MIoT device inputs $(TIBRK, sk_{\{ID\}}, RL\_ID \subseteq RL\_ID_a, \mathfrak{M}, \mathfrak{E})$, randomly chooses $r_3, r_4, r_5, r_6 \in \mathbb{Z}_q$, then computes

$$\sigma_0 = x_0 \cdot \vartheta^{r_3 \cdot H(ID)} \cdot \psi^{r_3} \cdot \varpi^{r_3} \cdot \mu^{r_4 \cdot H(RL\_ID)} \cdot \tau^{r_4} \cdot \chi^{r_5 \cdot H(\mathfrak{M} \| \mathfrak{E})} \cdot \kappa^{r_5} \cdot (x_1 \cdot g^{r_3})^{r_6}$$

$$= g_2^a \cdot \vartheta^{(r_1 + r_3) \cdot H(ID)} \cdot \psi^{r_1 + r_3} \cdot \varpi^{r_2 + r_3} \cdot \mu^{r_4 \cdot H(RL\_ID)} \cdot \tau^{r_4} \cdot \chi^{r_5 \cdot H(\mathfrak{M} \| \mathfrak{E})} \cdot \kappa^{r_5} \cdot$$

$$g^{(r_1 + r_3) \cdot r_6},$$

$$\sigma_1 = \vartheta^{H(ID)} \cdot \psi \cdot g^{r_6}, \sigma_2 = x_2 \cdot g^{r_3} = g^{r_2 + r_3},$$

$$\sigma_3 = g^{r_4}, \sigma_4 = g^{r_5}, \sigma_5 = x_1 \cdot g^{r_3} = g^{r_1 + r_3}.$$

Finally, this MIoT device outputs a traceable identity-based ring signature $\Phi = \{\sigma_0, \sigma_1, \sigma_2, \sigma_3, \sigma_4, \sigma_5\}$ and its data $\mathfrak{M}$ to the data collector.

4) TIBRS. *Verify*: The data collector receives and verifies the traceable identity-based ring signature Φ on the data $\mathfrak{M}$. The algorithm run by the data collector inputs $(TIBRK, RL\_ID, \mathfrak{M}, \mathfrak{E}, \Phi)$, and then the following computation is finished:

$$e(\sigma_0, g) = e(g_1, g_2) \cdot e(\sigma_1, \sigma_5) \cdot e(\varpi, \sigma_2) \cdot e(\mu^{H(RL\_ID)} \cdot \tau, \sigma_3) \cdot e(\chi^{H(\mathfrak{M} \| \mathfrak{E})} \cdot \kappa, \sigma_4).$$

If the above equation is correct, then the algorithm outputs *accept*, otherwise the algorithm outputs *reject*.

5) TIBRS. *Trace-Device*: The PKG system traces a signing MIoT device on two traceable identity-based ring signatures Φ_1 on $\mathfrak{M}_1$ and Φ_2 on $\mathfrak{M}_2$. The algorithm run by the PKG system inputs $(TIBRK, RL\_ID, \{\mathfrak{M}_1, \Phi_1\}, \{\mathfrak{M}_2, \Phi_2\}, \mathfrak{E})$, and then the following steps are finished:

a) For any potential identity $ID_1 \in RL\_ID$ and the tuple $\{\mathfrak{M}_1, \Phi_1\}$, the algorithm computes the equation:

$$e(\vartheta^{H(ID_1)} \cdot \psi, x_1 \cdot \frac{\sigma_2}{x_2}) =$$

$$\frac{e(\sigma_0, g)}{e(g_1, g_2) \cdot e(\frac{\sigma_1}{\vartheta^{H(ID_1)} \cdot \psi}, \sigma_5) \cdot e(\varpi, \sigma_2) \cdot e(\mu^{H(RL\_ID)} \cdot \tau, \sigma_3) \cdot e(\chi^{H(\mathfrak{M}_1 \| \mathfrak{E})} \cdot \kappa, \sigma_4)}.$$

If the above equation is correct, then the algorithm securely records the identity ID_1 of the true MIoT device, otherwise if the algorithm does not find the corresponding identity, the algorithm aborts; similarly, the same computation is finished for any potential identity $ID_2 \in RL\_ID$ and the tuple $\{\mathfrak{M}_2, \Phi_2\}$, and then the algorithm securely records the identity ID_2 of the true MIoT device, otherwise the algorithm aborts.

b) The algorithm outputs the following results according to the comparisons:

- *Result*="*Independent*",   if $ID_1 \neq ID_2$;
- *Result*="*Linked*",   else if $\mathfrak{M}_1 = \mathfrak{M}_2$;
- *Result*="ID_1",   otherwise.

4 Analysis of Our Proposed Scheme

4.1 Correctness

In our proposed scheme, the traceable identity-based ring signature is $\Phi = \{\sigma_0, \sigma_1, \sigma_2, \sigma_3, \sigma_4, \sigma_5\}$.

So, we have that

$$e(\sigma_0, g) = e(g_2^a \cdot \vartheta^{(r_1+r_3)\cdot H(ID)} \cdot \psi^{r_1+r_3} \cdot \varpi^{r_2+r_3} \cdot \mu^{r_4 \cdot H(RL\_ID)} \cdot \tau^{r_4} \cdot \chi^{r_5 \cdot H(\mathfrak{M}\|\mathfrak{E})} \cdot$$
$$\kappa^{r_5} \cdot g^{(r_1+r_3)\cdot r_6}, g)$$
$$= e(g_2^a, g) \cdot e(\vartheta^{(r_1+r_3)\cdot H(ID)} \cdot \psi^{r_1+r_3} \cdot g^{(r_1+r_3)\cdot r_6}, g) \cdot e(\varpi^{r_2+r_3}, g) \cdot e(\mu^{r_4 \cdot H(RL\_ID)} \cdot$$
$$\tau^{r_4}, g) \cdot e(\chi^{r_5 \cdot H(\mathfrak{M}\|\mathfrak{E})} \cdot \kappa^{r_5}, g)$$
$$= e(g_1, g_2) \cdot e(\sigma_1, \sigma_5) \cdot e(\varpi, \sigma_2) \cdot e(\mu^{H(RL\_ID)} \cdot \tau, \sigma_3) \cdot e(\chi^{H(\mathfrak{M}\|\mathfrak{E})} \cdot \kappa, \sigma_4).$$

4.2 Efficiency

We compare our proposed scheme with other traceable (or linkable) ring signature schemes proposed by [6–9,12]. Table 1 shows the comparisons of the traceable or linkable ring signature schemes. Compared with other schemes, our scheme is identity-based and constructed in the standard model, and has constant signature size in the comparison of the performance.

Table 1. Comparisons of the six schemes.

	Signature size	Identity-based	Traceability	Linking cost	Model
Scheme [7]	$O(n)$	No	No	$O(1)$	Random oracle model
Scheme [12]	$O(n)$	No	No	$O(1)$	Random oracle model
Scheme [9]	$O(\sqrt{n})$	No	Yes	$O(n \cdot \log n)$	Standard model
Scheme [8]	$O(n)$	No	Yes	$O(n)$	Random oracle model
Scheme [6]	$O(1)$	Yes	Yes	$O(1)$	Random oracle model
Our Scheme	$O(1)$	Yes	Yes	$O(n)$	Standard model

4.3 Security

In the section, we show our traceable identity-based ring signature scheme has a security reduction to the CDH assumption. In our scheme, any MIoT device cannot forge a traceable identity-based ring signature on any corrupted or fresh information. Second, the identity anonymity of MIoT device must be protected. Therefore, our traceable identity-based ring signature scheme must have the TIBRS unforgeability and anonymity (against *linkability attacks* and *exculpability attacks*) under the adaptive chosen message and identity attacks. Our proofs for the following theorems are based on the security framework proposed by [6,8] (The specific proof process can be found in [11]).

Theorem 1. *Our TIBRS scheme is $(\hbar, \varepsilon, q_g, q_s)$-unforgeable, assuming that the $(\hbar', \varepsilon')$-CDH assumption holds in $\mathbb{G}_1$, where:*

$$\varepsilon' = (1 - \frac{q_g}{q}) \cdot (1 - \frac{q_s}{q})^2 \cdot \frac{\varepsilon}{q^2},$$

$$\hbar' = \hbar + O(q_g \cdot (7 \cdot C_{exp} + C_{mul}) + q_s \cdot (18 \cdot C_{exp} + 14 \cdot C_{mul})),$$

and q_g is the maximal number of "Generate-Key" oracle queries, q_s is the maximal number of "Sign" oracle queries, C_{mul} and C_{exp} are respectively the time for a multiplication and an exponentiation in $\mathbb{G}_1$.

Theorem 2. *Our TIBRS scheme is a linkable (traceable) TIBRS scheme when it satisfies the following condition—this scheme is ($\hbar$, ε, q_g, q_s)-secure, assuming that the ($\hbar'$, ε')-CDH assumption holds in $\mathbb{G}_1$, where*

$$\varepsilon' = \left(1 - \frac{q_g}{q}\right) \cdot \left(1 - \frac{q_s}{q}\right)^2 \cdot \left(\prod_{i=0}^{i=t} \frac{1^k - i}{1^k \cdot q - i}\right)^2 \cdot \varepsilon,$$

$$\hbar' = \hbar + O(q_g \cdot (7 \cdot C_{exp} + C_{mul}) + q_s \cdot (18 \cdot C_{exp} + 14 \cdot C_{mul})),$$

and q_g is the maximal number of "Generate-Key" oracle queries, q_s is the maximal number of "Sign" oracle queries, t is the number of private keys possessed by adversary, C_{mul} and C_{exp} are respectively the time for a multiplication and an exponentiation in $\mathbb{G}_1$.

Theorem 3. *Our TIBRS scheme is exculpable when it satisfies the following condition—this scheme is ($\hbar$, ε, q_g, q_s)-secure, assuming that the ($\hbar'$, ε')-CDH assumption holds in $\mathbb{G}_1$, where*

$$\varepsilon' = (1 - \frac{q_g}{q}) \cdot (1 - \frac{q_s}{q})^2 \cdot \frac{\varepsilon}{q^2},$$

$$\hbar' = \hbar + O(q_g \cdot (7 \cdot C_{exp} + C_{mul}) + q_s \cdot (18 \cdot C_{exp} + 14 \cdot C_{mul})),$$

and q_g is the maximal number of "Generate-Key" oracle queries, q_s is the maximal number of "Sign" oracle queries, C_{mul} and C_{exp} are respectively the time for a multiplication and an exponentiation in $\mathbb{G}_1$.

Theorem 4. *Our TIBRS scheme is ($\hbar$, ε, q_g, q_s)-anonymous, assuming that the ($\hbar'$, ε')-CDH assumption holds in $\mathbb{G}_1$, where:*

$$\varepsilon' = (1 - \frac{q_{g_1}}{q}) \cdot (1 - \frac{q_{s_1}}{q})^2 \cdot (1 - \frac{q_{g_2}}{q}) \cdot (1 - \frac{q_{s_2}}{q})^2 \cdot \frac{\varepsilon}{q^2},$$

$$\hbar' = \hbar + O((q_{g_1} + q_{g_2}) \cdot (7 \cdot C_{exp} + C_{mul}) + (q_{s_1} + q_{s_2}) \cdot (18 \cdot C_{exp} + 14 \cdot C_{mul})),$$

q_{g_1} and q_{g_2} are respectively the maximal numbers of "Generate-Key" oracle queries in the Queries Phase 1 and 2, q_{s_1} and q_{s_2} are respectively the maximal numbers of "Sign" oracle queries in the Queries Phase 1 and 2, C_{mul} and C_{exp} are respectively the time for a multiplication and an exponentiation in $\mathbb{G}_1$.

5   Conclusions

In this paper, we propose a fully traceable identity-based ring signature scheme with constant size for MIoT devices. In our proposed scheme, the MIoT devices can anonymously issue their data by traceable identity-based ring signatures, where their identities are protected. On the other hand, if their identities need to be traced, then a trusted third party (private key generator) can trace the identities of these MIoT devices on their generated signatures. Based on the related security model, our proposed TIBRS scheme is proved to have a security reduction to the CDH assumption in the standard model, where this scheme has the anonymity with enough security to protecting the identities of MIoT devices. Compared with other related works, our proposed TIBRS scheme requires less computational overhead on MIoT devices, which generates constant size signatures.

References

1. He, Q., Xu, Y., Liu, Z., He, J., Sun, Y., Zhang, R.: A privacy-preserving Internet of Things device management scheme based on blockchain. Int. J. Distrib. Sens. Netw. **14**(11), 1–12 (2018)
2. Xiong, J., et al.: A secure data deletion scheme for IoT devices through key derivation encryption and data analysis. Future Gener. Comput. Syst. **111**, 741–753 (2020)
3. Rivest, R.L., Shamir, A., Tauman, Y.: How to leak a secret. In: Boyd, C. (ed.) ASIACRYPT 2001. LNCS, vol. 2248, pp. 552–565. Springer, Heidelberg (2001). https://doi.org/10.1007/3-540-45682-1_32
4. Abe, M., Ohkubo, M., Suzuki, K.: 1-out-of-n signatures from a variety of keys. In: Zheng, Y. (ed.) ASIACRYPT 2002. LNCS, vol. 2501, pp. 415–432. Springer, Heidelberg (2002). https://doi.org/10.1007/3-540-36178-2_26
5. Zhang, F., Kim, K.: ID-based blind signature and ring signature from pairings. In: Zheng, Y. (ed.) ASIACRYPT 2002. LNCS, vol. 2501, pp. 533–547. Springer, Heidelberg (2002). https://doi.org/10.1007/3-540-36178-2_33
6. Au, M.H., Liu, J.K., Susilo, W., Yuen, T.H.: Secure ID-based linkable and revocable-iff-linked ring signature with constant-size construction. Theor. Comput. Sci. **469**, 1–14 (2013)
7. Liu, J.K., Wong, D.S., et al.: Linkable ring signatures: security models and new schemes. In: Gervasi, O. (ed.) ICCSA 2005, Part II. LNCS, vol. 3481, pp. 614–623. Springer, Heidelberg (2005). https://doi.org/10.1007/11424826_65
8. Fujisaki, E., Suzuki, K.: Traceable ring signature. In: Okamoto, T., Wang, X. (eds.) PKC 2007. LNCS, vol. 4450, pp. 181–200. Springer, Heidelberg (2007). https://doi.org/10.1007/978-3-540-71677-8_13
9. Fujisaki, E.: Sub-linear size traceable ring signatures without random oracles. In: Kiayias, A. (ed.) CT-RSA 2011. LNCS, vol. 6558, pp. 393–415. Springer, Heidelberg (2011). https://doi.org/10.1007/978-3-642-19074-2_25
10. Branco, P., Mateus, P.: A traceable ring signature scheme based on coding theory. In: Ding, J., Steinwandt, R. (eds.) PQCrypto 2019. LNCS, vol. 11505, pp. 387–403. Springer, Cham (2019). https://doi.org/10.1007/978-3-030-25510-7_21

11. Gu, K., Dong, X., Wang, L.: Efficient traceable ring signature scheme without pairings. Adv. Math. Commun. **14**(2), 207–232 (2020)
12. Zheng, D., Li, X., Chen, K., Li, J., et al.: Linkable ring signatures from linear feedback shift register. In: Denko, M.K. (ed.) EUC 2007. LNCS, vol. 4809, pp. 716–727. Springer, Heidelberg (2007). https://doi.org/10.1007/978-3-540-77090-9_66

BSO-CMA-ES: Brain Storm Optimization Based Covariance Matrix Adaptation Evolution Strategy for Multimodal Optimization

Liang Qu, Ruiqi Zheng, and Yuhui Shi[✉]

Department of Computer Science and Engineering, Southern University of Science and Technology, Guangdong 518055, China
shiyh@sustech.edu.cn

Abstract. Recently, covariance matrix adaption evolution strategy (CMA-ES) and its variants have achieved great success in the continuous unimodal optimization tasks owing to its strong local search capabilities. However, it is precisely this capability that reduces the population diversity, which makes it unable to obtain the good performance on the multimodal optimization problems (MMOPs) aiming at locating all global optimal solutions during a single algorithm run. To address this problem, we first propose a swarm learning framework which is capable of collaboratively training multiple optimization algorithms (e.g., CMA-ES in this paper). Specifically, it introduces two objectives including individual objective and neighbor objective to balance the exploitation and exploration. The former guides each algorithm to locate at least one global optimal solution (exploitation), and the latter aims at maintaining the diversity of the different algorithms (exploration). Based on this framework, the brain storm optimization (BSO) is incorporated with multiple CMA-ES models, called BSO-CMA-ES, which makes the multiple CMA-ESs be collaboratively trained. To validate the effectiveness of the proposed method, several comparison algorithms are adopted and tested on typical MMOPs benchmark functions. Experimental results show that BSO-CMA-ES could obtain promising performance.

Keywords: Multimodal optimization · Brain storm optimization · Covariance matrix adaptation evolution strategy · Swarm learning

1 Introduction

Multimodal optimization refers to the problems that aim at locating all global optimal solutions during a single algorithm run, which is very important on many real-world problems. It can be formulated as follows:

$$x_1^*, x_2^*, \cdots, x_m^* = \arg min_{x \in R^D} f(x) \tag{1}$$

© Springer Nature Singapore Pte Ltd. 2021
Y. Tan et al. (Eds.): DMBD 2021, CCIS 1454, pp. 167–174, 2021.
https://doi.org/10.1007/978-981-16-7502-7_19

where $x_1^*, x_2^*, \cdots, x_m^*$ are a group of global optimal solutions for the minimization problems, and D and f are the dimension of the solutions and the evaluation function respectively. The main challenge of MMOPs lies in locating multiple optimal solutions simultaneously, which requires the search algorithms well balancing exploration (covering a large search space) and exploitation (searching in a local space).

Recently, population-based methods (PBMs) such as evolutionary algorithms [5], swarm intelligence algorithms [17] and evolution strategy [7] have shown promising performance on the unimodal optimization problems. However, the typical PBMs generally cannot obtain the good results on MMOPs owing to their single optimal solution objective. To apply these methods on the MMOPs, niching methods [12] are incorporated into the PBMs [3,9], which divides the population into multiple subpopulations to preserve the population diversity resulting in locating multiple optimal solutions. However, most existing niching based PBMs suffer from issues: (1) algorithm parameters such as the niching radius highly rely on expert knowledge to set. (2) the assumptions about the distribution or shape are not always satisfied in many practical MMOPs.

To address above issues, in this paper, we first propose a swarm learning framework which is capable of collaboratively training multiple population-based algorithms (e.g., CMA-ES [7] in this paper) such that different algorithms could locate different optimal solutions. Specifically, it introduces two objectives including individual objective and neighbor objective to balance the exploitation and exploration. The former guides each algorithm to locate at least one global optimal solution (exploitation), and the latter aims at maintaining the diversity of different algorithm (exploration). Based on this framework, the brain storm optimization algorithm (BSO) [15] is incorporated with multiple CMA-ES models, called BSO-CMA-ES, which makes the multiple CMA-ESs be collaboratively trained.

The contributions of this paper are summarized as follows:

- To address the MMOPs, we first propose a swarm learning framework which is capable of collaboratively training multiple population-based algorithms. In particular, it introduces the individual objective and the neighbor objective to balance the exploitation and exploration.
- Based on the swarm learning framework, we propose BSO-CMA-ES algorithm which trains multiple CMA-ES algorithms simultaneously and maintains the diversity of them by incorporating multiple training processes into BSO.
- To validate the effectiveness of the proposed method, we conduct the experiments on typical MMOPs benchmark functions and compare with several baseline methods. Experimental results show that the proposed method could obtain the promising performance.

The rest of paper is organized as follows. Section 2 will introduce related works. Section 3 will introduce the proposed method in detail. Section 4 will introduce the experimental settings and results followed by a conclusion in Sect. 5.

2   Related Work

2.1   Brain Storm Optimization (BSO)

Brain storm optimization algorithms (BSO) [4,13–15] are the promising swarm intelligence methods inspired by the brain-storming process of human. It introduces a clustering operator clustering the population into different clusters, which is suitable for addressing MMOPs. Self-adaptive Brain Storm Optimization (SBSO) [6] introduces a max-fitness grouping cluster method to divide the population into different sub-groups which could track different optimal solutions. BSO-OS [4] proposes to cluster the population in the objective space and the experimental results that BSO-OS could obtain good performance on MMOPs.

2.2   Covariance Matrix Adaptation Evolution Strategy (CMA-ES)

CMA-ES [7] is one of the most representative evolution strategy algorithms. It iteratively generates the population by sampling from a Gaussian distribution with several trainable parameters to update the distribution. Hansen et al. [8] evaluates the performance of CMA-ES on MMOPs, and experimental results showed that increasing the population size could effectively improve the CMA-ES performance on the MMOPs. RS-CMSA [1] proposes a new niching based CMA-ES method with repelling subpopulations for MMOPs. Specifically, it incorporates several existing techniques such as taboo points, normalized Mahalanobis distance, and the hill-valley function into CMA-ES. The main advantages of RS-CMSA are that it does not rely on any particular assumptions. Furthermore, restart strategy is also a common alternative method [2,11] for applying CMA-ES on MMOPs.

3   Proposed Method

This section will elaborate on the proposed method. It will start with the general swarm learning framework, and then the BSO-CMA-ES will be introduced in detail.

3.1   Swarm Learning

Recent years, with the rapid development of the real-world various applications, the optimization and learning problems in these applications get more and more complicated, and it is difficult to use a single algorithm to address these problems. Thus it is natural to think that using multiple algorithms collaboratively solves the challenging problems. For example, in the context of MMOPs, although using a single CMA-ES is capable of obtaining good performance on the unimodal optimization problems, it is difficult on MMOPs. Thus, it is necessary to explore how to collaboratively train multiple CMA-ES algorithms simultaneously such that different CMA-ES algorithms could locate at different optimal solutions. Based on this idea, we propose a general swarm learning (SL) framework. Specifically, it contains following steps:

– **Step 1:** set problem-dependent individual objective O_{indi} and neighbor objective O_{nei}.
– **Step 2:** initialize the parameters of P individuals. For example, in this paper, each individual is a CMA-ES algorithm, and the different individuals have different parameters such as the different covariance matrices. Furthermore, each CMA-ES individual can generate λ candidate solutions.
– **Step 3:** each individual independently learn M generations, and the individual objective O_{indi} is utilized to select the solutions with high fitness values.
– **Step 4:** neighbor individuals collaboratively learning between each other, and the neighbor objective is utilized to maintain the population diversity.
– **Step 5:** if the stop condition is not met, return Step 3.

3.2 BSO-CMA-ES

Based on the SL framework, we further propose the BSO-CMA-ES algorithm. Specifically, it contains P individuals (i.e., P CMA-ES algorithms with different parameters.), and each CMA-ES individual could sample λ solutions. Thus the total population size is $P \times \lambda$. For the maximum optimization problems, the individual objective O_{indi} is to maximize the evaluation values $f(x)$ for a given benchmark function f with respect to the candidate solutions x. Furthermore, the individual objective is utilized to select the parent solutions to update the parameters for each CMA-ES individual. For the neighbor individuals collaboratively learning process, we first define the central solution x_j^* for the j-th CMA-ES individual by selecting the solution with the highest fitness value among all solutions in the j-th CMA-ES individual, and then the distance $D(x_j^*, V)$ between the j-th CMA-ES individual and residual CMA-ES individuals is defined as follows:

$$D(x_j^*, V) = \sum_{u \in V} ||x_j^* - u||^2 \tag{2}$$

where V is the set of central solutions of residual CMA-ES individuals (i.e., excepting x_j^*). The BSO algorithm is utilized to generate new CMA-ES individuals by exchanging solutions within/between CMA-ES individuals. At last, the neighbor objective O_{nei} is utilized to select the CMA-ES individuals with the maximum distance away from other CMA-ES individuals. Thus, the BSO-CMA-ES can be implemented as following steps:

– **Step 1:** Set the individual objective $O_{indi} = max f(x)$ and neighbor objective $O_{nei} = max D(x_j^*, V)$
– **Step 2:** Randomly initialize the parameters of P CMA-ES individuals.
– **Step 3.1:** Sample the candidate solution x_i^t according to the formula (3) [7], for $i = 1, 2, ..., P$ and $t = 1, 2, ..., \lambda$

$$x_i^t \sim \mathcal{N}(m_i, \sigma_i^2 C_i) \tag{3}$$

where m_i, C_i, σ_i represent the mean value, covariance matrix and step size of the i-th CMA-ES individual respectively.

- **Step 3.2:** Evaluate each candidate solution $f(x_i^t)$, and select μ solutions with the highest fitness value for each CMA-ES individual.
- **Step 3.3:** Update mean value m_i according to formula (4) [7].

$$m_i^{g+1} = m_i^g + \sum_{b=1}^{\mu} \frac{1}{\mu}(x_{b:\lambda}^{g+1} - m^g) \tag{4}$$

where g represent the generations.
- **Step 3.4:** Update step-size control σ_i according to formula (5) [7].

$$\sigma_i^{g+1} = \sigma_i^g exp(\frac{c_\sigma}{d_\sigma}(\frac{||p_\sigma^{g+1}||}{E||\mathcal{N}(0,I)||} - 1)) \tag{5}$$

where c_σ, d_σ, I are learning rate, damping parameter and identity matrix respectively. p_σ^g is the evolution path calculated according to [7].
- **Step 3.5:** Update covariance matrix C_i according to formula (6) [7].

$$C_i^{g+1} = \frac{2}{dim^2}p_c^{g+1}(p_c^{g+1})^T + c_\mu \sum_{b=1}^{\lambda} \frac{1}{\lambda}\frac{x_{b:\lambda}^{g+1} - m^g}{\sigma^g}(\frac{x_{b:\lambda}^{g+1} - m^g}{\sigma^g})^T \tag{6}$$

where dim and c_μ are the dimension of problem solution and learning rate for rank-μ update. p_c^g is the covariance evolution path calculated according to [7].
- **Step 4.1:** Select the solution x_i^* with the highest fitness as the central solution for each CMA-ES individual.
- **Step 4.2:** Generate a random number $rand_1$ to compare with pre-defined parameter P_{in}. If the result is $rand_1 > P_{in}$, randomly select a CMA-ES individual and use non-center solution to replace the central solution.
- **Step 4.3:** Generate a random number $rand_2$ to compare with pre-defined parameter P_{ou}. If the result is $rand_2 > P_{ou}$, randomly select two CMA-ES individuals and exchange their central solutions.
- **Step 4.4:** Calculate the distance for each CMA-ES individual according to the formula (2) and preserve the P individuals with highest distance.
- **Step 5:** If the stop condition is not met, return Step 3.1.

4 Experiments

4.1 Benchmark Functions

We test the performance of the proposed BSO-CMA-ES on 8 typical MMOPs benchmark functions chosen from [10] as shown in the Table 1. The *#Global Optimal* represents the number of global optimal. *MaxFEs* represents the maximum function evaluations, and *Peak Height* represents the fitness values of the global optimal.

Table 1. The information of the benchmark functions.

Index	Function	#Global optimal	MaxFEs	Peak height
1	F1(1D)	2	5.00E + 04	200.0
2	F2(2D)	5	5.00E + 04	1.0
3	F3(1D)	1	5.00E + 04	1.0
4	F4(2D)	4	5.00E + 04	200.0
5	F5(2D)	2	5.00E + 04	1.031628
6	F6(2D)	18	2.00E + 05	186.730909
7	F7(2D)	36	2.00E + 05	1.0
8	F6(3D)	81	4.00E + 05	2709.093535

4.2 Comparison Method

We compare the proposed BSO-CMA-ES with BSO [15], CMA-ES [7] and IPOP-CMA-ES (i.e., CMA-ES with restart strategy) [2]. We implement these three comparison methods based on the source codes with the default parameters provided by the authors.

Table 2. The experimental results.

Algorithms	F1(1D)		F2(1D)		F3(1D)		F4(2D)	
	PR	*SR*	*PR*	*SR*	*PR*	*SR*	*PR*	*SR*
BSO	**1.000**	0.000	**1.000**	0.000	**1.000**	0.000	**1.000**	0.000
CMA-ES	**1.000**	0.000	**1.000**	0.000	**1.000**	0.000	**1.000**	0.000
IPOP-CMA-ES	**1.000**	1.000	**1.000**	1.000	**1.000**	1.000	**1.000**	1.000
BSO-CMA-ES	**1.000**	1.000	**1.000**	1.000	**1.000**	1.000	**1.000**	1.000
Algorithms	F5(2D)		F6(2D)		F7(2D)		F6(3D)	
	PR	*SR*	*PR*	*SR*	*PR*	*SR*	*PR*	*SR*
BSO	**1.000**	0.000	0.932	0.000	0.752	0.000	0.554	0.000
CMA-ES	**1.000**	0.000	0.954	0.000	0.801	0.000	0.613	0.000
IPOP-CMA-ES	**1.000**	1.000	**1.000**	1.000	0.884	0.147	0.857	0.000
BSO-CMA-ES	**1.000**	1.000	**1.000**	1.000	**0.913**	0.224	**0.895**	0.000

4.3 Experimental Setting

To evaluate the performance of above methods, we use *peak ratio* (PR) [16] and *success rate* (SR) [10] as the evaluation metrics. Furthermore, the *accuracy level* $\epsilon = 1.0E - 04$ is utilized to measure if a global optimal solution is found [10]. Each algorithm is run 50 times independently for each benchmark function, and the mean is reported for comparison.

4.4   Results and Discussion

The experimental results are shown in the Table 2, and the best results are marked in **bold**. From the results we can observe that: (1) Comparing with the unimodal optimization methods such as BSO and CMA-ES, the MMOPs methods IPOP-CMA-ES and BSO-CMA-ES could achieve the better performance on all benchmark functions in terms of SR metric. It is reasonable since that MMOPs methods utilize the various strategies to maintain the population diversity such that multiple global optimal solutions could be found during a single algorithm run. (2) The proposed BSO-CMA-ES could obtain the better performance on the complicated multimodal functions such as $F6$ and $F7$. It is reasonable since the IPOP-CMA-ES utilizes the restart strategy such that the different CMA-ES training processes are independent instead of being collaboratively trained like BSO-CMA-ES.

5   Conclusion

In this paper, to address the MMOPs, we first propose a general swarm learning (SL) framework which could effectively collaboratively train multiple CMA-ES algorithms and maintain the diversity of different algorithms. Furthermore, SL is capable of well balancing the exploration and exploitation during the learning process by optimizing two objectives including individual objective and neighbor objective. Based on SL framework, the BSO-CMA-ES algorithm is proposed to train multiple CMA-ES simultaneously by incorporating BSO into the training process. The experimental results on eight typical MMOPs benchmark functions show that the proposed BSO-CMA-ES could obtain promising results.

Acknowledgement. This work is partially supported by the Shenzhen Fundamental Research Program under the Grant No. JCYJ20200109141235597, National Science Foundation of China under Grant No. 61761136008, Shenzhen Peacock Plan under Grant No. KQTD2016112514355531, and Program for Guangdong Introducing Innovative and Entrepreneurial Teams under grant No. 2017ZT07X386.

References

1. Ahrari, A., Deb, K., Preuss, M.: Multimodal optimization by covariance matrix self-adaptation evolution strategy with repelling subpopulations. Evol. Comput. **25**(3), 439–471 (2017)
2. Auger, A., Hansen, N.: A restart CMA evolution strategy with increasing population size. In: 2005 IEEE Congress on Evolutionary Computation, vol. 2, pp. 1769–1776. IEEE (2005)
3. Barrera, J., Coello, C.A.C.: A review of particle swarm optimization methods used for multimodal optimization. In: Lim, C.P., Jain, L.C., Dehuri, S. (eds.) Innovations in Swarm Intelligence, pp. 9–37. Springer, Heidelberg (2009). https://doi.org/10.1007/978-3-642-04225-6_2

4. Cheng, S., Qin, Q., Chen, J., Shi, Y.: Brain storm optimization algorithm: a review. Artif. Intell. Rev. **46**(4), 445–458 (2016). https://doi.org/10.1007/s10462-016-9471-0
5. Fortin, F.A., De Rainville, F.M., Gardner, M.A.G., Parizeau, M., Gagné, C.: Deap: evolutionary algorithms made easy. J. Mach. Learn. Res. **13**(1), 2171–2175 (2012)
6. Guo, X., Wu, Y., Xie, L.: Modified brain storm optimization algorithm for multi-modal optimization. In: Tan, Y., Shi, Y., Coello, C.A.C. (eds.) ICSI 2014. LNCS, vol. 8795, pp. 340–351. Springer, Cham (2014). https://doi.org/10.1007/978-3-319-11897-0_40
7. Hansen, N.: The CMA evolution strategy: a tutorial. arXiv preprint arXiv:1604.00772 (2016)
8. Hansen, N., Kern, S., et al.: Evaluating the CMA evolution strategy on multi-modal test functions. In: Yao, X. (ed.) PPSN 2004. LNCS, vol. 3242, pp. 282–291. Springer, Heidelberg (2004). https://doi.org/10.1007/978-3-540-30217-9_29
9. Li, J.P., Li, X.D., Wood, A.: Species based evolutionary algorithms for multimodal optimization: A brief review. In: IEEE Congress on Evolutionary Computation. pp. 1–8. IEEE (2010)
10. Li, X., Engelbrecht, A., Epitropakis, M.G.: Benchmark functions for CEC 2013 special session and competition on niching methods for multimodal function optimization, Evolutionary Computation and Machine Learning Group, Australia, Tech. Rep. RMIT University (2013)
11. Loshchilov, I., Schoenauer, M., Sebag, M.: Alternative restart strategies for CMA-ES. In: Coello, C.A.C., Cutello, V., Deb, K., Forrest, S., Nicosia, G., Pavone, M. (eds.) PPSN 2012. LNCS, vol. 7491, pp. 296–305. Springer, Heidelberg (2012). https://doi.org/10.1007/978-3-642-32937-1_30
12. Mahfoud, S.W.: Niching methods for genetic algorithms. Ph.D. thesis, Citeseer (1995)
13. Qu, L., Duan, Q., Yang, J., Cheng, S., Zheng, R., Shi, Y.: BSO-CLS: brain storm optimization algorithm with cooperative learning strategy. In: Tan, Y., Shi, Y., Tuba, M. (eds.) ICSI 2020. LNCS, vol. 12145, pp. 243–250. Springer, Cham (2020). https://doi.org/10.1007/978-3-030-53956-6_22
14. Qu, L., Zhu, H., Shi, Y.: BSOGCN: brain storm optimization graph convolutional networks based heterogeneous information networks embedding. In: 2020 IEEE Congress on Evolutionary Computation (CEC), pp. 1–7 (2020). https://doi.org/10.1109/CEC48606.2020.9185532
15. Shi, Y.: Brain storm optimization algorithm. In: Tan, Y., Shi, Y., Chai, Y., Wang, G. (eds.) ICSI 2011. LNCS, vol. 6728, pp. 303–309. Springer, Heidelberg (2011). https://doi.org/10.1007/978-3-642-21515-5_36
16. Thomsen, R.: Multimodal optimization using crowding-based differential evolution. In: Proceedings of the 2004 Congress on Evolutionary Computation (IEEE Cat. No. 04TH8753), vol. 2, pp. 1382–1389. IEEE (2004)
17. Yang, J., et al.: Swarm intelligence in data science: applications, opportunities and challenges. In: Tan, Y., Shi, Y., Tuba, M. (eds.) ICSI 2020. LNCS, vol. 12145, pp. 3–14. Springer, Cham (2020). https://doi.org/10.1007/978-3-030-53956-6_1

A Generalized χ^2 Divergence for Multisource Information Fusion

Xueyuan Gao[1,2] and Fuyuan Xiao[2(✉)]

[1] School of Computer and Information Science, Southwest University,
Chongqing 400715, China
[2] School of Big Data and Software Engineering, Chongqing University,
Chongqing 401331, China
xiaofuyuan@cqu.edu.cn

Abstract. Divergence measure has been extensively applied in many fields. Basic probability assignment (BPA), instead of probability, is adopted to represent the belief degree of elements in Dempster-Shafer theory. But how to measure the divergence among $BPAs$ is still under research. This paper proposes a novel belief divergence measure based on classic χ^2 divergence. Comparing to the existing divergence, the new proposed divergence performs better in measuring discrepancy among $BPAs$. In addition, the proposed divergence is proved be a bounded, non-degenerated and symmetrical divergence measure. Numerical examples are presented to describe the effectiveness of proposed divergence measure.

Keywords: Dempster-Shafer (D-S) theory · Belief χ^2 divergence · Multi-source information fusion

1 Introduction

Moultisource information fusion [1] is an emerging technique, generating information from various sources to make a comprehensive evaluation. It is a popular research direction field applied in medial diagnosis [2], engineering optimization [3,4], health assessment [5], decision-making [6] and so on [7–9]. As we known, the real world is full of uncertainty, how to handle uncertain [10,11] and even conflicting [12] information is an open issue. A lot of models have been proposed, such as soft likelihood function [13,14], fuzzy set [15,16], intuitionistic fuzzy sets [17,18], pythagorean fuzzy sets [19], Z-number [20], D-number [21], and so on [22,23].

Among those models, a basic probability assignment(BPA) in D-S theory has many advantages in process uncertainty. Compared with probability distribution, the multi-element subset in D-S theory can be assigned a mass which represent the uncertainty of elements in the set. In addition, Dempster's combination rule is an effective way for information conflict. Due to the merits above,

Supported by the National Natural Science Foundation of China (No. 62003280).

D-S theory [24] and its extending works have widely applied in multi-criteria decision-making [25,26], risk analysis [27], classification [28,29] and evidential reasoning [30–32].

However, Demspter's combination rule will obtain counter-intuitive results when fusing highly conflicting evidences. Many solutions have been proposed which can be summarized into the following two groups: the modification the combination rule and the revision of evidences before fusion. In this work we adopt the second one. The most famous of existing works is Murphy's [33] simple average method. Later, Deng et al. [34] improved Murphy's method by allocating every piece of evidences a weight based on divergence. Furthermore, Xiao [35] offered belief Jensen-Shannon (BJS) divergence as a measure to modified evidence body. But, BJS divergence ignores the impact of multi-element subsets.

In this work, we first propose a new belief χ^2 divergence. It is a combination of χ^2 divergence, satisfying the property of symmetry. In order to consider the influence of multi-element subsets, then we improve χ^2 divergence by dividing number of subsets. In fact, the improved belief χ^2 ($\mathcal{IB}$) divergence is a generalization of $\mathcal{B}$ divergence. When $BPAs$ degenerate as probability distributions, The $\mathcal{IB}$ divergence degenerates as $\mathcal{B}$ divergence. Moreover, The $\mathcal{IB}$ is proved to be a bounded, non-degenerate and symmetrical divergence measure.

The main contributions of this work are summarized as below.

(1) A new belief χ^2 divergence is proposed to measure the discrepancy between $BPAs$.
(2) The proposed belief χ^2 divergence takes the number of all possible hypotheses into account. It also has some good properties including boundedness, non-degeneracy and symmetry which allow it be a convincing solution for measuring the discrepancy between $BPAs$.

2   Preliminaries

This section briefly introduces some fundamental preliminaries of D-S theory and divergence measures.

2.1   D-S Theory

D-S theory, raised by Dempster and extended by Shafer, is a generalization of Bayes probability theory. It satisfies a weaker conditional reasoning system because both single-element subsets and multi-element subset can be assigned.

Definition 1. (Framework of discernment)

Let Θ be a set containing N events which represent exclusive and exhaustive hypotheses:

$$\Theta = \{\mathcal{H}_1, \mathcal{H}_2, \cdots, \mathcal{H}_i, \cdots, \mathcal{H}_N\}. \tag{1}$$

Θ is the framework of discernment. Its power set (denoted as 2^Θ) is defined as:

$$2^\Theta = \{\emptyset, \{\mathcal{H}_1\}, ..., \{\mathcal{H}_N\}, \{\mathcal{H}_1, \mathcal{H}_2\}, ..., \{\mathcal{H}_1, \mathcal{H}_2, ..., \mathcal{H}_i\}, ..., \Theta\}, \qquad (2)$$

where $\emptyset$ indicates the empty-set.

Definition 2. (Mass function)

A mass function m (mapping from 2^Θ to $[0, 1]$) is defined as:

$$m : 2^\Theta \rightarrow [0, 1], \qquad (3)$$

which requires the following rules:

$$m(\emptyset) = 0, \sum_{A \in 2^\Theta} m(A) = 1. \qquad (4)$$

A mass function is also referred to as a basic probability function (BPA) which represents belief value of hypotheses. Since BPA can effectively model uncertainty, it has been deeply studied and extended, such as distance [36], entropy [37], negation [38], probability [39], association coefficient [40], complex mass function [41,42], and others [43].

Definition 3. (Dempster's combination rule)

Suppose two $BPAs$ m_1 and m_2 on discernment Θ. Denmpster's combination rule is described as:

$$\begin{cases} m(\emptyset) = 0, \\ m(A) = \frac{\sum_{B \cap C = \emptyset} m_1(B) m_2(C)}{1 - K}, \end{cases} \qquad (5)$$

and

$$K = \sum_{B \cap C = \emptyset} m_1(B) m_2(C), \qquad (6)$$

where $B, C \in 2^\Theta$ and K is mass assigned to emptyset.

2.2 Divergence Measure

As an generalization of probability, BPA is widely applied in information fusion flied. But how to measure uncertainty [44] of $BPAs$ remains an open issue. Some researchers introduces divergence measures of probability theory. Next we will introduce several of them.

Definition 4. (χ^2 Devergence [45])

Suppose two probability distributions $P = \{p_1, p_2, ..., p_n\}$ and $Q = \{q_1, q_2, ..., q_n\}$ with $\sum_i p_i = \sum_i q_i = 1$. The χ^2 divergence is defined as:

$$\chi^2(P, Q) = \sum_{i=1}^n \frac{(p_i - q_i)^2}{q_i}. \qquad (7)$$

Definition 5. (BJS Divergence [35])

Suppose two independent groups of $BPAs$ m_1, m_2 on discernment Θ, containing N collectively exclusive and mutually exhaustive hypotheses. A_i is a hypothesis of belief function m. The BJS divergence is defined as:

$$BJS(m_1, m_2) = \frac{1}{2}\left[DIV_{KL}(m_1, \frac{m_1 + m_2}{2}) + DIV_{KL}(m_2, \frac{m_1 + m_2}{2})\right], \quad (8)$$

where $DIV_{KL}(m_1, m_2)$ represents DIV_{KL} divergence with $DIV_{KL}(m_1, m_2) = \sum_i^n m_1(A_i)\log\frac{m_1(A_i)}{m_2(A_i)}$ and $\sum_i^n m_j(A_i) = 1$ $(j = 1, 2)$.

3   Proposed Method

In order to measure discrepancy among evidences, a novel belief divergence measure is proposed in this section.

3.1   Proposed Divergence

Definition 6. ($\mathcal{B}$ divergence measure)

Given two $BPAs$ m_1 and m_2 defined on discernment Θ, The $\mathcal{B}$ divergence is defined as below:

$$B(m_1, m_2) = \frac{1}{2}\left[\chi^2(m_1, \frac{m_1 + m_2}{2}) + \chi^2(m_2, \frac{m_1 + m_2}{2})\right], \quad (9)$$

where $\chi^2(m_1, m_2) = \sum_i^n \frac{(m_1(\theta_i) - m_2(\theta_i))^2}{m_2(\theta_i)}$ and $\sum_i^n m_j(A_i) = 1$ $(j = 1, 2)$.

$\mathcal{B}$ divergence, as a combination of χ^2 divergence, is a symmetric divergence measure while χ^2 divergence is not. Besides, $\mathcal{B}$ divergence can measure uncertain problems by utilizing mass function instead of probability distributions.

Definition 7. ($\mathcal{IB}$ divergence measure)

$$\mathcal{IB}(m_1, m_2) = \frac{1}{2}\left[\chi^2(\mathcal{M}_1, \frac{\mathcal{M}_1 + \mathcal{M}_2}{2}) + \chi^2(\mathcal{M}_2, \frac{\mathcal{M}_1 + \mathcal{M}_2}{2})\right], \quad (10)$$

where $\mathcal{M}(A_i) = \frac{m(A_i)}{2^{|A_i|} - 1}$ and $\sum_i^n m_j(A_i) = 1$ $(j = 1, 2)$. The $\mathcal{IB}(m_1, m_2)$ can be simplified as:

$$\mathcal{IB}(m_1, m_2) = \frac{1}{2}\sum_{A_i \in \Theta} \frac{(\mathcal{M}_1(A_i) - \mathcal{M}_2(A_i))^2}{\mathcal{M}_1(A_i) + \mathcal{M}_2(A_i)}. \quad (11)$$

As the formula shows, every belief mass of element A_i is divided by $(2^{|A_i|} - 1)$ which represents all possible combinations number of A_i. Compared with probability theory, element in evidence theory also includes multiple subsets, so multiple subsets is assigned as long as the single subset. It should be noted that the $\mathcal{IB}$ divergence is extension of $\mathcal{B}$ divergence. $\mathcal{IB}$ divergence turns into $\mathcal{B}$ divergence when BPA is degenerated into probability distribution. Besides, the $\mathcal{IB}$ divergence takes consideration of both multiple subsets and single subsets which makes it performs better than $\mathcal{B}$ divergence.

3.2 Properties

In this section, several important properties of $\mathcal{IB}$ divergence are proved.

Properties. Let m_1, m_2 and m_3 be three $BPAs$ in Θ. The $\mathcal{IB}$ divergence has properties (1)–(3) as below.

(1) **Boundedness:** $0 \le \mathcal{IB}(m_1, m_2) < 1$;
(2) **Non-degeneracy:** $\mathcal{IB}(m_1, m_2) = 0$ if and only if $m_1 = m_2$;
(3) **Symmetry:** $\mathcal{IB}(m_1, m_2) = \mathcal{IB}(m_2, m_1)$.

Proof. (1)

$$\mathcal{IB}(\mathcal{M}_1, \mathcal{M}_2) = \frac{1}{2} \sum_{A_i \in \Theta} \frac{(\mathcal{M}_1(A_i) - \mathcal{M}_2(A_i))^2}{\mathcal{M}_1(A_i) + \mathcal{M}_2(A_i)}$$

$$\le \frac{1}{2} \sum_{A_i \in \Theta} \frac{(\mathcal{M}_1(A_i) + \mathcal{M}_2(A_i))^2}{\mathcal{M}_1(A_i) + \mathcal{M}_2(A_i)}$$

$$= \frac{1}{2} \sum_{A_i \in \Theta} (\mathcal{M}_1(A_i) + \mathcal{M}_2(A_i))$$

$$< \frac{1}{2} \sum_{A_i \in \Theta} (m_1(A_i) + m_2(A_i))$$

$$= 1$$

Hence, the property of boundedness has been proved.

Proof. (2) Consider there are two $BPAs$ $m_1 = m_2$ in discernment Θ. According to Eq. (10):

$$m_1 = m_2 \Rightarrow m_1(A_i) = m_2(A_i)$$

$$\Rightarrow \mathcal{M}_1(A_i) = \mathcal{M}_2(A_i)$$

$$\Rightarrow \mathcal{M}_1(A_i) = \mathcal{M}_2(A_i) = \frac{\mathcal{M}_1(A_i) + \mathcal{M}_2(A_i)}{2}$$

$$\Rightarrow \chi^2(\mathcal{M}_1(A_i), \frac{\mathcal{M}_2(A_i) + \mathcal{M}_1(A_i)}{2}) = \chi^2(\mathcal{M}_2(A_i), \frac{\mathcal{M}_1(A_i) + \mathcal{M}_2(A_i)}{2})$$

$$= \chi^2(\mathcal{M}_1(A_i), \mathcal{M}_1(A_i)) = \sum_{\theta_i \in \Theta} \frac{(\mathcal{M}_1(A_i) - \mathcal{M}_1(A_i))^2}{\mathcal{M}_1(A_i)} = 0$$

$$\Rightarrow \mathcal{IB}(m_1, m_2) = 0.$$

Proof. (3) Given two independent $BPAs$ m_1 and m_2 in discernment Θ. By Eq. (10), we have:

$$\mathcal{IB}(m_1, m_2) = \frac{1}{2} \left[\chi^2(\mathcal{M}_1, \frac{\mathcal{M}_1 + \mathcal{M}_2}{2}) + \chi^2(\mathcal{M}_2, \frac{\mathcal{M}_1 + \mathcal{M}_2}{2}) \right],$$

$$\mathcal{IB}(m_2, m_1) = \frac{1}{2} \left[\chi^2(\mathcal{M}_2, \frac{\mathcal{M}_1 + \mathcal{M}_2}{2}) + \chi^2(\mathcal{M}_1, \frac{\mathcal{M}_1 + \mathcal{M}_2}{2}) \right].$$

It is obvious that:

$$\mathcal{IB}(m_1, m_2) = \mathcal{IB}(m_2, m_1).$$

Hence, the property of symmetry has been proved.

3.3   Numerical Examples

Examples are provided to explain the properties of IB divergence.

Example 1. Given two $BPAs$ m_1, m_2 defined in discernment $\Omega = \{X_1, X_2, X_3\}$ as follows.

$m_1 : m_1(\{X_3\}) = 0.1000, m_1(\{X_2, X_3\}) = 0.3000, m_1(\{X_1, X_2, X_3\}) = 0.6000;$
$m_2 : m_2(\{X_3\}) = 0.2000, m_2(\{X_2, X_3\}) = 0.5000, m_2(\{X_1, X_2, X_3\}) = 0.3000.$

By Eq. 11, we have:

$$IB(m_1, m_2) = IB(m_2, m_1) = 0.0321.$$

From Example 1, the value of IB divergence between m_1 and m_2 is equal to that of m_2 and m_1. So, the proposed IB divergence is symmetric which is of importance for measure difference among evidences.

Example 2. Given two $BPAs$ m_1, m_2 defined in discernment $\Omega = \{X_1, X_2, X_3\}$ as below.

$m_1 : m_1(\{X_1\}) = 0.5000, m_1(\{X_2, X_3\}) = 0.3000, m_1(\{X_1, X_2, X_3\}) = 0.2000;$
$m_2 : m_2(\{X_1\}) = 0.5000, m_2(\{X_2, X_3\}) = 0.3000, m_2(\{X_1, X_2, X_3\}) = 0.2000.$

By Eq. 11, we have:
$$IB(m_1, m_2) = 0.$$

Form Example 2, the belief divergence is zero for two same $BPAs$.

Example 3. Given two $BPAs$ m_1, m_2 defined in discernment $\Omega = \{X_1, X_2, X_3\}$ as below.

$m_1 : m_1(\{X_1\}) = 0.7000, m_1(\{X_2\}) = 0.2000, m_1(\{X_3\}) = 0.1000;$
$m_2 : m_2(\{X_1\}) = 0.5000, m_2(\{X_2\}) = 0.3000, m_2(\{X_3\}) = 0.2000.$

By Eq. 9, we have:
$$B(m_1, m_2) = 0.0433.$$

By Eq. 11, we have:
$$IB(m_1, m_2) = 0.0433.$$

From Example 3, the value of proposed IB divergence is equal to that of B divergence when only single subsets be assigned.

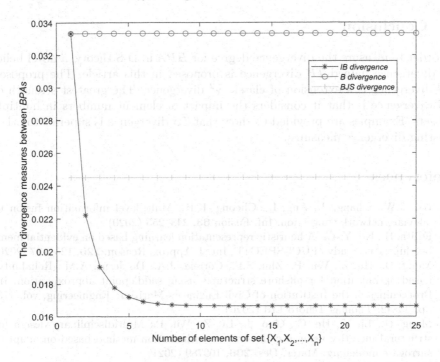

Fig. 1. A comparison of $\mathcal{IB}$ divergence, $\mathcal{B}$ divergence and BJS divergence.

Table 1. The value of two $BPAs$.

	X_1	X_2	$\{X_3, ..., X_n\}$
m_1	0.7000	0.1000	0.1000
m_2	0.7000	0.2000	0.2000

Example 4. Suppose two group of $BPAs$ modeled by senior reports as Table 1 shown.

See Fig. 1, the value of BJS divergence and $\mathcal{B}$ divergence remain unchanged as number of elements increase. The reason is that both of them ignore the influence of multiple subsets. While the value of $\mathcal{B}$ divergence is bigger explaining its more sensitive to measure discrepancy among evidences. Thus $\mathcal{B}$ divergence preforms better than BJS divergence. When there one element in the variable set. The $\mathcal{IB}$ divergence along with $\mathcal{B}$ divergence has the same and biggest value. While with the increase of element numbers, the $\mathcal{B}$ divergence remains unchanged while $\mathcal{IB}$ keeps decreasing and finally tends to be stable. This advantage indicates that $\mathcal{IB}$ divergence can reflect the influence of multiple subsets while $\mathcal{IB}$ divergence cannot.

4   Conclusion

In order to measure the divergence degree for BPA in D-S theory, a novel belief χ^2 divergence named $\mathcal{IB}$ divergence is proposed in this article. The proposed $\mathcal{IB}$ divergence is a extension of classic χ^2 divergence. The greatest strength of $\mathcal{IB}$ divergence is that it considers the impact of element numbers in multiple subsets. Examples are provided to show that $\mathcal{IB}$ divergence is superior to other existing divergence measures.

References

1. Lai, J.W., Chang, J., Ang, L., Cheong, K.H.: Multi-level information fusion to alleviate network congestion. Inf. Fusion **63**, 248–255 (2020)
2. Fujita, H., Ko, Y.-C.: A heuristic representation learning based on evidential memberships: case study of UCI-SPECTF. Int. J. Approx. Reason. **120**, 125–137 (2020)
3. Meng, D., Hu, Z., Wu, P., Zhu, S.P., Correia, J.A., De Jesus, A.M.: Reliability-based optimisation for offshore structures using saddlepoint approximation. In: Proceedings of the Institution of Civil Engineers-Maritime Engineering, vol. 173, pp. 33–42. Thomas Telford Ltd (2020)
4. Meng, D., Li, Y., He, C., Guo, J., Lv, Z., Wu, P.: Multidisciplinary design for structural integrity using a collaborative optimization method based on adaptive surrogate modelling. Mater. Des. **206**, 109789 (2021)
5. Zhou, Z., Feng, Z., Hu, C., Hu, G., He, W., Han, X.: Aeronautical relay health state assessment model based on belief rule base with attribute reliability. Knowl. Based Syst. **197**, 105869 (2020)
6. Liu, P., Zhang, X., Pedrycz, W.: A consensus model for hesitant fuzzy linguistic group decision-making in the framework of Dempster-Shafer evidence theory. Knowl. Based Syst. **212**, 106559 (2021)
7. Jiang, W., Huang, K., Geng, J., Deng, X.: Multi-scale metric learning for few-shot learning. IEEE Trans. Circuits Syst. Video Technol. **31**(3), 1091–1102 (2020)
8. Cheong, K.H., Koh, J.M., Jones, M.C.: Paradoxical survival: examining the parrondo effect across biology. BioEssays **41**(6), 1900027 (2019)
9. Lai, J.W., Cheong, K.H.: Parrondo effect in quantum coin-toss simulations. Phys. Rev. E **101**, 052212 (2020)
10. Meng, D., Xie, T., Wu, P., Zhu, S.-P., Hu, Z., Li, Y.: Uncertainty-based design and optimization using first order saddle point approximation method for multidisciplinary engineering systems, ASCE-ASME Journal of Risk and Uncertainty in Engineering Systems. Part A: Civil Eng. **6**(3), 04020028 (2020)
11. Meng, D., Xie, T., Wu, P., He, C., Hu, Z., Lv, Z.: An uncertainty-based design optimization strategy with random and interval variables for multidisciplinary engineering systems. Structures **32**, 997–1004 (2021)
12. Song, Y., Zhu, J., Lei, L., Wang, X.: Self-adaptive combination method for temporal evidence based on negotiation strategy. Sci. China Inf. Sci. **63**(11), 1–13 (2020). https://doi.org/10.1007/s11432-020-3045-5
13. Fei, L., Feng, Y., Liu, L.: Evidence combination using OWA-based soft likelihood functions. Int. J. Intell. Syst. **34**(9), 2269–2290 (2019)
14. Tian, Y., Liu, L., Mi, X., Kang, B.: ZSLF: a new soft likelihood function based on Z-numbers and its application in expert decision system. IEEE Trans. Fuzzy Syst. (2020)

15. Deng, J., Deng, Y.: Information volume of fuzzy membership function. Int. J. Comput. Commun. Control **16**(1) (2021)
16. Ramot, D., Milo, R., Friedman, M., Kandel, A.: Complex fuzzy sets. IEEE Trans. Fuzzy Syst. **10**(2), 171–186 (2002)
17. Wu, W., Song, Y., Zhao, W.: Evaluating evidence reliability on the basis of intuitionistic fuzzy sets. Information **9**(12), 298 (2018)
18. Alkouri, A.M.J.S., Salleh, A.R.: Complex intuitionistic fuzzy sets. In: AIP Conference Proceedings, vol. 1482, pp. 464–470. American Institute of Physics (2012)
19. Pan, L., Gao, X., Deng, Y., Cheong, K.H.: The constrained pythagorean fuzzy sets and its similarity measure. IEEE Trans. Fuzzy Syst. (2021)
20. Jiang, W., Cao, Y., Deng, X.: A novel Z-network model based on bayesian network and Z-number. IEEE Trans. Fuzzy Syst. **28**(8), 1585–1599 (2019)
21. Zhou, J., Su, X., Qian, H.: Risk assessment on offshore photovoltaic power generation projects in China using D numbers and ANP. IEEE Access **8**, 144704–144717 (2020)
22. Deng, Y.: Information volume of mass function. Int. J. Comput. Commun. Control **15**(6) (2020)
23. Wen, T., Cheong, K.H.: The fractal dimension of complex networks: a review. Inf. Fusion **73**, 87–102 (2021)
24. Yager, R.R.: Generalized Dempster-Shafer structures. IEEE Trans. Fuzzy Syst. **27**(3), 428–435 (2018)
25. Ni, L., Chen, Y.-W., de Brujin, O.: Towards understanding socially influenced vaccination decision making: an integrated model of multiple criteria belief modelling and social network analysis. Eur. J. Oper. Res. **293**(1), 276–289 (2021)
26. Zhou, M., Liu, X.-B., Chen, Y.-W., Yang, J.-B.: Evidential reasoning rule for MADM with both weights and reliabilities in group decision making. Knowl.-Based Syst. **143**, 142–161 (2018)
27. Pan, Y., Zhang, L., Wu, X., Skibniewski, M.J.: Multi-classifier information fusion in risk analysis. Inf. Fusion **60**, 121–136 (2020)
28. Liu, Z., Pan, Q., Dezert, J., Han, J.-W., He, Y.: Classifier fusion with contextual reliability evaluation. IEEE Trans. Cybern. **48**(5), 1605–1618 (2017)
29. Liu, Z., Zhang, X., Niu, J., Dezert, J.: Combination of classifiers with different frames of discernment based on belief functions. IEEE Trans. Fuzzy Syst. (2020)
30. Fu, C., Xue, M., Chang, W., Xu, D., Yang, S.: An evidential reasoning approach based on risk attitude and criterion reliability. Knowl.-Based Syst. **199**, 105947 (2020)
31. Xu, X., Zhang, D., Bai, Y., Chang, L., Li, J.: Evidence reasoning rule-based classifier with uncertainty quantification. Inf. Sci. **516**, 192–204 (2020)
32. Liao, H., Ren, Z., Fang, R.: A Deng-entropy-based evidential reasoning approach for multi-expert multi-criterion decision-making with uncertainty. Int. J. Comput. Intell. Syst. **13**(1), 1281–1294 (2020)
33. Murphy, C.K.: Combining belief functions when evidence conflicts. Decis. Support Syst. **29**(1), 1–9 (2000)
34. Yong, D., WenKang, S., ZhenFu, Z., Qi, L.: Combining belief functions based on distance of evidence. Decis. Support Syst. **38**(3), 489–493 (2004)
35. Xiao, F.: Multi-sensor data fusion based on the belief divergence measure of evidences and the belief entropy. Inf. Fusion **46**, 23–32 (2019)
36. Han, D., Dezert, J., Yang, Y.: Belief interval-based distance measures in the theory of belief functions. EEE Trans. Syst. Man Cybern. Syst. **48**(6), 833–850 (2016)
37. Babajanyan, S., Allahverdyan, A., Cheong, K.H.: Energy and entropy: path from game theory to statistical mechanics. Phys. Rev. Res. **2**(4), 043055 (2020)

38. Deng, X., Jiang, W.: On the negation of a Dempster-Shafer belief structure based on maximum uncertainty allocation. Inf. Sci. **516**, 346–352 (2020)
39. Han, D., Dezert, J., Duan, Z.: Evaluation of probability transformations of belief functions for decision making. IEEE Trans. Syst. Man Cybern. Syst. **46**(1), 93–108 (2015)
40. Jiang, W., Huang, C., Deng, X.: A new probability transformation method based on a correlation coefficient of belief functions. Int. J. Intell. Syst. **34**(6), 1337–1347 (2019)
41. Xiao, F.: Generalization of Dempster-Shafer theory: a complex mass function. Appl. Intell. **50**, 3266–3275 (2020)
42. Xiao, F.: CEQD: a complex mass function to predict interference effects. IEEE Trans. Cybern. (2021)
43. Xiao, F.: CED: a distance for complex mass functions. IEEE Trans. Neural Netw. Learn. Syst. **32**(4), 1525–1535 (2020)
44. Deng, Y.: Uncertainty measure in evidence theory. Sci. China Inf. Sci. **63**(11), 1–19 (2020). https://doi.org/10.1007/s11432-020-3006-9
45. Pearson, K.: X. on the criterion that a given system of deviations from the probable in the case of a correlated system of variables is such that it can be reasonably supposed to have arisen from random sampling. London Edinburgh Dublin Philos. Mag. J. Sci. **50**(302), 157–175 (1900)

Certificateless Proxy Authentication Scheme on Lattices Under the Background of Big Data

Siqi Yu, Yang Cui, and Fengyin Li[✉]

School of Computer Science, Qufu Normal University, Rizhao 276826, China

Abstract. As a special digital signature, proxy signature is becoming more and more important in electronic authentication. Compared with the insecurity of proxy signatures based on the decomposition of large integers and the difficulty of discrete logarithms, lattice-based cryptography have higher security and computational efficiency. This paper uses the pre-image sampling algorithm and trapdoor generation algorithm to construct a certificateless proxy signature scheme on lattices, and puts the scheme into the background of big data to realize authentication. The safety of the problem is proved by using the difficulty of small integer solutions on the lattices. Compared with other existing proxy signature schemes, it has low computational complexity and higher security.

Keywords: Lattice · Certificateless cryptography · Proxy signature · Big data · Small integer solution

1 Introduction

1.1 Background

With the rapid development of network technology, data has become diversified semi-structured or unstructured. Due to the large number of data types and the large volume of data, it is difficult to encrypt and authenticate network data. With the rapid increase in data volume, data security is also facing greater threats. Traditional authentication technologies and encryption algorithms are no longer able to solve the problem of network information security [11,12]. In the context of big data, network information data is more complex, and it also makes data encryption and authentication more difficult. This paper proposes a proxy signature scheme on lattices and applies it to data authentication to solve the problem.

In the development of computer technology, mobile terminal smart devices have been widely used in people's daily lives, and network information technology has also become an important way for people to obtain information. However, how to ensure information security in the process of information acquisition has become information technology Issues that researchers in the field focus on. Generally, there are two main types of information encryption technology and authentication technology to ensure information security, such as

© Springer Nature Singapore Pte Ltd. 2021
Y. Tan et al. (Eds.): DMBD 2021, CCIS 1454, pp. 185–193, 2021.
https://doi.org/10.1007/978-981-16-7502-7_21

AES encryption algorithm and digital signature. Among them, digital signature is an important form of user identity authentication, and digital signature with encryption. This authentication method is more safety. Difficulty in the management and maintenance of public key certificates is an inevitable problem in traditional PKI-based cryptographic systems. At the same time, the design of PKG in identity-based cryptographic systems has defects, that is, the issue of private key escrow. In order to overcome the above-mentioned problems, in 2003 Al. Riyami and Paterson proposed the concept of certificateless public key cryptography [1]. In the certificateless public key cryptosystem, in order to ensure that the user's private key is not maliciously stolen, the participation of PKI and PKG is not required. Instead, the Key Generation Center (KGC) first generates part of the user's private key, and then the user chooses A secret value of the user's private key is composed of these two parts.

In real life, we often encounter situations where the right to sign is granted to others. In 1998, Blaze, Bleumer, and Strauss first proposed the concept of proxy resignature [2]. Proxy re-signature has very good application prospects in digital rights management, certificate management, and construction of cross-domain operating systems. In 2005, Ateniese and Honenberger [3] gave a more specific definition of proxy resignature, and gave a specific proxy resignature scheme. Since it has not been discovered that the polynomial time quantum algorithm can solve the difficult problems on the lattice, it is currently believed that the lattice cipher can resist quantum attacks. In addition to the resistance to quantum attacks, the public key cipher scheme designed based on the lattice theory has some other advantages: The operation is simple and the degree of security is high. In 2012, Lyubasevsky proposed an efficient signature scheme with no trapdoor on the lattice under a random oracle [4]. Its security is based on the small integer solution problem (SIS) problem, which uses the Sampling technology makes it more efficient. On the basis of this signature, Tian M et al. proposed a certificate-free signature scheme in 2015 [5], which is smaller and more efficient than other schemes of the same type; in the same year, it was also constructed An identity-based two-way proxy re-signature scheme [6], but the proxy re-key of this scheme requires the private keys of the principal and the trustee to be generated.

1.2   Contribution

The main contribution of this paper is as follows:

- This paper proposes a lattice-based certificateless proxy signature scheme. In this paper, the trapdoor generation algorithm and the pre-image sampling algorithm are used to generate the public and private keys of the signers.
- Under the random oracle model, its safety is strictly proved.
- Compared with other existing proxy signature schemes, this scheme is simple in structure, the size of keys and signatures is shorter, and the efficiency is higher.

1.3 Organization

The survey is organized as follows:

- The first section introduces the main background and contribution of this paper;
- The second section is about the related work;
- The third section is about the authentication model in big data environment;
- The fourth section introduces is the core work of this paper. This section introduces a certificateless proxy signature based on the lattices;
- The fifth section is the safety analysis;
- The last section is conclusions.

2 Related Work

2.1 Lattices

Definition 1 (Lattice). Let $B = \{b_1, ..., b_m\} \in R^{m \times m}$ be a matrix constructed by m linearly independent vectors $\{b_1, b_2, ..., b_m\}$. The lattice L generated by B is defined as

$$\Lambda = L(B) = \left\{ Bc = \sum_{i=1}^{m} c_i b_i | c_i \in Z \right\}$$

Here $b_1, ..., b_m$ constitutes a set of bases of the lattice Λ.

Definition 2. Two special integer lattices modulo q:

$$\Lambda_q^{\perp}(A) = \{e \in Z^m | Ae = 0 \bmod q\}$$

$$\Lambda_q^u(A) = \{e \in Z^m | Ae = u \bmod q, u \in Z^n\}$$

where q is a prime number, $A \in Z_q^{n \times m}$.

2.2 SIS Problem

Definition 3 (Short Integer Solution ($SIS_{q,n,m,\beta}$)). From Reference [7], given m uniformly random vectors $a_i \in Z_q^n$, forming the columns of a matrix $A \in Z_q^{n \times m}$, find a nonzero integer vector $z \in Z^m$ of norm $|z|| \leq \beta$ such that

$$f_A(z) := Az = \sum a_i \cdot z_i = 0 \in Z_q^n$$

Definition 4 ($ISIS_{q,n,m,\beta}$). Given the positive integer parameters m, n, non-zero real number β, the matrix $A \in Z_q^{n \times m}$ is uniformly selected randomly, and any uniform random vector $u \in Z_q^n$, find the non-zero vector v, which satisfies $Av \equiv u \bmod q$, and its norm number $|v|| \leq \beta$.

2.3   Discrete Gaussian Distribution on Lattice

Definition 5 (Discrete Gaussian distribution). For any $c > 0$, real number $\sigma > 0$, an m-dimensional lattice Λ, the discrete Gaussian distribution on lattice Λ is defined as

$$\forall x \in \Lambda, D_{\Lambda,\sigma,c}(x) = \rho_{\sigma,c}(x)/\rho_{\sigma,c}(\Lambda)$$

2.4   Trapdoor Generation and Original Image Sampling Algorithm

Reference [8] gives the trapdoor generation algorithm and the pre-image sampling algorithm, and some of the results are shown in Lemma 1 and Lemma 2.

Lemma 1. Given an integer $n > 0, q > 1$ and $m = O(n \log q)$ there is an effective random algorithm $TrapGen(1^n, 1^m, q)$ that satisfies $(A, B) \leftarrow TrapGen(1^n, 1^m, q)$, where B is a trapdoor, and the distribution of the output matrix $A \in Z_q^{n \times m}$ is distinguished from the uniform distribution on the set $Z_q^{n \times m}$ with a probability not higher than $negl(n)$.

Lemma 2 (Pre-image sampling algorithm). Take the matrix $A \in Z_q^{n \times m}, B \in Z_q^{m \times m}$, the Gaussian parameter $s \geq ||\tilde{B}|| \cdot \omega(\sqrt{\log n})$, and a random value y on the uniform distribution of Z_q^n as input, and output $x \in \{x_i \in Z^m, ||x_i|| \leq s\sqrt{m}\}$ such that $f(x) = Ax = y \bmod q$ where x obeys the Gaussian distribution $D_{\Lambda_q^y(A),s}^m$.

Lemma 3 (General pre-image sampling algorithm). Take the matrix $A \in Z_q^{n \times m}, B \in Z_q^{m \times k}$, the Gaussian parameter $s \geq ||\tilde{B}|| \cdot \omega(\sqrt{\log n})$, and a random value U on the uniform distribution of $Z_q^{n \times k}$ as input, and output $S \in Z^{m \times k}$ such that $AS = U \bmod q$ where S obeys the Gaussian distribution $D_{\Lambda_q^U(A),s}^m$.

3   Authentication Model in Big Data Environment

At present, big data has a wide range of applications in the financial industry. The commercial application of big data in banks is dominated by its own transaction data and customer data. Bank data can be divided into four categories: transaction data, customer data, credit data, and asset data. Most of the bank data is structured data with strong financial attributes. It is stored in traditional relational databases and data warehouses. Through data mining, some of the knowledge hidden in transaction data with commercial value can be analyzed.

As shown in Fig. 1, in the certificateless proxy authentication scheme proposed in this paper, the user delegates his power to the proxy signer, and the proxy signer replaces him to complete the signature. The bank first authenticates the identity information of the proxy user to ensure the legitimacy of the identity information. Second, the bank authenticates the message signed by the proxy user to ensure the integrity of the message and verify that the message has not been tampered with or delayed during transmission or storage.

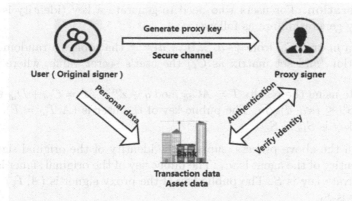

Fig. 1. Model of proxy authentication process in big data environment.

4 Certificateless Proxy Signature Based on the Lattices

4.1 Certificateless Proxy Signature Based on the Lattices

For the definition of each algorithm of the certificateless encryption scheme, please refer to the reference [9,10]. Our certificateless proxy signature scheme is shown as follow:

System Initialization. Enter the security parameter n, run TrapGen(n, m, q) and output a matrix $A \in Z_q^{n \times m}$ that obeys a random uniform distribution and a set of basis $B \in Z_q^{m \times m}$ on the lattice $\Lambda^{\perp}(A)$, where $AB = 0 \bmod q$, $|B|| \leq O(\sqrt{n \log q})$; Choosing hash function

$$H : \{0,1\}^* \to Z_q^{n \times k} \tag{1}$$

$$H_1 : id \to \{-1, 0, 1\}^{k \times k} \tag{2}$$

$$H_2 : \{0,1\}^* \to D_{H_2} = \left\{ c : c \in \{-1, 0, 1\}^k, ||c||_1 \leq \kappa \right\} \tag{3}$$

Public parameters $param = \{A, H, H_1, H_2, H_3\}$, the master private key is $sk = B$.

Partial Private Key Extraction. Assuming that KGC wants to generate a partial key value of a user whose identity is ID, the specific steps are as follows:

- Calculation $F = H(id)$.
- KGC runs the algorithm $SampleMat(A, B, s, F)$.
- Outputs the matrix $D_{id} \in Z_q^{m \times k}$, and then sends D_{id} to the user, where $AD_{id} = F, ||D_{id}|| \leq s\sqrt{m}$. D_{id} is part of the private key of the user, and send it to the user.

Key Generation. For users who need to generate a key (identity is id), the steps of key generation are as follows:

- Choose a matrix C_{id} from $\{-d, ..., 0, ..., d\}^{m \times k}$ that obeys a random uniform distribution, and set matrix as C_{id} the user's secret value, where $|C_{id}|| \leq d\sqrt{m}$.
- Calculate using the results $T = AC_{id} \bmod q \in Z_q^{n \times k}$, $S = C_{id} + D_{id} \in Z_q^{m \times k}$, where $|S|| \leq (s+d)\sqrt{m}$; The public key of the user is $(A, T_{id} = T)$, and the private key is $S_{id} = S$.

Through the above process, suppose the identity of the original signer is id and the identity of the agent is id_1. The public key of the original signer is (A, T), and the private key is S. The public key of the proxy signer is (A, T_1), and the private key is S_1.

Proxy Signing Key Generation. For proxy signer id_1, calculate $U_{id} = H_1(id_1) \in \{-1, 0, 1\}^{k \times k}$, $S_2 = C_{id} U_{id} \in Z_q^{m \times k}$, $T_2 = T U_{id} \bmod q$. The proxy signature key is S_2, and the corresponding public key is T_2. The original signer sends the proxy signature key to the proxy through a secure channel.

Proxy Signer Verification. After receiving the proxy signature key, the proxy signer checks whether $AS_2 = T U_{id} \bmod q$ is established, if established, then accepts the proxy signature key, otherwise rejects it.

Proxy Signature. Enter a message μ, the proxy signer's own private key is S_1, the Proxy signature key is S_2, and the signature is as follows:

- Select two vectors $y_1, y_2 \leftarrow D_\sigma^m$;
- Calculate $c_1 = H_2(Ay_1, \mu), c_2 = H_2(Ay_2, \mu)$;
- Calculate $z_1 = S_1 c_1 + y_1 \in Z_q^m$ $z_2 = S_2 c_2 + y_2 \in Z_q^m$;
- Output (z_1, c_1) with the probability of $(\frac{D_\sigma^m(z_1)}{M D_{S_1 c_1, \sigma}^m(z_1)}, 1)$, output (z_2, c_2) with the probability of $(\frac{D_\sigma^m(z_2)}{M D_{S_2 c_2, \sigma}^m(z_2)}, 1)$.

Verification. Enter the message μ and its corresponding signature (z_1, c_1), (z_2, c_2), matrix A, T_1, T_2, and verify whether $|z_i|| \leq 2\sigma\sqrt{m}$, $c_1 = H_2(Az_1 - (T_1 + F_1)c_1, \mu)$, $c_2 = H_2(Az_2 - T_2c_2, \mu)$ is valid at the same time. If it is valid, accept it; otherwise, reject it.

5   Safety Analysis

5.1   Correctness

For the message μ and its corresponding proxy signature $(z_1, c_1), (z_2, c_2)$, it is necessary to verify that $|z_i|| \leq 2\sigma\sqrt{m}$, $c_1 = H_2(Az_1 - (T_1 + F_1)c_1, \mu)$, $c_2 = H_2(Az_2 - T_2c_2, \mu)$ is valid at the same time. First

$$|z_i|| = ||S_i c_i + y_i|| \leq ||S_i c_i|| + ||y_i|| \leq 2\sigma\sqrt{m}$$

Then for signature (z_1, c_1):

$$Az_1 - (T_1 + F_1)c_1 = A(S_1c_1 + y_1) - (T_1 + F_1)c_1$$
$$= A(D_{id_1} + C_{id_1})c_1 + Ay_1 - (T_1 + F_1)c_1$$
$$= Ay_1$$

For signature (z_2, c_2):

$$Az_2 - T_2c_2 = A(S_2c_2 + y_2) - T_2c_2$$
$$= AC_{id}U_{id}c_2 + Ay_2 - TU_{id}c_2$$
$$= Ay_2$$

5.2 Security

Theorem 1. *Assuming that the hash function can be regarded as a random oracle, and it is difficult for small integers to solve the problem of SIS, then in the certificateless proxy signature scheme, the proxy signer's own id signs the message μ, if the attacked adversary A is successfully forged in polynomial time, there is an algorithm to crack the SIS problem with a non-negligible probability.*

Proof. Here we discuss the unforgeability of the malicious original signer (the attack ability of the malicious third party is weaker than that of the malicious original signer). Here we use a game played between the adversary A and the challenger C to show that the signature scheme is unforgeable. Assuming that the adversary A can forge the signature with a non-negligible probability in polynomial time, then the challenger C can use the signature forged by the adversary A to solve the SIS problem with a non-negligible probability.

The challenger first builds two lists. The first list T_1 stores (users id, $F = H(id)$, partial key value D, secret value C, public key P, private key S); The second list T_2 stores(users id, message μ, random value $y \leftarrow D_\sigma^m$, $c = H(Ay, \mu)$, signature $sign = (z, c)$).

When the system initialization has been carried out, challenger C can call the algorithm l for creating users: after entering the system's public parameters param, master private key B, and the user's identity id, first query the list T_1, and if there is an identity id in the table, exit; Otherwise, randomly extract F and secret value C from $Z_q^{n \times k}$ and $\{-d, ...0, ...d\}$, call algorithm $SampleMat(A, B, s, F)$ to obtain part of the key value D, then calculate the public key $P = AC \bmod q \in Z_q^{n \times k}$ and private key $S = C + D$ respectively, and finally save (ID, F, D, C, P, S) into the list T_1 and exit.

The steps for adversary A and challenger C to play the game are as follows:

System Establishment: Challenger C first chooses the safety parameter n, the prime number $q \geq 3$, $m \geq 5n \log q$. Run the algorithm $TrapGen(1^n)$ and output a matrix A that obeys a random uniform distribution and a set of basis $B \in Z_q^{m \times m}$ on the lattice $\Lambda^\perp(A)$, where $AB = 0 \bmod q$, $\|B\| \leq O(\sqrt{n \log q})$.

H Query: Adversary A sends id_i to challenger C, hoping to get the corresponding hash value $F_i = H(id_i)$. C first queries list T_1, if the user already exists in the list, then sends the corresponding F_i to A; otherwise, C calls algorithm l, enter the user's id_i, when the algorithm is completed, C queries the list T_1, and sends the F_i corresponding to the id_i directly to A.

H_2 *Query:* The adversary A sends a message μ_i to the challenger C, hoping to get the corresponding hash value. C first queries the list T_2, if the message μ_i already exists in the list, then directly sends the corresponding c_i to A; Otherwise, randomly select c_i in $\{c : c \in \{-1, 0, 1\}^\kappa, ||c||_1 \leq \kappa\}$ and send it to A, then randomly select $y \leftarrow D_\sigma^m$, and finally save (μ_i, y_i, c_i).

Partial Key Extraction Query: The adversary A sends id_i to the challenger C, hoping to obtain the partial key value of the user. C first queries the list T_1, if the user already exists in the list, then D_i directly sends the corresponding partial key value D_i to A; otherwise C call algorithm l, enter the user's identity id_i, when the algorithm is completed, C queries list T_1, and sends the partial key value D_i corresponding to id_i directly to A.

User Key Extraction Query: Adversary A sends id_i to challenger C, hoping to get the user's public and private keys (P_i, S_i). C first queries the list T_1, if the user already exists in the list, then sends the corresponding public and private keys (P_i, S_i) to A; otherwise C calls the algorithm l, enters the identity id_i, and after l runs, C queries the list T_1, and sends the public and private keys (P_i, S_i) corresponding to id_i to A.

When A's corresponding query is completed, A outputs the identity id^* of any user based on the existing experience.

At this time, after challenger C obtains the signature of user id^* on message μ^*, according to the general forking lemma [4], when challenger C reselects the H_2 query value corresponding to message μ^*, adversary A can also forge another signature $sig' = (z', c')$ of the user id^* to the message μ^* with a non-negligible probability, such that

$$\begin{cases} Az^* - (H(id^*) + Tid^*)c^* = Az' - (H(id^*) + Tid^*)c' \\ c' \neq c^* \end{cases}$$

According to the literature [4] Lemma 5.4, we have

$$A(z^* - z' + D_{id^*}(c' - c^*) + C_{id^*}(c' - c^*)) = 0$$

Now all we need to show is that $z^* - z' + D_{id^*}(c' - c^*) + C_{id^*}(c' - c^*) \neq 0$. Then according to Lemma 4.2 in [4], there is another secret value C'_{id} at least with a probability of $1 - 2^{-100}$, so that $AC_{id^*} = AC'_{id^*}$. It is clear that with this definition of C'_{id}, if $z^* - z' + D_{id^*}(c' - c^*) + C_{id^*}(c' - c^*) = 0$, then $z^* - z' + D_{id^*}(c' - c^*) + C'_{id^*}(c' - c^*) \neq 0$, the challenger C does not know whether secret value like C_{id^*} or like C'_{id^*} will use in the forged signature, so challenger C randomly select one of the two secret values will get a non-zero with probability at least $1/2$, since each key has an equal probability of being chosen. Therefore, challenger C solved the SIS problem with a non-negligible probability.

6   Conclusions

The paper is based on the trapdoor generation algorithm and pre-image sampling algorithm, then proposes a certificateless proxy signature scheme. Under the random oracle model, it is proved that the security is based on the SIS problem, which guarantees the scheme's security in the quantum environment. In the context of big data, the scheme realizes the authentication process. This scheme mainly adopts matrix multiplication in the calculation, and the calculation complexity is low.

References

1. Al-Riyami, S.S., Paterson, K.G.: International conference on the theory and application of cryptology and information security. Certificateless Cryptogr. J. **2**(5), 99–110 (2016)
2. Blaze, M., Bleumer, G., Strauss, M.: Divertible protocols and atomic proxy cryptography. In: Nyberg, K. (ed.) EUROCRYPT 1998. LNCS, vol. 1403, pp. 127–144. Springer, Heidelberg (1998). https://doi.org/10.1007/BFb0054122
3. Ateniese, G., Hohenberger, S.: Proxy re-signatures: new definitions, algorithms, and applications. In: Proceedings of ACM Conference on Computer and Communications Security, pp. 310–319. ACM (2005). https://doi.org/10.1145/1102120. 1102161
4. Lyubashevsky, V.: Lattice signatures without trapdoors. In: Pointcheval, D., Johansson, T. (eds.) EUROCRYPT 2012. LNCS, vol. 7237, pp. 738–755. Springer, Heidelberg (2012). https://doi.org/10.1007/978-3-642-29011-4_43
5. Tian, M.M., Huang, L.S.: Certificateless and certificate based signatures from lattices. Secur. Commun. Netw. **8**(8), 1575–1586 (2015). https://doi.org/10.1002/sec. 1105
6. Tian, M.M.: Identity-based proxy re-signatures from lattices. Inf. Process. Lett. **115**(4), 462–467 (2015). https://doi.org/10.1016/j.ipl.2014.12.002
7. Micciancio, D., Regev, O.: Worst-case to average-case reductions based on Gaussian measures. SIAM J. Comput. **37**(1), 267–302 (2007)
8. Gentry, C., Peikert, C., Vaikuntanathan, V.: Trapdoors for hard lattices and new cryptographic constructions. In: Proceedings of the 40th ACM Symposium on Theory of Computing (STOC 2008), pp. 197–206. ACM (2008). https://doi.org/10. 1145/1374376.1374407
9. Dent, A.: A survey of certificateless encryption schemes and security models. Int. J. Inf. Secur. **7**(5), 347–377 (2008). https://doi.org/10.1007/s10207-008-0055-0
10. Zhang, F.T., Sun, Y.X., Zhang, L., Geng, M.M., Li, S.J.: Research on certificateless public key cryptography. Comput. Knowl. Technol. (15), 33, 44 (2018)
11. Chen, D.M.: Discussion on big data security and privacy protection based on cloud computing. Comput. Knowl. Technol. (15), 33, 44 (2018)
12. Xie, J.: Research on big data security and privacy protection based on cloud computing. Commun. World (02), 112 (2017)
13. Jiang, M.M., Hu, Y.P., Wang, B.C., et al.: Efficient proxy signature on the lattices. J. Beijing Univ. Posts Telecommun. **37**(3), 89–92 (2014)
14. Chen, H., Hu, Y.P., Lian, Z.Z., et al.: Efficient certificateless encryption schemes from lattices. J. Softw. **27**(11), 2884–2897 (2016)

A Privacy-Preserving Anime Recommendation Method on Distributed Platform

Yuwen Liu(✉), Ying Miao, and Shengqi Wu

School of Computer Science, Qufu Normal University, Rizhao 276800, China

Abstract. The Japanese anime industry has directly promoted Japan's economic development. There are many anime works, which types are also various. How to recommend users' favorite anime from many anime has become a worthy problem. However, the anime recommendation methods face the following challenges. (1) Users tend to watch anime on multiple platforms and leave corresponding ratings. When using the similar users' preferences for recommendation, the existence of distributed platform will lead to the disclosure of users' privacy. (2) How to search similar users quickly and efficiently is also an urgent problem. Therefore, we use local-sensitive hashing (LSH) technology which can not only provide users with fast and efficient recommendation but also protect users' privacy. LSH can index users by users' rating data. Moreover, by projecting the index, similar users will be mapped to the same bucket. The time complexity of establishing offline indexes is O(1), and the target user can find similar users from the bucket directly. Therefore, we can achieve a privacy-aware anime recommendation. We use a real dataset provided by an anime website for experiment, and the experiment proves that our method is fast and effective.

Keywords: Privacy protection · Anime recommendation · Distribute platform · Locality-sensitive hashing

1 Introduction

With the massive growth of candidate items, it is difficult for users to choose the items that they are interested in. The emergence of recommendation system provides a solution to this challenge [14]. Recommendation systems are used in many industries [3,10,17]. For example, music software can recommend music to users according to popularity and user preferences, and e-commerce platforms (e.g., Taobao, Amazon) can recommend products to users according to their historical search records, so as to increase trading volume. At present, anime has occupied a large proportion in people's entertainment and leisure. Anime has also become a mainstream phenomenon in Japan and the United States [4]. Therefore, it is necessary to mine users' preferences and recommend anime for users. It can not only improve users' satisfaction with anime websites, but also promote the revenue of anime websites.

© Springer Nature Singapore Pte Ltd. 2021
Y. Tan et al. (Eds.): DMBD 2021, CCIS 1454, pp. 194–204, 2021.
https://doi.org/10.1007/978-981-16-7502-7_22

It is necessary to find users' preferences for anime to make anime recommendation. Users will watch the anime they are interested in, and leave the corresponding ratings. The ratings can well reflect the user's attitude towards anime (i.e., like, neutral, dislike). Therefore, we can mine users' preferences by using the records left by users in multiple anime websites [11]. However, it's not enough to just use users' historical records on a platform. A better way is to use the historical records left by users on multiple platforms, which can more comprehensively reflect users' interests. Collaborative filtering (CF) is a widely used method in recommendation system, which mainly uses the similar users' preferences for recommendation. This method is based on the assumption that similar users are likely to have similar anime preferences. Although these method can mine users' preferences, they will be faced with the problem of users' privacy disclosure when interacting with multiple platforms [23]. The platform has the obligation to protect users' browsing records on this platform, and users are unwilling to share their anime browsing data with other platforms. Therefore, it is a challenging problem to mine users' interests and protect users' privacy in distributed platforms.

To address this challenge, we propose to use Locality-Sensitive Hashing (LSH) [12] technology to find similar users under the condition of protecting users' privacy, and then we try to predict the anime score for users. Finally, the Top-K anime with the highest ratings are recommended to users. Our work of this paper is summarized as follows.

- We propose a privacy-aware anime recommendation method (*LSH_par*). We first use LSH technology for anime recommendation. It can only to protect users' privacy, but also find similar users in the distributed platforms. Combining the user's interests and similar users' interests, we can achieve fast and accurate anime recommendation.
- We analyze the real interaction data between users and the platforms, and carry out the experiment. The experiment accurately demonstrates the calculation process of our method, and verifies the accuracy and feasibility of our proposed method.

Other arrangements of this paper are as follows: first, we summarize the related work of this paper, review the anime recommendation and some widely used recommendation methods. Then, we introduce the motivation of our work and explain the necessity of our work. Next, we introduce our model and the corresponding experimental results. Finally, we summarize the work of this paper.

2   Related Work

Collaborative filtering [13] is one of the most widely used methods in recommendation system. Girsang et al. [7] used the least square method to judge the user similarity, and then mined the similar users' interest. They predicted the anime films ratings that the user has not watched, and then recommended the anime films with high ratings to the user. Li et al. [8] proposed a CF method that both considers score prediction and ranking prediction. However, the CF-based methods need enough similar users. In real scenarios, the user's rating data is often scarce. It may be difficult to find similar users. CF-based recommendation will face great obstacles because of sparse data. Qi et al. [15] combined CF with the social balance theory, and proposed an improved CF to reduce the search space for recommendation. This method can alleviate the obstacles caused by data sparsity.

Matrix factorization (MF) [2] is also widely used to predict the items' ratings. It realizes the decomposition process by dividing the user-item rating matrix into a user-feature matrix and an item-feature matrix. Then, the product of the two matrices after training is used to predict the user's ratings of the ungraded items. Through collaborative learning technology, Gao et al. [6] studied the relationship between users and application programming interfaces (APIs) in the Internet of things (IoT), and they proposed an enhanced matrix decomposition model by using the hidden information, which is used for API recommendation. Wang et al. [18] proposed a new MF-based recommendation model. This method is an improvement o traditional MF, and it can alleviate the data sparsity problem.

However, CF and MF can only use the historical display interactive information (i.e., ratings) between users and anime to make anime recommendation, and can not provide personalized recommendation for users. At present, deep learning has a great impact on the recommendation system [22]. Wibowo et al. [9] proposed a deep learning method to integrate auxiliary information from users and anime into a hybrid model. By learning potential features, the hybrid model can make personalized anime recommendations for users. To overcome the frustration of CF-based methods, Fu et al. [5] proposed a novel deep learning method. The method first learns the users' vectors and projects' vectors, and the vectors reflect the correlation between users and the correlation between projects respectively. Finally, they used a feed-forward neural network to simulate the interaction between users and projects and made recommendations for target users. Negative sampling [19] is a widely used method when neural network model is learning parameters. However, the computation cost of negative sampling is very expensive, and the parameters learned by negative sampling are difficult to achieve the best performance. Chen et al. [1] proposed to train a neural recommendation model without sampling. Through mathematical derivation, they put forward three parameter optimization methods. In this way, the parameters of the model can be learned efficiently. Next, they used the neural matrix decomposition model to complete the recommendation task.

However, the above methods are all based on the user's anime preferences on a certain platform, ignoring the user's anime preference on multiple platforms, which can obviously reflect the user's interests. Morever, users will leave records and rating records on the platforms. When using users' information in distributed platforms, users will face the problem of privacy leakage. Users' viewing and scoring records on the platform often belong to users' privacy and need to be protected. Therefore, how to protect users' privacy when mining users' anime preferences on distributed platforms is also a challenging problem.

There have been many researches devoted to user privacy protection [24–26]. Sun et al. [16] proposed a two-stage privacy protection mechanism based on blockchain to protect the employees' privacy in IoT. Xiao et al. [21] put forward a user profile perturbation scheme. The scheme used differential privacy to protect users' privacy, and used deep reinforcement learning against attackers. Yin et al. [27] developed a personalized recommendation technology that can protect users' privacy. They use differential privacy to prevent user privacy from leaking. However, the application of this method will reduce recommendation accuracy.

In order to better mine users' interest preference in anime, we propose a privacy-aware anime recommendation method. First of all, we preprocess the data and filter the users who have too few rating records. Secondly, we use LSH to find similar users in distributed environment. Finally, we predict the target user's anime ratings by using the similar users' anime preferences, and then recommend the Top-K anime to the target user. Our method can better mine users' preferences for anime and achieve better recommendation performance on the premise of protecting users' privacy.

3 Motivation

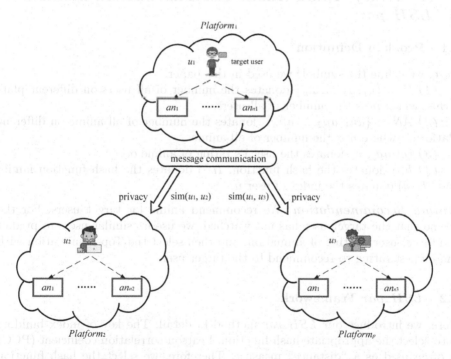

Fig. 1. Privacy-aware anime recommendationn: an example.

We use Fig. 1 to illustrate our research motivation. Users will watch anime through different platforms, and leave different ratings for the animae they have seen. User 1 watched $n1$ anime and left his rating records $an_1, an_2, ..., an_{n1}$ on platform 1. At present, there are many video playback platforms can play anime. For the users we want to recommend anime (i.e., target users), they often have their own historical rating records. Our recommendation is to make recommendations for target users by using the similar users' interests. Therefore, we need to find similar users by judging $sim(u_1, u_2)$ and $sim(u_1, u_3)$. However, when searching for similar users, there are often several challenges.

- Users are distributed on different platforms, and the CF-based methods need to make clarify the users' historical rating records when looking for similar users. This measure will expose the users' privacy.
- With the rapid development of the internet, network user data and rating data are huge. It is very time-consuming to find similar users in a large number of users.

Considering the above two challenges, it is necessary to propose an effective and privacy preserving anime recommendation method.

4 A Privacy-Aware Anime Recommendation Method: LSH_par

4.1 Problem Definition

Here, we define the symbols we used in this paper.

(1) $U = \{u_1, u_2, ..., u_m\}$ donates the number of all users on different platforms, where m is the number of all users.

(2) $AN = \{an_1, an_2, ..., an_n\}$ donates the number of all anime on different platforms, where n is the number of all anime.

(3) $rating_{io}$ = donates the user i's rating of anime o.

(4) $h(\cdot)$ donates the hash function, $H(\cdot)$ donates the hash function family and $H_k(u)$ donates the index of user u.

Anime Recommendation. We recommend anime for target users. For the anime that the target user has not watched, we use its similar users to predict the target user's rating of animation, and then select the Top-k animation with the highest rating to recommend to the target user.

4.2 *LSH_par* Framework

Here, we introduce our *LSH_par* method in detail. The key of index building is to select the appropriate hash function. Pearson correlation coefficient (PCC) is often used as a "distance" measure. Therefore, we select the hash function corresponding to PCC. For each user's rating data $\{an_1, an_2, ..., an_N\}$, we first need to transform it into an n-dimensional vector $\overrightarrow{u_k} = (an_1, an_2, ..., an_n)$. If the user has a rating on the anime, the corresponding value is the rating score. If the user has not watched the anime, or the user has watched the anime without rating, the corresponding value is 0. Next, we use the hash function $h(\cdot)$ to calculate the corresponding hash value. We initialize the n-dimensional vector $\vec{z} = (z_1, z_2, ..., z_n)$ randomly which range is in $[-1, 1]$. Then the hash value is obtained by (1) and (2).

$$h_k'(u) = (an_1, an_2, ..., an_n) \cdot (z_1, z_2, ..., z_n) \tag{1}$$

$$h_k(u) = \begin{cases} 1 & \text{if } \vec{u_k} \cdot \vec{z} > 0 \\ 0 & \text{if } \vec{u_k} \cdot \vec{z} \leq 0 \end{cases} \tag{2}$$

The more similar the hash values, the more similar the users are. Obviously, it's hard to guarantee that all similar users can be found through one hash function. Therefore, we initialize t hash functions as a hash family $H(\cdot)$. Therefore, for each user, a t-dimensional vector $H_k'(u)$ composed of t hash values can be obtained by (3). Then, the binary vector $H_k'(u)$ is converted to decimal $H_k(u)$ by weight expansion in (4).

$$H_k'(u) = (h_k^1(u), h_k^2(u), ..., h_k^t(u)) \tag{3}$$

$$H_k(u) = H_k'(u) \cdot weight_D \tag{4}$$

where $weight_D$ is the corresponding weight vector. Next, we need to find similar users through the hash index. For the convenience of calculation, here we will convert the user index vector from binary to decimal. For the target user, we can select the top-N users which are most similar to target user's index. Through the similar users' anime preferences, we can predict the anime ratings of the target user. Finally, the Top-K anime with the highest ratings can be recommended to the user. Through the rating function in (2), if we want to predict user j's rating of an unwatched anime o, we need to find top-N users who are most similar to user j, and then predict j's rating based on the N users' rating on anime o.

$$\text{rating}_{jo} = \frac{\sum_{i=1}^{N} sim_{ij}(u) \cdot \text{rating}_{io}}{\sum_{i=1}^{N} sim_{ij}(u)} \tag{5}$$

where $sim_{ij}(u)$ represents the similarity between user i and user j, and $rating_{io}$ represents the user i's rating on anime o. The overall framework of LSH_par is shown in Fig. 2.

5   Experiments

5.1   Dataset

The real dataset we use is collected through the MyAnimeList website [20]. We used the rating data in the dataset. Due to the huge dataset, the cold start problem will affect the model. Therefore, we filtered out anime with less than 300 views and users who watched less than 500 movies. The details before and after data preprocessing are shown in Table 1.

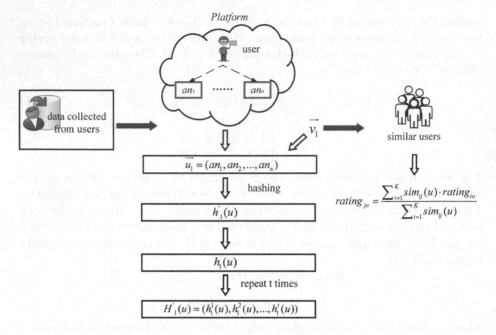

Fig. 2. The architecture of LSH_{par}.

Table 1. Details of anime data set before and after preprocessing

	Users	Anime	Records
Data before processing	73515	11200	7813137
Data after processing	1515	3103	1059518

5.2 Evaluation

Since our purpose is to predict anime ratings that users have not watched, we need an appropriate method to verify our method's performance. We erase the rating data according to a certain percentage, and then compare the predicted rating with the real rating. We use the mean absolute error (MAE) and root mean squared error (RMSE) to measure our model's performance. Here $PRErating_{io}$ represents the predicted value of $user_i$'s rating on $anime_o$, $TRUrating_{io}$ represents the real rating of $user_i$ on $anime_o$.

$$\text{MAE} = \frac{\sum_{i=1}^{N} |PRErating_{io} - TRUrating_{io}|}{n} \tag{6}$$

$$\text{RMSE} = \sqrt{\frac{1}{N} \sum_{i=1}^{N} (PERrating_{io} - TRUrating_{io})^2} \tag{7}$$

5.3 Parameters

In the process of recommendation, we need to decide the number of hash functions and hash tables. We choose the number of hash tables as 4, 6, 8, 10. And the number of hash functions as 4 and 8. We use different collocations to select the most appropriate parameters. The performance of the model is shown in Fig. 3 that both MAE and RMSE reach the minimum when the number of hash tables = 8 and the hash function = 4.

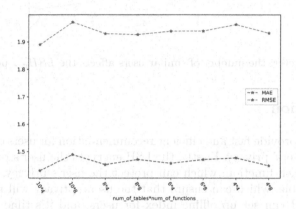

Fig. 3. Parameters: hash table and hash function affect the LSH_{par} performance.

For the anime ratings we want to predict, we use a weighted assignment method. That is, the ratings of similar users are assigned to anime according to the similarity ratio. Therefore, the number of similar users will also affect the recommendation accuracy. We select 2, 4, 6, 8 and 10 similar users to assign values to anime. The model performance is shown in Fig. 4. It can be seen that MAE and RMSE decrease with similar users increases. When k = 10, the model has the best performance.

5.4 Experimental Results and Analysis

Here, we analyze and summarize the experimental results. The first evaluation we use is MAE. For the model, the smaller the error, the better the model. When k = 10, hash table = 8, hash function = 4, the model's MAE = 1.4528. The MAE is less than 2, which shows that our model is basically correct in predicting user preferences. The second evaluation we use is RMSE, which is used to measure the deviation between the real value and the predicted value. The model's RMSE = 1.930, which can also prove the validity of the method.

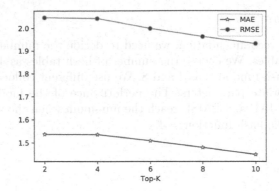

Fig. 4. Parameter: the number of similar users affects the LSH_{par} performance.

6   Conclusion

We use LSH to provide fast and efficient recommendation for users on the premise of protecting users' privacy. Firstly, the LSH encrypts the user's rating information through hash function, which can protect the user's privacy, and this process is irreversible, which can ensure that the users' privacy will not be leaked. Again, the LSH can set up offline index for users, and it's time complexity is O(1). Therefore, when searching for similar users for the target user, the search time is greatly shortened. Experiments on real dataset show that LSH_par is practical and effective.

In the future work, we will try to consider the user's comments, the correlation between items and other factors to improve recommendation performance. In addition, we will try to extend this method to other application scenarios to solve more problems.

Acknowledgment. This work was supported by the National Natural Science Foundation of China (No. 61872219).

References

1. Chen, C., Zhang, M., Zhang, Y., Liu, Y., Ma, S.: Efficient neural matrix factorization without sampling for recommendation. ACM Trans. Inf. Syst. (TOIS) **38**(2), 1–28 (2020)
2. Chen, L., Wu, Z., Cao, J., Zhu, G., Ge, Y.: Travel recommendation via fusing multi-auxiliary information into matrix factorization. ACM Trans. Intell. Syst. Technol. (TIST) **11**(2), 1–24 (2020)
3. Chi, X., Yan, C., Wang, H., Rafique, W., Qi, L.: Amplified locality-sensitive hashing-based recommender systems with privacy protection. Concurr. Comput. Pract. Experience, e5681 (2020)
4. Exner, N.: Anime-zing in North Carolina: library views of anime fans. North Carolina Librar. **70**(1), 7 (2012)

5. Fu, M., Qu, H., Yi, Z., Lu, L., Liu, Y.: A novel deep learning-based collaborative filtering model for recommendation system. IEEE Trans. Cybern. **49**(3), 1084–1096 (2019). https://doi.org/10.1109/TCYB.2018.2795041
6. Gao, H., Qin, X., Barroso, R.J.D., Hussain, W., Xu, Y., Yin, Y.: Collaborative learning-based industrial IoT API recommendation for software-defined devices: the implicit knowledge discovery perspective. IEEE Trans. Emerg. Top. Comput. Intell. 1–11 (2020). https://doi.org/10.1109/TETCI.2020.3023155
7. Girsang, A., Al Faruq, B., Herlianto, H., Simbolon, S.: Collaborative recommendation system in users of anime films. J. Phys. Conf. Ser. **1566**, 012057 (2020). IOP Publishing
8. Li, G., Chen, Q., Li, L.: Collaborative filtering recommendation algorithm based on rating prediction and ranking prediction. ACTA ELECTONICA SINICA **45**(12), 3070 (2017)
9. Nuurshadieq, Wibowo, A.T.: Leveraging side information to anime recommender system using deep learning. In: 2020 3rd International Seminar on Research of Information Technology and Intelligent Systems (ISRITI), pp. 62–67 (2020). https://doi.org/10.1109/ISRITI51436.2020.9315363
10. Qi, L., He, Q., Chen, F., Zhang, X., Dou, W., Ni, Q.: Data-driven web APIS recommendation for building web applications. IEEE Transactions on Big Data (2020). https://doi.org/10.1109/TBDATA.2020.2975587
11. Qi, L., Wang, R., Hu, C., Li, S., He, Q., Xu, X.: Time-aware distributed service recommendation with privacy-preservation. Inf.. Sci. **480**, 354–364 (2019)
12. Qi, L., Wang, X., Xu, X., Dou, W., Li, S.: Privacy-aware cross-platform service recommendation based on enhanced locality-sensitive hashing. IEEE Trans. Netw. Sci. Eng. (2020). https://doi.org/10.1109/TNSE.2020.2969489
13. Qi, L., et al.: Structural balance theory-based e-commerce recommendation over big rating data. IEEE Trans. Big Data **4**(3), 301–312 (2018). https://doi.org/10.1109/TBDATA.2016.2602849
14. Qi, L., Zhang, X., Li, S., Wan, S., Wen, Y., Gong, W.: Spatial-temporal data-driven service recommendation with privacy-preservation. Inf. Sci. **515**, 91–102 (2020)
15. Qi, L., Zhou, Z., Yu, J., Liu, Q.: Data-sparsity tolerant web service recommendation approach based on improved collaborative filtering. IEICE Trans. Inf. Syst. **100**(9), 2092–2099 (2017)
16. Sun, Z., Wang, Y., Cai, Z., Liu, T., Tong, X., Jiang, N.: A two-stage privacy protection mechanism based on blockchain in mobile crowdsourcing. Int. J. Intell. Syst. **36**(5), 2058–2080 (2021)
17. Wang, F., Zhu, H., Srivastava, G., Li, S., Khosravi, M.R., Qi, L.: Robust collaborative filtering recommendation with user-item-trust records. IEEE Trans. Comput. Soc. Syst. 1–11 (2021). https://doi.org/10.1109/TCSS.2021.3064213
18. Wang, R., Cheng, H.K., Jiang, Y., Lou, J.: A novel matrix factorization model for recommendation with LOD-based semantic similarity measure. Expert Syst. Appl. **123**, 70–81 (2019)
19. Wang, X., Xu, Y., He, X., Cao, Y., Wang, M., Chua, T.S.: Reinforced negative sampling over knowledge graph for recommendation. In: 2020 Proceedings of The Web Conference, pp. 99–109 (2020)
20. Wibowo, A.T., et al.: Leveraging side information to anime recommender system using deep learning. In: 2020 3rd International Seminar on Research of Information Technology and Intelligent Systems (ISRITI), pp. 62–67. IEEE (2020)
21. Xiao, Y., Xiao, L., Lu, X., Zhang, H., Yu, S., Poor, H.V.: Deep-reinforcement-learning-based user profile perturbation for privacy-aware recommendation. IEEE IoT J. **8**(6), 4560–4568 (2021). https://doi.org/10.1109/JIOT.2020.3027586

22. Xu, W., Zhou, Y.: Course video recommendation with multimodal information in online learning platforms: a deep learning framework. Br. J. Educ. Technol. **51**(5), 1734–1747 (2020)
23. Xu, X., et al.: An IoT-oriented data placement method with privacy preservation in cloud environment. J. Netw. Comput. Appl. **124**, 148–157 (2018)
24. Xu, X., Huang, Q., Zhang, Y., Li, S., Qi, L., Dou, W.: An LSH-based offloading method for IoMT services in integrated cloud-edge environment. ACM Trans. Multimedia Comput. Commun. Appl. **16**(3s), 1–19 (2021)
25. Xu, X., Liu, X., Yin, X., Wang, S., Qi, Q., Qi, L.: Privacy-aware offloading for training tasks of generative adversarial network in edge computing. Inf. Sci. **532**, 1–15 (2020)
26. Xu, X., et al.: An edge computing-enabled computation offloading method with privacy preservation for internet of connected vehicles. Future Gener. Comput. Syst. **96**, 89–100 (2019)
27. Yin, C., Shi, L., Sun, R., Wang, J.: Improved collaborative filtering recommendation algorithm based on differential privacy protection. J. Supercomput. **76**(7), 5161–5174 (2019). https://doi.org/10.1007/s11227-019-02751-7

Compound Fault Diagnosis of Industrial Robot Based on Improved Multi-label One-Dimensional Convolutional Neural Network

Ping Li[1], Hong Xiao[1(✉)], Wenchao Jiang[1], and Dongjun Ning[2]

[1] School of Computer Science and Technology, Guangdong University of Technology, Guangzhou 510006, China

[2] Taotall Technology Development Co., Ltd., Guangzhou 510635, China

Abstract. Industrial robot is one kind of complex infrastructure in industrial production and applications. Fault diagnosis is an important part of the intelligent application and monitoring of industrial robots. For multi-axis industrial robot compound fault prediction and diagnosis problem, this paper proposes a fault diagnosis model based on improved multi-label one-dimensional convolutional neural network (ML-SRIPCNN-1D). Firstly, the compound fault data set is enhanced by random sampling and Mixup. Then, the single fault data and compound fault data were trained end-to-end by the improved multi-label one-dimensional convolutional neural network. Finally, accurate diagnosis and prediction of compound faults of industrial robots are implemented. The compound fault data set was derived from a company's multi-axis industrial robot. The characteristic variables of fault diagnosis are torque, current, velocity, position, etc. Compared with SRIPCNN-1D, MLCNN, WT-MLCNN, T-FSM-MLCNN, ELM + AE + SVM, LMD + TDSF + ML-KNN models, the average diagnosis accuracy of ML-SRIPCNN-1D reached 98.67%. The model has good diagnosis effect and high accuracy for the prediction and diagnosis of industrial robot compound fault.

Keywords: Multi-axis industrial robot · Fault diagnosis · One-dimensional convolutional neural network

1 Introduction

Industrial robot are precision mechanical equipment with complex composition and numerous components. With the increase of industrial robot's service time, simultaneous failure of several different components may occur. Such as a shaft motor and reducer failure at the same time. Once a mechanical axis failure occurs in a multi-axis industrial robot, it will affect the operation of other axes as well. Compound fault refers to the fault of multiple components detected simultaneously in a complex system [1].

In the past few decades, most of the research objects of fault diagnosis have been focused on a single component, focusing on the fault of a single component or a different type of fault of an important component. In 2013, Li Rong et al. [2] proposed a fault

© Springer Nature Singapore Pte Ltd. 2021
Y. Tan et al. (Eds.): DMBD 2021, CCIS 1454, pp. 205–216, 2021.
https://doi.org/10.1007/978-981-16-7502-7_23

diagnosis method of variable speed gearbox based on order tracking, aiming at the problem of fault feature extraction and separation in fault vibration signal of variable speed gearbox. In 2014, Xu Yonggang et al. [3] proposed a fault diagnosis method combining DT-CWT and ICA to solve the problem that the fault signal features of rolling bearings were difficult to separate. In 2015, Fu Qiang et al. [4] applied the resonant sparse decomposition method to extract early fault information of planetary carrier bearing and planetary gear of wind turbine gearbox. Wang Hongchao et al. [5] proposed a sparse non-negative matrix decomposition method to extract effectively features from bispectral 3D images, thus realizing efficient and intelligent diagnosis of rolling bearing faults. Many scholars [6–13] have studied the problem of gearbox fault diagnosis. For example, in 2018, Yi Z et al. [14] proposed an improved frequency-domain deconvolution algorithm and studied its performance through rolling bearing fault diagnosis, using FD-SCA algorithm to reduce the complexity of noise signal separation. Dhamande LS et al. [15] proposed a gear and bearing fault identification method based on time-frequency method CWT and vibration signal DWT. First, new fault features are extracted from continuous and discrete wavelet transforms of vibration signals, after the extraction of time-frequency features, three different classifiers were used to compare their diagnostic potential with time-frequency domain features for fault identification. Qin A et al. [16] proposed a concurrent fault diagnosis method based on Bayesian discrimination and dimensionless time series analysis. The method is applied to fault diagnosis of centrifugal multistage impeller blowers with six states, including single and multiple faults of gears and bearings. In 2019, Liang P et al. [17] combined convolutional neural network with wavelet transform and multi-label classification. They designed a network architecture suitable for MLCNN model to realize fault diagnosis of gearbox, such as broken teeth in gears, seat rings of external worn bearings, shaft imbalance and looseness, etc. Miao Y et al. [18] proposed an improved parametric adaptive variational mode decomposition (VMD) with envelope spectrum analysis to extract locomotive bearing fault features. VMD can extract fault information more efficiently. In 2020, Liang P et al. [19] carried out fault diagnosis of transmission system by using wavelet transform and generative neural network. Yu C et al. [20] proposed a multi-label fault diagnosis method based on meta-learning. After extracting T - FSM characteristics of vibration signal, multi-label fault diagnosis was realized by MLCML.

All the above studies focus on the concurrent faults of a single key component, but there are relatively few studies on the multi-component compound fault diagnosis of complex mechanical systems. In 2018, Huang R et al. [21] proposed a deep decoupled convolutional neural network (DDCNN) for compound fault diagnosis of bearings and gears. In 2020, FA Jun Yu et al. [22] proposed a fault diagnosis method based on WPT and SRC for gearbox compound fault diagnosis. This method uses WPT to convert transmission vibration signals of unknown compound faults into frequency band components. According to the minimum of each selected frequency band component, the fault category corresponding to the error is reconstructed to diagnose the compound fault of gearbox. For the training data problem, many scholars try to train the model by single fault training data, then expand to compound fault diagnosis. For example, in 2017, ASR My et al. [23] used empirical mode decomposition (EMD), combined diagnosis of bearing and gear faults was carried out by statistical feature and Non-Naive

Bayes classifier. Only single fault state and health state data are used to train the classifier to obtain better compound fault diagnosis effect. In 2018, Li S et al. [24] studied a data-driven multi-label fault diagnosis method. The method is based on the multi-label support vector machine of solid oxide fuel cell system, it can effectively diagnose the compound faults during this period. In 2020, Dibaj A et al. [25] proposed an end-to-end hybrid method based on fine-tuning VMD and CNN. This method classifies machine health status, including health status, single fault and corresponding compound fault.

However, the comprehensive prediction and diagnosis of compound faults is still a difficulty in the application and monitoring of industrial robots. On the one hand, industrial robot fault data is difficult to obtain, most studies require additional sensors to collect data. Moreover, it needs to further use the knowledge of signal processing for feature extraction. On the other hand, most studies regard compound fault conditions as multiple single fault types without considering the correlation between multiple faults. They consider compound faults as simple concurrence of a single fault of a component and ignore the internal interaction when compound faults concurrence in mechanical systems.

To solve these problems, a compound fault diagnosis model based on improved multi-label one-dimensional convolutional neural network (ML-SRIPCNN-1D) is proposed. Firstly, there is no need to perform manual feature extraction and selection, but directly use the original operation data to carry out fault diagnosis in an end-to-end manner. It does not need to convert one-dimensional signal into two-dimensional time-frequency image, which reduces the dependence on expert knowledge and manual intervention. Then, unlike the single fault diagnosis model, ML-SRIPCNN-1D is suitable for compound fault prediction and diagnosis. Instead of simply treating the compound fault as a new fault mode, the algorithm gives multiple fault labels to the samples with compound fault. It uses multi-label learning model to input both compound fault and single fault into the model for fault diagnosis. In this paper, we take a company's multi-axis industrial robot as the experimental object. The characteristic variables of fault diagnosis are torque, current, velocity, position, etc. Compared with SRIPCNN-1D, MLCNN, WT-MLCNN, T-FSM-MLCNN, ELM + AE + SVM, LMD + TDSF + ML-KNN models. The experimental results show that the ML-SRIPCNN-1D has high accuracy in compound fault prediction and diagnosis of industrial robots.

2 Compound Fault Diagnosis Model

2.1 Improved Multi-label One-Dimensional Convolutional Neural Network

Multi-label classification is different from ordinary multi-label classification. In a multi-label classification task, a sample may have more than one label, for example, the label of a robot means 2-axis motor fault and 6-axis reducer fault. The traditional CNN model is suitable for two-dimensional data classification problems, it doesn't handle multi-label sorting. Therefore, this paper proposes a multi label one-dimensional convolutional neural network model (ML-SRIPCNN-1D). The label form and model structure are improved to be suitable for the multi-axis industrial robot compound fault diagnosis task. First, the traditional multi-classification task uses One-Hot Encoding, it extends the value of discrete features to Euclidean space, which makes the calculation of distance between features more reasonable with respect to multi-label form, we need to change the label vector form of each sample to Multi-Hot Encoding. The Multi-Hot Encoding label is 1 at multiple indexes. Second, ML-SRIPCNN-1D regards compound faults as multiple fault combinations, so the number of output layers is determined by the type of single fault samples. Compared with the traditional CNN model, the loss function of ML-SRIPCNN-1D is quite different. It uses multiple sigmoids as the activation function in combination with the binary cross-entropy loss function. The model considers that each fault category is independent of each other. It is not necessary to limit the sum of probabilities of all classes to 1. Each category has its own independent cross-entropy function.

Figure 1 is the schematic diagram of ML-SRIPCNN-1D using the improved multi label one-dimensional convolutional neural network structure. The input layer is the real-time operation data of the multi-axis robot, it is followed by multiple convolution layers and pooling layers. The output layer is a fully connected layer with multiple sigmoid activation functions, the number of neurons is the same as the number of single fault types.

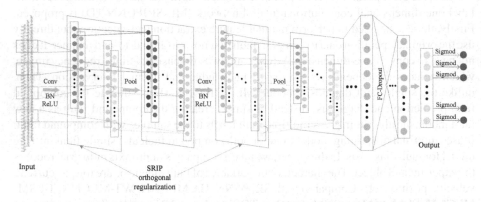

Fig. 1. Multi-label one-dimensional convolutional neural network model diagram.

2.2 Compound Fault Diagnosis Process

The real-time fault diagnosis process of industrial robot compound fault diagnosis model ML-SRIPCNN-1D is shown in Fig. 2. Fault diagnosis is divided into the following three steps.

(1) Data preprocessing stage. Firstly, the collected real-time operation data is cleaned and normalized. Then, the data is expanded by using random sampling and Mixup enhancement methods. Finally, the industrial robot fault data set is divided into three parts: verification set, training set and test set.

(2) Model training stage. Establish ML-SRIPCNN-1D fault diagnosis model. We use orthogonal initialization to avoid gradient explosion/vanishing. The ML-SRIPCNN-1D activation function is ReLU, it uses global maximum pooling to

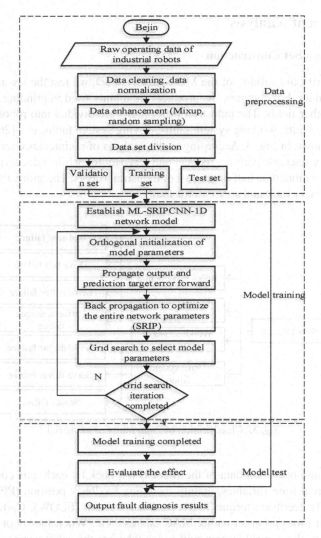

Fig. 2. Process of fault diagnosis model of industrial robot.

achieve dimensionality reduction. Sigmoid classifier is used to achieve the classification output. The model loss function is the cross-entropy loss function, as shown in Formula (1).

$$L = \frac{1}{N} \sum_i L_i = \frac{1}{N} \sum_i - \sum_C^M = 1 \, y_{ic} \, logp_{ic} \qquad (1)$$

In (1): M is the number of categories, y_{ic} is the indicator variable (0 or 1). If the category is the same as the sample i, it is 1, otherwise it is 0. P_{ic} is the predicted probability that the observed sample i belongs to category c.

(3) Model testing phase. Input the data to be diagnosed into the best trained model to verify the effect of the robot diagnosis model.

3 Experiment Analysis

3.1 Fault Data Set Construction

In order to verify the validity of the ML-SRIPCNN-1D, we test the six-axis industrial robot based on a robot company. Its products are mainly used in grinding, sorting, palletizing and other fields. The industrial robot faults are divided into robot body faults, control system faults, working system faults, driving system faults, etc. [26]. Fault classification is shown in Fig. 3. According to the analysis of maintenance record statistics [27], the most vulnerable parts are reducer and servo motor, while reducers and servomotors account for more than half of the cost of industrial robots. Therefore, the experiment focuses on reducer fault and servo motor fault.

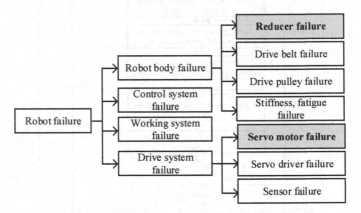

Fig. 3. Classification of main faults of industrial.

The real-time operation data of the robot is fed back by each axis control system. There are 38 real-time variables, mainly including feedback position (PFB), feedback velocity (VFB), feedback torque(TFB), feedback current (FLOW), Cartesian coordinates, creation time, program name, MAC address, etc. When the robot executes the action program, the control system will judge whether the robot can reach the designated position at the set speed. In the early stage of the fault, the robot can operate normally on the surface. The feedback speed and position of the malfunctioning robot are not significantly different from those of the normal robot, but its feedback torque and feedback current will have obvious changes. After a series of analysis and screening, the core characteristic variables of fault diagnosis are determined to be feedback torque (TFB), feedback current (FLOW), feedback velocity (VFB) and feedback position (PFB). Table 1 shows the compound fault data set.

Table 1. Compound fault data set of industrial robots.

Category	Variable	Axis	Data volume	Situation
1	tfb, flow, vfb, pfb	1–6	1,500,000	Normal
2	tfb, flow, vfb, pfb	1–6	180,000	1 axis reducer, 2 axis motor failure
3	tfb, flow, vfb, pfb	1–6	210,000	1, 3-axis reducer failure
4	tfb, flow, vfb, pfb	1–6	220,000	3, 4 axis reducer failure
5	tfb, flow, vfb, pfb	1–6	390,000	3-axis reducer failure
6	tfb, flow, vfb, pfb	1–6	420,000	2 axis motor failure
7	tfb, flow, vfb, pfb	1–6	350,000	4-axis reducer failure

As shown in Table 1, the data set contains normal sample data, single fault sample and compound fault sample. Different from single fault diagnosis sample labels, multi-label compound fault samples have multiple labels to represent rich fault information. The specific label setting method is to set 2-bit mark for each axis. For example, the (0,0) label represents the axis is anomaly, the (0,1) label represents the axis reducer anomaly, the (1,0) label represents the axis motor anomaly, the (1,1) label represents the axis reducer and motor are abnormal. By setting multiple tags in this way, we can use less and intuitive marking method to represent robot compound faults, and take the compound fault label as model input. For example, the compound fault of Category 3 in Table 1 can be expressed as: (1,0,0,0,1,0,0,0,0,0,0,0). The end of the multi-label convolutional neural network model has multiple sigmoid functions. Each sigmoid function can output judgment independently. Finally, the fault diagnosis results of six axis can be obtained.

Compared with single fault and normal data, the amount of compound fault data is less due to the long acquisition time. To avoid model bias caused by category imbalance, we use random sampling and Mixup data enhancement methods for data enhancement. The fault samples are expanded to 400000 pieces of data by multiple data enhancement.

3.2 Analysis of the Accuracy of Fault Diagnosis

If single fault label is used to mark compound fault, the data in Table 1 data set will be divided into seven independent tags. For multi-label compound fault, each fault is given a fixed label. Therefore, compound fault are represented by the combined form of labels. In order to diagnose compound fault, ML-SRIPCNN-1D takes fault label combination as input data. We compared ML-SRIPCNN-1D with single-label one-dimensional convolutional neural network, Table 2 shows the model comparison results.

In Table 2, although the traditional single fault diagnosis model has a high accuracy in single fault diagnosis, it is not competent for the task of compound fault diagnosis. This is because compound label will interfere with model training, such as 2-axis single fault and 2–3-axis compound fault. The compound fault is treated as a single new fault because both faults contain 2-axis fault and have no correlation in label categories. The model extracted 2-axis fault features but was trained for multiple separate tasks. Therefore, the accuracy of the single label method in SRIPCNN-1D for compound fault diagnosis is low, with an average accuracy of only 67%. ML-SRIPCNN-1D can effectively diagnose compound faults. The compound fault is regarded as a combination of multiple single fault labels, which ensures the consistency between fault features and labels. The average accuracy of the model is more than 98%.

Table 2. Comparison of multi-label and single-label convolutional neural networks.

Network model	Data enhancement method	Average diagnostic accuracy
SRIPCNN-1D	Random sampling + Mixup	67.18
ML-SRIPCNN-1D	Random sampling + Mixup	98.67

3.3 Model Validity Analysis

To further verify the validity of the ML-SRIPCNN-1D. We compared the model with multiple compound fault diagnosis models MLCNN [28], WT-MLCNN [17], T-FSM-MLCNN [20], ELM + AE + SVM [29], LMD + TDSF + ML-KNN [30]. The results are shown in Table 3. Among them, MLCNN, WT-MLCNN and T-FSM-MLCNN are compound fault diagnosis models based on CNN, while ELM + AE + SVM and LMD + TDSF + ML-KNN are fault diagnosis models based on the combination of multiple methods.

Table 3. Comparison of compound fault diagnosis models.

Network model	Data enhancement method	Average diagnostic accuracy
MLCNN	Random sampling + Mixup	90.97
WT-MLCNN	Random sampling + Mixup	91.27
T-FSM-MLCNN	Random sampling + Mixup	86.43
ELM + AE + SVM	Random sampling + Mixup	82.85
LMD + TDSF + ML-KNN	Random sampling + Mixup	85.27
ML-SRIPCNN-1D	Random sampling + Mixup + Mixup	98.67

As can be seen from Table 3, the ML-SRIPCNN-1D has higher diagnostic accuracy. MLCNN adopts multi-layer convolution and pooling, but the original data still needs to be converted into two-dimensional data to carry out fault diagnosis. WT-MLCNN needs to use wavelet transform(WT)to obtain time-frequency data, then input two-dimensional time-frequency data into MLCNN to realize single fault diagnosis and compound fault diagnosis. T-FSM-MLCNN has better feature extraction ability than wavelet transform in rare fault diagnosis. ELM + AE + SVM method uses local mean decomposition to extract features from original non-stationary and nonlinear data. It uses several extreme learning machines (ELMs) to recognize the number and type of faults. The LMD + TDSF + ML-KNN method still needs to carry out the time-domain statistical feature (TDSF) transformation, which requires multi-step processing and optimization process. Through comparison, it can be seen that the ML-SRIPCNN-1D adopts end-to-end training mode, without converting real-time data into two-dimensional data, which effectively improves the efficiency of fault diagnosis. Under the current compound fault data set, the fault diagnosis of multi-axis industrial robot has better diagnosis and prediction effect.

3.4 The Influence of Different Sampling Frequency and Sequence Length on Fault Diagnosis

In the actual industrial application, hundreds or even thousands of industrial robots will be connected to the fault diagnosis system to collect real-time data, such a large amount of operational data requires high network bandwidth and hardware resources for transmission and processing. High frequency data acquisition will also cause heavy load on the robot controller, even affect the operation and control of the robot program. Therefore, setting the appropriate data acquisition frequency can not only reduce the utilization rate of robot data processing resources, but also meet the requirements of actual fault monitoring and diagnosis.

In order to test the appropriate data collection frequency of the ML-SRIPCNN-1D, we set the sampling intervals as 4ms, 100ms, 1s and 10s to analyze the influence of different sampling frequencies on the robot operation status and fault diagnosis accuracy. Due to the difference in data volume caused by different collection intervals, all data were enhanced by random sampling and Mixup. Data samples at different intervals were enhanced to make the training set reach 400,000. According to experience, two different data sequence lengths of 200 and 3000 were set in the experiment. When the sequence length is 200, the corresponding data cycle of each sampling interval ranges from 0.016 to 40 cycles. When the sequence length is 3000, the data cycle corresponding to each sampling interval ranges from 0.24 to 600 cycles. Table 4 shows the experimental results.

Table 4. Fault diagnosis accuracy under different sampling intervals and sampling points.

Sampling interval	Sequence length	Average diagnostic accuracy	Sequence length	Average diagnostic accuracy
4 ms	200	94.13	3000	98.67
100 ms	200	93.91	3000	98.46
1 s	200	93.78	3000	97.11
10 s	200	93.04	3000	96.13

In Table 4, although the length accuracy of 3000 point sampling data is better, the acquisition time is longer. In the case of 200 sampling points, the accuracy of the training model obtained by using interval data in 4 ms is the highest, reaching 94.13%. When the acquisition interval was increased to 100 ms, 1 s, and 10 s, the accuracy of the training model decreased, but the diagnostic accuracy was above 93%. The coverage period of diagnosis data is different due to different data intervals, but the diagnosis accuracy is similar, which indicates that the fault diagnosis model is not sensitive to the action period. 10 s sampling interval can still obtain good diagnosis results, but the data time span required for fault diagnosis is long, which is difficult to meet the needs of real-time and fast diagnosis. Therefore, based on the experimental results in Table 4. Combined with the network configuration and database of the robot acquisition system. In order to balance data acquisition frequency and model diagnosis accuracy. The sampling interval of 1s will not cause heavy load on the acquisition system, but also can obtain rich prediction results with less data, so the fault diagnosis model has high accuracy.

4 Conclusion

In this paper, an improved multi-label one-dimensional convolutional neural network fault diagnosis model (ML-SRIPCNN-1D) is proposed to solve the compound fault diagnosis and prediction problem of multi-axis industrial robots. ML-SRIPCNN-1D improves the expression of data labels by using random sampling and Mixup data enhancement methods. Then, the single fault data and compound fault data were trained end-to-end by the improved multi-label one-dimensional convolutional neural network. The experimental results show that the ML-SRIPCNN-1D has good diagnostic effect and high accuracy for the prediction and diagnosis of industrial robot compound faults. The average accuracy rate reaches 98.67%. It can provide reliable fault diagnosis and prediction guarantee for industrial robot large-scale application.

Acknowledgement. This paper is supported by the Key Technology Project of Foshan City in 2019 (1920001001367), National Natural Science and Guangdong Joint Fund Project (U2001201), Guangdong Natural Science Fund Project (2018A030313061, 2021A1515011243), Research and Development Projects of National Key fields (2018YFB1004202), Guangdong Science and Technology Plan Project (2019B010139001) and Guangzhou Science and Technology Plan Project (201902020016).

References

1. Zhang, K., Zhou, D., Chai, Y.: Summary of compound fault diagnosis technology. Control Theor. Appl. **32**(9), 1143–1157 (2015)
2. Li, R.: Research on compound fault diagnosis method of gearbox. Hunan University (2013)
3. Xu, Y., Meng, Z., Zhao, G.: Research on bearing composite fault diagnosis based on dual-tree complex wavelet transform. Chin. J. Sci. Instrum. **35**(2), 447–452 (2014)
4. Fu, Q.: Research on early compound fault information extraction technology of wind power gearbox. Harbin Institute of Technology (2015)
5. Wang, H.: Weak fault diagnosis of rolling bearing based on sparse decomposition and image sparse representation. Shanghai Jiao Tong University (2015)
6. Wang, Z.: Research on several methods for feature extraction of gearbox compound fault diagnosis. Taiyuan University of Technology (2015)

7. Han, T., Yuan, J., Tang, J., et al.: Intelligent compound fault diagnosis method for rolling bearing based on MWT and CNN. J. Mech. Trans. **40**(12), 139–143 (2016)
8. Zhang, R.: Research on fault diagnosis of fan gearbox based on feature fusion and XGBOOST algorithm. Shanghai Institute of Electrical Engineering (2019)
9. Zhang, L., Jing, L., Xu, W., et al.: Research on compound fault diagnosis of gearbox combined with CNN and D-S evidence theory. Mech. Sci. Technol. Aerosp. Eng. **38**(10), 1582–1588 (2019)
10. Wang, P., Li, T., Gao, X., et al.: Rolling bearing composite fault feature extraction method based on LMD and MSEE. Bearing **472**(3), 63–69 (2019)
11. Zhang, J., Li, Y.: Compound fault diagnosis of motor rolling bearing based on particle swarms optimization blind source separation method. Mach. Tool Hydraulics **47**(1), 167–172 (2019)
12. Li, J., Cheng, J., Huang, Z., et al.: Gearbox composite fault diagnosis method based on SWD-AVDIF. Noise Vibr. Control **39**(1), 166–171 (2019)
13. Fan, G., Zhou, J., Zhu, K.: Acoustic diagnosis of bearing complex faults based on improved morphological wavelet threshold denoising. J. Vibr. Shock, **39**(12), 221–226, 288 (2020)
14. Yi, Z., Pan, N., Guo, Y.: Mechanical compound faults extraction based on improved frequency domain blind deconvolution algorithm. Mech. Syst. Sig. Process. **113**, 180–188 (2018)
15. Dhamande, L.S., Chaudhari, M.B.: Compound gear-bearing fault feature extraction using statistical features based on time-frequency method. Measurement **125**, 63–77 (2018)
16. Qin, A., Hu, Q., Lv, Y., et al.: Concurrent fault diagnosis based on Bayesian discriminating analysis and time series analysis with dimensionless parameters. IEEE Sens. J. **19**(6), 2254–2265 (2018)
17. Liang, P., Deng, C., Wu, J., et al.: Compound fault diagnosis of gearboxes via multi-label convolutional neural network and wavelet transform. Comput. Indus. **113**, 103132 (2019)
18. Miao, Y., Zhao, M., Lin, J.: Identification of mechanical compound-fault based on the improved parameter-adaptive variational mode decomposition. ISA Trans. **84**, 82–95 (2019)
19. Liang, P., Deng, C., Wu, J., et al.: Single and simultaneous fault diagnosis of gearbox via a semi-supervised and high-accuracy adversarial learning framework. Knowl.-Based Syst. **198**, 105895 (2020)
20. Yu, C., Ning, Y., Qin, Y., et al.: Multi-label fault diagnosis of rolling bearing based on meta-learning. Neural Comput. Appl. **33**(10), 5393–5407 (2020)
21. Huang, R., Liao, Y., Zhang, S., et al.: Deep decoupling convolutional neural network for intelligent compound fault diagnosis. IEEE Access **7**, 1848–1858 (2018)
22. Fa-jun, Y., Yi-cai, L., Qi-feng, Z.: Compound fault diagnosis of gearbox based on wavelet packet transform and sparse representation classification. In: Proceedings of the 32nd Chinese Conference on Control and Decision Making, vol. 2, pp. 1105–1109 (2020)
23. Asr, M.Y., Ettefagh, M.M., Hassannejad, R., et al.: Diagnosis of combined faults in rotary machinery by non-naive Bayesian approach. Mech. Syst. Sig. Process. **85**, 56–70 (2017)
24. Li, S., Cao, H., Yang, Y.: Data-driven simultaneous fault diagnosis for solid oxide fuel cell system using multi-label pattern identification. J. Power Sour. **378**, 646–659 (2018)
25. Dibaj, A., Ettefagh, M.M., Hassannejad, R., et al.: A hybrid fine-tuned VMD and CNN scheme for untrained compound fault diagnosis of rotating machinery with unequal-severity faults. Expert Syst. Appl. **167**, 114094 (2020)
26. Chen, S.: Research on condition monitoring and fault diagnosis system of industrial robot (2009)
27. Xiao, J.: Fault detection diagnosis and fault tolerant control of robot and its experimental research. Yanshan University (2010)
28. Zhu, J., Liao, S., Lei, Z., et al.: Multi-label convolutional neural network based pedestrian attribute classification. Image Vis. Comput. **58**, 224–229 (2017)

29. Yang, Z., Wang, X., Zhong, J.: Representational learning for fault diagnosis of wind turbine equipment: a multi-layered extreme learning machines approach. Energies **9**(6), 379 (2016)
30. Yang, Z., Wang, X., Wong, P.K.: Single and simultaneous fault diagnosis with application to a multistage gearbox: a versatile dual-elm network approach. IEEE Trans. Ind. Inf. **14**(12), 5245–5255 (2018)

A Class Imbalance Monitoring Model for Fetal Heart Contractions Based on Gradient Boosting Decision Tree Ensemble Learning

Chen Qin[1], Shaopeng Liu[2], Shengxiang Lin[2], Guangzhe Li[2], and Jiaming Hong[1,3](✉)

[1] School of Medical Information Engineering, Guangzhou University of Chinese Medicine,
Guangzhou, China
hjm@gzucm.edu.cn
[2] Department of Computer Science, Guangdong Polytechnic Normal University,
Guangzhou, China
[3] Guangdong Key Laboratory of Big Data Analysis and Processing, Guangzhou, China

Abstract. Aiming at the imbalance and cost-sensitive problem of sample categories in actual fetal monitoring, as well as actual needs, we proposed a category imbalance fetal contraction monitoring model based on GBDT (Gradient Boosting Decision Tree) combined learning. Subsets with balanced category were generated by random under-sampling and applied to train several GBDT base classifiers using the method of feature selection. We integrated the base classifiers by the simple average method and calculated the final prediction probability. In this study, AUC and cost-sensitive error rate were used as evaluation indicators to compare with the commonly used single learning models such as Decision Tree, Logistic Regression and combined learning models like Random Forest to verify the effectiveness of the model.

Keywords: Category imbalance · Cost sensitive · GBDT · Combined learning model

1 Introduction

In China, the liberalization of the comprehensive two-child policy has significantly increased the population of elderly parturient and newborns. People pay more attention to the health of fetuses and pregnant women. According to the National Bureau of Statistics [1], the birth rate in 2016 climbed up to 12.95%, a year-on-year raise of 0.88% thousand points. The latest data shows that the second child fertility rate of 35 to 39 year-old women in 2015 is 10.96%, a year-on-year increase of 1.25% thousand points. Research shows that one of the main causes of perinatal morbidity and death is fetal distress, and continuous fetal monitoring can greatly reduce the occurrence of fetal distress and neonatal asphyxia [2].

Fetal monitoring is an effective way to evaluate fetal development, divided into external and internal monitoring method. The internal monitoring method is complicated to operate and requires high safety indicators. In current clinical practice, doctors generally

© Springer Nature Singapore Pte Ltd. 2021
Y. Tan et al. (Eds.): DMBD 2021, CCIS 1454, pp. 217–227, 2021.
https://doi.org/10.1007/978-981-16-7502-7_24

use the external monitoring method. With the continuous development of science and technology, different methods of fetal monitoring are also appearing, such as electronic monitoring, imaging monitoring and amniotic fluid testing. Cardiotocography (CTG), as the main tool for fetal health monitoring [3] which has been introduced into clinical practice since the late 1960s, is not only low in price but also non-invasive.

Cardiotocography (CTG), also known as electronic fetal monitoring, is a technique for recording Fetal Heart Rate (FHR) and Uterine Contractions (UC) synchronously during pregnancy, typically in the third trimester to evaluate maternal and fetal well-being. It mainly used to diagnose fetal distress during pregnancy and delivery in order to improve the prognosis of newborns [4]. CTG can stably and accurately assess the baseline variation of Fetal Heart Rate, the change of Fetal Heart Rate during fetal movement and the change of Fetal Heart Rate during uterine contractions. According to the Fetal Heart Rate, variability and whether there is deceleration in fetal heart rate, and at the same time comparing the relationship between the deceleration and the time of uterine contractions, the FHR can be divided into 3 categories: normal class, suspicious class and pathologic class [5] (Fig. 1).

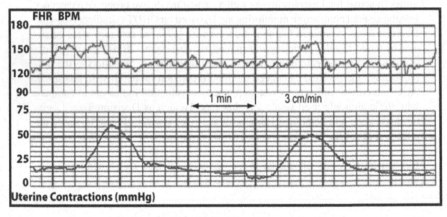

Fig. 1. Normal fetal heart contractions

In current clinical practice, the interpretation of CTG mainly depends on the experience and knowledge of doctors. Due to the various levels of experience of doctors, the diagnosis results might be subjective. Different experts have different interpretations of the same CTG data, even the same expert has different interpretations of the same CTG data at different times. Therefore, using modern computer technology and signal processing technology to recognize CTG intelligently can reduce the influence of subjective factors, and even more accurately evaluate the condition of fetuses, which help effectively improve the prognosis. In order to solve the problem of inconsistency CTG interpretation, this project is committed to establishing an intelligent fetal contraction monitoring model that predicts the health of fetus in the uterus.

Classification is one of the key points in machine learning research. A large number of theories and algorithm models have emerged, which can bring new methods and thing to the recognition of CTG data. Many scholars in foreign countries have applied machine learning methods in classifying CTG data (some related research is shown in Table 1. below). In references [6, 7], the fetal state prediction of CTG data is treated as a second-class classification problem, which is normal class and pathologic class. In references [8–14], fetal state is divided into three class, normal class, pathologic class and suspicious class.

Table 1. Related research in CTG classification

Classification research technology	Reference
Adaptive Neural-based Fuzzy Inference System	[6]
SVM and the Genetic Algorithm	[7]
Multi-layer Perceptron Neural Network	[8]
Probabilistic Neural Network	[8]
Generalized Regression Neural Network	[8]
Discriminant Analysis, Decision Tree, and Artificial Neural Network	[9]
BP Neural Network	[10]
Decision Tree Based Adaptive Boosting Approach	[11]
Random Forest	[12]
LS-SVM and Binary Decision Tree	[13]
Improved Adaptive Genetic Algorithm	[14]

Synthesize the domestic and oversea research mentioned above, experts mainly considered classification algorithms, fuzzy algorithms, integrated algorithms and hybrid algorithms, and among them, neural networks are more commonly used. Overall, it is accessible to establish a fetal heart contraction monitoring model based on machine learning methods. The baseline, variability, acceleration and deceleration in CTG data can be considered as input features for machine learning methods. After consulting a large number of papers, we found that there is a key problem in the existing research. There is a high error rate in the prediction of suspicious and pathologic category data mainly because the imbalance of CTG data is not considered, that is, the number of positive samples (pathologic or suspicious class) in clinic is small. Although the fetal heart contraction monitoring dataset rarely has unbalanced problem, that is, the pathologic and suspicious fetal states account for only a small number in real life, positive examples are still the focus of experts' attention which is of great significance.

The imbalanced CTG data brings considerable challenges and risks to machine learning, because the existing algorithms are designed based on samples in balanced distribution and maximum the accuracy of classification. When classifying unbalanced CTG data through traditional machining learning algorithms, the majority of normal categories will be over-learned, while the identification of a few pathological and suspicious samples is often very tough, making easier to predict them as normal samples. When pathologic and suspicious samples are misjudged as the normal class, the fetus will probably miss the best time for intervention and treatment, causing irreversible and serious consequences. Thus, we purposed to use the Gradient Boosting Decision Tree algorithm (GBDT) in this paper. GBDT is also applicable as a base classifier for combined learning.

2 Meterial and Methods

2.1 GBDT

GBDT utilizes the additive model and forward step-by-step algorithm to realize the optimization process of learning. When the loss function is square loss and exponential loss function, the optimization of each step is clear, for example, the square loss function learning residual regression tree. However, for general loss functions, it is not easy to optimize each step such as the absolute value loss function and the Huber loss function. To solve this problem, Freidman came up with a gradient boosting algorithm: applying the approximate method of steepest descent, which means, using the value of the negative gradient of the loss function in current model as the approximate value of the residual of the boosting tree algorithm to fit a regression tree. The procedure of GBDT algorithm is presented below:

1. Input: training set $T = \{(x_1, y_1), (x_2, y_2), \ldots\ldots (x_N, y_N)\}$
2. Initialize and estimate the value that minimizes the loss function which is a tree with only 1 root node.

$$F_0(x) = argmin_\rho \sum_{i=1}^{N} L(y, \rho) \tag{1}$$

where N represents the size of samples.
3. For m = 1 to M do:

   a. Calculate the value of the negative gradient of the loss function in the current model $F_{m-1}(x)$ and use it as the estimate of the residual.

$$\tilde{y} = -\left[\frac{\partial \phi(F(x))}{\partial F(x)}\right] F(x) = F_{m-1}(x) = y_i - F_{m-1}(x_i)$$
$$i = 1, 2, \ldots\ldots, N \tag{2}$$

   b. Estimate regression leaf node area to fit the approximate value of residual.
   c. Applying linear search to get the value of leaf node area, y_i learns the number m regression tree, and the corresponding node area is $\{R_j\}_1^J$ which minimizes the loss function.

$$\gamma_{m,j} = argmin_\gamma \sum_{x_i \in R_{m,j}} L(y_i, F_{m-1}(x_i) + \gamma) \tag{3}$$

   d. Update regression tree and get the best-fitting decision tree for this round is:

$$h_m(x; a) = \sum_{j=1}^{J} \gamma_{m,j} I(x \in R_{m,j}) \tag{4}$$

e. The strong basis learner obtained in this iteration is:

$$F_m(x) = F_{m-1}(x) + \sum_{j=1}^{J} \gamma_{m,j} I\left(x \in R_{m,j}\right) \tag{5}$$

f. Get the final model output.

Use the error rate of the latest iteration to update the weights of training set. and correct the samples that were misclassified in the previous iteration. The model will then focus on the misclassified samples. The strong learner after iteration is:

$$F_M(x) = \sum_{m-1}^{M} \sum_{j=1}^{J} \gamma_{m,j} I\left(x \in R_{m,j}\right) \tag{6}$$

2.2 GBDT Combined Learning Model

CTG data is characterized by data imbalance, thus this paper proposed a combined learning model based on GBDT. The model includes 3 parts:

1. Use the under-sampling method to balance the number of the majority class and minority classes in ever subst.
2. Use diverse training subsets and feature samplings to train various differentiated GBDT sub-models.
3. Simple average the predicted probability of each sub-model to get the final predicted probability.

The whole structure of the model has been showed below (Fig. 2):

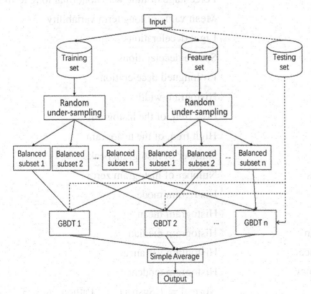

Fig. 2. Overall structure of the model

3   Experiment Analysis

In this study, we compared the performance of the common prediction models and the combined model based on GBDT by AUC and cost-sensitive error rate.

3.1   Dataset

Cardiotocography (CTG) dataset collected from the UCI Machine Learning Repository was used in the experiment [15, 16]. The dataset included measurements of uterine contraction (UC), fetal heart rate (FHR) features on Cardiotocograms classified by expert obstetricians. These features are obtained using the CTG analysis program SisPorto 2.0 [15, 17]. The CTG dataset consisted of 2126 instances, without abnormal or missing value, and every record of CTG data was made up of 21 numeric attributes, shown in Table 2.

Table 2. CTG data attribute decription

No.	Name of the feature	Decription
1	LB	Baseline value
2	AC	Accelerations
3	FM	Foetal movement
4	UC	Uterine contractions
5	ASTV	Percentage of time with abnormal short term variability
6	mSTV	Mean value of short term variability
7	ALTV	Percentage of time with abnormal long term variability
8	mLTV	Mean value of long term variability
9	DL	Light decelerations
10	DS	Severe decelerations
11	DP	Prolongued decelerations
12	Width	Histogram width
13	Min	Low freq. of the histogram
14	Max	High freq. of the histogram
15	Nmax	Number of histogram peaks
16	Nzeros	Number of histogram zeros
17	Mode	Histogram mode
18	Mean	Histogram mean
19	Median	Histogram median
20	Variance	Histogram variance
21	Tendency	Histogram tendency
22	NSP	Normal = 1;Suspect = 2;Pathologic = 3

The CTG data was classified as 3 distinct classes: Normal, Suspicious, and Pathologic. The number of the data labeled normal was 1655, accounting for 78% of the data, while 176 labeled suspicious class and 295 labeled Pathologic class, accounting for only 22%. Obviously, the class distribution of the dataset was highly imbalanced.

3.2 Data Pre-processing

Classifiers based on distance metrics are greatly sensitive to the magnitude of data. A large magnitude difference among the data can leads to the poor performance of the prediction classifier. To solve the problem, data was standardized at first, and z-scores were selected as the standard scores.

$$x^* = \frac{x - \bar{x}}{\sigma} \tag{7}$$

where $\bar{x}$ is the average of the raw data, and σ is referred to the standard deviation.

In this muti-class classification experiment, One-Hot Encoding was used to encode the label (Table 3).

Table 3. One-hot encoding example

NSP	NSP_1	NSP_2	NSP_3
1 (Normal)	1	0	0
2 (Suspicious)	0	1	0
3 (Pathologic)	0	0	1

3.3 Evaluation Indicators

In terms of imbalanced and cost-sensitive problems, using measures such as accuracy, precision, and recall to evaluate the model can cause misleading conclusions [3, 18]. Therefore, we adopted AUC and cost-sensitive error rate to assess the model.

AUC (Area under the Curve of ROC) is a statistical index varying between 0 and 1, calculated to evaluate discrimination power. When the value is greater than 0.5, the model performs better than the random prediction, otherwise, the model is uninformative. Since AUC is independent of threshold and misclassification costs, it is very suitable for imbalanced and cost-sensitive issues.

The definition of cost-sensitive error rate depends on the cost-sensitive matrix shown in the table below. $cost_{ij}$ represents the cost of predicting the i-th sample as the j-th sample. Generally, the value of $cost_{ii}$ is 0. $cost_{01}$ represents the cost of predicting the normal sample as the suspicious sample, and $cost_{10}$ is the cost of predicting the pathologic sample as the normal sample, and $cost_{20}$ means the cost of predicting the suspicious sample as the normal sample (Table 4).

Table 4. Matrix of three classification cost

True class	Prediction class		
	0	1	2
Class 0	0	$cost_{01}$	$cost_{02}$
Class 1	$cost_{10}$	0	$cost_{12}$
Class 2	$cost_{20}$	$cost_{21}$	0

The total cost is expected to be minimized in the condition of unequal cost,

$$E(f; D; cost)\frac{1}{m}(\sum_{x_i \in D_0} \prod (f(x_i) \neq y_i) \times \cos t_{01} + \sum_{x_i \in D_0} \prod (f(x_i) \neq y_i) \times \cos t_{02}$$
$$+ \sum_{x_i \in D_1} \prod (f(x_i) \neq y_i) \times \cos t_{10} + \sum_{x_i \in D_1} \prod (f(x_i) \neq y_i) \times \cos t_{12}$$
$$+ \sum_{x_i \in D_2} \prod (f(x_i) \neq y_i) \times \cos t_{20} + \sum_{x_i \in D_2} \prod (f(x_i) \neq y_i) \times \cos t_{21}) \qquad (8)$$

where D_0 is class 0, D_1 is class 1, D_2 is class 2.

But in practice, $cost_{10}$ and $cost_{20}$ are more sensitive, so as a condition of (8), $cost_{10}$ and $cost_{20}$ should achieve the largest weight as well as the smallest cost.

$$E_a(f; D; cost)\frac{1}{m}\left(\sum_{x_i \in D_1} \prod (f(x_i) \neq y_i) \times \cos t_{10} \sum_{x_i \in D_2} \prod \frac{(f(x_i) \neq y_i)}{\times \cos t_{20}}\right) \qquad (9)$$

3.4 Experiment Design

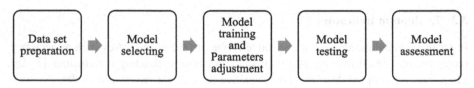

Fig. 3. Research roadmap

Ten-fold Cross validation was used to evaluate the performance of the GBDT combined learning model and measures mentioned above were calculated from 10 runs. Single models such as KNN, LR, SVM, DT are involved in the contrast experiment, so as combined learning models like Stacking, AdaBoost, GBDT, RF [17] (Fig. 3).

3.5 Experiment Results

AUC values. The average AUC for each model under 10-fold cross-validation is shown in Table 5. below.

Table 5. AUC values of different models

Model	AUC (avg)
kNN	0.8913
LR	0.8585
SVM	0.6065
DT	0.9398
Staking	0.8911
AdaBoost	0.9484
GBDT	0.9684
RF	0.9514

1. The GBDT combined learning model proposed in this paper has the highest value of AUC, which indicated the best predicting performance.
2. The prediction effect of the combined learning model is better than that of the single model. The reason is that Ensemble Learning can reduce the variance of the prediction results and improve the generalization ability of the model.

Cost Sensitive Error Rates. Taking the cost-sensitive error rate as an evaluation indicator, Table 6. shows the experimental results. Avg is the average of the cross-validation results in 10 times. We set the cost ratio on the basis of sample counts. According to the actual condition, we may predict the pathologic samples as suspicious samples, or judge the suspicious as pathologic. Patients need further examination, so the cost is lowest and the same. Judging normal as suspicious or normal as pathologic would cause a series of problems for the fetuses and pregnant women, and the cost is high. In the end, if the pathologic is predicted as normal or the suspicious as normal, it will miss the best intervention and treatment time for the fetus. Similarly, it is even more serious to predict the pathologic as normal than the suspicious as normal, so the cost rises. We set the cost ratios based on the analysis above:

$$cost_{01}:cost_{02}:cost_{10}:cost_{12}:cost_{20}:cost_{21} = 1:1:3:0.5:4:0.5$$

From the comparison of the models in Table 6, it can be seen that the cost-sensitive error rate of Decision Tree, Stacking, Adaptive Boosting (AdaBoost), and combined learning model of Gradient Boosting Decision Tree (GBDT) has been reduced, and the result of combined learning model of GBDT is better.

The above results intuitively reflect that GBDT has better effect than other models.

Table 6. Cost sensitive error rates of different models

Model	ER (%)	CSER (%)
KNN	7.75	8.25
LR	10.80	11.2
SVM	19.48	27.15
DT	7.75	5.9
Stacking	6.81	5.1
AdaBoost	9.62	8.3
GBDT	3.29	2.9
RF	3.76	4.5

Note: ER is error rate. CSER is cost sensitive error rate

4 Conclusion

Considering the imbalance of the CTG data, a combined learning model based on GBDT was applied to the experiment. Several balanced subsets were generated by splitting the training data with random under-sampling and utilized for training several base classifiers. Integrating the base classifiers ensured the integrity of the global sample information, and under-sampling enabled a random data distribution, which contributed to a better prediction model aiming at imbalanced data. In terms of improving performance, adopting GBDT as the base classifier and employing the method of samples and features to train model also conduce to a well-performed GBDT combined learning model. The experiment compared the AUC and cost-sensitive error rate of the GBDT combined learning model and the current common prediction model on the CTG data set of UCI. The results showed that the prediction model proposed in this paper has a higher AUC and a smaller cost-sensitive error rate. These improvements can play an important role in the prediction of fetal monitoring and protect the safety of mothers and fetuses.

Acknowledgment. This work is partially supported by a grant from the Natural Science Foundation of Guangdong Province (grant no. 2018A0303130055), the Opening Project of Guangdong Province Key Laboratory of Big Data Analysis and Processing at Sun Yat-sen University (No. 202001) and the Social Science Project of Guangzhou University of Chinese Medicine grants 2020SKYB05 and 2020SKXK25.

References

1. China Statistical Yearbook: China Statistical Publishing House, Beijing (2017)
2. Alfirevic, Z., Devane, D., Gyte, G.M.L.: Continuous cardiotocography (CTG) as a form of electronic fetal monitoring (EFM) for fetal assessment during labour. Cochrane Database Syst. Rev. **5**(3), CD006066 (2006)
3. Li-Jun, W., Ming-Quan, C., An-Bo, L.: Study of continuous electronic heart rate monitoring during delivery period in rural district. Chin. J. Obstet. Gynecol. Pediatrics (2007)

4. Umstad, M.P.: The predictive value of abnormal fetal heart rate patterns in early labour. Aust. N. Z. J. Obstet. Gynaecol. **33**(2), 145–149 (2010)
5. Fergus, P., Hussain, A., Al-Jumeily, D., Huang, D.-S., Bouguila, N.: Classification of cae-sarean section and normal vaginal deliveries using foetal heart rate signals and advanced machine learning algorithms. Biomed. Eng. Online **16**(1), 89 (2017)
6. Ocak, H., Ertunc, H.M.: Prediction of fetal state from the cardiotocogram recordings using adaptive neuro -fuzzy inference s ystems. Neural Comput. Appl. **23**(6), 1583–1589 (2013)
7. Ocak, H.: A medical decision support system based on support vector machines and the genetic algorithm for the evaluation of fetal well-being. J. Med. Syst. **37**(2), 9913 (2013)
8. Yılmaz, E.: Fetal state assessment from cardiotocogram data using artificial neural networks. J. Med. Biol. Eng. **36**(6), 820–832 (2016)
9. Huang, M.L., Hsu, Y.Y.: Fetal distress prediction using discriminant analysis, decision tree, and artificial neural network. J. Biomed. Sci. Eng. **05**(9) (2012)
10. Sundar, C., Chitradevi, M., Geetharamani G.: Classification of cardiotocogram data using neural network based machine learning technique. Int. J. Comput. Appl. **47**(14), 19–25 (2013)
11. Karabulut, E.M., Ibrikci, T.: Analysis of cardiotocogram data for fetal distress determination by decision tree based adaptive boosting approach. J. Comput. Commun. **02**(9), 32–37 (2014)
12. Arif, M.: Classification of cardiotocograms using random forest classifier and selection of important features from cardiotocogram signal. Biomater. Biomech. Bioeng. **2**(3), 173–183 (2015)
13. Yılmaz, E.: Determination of fetal state from cardiotocogram using LS-SVM with particle swarm optimization and binary decision tree. Comput. Math. Methods Med. **2013**(2), 487179 (2013)
14. Ravindran, S., Jambek, A.B., Muthusamy, H., et al.: A novel clinical decision support system using improved adaptive genetic algorithm for the assessment of fetal well-being. Comput. Math. Methods Med. **2015** (2015)
15. Lessmann, S., Baesens, B., Scow, H.V., et al.: Benehmarking state-of-the-art classification algorithms for credit scoring: an update of research. Eur. J. Oper. Res. **247**(1), 1(32) (2015)
16. Krebs, H.B., Petres, R.E.: Clinical application of a scoring system for evaluation of antepartum fetal heart rate monitoring. Am. J. Obstet. Gynecol. **130**(7), 765–72 (1978)
17. Sahin, H., Subasi, A.: Classification of the cardiotocogram data for anticipation of fetal risks using machine learning techniques. Appl. Soft Comput. **33**(C), 231–238 (2015)
18. Chawla, N.V., Japkowicz, N., Kotcz, A.: Editorial: special issue on learning from imbalanced data sets. ACM SIGKDD Explor. News·Lett. **6**(1), 1–6 (2004)

A Lattice-Based Anonymous Authentication for Privacy Protection of Medical Data

Yang Cui, Siqi Yu, and Fengyin Li[(✉)]

School of Computer Science, Qufu Normal University, Rizhao 276826, China

Abstract. With the process of informatization of medical institutions, the issue of protecting patients' personal privacy information has also attracted more and more attention. At the same time, the development of quantum computers has also caused people's attention post-quantum encryption algorithms. Lattice-based cryptography is a typical post-quantum encryption algorithm. In order to protect the privacy of medical information in the quantum computer environment, a medical information collection model that resists quantum attacks is proposed in this paper. The model is based on lattice-based anonymous identity authentication scheme. The lattice-based anonymous authentication scheme proposed in this paper has proved its security in the random oracle model.

Keywords: Lattice-based · Anonymous authentication · Privacy protection · Medical data

1 Introduction

Based on lattice-based anonymous authentication technology, this paper proposes a medical data collection model that can effectively resist quantum attacks. The anonymous authentication scheme in this article is mainly based on the identity authentication scheme of Lyu09 [20]. Another part of the contribution of this article is the application of anonymous authentication schemes in the medical data environment.

1.1 Background

By using technologies such as big data and cloud platforms, the information processing capabilities of the medical system have been improved. At the same time, the efficiency of medical data processing and utilization has been improved [1]. The information obtained by medical data processing can play an important role in drug research and clinical treatment [2]. Therefore, the collection and utilization of medical data has a good development prospect.

However, medical data often involves some personal privacy information. In many cases, the process of information collection and use also brings the risk of

Y. Tan et al. (Eds.): DMBD 2021, CCIS 1454, pp. 228–238, 2021.
https://doi.org/10.1007/978-981-16-7502-7_25

privacy leakage. Therefore, in order to ensure the patient's private information will not be maliciously leaked in the process of the application of data analysis in medicine. We have to use some anonymous authentication.

Most of the existing anonymous authentication schemes are based on the integer factorization problem and the discrete logarithm problem. However, Shor proposed an effective quantum algorithm to solve these two difficult problems in 1997 [3]. With the development of quantum computers [4], existing anonymous authentication schemes have some security problems. Existing quantum algorithms do not have polynomial time solving algorithms for difficult problems on lattices. In 2020, there are 26 candidate schemes in the second round of the NIST post-quantum cryptography standardization process screening results, among which there are 12 kinds of lattice-based schemes [5].

1.2 Contribution

The main contribution of this paper is as follows:

1. We constructed a lattice-based anonymous authentication scheme, and its security is proved in the random oracle model.
2. We apply the aforementioned anonymous authentication scheme to the process of collecting medical information in a big data environment to ensure anonymity and privacy during the collection process. At the same time, theoretical quantum security is guaranteed.

1.3 Organization

The survey is organized as follows:

- The first section introduces the motivation, main background and contribution of this paper;
- The second section is about the related work;
- The third section is preliminaries, mainly about the definitions and properties of the lattice, the security model, and the random oracle;
- The fourth section introduces the medical data collection model proposed in this paper;
- The fifth section is the core work of this paper. This section introduces a lattice-based anonymous authentication scheme and proves its safety.
- The last section is Conclusions.

2 Related Work

According to the main content of this paper, the following mainly introduces the research status of lattice Cryptography (especially lattice signature).

In 1996, Ajtai groundbreakingly proved the reduction from the lattice problem in the average case to the lattice problem in the worst case [6]. This proof laid the foundation for the research of lattice cryptography. The early encryption schemes GGH [7] and NTRU [8, 9] both had signature versions, but they were later found to be unable to achieve security proofs, and both had certain flaws. Lattice signature schemes can be divided into two categories. One type lattice-based signature scheme is the hash-and-sign structure. The representative of this type is the application of the trapdoor generation function proposed by Gentry et al. [10]. This type of scheme is to use the trapdoor generation algorithm to generate the key, and the sampling algorithm to construct the signature. After scheme of Gentry et al., there are many improved schemes for trapdoor generation algorithms, such as [11]. In addition, there are various extended lattice signatures, such as identity-based signatures [12]. Another type of lattice-based signature scheme is Fiat-Shamir structure. Representative work is "lattice-based signature without trapdoor" (Lyu12 [13]). In fact, most of this type of scheme are constructed by Lyubashevsky et al. The lattice signature scheme without trapdoor has advantages in both signature and key length. The anonymous authentication protocol in this paper is inspired by the schemes of Lyu et al. [14] And Chen et al. [15].

3   Preliminaries

In this section, we will introduce some basic knowledge [18] related to the scheme in this paper.

3.1   Notations

The notations used in this paper will be presented in the form of tables (Table 1).

Table 1. Symbol description

Notations	Description
$\mathbb{R}, \mathbb{Z}$	Set of real numbers (integers)
k	Security parameter
R	A degree-n polynomial ring of the form $R = \mathbb{Z}[X]/(f(X))$
R_q	$R_q := R/_qR = \mathbb{Z}_q[X]/(f(X))$
D	A subset of R_q
$poly(n)$	Polynomial order of n
mpk, msk	Master public key and master private key of PKI
id	Identity of user
S_{id}	Private key of Signer
μ	Message
σ	Signature of message (in sampling and Gaussian distribution, it is the standard deviation)

Theorem 1. *RejectionSample(zS, σ, k) [14]:*

1. With the probability $\frac{D_\sigma^k(z)}{M \cdot D_{S,\sigma}^k(z)}$, *output 1, Else output 0.*

3.2   Lattice

Definition 1. *Lattice [19]*
If $B = (b_1, b_2, \ldots, b_m)$ by R^n is composed of m linearly independent vectors, then $\mathcal{L}(B)$ is defined as the linear combination of all integer coefficients of this group of vectors, denoted as

$$\Lambda = \mathcal{L}(B) = \left\{ \sum_{i=1}^{m} x_i b_i \,|\, x_i \in \mathbb{Z} \right\} \tag{1}$$

Let n be the dimension of the lattice $\mathcal{L}(B)$, m is the rank, and B is a set of bases of the lattice.

Definition 2. *(Approximate Shortest Vector Problem (SVPγ)) [18]*
Given a basis B of an n-dimensional lattice $\mathcal{L} = \mathcal{L}(B)$, find a nonzero vector $v \in \mathcal{L}$ for which $|v| \leq \gamma(n) \cdot \lambda_1 \mathcal{L}$

3.3   Lyubashevsky's Hash Functions

Definition 3. *Family of hash functions [15]*
For $D \subset R$ and any integer m, $\mathcal{H}(R, D, m) = \{h_A : h_A(Z) = A \cdot Z, Z \in R^m, Z \in D^m\}$ is the hash function family, where all operations are executed in the ring $Zp[x]/ < x^n + 1 >$. Given an element $h \in \mathcal{H}(R, D, m)$, for any y, $z$in R^m and $c \in R$, two equations, i.e., $h(Y + Z) = h(Y) + h(Z)$ and $h(Yc) = h(Y)c$, hold.

Definition 4. *Collision problem Col(h, D)*
Given $D \subset R$ and an element $h \in \mathcal{H}(R, D, m)$, the goal of Col(h, D) is to find two distinct vectors $z_1, z_2 \in D^m$ such that $h(z_1) = h(z_2)$.

Theorem 2. *(Lyubashevsky, 2009)*
If there exists a polynomial time algorithm that can solve the Col(h, D) problem for a random $h \subset H(R, D, m)$ with a non-negligible probability, then there exists a polynomial time algorithm that can solve $SVP_\gamma(\Lambda)$ for every $(x^n + 1)$-cyclic lattice Λ, where $\gamma = 16dmn \log^2 n$.

4   A Lattice-Based Anonymous Authentication Scheme

In this part, we mainly introduce a lattice-based anonymous authentication scheme. The main content is about anonymous authentication, correctness, and security.

4.1   Construction

In this section, we propose a lattice-based anonymous authentication scheme this scheme consists of the following five parts: GenKey(1^λ), Extract(id, msk), VerifyKey(S_{id}, Q_{id}), Sign(μ, S_{ID}, Q_{ID}), Verify(mpk, σ, μ). The random oracle used in this scheme is defined by Definition 3.

GenKey(1^λ): Genkey algorithm is used to generate medical institution's master public key (mpk) and master private key (msk).

$$
\begin{aligned}
&\text{GenKey}(1^\lambda) = (\text{mpk,msk}) \\
&1.\text{Generate } \hat{s} \xleftarrow{\$} D_s^m \\
&2.\text{Generate } h \xleftarrow{\$} \mathcal{H}(R, D, m), S \leftarrow h(\hat{s}) \; ; \\
&3.\text{mpk} \leftarrow S, \text{msk} \leftarrow \hat{s}.
\end{aligned}
$$

Extract(id,msk): Extract algorithm is used to generate the public key(Q_{id}) and private key(S_{id}) of the signing user.

$$
\begin{aligned}
&\text{Extract}(\text{id,msk}) = (S_{id}) \\
&1.\text{Computer } e := h(id); (id \in D^m) \\
&2.\text{Computer } S_{id} := \hat{s} \cdot e + id.
\end{aligned}
$$

VerifyKey(S_{id}, Q_{id}): VerifyKey algorithm is used to verify whether the received key is valid.

$$
\begin{aligned}
&\text{VerifyKey}(S_{id}, id) = (\text{yes or no}) \\
&1.\text{Verify } h(S_{id}) \stackrel{?}{=} S \cdot h(id) + h(id).
\end{aligned}
$$

Sign(μ, S_{ID}, Q_{ID}): The signer signs the message using the following algorithm.

$$
\begin{aligned}
&\text{Sign}(\mu, S_{id}, id) = \sigma \\
&1.\text{Generate } y \leftarrow D^m, \text{computer } Y := h(y); \\
&2.\text{Computer } c := H(\mu, Y); \\
&3.\text{Computer } z := S_{id} \cdot c + y; \\
&4.\text{b} := \text{RejectionSample}(z, S_{id}); \\
&5.\text{If b} = 1, \text{Return } \sigma = (z, Y); \text{ else, return step 1.}
\end{aligned}
$$

Verify(mpk, σ, μ)=(yes or no): The verifier uses the following algorithm to verify the signature.

$$
\begin{aligned}
&\text{Verify}(\text{mpk}, \sigma, \mu) = (\text{yes or no}) \\
&1.\text{Computer } a = S \cdot h(id) \cdot H(\mu, Y) + h(id) \cdot H(\mu, Y) + Y; \\
&2.\text{Verify } h(z) \stackrel{?}{=} a.
\end{aligned}
$$

4.2   Correctness

If the following equation holds, then the scheme is obviously correct.

$$
\begin{aligned}
h(z) &= h(S_{id} \cdot c + y) \\
&= h(S_{id} \cdot c) + h(y) \\
&= h(\hat{s} \cdot e + y) \cdot c + Y \\
&= S \cdot h(id) \cdot H(\mu, Y) + h(id) \cdot H(\mu, Y) + Y
\end{aligned}
\tag{2}
$$

4.3   Security

In order to prove the security of the signature scheme, we construct two hybrid sign schemes.

HybridSign1$(\mu, S_{id}, h())$
1. Choose $Y \leftarrow D^m$;
2. Choose $c \leftarrow R^m$;
3. Computer $Z \leftarrow S_{id} \cdot c + y$;
4. With the probability $\frac{D_\sigma^m(z)}{M \cdot D_{S_{id}c,\sigma}^m(z)}$ output signature $\sigma = (z, Y)$;

program $H(\mu, Y) = c$.

HybridSign2$(\mu, S_{id}, h())$
1. Choose $Y \leftarrow D^m$;
2. Choose $z \leftarrow R^m$;
3. With the probability $\frac{1}{M}$ output signature $\sigma = (z, Y)$;
program $H(\mu, Y) \cdot h(S_{id}) = h(z) - Y$.

Theorem 3. *If there is a polynomial time adversary, it can attack the scheme with a probability of ϵ. The adversary can perform at most t_1 queries to the random oracle, t_2 queries to extract orcale and t_3 queries to sign orcale.($t = t_1 + t_2 + t_3$) Then we can construct a simulator B, which can use the adversary's ability to solve the SVP_γ roblem.*

Proof. For the proof of Theorem 3, we choose to use a set of lemmas and Theorem 2. Lemma 1 proves that the output of our scheme is indistinguishable from that of HybridSign2. Lemma 2 proves that if there is an adversary who can break the HybridSign2 scheme, then the adversary's ability can be used to solve the Collision problem. According to the conclusion of Theorem 2, if the adversary can break through the HybridSign2, the SVP_γ problem can be solved. The structure of proof is shown in Fig. 1.

Lemma 1. *The reduction from Sign to HybridSign2. The real signature scheme and HybridSign2 are indistinguishable.*

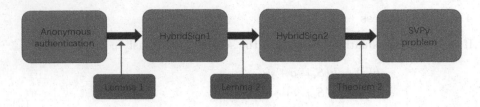

Fig. 1. The structure of proof

Proof. The real signature scheme and HybridSign1 differ only in the generation process of Y and C. The advantage that distinguishes output of real signature scheme and output of HybridSign1 is at most $t_3(t) \cdot 2^{-n+1}$. The statistical distances [17]of output by HybridSign1 and HybridSign2 are indistinguishable. So, We can use HybridSign2 to replace the real signature scheme for security proof.

Lemma 2. *The reduction from HybridSign2 to Collision problem. Assuming that there is an adversary $\mathcal{A}$ that can break through HybridSign2 with the probability of ϵ, then there is a simulator $\mathcal{B}$ that can use the ability of adversary $\mathcal{A}$ to solve the Collision problem with the probability of $\frac{\epsilon}{2}$.*

Proof. The proof is mainly divided into five parts: Setup, Random oracle query, Extract query, Signature query, and Forgery.

Setup: The simulator $\mathcal{B}$ sets the system parameters.

Setup(1^λ) = (mpk,msk)
1.Generate $\hat{s} \xleftarrow{\$} D_s^m$
2.Generate $h \xleftarrow{\$} \mathcal{H}(R, D, m), S \leftarrow h(\hat{s})$;
3.mpk $\leftarrow S$,msk$\leftarrow \hat{s}$.

Random oracle query: The simulator $\mathcal{B}$ allows adversary $\mathcal{A}$ to query random oracles.

Random oracle query:
1.$\mathcal{B}$ constructs an empty list, each line contains three items (μ, Y, c).
2.$\mathcal{A}$ query the random oracle. If the message μ^* to be queried is in the list ,$\mathcal{B}$ will directly take it out and send it to $\mathcal{A}$.
3.Adversary $\mathcal{A}$ query the random oracle. If the message μ^* to be queried is not in the list , $\mathcal{B}$ will randomly select a $Y \in D_m$ and program $H(\mu, Y) = c$. Send the result to the adversary $\mathcal{A}$ and add the record to the list.

Extract query: The simulator $\mathcal{B}$ allows adversary $\mathcal{A}$ to query Extract orcale.

Extract query:
1.$\mathcal{B}$ constructs an empty list, each line contains three items (id, e, S_{id}).
2.$\mathcal{A}$ query the Extract orcale.
- If the identity id^* to be queried is in the list, $\mathcal{B}$ will directly take it out and send it to the adversary $\mathcal{A}$.
- If the identity id^* to be queried is not in the list, $\mathcal{B}$ will compute $e = h(id)$, and $S_i d = \hat{s} \cdot e + id$. $\mathcal{B}$ send the result to $\mathcal{A}$ and add the record to the list.

Sign query: The simulator $\mathcal{B}$ allows adversary $\mathcal{A}$ to query Sign orcale.

Sign query:
1.$\mathcal{B}$ constructs an empty list, each line contains five items (μ, id, z, Y, c).
2.$\mathcal{A}$ query the sign orcale. If the message μ^* to be queried is in the "Random oracle query" list, and the id id^* to be queried is in the "Extract query" list. $\mathcal{B}$ will directly take it's $c, Y, e, S_i d$ out, compute $z = S_i d \cdot c + Y$. After this, $\mathcal{B}$ send (z, Y) to the adversary $\mathcal{A}$.
3.If,id or μ is ont been queried. $\mathcal{B}$ will call the oracle, add the corresponding record to the list. After this, $\mathcal{B}$ compute $z = S_{id} \cdot c + Y$, and send (z, Y) to the adversary $\mathcal{A}$.

Forgery: Assume that the adversary can forge a signature σ' and satisfy $Z' = S_{id} \cdot c' + Y$.

Bcause of this scheme is perfectly witness-indistinguishable [20](if there are two different legal secret keys, the adversary cannot tell which key is used for encryption). There is another $s'_{id} \in D_s^m$ with probability $1 - 2^{-128}$ such that $h(s_{id}) = h(s'_{id})$, for a randomly-picked $s_{id} \in D_s^m$.

So, we can extract a collision in h from the signature of adversary. As we know $y' = z - S'_{id}c = y + S_{id}c - S'_{id}c = y + (S_{id} - S'_{id})c$. Due to the above-mentioned relationship between S and s'and s, we can draw the following conclusions, $s \neq s' \longrightarrow S_{id} \neq S'_{id} \longrightarrow y \neq y'$. In summary, we have at least a half probability of getting a hash function collision (y, y'). Because the adversary's used the s or s' for forging signature with the probability of $\frac{1}{2}$ (s and s' are indistinguishable).

The Lemma 2 is proved.

5   Model of Medical Data Collection

This section introduces a model of medical data collection, there are three main entities in this model: patients, medical institutions, and databases.

5.1   Problems in Quantum Computer Environment

In the process of data transmission, the plaintext of data is not directly transmitted in the process of data transmission. In this process, a certain encryption algorithm needs to be used to encrypt the message. The information transmitted in the channel is ciphertext of data. The advantage of this is that even if the Eve(eavesdropper) steals the ciphertext through the channel, he still cannot obtain information from it.

But most of the existing encryption algorithms are not resistant to quantum attacks. Therefore, if the current eavesdropper is an adversary with quantum computing capabilities. At this time, most of the existing encryption algorithms cannot guarantee that the adversary cannot obtain information from the ciphertext. This makes it impossible to guarantee the privacy of the patient's personal information during the transmission process. In order to protect the personal privacy of patients, we propose a lattice-based anonymous authentication scheme to resist quantum attacks.

5.2   Medical Data Collection Model

In the medical data collection model proposed here, we assume that all patients are honest. In other words, there is no malicious adversary who pretends to be a patient and adds wrong information to the database to carry out similar data poisoning attacks.

In this model, the medical institution generates a pair of master keys (mpk, msk) in first. After having msk, the medical institution can generate a key S_{id} for the patient's pseudonym id. The pseudonym of the patient is generated by himself, and even medical institutions cannot know the correspondence between the true identity of a patient and his pseudonymsid. After receiving the key pair from the medical institution, the patient can verify the validity of the key S_{id}. After confirming that the key S_{id} is valid, use S_{id} to sign the medical data. The message is sent to the database with the signature. The database can get the id the pseudonym of patient from the medical institution. The database can verify the signature and add the message to the database after confirming that the signature is legal. This completes a collection of medical data.

The model introduction diagram is shown in Fig. 2.

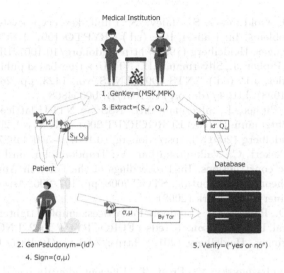

Fig. 2. Medical data collection model

6   Conclusions

This paper proposes a lattice-based anonymous authentication scheme, and reduces its security to the difficulty of the approximating-SVP problem in the random oracle model. Another work of this paper is to construct a medical data collection model based on the anonymous authentication scheme to protect the privacy of patients.

Future Work: In the medical information collection model, we set the assumption that all patients are honest. This assumption can be eliminated using zero-knowledge proof or other methods. We will solve this problem in the next work.

References

1. Tang, W., Ren, J., Zhang, Y.: Enabling trusted and privacy-preserving healthcare services in social media health networks. IEEE Trans. Multimedia (2018)
2. Obermeyer, Z., Emanuel, E.J.: Predicting the future - big data, machine learning, and clinical medicine. N. Engl. J. Med. **375**(13), 1216–1219 (2016)
3. Shor, P.W.: Polynomial-time algorithms for prime factorization and discrete logarithms on a quantum computer. SIAM Rev. **41**(2), 303–332 (1999)
4. Zhong, H.-S., et al.: Quantum computational advantage using photons. Science **370**(6523), 1460–1463 (2020)
5. Moody, D., et al.: Status report on the second round of the NIST post-quantum cryptography standardization process, 2020–07–22 (2020)
6. Ajtai, M.: Generating hard instances of lattice problems (extended abstract). In: Proceedings of the Twenty-Eighth Annual ACM Symposium on Theory of Computing, STOC 1996, pp. 99–108. Association for Computing Machinery, New York (1996)

7. Goldreich, O., Goldwasser, S., Halevi, S.: Public-key cryptosystems from lattice reduction problems. In: Kaliski, B.S. (ed.) CRYPTO 1997. LNCS, vol. 1294, pp. 112–131. Springer, Heidelberg (1997). https://doi.org/10.1007/BFb0052231

8. Hoffstein, J., Pipher, J., Silverman, J.H.: NTRU: a ring-based public key cryptosystem. In: Buhler, J.P. (ed.) ANTS 1998. LNCS, vol. 1423, pp. 267–288. Springer, Heidelberg (1998). https://doi.org/10.1007/BFb0054868

9. Hoffstein, J., Pipher, J., Silverman, J.H.: NSS: an NTRU lattice-based signature scheme. In: Pfitzmann, B. (ed.) EUROCRYPT 2001. LNCS, vol. 2045, pp. 211–228. Springer, Heidelberg (2001). https://doi.org/10.1007/3-540-44987-6_14

10. Gentry, C., Peikert, C., Vaikuntanathan, V.: Trapdoors for hard lattices and new cryptographic constructions. In: Proceedings of the Fortieth Annual ACM Symposium on Theory of Computing, STOC 2008, pp. 197–206. Association for Computing Machinery, New York (2008)

11. Micciancio, D., Peikert, C.: Trapdoors for lattices: simpler, tighter, faster, smaller. In: Pointcheval, D., Johansson, T. (eds.) EUROCRYPT 2012. LNCS, vol. 7237, pp. 700–718. Springer, Heidelberg (2012). https://doi.org/10.1007/978-3-642-29011-4_41

12. Ducas, L., Lyubashevsky, V., Prest, T.: Efficient identity-based encryption over NTRU lattices. In: Sarkar, P., Iwata, T. (eds.) ASIACRYPT 2014. LNCS, vol. 8874, pp. 22–41. Springer, Heidelberg (2014). https://doi.org/10.1007/978-3-662-45608-8_2

13. Lyubashevsky, V.: Lattice signatures without trapdoors. In: Pointcheval, D., Johansson, T. (eds.) EUROCRYPT 2012. LNCS, vol. 7237, pp. 738–755. Springer, Heidelberg (2012). https://doi.org/10.1007/978-3-642-29011-4_43

14. Lyubashevsky, V.: Digital signatures based on the hardness of ideal lattice problems in all rings. In: Cheon, J.H., Takagi, T. (eds.) ASIACRYPT 2016. LNCS, vol. 10032, pp. 196–214. Springer, Heidelberg (2016). https://doi.org/10.1007/978-3-662-53890-6_7

15. Chen, J.S., Hu, Y.P., Liang, H.M., Gao, W.: Novel efficient identity-based signature on lattices. Frontiers Inf. Technol. Electron. Eng. **22**, 244–250 (2020)

16. Bellare, M., Neven, G.: Multi-signatures in the plain public-key model and a general forking lemma. In: Proceedings of the 13th ACM Conference on Computer and Communications Security, CCS 2006, pp. 390–399. Association for Computing Machinery, New York (2006)

17. Aguilar Melchor, C., Bettaieb, S., Boyen, X., Fousse, L., Gaborit, P.: Adapting Lyubashevsky's signature schemes to the ring signature setting. In: Youssef, A., Nitaj, A., Hassanien, A.E. (eds.) AFRICACRYPT 2013. LNCS, vol. 7918, pp. 1–25. Springer, Heidelberg (2013). https://doi.org/10.1007/978-3-642-38553-7_1

18. Peikert, C.: A decade of lattice cryptography. Found. Trends Theor. Comput. Sci. **10**(4), 283–424 (2016)

19. Micciancio, D.: Lattice-based cryptography, pp. 713–715. Springer, Boston (2011)

20. Lyubashevsky, V.: Fiat-Shamir with aborts: applications to lattice and factoring-based signatures. In: Matsui, M. (ed.) ASIACRYPT 2009. LNCS, vol. 5912, pp. 598–616. Springer, Heidelberg (2009). https://doi.org/10.1007/978-3-642-10366-7_35

Defend Against Poisoning Attacks in Federated Learning

Changchang Zhu, Jiangtao Ge, and Yan Xu[✉]

School of Computer Science and Technology, Anhui University, Hefei, China
xuyan@ahu.edu.cn

Abstract. The rapid development of artificial intelligence not only brings convenience to people's lives, but also leads to many privacy leaks. In order to resolve the contradiction between data availability and privacy protection, Google proposed the framework of federated learning. In federated learning, local clients upload model update values to the server, and the server aggregates all update values to obtain a new global model. However malicious attackers can upload malicious update values to perform poisoning attacks, making the global model unavailable or introducing a backdoor. In this paper, we deploy an AutoEncoder on the server side to calculate the reconstruction error of model update values. According to the size of the reconstruction error, we remove malicious update values and retain benign update values. Finally, the server aggregates all benign update values to obtain a new global model. Experimental results show that our scheme can effectively defend against poisoning attacks.

Keywords: Federal learning · Poisoning attacks · AutoEncoder · Deep learning

1 Introduction

Deep learning has been widely used in many aspects of the society. While brings convenience deep learning also leads to many privacy leaks. As privacy become more and more concerned, several laws are introduced to protect users' private data, such as the EU's GDPR, which leads to the creation of data islands. In order to solve the contradiction between data availability and privacy protection, Shokr et al. [13] first proposed a distributed deep learning framework. The client trains the model locally, and then uploads the update value to the server. Google proposed a federated learning framework in 2017 [9], which includes a server and multiple clients. The server and clients train a global model collaboratively, and the final global model is obtained after multiple rounds of iterations.

Federated learning is proposed to protect users' private data, but it faces serious security problems. Recent studies have shown that federated learning is vulnerable to inference attacks [2,7,10,14] and poisoning attacks [3,6,8,12]. A malicious client can upload a malicious model update value to perform poisoning attack, causing the final global model to be unavailable or there is a backdoor. Many defense schemes against poisoning attacks have been proposed.

© Springer Nature Singapore Pte Ltd. 2021
Y. Tan et al. (Eds.): DMBD 2021, CCIS 1454, pp. 239–249, 2021.
https://doi.org/10.1007/978-981-16-7502-7_26

Auror [12] found the indicator features of the abnormal model, and then used k-means clustering to distinguish between normal and abnormal. But it has the lower detection accuracy. Krum [5] calculated the Euclidean distance between each gradient, and the sum of the gradient distances to specified neighbors, and finally select the gradient with the smallest distance sum as the aggregation value. The algorithm only retains one gradient as the aggregation result in each round. Obviously, it discards many benign update values, which results in lower model accuracy and longer training time. Recently, Zhao et al. [15] delegated the detection task to some selected clients. These clients test other clients' model updates and send the feedback results to the server. This scheme has the problem that malicious clients may report false results. FoolsGold [6] used cosine similarity to judge whether the update value is normal or abnormal, but it can be evaded by a single-client attack or by decomposing the update value as an orthogonal vector.

In this paper, we propose a defense scheme with higher detection accuracy, which can defend against targeted poisoning attack and untargeted poisoning attack. The main idea of our defense scheme is to use an AutoEncoder on the server side to calculate the reconstruction error of clients' update values. According to the size of reconstruction error, we remove malicious update values, and then the server aggregates benign update values to obtain a new global model.

2   Background

In this section, we will introduce the background knowledge of federated learning, poisoning attacks, and AutoEncoder.

2.1   Federated Learning

Federated learning was proposed by Google in 2017 [9], which is used to train the model while protecting user privacy. Figure 1 illustrates the framework of federated learning. In federated learning, clients only need to train the model locally, and then upload the model update values to the server, without uploading their own data. Therefore, the privacy of clients can be protected. The training process of federated learning follows Eq. 1 and 2. In the t-th round, the server randomly selects N clients, and then sends the current round's global model M_t to the selected clients. These clients use their local dataset to train the local model $M_{t,i}$, then calculate and send the update value $u_{t,i}$ to the server. Finally, the server aggregates all update values to obtain a new global model M_{t+1} for the next round.

$$u_{t,i} = M_{t,i} - M_t \tag{1}$$

$$M_{t+1} = M_{t+1} + \frac{1}{N} \sum_{i=1}^{N} u_{t,i} \tag{2}$$

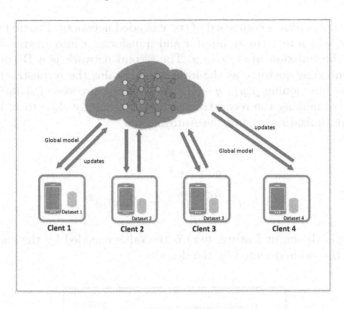

Fig. 1. The framework of federated learning

2.2   Poisoning Attacks

According to the attacker's purpose, poisoning attacks can be classified into two types: untargeted attack and targeted attack. Untargeted attack which reduce the test accuracy of the global model and target attack which achieve the attacker-chosen subtask, i.e. backdoor, while test accuracy of the main task is not greatly reduced. The attacks defended in this paper are as follows:

Sign-Flipping Attack [8]: Sign-flipping attack is an untargeted attack. The attacker modifies the sign of the update value so that the global model converges in the opposite direction. Assuming that the attacker's update value is $\tilde{u}$ after training the model, the attacker sends $u = \sigma\tilde{u}$ as the update value to the server. σ is a hyperparameter that controls the modification degree of the update value. Here we set $\sigma = -5$.

Label-Flipping Attack [4]: Label-flipping attack is a targeted attack. The attacker modifies the real label of a certain type of data into the target label, and then uses the modified data for training. For example, for handwritten digit recognition tasks, the attacker's subtask is to recognize handwritten digits 1 as 3, then the attacker changes the real label 1 to 3 during training, eventually the global model has a high probability of classifying handwritten digits 1 into 3.

2.3   AutoEncoder

AutoEncoder was first proposed by Rumelhart [11], which can remove redundant features while retaining effective features. The architecture of the AutoEncoder is shown in Fig. 2, which is composed of two cascaded networks. The first network is an Encoder, which receives an input x and transforms x into an encoding vector y through the function $h(x) : x \to y$. The second network is a Decoder, which takes the encoding vector y as the input, and obtains the reconstructed data $\tilde{x}$ through the functioning $g(y) : y \to \tilde{x}$. The training process of AutoEncoder is the process of making the reconstructed data $\tilde{x}$ infinitely close to x. Equation 5 shows the optimization goal of the AutoEncoder.

$$h : x \to y \tag{3}$$

$$g : y \to \tilde{x} \tag{4}$$

$$h, g = \frac{argmin}{h, g} \|x - g(h(x))\|^2 \tag{5}$$

where x is the input feature, $h(x)$ is the value encoded by the encoder, and $g(h(x))$ is the value decoded by the decoder.

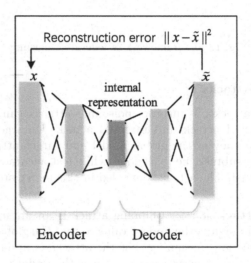

Fig. 2. The architecture of AutoEncoder

3   Adversary Goal

Subtask Accuracy: The attacker's goal is to achieve high prediction accuracy in specific target samples. Assuming the real label of samples are *source*, the attacker hopes to predict it as the specified *target*. The attacker's subtask accuracy is the ratio of the number of predicted *target* in the *source* to the total number of *source*, that is *subtask accuracy* $= \frac{N_{source \to target}}{N_{source}}$.

Main Task Accuracy: The prediction accuracy of the global model on the testset.

For sign-flipping attack, the attacker has no subtask, and the attacker's goal is to significantly reduce the accuracy of the main task. For label-flipping attack, the attacker must ensure that the accuracy of the main task is not greatly reduced while achieving the high accuracy of the subtask.

4   Method

We will give an overview of our proposed scheme in Sect. 4.1, and introduce the detail of scheme in Sect. 4.2. We summarize the important symbols in Table 1.

Table 1. Important symbols

Notation	Description
t	The t-th training round
C	The proportion of randomly selected clients
K	The total number of clients
S_N	The set of N clients for training
M_t	The global model in the t-th round
$u_{t,i}$	The update value of the i-th client in t-th round
$Dist$	The distance matrix
S_f	The set of f benign clients
$error_{t,i}$	The reconstruction error of the i-th client in t-th round
$threshold_t$	The threshold in the t-th round
D_{local}	The local dataset

4.1   Overview of the Proposed Scheme

If an attacker wants to carry out poisoning attacks, he needs to modify his dataset or model update value. Intuitively, the distribution difference between malicious update values and benign update values is greater than the distribution difference between benign update values. The stronger the attack effect is, the greater the difference is. Based on this observation, we propose deploying an AutoEncoder on the server to measure the distribution difference between update values. Since the update value is closely related to the model structure and difficult to be trained, we use the indicative features to train the AutoEncoder following the Ref. [12].

Figure 3 shows the framework of our defense scheme. The server first calculates the distance matrix for the update values of clients. The distance matrix represents the distance from each client to other clients. The server select the smallest f clients in the distance matrix as trusted update values, and then use the indicative features of these update values to train an AutoEncoder. The server removes malicious update values according to threshold. Finally, the server aggregates remaining update values to obtain a new global model.

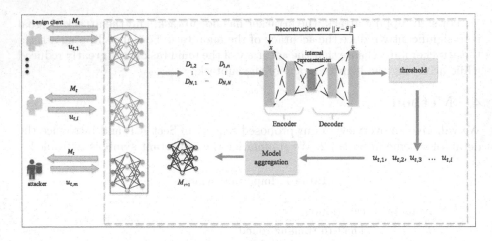

Fig. 3. The framework of the proposed scheme

4.2   Detail of the Proposed Scheme

Specifically, in each global round t, the server sends the global model M_t to a set of clients S_N. Theses clients use the global model M_t to train local models, calculate update values $(u_{t,1}, u_{t,2}, u_{t,3}, \ldots, u_{t,N})$ and send them to the server. The server calculates the distance matrix $Dist$ of client update values. $Dist_{i,j}$ represents the distance between the update value of client i and client j. Here we use Euclidean distance for the distance measurement method. The server then calculates the sum of the distances D_i from client i to other clients, that is $D_i = \sum_{j=1, i!=j}^{N} D_{i,j}$. The server selects f clients with the smallest D_i, and then uses indicative features of these clients' update values to train an AutoEncoder, which purpose is to make the AutoEncoder learn the distribution of benign update values. If the indication feature of the update value of the malicious client is input to the AutoEncoder, the output reconstruction error will be large [1]. Finally, the indication features of the remaining $N - f$ update values are sent to the AutoEncoder to calculate the reconstruction error. Then, we use the average reconstruction error of all update values as the threshold for each round. For update values that exceed the threshold are discarded directly, and the server only aggregates those update values that are below the threshold. Algorithm 1 describes the specific process of defense schem. The threshold is calculated as Eq. 6:

$$threshold_t = mean\left(error_{t,1},\ error_{t,2}, error_{t,3},\ \ldots\ error_{t,i}\right) \qquad (6)$$

where $error_{t,i}$ is the reconstruction error of the update value of the i-th client in the t-th round. The $threshold_t$ is the threshold of the t-th round.

Algorithm 1. The Defense Scheme

ServerExecutes:

1: **for** round $i = 1$ to T **do**
2:     $N = max(C * K, 1)$
3:     $S_N \leftarrow$ Randomly select N clients
4:     **for** each client $i \in S_N$ **do**
5:         $u_{t,i} \leftarrow$ ClientUpdate(i, M_t)
6:     **end for**
7: **end for**
8: $Dist \leftarrow Distance(u_{t,1}, u_{t,2}, \ldots, u_{t,i})$
9: $S_f \leftarrow$ select the first f clients with the smallest distance
10: Train the AutoEncoder by using the indicative features of S_f
11: $error_{t,i} \leftarrow$ Calculate the reconstruction error of each client in$(S_N - S_f)$
12: $threshold_t = mean(error_{t,1}, error_{t,2}, \ldots, error_{t,i})$
13: $S_M \leftarrow$ Clients whose reconstruction error is less than the $threshold_t$
14: $M_{t+1} = M_t + \frac{1}{M} \sum_{i=1}^{M} u_{t,i}$

ClientUpdate(i, M_t):

1: **for** iteration $k = 1$ to E **do**
2:     **for** batch data $B \in D_{local}$ **do**
3:         $M_{t,i} = M_t - \eta \bigtriangledown l(M_t, B)$
4:     **end for**
5: **end for**
6: $u_{t,i} = M_{t,i} - M_t$
7: **return** $u_{t,i}$ to server

5 Experimental Evaluation

To evaluate the proposed defense scheme, we conduct experiments on two well-known datasets MNIST and Fashion-MNIST. We follow the general setting of federated learning [9]. We set $K = 100$, $C = 30\%$, $T = 100$, and the proportion of attackers is 30%. We randomly assign samples of 8 categories to each client, randomly select 1000 samples for each category. Each client uses the SGD optimizer to train the local model, local epoch $E = 100$, local batch size $B = 50$, learning rate $\eta = 0.01$, $momentum = 0.9$. In this paper, we set $f = 10$. We use pytorch to implement our scheme and build CNN models for MNIST and Fashion-MNIST respectively.

5.1 Defend Sign-Flipping Attack

For sign-flipping attack, we evaluate the accuracy of the global model without defense and with defense. It can be seen from Fig. 4 that in 100 rounds, the accuracy of the global model in both MNIST and Fashion-MNIST is maintained at around 10%, and the model without defense is no longer available. After the defense, the accuracy of the global model reached 99.19% on MNIST and 92.06%

on Fashion-MNIST. It is shown that our defense scheme is very effective against sign-flipping attack.

5.2 Defend Label-Flipping Attack

For label-flipping attack, we evaluate the accuracy of the attackers' main tasks and subtasks. Figure 5 and Fig. 6 show the accuracy of MNIST and Fashion-MNIST without defense and with defense respectively. It can be seen from Fig. 5(a) and Fig. 6(a) that the subtask accuracy of the label-flipping attack is constantly changing and fluctuating, because the attackers cannot guarantee that they will be selected for training in each round. According to [8], even if the attacker cannot guarantee high subtask accuracy in each round, such attacks are still dangerous. It can be seen from Fig. 5(b) and Fig. 6(b) that the accuracy of the subtask in MNIST and Fashion-MNIST have been reduced to 0.11% and 7.43%, respectively, while the accuracy of the main task reached 99.07% and 91.08%, respectively. This shows that our method can effectively defend against label-flipping attack.

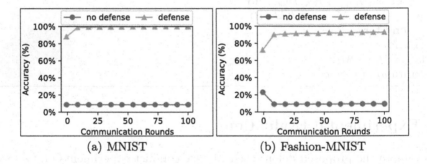

(a) MNIST   (b) Fashion-MNIST

Fig. 4. Accuracy of global model without and with defense.

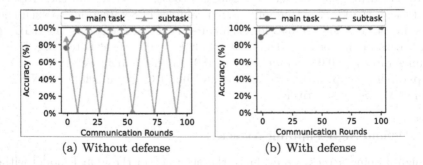

(a) Without defense   (b) With defense

Fig. 5. Accuracy of MNIST without and with defense.

5.3 Compared with Other Defense Methods

For sign-flipping attack and label-flipping attack, we evaluated the defense effects of different methods. The experimental results are shown in Table 2 and Table 3. It can be seen from these two tables that our defense method is superior to other methods. We analyze the reasons for this result. Auror [12] assumes that the attacker can perform attack in each round, but this is not consistent with the actual situation. Because attackers can't guarantee that they can be selected by the server in each round, Auror [12] will mistakenly classify benign clients as attackers, which leads to lower accuracy. Krum [5] only aggregates global model with an update value and discards other update values, which leads to the reduction of model accuracy.

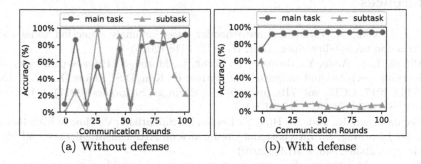

(a) Without defense   (b) With defense

Fig. 6. Accuracy of Fashion-MNIST without and with defense.

Table 2. The performance of different defense methods against sign-flipping attack

Dataset	MNIST	Fashion_MNIST
	Main task accuracy	Main task accuracy
Attacked	9.80%	9.94%
Auror [12]	98.05%	88.23%
Krum [5]	98.32%	88.54%
Ours	99.19%	92.06%

Table 3. The performance of different defense methods against label-flipping attack

Dataset	MNIST		Fashion-MNIST	
	Main task accuracy	Subtask accuracy	Main task accuracy	Subtask accuracy
Attacked	89.55%	99.48%	82.69%	90.20%
Auror [12]	95.46%	6.16%	87.26%	11.42%
Krum [5]	98.14%	0.41%	88.62%	9.41%
Ours	99.07%	0.11%	91.08%	7.43%

6   Conclusion

In this paper, we study two types of poisoning attacks in federated learning: untargeted attack and targeted attack. To defend against these two attacks, we propose a novel defense scheme. In the scheme, the server uses an AutoEncoder to calculate the reconstruction error of model update values. According to the reconstruction error, the server calculates a dynamic threshold, and then uses the threshold to remove malicious update values and retain benign update values. Finally, the server aggregates benign update values to obtain a new global model. Experiments show that our proposed defense scheme can effectively defend against poisoning attacks in federated learning.

References

1. An, J., Cho, S.: Variational autoencoder based anomaly detection using reconstruction probability. Spec. Lect. IE **2**(1), 1–18 (2015)
2. Phong, L.T., Aono, Y., Hayashi, T., Wang, L., Moriai, S.: Privacy-preserving deep learning: revisited and enhanced. In: Batten, L., Kim, D.S., Zhang, X., Li, G. (eds.) ATIS 2017. CCIS, vol. 719, pp. 100–110. Springer, Singapore (2017). https://doi.org/10.1007/978-981-10-5421-1_9
3. Bagdasaryan, E., Veit, A., Hua, Y., Estrin, D., Shmatikov, V.: How to backdoor federated learning. In: International Conference on Artificial Intelligence and Statistics, pp. 2938–2948. PMLR (2020)
4. Barreno, M., Nelson, B., Joseph, A.D., Tygar, J.D.: The security of machine learning. Mach. Learn. **81**(2), 121–148 (2010). https://doi.org/10.1007/s10994-010-5188-5
5. Blanchard, P., El Mhamdi, E.M., Guerraoui, R., Stainer, J.: Machine learning with adversaries: byzantine tolerant gradient descent. In: Proceedings of the 31st International Conference on Neural Information Processing Systems, pp. 118–128 (2017)
6. Fung, C., Yoon, C.J., Beschastnikh, I.: The limitations of federated learning in Sybil settings. In: 23rd International Symposium on Research in Attacks, Intrusions and Defenses ({RAID} 2020), pp. 301–316 (2020)
7. Hitaj, B., Ateniese, G., Perez-Cruz, F.: Deep models under the GAN: information leakage from collaborative deep learning. In: Proceedings of the 2017 ACM SIGSAC Conference on Computer and Communications Security, pp. 603–618 (2017)
8. Li, L., Xu, W., Chen, T., Giannakis, G.B., Ling, Q.: RSA: Byzantine-robust stochastic aggregation methods for distributed learning from heterogeneous datasets. In: Proceedings of the AAAI Conference on Artificial Intelligence, pp. 1544–1551 (2019)
9. McMahan, B., Moore, E., Ramage, D., Hampson, S., Arcas, B.A.: Communication-efficient learning of deep networks from decentralized data. In: Artificial Intelligence and Statistics, pp. 1273–1282. PMLR (2017)
10. Melis, L., Song, C., De Cristofaro, E., Shmatikov, V.: Exploiting unintended feature leakage in collaborative learning. In: 2019 IEEE Symposium on Security and Privacy (SP), pp. 691–706. IEEE (2019)
11. Rumelhart, D.E., Hinton, G.E., Williams, R.J.: Learning representations by backpropagating errors. Nature **323**(6088), 533–536 (1986)

12. Shen, S., Tople, S., Saxena, P.: AUROR: defending against poisoning attacks in collaborative deep learning systems. In: Proceedings of the 32nd Annual Conference on Computer Security Applications, pp. 508–519 (2016)
13. Shokri, R., Shmatikov, V.: Privacy-preserving deep learning. In: Proceedings of the 22nd ACM SIGSAC Conference on Computer and Communications Security, pp. 1310–1321 (2015)
14. Wang, Z., Song, M., Zhang, Z., Song, Y., Wang, Q., Qi, H.: Beyond inferring class representatives: user-level privacy leakage from federated learning. In: IEEE INFOCOM 2019-IEEE Conference on Computer Communications, pp. 2512–2520. IEEE (2019)
15. Zhao, L., et al.: Shielding collaborative learning: mitigating poisoning attacks through client-side detection. IEEE Trans. Dependable Secure Comput. (2020)

SOBC: A Smart Ocean Oriented Blockchain System for Cross-organizational Data Sharing

Yuchen Tian[1], Yansong Wang[1], Weiguo Tian[1], Haiwen Du[2], Xiaofang Li[3], and Dongjie Zhu[1(✉)]

[1] School of Computer Science and Technology, Harbin Institute of Technology, Weihai 264209, China
zhudongjie@hit.edu.cn
[2] School of Astronautics, Harbin Institute of Technology, Harbin 150001, China
[3] Department of Mathematics, Harbin Institute of Technology, Weihai 264209, China

Abstract. The refinement of the division of labor among organizations in the field of ocean exploration has made the cross-organizational data sharing a common phenomenon. Although the blockchain system can solve the trust problem among organizations, the unstable Underwater Wireless Sensor Network (UWSN) and high network traffic costs of satellite network hindered the application of blockchain in the smart ocean. In this paper, we propose the smart ocean blockchain architecture (SOBC) that supports high transaction concurrency and saves network traffic to achieve trusted cross-organizational data sharing in the ocean exploration field. First, we design the SOBC architecture and use channels to isolate different businesses to ensure data privacy and high transaction concurrency. Second, we design blockchain smart contracts to implement data transmission rules among regulatory agencies, data providers and data demanders to achieve trusted data sharing. Finally, we design a channel-based consistency protocol to reduce the network traffic consumption when nodes reconnect to the core network. We use data collected from the spectrum detection platform to verify the effect of SOBC by simulating the ocean exploration network conditions. The experimental results show that the SOBC is superior to the Ethereum-based blockchain architecture in transactions concurrency supporting. Besides, compared with Ethereum, the SOBC reduces network traffic consumption by 70% under unstable network conditions.

Keywords: Blockchain · Cross-organizational data sharing · Underwater wireless sensor network · Internet of underwater things · Ocean exploration · Smart ocean

1 Introduction

Exploration for valuable natural resources from oceans is now active in many parts of the world. As a source of ocean observing data, Underwater Wireless Sensor Networks (UWSN) is an important part of ocean exploration. However, complex underwater environments, such as tides, ocean currents, etc., may cause network unstable. It makes the

© Springer Nature Singapore Pte Ltd. 2021
Y. Tan et al. (Eds.): DMBD 2021, CCIS 1454, pp. 250–262, 2021.
https://doi.org/10.1007/978-981-16-7502-7_27

traditional Internet of Things (IoT) technology cannot provide stable data transmission efficiency in this scenario [11]. To address these problems, researchers built the Internet of Underwater Things (IoUT) using different communication technologies [3]. However, the division of labor in the field of ocean exploration is dispersed. Equipment development, equipment manufacturing, and detection works are mostly performed by different organizations. Most of the work needs wireless sensor data provided by other organizations, which makes cross-organizational data sharing in this field the norm [13]. Among them, the authority and accuracy of data affect the R&D and manufacturing process, and inaccurate and wrong data can cause significant economic losses. Besides, some data sharing involving security and economic benefits require authorization from the relevant regulatory agency. Therefore, how to establish a safe, reliable, and efficient data management framework is a hot topic in the field of ocean exploration. Most existing data management architectures in the field of IoT and ocean exploration use the method of cloud data centers [18, 19] or independent data server [14] to manage ocean observing data. Various organizations access the unified cloud platform for data management and behavior authorization. However, as a centralized architecture, the authority of each organization is opaque. Accounts and organizations with relevant rights can still modify data arbitrarily without the reluctance of other organizations, seriously threatening data security. Therefore, how to solve the trust problem among organizations in data sharing scenarios is the key issue for next-generation smart ocean systems.

To solve the trust problem among network participants, the blockchain system came into being. It stores the hash of transactions in the block structure. Each block includes the cryptographic hash of the prior block in the blockchain. This iterative process confirms the integrity of the previous block, all the way back to the original genesis block. Therefore, the blockchain technology can solve the problem of trust between the regulatory agency and scientific research institutions in the process of cross-organizational data sharing [15]. However, unlike urban IoT and industrial IoT [6], underwater wireless sensor nodes and AUVs rely on fixed point base stations (such as offshore drillings) and mobile base stations (such as unmanned surface vehicles) for network interaction (see Fig. 1) [1]. It makes the observing data need to be transmitted through the satellite network. In addition, underwater obstacles and the displacement of sensors can make the nodes temporarily disconnect from the core network. However, the existing blockchain architectures are designed for stable network condition environments. The nodes needs synchronize all the missed blocks of the entire core network when rejoining the blockchain system. It generates too much network traffic, thereby leading to low transaction concurrency for ocean exploration.

In this paper, we propose the smart ocean blockchain architecture (SOBC) to solve the trust problem in data sharing under unstable network conditions in the ocean exploration field. We design smart contracts to implement trusted data sharing business among ocean exploration organizations. Further, we implement a channel-based data consistency protocol to reduce network traffic under unstable network conditions.

The later parts of paper are organized as follows. In Sect. 2, we introduce the background and motivation of our work. In Sect. 3, we detail the SOBC architecture, smart contract and channel based consistent protocol. We verify the performance of SOBC in Sect. 4 and conclude our work in Sect. 5.

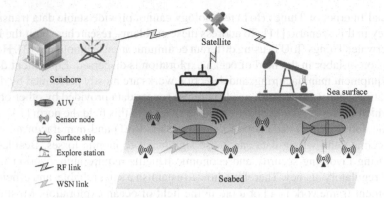

Fig. 1. The network model of ocean exploration environment.

2 Background and Motivation

2.1 Trust Problems in Smart Ocean

Due to the different professional fields between organizations, the construction of a smart ocean requires collaboration between organizations on data and compliance with data sharing rules to ensure the authenticity and reliability of data. However, electromagnetic waves cannot propagate over a long distance in underwater environments. Organizations have to build UWSN and use AUVs to collect underwater wireless sensor data [5]. It makes the observing data managed by its owner organization, forming information isolated islands.

To address this problem, researchers build cloud storage systems to manage such unstructured observing data, and there are a large number of optimization cases for such data access optimization strategies [16, 17]. This architecture is to store data in virtualized storage devices. The data demander and provider access platform, and perform data transmission with authorization [8]. It can greatly simplify the process of data exchange between organizations and facilitate the scientific calculation of data on the cloud platform [9]. However, the data management of the cloud platform is centralized, and its managers have very high authority to modify the data in the platform arbitrarily (see Fig. 2). Therefore, it is impossible to guarantee whether the data has tampered in storage systems. Although the researchers have proposed follow-up tracing methods such as data auditing, the trust problem among organizations remains due to its centralized nature.

2.2 Application of Blockchain

Blockchain technology solves the problem of trust among system participants. It uses consensus protocols to enable each sensitive operation in the system to be approved by the related participants of the blockchain system. Yang's research shows that it has a good effect on inter-organizational trust in the field of ocean exploration by improving the reliability of data [15]. However, the existing researches of the blockchain are in the stage of theoretical analysis in the field of ocean exploration. To implement the smart ocean blockchain system, we discuss the different blockchain systems in this section.

According to the different types of participants, the blockchain system is divided into a public chain and a private chain.

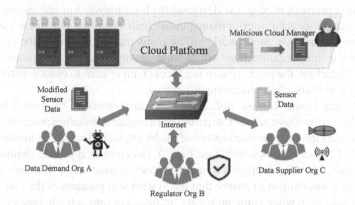

Fig. 2. Schematic diagram of malicious cloud manager tampering with wireless sensor data.

Network participants in the public chain are anonymous. They have equal status and can join the network at any time. To ensure that the data in the blockchain system cannot be tampered with, the public chain needs to strictly control the reach of consensus, and encourage all of the honest nodes on the network to participate in the consensus reaching process. For example, the PoW consensus protocol in the Bitcoin network sets up a difficult hashing problem, so that nodes need to use random hash collision to obtain the transaction packaging right. This makes the attacker need to obtain more than 50% of the computing power of the entire blockchain network [10]. Therefore, the PoW mechanism guarantees the unalterable of the block content by computing power. It makes blockchain systems can tolerate anonymous nodes joining and exiting the network at any time while most nodes are honest. However, this type of blockchain system needs too much hardware resources and energy consumption for sensors. To reduce the cost of computing power, Ethereum proposed a PoS mechanism [12]. It introduces the concept of Stake so that the transaction packaging right is no longer determined by solving mathematical problems, but the stake value calculated by the number and duration of tokens held, and the packaging node is determined based on the amount of stack. However, the PoS mechanism is based on accounts, which makes Bribe Attacks and Long Range Attacks more likely to occur. Therefore, PoS consistency protocol reduces the computational cost at the expense of security [7].

Whether it is a public chain system based on PoW, PoS, or other consensus protocol, its design target is to ensure the security of the blockchain system in an anonymous and open environment. The complex security mechanism has led to low transaction processing speed.

The main difference between the private chain (the alliance chain) and the public chain is that the participants in the private chain are not anonymous. All participating nodes need to obtain identity authentication from the Certificate Authority (CA). Besides, the consensus protocol it adopts is designed for high transaction processing speed, its anti-attack capability is far inferior to the public chain. However, due to the transparency of the identity, attacks on the network will be easily traced. Therefore, the private chain is designed for inter-organizational trusts, such as supply chain, insurance, and other industries. Therefore, the private chain is a blockchain system to ensure distributed data consistency and transaction processing efficiency.

Hyperledger Fabric 1.0 use Kafka's master-slave structure to publish blocks [2]. Although the master-slave network structure has a higher transaction processing speed, it completely loses the decentralized nature of the blockchain. That is, the master node still has control of the entire blockchain (see Fig. 3). Decentralized private chains generally use PBFT, raft, and other protocols to achieve block consistency [4]. It uses a dynamic leader election mechanism to ensure that the system still guarantees the consistency of blockchain data even when some nodes are untrusted or unreachable (see Fig. 4).

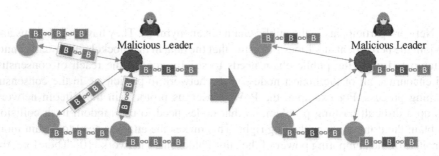

Fig. 3. When the leader node is malicious, even if the blockchain is distributed on each child node, the leader can change the transactions data by republishing the generated block, because the slave node is unconditional trust the leader.

However, existing blockchain systems require stable network conditions to ensure data consistency. The data transmission method for ocean sensors is generally implemented by establishing UWSN. The unstable network may cause some nodes to temporarily disconnect from the core network. It makes the nodes have to synchronize all the missed blocks of the entire core network when rejoining the blockchain system. This will generate large-scale instantaneous network traffic and severely increase network operating costs.

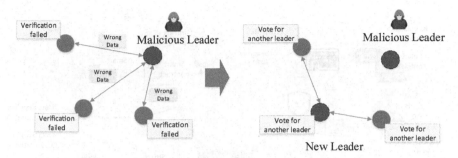

Fig. 4. When the leader node republishes sensitive blocks, the slave node will check its own data to determine whether the leader node is still trusted. If it is not trusted, it will give up following the leader node and vote to generate a new leader node.

3   Smart Ocean Blockchain Based on Hyperledger Fabric

As we discussed in Sect. 2, the ocean exploration blockchain should be able to ensure the unalterable of data under unstable network conditions. Therefore, we propose a smart ocean blockchain (SOBC) architecture based on Hyperledger Fabric, an open source blockchain system developed by IBM and is used by Anthem, Amazon, PayPal, etc. to achieve trusted cross-organizational business. Then, we design smart contracts to implement trusted data sharing business among ocean exploration organizations. Further, we implement a channel-based data consistency protocol to reduce network under unstable network conditions.

3.1   Architecture Design of SOBC

Due to the confidentiality of data in the field of ocean exploration, some data sharing among organizations requires authorization from the regulatory agency. Therefore, we design three roles of participants: regulatory agency, data providers, and data demanders. The regulatory agencies are responsible for defining the behavior rules of data providers and demanders, and participates in the process of data sharing and authorize; data providers are responsible for collecting and providing wireless sensor data; The data demanders is responsible for submitting the data request and get the data in the blockchain after the data provider uploads the completed data. Of course, an organization may have more than one role. Our blockchain system operates on the nodes of the regulatory agency, the network participating nodes of data providers (including AUVs and other internet-connected nodes), and the nodes of data consumers. The blockchain data is stored on channel participating nodes, which allows these nodes to verify all transactions in the channel, thus ensuring any transaction among participating organizations is transparent. The network design is shown in Fig. 5.

For different business types, the participants are different. Some of the private data is not shared with all of the nodes. For example, the transactions between organization A and organization B involves private data, and organization C is not expected to know its contents. At this time, a new channel containing organization A and organization B can be established by an organization that has management authority. The data in

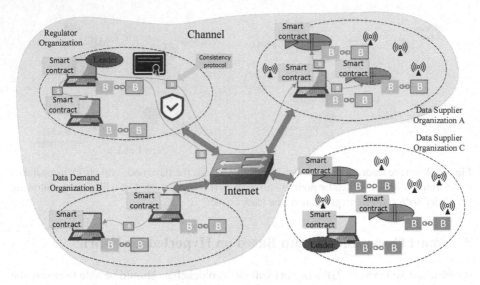

Fig. 5. Schematic diagram of SOBC network structure.

this channel is invisible to organization C, thereby protecting private data. Besides, the isolated channels make the blocks only need to be synchronized with the nodes within the channel. It greatly reduces the time required to achieve consistency, making it support higher transaction concurrency. Therefore, the next key issue is to establish smart contracts which detail the process for trusted cross-organizational wireless sensor data sharing.

3.2 Smart Contract for Wireless Sensor Data Sharing

As a core business in the field of ocean exploration, we designed smart contracts for cross-organizational data sharing. Smart contracts are implemented with chaincode, which can be packaged and deployed to nodes in the blockchain system. For a node that deploys a chaincode, it can use its identity (obtained from CA) to submit a proposal, endorse and verify the execution result of chaincode. When a node endorses a proposal, it needs to execute this chaincode to verify it. If the verification is passed, it will return the endorsement to the Client. This means that its organization has approved this proposal. Therefore, we propose the following three smart contracts:

Wireless sensor data request: The client that submitted the request in organization A packages the data information it wants to request into a proposal. After the proposal is endorsed by peer nodes of organization A, regulatory agency B, and data providing organization C, the data request can be written to the blockchain (see Fig. 6). It ensures that all requests comply with the agreement of the participants and the regulator.

Data uploading authentication: When a node receives a proposal that needs to provide data by itself, it needs to package the target data into an upload proposal and store it in the blockchain system. The content of the data will be stored in the state database for the applicant to obtain. The summary information of the stored data is directly stored in

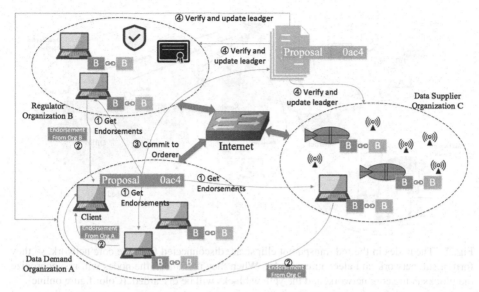

Fig. 6. Smart contract execution process of SOBC within a channel.

the block. Proposal submission and endorsement processes are the same as the wireless sensor data request.

Data reading authentication: When the client applying for data acquisition learns that the target data has been transmitted in the blockchain system, it will submit a data authentication proposal to read the target data from the blockchain system. If its data reading proposal passes the endorsement and verification, it will be allowed to download data from the state database. Finally, it verifies that the data summary is the same as the data summary in the block. If they are the same, the proposal is completed. Otherwise, the data may have been tampered with.

3.3 Channel Based Consistent Protocol

Since the nodes in the private chain need to obtain certification from the CA, their behavior is not anonymous. This makes the consistency protocol of our blockchain architecture need not consider security issues such as fork attacks, and its main purpose is to verify and trace data. Therefore, we adopt the raft consistency protocol to maintain the consistency of blockchain data. The reason is that the raft protocol has a stronger ability to tolerate offline nodes. This is critical for the ocean exploration scenario because high latency and sensor offline often occur. In addition, the Raft protocol is simple to implement and has strong portability. It can greatly reduce the hardware requirements of the devices for the operation of the blockchain system.

As shown in Fig. 7, when some devices are disconnected from the core network, it will form a new blockchain network. Since these nodes cannot communicate with other nodes, they cannot be able to respond to transactions submitted by clients.

In traditional blockchain networks, the nodes that temporarily disconnected from the core network needs to synchronize the missed blocks in the entire blockchain network

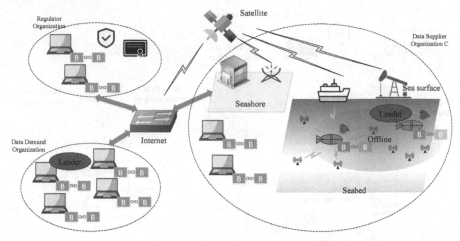

Fig. 7. The nodes in the red transparent ellipse are disconnected from the core network, so they form a sub-network and elect a new leader. When they reconnect, the nodes will resynchronize the blocks in the core network, and the yellow blocks will be discarded. (Color figure online)

when reconnected to the network, regardless of whether these blocks are related to it. It consumes a lot of network resources. To avoid this problem, the node in our architecture has a leader in each channel (see Fig. 8). It makes the blockchain only need to synchronize the block with the leader inside the channel, which greatly reduces the amount of data transmission. And this effect will become more prominent as the number of blocks and channels in the network increase.

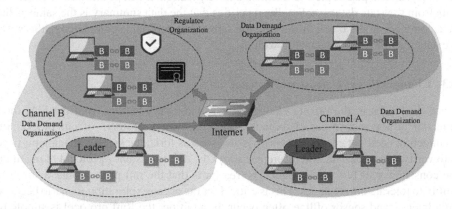

Fig. 8. Channel A and Channel B each have their own leader. Nodes that belong to two channels maintain two blockchains.

4 Experiments and Analysis

To verify the performance of the proposed architecture, we implemented it using Hyperledger Fabric 1.4.4. The experiment uses docker 19.03 version as a container to simulate the running node. We established data sharing channels, create data demander Org_Req_1, Org_Req_2, regulatory agency Org_Mng_1, Org_Mng_2, data provider Org_Res_1, Org_Res_2. Data provider Org_Res_1, Org_Res_2 have 20 nodes for providing underwater spectrum data. The data format is 1440 8-bit long floating-point numbers separated by commas, and jpeg format images with a resolution of 1440 * 900. Org_Req_1 and Org_Req_2 each have 50 nodes to submit data requests. Org_Mng_1 and Org_Mng_2 each have 50 nodes for node authenticating and participating in the execution of proposals. The hardware environment is shown in Table 1.

Table 1. Experiment environment.

Property	Type
CPU	Xeon E5-2620 v4
DRAM	64 GB 2400 MHz
HDD	4 TB 7200RPM SATA 4096-byte block size
Operation system	Centos Linux release 7.5.1804, 64 bit

We established two channels. Channel A is composed of Org_Req_1, Org_Mng_1, Org_Mng_2, Org_Res_1, and Channel B is composed of Org_Req_2, Org_Mng_1, Org_Mng_2, Org_Res_2. They simulate the execution of ocean spectrum wireless sensor data sharing transactions. In smart contracts, all proposals must get at least 2 endorsements by each organization in the Channel. The dataset uses the 421,350 spectral data collected from our spectral detection platform from April 25 to May 15, 2019, and the data read-write ratio is 9: 1.

We compared the proposed architecture with the public chain based on Ethereum and the cloud platform based on OpenStack. In terms of transaction processing capabilities, the proposed blockchain architecture is much higher than that based on Ethereum and is close to the cloud platform (see Fig. 9 (a)).

For network traffic consumption, the architecture proposed is slightly higher than the cloud platform, which is caused by the heartbeat packet, block synchronization process when running the raft protocol, and the smart contract processing overhead. Compared with Ethereum, the proposed architecture requires less network resources. The reason is that Ethereum has no channel design, resulting in the need for blocks to be synchronized across the entire blockchain network (see Fig. 9 (b)).

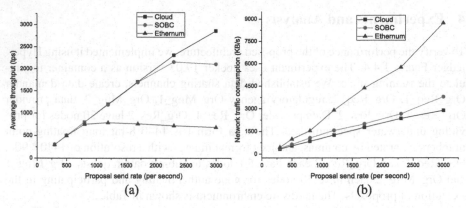

Fig. 9. Average throughput and network traffic consumption with proposal send rate.

For the performance of consistency protocol, we randomly select several nodes every 5 s and disconnect their network for 3 s. We count the network traffic after reconnecting to the core network and simulate different numbers of channels to test the network traffic consumption for consistency maintenance. The experimental results show that when transaction send rate is 500 proposals per second, our model can greatly reduce the network traffic consumption when the node reconnect to core network compared to raft and PoS (see Fig. 10).

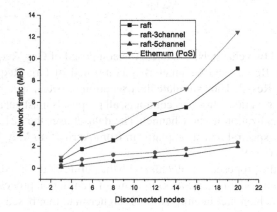

Fig. 10. The network traffic consumption when nodes reconnect to blockchain network.

5 Conclusion

We proposes the SOBC architecture, which implements trusted cross-organizational data sharing in the field of ocean exploration. In addition, the experimental results show that the proposed architecture supports higher transaction concurrency and reduces network traffic consumption compared to existing public blockchain platforms. Although our experiment is simulated in docker environment, it can be integrated into sensor embedded devices through further development. In the experiments, we just designed and implemented the data sharing business in detail. In the next stage, we will implement more business scenarios in the field of ocean exploration, and devote to using blockchain platforms to solve more issues in this field. In addition, for the complexity of the underwater network environment, although Raft protocol can flexibly and quickly achieve blockchain consistency. However, it will still incur additional network overhead when the network is unstable. Therefore, developing new consistency protocols is an important direction of the construction of the ocean exploration blockchain platform, and is also the core technology for the construction of the next-generation smart ocean platform.

References

1. Albiez, J., et al.: Flatfish-a compact subsea-resident inspection AUV. In: OCEANS 2015-MTS/IEEE Washington, pp. 1–8. IEEE (2015)
2. Androulaki, E., et al.: Hyperledger fabric: a distributed operating system for permissioned blockchains. In: Proceedings of the Thirteenth EuroSys Conference, pp. 1–15 (2018)
3. Domingo, M.C.: An overview of the internet of underwater things. J. Netw. Comput. Appl. **35**(6), 1879–1890 (2012)
4. Huang, D., Ma, X., Zhang, S.: Performance analysis of the raft consensus algorithm for private blockchains. IEEE Trans. Syst. Man Cybern. Syst. (2019)
5. Javaid, N., Hafeez, T., Wadud, Z., Alrajeh, N., Alabed, M.S., Guizani, N.: Establishing a cooperation-based and void node avoiding energy-efficient underwater WSN for a cloud. IEEE Access **5**, 11582–11593 (2017)
6. Korpela, K., Hallikas, J., Dahlberg, T.: Digital supply chain transformation toward blockchain integration. In: Proceedings of the 50th Hawaii International Conference on System Sciences (2017)
7. Košt'ál, K., Krupa, T., Gembec, M., Vereš, I., Ries, M., Kotuliak, I.: On transition between pow and PoS. In: 2018 International Symposium ELMAR, pp. 207–210. IEEE (2018)
8. Liu, J., Guo, K., Cui, J.: Cloud-ocean computing: a new scheme of marine data processing. In: Proceedings of the Thirteenth ACM International Conference on Underwater Networks & Systems, pp. 1–2 (2018)
9. Lu, H., et al.: CoNet: a cognitive ocean network. IEEE Wirel. Commun. **26**(3), 90–96 (2019)
10. Nakamoto, S.: Bitcoin: a peer-to-peer electronic cash system. Technical report, Manubot (2019)
11. Qiu, T., Zhao, Z., Zhang, T., Chen, C.: Underwater internet of things in smart ocean: system architecture and open issues. IEEE Trans. Ind. Inform. (2019)
12. Saleh, F.: Blockchain without waste: proof-of-stake. Available at SSRN 3183935 (2020)
13. Vance, T.C., et al.: From the oceans to the cloud: opportunities and challenges for data, models, computation and workflows. Front. Marine Sci. (2019)
14. Wang, H., Yang, W., Xin, Y., Zhang, S.: A data management method for remote and long-term seafloor observation system. Mar. Geodesy **43**(1), 1–22 (2020)
15. Yang, Z., Xie, W., Huang, L., Wei, Z.: Marine data security based on blockchain technology. In: IOP Conference Series: Materials Science and Engineering, vol. 322, p. 052028. IOP Publishing (2018)
16. Zhu, D., Du, H., Cao, N., Qiao, X., Liu, Y.: SP-TSRM: a data grouping strategy in distributed storage system. In: Vaidya, J., Li, J. (eds.) ICA3PP 2018. LNCS, vol. 11334, pp. 524–531. Springer, Cham (2018). https://doi.org/10.1007/978-3-030-05051-1_36

17. Zhu, D., et al.: Massive files prefetching model based on LSTM neural network with cache transaction strategy. Comput. Mater. Continua **63**(2), 979–993 (2020)
18. Zhu, D., Du, H., Wang, Y., Peng, X.: An IoT-oriented real-time storage mechanism for massive small files based on swift. Int. J. Embed. Syst. **12**(1), 72–80 (2020)
19. Zhuang, Y., et al.: D-ocean: an unstructured data management system for data ocean environment. Front. Comput. Sci. **10**(2), 353–369 (2016)

Personalized Recommendation System of Web Academic Information Based on Big Data and Quality Monitoring Technology

Jieli Sun, YanXia Zhao$^{(\boxtimes)}$, Pei Liu, JianKe Li, and Hao Wen Zhai

Information and Technology College, Hebei University of Economics and Business, Shijiazhuang, China

Abstract. This paper mainly studies personalized recommendation system of web academic information based on big data and quality monitoring technology. Starting with big data technology and information quality monitoring, take web academic information recommendation as the application background, conduct in-depth research on information quality monitoring methods, build an information quality monitoring system suitable for the information recommendation system, and provide users with high-quality web academic information recommendation services.

Keywords: Big data · Information quality monitoring · Personalized recommendation system

1 Introduction

Today is in the era of big data, with a huge number of users using the network to obtain information. According to the 47th Statistical Report on China Internet Development released in February 2021, by December 2020,989 million, 770 million search engine users and 768 million mobile search engine users. In terms of personalized recommendation services, Internet enterprises have gradually strengthened diversified and differentiated services to users [1]. In the era of big data, the huge number of academic information, some good and some bad, rich sources, unguaranteed information quality, difficulty to obtain accurate academic information, urgently need to provide users with high-quality academic information recommendation services. The use of big data technology and information quality monitoring, to provide users with high-quality information recommendation service, can improve the user's work efficiency and satisfaction, with a wide range of application prospects.

2 Research Status and Analysis at Home and Abroad

From the perspective of information quality, the quality monitoring of academic information can improve the correctness of the recommended information and meet the needs

© Springer Nature Singapore Pte Ltd. 2021
Y. Tan et al. (Eds.): DMBD 2021, CCIS 1454, pp. 263–274, 2021.
https://doi.org/10.1007/978-981-16-7502-7_28

of academic research rigor. From the perspective of the efficiency of data acquisition, using parallel computing, data mining, machine learning and other technologies to recommend information for users can meet the needs of users to quickly obtain the required information

Personalized recommendation refers to recommending to the user the information and goods that may be valuable to the user by analyzing the relevant historical behavior log information and the user's potential connection with the information or item. Personalized recommendation was presented in 1994 [2]. It is proposed that the research of the recommendation system focus on two aspects: recommendation algorithms and engineering practice. In terms of recommendation algorithm research, common recommendation algorithms include: Common recommendation algorithms include: recommendation algorithms based on collaborative filtering, content, knowledge, semantic and hybrid recommendation algorithms. In terms of engineering practice, the recommended system is mainly used for online e-commerce, information retrieval, mobile applications and other fields. At present, Internet companies, e-commerce enterprises and other companies provide users with the required information and commodities through the recommendation system. In the era of big data, the network data presents the characteristics of huge data volume, complex type, fast generation speed, huge value, low density, and different level of information quality, puts forward new challenges to the research of personalized recommendation, big data technology and information quality monitoring application in the recommendation system has become a new research hotspot and achieved certain research results.

2.1 Research on the Application of Big Data Technology in Personalized Recommendation

Big data was proposed in 2000, McKinsey gave the definition of big data: big data refers to datasets that exceed the size of conventional database tools to acquire, store, manage, and analyze capabilities, but pointed out that data not more than TB is big data. Big data has three characteristics: large problem, multi-dimension and sigmacompleteness [3]. Big data technologies related to personalized recommendation technologies mainly include Hadoop, MapReduce, Spark, Mahout.

At present, many researchers have used research on big data methods to carry out personalized recommendation research, and some companies have also launched their own academic information recommendation products. Literature [4] utilizes MapReduce to address the lack of user similarity computational performance. Document [5] uses Mahout, MLlib to construct off-line, near-line, real-time recommendation structure, and realizes elastic big data processing capabilities through Spark, Hadoop technology. Many Internet companies have also introduced academic information recommendation products. For example, Baidu launched the "Baidu Academic".

2.2 Research on the Application of Information Quality Monitoring in Personalized Recommendation System

Information quality Research in information quality involves multiple areas that is based on data quality. When the data is given a certain context and structure, it becomes the information. The quality of information research focuses on user needs and has no unified definition. The quality of the information is divided into four dimensions: accuracy, integrity, consistency, and timeliness [6]. From the perspective of the user's process of using information, the information quality dimensions are divided into accessibility, comprehension, usefulness, and credibility [7]. The research on information quality mainly focuses on the information quality structure system, information quality analysis tools, information quality evaluation, information quality management, etc. Research on the assessment of information quality, mainly by Lee et al. [8]. The AIMQ Information Quality Assessment Method and Lee [9]. The proposed two specific criteria for evaluating the quality of information (robustness and comprehensiveness of information sources) and automated evaluation methods based on information source sampling.

Information quality monitoring research in academic information personalized recommendation is mainly trust-based research and the establishment of recommendation quality evaluation system. Literature [10] proposes a trust model for recommender systems modeled using ontologies and fuzzy languages. The evaluation system of recommended information quality is generally determined by researchers for a specific environment information, without a recognized system [10]. Document [11] proposed an idea of judging the quality of book recommendation, and designed an iterative algorithm based on the dipartite network structure of measuring book recommendation quality [11].

3 Key Problems Existing in the Current Information Recommendation System

Although numerous studies on personalized recommendations by scholars at home and abroad, there are still some key issues to be addressed.

3.1 The Real-Time Growth of Information Cannot Be Recommended Quickly

In addition to the official data such as CNKI and ACM (American Computer Association) database, academic information also has data from microblogs, forums and other channels, which belongs to big data. Processing this data quickly and thus enabling quick recommendation is a very tricky problem. There are two ways to improve the recommendation efficiency: exact algorithm and approximate algorithm [12]. The exact algorithm can be implemented by both algorithms with low spatial and temporal complexity or parallelization [12]. Approximation algorithm is generally based on incremental calculation, only based on newly added nodes and continuous edge of the local information calculation [13]. Incremental algorithms have already applications. For example, the percentage point recommendation engine uses the incremental algorithm to quickly update the recommendation list. However, the incremental algorithm causes error accumulation, and the whole data needs to be recalculated at some time. The way to avoid error accumulation is to utilize adaptive algorithms, but it is difficult to design. Currently, adaptive algorithms can only be implemented on relatively special algorithms, not used by large-scale generalization [14, 15].

3.2 Cannot Guarantee the Recommended Information Quality Issues

Academic information has wide sources, and information quality cannot be guaranteed. The rigor of academic information requires quality monitoring of information. Most personalized recommendation studies use trust relationships to ensure the quality of recommendation information [10]. In addition, some scholars have studied the impact of information quality on user academic information search behavior. Literature [16] used information quality (central path) and source credibility (edge path) to study users' academic information searching behavior in the microblog environment. At present, monitoring of recommended information quality is not ideal and requires further research.

3.3 The Recommended Results Do not Meet the Personalized Needs of Different Users

In the current study, the recommended results do not meet the following needs:

① can hardly recommend different academic information to users with different research levels.
② When users input keywords with multiple semantics, it is difficult to accurately recommend their academic information to users in different research fields.
③ recommends relevant research literature in recent years to users, and can not simultaneously recommend early literature that plays an important role in these studies.
④ does not guarantee that the recommended information meets both accuracy and diversity.

For ① related research, although CNKI provides the function to search lists by "research level", the effect is not ideal.

A study of ②, need to consider the historical search and attention behavior, recommend the information most consistent with their identity. Google has achieved some results, but domestic applications are not yet to meet this demand.

For ③ related research, the time factors need to be considered. By studying temporal information retrieval, the researchers combine document correlation and temporal information, define temporal correlation, and produce recommended results according on the temporal correlation between query text and documents. A retrieval model including temporal representations is presented [17]. However, just ordering the recommended results by time, the information requirements have not changed. Document [18] believes that information demand refers to the results of the user on different time dimensions (information demand changes), proposed the Chronological Citation Recommendation (CCR) method, can generate a list of references recommended on different time slices. However, there are some deficiencies: long training time; evaluation accuracy to be improved; metadata quality needs to be improved [18].

For ④ related research, the better solution is to design the accuracy and diversity of the recommendations. The literature [19] guarantees the recommended accuracy and diversity by using hybrid energy diffusion and heat transfer algorithms. But the relationship between the two is complex, and there is no good way to guarantee both the accuracy and diversity of the recommendations.

3.4 Insufficient Attack Resistance Problem of the Recommended System

When someone maliciously reviews some scholars' microblogs and papers, it need to improve the robustness of the recommendation system to resist these malicious attacks. Some of the existing studies are to analyze and compare the differences in the scoring behavior patterns between the real users and the suspected malicious users, judge the malicious behavior, and prevent the suspected malicious users from entering the system or giving them a relatively low influence [20]. There is relatively little research and a lack of systematic analysis.

4 Personalized Recommendation System for Web Academic Information Based on Big Data and Quality Monitoring

As of December 2020, China had reached 989 million mobile netizens and 986 million, including 770 million search engine users and 768 million. In the era of big data, there is a large number of information, information quality is difficult to ensure, and it is urgent to provide high-quality information recommendation services for network users. The use of big data technology and information quality monitoring, to provide users with high-quality information recommendation service, can improve the user's work efficiency and satisfaction, with a wide range of application prospects. See Fig. 1 for the research framework of personalized recommendation system for web academic information based on big data and quality monitoring technology.

The research framework of personalized recommendation system for web academic information based on big data and quality monitoring technology includes four parts (see Fig. 1), information recommendation system resource database based on big data and information quality monitoring technology, research content of information recommendation system based on big data and information monitoring technology, and information recommendation system evaluation index system based on big data and quality monitoring technology. The information recommendation system architecture based on big data and quality monitoring technology will clearly recommend the levels included in the system, the logical relationship between the layers and the software and hardware or the main modules required by each layer. The information recommendation system based on big data and information quality monitoring technology studies the data sources of the recommendation system. The recommendation data is obtained through multiple sources. The main data sources include open journals, open knowledge bases, academic websites, academic forums, microblogs and blogs, etc. Data obtained through these channels is written to the recommended system resource repository. The research content of information recommendation system based on big data and information monitoring technology mainly includes research on information quality monitoring method, information user clustering and classification method research based on big data technology, academic information personalized recommendation algorithm research based on big data technology, and personalized recommendation algorithm research based on big data and quality monitoring technology. Research on the evaluation index system and evaluation system based on big data and quality monitoring technology includes the evaluation index after introducing big data and quality monitoring into the recommendation system, putting forward the evaluation system of the recommendation system, and designing the evaluation system of the recommendation system.

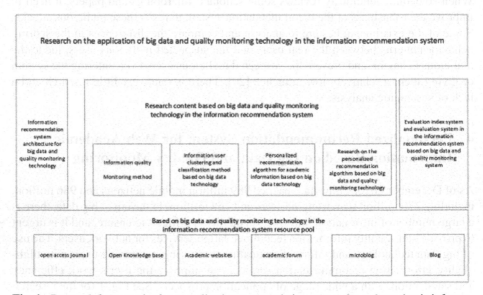

Fig. 1. Research framework of personalized recommendation system for web academic information based on big data and quality monitoring technology

4.1 Application of Big Data Technology in Personalized Recommendation System

Through big data technology to ensure the accuracy and diversity of recommendation results, the application of big data in personalized recommendation, the method is transformed from the original follow causality to the strong correlation of exploiting data features. When determining the strong correlation, the comprehensive use of the large volume, multi-dimensional and sigmacompleteness of big data can meet the accurate and diverse needs of user requirements and recommendation results to a certain extent.

Academic information grows rapidly, and the number of users and the behavior data of the recommended system are also increasing sharply. The traditional serial clustering algorithm has defects of slow clustering speed and low efficiency. In the face of a large scale of massive data, it is limited by memory capacity and cannot operate effectively. When there are large cluster groups, the classifier judgment is also time-consuming respectively, so it is necessary to use big data technology to study the parallelization implementation method of clustering and classification algorithms.

Clustering algorithms serve as unsupervised learning methods, It is a common technology for personalized recommended preprocessing of association rule preprocessing, For recommendation item classification and similar user determination for incremental data, The classifier principle in supervised learning can be utilized, Each cluster is grouped for one category, Data involved in clustering for learning samples, The resulting classifier is used to determine which cluster group the incremental data fits; Recommended common association rule algorithms in real time, This algorithm needs to be based on the massive historical data mining association rules, algorithm efficiency is a focus for the association rule mining, the application of big data technology for mining needs to study the study of heterogeneous data acquisition, massive data storage, rapid retrieval and parallelization implementation of related rules mining algorithm; Collaborative recommendation based on user behavioral data and social relations chains requires finding similarities between and between users of different information sources of academic information, as well as correlations between recommendation items and users, Based on the recommended items and user clustering and classification work, a hybrid personalized recommendation algorithm implementation scheme combining big data technology can be designed.

From the perspective of the efficiency of data acquisition, using parallel computing, data mining, machine learning and other technologies to recommend information for users can meet the needs of users to quickly obtain the required information. The existing Web academic information personalized recommendation system can not guarantee fast real-time recommendation and high information quality. In order to solve this problem, we also need to change our ideas. The application of big data technology and information quality monitoring to Web academic information personalized recommendation can improve the user satisfaction of personalized recommendation.

4.2 Application of Information Quality Monitoring Technology in Personalized Recommendation System

At present, the effect of Web academic information personalized recommendation can not satisfy the correctness, accuracy and diversity, which makes users take a long time to search and choose to obtain the required academic information. Quality monitoring can ensure the correctness of the recommended results.

Quality monitoring of Web academic information quality can ensure the correctness of the recommended information and meet the needs of academic research rigor. According to the multidimensional characteristics of academic information and user behavior data and information quality monitoring index system, excavate academic information quality characteristics, common K-Means algorithm is sensitive to noise and outliers and academic information quality monitoring indicators and monitoring methods can be applied to data noise deletion and outlier monitoring. When applying parallel cluster classification algorithm, study big data file storage and access control strategy; distinguish effective users and malicious users according to user behavior data, and improve the anti-attack ability of the recommended system.

4.3 Personalized Recommendation System for Web Academic Information Based on Big Data and Quality Monitoring Technology

There are three main challenges in personalized recommendation research: first, massive users, data and behavior; the second is real-time, and the third is precision. The application of big data technology can greatly shorten the academic information recommendation time and improve the user work efficiency. Quality monitoring of Web academic information can provide users with high-quality recommendation services. Personalized recommendation based on big data and information quality monitoring technology can accurately identify user needs, realize the rapid recommendation of Web academic information, improve the information quality of personalized recommendation and the user satisfaction of personalized recommendation, and enhance the anti-attack ability of the recommendation system. See Fig. 2 for research process schematic diagram of personalized recommendation system for web academic information based on big data and quality monitoring technology.

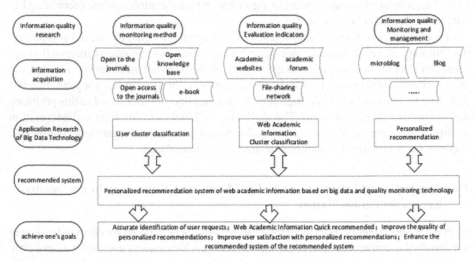

Fig. 2. Research process schematic diagram of personalized recommendation system for web academic information based on big data and quality monitoring technology

The research process of personalized recommendation system of web academic information based on big data and quality monitoring technology is divided into five steps (see Fig. 2). Step 1, Information quality research. Information quality research includes research on information quality monitoring methods, information quality evaluation indicators, and information quality monitoring and management. The research of information quality monitoring method is mainly aimed at the uneven situation of academic information quality levels obtained from different network channels. Through the combination of machine learning and artificial methods, the obtained academic data found the common inaccurate or irregular academic statements, sort out the correct expression, and then establish a common error expression correction database. The corresponding algorithm is designed to enable the recommendation system to automatically identify incorrect representations in the obtained Web academic information and correct them to its accurate representation.

On this basis, other information quality monitoring and correction of their wrong statements are studied. The research of information quality evaluation indicators is mainly to study which indicators can conduct comprehensive evaluation of information quality, can use system dynamics and other methods to study the relationship between the information quality, and choose the evaluation indicators that can most reflect the information quality. Information quality monitoring management refers to the management of information quality monitoring. When the problems of information quality monitoring occur should have corresponding treatment measures. When the information quality monitoring method has been unable to adapt to the new and changed Web academic information, we should timely organize technicians to improve the information quality monitoring method. The second step, information acquisition. We study methods for obtain recommended data from network resources such as different network data storage structures and types. Design corresponding data acquisition methods for different sources. For example,

From different data sources such as open journals, academic forums and professional databases, the way of storage and the data types of the data stored may be different. Getting the recommended data from these data sources needs to design appropriate collection methods. The third step, the application of big data technology research. The application research content of big data technology includes user clustering or classification algorithm based on big data technology, Web academic information clustering or classification algorithm based on big data technology, and research on Web academic information personalized recommendation algorithm based on big data and quality monitoring technology. Step 4, the recommended system. Based on the first three steps of research results, the Web academic information personalized recommendation system based on big data and quality monitoring technology is designed. Step 5, to achieve the goal. Through the first five steps, finally complete the goal that the Web academic information personalized recommendation system hopes to achieve, namely accurately identify the user request; Web academic information rapid recommendation; improve the quality of personalized recommendation information; improve the user satisfaction of personalized recommendation; and enhance the anti-attack capability of the recommendation system. The goal of step 5 is not reached before the research process can be recycled in Fig. 2, knowing that the research goal of step 5 is reached.

See Fig. 3 for the architecture of the personalized recommendation system for web academic information based on big data and quality monitoring technology. The database of the data layer provides data for the Web academic information personalized recommendation system, and conducts data interaction with the system function layer through the calling interface. The Web Academic Information Resource database is used to store the data resources required by the Web academic information personalized recommendation system. The functional layer realizes the core functions of the Web academic information personalized recommendation system. The application layer realizes the recommendation center of the Web academic information personalized recommendation system, the Web academic information display and search module.

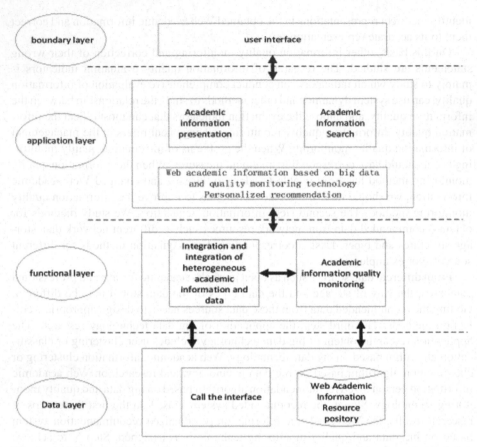

Fig. 3. Architecture diagram of personalized recommendation system for web academic information based on big data and quality monitoring technology

The functional model of the personalized recommendation system based on big data and information quality monitoring technology is shown in Fig. 4. It includes the recommendation center of the front desk module, the Web Academic Information Display and Search module, and the background module includes the recommendation center management, the academic information management, the search module management, and the information quality management module.

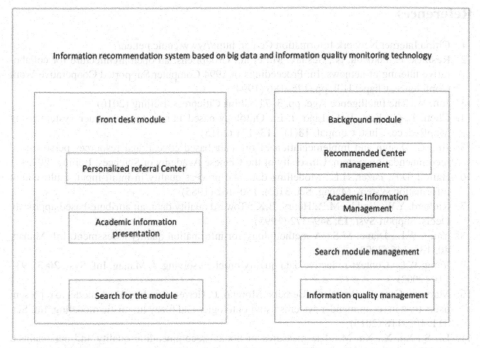

Fig. 4. The functional model of personalized recommendation system for web academic information based on big data and information quality monitoring technology

5 Conclusion

This paper studies the personalized recommendation system for web academic information based on big data and information quality monitoring technology, Analysis and research on Web academic information quality monitoring and personalized recommendation related issues, Based on information quality monitoring and big data technology, Integrate personalized recommendation methods and techniques, Including Web academic information society network analysis, user information behavior analysis, Web academic information content analysis, and a personalized recommendation algorithm based on information quality monitoring, Personalized recommendation system architecture based on information quality monitoring and integrated big data technology, And explore the application of information quality monitoring and big data technology in the Web academic information personalized recommendation.

Acknowledgment. This work is supported by the New engineering development mode of information technology for new finance – takes Hebei University of Economics and Trade as an example (E-JSJRJ20201310) and Information Technology Theory and Practice Teaching Research Supporting the New Finance Education Reform- -Take Hebei University of Economics and Trade as an example (2020GJJG140). Scientific Research Fund Project of Hebei University of Economic and Trade (2020PY10).

References

1. China Internet Network Information Center. http://www.cnnic.net.cn/
2. Resnick, P., Iakovou, N., Sushak, M., et al.: GroupLens: an open architecture for collaborative filtering of netnews. In: Proceedings of 1994 Computer Supported Cooperative Work Conference, Chapel Hill, pp. 175–186 (1994)
3. Jun, W.: The Intelligence Age, pp. 3–71. China Citicpress, Beijing (2016)
4. Chen, L.-C., Kuo, P.-J., Liao, I.-E.: Ontology-based library recommender system using MapReduce. Clust. Comput. **18**(1), 113–121 (2015)
5. Jin, Z.: Design and implementation of big data-based educational resources personalized recommendation system. University of the Chinese Academy of Sciences, Beijing (2015)
6. Ballou, D.P., Pazer, H.L.: Modelling data and process quality in multi-input, multi-output information system. Manag. Sci. **31**(2), 150–162 (1985)
7. Richard, Y.W., Reddy, M.P., Henry, B.K.: Toward quality data: an attribute-based approach. Decis. Support Syst. **13**, 349–372 (1995)
8. Yang, W.L., Diane, M.S.: A methodology for information quality assessment. Inf. Manag. **40**, 133–146 (2002)
9. Yang, W.L.: Context-reflective data quality problem solving. J. Manag. Inf. Syst. **20**(3), 93–119 (2003)
10. Martinez-Cruz, C., Porcel, C., Bernabe-Moreno, J., Herrera-Viedma, E.: A model to represent users trust in recommender systems using ontologies and fuzzy linguistic modeling. Inf. Sci. **311**, 102–118 (2015)
11. Li, S., Xu, X., Xu, M.: The measures of books' recommending quality and personalized book recommendation service based on bipartite network of readers and books' lending relationship. J. Libr. Sci. China **38**(205), 83–95 (2013)
12. Zhou, T.: Top ten challenges for personalized recommendations. Commun. CCF **8**(7), 48–61 (2012)
13. Sarwar, B., Konstan, J., Riedl, J.: Incremental singular value decomposition algorithms for highly scalable recommender systems. In: International Conference on Computer and Information Science, pp. 27–28 (2002)
14. Chu, X., Cai, F., Cui, C., Hu, M., Li, L., Qin, Q.: Adaptive recommendation model using meta-learning for population-based algorithms. Inf. Sci. 192–210 (2019)
15. Wang, D., Liang, Y., Xu, D., Feng, X., Guan, R.: A content-based recommender system for computer science publications. Knowl. Based Syst. 1–7 (2019)
16. Zha, X., Zhang, J., Yan, Y.: Impacting factors of users' academic information seeking behavior in the context of microblogs: a dual-route perspective of information quality and information source credibility. J. Libr. Sci. China **41**(217), 71–86 (2015)
17. Kalczynski, P.J., Chou, A.: Temporal document retrieval model for business news archives. Inf. Process. Manag. **41**(3), 635–650 (2005)
18. Jiang, Z.: Chronological citation recommendation technology based on information-need shifting. Dalian Maritime University, Dalian (2015)
19. Zhou, T., Kuscsik, Z., Liu, J.-G., Medo, M., Wakeling, J.R., Zhang, Y.-C.: Solving the apparent diversity-accuracy dilemma of recommender systems. Proc. Natl. Acad. Sci. **107**(10), 4511–4515 (2010)
20. Shi, C., Kaminsky, M., Gbbons, P.B., Xiao, F.:Dsybil: optimal sybil-resistance for recommendation systems. In: Proceeding of the 30th IEEE Symposium on Security and Privacy, pp. 281–298. IEEE Press (2009)

Population Learning Based Memetic Algorithm for Community Detection in Complex Networks

Xin Sun[1], Yifei Sun[1(✉)], Shi Cheng[2], Kun Bian[1], and Zhuo Liu[1]

[1] School of Physics and Information Technology, Shaanxi Normal University, Xi'an, China
{sunxin_,yifeis,biankun,zhuoliu}@snnu.edu.cn
[2] School of Computer Science, Shaanxi Normal University, Xi'an, China
cheng@snnu.edu.cn

Abstract. Community structure property is indispensable to discover the potential functionality of complex systems. Community detection (community discovery) is a technology for revealing the behavior of nodes aggregation in complex networks. To uncover the community structure of networks in a fast and effective way, in this paper, we propose a novel memetic algorithm called memetic algorithm with population learning (MAPL) based on the optimization of modularity. The proposed MAPL consists of a new initialization method, which can improve the population quality and accelerate the convergence of the algorithm to the optimal solutions, genetic operations and a local search using population learning to guide the direction of the optimization process. Extensive experiments on both synthetic networks and real-world networks demonstrate that compared with the five classic algorithms, the proposed MAPL has effective performance on discovering the community structure of complex networks.

Keyword: Complex networks · Community detection · Memetic algorithms · Local search · Population learning

1 Introduction

In our real life, many complex systems can be modeled as a complex network for analysis, such as the common power network, aviation network, computer network and social network. Its characteristics are mainly embodied in the following three aspects: small world characteristics [1], scale-free characteristics [2] and community structure characteristics [3, 4]. The network is represented by a graph. Points represent objects and edges represent connections between nodes. Community is a collection of nodes with the same characteristics. The nodes inside the community are closely connected, while the nodes outside the community are sparsely connected [5]. Social network analysis performs better with community detection [6]. Community detection is of great significance in recommendation system, the users who have same characteristics in the online shopping system are divided into the same community, confirming these user groups with the same interests can establish an effective recommendation system [7].

Community detection is a typical NP-hard problem, many algorithms were proposed by scholars to reveal the structure of complex networks. In 2002, Newman and Girvan

© Springer Nature Singapore Pte Ltd. 2021
Y. Tan et al. (Eds.): DMBD 2021, CCIS 1454, pp. 275–288, 2021.
https://doi.org/10.1007/978-981-16-7502-7_29

proposed GN algorithm to detect community with diving method and the objective function called modularity to evaluate the quality of community division [8]. Furthermore, Newman proposed FN algorithm based on GN algorithm [9]. Clauset proposed CNM algorithm to detect large-scale community structure based on modularity optimization [10]. In recent years, researchers proposed the evolutionary algorithm to the community detection problem. Pizzuti proposed a single objective evolutionary algorithm called GA-net [11]. Gong proposed a network clustering method based on meme algorithm [12]. Pizzuti proposed a multi-objective evolutionary algorithm called NSGAII-net [13]. In [14], author also proposed a multi-objective evolutionary algorithm called MOEA/D-net. Liang proposed a distributed multi-objective community detection (DMOCD) to detect community [15].

We propose a new memetic algorithm, and transform the community detection problem into the optimization of the modularity. We use a similarity between nodes and a probability matrix for step-by-step transition to initialize the population, Compared with generating candidate solutions of each allele directly in the neighbor nodes, this initialization method is more efficient. We give different weights to the elite individuals of each generation. With the increase of the number of iterations, the weight also increases. This weight is used to guide the local search direction of the population. MAPL algorithm uses two-points crossover operation, each crossing operation is carried out in two individuals with great difference. Compared with single-point crossover operator, the multi-point crossing increases the diversity of individuals and improves the quality of understanding.

In this article, we use MAPL algorithm to test three real world networks and eleven synthetic networks. The experimental results show that the accuracy of MAPL algorithm is higher than that of classic algorithm.

The remaining paper is organized as follows. We introduce the work related to community detection in Sect. 2. Section 3 introduces the details of MAPL algorithm. The experimental results and analysis are presented in Sect. 4. Finally, Sect. 5 summarizes this paper and identifies the future work.

2 Background

2.1 Modularity Function

A graph $G(V, E)$ is used to represent a complex network. V represents the set of nodes and E represents the set of edges. Each edge in the graph corresponds to two different nodes, indicating that there is a relationship between the two nodes. If the same edge exists from node A to node B and from node B to node A, then G is called an undirected graph, otherwise it is a directed graph. If the weight of each side is different, it will be a weighted graph, otherwise it is called the unweighted graph. This paper studies the undirected and unweighted graph.

Newman defines the function to measure the standard of community division, modularity, and its calculation formula is like this [8]. Modularity is an index function to evaluate the community division. The larger the modularity is, the more obvious the community division is. Generally speaking, the value of modularity is between 0.3 and

0.8. The problem of community detection is to find the community division with the highest modularity.

The calculation formula of modularity is defined as

$$Q = \sum_{i=1}^{m} [\frac{l_i}{L} - \left(\frac{d_i}{2L}\right)^2]$$

(1)

For a divided network, it is composed of m communities. L is the sum of the edges in the community, d_i is the sum of all the node degrees in community, and l_i is the total number of edges in community i.

In this work, modularity is the fitness function for MAPL. The selection operation is to retain the individual with high modularity.

2.2 Normalized Mutual Information

In order to evaluate the quality of solutions, we introduce an evaluation index function, normalized mutual information (NMI), proposed by Leon Danon [16], NMI is used to calculate the similarity between the solution and the real partition. The value of NMI is between 0 and 1. The closer to 1, the closer to the real partition.

Two partitions of a given network A and B, C is a confusion matrix, C_{ij} is the number of nodes in community A and community B. NMI is defined as

$$NMI(A, B) = \frac{-2 \sum_{i=1}^{C_A} \sum_{j=1}^{C_B} C_{ij} \log(C_{ij}N/C_{i.}C_{.j})}{\sum_{i=1}^{C_A} C_{i.} \log(C_{i.}/N) + \sum_{j=1}^{C_B} C_{.j} \log(C_{.j}/N)}$$

(2)

Where $C_A(C_B)$ is the number of communities divided into $A(B)$, $C_{i.}(C_{.j})$ is the sum of the elements in line i(column j), and N is the number of nodes.

3 Descriptions of MAPL

3.1 Coding Strategy

We adopt the coding method based on the locus-Based adjacency representation [4] of the adjacency table. This coding method has been applied to evolutionary multi-objective clustering.

Figure 1 shows this coding method, each individual contains n allele's gene, where n represents the number of nodes in the whole network. When the allele of the *No.i* locus is j, it means that node i and node j are in the same community. The advantage of this method is that it can automatically divide the number of communities without setting in advance. The algorithm complexity of decoding process is not high and can be completed in linear time [17].

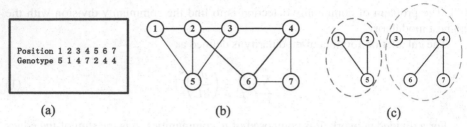

Fig. 1. An example of individual coding (a) a possible genotype (b) the connection relationship of nodes (c) the result of community divided by individuals of seven nodes

3.2 Individual initialization

The traditional initialization method is that each individual takes the node directly connected to the *No.1* gene as the allele gene. In Sect. 4, we name this coding method with neighbor nodes (NN). For the network with a small number of nodes, the performance of this initialization method is slightly better, but with the increase of the number of nodes, the performance of this method is very poor, far from being used as an initialization method.

By calculating the common node of two nodes and sorting them, the top node similarity value can be obtained, which can reduce the candidate solution of each allele and improve the efficiency of the algorithm.

For a social network $G = (V, E)$, $N(u) = \{\exists v \in V, vu \in E\}$ represents the neighbor of $u \in V$ node, structural similarity of two nodes (SSTN) u and v is defined as [18]

$$s(u, v) = \frac{|NB(u) \cap NB(v)|}{\sqrt{|NB(u)| * |NB(v)|}} \tag{3}$$

$NB(u) = \{u|u \cup N(u)\}$ represents a set of nodes including node u and its neighbors, $|NB(u)|$ represents the number of nodes in the node set.

The formula can evaluate the similarity of two nodes, that is, the overlapping degree of neighbor nodes.

Better than the node similarity is the step-by-step transition probability. We propose a method based on node transfer probability matrix as initialization population [19, 20]. P represents the step-shift probability matrix, element values of transition probability matrix $P(i, j)$ is the ratio of the weight value to the total weight value of all edges associated with vertex I. The transition probability can be expressed as

$$P_{ij} = 1/d_i \tag{4}$$

d_i is the degree of node i. Generally, the third party of P is the three-step transfer probability matrix (TPM) P^3 which can better represent the degree of connection tightness of nodes. The higher the three-step transfer probability indicates the closer the connection between the two nodes. Usually, we take the first three or four nodes of node i's three-step transition probability as candidate solutions. This is based on experience. Sometimes this will include node i itself. Obviously, we need to remove this meaningless candidate solution.

3.3 Selection Operator

To keep the good individuals, we should design a good selection operation. Roulette selection algorithm is one of the methods. The characteristic of the algorithm is that the higher the fitness, the higher the probability of being selected. But this does not mean that the lower fitness individuals will not be selected. In this way, the excellent population can be selected and the diversity of the population can be ensured. The specific steps are as follows:

Step 1: Calculate the fitness of each individual $Q_1, Q_2, Q_3 \cdots$.
Step 2: Add the fitness of individuals together to get Q_{sum}.
Step 3: The fitness of each individual divided by the total fitness Q_{sum}.
Step 4: Calculate the cumulative probability of the individual.
Step 5: Generate a random number from 0 to 1, and the individuals in the corresponding interval will be selected.

3.4 Crossover and Mutation Operator

We use the method of multi-point crossover to select the same allele in different gene positions on father's and mother's chromosomes, and randomly select one fourth of them. At the same time, we propose multi-point crossover operation [21], so that two new individuals can be generated by father and mother, and these two new individuals inherit the characteristics of father and mother. Figure 2 show the third gene of parents is the same, so they will not be selected to do crossover operation. Several other genes will be randomly selected to do crossover operation. The specific steps are as follows:

Step 1: Two individuals were randomly selected to calculate I_{diff} (the number of different genes in the same allele).
Step 2: If $I_{diff} \geq 0.25 I_{length}$, go to Step 3.
    Else go to Step 1 (I_{length} is the gene length of an individual).
Step 3: Two new individuals were generated by randomly selecting a quarter of the alleles with differences (Fig. 2).

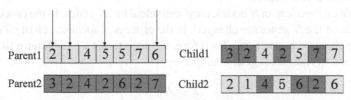

Fig. 2. An example of multi-point crossover operator

Mutation operation are partial allele alterations in randomly selected individuals, and candidate solutions include neighbor nodes of nodes and nodes with a high probability of transition to reduce unnecessary mutations.

3.5 Local Search Strategy

Learn Probability Initialization

The renewal of learning probability is very important for the generation of offspring individuals, the probabilities of learning have a directive effect on the generation of offspring. During initialization, g_i is the *ith* gene of an individual, each gene has M allele's j, genes j are generated in the process of individual initialization. P_{ij} is the learning probability, each allele has a learning probability, which we define as

$$P_{ij} = 1/M \tag{5}$$

This shows that alleles of the same gene have the same learning probability. These learning probabilities change with evolution, but the sum of all alleles in the same gene is always 1.

Learning Probability Update

First, we generate the first generation individuals using the method in Sect. 3.3, then calculate the fitness of each individual. The top 5% of individuals with the highest fitness were selected in the population, and the learning probability P_{ij} was modified according to the allele j of these individuals in gene i.

Take 100 individuals in the population as an example, there are five alleles j_1, j_2, j_3, j_4, j_5 in the *ith* gene of the five individuals with the highest fitness in the population, P_{ij_n} is updated to

$$P_{ij_n} = P_{ij_n} \varepsilon (n = 1, 2, 3, 4, 5) \tag{6}$$

Where ε is a random perturbation operator, ranging from 1.2 to 1.05 with a step of 0.03. Finally, the learning probability should be normalized,

$$P_{ij} = P_{ij} / \sum_{i=1}^{M} P_{ij} \tag{7}$$

Framework of Local Search

For a complex network with N nodes, each individual has N genes. In the process of local search, some of the N genes are changed. In the process of local search of an individual, k genes are changed at one time. Therefore, we need to set a parameter η to determine the proportion of individual gene changes

$$k = N\eta \tag{8}$$

The gene of the node with higher degree needs to be changed, because the higher the degree of the node, the more fuzzy the community division of the node. Through the local search of individuals, if the individuals obtained after the search are better, the former individuals will be replaced, so that the quality of the solution can be improved and the convergence speed can be accelerated. The specific steps are as follows:

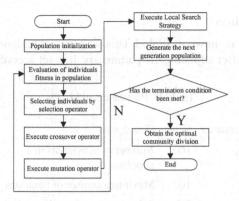

Fig. 3. MAPL algorithm flow chart

Step 1: The degree of each node in the complex network is calculated and sorted in descending order. The probability of allele j replacement of the individuals corresponding to the nodes with higher degree increases.

Step 2: The fitness of each individual was calculated and arranged in descending order.

Step 3: Take the top five percent fitness individuals and change the probability P_{ij} of each individual's gene value being selected in order.

Step 4: k genes of each individual in the population are changed, and the probability P_{ij} of change is based on the step 3.

Step 5: If the fitness of the new individual is better than that of the original individual, the new individual is used to replace the original individual.

Step 6: New individuals are used to generate new populations.

3.6 Framework of MAPL

We select the excellent individuals in the population, cross mutate these excellent individuals and conduct local search operation to generate a new generation of population, input is network adjacency matrix, and output is community division of complex network. Figure 3 is the flow chart of the algorithm.

4 Experiments and Analysis

4.1 Experiment Description

The performance of the algorithm is tested in three real networks and artificial random networks, and compared with several classical algorithms genetic algorithm (GA) [22], Girvan-Newman (GN) [23], multi-objective evolutionary algorithm with decomposition (MOEA/D) [24], multi-objective genetic algorithm (MOGA) [14], and memetic algorithm (Meme) [12]. The real network includes Zachary's karate club network, Dolphin social network and American college football network club network.

4.2   Parameter Settings

The parameter setting is shown in Table 1.This is a group of parameter setting with good experimental results after adjusting the parameters. It is set according to experience.

Table 1. Parameters of MAPL

Parameter	Value	Description
Pop	100	Number of individuals in a population
N	100	Maximum number of iterations
P_S	0.5	Selection rate of excellent individuals
P_C	0.8	The ratio of crossed individuals
V	0.05	The rate of variation in the population
η	0.15	The proportion of individual gene changes

4.3   Experimental Results and Analysis

Description of Real Network

Table 2. The scale of the real network in the experiment

Network name	Number of nodes	Number of edges
Zachary's karate club	34	78
Dolphin sociality	62	159
American college football	115	613

As shown in Table 2, we use Zachary karate club network [25], Dolphin social network [26] and American football club [22] to test the algorithm.

(1) Zachary karate club network: this network was obtained by Zachary by observing a 34 member karate club in two years. In the course of the study, there was a disagreement between the club manager and the coach, which eventually led to the departure of the coach and took away about half of the club members.

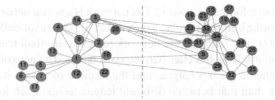

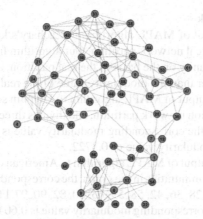

Fig. 4. Community partition result of Zachary's karate club network using MAPL

Fig. 5. Community partition result of Dolphin social network using MAPL

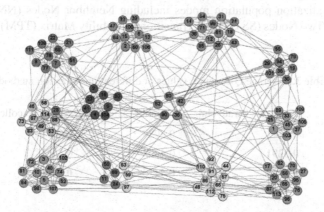

Fig. 6. Community partition result of American college football network using MAPL

(2) Dolphin social network: this network was obtained by Lusseau. Through observing the behavior of 62 dolphins living in Doubltill Sound in New Zealand for seven years, the connection between the two sea knees indicates that there is a significant contact frequency between them. The number of connections in this network is 159, which naturally forms two large communities.

(3) American college football network: The network is a social network constructed by Newman according to the regular season plan of American college football team in autumn 2000. The nodes in the network represent football teams, and the edges represent regular season matches between two teams. The network usually consists of 8 to 12 teams to form a league, and the number of games between the league teams is more than that between different league teams. Each league represents a real network.

Results of Real Network

Figure 4 shows the output of MAPL algorithm to Zachary's karate club network. The dotted line indicates the real network partition. Our algorithm finds the smaller community in the known community on the basis of the real partition, and the modularity value is 0.4198, which is higher than the modularity value of the real partition of 0.3715.

Figure 5 shows the output of MAPL algorithm to Dolphin social network. Our algorithm finds the real partition network partition, and divides three smaller communities in the above communities, the corresponding modularity value is 0.5216, which is higher than the real partition modularity value of 0.3722.

Figure 6 shows the output of MAPL algorithm to American college football network. Our algorithm finds 11 communities in the graph, the corresponding NMI value is 0.9095, the wrong nodes include 28, 36, 42, 58, 59, 63, 80, 82, 90, 97,110, and the result is close to the real partition, the corresponding modularity value is 0.6046, the same as the above network, higher than the modularity of the real partition of 0.5518.

The following table shows NMI of real network and artificial random network in different initialization population modes including Neighbor Nodes (NN), Structural Similarity of Two Nodes (SSTN) and Transition Probability Matrix (TPM) as candidate solutions.

Table 3. Average Q-function values of different initialization methods

Network name	Zachary's karate club	Dolphin sociality	American college football
NN	0.2111	0.3088	0.3071
SSTN	**0.3291**	0.4303	0.4751
TPM	0.2337	**0.4433**	**0.5004**

From Table 3, we can see that the latter two initialization methods are more efficient than the first. For different networks, the effect of SSTN and TPM is slightly different. SSTN has better performance in Dolphin sociality network and TPM has better performance in American college football network. Both of them can improve the efficiency of the algorithm.

The algorithms has been run for 50 times, and the average modularity is shown in Table 4. We can see that MAPL algorithm has better performance in three kinds of networks.

Table 4. Average Q-function values of different algorithm running on 3 real social networks

Network name	Zachary's karate club	Dolphin sociality	American college football
Meme	0.4020	0.5155	0.5888
GA	0.4059	0.4946	0.5830
MOGA	0.4160	0.5215	0.5173
MOEA/D	**0.4198**	**0.5226**	0.5802
GN	0.2330	0.4060	0.5350
MAPL	**0.4198**	0.5216	**0.6046**

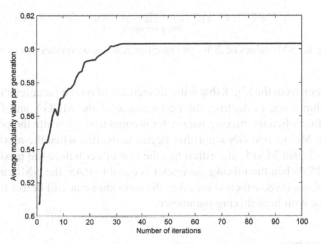

Fig. 7. Convergence of MAPL running on American college football network

For real networks, MAPL algorithm converges faster. For example, the effect of MAPL algorithm running on the football network is shown in Fig. 7.

Artificial Random Network

Here we use the benchmark network proposed by landchinetti [27]. Lancichinetti benchmark network consists of 128 nodes, 4 communities, and 32 nodes per community. The average degree of each node is 16, and the proportion of exteriority is controlled by mixed parameters. We adjust the value of the mixing parameter μ to generate 11 networks with the ratio from 0 to 0.5, and use NMI to measure the similarity between the real network partition and the detection results. The larger the μ is, the larger the connection ratio between nodes and nodes outside the community is, and the fuzzier the community structure is. For example, when 0.5 is taken, half of the connections of each node point to the nodes outside the community, and the community structure is fuzzy. When $\mu < 0.5$, the proportion of external degree is less than that of internal degree, so a good algorithm should be able to find the community structure in the network. Figure 8 shows the test results of synthetic network on different algorithms.

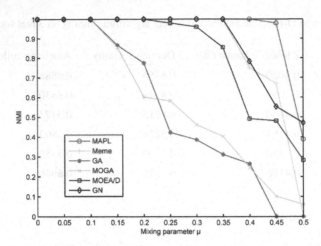

Fig. 8. NMI values of different algorithm running on synthetic networks

It can be seen from the Fig. 8 that with the increase of mixed parameters, the accuracy of the algorithm tends to decline, the performance of the MOGA and GA algorithm begins to decline when the mixing parameter is equal to 0.15, while the performance of the MOEA\D, Meme, and GN algorithm begins to decline when the mixing parameter is equal to 0.35. But MAPL algorithm has the best effect before the mixing parameter is equal to 0.45. When the mixing parameter is equal to 0.45, the NMI value of MAPL algorithm is about 0.98, which shows that the algorithm can still detect the real results on the network with high mixing parameter.

5 Conclusions

In the community detection algorithm for complex networks, MAPL algorithm can automatically divide the community in the way that the generated individuals use gene nearest neighbor coding. And MAPL considers the degree of association between nodes when initializing the population, which improves the convergence speed. In the local search process of MAPL, the direction of evolution is continuously adjusted according to the genes of optimal individual, so that it can move towards the optimal direction. The experiments have demonstrated that MAPL has better modularity in real network and has better NMI in synthetic network than other algorithms including GA, MOGA, MOEA/D, GN and Meme. Therefore, it is a simple and effective genetic algorithm for community detection in complex networks.

For the further study, we need to use MAPL and local search strategy to run more complex networks and signed network to identify if the MAPL still has advantages. And we would like to use niching technologies in population to accelerate the pace of converging to optimal solution.

Acknowledgement. This work was supported by the National Natural Science Foundation of China (Grant No. 61703256, 61806119), Natural Science Basic Research Plan in Shaanxi Province of China (Program No. 2017JQ6070) and the Fundamental Research Funds for the Central Universities (Program No. GK201803020).

References

1. Watts, D.J., Strogatz, S.H.: Collective dynamics of 'small-world' networks. Nature **393**(6684), 440–442 (1998)
2. Barabási, A.L., Albert, R.: Emergency of scaling in random networks. Science **286**(5439), 509 (1999)
3. Rosvall, M., Bergstrom, C.T.: An information-theoretic framework for resolving community structure in complex networks. Proc. Natl. Acad. Sci. **104**(18), 7327–7331 (2007)
4. Steinhaeuser, K., Chawla, N.V.: Identifying and evaluating community structure in complex networks. Pattern Recogn. Lett. **31**(5), 413–421 (2010)
5. Li, Q., Zhong, J., Cao, Z., Wang, C.: Enhancing network embeddingwith implicit clustering, 452–467 (2019)
6. Moscato, V., Sperlì, G.: A survey about community detection over on-line social and heterogeneous information networks. Knowl. Based Syst. **224**, 107112 (2021)
7. Chen, J., Wang, B., U.L.: Personal recommender system based on user interest community in social network model. Phys. A Stat. Mech. Appl. **526**, 120961 (2019)
8. Newman, M.E.J., Girvan, M.: Finding a devaluating community structure innetworks. Phys. Rev. E **69**(2), 026113 (2019)
9. Newman, M.E.J.: Fast algorithm for detecting community structure in networks. Phys. Rev. E **69**(6), 066133 (2004)
10. Clauset, A., Newman, M.E.J., Moore, C.: Finding community structure in very large networks. Phy. Rev. E **70**(6), 066111 (2004)
11. Pizzuti, C.: A genetic algorithm for community detection in social networks. In: Rudolph, G., Jansen, T., Beume, N., Lucas, S., Poloni, C. (eds.) PPSN 2008. LNCS, vol. 5199, pp. 1081–1090. Springer, Heidelberg (2008). https://doi.org/10.1007/978-3-540-87700-4_107
12. Gong, M., Fu, B., Jiao, L.: Memetic algorithm for community detection in networks. Phys. Rev. **84**(5), 056101 (2011)
13. Pizzuti, C.: A multi-objective genetic algorithm to find communities in complex networks. IEEE Trans. Evol. Comput. **16**(3), 418–430 (2012)
14. Gong, M., Ma, L., Zhang, Q.: Community detection in networks by using multiobjective evolutionary algorithm with decomposition. Physica A **391**(15), 4050–4060 (2012)
15. Pizzuti, C.: A multiobjective genetic algorithm to find communities in complex networks. IEEE Trans. Evol. Comput. **16**(3), 418–430 (2012)
16. Liang, S., Li, H., Gong, M.: Distributed multi-objective community detection in large-scale and complex networks, 201–205 (2019)
17. Danon, L., Diaz-Guilera, A., Duch, J., Arenas, A.: Comparing communitystructure identification. J. Stat. Mech. P09008 (2005)
18. Handl, J., Knowles, J.: An evolutionary approach to multiobjective clustering. IEEE Trans. Evol. Comput. **11**(1), 56–76 (2007)
19. Chen, Y.C., Zhu, W.Y., Peng, W.C.: CIM: community-based influence maximization in social networks. ACM Trans. Intell. Syst. Technol. (TIST) **5**(2), 25 (2014)
20. Lambiotte, R., Delvenne, J., Barahona,M.: Laplacian dynamics and multiscalemodular structure in networks. arXiv preprint arXiv:0812.1770 (2008)
21. Evans, T., Lambiotte, R.: Line graphs, link partitions, and overlappingcommunities. Phys. Rev. E **80**, 016105 (2009)

22. Pizzuti, C.: A genetic algorithm for community detection in social networksparallel problem solving. Nature-PPSN X Springer, 1081–1090 (2008)
23. Tasgin, M., Bingol, H.: Community detection in complex networks using genetic algorithm. ArXiv Condensed Mattere-prints, 4419 (2006)
24. Girvan, M., Newman, M.E.J.: Community structure in social and biological networks. Proc. Natl. Acad. Sci. **99**(12), 7821–7826 (2002)
25. Zachary, W.W.: An information flow model for conflict and fission in small groups. J. Anthropol. Res. 452–473 (1997)
26. Lusseau, D., Schneider, K., Boisseau, O.J.: The bottlenose dolphin community of doubtful sound features a large proportion of long-lasting associations. Behav. Ecol. Sociobiol. **54**(4), 396–405 (2003)
27. Lancichinetti, A., Fortunato, S., Radicchi, F.: Benchmark graphs for testing community detection algorithms. Phys. Rev. E **78**(4), 046110 (2008)

An Improved Bacterial Foraging Optimization for Global Optimization

Tongtong Xing, Mengjie Wan, Sili Wen$^{(\boxtimes)}$, Li Chen$^{(\boxtimes)}$, and Hong Wang

College of Management, Shenzhen University, Shenzhen, China

Abstract. This paper presents an Improved Bacterial Foraging Optimization (IBFO) to solve the high computational complexity and less conductive search capability of the original BFO. A single loop implementation structure is adopted to reduce the computational complexity of the original algorithm with a triple-nested implementation structure. We adopt a cuckoo search in chemotaxis operation to increase the randomness of step size and improve search efficiency. Additionally, a new reproduction strategy is explored by employing the Lévy flight strategy to generate new individuals to replace the less conductive ones evaluated and sorted according to the current fitness values rather than accumulated fitness cost. Finally, the candidate mechanism is introduced into reproduction and elimination-dispersal events for comparing and obtaining a better solution. The proposed algorithm's effectiveness is compared with 6 well-known heuristic algorithms on 12 benchmark functions. The results indicate that the proposed IBFO outperforms other algorithms significantly in most cases.

Keywords: Bacterial foraging optimization · Cuckoo search · Lévy flight strategy

1 Introduction

Swarm Intelligence (SI) is a part of the artificial intelligence discipline, which is inspired by the collective intelligence of social animals or insects. In recent decades, SI algorithms have been attracted scholars' attention including Particle Swarm Optimization (PSO) [5], Cuckoo Search (CS) [17], Hydrological Cycle Algorithm (HCA) [16], etc. These algorithms are widely used for optimization since they can get better results by setting a few parameters.

Inspired by bacterial foraging behavior, K.M. Passino proposed Bacterial Foraging Optimization (BFO). It's a powerful tool to solve optimization problems due to its strong environmental adaptability and global search ability [3, 6, 7]. Although some encouraging results have been achieved in engineering and management [4], BFO still has some inherent shortcomings which severely restrict its development and application in global optimization.

As an essential parameter in BFO, chemotaxis step size is often set to a fixed value based on subjective experience, which leads to the local optima or slower convergence

© Springer Nature Singapore Pte Ltd. 2021
Y. Tan et al. (Eds.): DMBD 2021, CCIS 1454, pp. 289–302, 2021.
https://doi.org/10.1007/978-981-16-7502-7_30

rate. Sathya et al. proposed a modified bacterial foraging optimization that the best bacteria among all the chemotactic steps are passed to the subsequent generations [13]. Chen et al. proposed a novel adaptive chemotaxis bacterial foraging optimization algorithm and used it to deal with feature selection problems effectively [1]. Pang et al. used the stochastic flight lengths of the improved Lévy flight to determine the step size of BFO, making the bacteria transform from global search to local search and improving the global search ability of the algorithm [11]. However, these methods are highly dependent on problems or conditions and are not universally applicable to optimization techniques. So far, there has been a lack of systematic guidance on parameter settings.

In the process of reproduction, the population is usually sorted ascending using accumulated fitness values. Each of the healthiest bacteria splits into two bacteria while the bacteria with the least healthy die. Tripathy et al. proposed measuring health status according to the best fitness value of all the positions of the individual bacteria instead of accumulated fitness value [14]. Wang et al. developed a basic framework of BFO, which used a population diversity-based reproductive strategy to assess individual health and avoided falling into local optimality [15]. Although the reproduction operation helps speed up the convergence rate, it significantly impaired the diversity of the population.

In BFO, once the random number is less than the elimination-dispersal probability, bacteria will migrate. The elimination-dispersal operation based on a certain probability reduces the population diversity, resulting in the loss of the optimal solution of the algorithm. Devi et al. proposed a modified BFO called MBFO and randomly initialized the selected bacterium to replace the original probability operation in the elimination and dispersal events. Experimental results show that MBFO converges faster than BFO algorithm [2]. Sahib et al. proposed an elimination-dispersal operation that uses a non-uniform probability distribution, which was realized by replacing the conventional constant distribution with linear and non-linear probability distributions [12]. The setting of elimination-dispersal probability has been improved in the above papers. However, there is still the possibility to eliminate the better individuals.

Based on the above literature, this paper proposes an Improved Bacterial Foraging Optimization (IBFO). Some modifications have been presented, including the redesigned structure, a cuckoo search in chemotaxis, and a new reproduction strategy based on Lévy flight. The main contents and innovations are as follows.

- The proposed IBFO is developed for global optimization to solve the original algorithm's computational complexity and search capability by integrating some strategies in the redesigned structure.
- To improve the convergence rate, we employ a cuckoo search to obtain the randomness of step size.
- The Lévy flight strategy and the candidate mechanism are introduced into reproduction operation to ensure the population diversity and convergence rate.

The rest of this paper is organized as follows. Section 2 describes the details of BFO algorithm. The proposed IBFO is presented in detail in Sect. 3. Section 4 simulates the comparative experiments between IBFO and other algorithms. Finally, the conclusions are summarized in Sect. 5.

2 Bacterial Foraging Optimization

The original BFO algorithm simulates the foraging behavior of E.coli, and it can update the location and search the optimal solution by three operators based on three behaviors of chemotaxis, reproduction and elimination-dispersal.

2.1 Chemotaxis

This process is mainly to simulate the movement mode of E. coli. Bacteria can get two different movement modes of tumbling and swimming. Bacteria can choose to swim in the same direction or tumble over in a certain period of time according to their adaptability to the environment or alternate between the two modes of motion throughout the life cycle. If the fitness value is not improved after a tumble, it will jump out of the cycle. Otherwise, it will continue to move several steps in the same direction until the termination condition is reached. Theoretically, $P^i(j, k, l)$ represents the position of each member in the population of the S bacteria at the j th chemotactic step, k th reproduction step, and l th elimination-dispersal event. The direction of the bacteria after tumbling $\phi(i)$ can be expressed as

$$\phi(i) = \frac{\Delta(i)}{\sqrt{\Delta(i)^T \Delta(i)}} \tag{1}$$

where $\Delta(i), i = 1, 2, \ldots, S$ is a random vector, every component $\Delta_m(i), m = 1, 2, \ldots, p$ is a random number between -1 and 1, the formula for updating the position of bacteria is shown in

$$P^i(j, k, l) = P^i(j, k, l) + c(i)\phi(i) \tag{2}$$

where $c(i), i = 1, 2, \ldots, S$ denotes a primary chemotactic step size. Simultaneously, the bacteria will carry out signal transmission between each other in the process of movement. If a bacterium finds a nutritious area, it will release chemicals to attract other bacteria. On the contrary, if the bacteria reach the harmful area, they will release chemicals to produce repulsion. The definition of social behavior is shown in (3). In the equation, $Jcc(P^i(j, k, l))$ denotes the combined cell-to-cell attraction and repelling effects, and $d_{attract}$, $\omega_{attract}$, $h_{repellent}$ and $\omega_{repellent}$ are different coefficients that should be appropriately chosen.

$$Jcc(P^i(j, k, l)) = \frac{\sum_{i=1}^{S}\left[-d_{attract}\exp\left(-\omega_{attract}\sum_{m=1}^{p}\left(P_m(j, k, l) - P_m^i(j, k, l)\right)^2\right)\right]}{+\sum_{i=1}^{S}\left[-h_{repellant}\exp\left(-\omega_{repellant}\sum_{m=1}^{p}\left(P_m(j, k, l) - P_m^i(j, k, l)\right)^2\right)\right]} \tag{3}$$

2.2 Reproduction

After chemotaxis steps, bacteria are arranged in descending order according to cumulative cost which represents health status. The higher the cost is, the less nutrition the bacteria get in the process of foraging. Therefore, the least healthy bacteria die, and the healthiest ones reproduce and are placed at the same location to keep a constant population quantity. Theoretically, assuming S is a positive even number, Sr is the number of bacteria with sufficient nutrition.

2.3 Elimination and Dispersal

With the gradual change of living environment (such as the consumption of nutrients) or mutation caused by some factors, bacteria may die or migrate to other new places. This process is simulated by dispersing in a small probability. At the same time, some new bacteria are produced to replace.

3 Improved Bacterial Foraging Optimization

This paper makes corresponding improvements to the intrinsic limitations of BFO based on an integrated idea and proposes a heuristics algorithm, namely Improved Bacterial Foraging Optimization (IBFO). In the proposed IBFO, the Lévy flight strategy, nest parasitism mechanism, candidate mechanism and algorithm structure redesign method are incorporated into the standard BFO method.

3.1 Redesign of Algorithm Structure

Inspired by SRBFO [8], we design a single loop implementation structure shown in Fig. 1 to simplify the original triple-nested loops on the premise of ensuring that it does not violate the original algorithm idea. In this paper, the three operations of chemotaxis, reproduction and elimination-dispersal events are performed in the sequence which is judged by the relationship among three parameters of the frequency of reproduction (Fre), the frequency of elimination-dispersal events (Fed), and the current number of iterations (Iter). Chemotaxis with cuckoo search, reproduction with Lévy flight and candidate mechanism and elimination-dispersal events with candidate mechanism are explained in detail in the following sections.

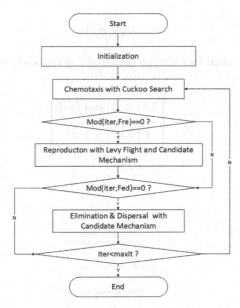

Fig. 1. The flowchart of IBFO.

3.2 Chemotaxis with Cuckoo Search

Cuckoo Search can get an optimal nest to hatch its eggs to achieve an efficient optimization mode. Its core operations are Lévy flight strategy and nest parasitism mechanism. Therefore, we introduce these operations to replace the original chemotaxis assuring randomization of step size, search efficiency and convergence accuracy and realize the real chemotaxis with cuckoo search.

Lévy Flight Operation. As one of the most effective methods to find the target solution, the Lévy flight strategy can obtain more effective randomization of step size by alternating long and short step sizes and achieve a promising global search effect. Therefore, aiming to avoid setting step size based on experience and the randomness of direction in tumbling behavior, it replaces the tumbling operation in BFO to update the bacteria's position. The specific definition is shown in

$$X^{t+1}(i) = X^t(i) + \alpha \oplus Le'vy(\beta) \tag{4}$$

$$Le'vy(\beta) = \frac{\mu}{|v|^{1/\beta}} \tag{5}$$

where $X^t(i)$ represents the position of i th member in the population of the S bacteria at the t th iteration, α is the step length, $Le'vy(\beta)$ shown in (5) is the Lévy random path, μ, v obey the normal distribution,

$$\mu \sim N\left(0, \sigma_\mu^2\right) \tag{6}$$

$$v \sim N\left(0, \sigma_v^2\right) \tag{7}$$

where σ_μ^2, σ_v^2 are calculated by formulas (8) and (9), β is usually taken as 1.5, and $\Gamma(z)$ is the gamma function.

$$\sigma_u = \left\{ \frac{\Gamma(1+\beta)\sin\left(\frac{\pi\beta}{2}\right)}{\Gamma\left[\frac{1+\beta}{2}\right] \times 2^{\frac{\beta-1}{2}}} \right\} \tag{8}$$

$$\sigma_v = 1 \tag{9}$$

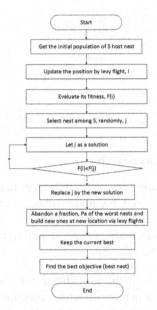

Fig. 2. The flow chart of chemotaxis with cuckoo search.

Nest Parasitism Mechanism. The nest parasitism mechanism of CS is used to abandon a small part of the worse nest and build the better nest by formula (10). In this equation, *rand*, ε are random numbers with uniform distribution, and *Heaviside*(z) is the Heaviside function.

$$X^{t+1} = X^t + rand \otimes Heaviside(Pa - \varepsilon) \otimes \left(X_i^t - X_j^t\right) \tag{10}$$

The mechanism reduces the use of swimming behavior and other parameters. It uses the elitism idea to retain the optimal solution in the iterative process and improve the local search capability.

The main searching process in chemotaxis with cuckoo search is clearly illustrated in Fig. 2.

3.3 Reproduction with Lévy Flight and Candidate Mechanism

In the reproduction step of the proposed IBFO, the sorting criterion is modified to reduce the computational complexity and avoid eliminating the bacteria with better fitness value. Based on the current fitness values, a new reproduction strategy is proposed to ensure diversity and reduce the risk of falling into the local optimum. The specific improvements are as follows.

Modified Criterion of Sorting. To ensure that the next generation of bacteria with the best fitness value can be retained and to improve the algorithm's convergence speed, the current fitness values of bacteria are used as the measure of health status instead of accumulated cost.

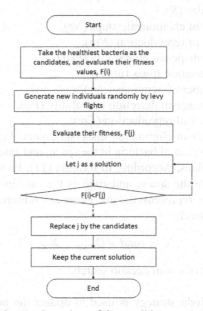

Fig. 3. The flow chart of the candidate mechanism.

Reproduction with Lévy Flight and Candidate Mechanism. It is the core operation in the reproduction step for the Sr healthiest bacteria to reproduce and replace the eliminated bacteria. To ensure the population diversity and improve convergence accuracy, this paper also changes the way of generating new individuals by Lévy flight strategy and introduces the candidate mechanism.

The Sr unhealthiest bacteria die and the Sr healthiest ones split in two, which are placed at the same location as candidates. At the same time, the Lévy flight strategy shown in formula (4)–(9) is used to generate new individuals for enhancing the diversity of the population, and the fitness values obtained are compared with those of the candidates. The better ones are selected to replace the eliminated bacteria for keeping the constant population size. The idea of comparison is called Candidate Mechanism in this paper, and its specific process is shown in Fig. 3.

Similarly, in the elimination and dispersal operation of IBFO, this paper takes the selected individuals as the candidates, updates the individual position. The better can survive in the bacterial population and ensure the algorithm's accuracy and avoid missing the global optimum.

3.4 The Algorithm Framework

In what follows, we illustrate the framework of the proposed IBFO step by step.

Step 1. Initialize parameters p, S, Nc, Nre, Ped, max $It, iter, Pa, Fre, Fed$. Where
   Initial search space dimension (p),
   Population size (S),
   The number of chemotactic steps (Nc),
   The number of reproduction (Nre),
   Elimination-dispersal probability (Ped),
   Maximum iteration times (max It),
   Current number of iterations ($iter$),
   Bacterial parasitism detection probability (Pa),
   The frequency of reproduction (Fre),
   The frequency of elimination-dispersal events (Fed).

Step 2. Initialize the position of bacteria in the space, and calculate the corresponding initial fitness values. According to formula (11), bacteria randomly initialize their positions in the space, and *rand* is the random number of the interval $[0, 1]$, X_{max}, X_{min} represents the maximum and minimum value of the bacterial position, respectively.

$$X = rand * (X_{max} - X_{min}) + X_{min} \qquad (11)$$

Step 3. Perform chemotaxis with cuckoo search.

   1) The Lévy flight strategy is used to update the position of bacteria. The formula of bacterial renewal position is shown in (4)–(9).
   2) The new position of bacteria produced by Lévy flight is compared with the bacteria's before updating. The position before updating is set as the host nest. If the new fitness value is better, the new position will replace the position of the host nest, that is, the solution represented by the new position of bacteria and the corresponding fitness values are assigned to the host nest.
   3) Judge whether the host nest discoveries the new bacteria. If $rand > Pa$, the host nest will be abandoned and a new nest will be built by the bias random walk formula shown in (10), otherwise it is not changed.
   4) According to the current position of bacteria, the corresponding fitness values are calculated.

Step 4. If mod ($iter, Fre$) $== 0$, the reproduction operation will be started. The bacteria individuals are ranked according to their current fitness values. The Sr least healthy bacteria die, and the other Sr healthiest bacteria perform the splitting operation, acting as the candidates to replace the eliminated bacteria. The Lévy flight strategy updates the position of the less conductive bacteria according to formula (4). The fitness values obtained are compared with the candidates', and then the Sr better individuals and the other Sr healthiest bacteria form a new population to keep a constant population size.

Step 5. If mod($iter, Fed$) == 0, the elimination-dispersal events will be performed. The bacterial individuals that meet the elimination-dispersal probability Ped are selected as candidates. The bacterial individuals are randomly initialized by formula (11), and the corresponding fitness values are calculated. The better ones can survive in the bacterial population.

Step 6. If $iter <$ max It, then go to step 3; otherwise, end.

4 Experiments and Analyses

Table 1. Descriptions of 12 benchmark functions selected in the experiments.

No.	Func	Domain	Minimum	No	Func	Domain	Minimum
f_1	DixonPrice	$[-10, 10]$	0	f_7	Rastrigin	$[-5.12, 5.12]$	0
f_2	Schwefel	$[-500, 500]$	0	f_8	Ackley	$[-32, 32]$	0
f_3	Rosenbrock	$[-2.048, 2.048]$	0	f_9	Griewank	$[-600, 600]$	0
f_4	Sphere	$[-5.12, 5.12]$	0	f_{10}	Apline	$[-10, 10]$	0
f_5	Step	$[-100, 100]$	0	f_{11}	NCRastrigin	$[-5.12, 5.12]$	0
f_6	Quartic	$[-50, 50]$	0	f_{12}	Penalized1	$[-50, 50]$	0

In this section, the proposed IBFO has been compared with other 6 swarm intelligence algorithms over 12 well-known benchmark functions. All experiments are performed in Matlab R2018a on an Intel Core i5, with 3.1 GHz, 8 GB RAM in a Win 10 environment.

4.1 Experimental Parameters Setting

To verify the performance of the proposed IBFO, we employ 12 known benchmark functions shown in Table 1 to test the proposed algorithm. These benchmark functions are simply categorized into two types according to their forms: 6 basic unimodal functions ($f_1 - f_6$), 6 basic multimodal functions ($f_7 - f_{12}$). The unimodal benchmark function has only one optimal solution, which is used to test the algorithm's convergence speed and optimization accuracy. The multimodal test function often has two or more local optimal solutions; it can be used to test the global search ability of the algorithm. Note that all functions need to be minimized in the experiments.

As the proposed IBFO is a variant of BFO, we compare the proposed algorithm with some other well-known SI algorithms, including PSO [5], CS [17] and HCO [16]. We also choose BFO and its variants like BFOLIW [9] and BFONIW [10]. For making fair comparisons, all involved algorithms have the same initialization positions on each benchmark function and the recommended parameter settings are adopted for the comparison algorithms. For example, for all the competitive algorithms, the dimension of benchmark functions is set to 30, the population size is 50, and the maximum number of iterations is 10000. The parameter settings of the comparison algorithms are consistent with the corresponding articles. For our proposed IBFO, the other relative parameters are set as follows:$Nc = 1000, Nre = 5, Ped = 0.25$, max $It = 10000$, $Pa = 0.25$, $Fre = 1000$, $Fed = 5000$.

Table 2. Mean values and standard deviation (in parenthesis) of the 15 runs of the seven algorithms on benchmark functions $f_1 - f_{12}$ (30-D).

Func	Metrics	PSO	CS	HCO	BFO	BFOLIW	BFONIW	IBFO
f_1	Mean	6.14E−02	2.20E−01	4.86E+00	7.59E+00	7.20E−01	7.66E−01	**1.26E−02**
	Std	2.38E−01	**2.13E−02**	3.64E+00	9.63E−01	3.01E−02	4.86E−02	4.88E−02
f_2	Mean	4.71E+02	2.05E+03	5.83E+03	3.28E+03	3.17E+03	2.77E+03	**1.59E+01**
	Std	1.82E+03	3.68E+02	5.05E+02	3.57E+02	3.57E+02	4.30E+02	**6.15E+01**
f_3	Mean	1.85E+00	1.47E+01	2.94E+01	7.25E+01	2.42E+01	2.33E+01	**5.45E−01**
	Std	7.17E+00	**9.22E−01**	1.12E+00	5.61E+00	1.06E+00	1.17E+00	2.11E+00
f_4	Mean	6.53E−07	2.03E−19	1.74E−02	3.64E−01	4.88E−03	5.99E−03	**4.61E−27**
	Std	2.53E−06	2.10E−19	1.47E−02	4.21E−02	6.21E−04	7.13E−04	**1.79E−26**
f_5	Mean	6.93E−03	1.84E−18	1.08E+01	3.90E−01	4.65E−03	5.59E−03	**4.48E−26**
	Std	2.68E−02	1.53E−18	7.97E+00	3.98E−02	4.27E−04	7.56E−04	**1.73E−25**
f_6	Mean	2.49E−11	2.53E−24	5.48E+02	2.62E−01	3.47E−05	5.76E−05	**1.90E−40**
	Std	9.63E−11	6.17E−24	5.77E+02	5.15E−02	1.38E−05	1.67E−05	**7.37E−40**
f_7	Mean	6.17E+00	5.26E+01	3.04E+01	1.38E+02	7.74E+01	1.73E+02	**1.25E+00**
	Std	2.39E+01	1.15E+01	1.05E+01	1.59E+01	9.05E+00	2.21E+01	**4.83E+00**
f_8	Mean	1.63E−03	1.94E−09	2.66E+00	1.92E+01	1.86E+01	1.15E+01	**3.99E−14**
	Std	6.31E−03	1.11E−09	9.47E−01	2.35E−01	3.11E−01	7.31E+00	**1.54E−13**
f_9	Mean	4.27E−03	3.33E−13	1.01E+00	1.41E+02	1.95E+02	4.85E−04	**0**
	Std	1.65E−02	8.08E−13	1.10E−01	3.73E+01	3.74E+01	1.00E−04	**0**

(*continued*)

Table 2. (*continued*)

Func	Metrics	PSO	CS	HCO	BFO	BFOLIW	BFONIW	IBFO
f_{10}	Mean	1.61E−01	3.07E+00	3.88E−01	1.00E+01	2.17E+00	5.05E+00	**8.62E−04**
	Std	6.24E−01	1.92E+00	5.85E−01	1.02E+00	4.13E−01	8.10E−01	**3.34E−03**
f_{11}	Mean	5.28E+00	5.21E+01	2.70E + 01	1.83E + 02	1.78E+02	3.63E+02	**1.40E + 00**
	Std	2.05E+01	1.13E+01	7.97E+00	1.94E+01	2.08E + 01	2.24E+01	**5.44E + 00**
f_{12}	Mean	4.51E−02	1.70E+00	5.68E + 00	1.39E+01	9.45E+00	2.26E+00	**1.49E−07**
	Std	1.75E−01	5.61E−01	1.20E + 00	1.80E+00	8.66E−01	3.40E−01	**5.78E−07**

4.2 Experimental Results and Analyses

In the experimental environment mentioned in the foreword of this section, 7 competitive algorithms are performed to get optimal numerical results for 12 benchmark functions shown in Table 1. The mean values and the standard deviation of best numerical results obtained in 15 runs using the 7 algorithms on the 12 benchmark functions are collated in Table 2. The best results of all the numerical values obtained by the 7 algorithms are emphasized using a bold type.

From the experimental results shown in Table 2, it can be seen that the overall performance of the proposed IBFO is better than other comparative algorithms. In general, the proposed IBFO increases 1–42 orders of magnitude than other comparative algorithms on unimodal benchmark functions and 1–15 orders of magnitude than other comparative algorithms on multimodal functions when comparing the mean value and standard deviation value, respectively. When dealing with functions 4, 5, 6, 8 and 9, IBFO can significantly enhance the quality of solutions compared with the other 6 algorithms. When solving functions 1 and 3, CS obtains a smaller standard deviation value than IBFO, but the difference between the results obtained by CS and IBFO is slight. According to the mean of the optimal fitness values through 15 runs for each algorithm, Fig. 4 can be obtained.

The convergence curves shown in Fig. 4 show that the proposed IBFO can enhance the global search ability and has good convergence speed and accuracy in most cases. For example, when the number of iterations is about 7000, the proposed algorithm can approximately reach the global optimal value on the Griewank function. However, the PSO algorithm and BFO algorithm fall into the local optimal value.

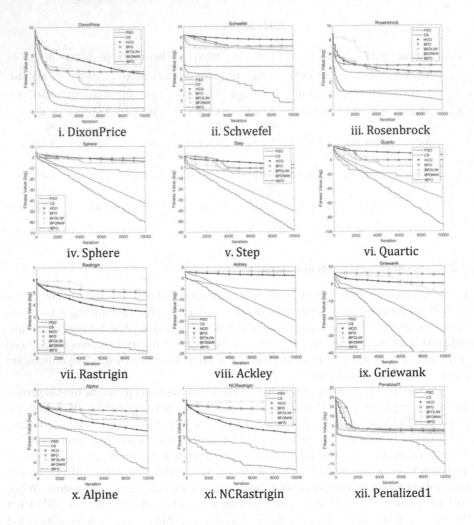

Fig. 4. Convergence curves of costs with increasing Iteration on 12 30-D functions.

5 Conclusions

Aiming at tackling the problems of BFO algorithm, this paper proposes an Improved Bacterial Foraging Optimization (IBFO). In chemotaxis operation, we introduce the cuckoo search to replace the original tumbling and swimming behaviors. Then the bacterial individuals are ranked according to the current fitness values, the Lévy flight strategy is used to generate new individuals, and the candidate mechanism is proposed to select the better individuals. Similarly, we introduce the candidate mechanism into the operation of elimination and dispersal. Finally, we redesign the structure of BFO as a simplified version for reducing computational complexity. The experimental results illustrate that the proposed IBFO outperforms the comparative algorithms on most functions with respect to search efficiency and convergence performance. In the future, more comprehensive analyses of the proposed strategies will be employed, especially from mathematics. Additionally, our algorithm will be further improved for multiple optimization problems.

Acknowledgments. This work is partially supported by The National Natural Science Foundation of China (Grants Nos. 71901152), Natural Science Foundation of Guangdong Province (2020A1515010752), Natural Science Foundation of Shenzhen University (85303/00000155), and Scientific Research Team Project of Shenzhen Institute of Information Technology (SZIIT2019KJ022), Guangdong Basic and Applied Basic Research Foundation (Project No. 2019A1515011392).

References

1. Chen, Y., et al.: A novel bacterial foraging optimization algorithm for feature selection. Expert Syst. with Appl. **83**(1) (2017)
2. Devi, S., Geethanjali, M.: Application of modified bacterial foraging optimization algorithm for optimal placement and sizing of distributed generation. Expert Syst. Appl. **41**, 2772 (2014)
3. Elattar, E.E.: A hybrid genetic algorithm and bacterial foraging approach for dynamic economic dispatch problem. Int. J. Electr. Power Energy Syst. **69**(18) (2015)
4. Guo, C., Tang, H., Niu, B., Boon Patrick Lee, C.: A survey of bacterial foraging optimization. Neurocomputing (2021)
5. Kennedy, J., Eberhart, R.: Particle swarm optimization. In: Proceedings of ICNN 1995 - International Conference on Neural Networks, vol. 4, p. 1942 (1995)
6. Passino, K.M.: Biomimicry of bacterial foraging for distributed optimization and control. IEEE Control Syst. Mag. **22**, 52 (2002)
7. Liu Y., Passino K.M.: Biomimicry of social foraging bacteria for distributed optimization: models, principles, and emergent behaviors. J. Optim. Theory Appl. **115**, 603 (2002)
8. Niu, B., Bi, Y., Xie, T.: Structure-redesign-based bacterial foraging optimization for portfolio selection. In: Huang, D.-S., Han, K., Gromiha, M. (eds.) ICIC 2014. LNCS, vol. 8590, pp. 424–430. Springer, Cham (2014). https://doi.org/10.1007/978-3-319-09330-7_49
9. Niu, B., Yan, F., Pei, Z., Bing, X., Chai, Y.: A novel bacterial foraging optimizer with linear decreasing chemotaxis step. IEEE (2010)
10. Niu, B., Hong, W., Tan, L., Li, L.: Improved BFO with adaptive chemotaxis step for global optimization. In: Seventh International Conference on Computational Intelligence and Security, CIS 2011, Sanya, Hainan, China, 3–4 December 2011 (2012)
11. Pang, B., Song, Y., Zhang, C., Wang, H., Yang, R.: Bacterial foraging optimization based on improved chemotaxis process and novel swarming strategy. Appl. Intell. **49**(4), 1283–1305 (2018). https://doi.org/10.1007/s10489-018-1317-9
12. Sahib, M.A., Abdulnabi, A.R., Mohammed, M.A.: Improving bacterial foraging algorithm using non-uniform elimination-dispersal probability distribution. AEJ Alex. Eng. J. **57**,. 3341 (2018)
13. Sathya, P.D., Kayalvizhi, R.: Modified bacterial foraging algorithm based multilevel thresholding for image segmentation. Eng. Appl. Artif. Intell. **24**,. 595 (2011)
14. Tripathy, M., Mishra, S.: Bacteria foraging-based solution to optimize both real power loss and voltage stability limit. IEEE Trans. Power Syst. **22**,. 240 (2007)
15. Wang, L., Zhao, W., Tian, Y., Pan, G.: A bare bones bacterial foraging optimization algorithm. Cogn. Syst. Res. **52**(301) (2018)

16. Wedyan, A., Whalley, J., Narayanan, A.: Hydrological cycle algorithm for continuous optimization problems. J. Optim. **2017**, 1 (2017)
17. Yang, X.S., Deb, S.: Cuckoo search via Lévy flights. In: 2009 World Congress on Nature & Biologically Inspired Computing (NaBIC), vol. 210 (2009)

A Security Data Sharing Model for Cloud Network

Kunyuan Zhao[1], Qikun Zhang[1], Yimeng Wu[2], Liang Zhu[1], Hongfei Zhu[3], and Ruifang Wang[4](✉)

[1] School of Computer and Communication Engineering, Zhengzhou University of Light Industry, Zhengzhou 450001, China
[2] Zhengzhou Technical College, Zhengzhou 450000, China
[3] College of Computer and Technology, Chongqing University of Posts and Telecommunications, Chongqing 400065, China
[4] Department of System Technology, Zhengzhou University of Light Industry, Zhengzhou 450000, China

Abstract. With the continuous development and wide application of cloud computing technology, its security threats are also increasing, especially in data security sharing and user privacy security protection. Therefore, it is very necessary to establish a security and reliable data sharing model. Combined with blockchain technology, this paper proposes a security data sharing model for cloud network. Blockchain has the characteristics of non-forgery and traceability. By storing the user identity information into the blockchain, not only the authentication efficiency of the user identity can be improved, but also the security of the data sharing system can be improved. At the same time, bilinear mapping and attribute signature technology are used to realize mutual authentication among different entities in domains, secure data sharing and secure interoperability among domains are protected. In addition, the sharing model has the characteristics of low network delay, supporting massive data access and elastic infrastructure. After proof and analysis, the scheme has better security and performance than other references.

Keywords: Blockchain · Cloud network · Data sharing · Identity Authentication

1 Introduction

In recent years, with the rapid development and widespread popularization of the Internet of Things (IoT) and 5G wireless network technology, new service methods and businesses such as smart cities, smart transportation, and mobile payment have continued to appear, and the Internet of Everything (IoE) has become a reality. The number of smart phones, Pads, wearable devices, and other smart terminal devices will increase rapidly, showing an explosive growth trend, and the data generated by edge devices will increase exponentially. How to ensure the security and privacy of user' interactive information has attracted more and more attention. In response to these problems, this paper proposes a cloud security data sharing model based on blockchain. This solution supports

© Springer Nature Singapore Pte Ltd. 2021
Y. Tan et al. (Eds.): DMBD 2021, CCIS 1454, pp. 303–315, 2021.
https://doi.org/10.1007/978-981-16-7502-7_31

mutual authentication between entities in different domains, protects the privacy of entities and the security of interactions between domains, and improves the efficiency of secure sharing.

Through the integration of various wired and wireless networks and the Internet, real-time and accurate transmission of object information. However, in practical applications, the number of terminal nodes is huge and the data information is complex, which is in contradiction with limited energy. Therefore, this paper proposes a security data sharing model for cloud network. In this mode, in order to ensure the security of data sharing, most of the information is stored on the cloud server in encrypted form. There is a large amount of complex data in the Industrial Internet of Things (IIoT), and storing it directly on the blockchain will cause a huge storage burden. Therefore, this model combines cloud server storage. Massive source data is stored in the cloud server, and the storage address and data index are stored on the blockchain to achieve more convenient and efficient storage. At the same time, a flexible access strategy is designed so that terminals that meet certain conditions can access shared information. It also ensures the security of data information, avoids the leakage of sensitive information, and realizes secure data sharing between terminals.

2 Related Work

Due to the open features of edge computing, such as content awareness, real-time computing, parallel processing and so on, the existing data security and privacy problems in the cloud computing environment have become more prominent. A policy based file access control scheme is proposed in References [1] and [2]. The scheme realizes the exchange of confidential data, the sharing data access control, the resolution conflicts, and the audit and the verification data access. A secure data sharing architecture for distributed multi-party based on blockchain is proposed in References [3] and [4]. This architecture can improve the utilization of resources in manufacturing network through dynamic sharing, provide these services flexibly, and improve the efficiency of industrial resource sharing.

A certificateless multi-domain authentication technology for IoT is proposed in Reference [5]. Bilinear mapping and short signature technology are used to realize mutual authentication among entities in different domains, which ensures secure data sharing and secure interoperability between domains. Certificateless multi-domain authentication can avoid the inherent security risk of key escrow in the existing identity based authentication, and solve the complex certificate management and network bottleneck problems in the traditional certificate based authentication. The scheme has good security and performance, supports anonymous authentication between entities, and is suitable for large-scale distributed network security alliance authentication mechanism. A secure data sharing strategy based on traceable attributes in mobile medical network is proposed in Reference [6]. It enhances the fine-grained access control of encrypted shared data in mobile medical network. The scheme accords with the one to many application characteristics of attribute based encryption mechanism and protects the anonymity of users. The scheme is effective without reducing the security. In Reference [7], a secure sharing method based on attribute ciphertext strategy and blockchain is proposed. This method uses smart contract and serialization method to store system public key, user attribute, ciphertext and user key of the solution in chain database. At the same time, set the access rights of the database, register the authentication data set, and realize the fine-grained data sharing. In References [8] and [9], the latest access control model and architecture are introduced in detail, and the access control requirements in industrial Internet of things are studied respectively. On this basis, an access control architecture is proposed, which adopts a hierarchical approach and realizes access control in the industrial Internet of things based on the existing virtualization concept.

A medical data privacy protection and security sharing scheme based on blockchain is proposed in Reference [10], which realizes the security sharing of medical data among patients, research institutions, semi-trusted cloud servers and other entities. At the same time, the availability and consistency of the data between the patient and the research institution are realized. Without leaking the patient's privacy, the zero-knowledge proof is used to verify whether the patient's medical data meets the specific requirements of the research institution, then use proxy re-encryption technology to ensure that research institutions can decrypt the intermediate ciphertext. The scheme can meet the security and privacy requirements of confidentiality, integrity and availability. A secure and efficient data sharing scheme based on blockchain in the industrial Internet of things is proposed in Reference [11]. The scheme designed a secure data sharing framework based on identity authentication and Hyperledger structure to ensure the security of data sharing. At the same time, a community detection algorithm is proposed, which divides the client into different data sharing communities according to the similarity of label data. The range of data sharing can be effectively reduced and the efficiency of data sharing can be improved by selecting the data sharing range according to the community detection results of sharing degree evaluation. The scheme considers the security and efficiency of data sharing, and effectively realizes the safe and efficient data sharing between different clients. A data security sharing model based on privacy protection for blockchain-enabled IIoT is proposed in Reference [12]. In order to ensure the security of data sharing, most of the information is stored in the blockchain in encrypted form. There are a large amount of complex data in IIoT, and if it is directly stored on the blockchain, it will cause a great storage burden. Therefore, this model combines on-chain and off-chain storage to achieve more convenient and efficient storage. At the same time, a flexible access strategy is designed so that terminals that meet certain conditions can access shared information. It also ensures the security of data information, avoids the leakage of sensitive information, and realizes secure data sharing between terminals.

In order to achieve efficient authentication and information sharing between different platforms, A distributed trusted authentication system based on blockchain and edge computing is proposed in Reference [13], aiming to improve authentication efficiency. A mutual authentication and key agreement protocol based on blockchain for smart grid system based on edge computing in Reference [14]. The protocol uses blockchain to support effective conditional anonymity and key management without other complex encryption primitives. The protocol achieves reasonable security assurance. A secure access method for the IoT is proposed in Reference [15]. This method stores fingerprint information in the blockchain, and terminal members access the information after verifying their identity, ensuring the security of the terminal's access to the cloud. A multiauthority encrypted access control scheme is proposed in Reference [16]. The scheme uses the built-in policy to protect the security of data and the confidentiality of access policy, and uses the linear secret sharing scheme to achieve reachable secret sharing. A certification model for IIoT devices with limited resources is proposed in References [17–19], in which only 4 messages are exchanged between subjects for authentication. It has lower execution time and communication cost.

In References [20], a multi-authority encrypted access control scheme is proposed. The scheme protects the security of data and the confidentiality of access policies by using the built-in policies of the system. A multi-access edge computing Internet network location privacy protection scheme is proposed in Reference [21], which is a scalable system built on public cloud services, it can hide the network location and traffic of mobile users from communication peers. Internet users can get ubiquitous Internet mobility support, while network location privacy is well protected, performance overhead is minimal, and operating costs are the lowest. A security protocol design for edge server authentication without the requirement of a trusted third party is proposed in Reference [22]. Mobile edge computing needs an accurate and efficient authentication mechanism, a mutual authentication and key agreement scheme without the participation of trusted third party is constructed, which ensures the mutual authentication between users and edge server, and generates a secure session key. The scheme realizes some important security attributes such as secure communication, user anonymity in mutual authentication and session key negotiation. The protocol is secure against known attacks and has high efficiency.

Through the analysis of the above-mentioned related literature, many scholars have made different contributions in data resource security sharing and access control, which has laid a solid foundation for the research of this paper. However, in these documents, there are disadvantages in the leakage of personal privacy information, and the storage of shared resources also has disadvantages in terms of security and cost. They are not suitable for complex application environments. Therefore, there is an urgent need for a secure and flexible resource sharing scheme to protect personal privacy and secure data sharing, and realize the safe and efficient data sharing between different terminals. This paper proposes a secure sharing scheme of cloud network for blockchain. Compared with other literatures, this scheme improves the flexibility and security of network resource sharing. While sharing resources safely, it can protect the privacy of the terminal and improve the efficiency of data sharing. The security proof and performance analysis of the scheme are also given.

3 Basic Theory

3.1 Bilinear Mapping

The basic knowledge of bilinear mapping used in this paper is shown as below:

The definition of bilinear mapping is given. Assumed that G_1 and G_2 are an additive group and a multiplicative group with the common prime order q, respectively. And $q \geq 2^\kappa + 1$, κ is a security parameter. It is difficult to compute the discrete logarithm over G_1 and G_2, groups G_1 and G_2 are a pair of bilinear groups. g_1 is generated by G_1, that means $G_1 = \langle g_1 \rangle$. We call e a computable bilinear map, $e : G_1 \times G_1 \to G_2$, it meets the following characteristics:

1. Bilinearty: For all $\omega, \rho \in G_1$ and $a, b \in \mathbb{ZZ}_q^*$, and the equation $e(a\omega, a\rho) = e(\omega, \rho)^{ab}$ holds.
2. Nondegeneracy: Two numbers ω and ρ randomly selected from G_1, such that $e(\omega, \rho) \neq 1$.
3. Computability: For all $\omega, \rho \in G_1$, there exits a efficient way to calculate $e(\omega, \rho)$.

Inference 1. For all $\rho_1, \rho_2, \omega \in G_1$, there is $e(\rho_1 + \rho_2, \omega) = e(\rho_1, \omega)e(\rho_2, \omega)$.

Definition 1. Discrete Logarithm Problem (DLP). Given an equation $Y = aQ$, where Y and Q are two elements in additive group G_1 and a $\in \mathbb{ZZ}_q^*$. If a and Q are given, it is easy to calculate Y. But if Y and Q are given, it will be difficult to calculate a.

Definition 2. Inverse Computational Diffe–Hellman (ICDH) Problem. The ICDH problem is given g_1, ag_1 and abg_1, for $a, b \in Z_q^*$, so that $\left(\frac{ab}{a}\right)g_1$ can be calculated.

3.2 The Chinese Remainder Theorem (CRT)

Assumed that a series of mutually prime positive integers sequence $d_1, d_2, ..., d_n$, $(\gcd(d_i, d_j) = 1$, for every $i \neq j)$, $d = d_1 d_2 ... d_n = d_i D_i$, where $D_i = d_1 d_2 ... d_{i-1} d_{i+1} ... d_n$. Given the following system of equations as

$$\begin{cases} x = l_1 \bmod d_1, \\ x = l_2 \bmod d_2, \\ ... \\ x = l_n \bmod d_n, \end{cases}$$ There is a unique solution as $x = \left(\sum_{i=1}^{n} l_i \cdot y_i \cdot D_i\right) \bmod d$, where $y_i \cdot D_i \bmod d_i = 1, i = 1, 2, ..., n$.

4 The Design of Data-Sharing Model

4.1 System Model

The system mainly realizes the security sharing of data information and the privacy protection of terminal members from the aspects of authentication of terminal members, encryption storage of data resources, access of terminal members to data resources and so on. Figure 1 shows the resource sharing model frame for cloud network.

The cloud server is mainly to generate the parameters required by the system for user and authenticate the terminal members in the domain.

The data sharers encrypt the shared resources, and then store the encrypted ciphertext in the cloud server. Finally, the storage address and ciphertext resource index information are stored on the blockchain.

The data requesters first check the index information on the blockchain, and determine the storage address of the resource, then they obtain the ciphertext resource based on the address and calculate the key to decrypt it. Finally, they obtain the plaintext of the shared resource.

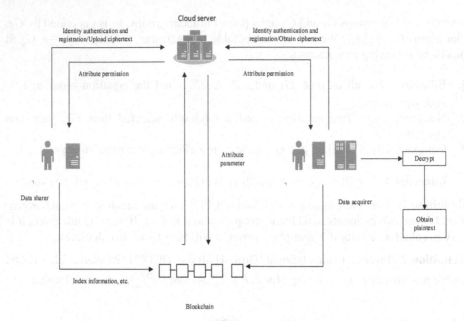

Fig. 1. The system model

4.2 Initialization

This section describes the basic parameters required by the technology and initializes a security data sharing model for cloud network. The system consists of cloud server and network terminal users. The cloud server is mainly used for identity authentication of terminal members to prevent impersonation attacks by illegal members.

Assume that there are n network terminals in this model, we use $U = \{u_1, u_2, ..., u_n\}$ to represent the set of terminal members and use $ID = \{id_{u_1}, id_{u_2}, ..., id_{u_n}\}$ to represent the identity set of terminal members. The cloud server defines an ordered network attribute sequence $ATTR = A_1|A_2|...|A_R$ and the corresponding ordered network attribute set $Attr = \{A_1, A_2, ..., A_j, ...A_R\}$, where $A_j < A_{j+1}(j < r)$ and $R(R \in N^*)$ represents the total number of attributes in the network attribute set. The cloud server defines an ordered network attribute sequence $attr_i = a_{i,1}|a_{i,2}|null|...|a_{i,r}|null$ and the corresponding ordered attribute set of the terminal u_i is $Attr_i = \{a_{i,1}, a_{i,2}, ..., a_{i,r}\}$, where $attr_i \subseteq Attr$, $r \in N^*$, $r \le R$, $a_{i,r-1} < a_{i,r}$ and r denotes the rth attribute of u_i.

KeyGen: $KeyGen(1^\lambda) \rightarrow (PK_A, SK_A)$. The cloud server runs the key generation algorithm $KeyGen(1^\lambda)$ to obtain the key pair (SK_A, PK_A), where $SK_A \in Z_q^*$ and $PK_A = SK_A g_1$.

Any member $u_i \in U(1 \le i \le n)$ calculates $sk_{u_i} = H_1(id_{u_i})s_{u_i}$, $s_{u_i} \in Z_q^*$. There is the private key sk_{u_i} and the public key pk_{u_i}, and $pk_{u_i} = g_1 sk_{u_i}$. The basic parameters of the system are params $= (PK_A, q, G_1, G_2, g_1, e, H_1, H_2)$.

Suppose G_1 and G_2 are an additive group and a multiplicative group on the elliptic curve, where G_1 and G_2 have respectively the order q. The discrete logarithm of G_1 and G_2 are difficult to compute. The generator $g_1 \in G_1$ is generated by the group G_1. Among them, there is a computable bilinear map $e : G_1 \times G_1 \rightarrow G_2$ and two hash functions $H_1 : \{0, 1\}^* \rightarrow Z_q^*, H_2 : G_1 \rightarrow Z_q^*$.

4.3 Authentication and Registration of the Terminals

Below is the terminal users authentication and registration process, below are the detailed steps:

The cloud server randomly selects a sequence of pairwise coprime positive integers $p_1, p_2, ..., p_R$, the cloud server broadcasts network attributes set and corresponding sequence numbers and positive integers $\{(A_1, S_1, P_1), (A_2, S_2, P_2), ..., (A_R, S_R, P_R)\}$, where $A_i(1 \leq i \leq R)$ represents attribute and S_i represents the serial number corresponding to the attribute A_i.

Each terminal u_i has an ordered attribute set $attr_i = \{a_{i,1}, a_{i,2}, ..., a_{i,r}\}$, where $a_{i,j} < a_{i,j+1}(1 \leq j < r)$. Each terminal user u_i calculates $\vartheta_{i,1} = s_{u_i} a_{i,1} g_1, \vartheta_{i,2} = s_{u_i} a_{i,2} g_1, ..., \vartheta_{i,r} = s_{u_i} a_{i,r} g_1, o_i = s_{u_i} H_2(\vartheta_{i,1} || \vartheta_{i,2} || ... || \vartheta_{i,r}) PK_A$. Then, u_i sends $\{id_{u_i}, pk_{u_i}, o_i, (\vartheta_{i,1}, A_1, S_1), (\vartheta_{i,2}, A_2, S_2), ..., (\vartheta_{i,r}, A_r, S_r)\}$ to the cloud server.

After received the messages u_i sends $\{id_{u_i}, pk_{u_i}, o_i, (\vartheta_{i,1}, A_1, S_1), (\vartheta_{i,2}, A_2, S_2),$

$..., (\vartheta_{i,r}, A_r, S_r)\}$, the cloud server calculates $\eta_i = SK_A^{-1} o_i = s_{u_i} H_2 \begin{pmatrix} \vartheta_{i,1} || \vartheta_{i,2} || \\ ... || \vartheta_{i,r} \end{pmatrix} g_1,$

then, it verifies the identity of u_i by the equation $H_1(id_{u_i}) \eta_i = ? H_2(\vartheta_{i,1} || \vartheta_{i,2} || ... || \vartheta_{i,r}) pk_{u_i}$. If it holds, the cloud server selects a random number $\iota_{i,k} \in Z_q^*(1 \leq k \leq r)$ for each attribute $a_{i,k}$ and calculates $\chi_{i,k} = \iota_{i,k} \vartheta_{i,k}$ as its permission parameter. Then, the cloud server sends messages $\{PK_A \delta_i, (\chi_{i,1}, \chi_{i,2}, ..., \chi_{i,r})\}$ to the terminal u_i being registered, where $\delta_i = SK_A(\iota_{i,1} a_{i,1} + \iota_{i,2} a_{i,2} + ... + \iota_{i,r} a_{i,r}) g_1$.

After receiving the messages $\{PK_A \delta_i, (\chi_{i,1}, \chi_{i,2}, ..., \chi_{i,r})\}$ from the cloud server, u_i calculates $T_{i,1} = s_{u_i}^{-1} \chi_{i,1} = \iota_{i,1} a_{i,1} g_1, T_{i,2} = s_{u_i}^{-1} \chi_{i,2} = \iota_{i,2} a_{i,2} g_1, ..., T_{i,r} = s_{u_i}^{-1} \chi_{i,r} = \iota_{i,r} a_{i,r} g_1$ and $\Phi_i = (T_{i,1} + T_{i,2} + ... + T_{i,r})$. Then, u_i verifies the identity of the cloud server and attribute permission $T_{i,k}$ of $a_{i,k}$ by calculating $e(\delta_i, g_1) = e(\Phi_i, PK_A)$. If it holds, u_i obtains the attribute permission $T_{i,k}$ corresponding to each of its attribute $a_{i,k}$. It shows that each terminal has successfully registered.

Finally, the cloud server stores the information $\{pk_{u_i}, (\chi_{i,1}, p_1, S_1), (\chi_{i,2}, p_2, S_2), ..., (\chi_{i,r}, p_r, S_r)\}$ in block of u_i.

4.4 Calculating Encryption Keys and Storing Shared Resources

The blockchain is a data structure that combines effective data blocks in a chain form through time sequence, and guarantees its non-tampering, non-repudiation, and decentralization through cryptographic methods. Based on these characteristics of the blockchain, fine-grained access control of data resources can be realized and the safety and reliability of data resources can be ensured. The blockchain uses cryptography, time stamps and consensus algorithms to ensure the consistency of information in the database of each node, so that transaction records can be verified instantly, transparently and traceable, undeniable and difficult to tamper with.

In order to prevent attackers from viewing, tampering or forging data, the data is encrypted before being stored on the cloud server. At the same time, in order to achieve lightweight storage and computing, the storage process is cloud server storage. Therefore, each terminal member sharing data first calculates the key and encrypts the information, and then each member uploads the ciphertext to the cloud server. Finally, the storage address of the ciphertext and related index information are uploaded to the blockchain. The encrypted storage of shared resources is cloud server storage. The user's shared resources are stored in the cloud server in cipher text to ensure data security.

The detailed steps for cloud server storage are as follows:

Each terminal u_i with attribute set $\{a_{i,1}, a_{i,2}, ..., a_{i,r}\}$ to share its resources, it selects the network attribute parameter $\{p_1, p_2, ..., p_r\}$ corresponding to the encrypted attribute $\{a_{i,1}, a_{i,2}, ..., a_{i,r}\}$ according to the attribute serial number $\{S_1, S_2, ..., S_r\}$, then it com-

putes $\begin{cases} x_i \equiv T_{i,1}(\bmod p_1) \\ x_i \equiv T_{i,2}(\bmod p_2) \\ ... \\ x_i \equiv T_{i,r}(\bmod p_r) \end{cases}$ by using the standard the CRT. A unique solution x_i is given

as $x_i = \left(\sum_{v=1}^{r} T_{i,v} \cdot y_v \cdot \frac{p}{p_v}\right) \bmod p_v$, where $p = p_1 \times p_2 \times \cdots \times p_r = \prod_{v=1}^{r} p_v$, and $y_v \cdot \frac{p}{p_v} \bmod p_v = 1$. $group_{key} = x_i = \left(\sum_{v=1}^{r} T_{i,v} \cdot y_v \cdot \frac{p}{p_v}\right) \bmod p_v$ can be used as a group key for encryption and decryption of group shared data, it can guarantee the security of data sharing among group terminals.

After each u_i has calculated the key, if it wants to share some resources $m \in M^*$, M^* represents the plaintext space, u_i encrypts the resource m by computing $c_{i,m} = m \oplus H_2(x_i)$. Then, u_i uploads the shared ciphertext information $c_{i,m}$ to the cloud server. Finally, the storage address $Address_{u_{i,m}}$ of the ciphertext is returned to the blockchain.

4.5 Download and Decrypt Shared Resources

If a user $u_j (1 \leq j \leq n)$ want to access resources, it can look for the corresponding ciphertext based on the index information in the block of any terminal user $u_k (1 \leq k \leq n)$, and u_j can view the attribute sequence used by the resource owner to encrypt the resource, and determine the attribute set required to decrypt the resource.

After u_j determines the resource it wants to access, it needs to obtain the corresponding attribute serial number $(S_{1,m}, S_{2,m}, ..., S_{r,m})$ from the index information in the block of u_k and send the messages $\left\{pk_{u_j}, (\chi_{j,1}, \chi_{j,2}, ..., \chi_{j,r}), Sig_j\right\}$ to u_k, where $Sig_j = H_2(\chi_{i,1}||\chi_{i,2}||...||\chi_{i,r})/sk_{u_j})g_1$. Then, u_k calculates $\mu_k = H_2(\chi_{j,1}||\chi_{j,2}||...||\chi_{j,r})$ and verifies the identity of u_j by verifying whether equation $e(sig_j, pk_{u_j}) = e(u_k g_1, g_1)$ is true. If it is true, u_j can obtain the storage address $Address_{u_{i,m}}$ on the blockchain.

u_j downloads the corresponding ciphertext resource $c_{k,m}$ from the cloud server according to the storage address $Address_{u_{i,m}}$. According to attribute serial number $(S_{1,m}, S_{2,m}, ..., S_{r,m})$, u_j calculates decryption key $x_j = \left(\sum_{v=1}^{r} T_{j,v} \cdot y_v \cdot \frac{p}{p_v}\right) \bmod p_v$ for ciphertext resource with its attribute permissions $\{T_{j,1}, T_{j,2}, ..., T_{j,r}\}$, u_j can obtain the plaintext resources by computing formula $m = c_{k,m} \oplus H_2(x_j)$.

5 Security Analysis

The security data sharing model proposed in this paper is based on the blockchain. We prove the safety and feasibility of the proposed scheme in the key process of implementation.

Theorem 1. Any legal terminal member u_i has an attribute $a_{i,r}$, and it can obtain the attribute permission $T_{i,r}$ corresponding to the attribute $a_{i,r}$. On the contrary, if there is no attribute $a_{i,r}$, the corresponding attribute permission $T_{i,r}$ cannot be obtained.

Proof. If the terminal member who owns the attribute $a_{i,r}$ wants to obtain the attribute permission $T_{i,r}$ corresponding to the attribute, u_i need to compute $\vartheta_{i,1} = s_{u_i}a_{i,1}g_1$, $\vartheta_{i,2} = s_{u_i}a_{i,2}g_1, ..., \vartheta_{i,r} = s_{u_i}a_{i,r}g_1$ and $o_i = s_{u_i}H_2(\vartheta_{i,1}||\vartheta_{i,2}||...||\vartheta_{i,r})PK_A$. After the cloud server received messages $\{id_{u_i}, pk_{u_i}, o_i, (\vartheta_{i,1}, A_1, S_1), (\vartheta_{i,2}, A_2, S_2), ..., (\vartheta_{i,r}, A_r, S_r)\}$ sent by u_i, the cloud server calculates $\eta_i = SK_A^{-1}o_i = s_{u_i}H_2(\vartheta_{i,1}||\vartheta_{i,2}||...||\vartheta_{i,r})g_1$, then, it verifies the identity of u_i by the equation $H_1(id_{u_i})\eta_i =?H_2(\vartheta_{i,1}||\vartheta_{i,2}||...||\vartheta_{i,r})pk_{u_i}$ and computes $\chi_{i,r} = \iota_{i,r}\vartheta_{i,r}$, where $\iota_{i,r}$ is a random positive integers selected by the cloud server, the cloud server sends $\chi_{i,r}$ to u_i, u_i calculates $T_{i,r} = s_{u_i}^{-1}\chi_{i,r} = \iota_{i,r}a_{i,r}g_1$.

The above proof indicates that only terminals with legal attributes can obtain attribute permissions, and terminals that do not possess certain attributes cannot obtain corresponding permissions for these attributes.

Theorem 2. If two terminal members u_i and u_j have the same attribute set $\{a_{i,1}, a_{i,2}, ..., a_{i,r}\}$, u_j can calculate the decryption key $x_i = \left(\sum_{v=1}^{r} T_{i,v} \cdot y_v \cdot \frac{p}{p_v}\right)$ mod p_v, x_i represents the decryption key of u_i's shared resource ciphertext. Conversely, if they don't have the same attributes $\{a_{i,1}, a_{i,2}, ..., a_{i,r}\}$, u_j cannot calculate the decryption key x_i.

Proof. If the terminal member u_j has determined that it wants to access the shared resource of u_i, it downloads the ciphertext of the resource shared by u_i through the storage address of the resource ciphertext, and u_j selects the corresponding attribute permission $\{T_{j,1}, T_{j,2}, ..., T_{j,r}\}$ and the corresponding network attribute parameter $(p_1, p_2, ..., p_r)$.

Then it calculates $\begin{cases} x_j \equiv T_{j,1}(\text{mod} p_1), \\ x_j \equiv T_{j,2}(\text{mod} p_2), \\ ... \\ x_j \equiv T_{j,r-1}(\text{mod} p_{r-1}), \end{cases}$ according to the CRT, x_j computes a unique

solution $x_j = \left(\sum_{v=1}^{r} T_{j,v} \cdot y_v \cdot \frac{p}{p_v}\right)$ mod p_v.

6 Performance Analysis

For the design of the whole technology, besides security, computing complexity, computing time and communication cost are also important indicators to measure resource sharing. Therefore, when we design this model, we compare our sharing model with several recent literatures. We compared our model with related literature [7] and [16]. The execution time shown in Table 1. In terms of time consumption, we use the Java-based encryption library JPBC library, using the Java programming language. The computer is configured with Intel(R) Core(TM)2 i5–7500 CPU, 3.40 GHz, and running the Windows 10 operating system.

Table 1. Execution time of each algorithm

Type of algorithm	Execution time
Modular inverse operation (T_{inv})	$T_{inv} \approx 0.0042$ ms
Multiplication operation (T_{mul})	$T_{mul} \approx 0.0011$ ms
Exponentiation operation ($T_{\exp}$)	$T_{\exp} \approx 6.6432$ ms
Elliptic curve point addition (T_{pa-ecc})	$T_{pa-ecc} \approx 0.003$ ms
Elliptic curve point multiplication (T_{sm-ecc})	$T_{sm-ecc} \approx 0.0036$ ms
Hash operation (T_h)	$T_h \approx 0.0001$ ms
Bilinear pairing (T_{bp})	$T_{bp} \approx 4.3183$ ms
Bilinear pairing point addition (T_{pa-bp})	$T_{pa-bp} \approx 0.0014$ ms
Bilinear pairing scalar multiplication (T_{sm-bp})	$T_{sm-bp} \approx 0.2038$ ms

We analyzed the computational cost of this model and the other two methods, where r represents the minimum number of attributes required by the terminal participating in the group key calculation. Table 2 lists the computational complexity of our shared model and the other two shared models. Comparing the computational complexity of these three shared models, our model has the smallest computational complexity.

Table 2. Computational complexity of our model and the models in the other two protocols

	Xue. et al. [7]	Zhong. et al. [16]	Ours
Setup	$(2r+4)T_{\exp} + T_{bp}$	$2rT_{\exp} + T_{bp}$	$(r-1)T_{pa-ecc} + (r+1)T_{mul} +$ $T_h + 2T_{\exp} + rT_{inv}$
Encrypt	$(4r+1)T_{\exp} + T_{bp}$	$4T_{\exp} + 4T_{bp}$	$T_{mul} + T_h$
Decrypt	$3rT_{bp}$	$T_{\exp} + 3T_{bp}$	$2T_{bp} + T_{mul} + T_h$

We compared the computational time required by our model with the other two protocol models. The results of the comparison in the registration phase is shown in the Fig. 2. According to the Fig. 2, it can be seen that the calculation time of our model is the smallest, the time consumption of Xue. et al. [7] is relatively small, and the time consumption of Zhong. et al. [16] is the largest.

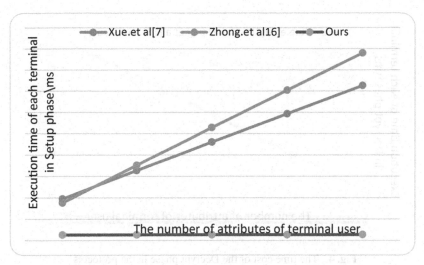

Fig. 2. The time cost of the Setup phase in the protocols

The results of the time consumption comparison in the encryption phase is shown in the Fig. 3. According to the Fig. 3, it can be seen that the calculation time of our model is the smallest, the time consumption of Zhong. et al. [16] is relatively small, and the time consumption of Xue. et al. [7] is the largest.

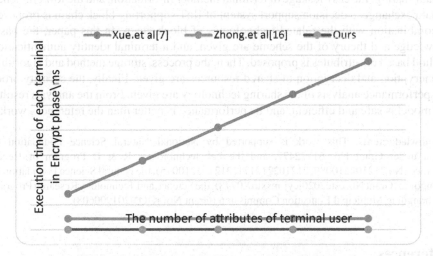

Fig. 3. The time cost of the Encrypt phase in the protocols

The results of the time consumption comparison in the decryption phase is shown in the Fig. 4. According to the Fig. 4, it can be seen that the calculation time of our model is the smallest, the time consumption of Zhong. et al. [16] is relatively small, and the time consumption of Xue. et al. [7] is the largest.

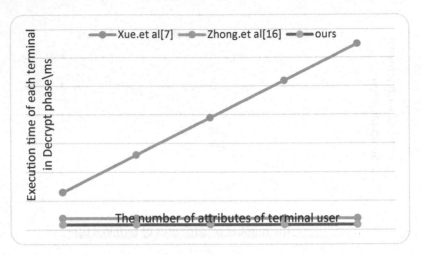

Fig. 4. The time cost of the Decrypt phase in the protocols

7 Conclusion

In this paper, we studied a security data sharing model for cloud network, and analyzed the contribution and existing problems of the current research on resource sharing. In view of the complexity of communication between terminal devices, the hidden danger of data sharing, the easy leakage of terminal member information, and the low efficiency of data exchange, a decision support system of IIoT supporting block chain is proposed in combination with the related technologies of block chain. In this paper, the basic knowledge and theory of the scheme are given, and a terminal identity authentication method based on attributes is proposed. Then, the process, storage method and algorithm of encryption and decryption of shared resources are given. Finally, the security proof and performance analysis of the sharing technology are given. From the analysis results, our model is safe and efficient, and its performance is better than the references works.

Acknowledgments. This work is supported by National Natural Science Foundation of China under Grant No. 61772477, and the key technologies R & D Program of Henan Province (No.212102210089, 212102210171, 212102210075), the Natural Science Foundation of Chongqing (Grant No. cstc2020jcyj-msxmX0778), the Science and Technology Research Program of Chongqing Municipal Education Commission (Grant No. KJQN201900608).

References

1. Guan, Z., Liu, X., Wu, L., et al.: Cross-lingual multi-keyword rank search with semantic extension over encrypted data. Journal **514**, 523–540 (2020)
2. Wang, W., Deng, Z., Wang, J., et al.: Securing cryptographic chips against scan-based attacks in wireless sensor network applications. Journal **19**(20), 4598 (2019)
3. Simeone, A., Caggiano, A., Boun, L., et al.: Intelligent cloud manufacturing platform for efficient resource sharing in smart manufacturing networks. Journal **79**, 233–238 (2019)

4. Lu, Y., Huang, X., Dai, Y., et al.: Blockchain and federated learning for privacy-preserved data sharing in industrial IoT. Journal 16(6), 4177–4186 (2019)
5. Zhang, Q., Zhao, K., Kuang, X., et al.: Multidomain security authentication for the Internet of things. Journal 2020(5), e5777 (2020)
6. Liu, X., Luo, Y., Yang, X.: Traceable attribute-based secure data sharing with hidden policies in mobile health networks. Journal 2020(5), 1–12 (2020)
7. Xue, Y., Xue, K., Gai, N., et al.: An attribute-based controlled collaborative access control scheme for public cloud storage. Journal 14(11), 2927–2942 (2019)
8. Salonikias, S., Gouglidis, A., Mavridis, I., Gritzalis, D.: Access control in the industrial Internet of Things. In: Alcaraz, C. (ed.) Security and Privacy Trends in the Industrial Internet of Things. ASTSA, pp. 95–114. Springer, Cham (2019). https://doi.org/10.1007/978-3-030-12330-7_5
9. Li, B., Huang, D., Wang, Z., et al.: Attribute-based access control for ICN naming scheme. Journal 15(2), 194–206 (2018)
10. Huang, H., Zhu, P., Xiao, F., et al.: A Blockchain-based scheme for privacy-preserving and secure sharing of medical data. Journal 99, 102010 (2020)
11. Chi, J., Li, Y., Huang, J., et al.: A secure and efficient data sharing scheme based on blockchain in industrial Internet of Things. Journal 167, 102710 (2020)
12. Zhang, Q., Li, Y., Wang, R., et al.: Data security sharing model based on privacy protection for blockchain-enabled industrial Internet of Things. Journal 36(1), 94–111 (2021)
13. Guo, S., Hu, X., Guo, S., et al.: Blockchain meets edge computing: a distributed and trusted authentication system. Journal 16(3), 1972–1983 (2019)
14. Wang, J., Wu, L., Choo, K., et al.: Blockchain-based anonymous authentication with key management for smart grid edge computing infrastructure. Journal 16(3), 1984–11992 (2019)
15. Cheng, Y., Lei, M., Chen, S., et al.: IoT security access authentication method based on blockchain. In: International Conference on Advanced Hybrid Information Processing, pp. 229–238. Springer, Cham (2019). https://doi.org/10.1007/978-3-030-36405-2_24
16. Zhong, H., Zhu, W., Xu, Y., Cui, J.: Multi-authority attribute based encryption access control scheme with policy hidden for cloud storage. Soft. Comput. 22(1), 243–251 (2016). https://doi.org/10.1007/s00500-016-2330-8
17. Lara, E., Aguilar, L., Sanchez, M., et al.: Lightweight authentication protocol for M2M communications of resource-constrained devices in industrial internet of things. Journal 20(2), 501 (2020)
18. Caviglione, L., Podolski, M., Mazurczyk, W., et al.: Covert channels in personal cloud storage services: the case of dropbox. Journal 13(4), 1921–1931 (2016)
19. Zhang, Q., Li, Y., Zhang, Q., et al.: A self-certified cross-cluster asymmetric group key agreement for wireless sensor networks. Journal 28(2), 280–287 (2019)
20. Li, Y., Wang, Y., Wang, Y., et al.: A feature-vector generative adversarial network for evading PDF malware classifiers. Journal 523, 38–48 (2020)
21. Zhang, P., Durresi, M., Durresi, A.: Internet network location privacy protection with multi-access edge computing. Computing 103(3), 473–490 (2020). https://doi.org/10.1007/s00607-020-00860-3
22. Mishra, D., Dharminder, D., Yadav, P., et al.: A provably secure dynamic ID-based authenticated key agreement framework for mobile edge computing without a trusted party. Journal 55, 102648 (2020)

A Dynamic Compression Method for Database Backup Files in Cloud Environments

Dongjie Zhu[1], Yulan Zhou[1], Shaozai Yu[2(✉)], Tianyu Wang[2], Yang Wu[2], Hao Hu[1], and Haiwen Du[3]

[1] School of Computer Science and Technology, Harbin Institute of Technology, Weihai 264209, China
[2] Kingsoft Cloud Inc., Beijing 100085, China
yushaozai@kingsoft.com
[3] School of Astronautics, Harbin Institute of Technology, Harbin 150001, China

Abstract. With the progress of society and the improvement of the degree of information technology, the data storage capacity of enterprise business is becoming larger. More and more enterprises choose to hand over the storage business to specialized cloud manufacturers. Generally, for the security and reliability of user data, cloud service providers (CSP) will conduct incremental or full backups of user data frequently. However, with the expansion of business and the increase of user data volume, the burden of data backup required by CSPs is becoming heavier. At present, most CSPs use open-source Xtrabackup for hot database backup and recovery, but Xtrabackup has shortcomings in compression rate and decompression speed.

To better improve Xtrabackup, we analyzed the backup and recovery process of Xtrabackup and fully explored the factors that affect its compression rate and decompression speed. Finally, an optimization strategy is proposed to optimize the original Xtrabackup. Experiments show that the proposed optimization scheme can increase the compression rate by 30%–50%, reduce the recovery time by 40%, and the total compression time by 25%.

Keywords: Compression rate · Decompression speed · Dynamic assignment · Double buffering model

1 Introduction

With the development of information technology and the arrival of the era of mobile Internet, the data storage capacity presents explosive growth [1, 2]. However, traditional storage solutions cannot meet complex, diverse, and large-scale storage needs [3]. More enterprises choose to save their data to cloud storage systems [4]. The explosion of cloud data has brought new challenges to the backup storage systems of CSPs [5]. The existing cloud storage backup scheme is mainly completed through Xtrabackup [6], but Xtrabackup has many shortcomings and deficiencies as follows:

The first is the low compression ratio of Xtrabackup backup compression. The default compression algorithm used by Xtrabackup is QuickLZ [7], which is an extremely fast

© Springer Nature Singapore Pte Ltd. 2021
Y. Tan et al. (Eds.): DMBD 2021, CCIS 1454, pp. 316–327, 2021.
https://doi.org/10.1007/978-981-16-7502-7_32

decompression algorithm. The latest version of QuickLZ was updated in January 2011. Although the decompression speed of this algorithm is fast, it was released 10 years ago, and the compression rate is lower than that of the newly released compression algorithms. Second, Xtrabackup sets a fixed value to key parameters, such as the output of the producer during the compression process – the read buffer size and the chunk size of the worker thread per compression. As a result, the program in some cases has low thread utilization and too slow compression speed. Finally, Xtrabacukp uses a pipeline model to implement compression, streaming, and encrypted backup of the database. When the upstream pipeline generates data and wants to write it to the downstream pipeline, if the downstream pipeline is executing file I/O at this time and has been locked, the upstream producer can only be forced to wait. This situation will greatly affect the overall system throughput and reduce the backup compression speed. Based on the above analysis, the shortcomings and deficiencies of the existing Xtrabackup will lead to a large waste of storage space and hardware resources, which in turn increases the total cost of ownership of cloud platform data (storage, acquisition, and migration costs).

To address the problems, we analyzed the principle and workflow of Xtrabackup. We make an in-depth analysis of its system architecture, program design, and propose an optimized scheme to improve the system from the following three aspects.

First of all, we test the default compression algorithm used by Xtrabakcup, and make a comprehensive comparison with the popular compression algorithms. Then, we decide to replace the original Qpress compression algorithm with the ZSTD [8] algorithm to improve the compression rate. At the same time, ZSTD only supports multithreaded compression but does not support multi-thread decompression. To further utilize the advantages of multi-thread and give full play to the hardware performance, we added additional skippable frames for each individually compressed block in the compression process, which is used to record the relevant information of the compressed block. In the subsequent decompression process, the information is used to realize multi-thread decompression of ZSTD, so as to further improve the decompression speed.

Secondly, through the analysis of the multi-thread model of the Xtrabackup compression process, we find that the original Xtrabackup ignores the relationship between upstream producers and consumers, and the characteristics of table files of different database instances. It leads to the mismatch between upstream producers' production volume and downstream consumers' consumption data volume in some cases. As a result, some producers or consumers generate more wait time, and the overall load of the threads is unbalanced, ultimately slowing down the compression speed of Xtrabackup. In this paper, a parameter setting method is designed to correlate the production data volume of upstream producers with the consumption capacity of downstream consumers. Besides, it dynamically adjusts the workload of a single worker thread that is assigned downstream based on the actual production volume of upstream. Therefore, it can ensure thread load balance and improve the compression efficiency of the system.

Finally, we provide an in-depth analysis of Xtrabackup's pipeline model and data flow. Then we optimize it for its most common business scenario: compressed streaming backup. In detail, the streaming pipe has its own independent buffer, so it does not need the additional buffer pipe set by the original Xtrabackup. At the same time, the file I/O step of the last link of the pipe is synchronous. When consumers read the contents in the buffer and unload the disk, other producers will be blocked, resulting in a lower throughput rate of the system. In this paper, the original Xtrabackup pipeline model is optimized, and the synchronous file I/O is changed to asynchronous by using double buffering, which reduces the contention of lock resources and improves the overall throughput rate of the system.

2 Compression Algorithm Replacement

The QuickLZ algorithm was first released in 2009. However, with the development of the times, more and more excellent compression algorithms have emerged in recent years. We selected some of these compression algorithms and tested them with Kingsoft Cloud's online data set. The test results are shown in Table 1, Table 2 and Table 3.

Table 1. Dataset 1 (34 GB) test results

	Quciklz	Quick-T4	ZSTD	ZSTD-T4-fast=1	ZSTD-T4-L7	ZSTD-MT4-14	MT4-ZSTD
compression ratio	3.09	3.09	6.18	4.3	6.8	6.18	6.18
compression time	117s	30s	199s	27s	135s	15s	37s
compression speed	298MB/s	1228MB/s	179MB/s	1289MB/s	257MB/s	2321MB/s	870MB/s
decompression time	100s	29s	70s	62s	77s	70s	26s
decompression speed	577MB/s	1094MB/s	453MB/s	512MB/s	412MB/s	453MB/s	1339MB/s

Based on the test results, we finally choose the ZSTD as the replacement algorithm. ZSTD compression algorithm is an open-sourced fast lossless compression algorithm contributed by Facebook. It provides a better compression rate for zlib level real-time compression scenarios. It is supported by the fast entropy phase provided by the Huff0 and FSE libraries.

To replace the compression algorithm correctly, the original Xtrabakcup decompression flow needs to be defined first.

For the compression process, Xtrabackup runs in the form of a pipeline, and the compressing process is one of the pipelines. In the pipeline initialization process, the *compress_open* method will be executed first to open the target file to be compressed. Then, it obtains the relevant information such as the handle of the target file and adds the suffix.*qp* to identify the compressed file type for file decompression. Then the compress pipeline will execute the *compress_write* method to compress the data read by the upstream producer. Finally, in the actual compression backup process, the compress pipeline needs to pass the compressed data to the downstream pipeline—buffer pipeline

Table 2. Dataset 2 (31 GB) test results

	Quciklz	Quick-T4	ZSTD	ZSTD-T4-fast=1	ZSTD-T4-L7	ZSTD-MT4-14	MT4-ZSTD
compression ratio	4.63	4.63	6.66	5.25	6.59	6.62	6.07
compression time	103s	20s	180s	20s	120s	16s	37s
compression speed	308MB/s	1586MB/s	176MB/s	1584MB/s	264MB/s	1984MB/s	858MB/s
decompression time	100s	30s	70s	54s	77s	54s	20s
decompression speed	317MB/s	1058MB/s	453MB/s	588MB/s	412MB/s	587MB/s	1578MB/s

Table 3. Dataset 3 (7 GB) test results

	Quciklz	Quick-T4	ZSTD	ZSTD-T4-fast=1	ZSTD-T4-L7	ZSTD-MT4-14	MT4-ZSTD
compression ratio	5.38	5.38	8.177	8.102	8.9	8.1	8.38
compression time	14s	6s	31s	4s	21s	3s	6s
compression speed	512MB/s	1194MB/s	231MB/s	1792MB/s	341MB/s	2389MB/s	1194MB/s
decompression time	11s	5s	13s	10s	12s	13s	5s
decompression speed	651MB/s	1433MB/s	551MB/s	716MB/s	597MB/s	551MB/s	1433MB/s

in order. We found that the QuickLZ algorithm api called by the *compress_write* method is basically the same as the ZSTD algorithm api, but the ZSTD compression algorithm has included the encapsulation steps such as writing header and trail in the compression process. Then, ZSTD does not need to write additional flag bits in the *compress_open* and *compress_end* stages like the original Xtrabackup. Therefore, the redundant operations in the original Xtrabackup need to be deleted before replacing the compression algorithm API. Finally, thanks to the pipeline architecture design of Xtrabackup, the functions of each pipeline are black box compared to other pipelines. Modifying the compress pipeline compression algorithm will not affect other functions such as xbstream and buffer pipelines. It reduces the difficulty of replacing the compression algorithm in Xtrabackup.

For the decompression process, Xtrabackup implements it through the qpress decompression tool and the bash pipeline. First, Xtrabackup executes the cat command to read the target file and output to STDOUT. Then, it determines in turn whether the file is an encrypted file ending with.*xbcrypt*. If it is, it performs the decryption process first. Then, it determines whether the file is a compressed file with.qp or.qp.xbcrypt suffix, and if so, it executes the decompression process (note: the.*qp.xbcrypt* file has been decrypted in the previous step). The decompression process of the original Xtrabackup is as follows: First, the data stream processed in the previous step is redirected to qpress through the | redirection symbol. Then qpress reads from standard input by setting command line parameters, then compresses the data, and outputs it to STDOUT. Finally, it outputs the decompressed content to the current path (that is, the original compressed file path with the.*qp* suffix removed) through the output redirection character ">". The final command is equivalent to "cat filepath | qpress -dio> dest_filepath". After the above analysis, it can be seen that the core step of the decompression process is to call the qpress tool to decompress. Since ZSTD provides executable programs and can support standard input and output, we can directly replace the calling tool and modify the suffix information recognized by the program.

Through the above scheme, we can directly realize the replacement of the compression algorithm. However, since the official ZSTD executable program only supports single-thread decompression, in order to make full use of system resources and take advantage of multi-threading, the decompression speed can be improved. We introduced a multi-threaded version of ZSTD, called pZSTD.

First, in order to achieve multi-threaded parallel decompression of a single compressed file, we need to divide a file into different independent blocks during compression, and then compress them separately. At the same time, it needs to be marked so that the program can recognize different blocks during subsequent decompression to achieve parallel decompression. In order to record the information of each independently compressed block, we introduced the skippable frame structure supported by the ZSTD algorithm. Skippable frames allow the insertion of user-defined metadata into a flow of concatenated frames. The structure of skippable frames is shown in the figure:

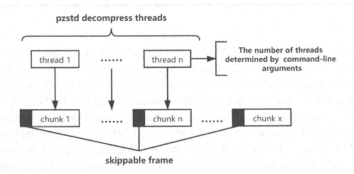

We can insert this structure into the header of the compressed block to identify the starting position of the compressed block. At the same time, the length information of the compressed block is recorded in User data, so that the program can quickly locate the skippable frame position of the next compressed block.

Magic_Number	Frame_Size	User_Data
4 bytes	4 bytes	n bytes

- Magic_Number: 4 bytes, little-endian, used to identify the structure as a skippable frame
- Frame_Size: 4 bytes, little-endian, used to indicate the size of subsequent User_Data
- User_Data: 4 bytes, user-defined data (used here to indicate the compressed block size)

Through the above method, the pZSTD executable program can quickly identify different compressed blocks, and use multiple threads to decompress different compressed blocks in parallel.

3 Parameter Setting Optimization

The Xtrabackup compression process uses a producer-consumer model. The upstream producer is the data copy thread, the number of which is set by the parameter parallel. The producer is mainly responsible for reading the files to be compressed and making relevant preparations to allow downstream consumers to compress them. The downstream consumer is Xtrabackup compress thread, the number of which is set by the parameter compress-threads. The consumer is mainly responsible for invoking the compression algorithm to compress the block to be compressed.

The specific interaction process of the producer-consumer model is shown in the figure:

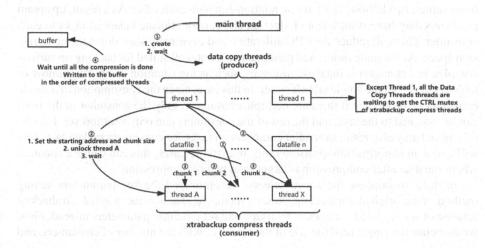

(1) First, the main thread creates several data copy threads according to the user input parameter parallel.
(2) Data copy threads first obtain a pointer to the file to be compressed, and then execute the while loop. It compresses a part of files each time (the length is fixed value len = 10 MB). Then the *compress_write* method tries to obtain the ctrl mutex of Xtrabackup compress threads (consumers) (note: once the copy thread acquires the first lock of the compress thread, it will block all other data copy threads and subsequent compress locks (ctrl mutex) can only be obtained by the data copy thread), and block the content of this part again (the length does not exceed the COMPRESS_CHUNK_SIZE set by the parameter –compress-chunk-size), and assign each block to a Xtrabackup compress thread to perform compression.
(3) Xtrabackup compress threads receives the starting address, block size and unlock signal of the content to be compressed, and then starts to perform the compression task. After completing the task, it sets the semaphore and sends a signal notification to the data copy thread that assigns the task.
(4) The data copy thread will wait for the Xtrabackup compress threads to complete the task in order (that is, the order when the compression task was allocated before) through the *for* loop (that is, if the compression thread 2, 3… has completed the compression task, but the compression thread 1 has not completed. They can only wait for the completion of compression thread 1 before proceeding to the next step, because it is necessary to ensure that the compressed content is written in the order of the original file). After receiving the completion signal, the compressed content of the thread is written to the next pipeline (buffer), and the ctrl mutex of the thread is released. After the *for* loop is completed (that is, the tasks assigned by the current data copy thread to Xtrabackup compress threads have been completed and written to the next pipeline in order), repeat the steps from the next data copy thread that gets the ctrl mutex (2)–(4).

Through the above process, we found that the single production volume of the original Xtrabackup producer (ie, the single read file size len), the number of downstream consumers, and the single consumption volume (COMPRESS_CHUNK_SIZE) are all fixed values. In addition, they have no relationship with each other. As a result, upstream producers may have insufficient production and cannot allocate balanced tasks to each consumer. This will reduce the CPU utilization and eventually slow down the compression speed. At the same time, fixed parameters are not well suited for backing up various complex and changeable database instances, such as the situation where the number of tables is large, but the single table is small. In this case, since the consumption of a single consumer is fixed, even if there are multiple consumers, only the consumer in the front can be assigned to the task, and the rest of the consumers can only wait forever. Finally, this model may also result in smaller compression tasks for consumers ranked last. This will cause an abnormal compression ratio. In extreme cases, this can cause a situation where the data after compression is larger than before compression.

In order to improve the above defects, we optimized the key parameters setting method of the original Xtrabackup. Among them, we abandon the original Xtrabackup scheme of setting fixed parameters by users, and set dynamic parameters instead. First, we associate the single read file size of the producer with the number of consumers, and assign values in the initialization phase of the program. Second, set a strategy to match the amount of work done by a producer (data copy thread) with the amount of work done by multiple consumers (compress threads) when all of them are allocated a balanced amount of work. Then, in the *compress_write* stage, before assigning tasks to consumers, determine whether the current read byte length can exceed the workload required for 3/4 thread work. If so, set it directly to the established chunk size, otherwise, divide it by the number of consumer threads for reallocation (note: rounding up is needed to avoid the remaining few bytes, and an additional compression is added) to ensure that all threads are load balanced. Finally, compare the calculated chunk size with 64k to avoid the size is too small and the compression rate is abnormal.

4 Double Buffering

Xtrabackup uses the pipeline model to achieve a combination of various backup scenarios. The pipeline data flow of the most common streaming compression backup is shown in the figure:

A single pipeline obtains the specific data file through the *ds_file_t->ptr* pointer, and then locates the next pipeline through the data file *dest_file* pointer.

The workflow of the streaming compression backup pipeline is as follows:

1. The *data_copy_thread* thread calls the *compress_write* method and waits for the compression to complete.
2. After the *Xtrabackup_compress_threads* thread finishes compression, modify the value of thd- > data_avail to FALSE, and notify *data_copy_thread* to continue the next step.
3. *data_copy_thread* calls the *buffer_write* method to write the compressed data into the buffer pipeline.
4. The *xb_stream_write_data* method writes the data converted to *xbstream* format into the buffer of the *xbstream* pipeline. If the buffer is full (the chunk buffer size is defined by the XB_STREAM_MIN_CHUNK_SIZE macro, the default is 10 MB), execute the *xb_stream_flush* method to flush the data to STDOUT in advance In the buffer of the pipeline.
5. Finally, when the data in the STDOUT pipeline reaches 10 MB, the data will be written to the disk through the ">" redirection symbol to complete the data placement.

From the above analysis, it can be seen that every time the STDOUT buffer data exceeds 10 MB, a data placement will be performed. When placing the order, because the upstream producer has already occupied the control lock of the downstream consumer, this stage will block other threads from placing the disk and entering the subsequent data compression process. It will eventually affect the overall throughput rate of the system.

In order to solve the above problems, we decided to adopt the double buffer model as shown in the figure. It uses the speed difference between upstream producers and downstream consumers to change synchronous I/O into asynchronous. It can reduce contention for lock resources, thereby increasing the overall throughput of the system.

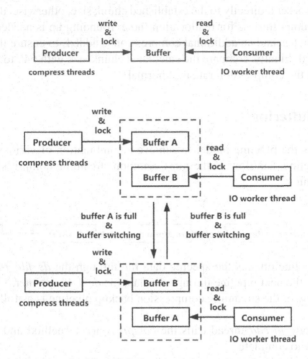

First, we initialize two buffers with the same size and mark their status with two tag variables (TRUE for available and FALSE for unavailable), and then create a pointer to the buffer currently in use.

The specific workflow is as follows:

1. When the upstream writes data to the STDOUT pipeline, determine whether the currently used buffer space is enough, if it is enough, write directly, if it is insufficient, temporarily switch to the backup buffer.
2. Before switching to the backup buffer, make sure that it is in a usable state, that is, the I/O worker thread has completed the cleaning of the backup buffer.
3. When it has been ensured that the spare buffer is available, mark the current buffer as unavailable and record its address information.
4. Wake up the I/O worker thread to clear the current buffer.
5. Switch to the backup buffer and save the data in it.

The final pipeline process changes are shown in the following figure:

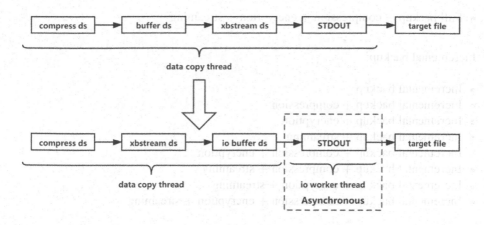

5 Experiments

In the experiment, we deployed the improved version of Xtrabackup and the original version of Xtrabackup to the same machine for testing. The test environment is as follows (Table 4):

Table 4. Dataset 2 (31 GB) test results

	Property
Operating system	CentOS 7.6
CPU	Intel(R) Xeon(R) Gold 6240 CPU @ 2.60 GHz
Memory	377.8 GB
Hard disk	Intel® SSD DC P4510 Series 2.0 TB
GLIBC	glibc-2.12-1.166.el6_7.7.x86_64

First, we verified the system correctness of the improved version of Xtrabackup. We permuted and combined all the scenarios of the Xtrabackup tool as follows:

Full backup:

- Full backup
- Full backup + compression
- Full backup + encryption
- Full backup + streaming
- Full backup + compression + encryption
- Full backup + compression + streaming
- Full backup + encryption + streaming

- Full backup + compression + encryption + streaming

Incremental backup:

- Incremental backup
- Incremental backup + compression
- Incremental backup + encryption
- Incremental backup + streaming
- Incremental backup + compression + encryption
- Incremental backup + compression + streaming
- Incremental backup + encryption + streaming
- Incremental backup + compression + encryption + streaming

After experimentation, the function of the improved version of Xtrabackup is correct. Because our modification to the compression pipeline is transparent to other steps of the pipeline, it will not affect other functions of the system.

Then, in order to prove that the optimization scheme we proposed can be applied to various real backup scenarios. We used multiple real data sets on Kingsoft Cloud online environments to evaluate the effect of the improved version of Xtrabackup and the original version of Xtrabackup.

The first database instance comes from Cheetah online data. Its database instance is characterized by a small number of tables (less than 100), but a single table.ibd file is large (above 10 GB).

The second database instance comes from Kingdee. Its database instance is characterized by a large number of tables (100,000 level), but a single table.ibd file is small (mostly empty tables, only 96 kb).

We mainly tested the most common usage scenario of Xtrabackup-compressed streaming backup, and performed statistics on key parameters such as compression rate, decompression time, and system resource consumption. The experimental results are shown in the table (Table 5):

Table 5. Dataset 2 (31 GB) test results

Version	Compressed size	Compression ratio	Compression time	Restoring time	Unpack time	Preparing time	Recovery time	Total time
Old	168 GB	2.58	56 m39 s	12 m27 s	17 m24 s	1.3 s	29 m52 s	86 m31 s
New	114 GB	3.81	37 m1 s	7 m58 s	12 m47 s	1.3 s	20 m46 s	57 m47 s
Version	Compressed size	Compression ratio	Compression time	Restoring time	Unpack time	Preparing time	Recovery time	Total time
Old	7.1 GB	9.43	39 m49 s	1 m1 s	5 m15 s	2 m50 s	9 m6 s	48 m55 s
New	4.0 GB	16.75	29 m24 s	0 m53 s	10 m13 s	2 m50 s	13 m56 s	43 m20 s

6 Conclusion

First of all, through experimental verification, it can be known that the optimization scheme proposed in this paper can ensure the correctness of the system functionality. And the system resource overhead (CPU utilization, memory) brought by the ZSTD compression algorithm and double buffer structure is within a controllable range. Secondly, the ZSTD algorithm API library does not depend on the high-version glibc environment or other third-party libraries, and because the modification of this optimization solution is completely transparent to the user application layer, the user can use it directly without modifying the original command or script. Finally, through testing on real online data sets, it can be seen that this optimization solution can increase the compression rate by 30%–50%, reduce the total compression time by 25%, and reduce the total recovery time by 40%.

In general, the optimization solution we proposed has significantly improved compression rate and decompression time-consuming compared with the original Xtrabackup, which can effectively reduce the backup cost of cloud vendors and improve company efficiency.

Acknowledgement. This research is based upon works supported by the Sanming University (19YG02), the Fundamental Research Funds for the Central Universities (Grant No. HIT.NSRIF.201714), Weihai Science and Technology Development Program (2016DXGJMS15), Key Research and Development Program in Shandong Provincial (2017GGX90103) and Weihai Scientific Research and Innovation Fund (2020).

References

1. Zhu, D., et al.: Massive files prefetching model based on LSTM neural network with cache transaction strategy. Comput. Mater. Continua **63**(2), 979–993 (2020)
2. Wu, J., Ping, L., Ge, X., Wang, Y., Fu, J.: Cloud storage as the infrastructure of cloud computing. In: 2010 International Conference on Intelligent Computing and Cognitive Informatics, pp. 380–383. IEEE (2010)
3. Zhu, D., Du, H., Wang, Y., Peng, X.: An IoT-oriented real-time storage mechanism for massive small files based on Swift. Int. J. Embedded Syst. **12**(1), 72–80 (2020)
4. Zhu, D., Haiwen, D., Cao, N., Qiao, X., Liu, Y.: SP-TSRM: a data grouping strategy in distributed storage system. In: Vaidya, J., Li, J. (eds.) ICA3PP 2018. LNCS, vol. 11334, pp. 524–531. Springer, Cham (2018). https://doi.org/10.1007/978-3-030-05051-1_36
5. Dzhagaryan, A., Milenkovic, A.: On effectiveness of compressed file transfers to/from the cloud: an experimental evaluation. In: PECCS, pp. 173–184 (2018)
6. Kim, H., Yeom, H.Y., Son, Y.: An efficient database backup and recovery scheme using write-ahead logging. In: 2020 IEEE 13th International Conference on Cloud Computing (CLOUD), pp. 405–413. IEEE (2020)
7. Wang, R., Wang, C., Zha, L.: PACM: A prediction-based auto-adaptive compression model for HDFS. In: 2016 IEEE International Parallel and Distributed Processing Symposium Workshops (IPDPSW), pp. 1617–1626. IEEE (2016)
8. Facebook/Zstd: Facebook, GitHub. https://github.com/facebook/zstd (2015)

Research on Fault Detection and Diagnosis Method of Diesel Engine Air System Based on Deep Learning

Yanyan Wang[1], Ning Ren[1(✉)], Jin Li[2], Bin Liu[2], Qingtao Si[2], and Ruitian Zhang[1]

[1] Harbin Institute of Technology, Weihai 264209, People's Republic of China
wangyanyan@hit.edu.cn

[2] Faw Jiefang Automotive Company, Changchun 130033, People's Republic of China
{lijin,liubin1,siqingtao}@rdc.faw.com.cn

Abstract. In order to meet the requirements of multi-parameter and real-time fault diagnosis of China VI vehicle emission standards diesel engine air system, this paper focuses on the research of the diesel engine air system fault detection and diagnosis method based on deep learning to improve the operational safety and fault diagnosis efficiency. In this paper, the air system fault detection and diagnosis are completed based on the AE model and the CNN model, combined with the actual operation of the diesel engine. Among them, the AE model successfully detected all real-time operation faults, and the false detection rate on the health data was 0.1162%; the CNN model obtained a 90.77% fault diagnosis accuracy rate on the test set of the real-time operation data set. The results show that the model has high accuracy in the diagnosis of diesel engine faults, which is of great significance to the application of deep learning based on big data processing.

Keywords: Diesel engine · Fault diagnosis · Deep learning · Autoencoder · CNN

1 Introduction

In order to control and monitor the status of each component of the diesel engine air system, the monitoring parameters of diesel engine have reached more than 80 kinds, so a large number of high dimensional real-time operation data have been generated. And the development of Internet of Vehicle and deep learning makes it possible to mine the high-dimensional real-time operation data of diesel engine. Deep learning has been applied in image analysis [1,2], speech recognition [3,4], text understanding [5] and other fields [6]. Big data and deep learning complement each other. Therefore, in the face of the big data transmitted by diesel engine sensors, using deep learning to mine these data is the most efficient method.

In the field of fault detection and diagnosis, the commonly used deep learning models include deep belief networks (DBN), convolutional neural networks (CNN), autoencoder (AE) and the variants of each network [7]. Since the AE

© Springer Nature Singapore Pte Ltd. 2021
Y. Tan et al. (Eds.): DMBD 2021, CCIS 1454, pp. 328–341, 2021.
https://doi.org/10.1007/978-981-16-7502-7_33

model does not need to use the fault data to train the model, it indirectly solves the problem of insufficient fault data; while the CNN fault diagnosis model can extract the spatial feature information of the data, and it has a good noise filtering ability. Therefore, AE and CNN are selected as fault detection and diagnosis models in this paper.

At present, fault detection methods based deep learning have been deeply studied in the fields of bearing wear [8], motor failure [9], aero-engine failure [10], fan blade failure [11] and so on. But it is still difficult to obtain fault data in the industrial field. At the same time, compared with other fields, the diesel engine sensor data fluctuation range is large, the working condition changes frequently, and the fault diagnosis is difficult.

Therefore, this paper cooperated with automobile enterprises to obtain a large number of real-time operation data of diesel engines. According to the characteristics of diesel engine data, a fault diagnosis algorithm based on condition fusion is proposed to solve the problem of low accuracy of single condition fault.

In order to realize the fault diagnosis of the air system, this paper selects 12 parameters from more than 80 monitoring parameters of the diesel engine to analyze three faults of the air system, namely, too low boost pressure, EGR valve communication timeout, EGR closed-loop monitoring fault. At the same time, according to the fuel injection rate, the diesel engine is divided into three operating conditions: low, medium and high operating conditions.

2 Fault Detection of Diesel Engine Air System Based on Autoencoder

2.1 Selection of Reconstruction Error of Autoencoder

The fault detection method based on the autoencoder belongs to the semi-supervised learning method based on deviation. For the autoencoder model, the deviation refers to the reconstruction error. The current fault is determined by calculating whether the reconstruction error between the input and output data of the model exceeds the given threshold.

The reconstruction error calculation method will directly affect the effect of model fault detection. Solving the reconstruction error between the health data and the fault data is to solve the distance between the two sets of data. Currently commonly used distance solving algorithms can be roughly divided into two categories. One category includes Minkowski distance and Mahalanobis distance to find the geometric distance between two points. The other category includes KL divergence and its variants JS Divergence algorithm for solving the probability distribution distance between two sets of data. Among them, since the Mahalanobis distance needs to calculate the inverse matrix of the covariance, but the covariance matrix is often irreversible, the Mahalanobis distance is no longer considered.

In this paper, the EGR valve position and EGR branch flow data of health data are used to train the model, and the EGR valve position and EGR branch flow data of the EGR valve closed-loop monitoring fault on 2020/09/03 are used to verify the model. Then use each distance measurement algorithm to calculate the distance between health data input and its reconstructed data, and the distance between fault data input and its reconstructed data. The results are shown in Fig. 1.

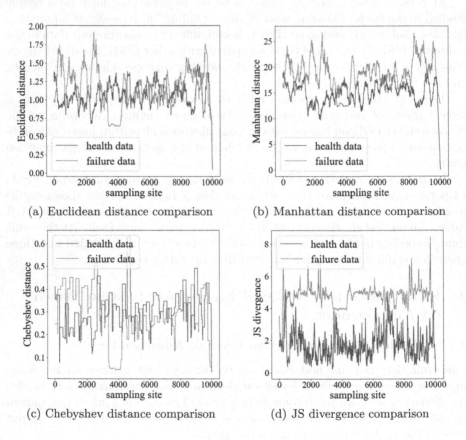

(a) Euclidean distance comparison

(b) Manhattan distance comparison

(c) Chebyshev distance comparison

(d) JS divergence comparison

Fig. 1. Comparison of health data and failure data.

As can be seen from the figure, Euclidean distance, Manhattan distance and Chebyshev distance did not separate the health data from the fault data, but the JS divergence successfully separated the health and fault data. Therefore, this paper will take JS divergence as the calculation method of reconstruction error.

2.2   Evaluation Criteria for Fault Detection Results

In this paper, the effect of the model is measured by four standards: the relative difference of average JS divergence between health data sets $H_{JS_{average}}$ and fault data sets $F_{JS_{average}}$, the false detection rate of health data $Rate_{mis}$ and the detection rate of fault data $Rate_{out}$. The calculation methods for the above parameters are as follows:

With health data $H_x = (hx_1, hx_2, ..., hx_n)$, fault data $F_x = (fx_1, fx_2, ..., fx_n)$, the model output health data JS dispersion $H_x = (hx_{JS1}, hx_{JS2}, ..., hx_{JSn})$, and the fault data JS dispersion $F_x = (fx_{JS1}, fx_{JS2}, fx_{JS3}, ..., fx_{JSn})$, then the average JS dispersion of health data as Eq. 1:

$$H_{JS_{average}} = \frac{\sum_1^n hx_{JSi}}{n} \tag{1}$$

The average JS dispersion of fault data is as Eq. 2:

$$F_{JS_{average}} = \frac{\sum_1^m fx_{JSi}}{m} \tag{2}$$

The JS dispersion relative difference of health data and fault data is as Eq. 3:

$$RE_{JS} = \frac{F_{JS_{average}} - H_{JS_{average}}}{H_{JS_{average}}} \tag{3}$$

Suppose the JS divergence threshold is T, and $y = N(x)$ represents the number of data points contained in x, then the health data false detection rate is the ratio of the number of health data points whose JS divergence value exceeds the threshold to the total number, as shown in Eq. 4:

$$Rate_{mis} = \frac{N(Hx_{JS} > T)}{n} \tag{4}$$

The fault data detection rate is the ratio of the number of fault data points whose JS divergence exceeds the threshold to the total number of fault data, as shown in Eq. 5:

$$Rate_{out} = \frac{N(Fx_{JS} > T)}{m} \tag{5}$$

2.3 The Determination of Structural Parameters and Activation Function of Fault Detection Model

The structural parameters of the model include the number of layers and the number of nodes of the model. The optimal number of layers and the number of nodes should be determined to obtain a better fault detection effect of the model. This paper constructs five model structures as shown in Table 1.

Use real-time collected health and fault data to verify the fault detection effects of different model structures. Finally, the JS divergence relative difference (DRD) of each fault is shown in Fig. 2. As can be seen from Fig. 2, model 4 has the largest JS divergence relative difference among faults and the model has the best performance.

Because the error detection rate of model 1 can reach more than 70%, far higher than the mis-detection rate of model 2, 3, 4, in order to avoid its effect

Table 1. Five model structures..

The model code	Model structure (Input - coding - intermediate - decoding - output layer)	Total number of model parameters
Model 1	12-2-12	62
Model 2	12-5-2-5-12	164
Model 3	12-10-2-10-12	314
Model 4	12-13-5-2-5-13-12	512
Model 5	12-19-5-2-5-19-12	728

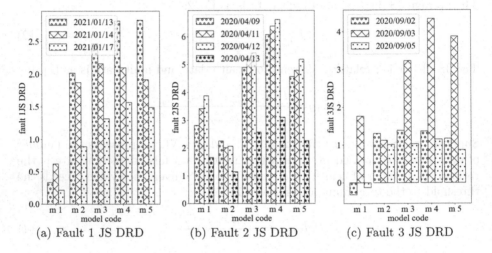

(a) Fault 1 JS DRD   (b) Fault 2 JS DRD   (c) Fault 3 JS DRD

Fig. 2. The JS DRD of fault 1, 2 and 3 under different model structural parameters.

on the observation of other model effects, Fig. 3 draws the false detection rate and fault detection rate of model 2, 3, and 4. Figure 3 shows the detection rate and false detection rate of each model when the JS divergence thresholds are respectively defined as 7, 6, 5, 4, 3, and 2. According to the figure, model 4 can obtain the highest fault detection rate while ensuring a low false detection rate. Through comprehensive analysis of JS divergence relative difference, model detection rate and false detection rate, model 4 is determined to be the optimal model structure.

Change the model activation function to Relu, and get the relative difference of JS divergence as shown in Fig. 4. As can be seen from the figure, except for the data on Days 2021/01/14 of fault 1, the JS divergence relative difference with Relu as the activation function is significantly smaller than the relative difference with Tanh as the activation function. Therefore, this paper chooses the Tanh function as the activation function of the model.

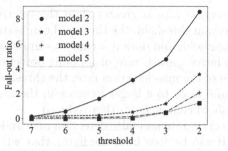
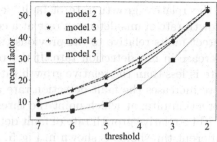

(a) health data fall-out ratio of different   (b) Recall factor under different models
models

Fig. 3. The fall-out ratio and recall factor ratio under different delimit thresholds.

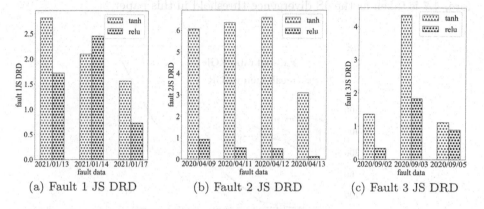

(a) Fault 1 JS DRD   (b) Fault 2 JS DRD   (c) Fault 3 JS DRD

Fig. 4. The JS DRD of fault 1, 2 and 3 under different model activation function.

2.4   The Determination of JS Divergence Threshold

After determining the model structure and working condition interval, it is necessary to further determine the JS divergence threshold according to the model output results. JS divergence delineation principles include the following two:

1. Improve the fault detection rate as much as possible;
2. Reduce the rate of health data mistesting as much as possible on the basis of the realization of Principle 1.

Suppose the ratio of the fault detection rate to the false detection rate of health data is Rate, and the relative growth rate of the ratio of the detection rate to the false detection rate is 1. With JS divergence thresholds T1 and T2, the ratio of the detection rate and the false detection rate under the T2 threshold corresponding to the relative growth rate of the ratio of the detection rate and the false detection rate under the T1 threshold is defined as:

$$Rate = \frac{Rate_{T2} - Rate_{T1}}{Rate_{T1}} \qquad (6)$$

If the relative growth rate of fault detection rate is greater than the relative growth rate of mis-detection rate at a certain threshold, the threshold can better detect faults relative to the previous threshold, and does not cause a significant increase in mis-detection rate. If the relative growth rate of its fault detection rate is less than the relative growth rate of the mis-detection rate, the threshold here increases the fault detection rate and leads to a larger increase in the mis-detection rate, at which point the threshold cannot be further reduced.

The relative growth rate of fault detection rate and false detection rate under different thresholds is shown in Fig. 5. It can be seen from the figure that when the threshold is slightly greater than 4.7, the relative growth rate of the fault detection rate and the false detection rate are equal, but after this point, as the threshold decreases, the increase rate of the relative growth rate of the false detection rate is greater than the increase rate of the fault detection rate. Therefore, 4.7 is taken as the JS divergence threshold in this paper.

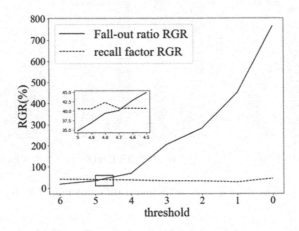

Fig. 5. The relative growth rate of false detection rate/detection rate under different thresholds.

2.5   Fault Detection Result

When the JS divergence threshold is 4.7, all real-time monitoring faults are successfully detected, and the fault and health data detection results are shown in Fig. 6, for example. Figure 7 shows the detection results of 750,000 health data, and meanwhile the false detection rate of health data is 0.1162%. Although the health data has a certain false detection rate, the JS divergence of the health data does not exceed the threshold for a long time like the fault data, but only exceeds the threshold at some point in time.

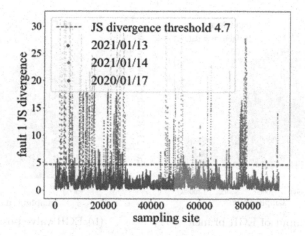

Fig. 6. Real-time fault monitoring of the final fault 1 detection results.

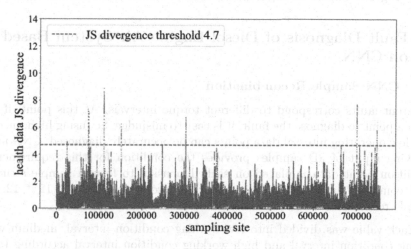

Fig. 7. Real-time monitoring of health data test results.

2.6   Visual Analysis of Fault Detection Models

In order to have a more intuitive understanding of the reconstruction effect of the autoencoder model, Fig. 8 draw the comparison diagram between the pre-processed input data of fault 2 and the reconstruction results of the autoencoder model.

Figure 8 shows the reconstruction result of fault 2. The reconstruction results of EGR valve opening and EGR branch flow by the model are significantly higher than the actual values of opening and flow, but because only two variables have large reconstruction errors, its JS divergence is slightly larger.

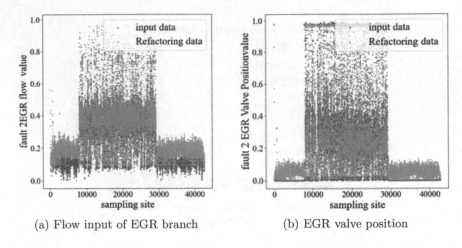

(a) Flow input of EGR branch   (b) EGR valve position

Fig. 8. Compare the input data of fault 2 with the reconstruction result.

3 Fault Diagnosis of Diesel Engine Air System Based on CNN

3.1 CNN Sample Recombination

Different faults correspond to different torque intervals. At this point, if only from a point to diagnose the fault, it is easy to misjudge. So fusing high, medium and low operating interval data points can be accurately diagnosed. CNN model allowing input of 3D samples provides the condition for this requirement: a condition point data is placed on each dimension to form a sample structure that combines data from different operating conditions by 3 * 12 * 12. The sample recombination method is as follows:

1. Each value was divided into low working condition interval, medium working condition interval and high working condition interval according to the injection amount of 0–100/cycle, 100–180/cycle and 180–300/cycle.
2. Assume that the original data contains a total of 12 variables from A to L. Assuming that time 1 is the data point of high working condition, time 4 is the data point of medium working condition, and time 7 is the data point of low working condition, rearrange each working condition point into a CNN input sample form of 3 *12 * 12 according to the Fig. 9. The first variable is A, and the following n variables are $\sum_k^{n-1}$ k values sliding backward from A [12]; for example, when $n = 4$ and $\sum_k^{n-1}$ k, sliding 6 backward from A, it is variable G. In the CNN reconstruction sample, in order that each variable can be located in the same CNN receptive field with all other variables, the variables are arranged from top to bottom in the order of A-B-D-G-K-D-J-E-A-J-H-G.

From the high working condition data layer after sample reorganization in Fig. 9, 6 CNN receptive fields centered on C1 can be seen. These 6 receptive fields make C1 have connections with A1, B1, D1, E1, F1, G1, H1, I1, J1, K1, and L1. In the original value of each variable, C1 is only adjacent to B1 and D1.

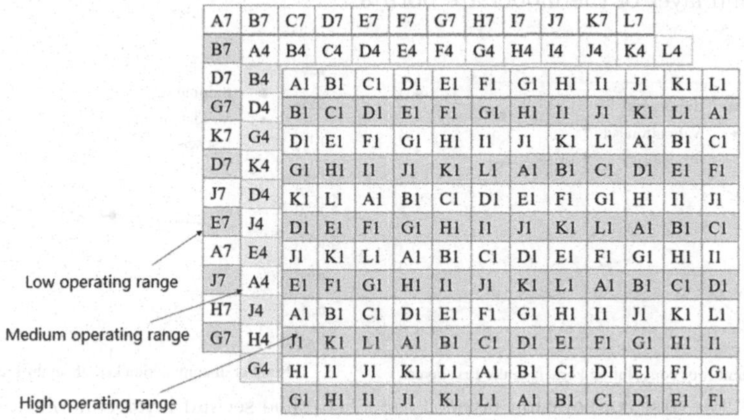

A7	B7	C7	D7	E7	F7	G7	H7	I7	J7	K7	L7	
B7	A4	B4	C4	D4	E4	F4	G4	H4	I4	J4	K4	L4
D7	B4	A1	B1	C1	D1	E1	F1	G1	H1	I1	J1	K1	L1
G7	D4	B1	C1	D1	E1	F1	G1	H1	I1	J1	K1	L1	A1
K7	G4	D1	E1	F1	G1	H1	I1	J1	K1	L1	A1	B1	C1
D7	K4	G1	H1	I1	J1	K1	L1	A1	B1	C1	D1	E1	F1
J7	D4	K1	L1	A1	B1	C1	D1	E1	F1	G1	H1	I1	J1
E7	J4	D1	E1	F1	G1	H1	I1	J1	K1	L1	A1	B1	C1
A7	E4	J1	K1	L1	A1	B1	C1	D1	E1	F1	G1	H1	I1
J7	A4	E1	F1	G1	H1	I1	J1	K1	L1	A1	B1	C1	D1
H7	J4	A1	B1	C1	D1	E1	F1	G1	H1	I1	J1	K1	L1
G7	H4	J1	K1	L1	A1	B1	C1	D1	E1	F1	G1	H1	I1
	G4	H1	I1	J1	K1	L1	A1	B1	C1	D1	E1	F1	G1
		G1	H1	I1	J1	K1	L1	A1	B1	C1	D1	E1	F1

Low operating range — Medium operating range — High operating range

Fig. 9. Sample recombination.

3.2 The Determination of Structural Parameters and Activation Function

In the CNN model, the number of convolutional layer kernel function and activation function have great influence on the final effect of the model, which are the parameters to be determined in. Firstly, set the size of the first layer of convolution kernel x_1 to 1, 3, 5, 8 and 12 respectively, set the number of the second layer of convolution kernel x_2 to 1, and set the activation function to Relu function. In order to ensure the effect of model training, the data volume of each failure training set should be balanced. Therefore, set the data of each failure training set and verification set to about 5000, in which the ratio of training set and verification set data is 1:1.

Finally, the accuracy rates of the training set, validation set, and test set corresponding to the different numbers of convolution kernels in the first layer are shown in Fig. 10(a). It is found by Fig. 10(a) that with the increase of the size of the first layer convolutional core, the accuracy of the training set is gradually increased, the accuracy of the verification set is increased first, and then gradually stabilizes at around 96%, while the test set accuracy is highest when the number of convolutions is 3. When the number of convolutions is greater than 5, although the accuracy of the training set is gradually increasing, the accuracy of the validation set is no longer greatly increased, and the accuracy of the test set is gradually decreasing, and the model has been fitted. Therefore, set the number of convolutional nuclei in the first layer of the model to 3.

Set the number of second-layer convolution kernels to 1, 3, and 5 respectively, and the accuracy of the model is shown in Fig. 10(b). It can be seen from the figure that when the number of second-layer convolution kernels is 3, the test set has the highest accuracy, which is 98.71%. So it is determined that the number of convolution kernels in the first layer and the number of convolution kernels in the second layer of the model are both 3.

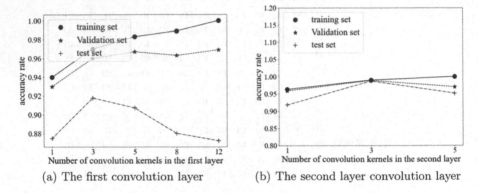

(a) The first convolution layer   (b) The second layer convolution layer

Fig. 10. Accuracy of different number of convolution kernel in layer convolution layer.

Set the model activation functions to Tanh and Relu respectively, and get the accuracy as shown in Fig. 11. It is found that the accuracy of the test set obtained by using Relu as the activation function is higher than that of the Tanh activation function. In addition, in the process of repeated training, it was found that when Tanh was used as the activation function, the final result of the model was less stable, and the accuracy of the test set fluctuated within the range of 89%–93%, while the training results of Relu activation function were relatively stable, and the accuracy difference was less than 2% after repeated training. So set the model activation function to Relu.

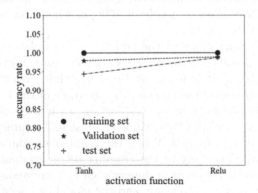

Fig. 11. The accuracy of different activation functions.

3.3 Fault Diagnosis Result

Based on the above analysis, the CNN model is set to two layers, and layer convolutional function number is both set to 3, and use Relu function as the activation function, while setting the CNN sample is 3 * 12 * 12, and the sample order is A-B-D-G-K-D-J-E-A-J-H-G. This section troubleshoots real-time acquisition data based on this model structure. The troubleshooting confusion matrix and accuracy are shown in Fig. 12.

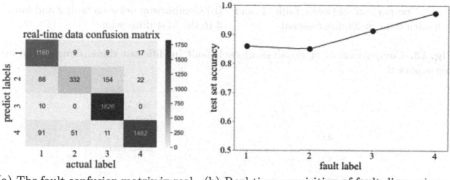

(a) The fault confusion matrix in real time

(b) Real-time acquisition of fault diagnosis accuracy

Fig. 12. Real-time acquisition of fault confusion matrix and diagnostic accuracy.

3.4 CNN Model Visualization

In order to understand the feature extraction results of the CNN model, this paper visualizes the various dimensions of the new feature space S after convolution and pooling of the CNN model. It is found that in the new feature space S, each fault can be distinguished in pairs in some dimensions. Figure 13 shows the comparison of the distribution of each fault feature point on the 28th, and 51st dimensions of the feature space S.

The fully connected layer uses the feature values in the feature space S to classify, and the fully connected layer uses the principal component analysis (PCA) to map and visualize the two-dimensional space. Figure 14 shows the distribution of each fault and health data in this two-dimensional space. In this space, each fault and health data has been clustered separately, and a small number of data points are confused at the boundary of each category.

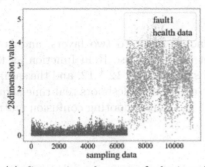 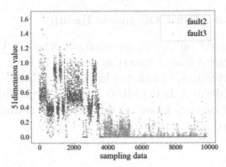

(a) Comparison between fault 1 and health data in 28 dimensional

(b) Comparison between fault 2 and fault 3 in the 51st dimension

Fig. 13. Comparison of eigenvalues of each fault in different dimensions of the new eigenspace S.

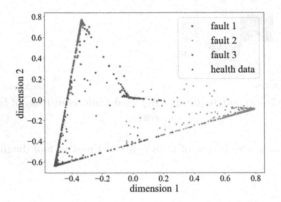

Fig. 14. Full connection layer two-dimensional mapping.

4   Conclusion and Future Work

In this paper, the fault detection model based on the AE successfully detects three real-time monitoring faults, and the false detection rate on the health data is 0.1162%. This paper proposes to recombine the original time series data into 3 * 12 * 12 3D CNN input sample data integrating different working conditions. Compared with the sample data of 1 * 12 * 12 without considering the working conditions, it proves the validity of the sample structure. Meanwhile, the diagnosis accuracy of CNN based fault diagnosis model for three real-time monitoring fault test sets is 90.77%. In this paper, the fault detection model based on the autoencoder and the fault diagnosis model based on CNN have high accuracy for the fault detection of the diesel engine air system, which is of great significance for its diagnosis.

In future work, it is possible to establish an accurate correspondence between the size of the reconstruction error of the autoencoder and the severity of the current fault to evaluate the current health of the air system; at the same time, the fault diagnosis model can be verified on more kinds of faults.

References

1. Islam, S.S., Rahman, S., Rahman, M.M., et al.: Application of deep learning to computer vision: a comprehensive study. In: 2016 5th International Conference on ICIEV, pp. 592–597. IEEE (2016)
2. Mohanty, S.P., Hughes, D.P., Marcel, S.: Using deep learning for image-based plant disease detection. Front. Plant Sci. **7**, 1419 (2016)
3. Zhang, Z., Geigere, J., Pohjalainen, J., et al.: Deep learning for environmentally robust speech recognition: an overview of recent developments. ACM Trans. Intell. Syst. Technol. **9**(5), 1–28 (2017)
4. Majumder, N., Poria, S., Gelbukh, A., et al.: Deep learning-based document modeling for personality detection from text. Intell. Syst. IEEE. **32**(2), 74–79 (2017)
5. Liang, H., Sun, X., Sun, Y., et al.: Correction to: text feature extraction based on deep learning: a review. EURASIP J. Wirel. Commun. Netw. **2018**(1), 42 (2018). https://doi.org/10.1186/s13638-018-1056-y
6. Saufi S R, Ahmad Z A B, Lenog M S, et al.: Challenges and opportunities of deep learning models for machinery fault detection and diagnosis: a review. IEEE Access (2019)
7. Zhang, Q., Yang, L.T., Chen, Z., et al.: A survey on deep learning for big data. Inf. Fusion **42**, 146–157 (2018)
8. Junbo, T., Weining, L., Juneng, A., et al.: Fault diagnosis method study in roller bearing based on wavelet transform and stacked auto-encoder, pp. 4608–4613. IEEE (2015)
9. Han, J., Choi, D., Hong, S., et al.: Motor fault diagnosis using CNN based deep learning algorithm considering motor rotating speed, pp. 440–445. IEEE (2019)
10. Verstraete, D., Ferrada, A., Drouuett, E.L., et al.: Deep Learning Enabled Fault Diagnosis Using Time-Frequency Image Analysis of Rolling Element Bearings. Shock and Vibration, pp. 1–17 (2017)
11. Li, Y.: A Research and application for wind turbine health condition monitoring based on data-driven. University of Electronic Science and Technology of China, pp. 1523–1631 (2019)
12. Liu, W., Hu, Z: Aero-engine sensor fault diagnosis based on convolutional neural network. In: 2019 Chinese Control and Decision Conference (CCDC), pp. 42–47 (2019)

A Multi-objective Structure Variant Bacterial Heuristic Feature Selection Method in High-dimensional Data Classification

Hong Wang, Yikun Ou, and Yixin Wang[✉]

College of Management of Shenzhen University, Shenzhen, China
wangyixin2020@email.szu.edu.cn

Abstract. Feature selection (FS) has been studied as a multi-objective problem in recent years to improve the classification effect. In this paper, to expand the ability of Bacterial Foraging Optimization (BFO) in feature selection problems for classification, a Multi-objective Adapting Chemotaxis Bacterial Foraging Optimization (abbreviated as MOACBFO) is proposed. In MOACBFO, a structural variation strategic model is proposed to reduce the computational complexity for multi-objective problems and applied with a dynamically updated external matrix to record the performance of bacteria on two objectives. In addition, an adaptive chemotaxis step mechanism is designed to help the bacteria jump out of the local optimality. To further enhance the diversity of bacteria searching capability, a feature subset updating strategy is developed. The optimal feature subset and fitness value are stored in the external matrix continuously by comparing them with the historical value records. The performance of the proposed algorithm is demonstrated by comparing it with four other advanced swarm intelligent algorithms on 11 high-dimensional microarray datasets. The results indicate that the MOACBFO performs better in achieving a lower classification error rate using a small number of features.

Keywords: Bacterial foraging optimization · Feature selection · Structural variation · Adaptive chemotaxis step size

1 Introduction

Iterative updates in information technology increase the amount of data generated and retrieved, resulting in most of the data becoming high-dimensional. To deeply uncover the effective information hidden in the data, researchers are trying to design various advanced data mining methods. In this context, feature selection has become a widely studied method as it can reduce the dimensionality of data, using a small combination of features to express the most information of the primal high-dimensional data.

This paper is submitted to Special Session on Intelligent Data Mining: Techniques and Applications (Session Chair: Ben Niu, Hong Wang)

© Springer Nature Singapore Pte Ltd. 2021
Y. Tan et al. (Eds.): DMBD 2021, CCIS 1454, pp. 342–357, 2021.
https://doi.org/10.1007/978-981-16-7502-7_34

Most of the features in the high-dimensional data are not always valid and necessary. It may contain a large number of redundant, and invalid information [1], which will significantly affect the effect of data analysis. For example, redundant features may increase the computation cost while invalid information may decrease the classification accuracy. Therefore, an appropriate method of feature selection can improve the reliability and validity of data analysis. At present, the FS for high-dimensional data has been applied in many fields, such as customer relationship management in enterprises [2], disease prediction [3] in modern medical diagnosis technologies, and customer recommendation [4] in electronic commerce.

FS is a preprocessing process, using certain evaluation criteria to select subsets from the original feature space [5]. The process of basic FS is followed in Fig. 1.

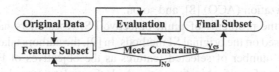

Fig. 1. General flow of basic FS.

In the process of FS, the feature subsets are generated according to some regulations or strategies [1]. Then, the fitness criteria are used to evaluate the effectiveness of the subsets, and the better performance features are stored in the final feature subset. The purpose of selecting feature subsets is to filter out invalid, incomplete, and redundant features as much as possible [2]. In other words, a good feature subset can use fewer features to present most of the attributes of the original data. Therefore, the information conveys by the original data can be better retained. From the processing, it can be seen that FS is also a typical optimization problem. In consequence, FS is now being studied extensively.

Aiming at reducing feature redundancy, J. Lee [3] designed a multi-variate feature ranking mechanism for FS in high-dimensional microarray data. This mechanism not only considers the relevance of features and targets but also considers the redundancy of repeating features. The ranking mechanism filters out the high-quality feature to generate new subsets. E. S. Hosseini and M. H. Moattar [4] also noticed the imbalance of the data features and instances. The candidate feature subsets were formed and evaluated by a multi-interactive information strategy to reduce the analysis bias caused by the imbalanced data.

In addition to data redundancy and imbalance, FS should also consider the computational complexity. In this regard, some studies used the differential evolution method to filter features, enhancing the ability of FS to select feature combination [5]. F. Aghaeipoor and M.M. Javidi [6] adopted a hybrid FS method of filter and wrapper methods, and selected feature subsets by mRMR and fuzzy rules to improve estimation accuracy and decrease the computing time.

Many researchers regard FS as a single objective task in the past. However, there are increasing amounts of researchers who beginning to pay attention to the interpretability and rationality of the feature subsets generated by FS. The inner connection of each feature in a subset needs to be considered. Especially, when classifying high-dimensional data, the algorithm may generate some large feature subsets without removing the redundant features, which is antithetical to the original intention of FS to reduce the dimension of data. Nevertheless, if the feature subsets are too small, it may filter out a lot of information. To make the subsets more concise with low dimensions, it is wise to consider FS as a multi-objective problem. This paper takes error rates of classification and size of feature subsets as the objective of FS.

The swarm intelligence (SI) algorithms are widely used in multi-objective FS due to their characteristics of simple structure and fewer mathematical rules. SI algorithms imitate the evolution processes of the biological population to construct systems with functions of search optimal solutions. It means to use the population to search a large number of solutions to a given problem and find out the optimal one. Common SI algorithms are artificial bee colony (ABC) [7], particle swarm optimization (PSO) [8], ant colony optimization (ACO) [8], and so on.

Focusing on the problems of multi-objective FS, researchers have made various improvements based on the original SI methods. In [9], the authors take the classification accuracy and the number of selected features as the objectives of FS. To reduce the computational cost of multi-objectives, it embeds the updating mechanism of PSO into the ABC to control the displacement of search individuals. Besides, a ladder-like sample combinations strategy is developed to increase search efficiency. Considering reducing the size of the subsets, Y. Zhou, et al. [10] chose to use the discrete method to compress the search space of the particle swarm, and set the size of particle population by a flexible cut-point method to better search optimal solutions.

Only reducing the size of the subsets can easily make the algorithms fall into the situation of local optimum. To escape the local optimum, W. Wei, et al. [11] design a vector-based elite learning rule and applied it to the immune algorithm to remove redundant features in the data being analyzed. However, elite learning often brings about the problem of premature convergence. To control the algorithms' speed of convergence, A. Santiago, et al. [12] propose a fuzzy selection of operators. All in all, SI methods are applied to multi-objective FS and they can be modified variously.

Except for the SI algorithms mentioned above, bacterial foraging optimization (BFO) is also a widely studied SI algorithm. BFO has been used to deal with a variety of complex optimization problems because of its outstanding searchability and versatility. Inspired by the foraging activities of E. coli, BFO simulates the life process of bacteria, Sect. 2 will give more details.

The common researches of BFO mainly focus on the improvement strategies of the algorithm, the problems of combinatorial optimization, and optimization scheduling. The improvement strategies mainly include parameters optimization, bacteria chemotaxis process optimization, and population structure optimization. For example, H. Chen et al. [13] designed a chaotic local search strategy to better control the convergence speed of BFO and the defect of the constant step length of bacteria chemotaxis, which increased the search diversity by dynamically changing the chemotaxis step length. In addition, the introduction of chaotic strategies has also expanded the search area of the bacteria population.

Except for the algorithm strategies' improvements, BFO also has multiple applications. B. Turanoğlu and G. Akkaya [14], aiming at the problem of dynamic facility layout, design a hybrid algorithm combining BFO and simulated annealing (SA) to solve such complex optimization problems. In addition to the problem of the dynamic facility, M. Kaur and S. Kadam [15], in the optimal scheduling problem, propose a multi-objective flora optimization algorithm to find the scheme closest to the optimal scheduling solution. However, the size of the population will significantly influence the search effect of BFO. For modulating the search population of the algorithm, H. Wang, et al. [16] design a multi-dimensional population mechanism of BFO based on the FS method. The algorithm can generate populations in different sizes, thereby generating different feature subsets in classification tasks to increase the variety of solutions. At present, there is very little research that focuses on BFO-based multi-objective FS, but it can be found from those existing studies that this area is very useful and meaningful because BFO performs well in multi-objective problems [17–19].

1.1 Goals

This research aims to reduce the dimensionality of high-dimensional data when doing classification tasks. So we design a modified BFO with the improved strategies of adaptive foraging process, structural variation, and update search bacteria population based on multi-objective FS. The specific contributions are as follows:

- Design a multi-objective BFO with structural variation to improve the problem of slow convergence of the original algorithm.
- Adaptively adjust the process of chemotaxis, replication, and elimination-dispersal of the improved BFO to increase the diversity of the search process.
- Design a feature subsets updating mechanism to identify features that can retain better classification effects and eliminate features that will weaken the classification accuracy.
- Combine the proposed algorithm with the KNN classifier to form a wrapper FS method to achieve efficient classification effects.

1.2 Organization

The rest of this article is structured as follows: Sect. 2 describes the principle of the basic BFO. The proposed algorithm and its improvement strategies are described in Sect. 3. Section 4 shows the experimental results and analysis, and the conclusion is placed in Sect. 5.

2 Basic Bacterial Foraging Optimization

The basic Bacterial Foraging Optimization (BFO) was proposed by K.M. Passino, which mimics the biological habits of E. coli. He designed chemotaxis, replication, and elimination-dispersion three main processes for the BFO algorithm. In addition, each bacterium involved activities of swimming, turning, attraction, and repulsion. It can be seen that BFO is a biological heuristic algorithm, and the researches show that this algorithm has strong searchability [20].

The process of bacterial foraging is called chemotaxis. In the chemotaxis, bacteria swarm towards the place with a high concentration of nutrients. One chemotaxis contains two steps: tumbling and swimming. Bacteria select a random direction by tumbling to find a place with a high nutrient concentration. By swimming, bacteria continuously exploit the direction with high nutrient concentration. In addition, the bacteria colony also has a cell-to-cell signaling communication mechanism via special pheromone. Once a unit finds a good place, it will release an attraction pheromone to inform other units. On the contrary, if a bacterium is exposed to a lower nutrient concentration place or a noxious one, it will release a repulsive pheromone to warn other units to avoid approaching. In the BFO algorithm, this mechanism speeds up the convergence and finds the global optimum more efficiently. The position updating of bacterial foraging optimization during the chemotaxis stage is [20]:

$$\theta^i(j+1,k,l) = \theta^i(j,k,l) + C(i)\frac{\Delta(i)}{\sqrt{\Delta^T(i)\Delta(i)}} \tag{1}$$

The $\theta^i(j,k,l)$ presents the position of i_{th} bacterium in j_{th} chemotaxis, k_{th} and l_{th} stand for the process of reproduction elimination-dispersal, respectively. $C(i)$ means the step of chemotaxis and $\Delta(i)$ is a manually setting parameter that controls the actives of i_{th} bacterium. As there are attraction and repulsion actives between bacteria, the formula is followed:

$$J_{cc}\big(\theta^i(j,k,l), P(j,k,l)\big) = \sum_j^S J_{cc}\big(\theta^i(j,k,l), \theta^j(j,k,l)\big) \tag{2}$$

Where $J_{cc}\big(\theta^i(j,k,l), P(j,k,l)\big)$ denotes the cell-to-cell signaling of i_{th} bacterium among other bacteria. $J_{cc}\big(\theta^i(j,k,l), \theta^j(j,k,l)\big)$ controls the communication level of attractant or repellant between i_{th} and j_{th} bacterium. Therefore, the i_{th} the bacterium will be updating with swarming effect not just its fitness $J(i,j,k,l)$:

$$J(i,j,k,l) = J(i,j,k,l) + J_{cc}\big(\theta^i(j,k,l), P(j,k,l)\big) \tag{3}$$

Reproduction simulates the most basic criteria in the natural world that is survival of the fittest. It improves the superiority of bacterial colonies and thus accelerates the convergence of BFO. Firstly, bacteria colonies are ranked according to the health level of each bacterium. Secondly, half of the bacteria with lower health levels are replaced by the half with higher. As a result, the overall health level in next-generation is improved. The health of bacteria are as follow:

$$J^i_{health} = \sum_{j=1}^{N_c+1} J(i,j,k,l) \tag{4}$$

Where the J^i_{health} is the health level of i_{th} the bacterium, it is calculated by adding up each fitness value in N_c chemotaxis processes.

Elimination-dispersal emulates uncertainty in nature. In the life cycle of a bacteria colony, each bacterium could die abruptly or be transported to somewhere else randomly since the uncertain natural disasters. In BFO, the position of bacteria will be reset in a custom probability P_{ed}, which helps the optimization algorithm reduce premature convergence.

3 The Proposed Multi-objective Adapting Chemotaxis BFO Method

Although the basic BFO can realize solving optimization problems. However, the algorithm's computational time cost of BFO will be increased when faced with high-dimensional data. In addition, the original algorithm is more suitable for single-objective problems. In this paper, we regard FS as a multi-objective problem with two objectives, which are "minimize the size of feature subset" and "maximize classification effect (minimum error rate)".

This paper proposes an effective algorithm, multi-objective adapting chemotaxis bacteria foraging optimization (MOACBFO), the general flow of MOACBFO is shown in Fig. 2. '*h*' represents the running time of the program, '*iter*' means the iteration times of each running. '*m*' is the swimming number of times of each bacteria.

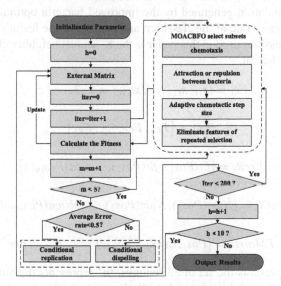

Fig. 2. General flow of MOACBFO.

Based on the original BFO, MOACBFO has four improved strategies, including *structural variation* (structure mutation of the basic BFO), *external matrix* mechanisms, *adaptive foraging* processes, and *feature subsets updating* mechanism.

3.1 Structure Variation

Traditional BFO is a multi-layer nested structure algorithm, when the bacterial population faces a high-dimensional search space, many calculation processes will be generated. However, as the scale of data analysis increases, many repetitive calculation results will be generated, which does not conform to the original intention of creating a concise and efficient algorithm. Therefore, this paper disassembled the nested structure of BFO, setting the three processes (chemotaxis, replication, and elimination-dispersal) to be carried out sequentially instead of being nested. We canceled the original nested loop structure of BFO and carried out serial and parallel transformations.

As Fig. 2 shows, in the search process of bacteria, the chemotaxis operation is performed first, and the classification effect of the intermediate process is used to decide whether the algorithm goes to replication operation or elimination-dispersal operation in the next stage of the algorithm. It is worth noting that replication or elimination-dispersal is not performed in every iteration, only if the conditions are met will one of the activities take place.

3.2 External Matrix

To make BFO more suitable for solving multi-objective problems, we introduce an external matrix (*EMatrix*) [21]. In each iteration, the matrix is used to store the location information of the population generated by the improved bacteria optimization algorithm, the classification error rate of the classifier, and the size of the feature subset generated each time. The classifier used in this paper is the K-nearest neighbor classifier, which is lightweight and efficient.

$$Fe_i = [x_{i1}, x_{i2}, \ldots, x_{in}], i = 1, 2, \ldots, z. \tag{5}$$

$$Pos_j = \left[Fe_1', Fe_2', \ldots, Fe_k'\right] \tag{6}$$

$$ErrR_j = \left[fit(Pos_1), fit(Pos_2), \ldots, fit(Pos_{iter})\right] \tag{7}$$

$$FitN_j = [Num(Pos_1), Num(Pos_2), \ldots, Num(Pos_{iter})] \tag{8}$$

$$EMatrix = \left[Pos_j, ErrR_j, FitN_j\right], j = 1, 2, \ldots, iter \tag{9}$$

Formula 5 represents the set of all features, *'n'* represents the number of features, and *'z'* represents the number of samples. *'Pos'* records the feature information of the jth generation of bacterial colony search, and *'k'* represents the number of selected features, see *Formula* 6. *'ErrR'* represents the classification error rate obtained by training the feature subset generated by the jth generation of flora into the classifier, see *Formula* 7 and *'iter'* represents the number of iterations. *'FitN'* represents the size of the feature subset generated by the jth generation of flora, see *Formula* 8.

3.3 Adapting Foraging Process

The adaptive bacterial foraging process is mainly the adaptive change of the step length of bacterial chemotaxis. In addition, there are adaptive options for replication and elimination-dispersal. The basic step length of chemotaxis in BFO is invariable, but the movement of bacteria is not rigid in the real world. The fixed-step makes the bacteria easy to be caught in the same local place which is not beneficial for the diversified development of the population. In other words, the lack of diversity of the bacterium will lead to the results becoming incomplete. In this paper, a simple adaptive chemotaxis step-changing method is adopted [22]. In the MOACBFO, the initial step control mechanism for each bacterium is followed *formula* (10–11):

$$\gamma = \left|\left(1 - \frac{i}{Swarm}\right) * (Che_{start} - Che_{end}) + Che_{end}\right| \tag{10}$$

$$Che_{start} = \frac{|J_{new}(i,j)|}{|J_{new}(i,j)|+\gamma} = \frac{1}{\left(1+\frac{\gamma}{|J_{new}(i,j)|}\right)} \tag{11}$$

'γ' is an adaptive parameter following *formula* (10), it controls the step length of chemotaxis ('Che_{st}'). $J_{new}(i,j)$ is the variation of *formula* (3). It removes 'k' and 'l' because the structure of BFO has been changed and the new strategy has followed the *formula* (14).

One bacterium may do reduplicative work if there is no communication between bacteria and the population. To reduce the computation cost, this paper introduces a learning strategy from PSO, see *formula* (12).

$$Che_{end} = Che_{start} + c_aR_a(PB_i - P_i) + c_bR_b(B - P_i) \tag{12}$$

'PB_i' stands for the best solution of ith bacterium and 'B' is the best location searched by the entire bacteria groups. Table 1 shows the pseudo-code of MOACBFO.

Table 1. The pseudo-code of MOACBFO

Initialize the parameters (S=45, Nc =4,Ns=5,h=10)

    Swimming: input dynamic quantity characteristics
    If the *number of data features* < 30
    | Input feature number = 1:1: number of data features
    Else
    | Input feature number = 1:5:50
    End *(This step is to control the number of features)*
    For *j=1:Nc*
        i=1:S
        Do the chemotaxis (10-12); Record bacteria search information by (9); Get a fitness by (13)
        If *new fitness* < *original fitness*
        | Record the best fitness, number of features, and position of bacteria
        End
        Replication:
    While *m<Ns(tumbling times)*
        Take tumble action in BFO, get fitness by (10-13), and updating the EMatrix.
        If *fitness* < *threshold value*
        | Do *Feature Subsets Updating Strategy*, and then do replication.
        Elimination:
        Else (error rate doesn't meet expectations, no need to replication)
        |Do elimination-dispersal by updating the position of bacteria. (see, TableII)
        End
    End
    End

When the error rate is over 50%, the bacteria population will do the elimination-dispersal operation. A high error rate means the combination of features in the subset cannot reflect most information of the data. To save the computation resources, we set the MOACBFO only do elimination-dispersal instead of replication. On the contrary, if the error rate is small, the MOACBFO will take the replication activity.

3.4 Feature Subsets Updating Strategy

High dimensional data always bring thousands or more instances with many features. If the search population has been the same all the time, the diversity of feature subsets will lack change. This paper proposes a feature subsets updating strategy, see Table 2.

Before updating the features in a subset, the position of each bacterium 'P' needs to be found. The basic position updating formula is followed:

$$P(i, j + 1) = Pos(i, j) + C_{en}(i)\frac{\Delta(i)}{\sqrt{\Delta^T(i)\Delta(i)}} \tag{13}$$

After recording the information of position into *EMatrix*, the fitness (error rate) must be calculated and saved into *EMatrix*. The fitness value $J_{new}(i, j)$ is acquired by *formula* (14). It uses the K-nearest neighbor to be the classifier, which takes the 'P' as the input value.

$$J_{new}(i, j) = Classifier_{KNN}(P(i, j + 1)) \tag{14}$$

The pseudo-code of feature subsets updating strategy is below.

Table 2. The pseudo-code of feature subsets updating

Calculate the position and best fitness by (13);
    If $J_{new}(i,j) < J_{PBest}$
        $J_{PBest} = J_{new}(i,j)$ *for individual bacterium*
    End
Cell to cell attraction and repulsion:
    If cellsig=0 (signals from a cell, manually control)
        Calculating the bacteria J_{health}^t *by (4);*
    End
Recording the classification effect of classifier in each run;
    If *fitness > 0.5 (error rate)*
        Delete the bad performance features and add new features instead
            In *times of bad performance combination >0*
                Delete the combination and create a new combination
        End
    End

---

4 Experiments and Analysis

In this section, the proposed algorithm is compared with four derived versions of traditional swarm intelligent algorithms. The experiment is carried on 11 microarray data.

4.1 Experiment Design and Parameter Initialization

The comparing algorithms are BPSO [23], BFO [20], BFOLIW [24] and BWFS [21]. Table 3 records the characteristics of the comparing algorithms. To compare the MOACBFO to the multi-objective algorithm, the comparing algorithms in this paper are all added to the external matrix mechanisms used in this paper. As for this, the final comparison algorithms are BPSO, BFO, BFOLIW, and BWFS in a multi-objective version.

Table 3. Algorithms for comparison

Basic algorithms	Characteristic
BPSO	FS can be treated as a 0/1 problem. For the features, 0 stands for unselected and 1 stands for selected. The binary particle swarm algorithm is a classical algorithm and is suitable for solving 0/1 problems
BFO	As the basis of the improved method (MOACBFO) in this paper, it is necessary to show the capacity of BFO in classification targets based on FS
BFOLIW	BFOLIW integrates the liner weight strategy to the basic BFO
BWFS	BWFS imports the roulette wheel mechanism into BFO to increase bacterial diversity

To make the comparison experiment more fair and reliable, the parameters set was referred to most of the literature. As the popular size S is usually 30 to 50, this paper takes 45 as the popular size and dimension. The maximum iterations are 200. The running time of the program is 10.

4.2 Data Sources

The testing datasets are 11 microarray data from the UCI machine learning repository [24]. The microarray datasets are high-dimension data about cancer, which have two or more categories and more than 5,000 features. The experiment compares the error rate and the size of the subset of the algorithm.

Table 4. Microarray datasets

Datasets	Features	Instance	Class
9_Tumors	5726	60	9
11_Tumors	12,533	174	11
14_Tumors	15,009	308	26
Brain_Tumor_1	5920	90	5
Brain_Tumor_2	10367	50	40
Leukemia_1	5328	72	3
Leukemia_2	11225	73	3
Lung_Cancer_I	12600	203	5
SRBCT	2309	83	4
DLBCL	5470	77	2
Prostate_Tumor	10509	102	2

4.3 Experiment Results and Analysis

Figure 3 and Fig. 4 show the experiment results of the comparisons. The abscissa axis represents the size of the subsets generated by the algorithms, and the axis of ordinates records the error rate of classification. From the results, MOACBFO always gets a minimum error rate. It reflects that the MOACBFO has a good ability in searching the optimization result.

Besides, MOACBFO can get a small number of features in a subset with a lower error rate compared with other methods. The results in Fig. 3 and Fig. 4 prove that MOACBFO has a better comprehensive performance. Especially in the datasets DLBCL, Lung-Cancer, Prostate-Tumor, Brain-Tumor2, Leukemia1, and SRBCT, MOACBFO gets better diversity of results.

To compare the effect of the algorithms in more detail, Table 5 shows the numerical results of average error rates and subsets' size of all methods. As shown in the Table 5, the MOACBFO can generally reach an error rate of less than 0.005. Although the number of features in each dataset is not the smallest one, the error rate of MOACBFO is low. Since the results need to fit the two objectives (minimize error rates and feature subsets).

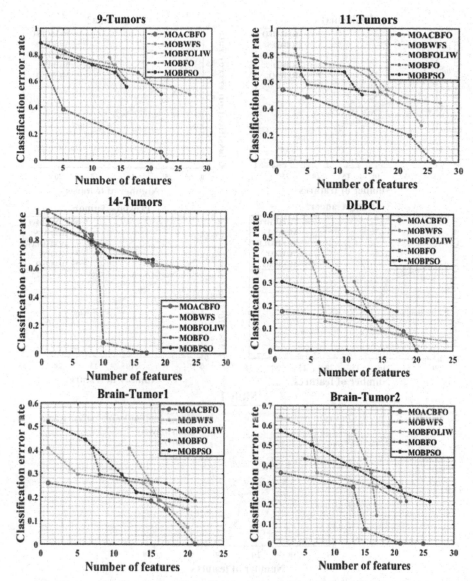

Fig. 3. Experiments results of all algorithms in comparison on microarray datasets.

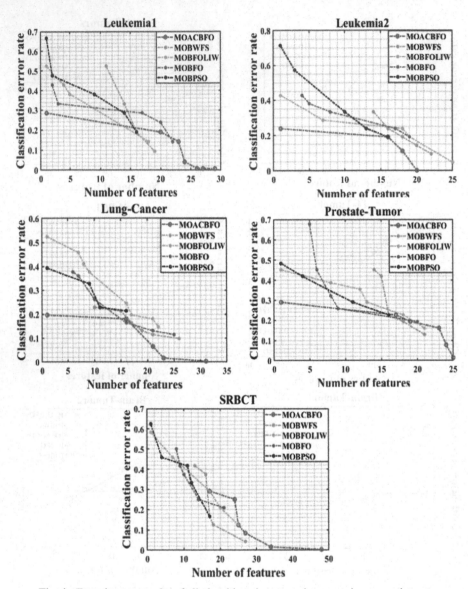

Fig. 4. Experiments results of all algorithms in comparison on microarray datasets.

Table 5. Average error rate and subset size of all algorithms

Datasets	Average	Algorithms				
		MO-B-PSO	MO-BFO	MO-LIW-BFO	MO-BWFS	MO-AC-BFO
		(Binary)	(Original)	(Linearly weight)	(Roulette wheels)	(Improved method in this paper)
9_Tumors	A_Size	**16**	22	**16**	27	23
	A_Error	0.556	0.500	0.611	0.500	**0.003**
11_Tumors	A_Size	**14**	16	27	24	26
	A_Error	0.500	0.519	0.442	0.269	**0.002**
14_Tumors	A_Size	18	18	24	30	**17**
	A_Error	0.663	0.640	0.596	0.596	**0.004**
Brain_Tumor_1	A_Size	20	21	20	20	21
	A_Error	0.185	0.185	0.074	0.148	**0.003**
Brain_Tumor_2	A_Size	26	22	21	**17**	25
	A_Error	0.214	0.214	0.214	0.143	**0.002**
DLBCL	A_Size	**14**	17	24	21	20
	A_Error	0.130	0.174	0.043	0.043	**0.005**
Leukemia_1	A_Size	**16**	22	18	19	29
	A_Error	0.190	0.143	0.143	0.095	**0.008**
Leukemia_2	A_Size	**16**	19	25	22	20
	A_Error	0.190	0.190	0.048	0.095	**0.002**
SRBCT	A_Size	**17**	21	25	27	48
	A_Error	0.167	0.208	0.125	0.417	**0.003**
Lung_Cancer_I	A_Size	**16**	25	22	26	31
	A_Error	0.213	0.115	0.148	0.098	**0.003**
Prostate_Tumor	A_Size	**16**	20	21	21	25
	A_Error	0.226	0.194	0.161	0.129	**0.013**

5   Conclusions

In general, this paper proposes a modified FS method MOACBFO and receives good performance in comparing with four swarm intelligence algorithms on 11 high-dimensional microarray datasets. MOACBFO effectively improves the classification results of the modified BFO method in a multi-objective optimization perspective. In addition, it achieves the four goals proposed in this paper. MOACBFO has a good convergence effect, better diversity of searching results, higher classification accuracy, and better effect during the multi-objective FS process in the target of classification. However,

MOACBFO needs more comparison to become more stable. In the future, we should pay more attention to the application of MOACBFO and its modified version on practical problems.

Acknowledgment. This work is partially supported by The National Natural Science Foundation of China (Grants Nos. 71901152), Natural Science Foundation of Guangdong Province (2020A1515010752), and Natural Science Foundation of Shenzhen University (85303/00000155).

References

1. Guan, B., Zhao, Y., Yin, Y., Li, Y.: A differential evolution based feature combination selection algorithm for high-dimensional data. Inf. Sci. (Ny) **547**, 870–886 (2021)
2. Gangavarapu, T., Patil, N.: A novel filter–wrapper hybrid greedy ensemble approach optimized using the genetic algorithm to reduce the dimensionality of high-dimensional biomedical datasets. Appl. Soft Comput. J. **81**, 105538 (2019)
3. Joloudari, J.H., Saadatfar, H., Dehzangi, A., Shamshirband, S.: Computer-aided decision-making for predicting liver disease using PSO-based optimized SVM with feature selection. Inf. Med. Unlocked **17**, 100255 (2019)
4. Wang, H., Niu, B., Tan, L.: Bacterial colony algorithm with adaptive attribute learning strategy for feature selection in classification of customers for personalized recommendation. Neurocomputing **452**, 747–755 (2021)
5. Jain, D., Singh, V.: Feature selection and classification systems for chronic disease prediction: a review. Egypt. Informat. J. **19**(3), 179–189 (2018)
6. Kalimuthan, C., Arokia Renjit, J.: Review on intrusion detection using feature selection with machine learning techniques. Mater. Today Proc. **33**, 3794–3802 (2020)
7. Khaire, U.M., Dhanalakshmi, R.: Stability of feature selection algorithm: a review. J. King Saud Univ. Comput. Inform. Sci. (2019). https://doi.org/10.1016/j.jksuci.2019.06.012
8. Lee, J., Choi, I.Y., Jun, C.H.: An efficient multivariate feature ranking method for gene selection in high-dimensional microarray data. Expert Syst. Appl. **166**, 113971 (2021)
9. Hosseini, E.S., Moattar, M.H.: Evolutionary feature subsets selection based on interaction information for high dimensional imbalanced data classification. Appl. Soft Comput. J. **82**, 105581 (2019)
10. Aghaeipoor, F., Javidi, M.M.: A hybrid fuzzy feature selection algorithm for high-dimensional regression problems: an mRMR-based framework. Expert Syst. Appl. **162**, 113859 (2020)
11. Karaboga, D., Basturk, B.: On the performance of artificial bee colony (ABC) algorithm. Appl. Soft Comput. J. **8**(1), 687–697 (2008)
12. Okwu, M.O., Tartibu, L.K.: Particle swarm optimisation. In: Metaheuristic Optimization: Nature-Inspired Algorithms Swarm and Computational Intelligence, Theory and Applications. SCI, vol. 927, pp. 5–13. Springer, Cham (2021). https://doi.org/10.1007/978-3-030-61111-8_2
13. Wang, X., Zhang, Y., Sun, X., Wang, Y., Du, C.: Multi-objective feature selection based on artificial bee colony: an acceleration approach with variable sample size. Appl. Soft Comput. J. **88**, 106041 (2020)
14. Zhou, Y., Kang, J., Sam Kwong, X., Wang, Q.Z.: An evolutionary multi-objective optimization framework of discretization-based feature selection for classification. Swarm Evol. Comput. **60**, 100770 (2021)
15. Wei, W., Chen, S., Lin, Q., Ji, J., Chen, J.: A multi-objective immune algorithm for intrusion feature selection. Appl. Soft Comput. J. **95**, 106522 (2020)

16. Santiago, A., Dorronsoro, B., Fraire, H.J., Ruiz, P.: Micro-genetic algorithm with fuzzy selection of operators for multi-Objective optimization: μFAME. Swarm Evol. Comput. **61**, 100818 (2021)

17. Chen, H., Zhang, Q., Luo, J., Xu, Y., Zhang, X.: An enhanced bacterial foraging optimization and its application for training kernel extreme learning machine. Appl. Soft Comput. J. **86**, 105884 (2020)

18. Turanoğlu, B., Akkaya, G.: A new hybrid heuristic algorithm based on bacterial foraging optimization for the dynamic facility layout problem. Expert Syst. Appl. **98**, 93–104 (2018)

19. Kaur, M., Kadam, S.: A novel multi-objective bacteria foraging optimization algorithm (MOBFOA) for multi-objective scheduling. Appl. Soft Comput. J. **66**, 183–195 (2018)

20. Wang, H., Tan, L., Niu, B.: Feature selection for classification of microarray gene expression cancers using bacterial colony optimization with multi-dimensional population. Swarm Evol. Comput. **48**, 172–181 (2019)

21. Passino, K.M.: Biomimicry of bacterial foraging for distributed optimization and control. IEEE Control Syst. **22**(3), 52–67 (2002)

22. Niu, B., Yi, W., Tan, L., Geng, S., Wang, H.: A multi-objective feature selection method based on bacterial foraging optimization. Nat. Comput. **20**(1), 63–76 (2019)

23. Majhi, R., Panda, G., Majhi, B., Sahoo, G.: Efficient prediction of stock market indices using adaptive bacterial foraging optimization (ABFO) and BFO based techniques. Expert Syst. Appl. **36**(6), 10097–10104 (2009)

24. Too, J., Abdullah, A.R., Saad, N.M.: A new co-evolution binary particle swarm optimization with multiple inertia weight strategy for feature selection. Informatics **6**(2), 21 (2019)

FAA Transition Away from Radar and Towards ADS-B Aircraft Communication-Based on Accuracy

Juan Manuel Nzamio Mba Andeme, Qingling Liu$^{(\boxtimes)}$, and Abdul Hadi

Laboratory 304, College of Information and Communication Engineering,
Harbin Engineering University, Harbin, China
liuqingling@hrbeu.edu.cn

Abstract. Communication is the most important thing for aviation security, remotes incidents that happened in the aviation industry are based on low accuracy on tracking airplanes. The Next Generation Transportation plan intends to transform the aviation industry increasing high accuracy and safety. To avoid this issue, this paper gives an overview of radar and the modern communication implemented by the Federal Aviation Administration; Automatic Dependent Surveillance-Broadcast (ADS-B) and compares their performance. Following the analyzes, the benefits of the transition from Radar towards ADS-B technology are demonstrated, not only to prevent incidents but also to provide updates during the fight, and avoid mid-air collisions. The method MST processing is used to fuses multiples sensors to generate the most accurate surveillance image. Our research analyzes an important incident that happens on 8 March 2014 when Malaysia Airline Flight MH370 disappeared from the controller's radar screen; the incident is pointed in this paper to better understand why the use of ADS-B was mandatory by the FAA to airlines that intend to flight over transoceanic since January 2020.

Keywords: Radar overview · ADS-B technology · MH370 disappearance · ACARS system · FAA NextGen

1 Introduction

The aviation industry is nowadays the most accurate and safe way to move millions of passengers around the world, to maintain this industry safe with error-free, communication has become the most crucial way to keep the successful journey of many flights. It needs a lot of effort from different departments that are working in this area to coordinate different tasks from the based ground station and air-to-air. It is essential to remind that its coordination should be error-free to avoid any kind of incidents. Aviation has been using two types of information transmission between airplanes and ground stations; voice communication and data link communication, which can be exchanged between the pilots and air controllers to monitoring the takeoffs, landings, provide crew members meteorological information, ensuring flight path interval, prevents collisions

© Springer Nature Singapore Pte Ltd. 2021
Y. Tan et al. (Eds.): DMBD 2021, CCIS 1454, pp. 358–374, 2021.
https://doi.org/10.1007/978-981-16-7502-7_35

and any other additional information support for pilots to ensure the safety and reliably of flight operations [1].

Traditional radar technology has been the primary use system to help controllers and pilots to manage the airspace for decades since it can detect the aircraft position from a long-range distance through satellites and GPS. The radar detects aircraft position based on the reflecting electromagnetic waves from the target and sends back the electromagnetic waves providing certain information to the ground station such as speed and location of the aircraft, the aircraft transponder interact after capturing the signal and respond with a new signal that supply additional information showing the aircraft altitude and identification number [1].

This technology has seven decades-old since has been improved. After reviewing some incidents that happen in the aviation industry, the radar still has some issues that need to be solved such as inaccuracies, time lags, search rescue limitations, less precision on tracking aircraft, high delayed to refresh on controller's radar screen, usually takes more than twelve seconds to show where the aircraft is located in exacted time and planes are not where they appear. These issues become interrogative when controllers want to monitor the sky using radar. The challenge of radar's limitations was showed when flight MH370 of Malaysia Airlines disappeared on the radar screen several minutes after takeoff from Kuala-Lumpur, Malaysia and ended in the Indian Ocean without the possibility of tracking where exactly the airplane crashed. This disappearance showed that radar still has some limitations on tracking airplanes when there are flying in transoceanic and dead zone areas.

The impact over the world caused by the missed of Malaysia Airline Flight MH370 opened a need of looking for an alternative technology based on tracking aircraft in real-time, so the new technology that was developed immediately to replace radar to solve similar mysteries was Automatic Dependent Surveillance-Broadcasting (ADS-B), it becomes a technique for better tracking tools across international borders. Scientists and researchers assure that if Automatic Dependent Surveillance-Broadcasting (ADS-B) had been developed during the moment of the tragedy; money, time, and lives could have been saved. More than six years after the fact, still unclear to determine what happened with the missing aircraft. It raised many theories that arose speculating that murder-suicide, terrorist hijacking, an attack by malicious hackers, or fire on board the aircraft has caused the vanish in March 2014, killing 239 passengers on board the aircraft. The aircraft transponder, ACARS, and other transmission systems were switched off and the need for ADS-B technology becomes very apparent to replacing the traditional radar that air traffic control has been using for a long time.

2 Radar System Overview

2.1 History

Radar was the first traditional technology used by several nations during World War II to detect and tracking military enemy aircraft [1]. The troops should be used correctly the radar sensors to make sure that everyone is on the right side of the war. In 1940 United States Navy created the term radar as an acronym for Radio Detection And Ranging [2]. Two types of radar have been developed: one is Primary Surveillance Radar, which is a system that used ground-based antenna transmitting radar pulse that could identify the position of the aircraft, another one is Secondary Surveillance Radar, in which the aircraft transponder captures the signal and convert it into a new, illustrating the aircraft identity, altitude and other further information which normally rely on its chosen mode [1].

2.2 Basic Concepts

The radar is an electromagnetic detection system that uses audio waves to precise the angle, range, direction, or velocity of the target, which can be fixed and moving objects. It detects ships, aircraft, weather phenomena, missiles, motor vehicles, and spacecraft. A lot of frequency bands are used in radar systems but a radar system usually operates in the UHF (Ultra High Frequency) or RF (Radio Frequency) spectrum. The frequency of electromagnetic waves used by radar is unaffected in certain weather conditions such as falling snow, fog, rains, clouds, and sleet when designing radar, except when their detection is intended. The information provided by radar can be used for different applications such as spacecraft detection, ground mapping, surface search, air search, tracking, weather predictions, SAR, and range, which is important for many fields that the need of such positioning are essential for their operations (Fig. 1).

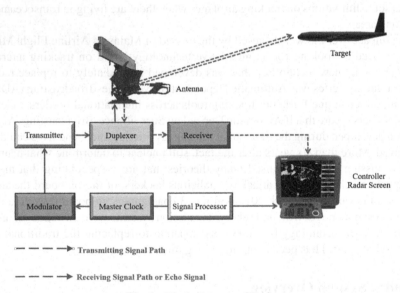

Fig. 1. Block diagram of Radar.

The basic design of radar is very easy to understand, the source or transmitter signal generates a pulse of energy, usually short duration of high power radio frequency (RF) that is transmitted to the radar antenna, and the signal is transferred to the target with required distribution and efficiency. The target sends back an echo signal to the radar antenna which is transferred to the duplexer. The button duplexer is essential because the high power pulse can destroy the receiver if the power were allowed to access the receiver. The receiver demodulates the echo signal or received radio frequency signal to provide the Air Traffic Control a video display signal where they can monitor the controlled airspace.

2.3 Limitation Factors

The safety of civilian aircraft is affected by the quality of the solution of the aircraft surveillance problems. In this case, the radar should be able to help aircraft dispatchers to separate all those aircraft that are flying closer, the accuracy of positioning the plane must prevent the dangerous proximity or their collision. It is demonstrated that there are three important characteristics to determine the quality of radar working area; the operational range, its resolution, and accuracy. In [3] use the MSPSR to analyze the problem of surveillance for those aircraft that are not equipped with the new ADS-B technology. The methods of angular and the range measurements are the key components to determine the location of the aircraft, based on the determination of the position of the object as its intersection point of three surfaces of position: elevation of the plane, the equal range surface, and the azimuth plane [3].

The problem of tracking aircraft has been improved several times for application in sonar, air traffic control systems, and military surveillance. A new performance of NL-GMKF was applied to help solve the problem of radar tracking with non-Gaussian glint noise. The performance on tracking airplanes can achieve incorporating information about altitude in the filter tracking as well as position. As the intensity of flights is constantly increasing, the visibility, tracking, and accuracy are drastically reducing. The aviation security needs an effective and high quality of radar information which consist on detecting and tracking target from long-range distances. In [4] said that one of the main issues to determine a possibility to develop such a system consist in assure simultaneously surveillance of space by all spatial positioned radars. The paper analyzes possibilities for maximizing the accuracy and high quality of radar information by finding 2D coordinate estimation to determine the airspace in a low-based MIMO radar based on two-coordinate radars.

Finally, the repeat radar jammers have taken part in one of the disadvantages over the last decades, which usually transmits jamming signals to diminish and get worse the radar system performance. The main challenge comes when the jamming wants to clear and efficiently decide the true or false target, which means the cross-correlation side lobes between repeat jamming signals and the angular waveforms should completely be suppressed to reduce the ill-reaction of repeat jamming signals. All these limitations become questionable with the tragedy of the Malaysia Airline MH370.

This paper is organized as follows: Sect. 3 as the next section briefly describes the implemented ADS-B technology, showing the operational works and some particular advantages. Section 4 discusses the case of Malaysia Airline Flight MH370 as the biggest impact that asked for a needed of an alternative method for transoceanic aircraft tracking system. Section 5 compares the traditional radar versus ADS-B. In Sect. 6 we give our contributions to ensure the accuracy and safety of aviation. The last section concludes our paper and answers the question: why of the transition from radar and towards ADS-B?

3 ADS-B Aircraft Technology

3.1 ADS-B Overview

Automatic Dependent Surveillance-Broadcast is the key component that has come in response to the need for a better tracking system and accuracy of the airplanes during the flight and on the ground (terminal airport). Its implementation is a result of a crucial plan of Federal Aviation Administration (FAA) Next Generation Air Transportation (NextGen) of the United States to substitute the ancient capabilities. With ADS-B, Air Traffic Control and the pilots have almost the same view on their display board. An exact traffic data information from a satellite which aircraft trajectory is cleared detailed with the constant broadcast of their exact position, speed, altitude, flight identification number, emergency estimation to nearby flights, and any other necessary information about the flight over encrypted data links that help to put on view a precise air traffic image for the air traffic management in real-time. It is important to remind that the design of ADS-B is to reinforce collision avoidance, runway incursion avoidance, air traffic controller situational awareness, and non-radar air space such as dead zones, north pole, and transoceanic.

3.2 ADS-B Working Performance

Automatic Dependent Surveillance-Broadcasting is extremely more accurate than the traditional radar, there was uncertainty supplied by radar forced Air Traffic Control to set up more extended flight paths, as consequence, less direct flight paths. ADS-B comes out to reduce that uncertainty, which normally gives air traffic control to direct aircraft to fly closer but maintaining safe separation between them. Set up more direct flight paths signify that aircraft are traveling less range, expend less time, generate less emission, and burn less fuel. The system capabilities become very essential in whole flight operation: push back, taxi and departure, descend and approach, landing, climb and cruise, taxi and arrival [5] (Fig. 2).

3.3 ADS-B System Architecture

Three principles components are interconnected to exchange data from the satellite. Divided in ADS-B OUT transmitter, ADS-B IN receiver, and the ground station operation system.

- ADS-B OUT which covers the capability for airplane or surface vehicle to periodically generate broadcast information about aircraft current position, velocity, identity and altitude to Air Traffic Control provided by the onboard transmitter in real-time and more accurate.
- ADS-B IN includes the capability that allows airplanes to receive and display data from ADS-B OUT of another airplane, usually traffic information such as; surface indicators, alerts, confliction guidance, airborne conflict, and graphical display of horizontal and vertical position. Adding that ADS-B IN enables the airplane to receive information supplied by the base ground stations (weather updates) [5] (Fig. 3).

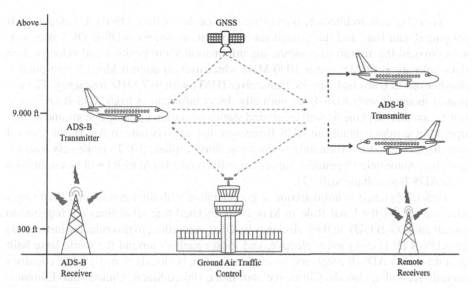

Fig. 2. ADS-B working performance. Figure 2 gives us an entire view of the working performance of ADS-B. The aircraft first provide its accurate position through GPS. The position source along with identification, speed vector, altitude, and vertical rate are automatically broadcast with the use of a Mode S transponder onboard the airplane. ADS-B-based ground stations within a certain range receive the broadcast and relay the source via networked backbone to Air Traffic Control. Those airplanes equipped within range can properly receive the broadcast.

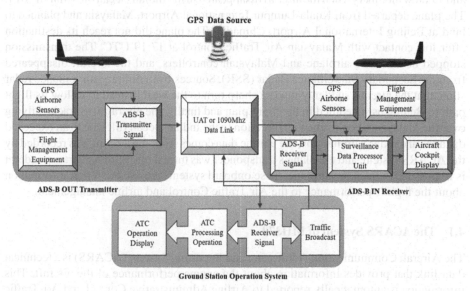

Fig. 3. ADS-B system architecture protocol

ADS-B system architecture is an entire functionality of the ADS-B OUT, and ADS-B IN paired data link, and the ground station operation system. ADS-B OUT uses sensors onboard the aircraft to compute the information about position and velocity. Two data links are available: one is 1090 MHz which uses an aircraft Mode S transponder, another one is Universal Access Transceiver (UAT) with 987 MHz frequency. The airplanes mounted with ADS-B IN normally detect information from ADS-B OUT sent out by another airplane as well as ground station operation system. The ground station operation system contains an ADS-B receiver that delivers data to Air Traffic Control and dispatches extra information to the transmitted airplane [6]. To make easy interoperability, Automatic Dependent Surveillance-Rebroadcast (ADS-R) will be established with ADS-B simultaneously [5].

Federal Aviation Administration in collaboration with the International Civil Organization set out the Final Rule in May 2010, dictated that all airlines are required to install an ADS-B OUT in their airplanes by 2020. According to this rule, the installation of ADS-B IN is completely elective, and most countries around the world have built ground station ADS-B receivers. Its implementation is already done by some countries include Australia, Canada, China, Iceland, India, United States, United Arab Emirates, Sweden, and so on.

4   The Missing of Malaysian Airline MH370

The disappearance of Malaysian Airline Flight MH370 is considered the biggest mystery of the aviation industry over the last decade after the missing of Amelia Earhart. The Boeing triple seven carried on board 227 passengers, where 154 were Chinese citizens and 12 crew members when the aircraft disappeared in the Indian Ocean on 8 March 2014. The plane departed from Kuala-Lumpur International Airport, Malaysia and planned to land at Beijing International Airport, China [7]. The plane did not reach its destination after lost contact with Malaysian Air Traffic Control at 17:19 UTC. The transmission stopped between the airplane and Malaysian controllers, and the aircraft disappeared from the Secondary Surveillance Radar (SSR). Sources from military surveillance radar show that the aircraft suddenly made a sharp turn to the west instead to follow its flight path to Beijing as scheduled in the flight plan and finally, the aircraft was tracked flying over the Malaysian Peninsula with direction to the Indian Ocean [8]. Due to an exceeded distance and radar's limitations, the unique data comes from the aircraft was recorded by the ACARS system, and the plane's transponder was turned off. Without a transponder it is impossible to track the airplane; these onboard systems are used to report information about the flight's performance to the Air Traffic Control and airline management.

4.1   The ACARS System of MH370

The Aircraft Communication Addressing and Reporting System (ACARS) is a technical data link that provides information about the engine performance of the aircraft. This information is automatically reported to Airline Administrative Control and Air Traffic Management to help fix up any technical issue.

The researchers focused their attention on Satellite Communication (SATCOM) link with the Inmarsat Satellite and discover that the aircraft's ACARS was automatically emitting signals technically called pings six hours after vanishing from the radar, indicating that the aircraft engine was operating until burned all the fuel onboard. Through this analysis, Inmarsat of the SATCOM suggested that probably the aircraft flew into the Southern Indian Ocean as mentioned without any accurate location [9] (Table 1 and Fig. 4).

Table 1. Analysis of SATCOM data used for MH370

Time (UTC)	Measurement	BTO	Events recorded by Inmarsat
2:25	R1200	Y	Log-on Ping
3:41	R1200	Y	Second Ping
4:41	R1200	N	Third Ping
5:41	R1200	Y	Fourth Ping
6:41	R1200	N	Fifth Ping
8:10	R1200	Y	Sixth Ping
8:19	R1200	Y	Last Short Ping

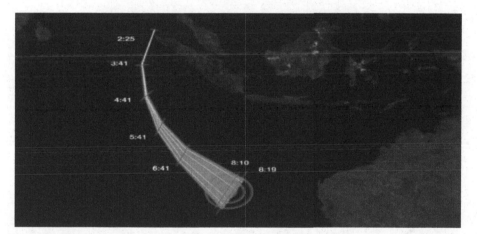

Fig. 4. Ping signal emitted by ACARS system of the MH370, the illustration is obtained from Google Earth, indicating that the aircraft engine was working after the last point of contact with Malaysian controllers. The automated ping starts from 2:25, 3:41, 4:41, 5:41, 6:41, 8:10 to the last short ping 8:19 (Local Time). This crucial data was found by a group of engineers of Inmarsat to follow up the final location of the MH370. On March 18, an intensive search and rescue were conducted immediately by many countries: Australia, Malaysia, China, United States, Japan, and United Kingdom took part in the investigation.

4.2 The Search of MH370

We describe the equation of motion to simulate the trajectory of the aircraft, the vehicle will be considered as a point-mass object with three degrees of translational motion: X, Y, and Z Position, where the axes XYZ denotes the inertial frame. The aircraft position vector $(\vec{R_A})$ is expressed as follow

$$\vec{R_A} = X_A\hat{I} + Y_A\hat{J} + Z_A\hat{K} \tag{1}$$

Where $\hat{I}, \hat{J}, \hat{K}$ denote unit vectors for the inertial frame. Note that axes X, Y, and Z indicate the corresponding North West, and Up direction.

The velocity frame is derived from the inertial frame by a sequence of two rotations; the angle χ about Z and the angle γ about the y_v axis. The aircraft velocity vector is given by

$$\vec{V_A} = \dot{X_A}\hat{I} + \dot{Y_A}\hat{J} + \dot{Z_A}\hat{K} \tag{2}$$

$$\vec{V_A} = V\hat{i_v} \tag{3}$$

Where $\hat{i_v}$ is the unit vector along χ_V (Fig. 5).

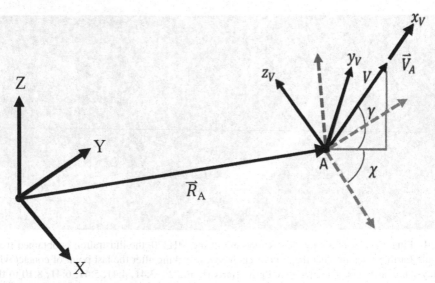

Fig. 5. Inertial and velocity frames visualization [10].

This method is extremely useful when following a flight path provided to the aircraft and the velocity frame becomes essential to calculate the direction of the target. The researchers began an aerial search to find any floating debris in the Southern Indian Ocean. In [7] reported that the flight ended in the Indian Ocean, although the exact location was unclear and no debris was found. A lot of effort, analysis, and simulations have been done to solve the mystery. Inmarsat added a contribution with an important article published concerning its contribution to the flight trajectory reconstruction effort [9].

On 29 July 2015, a section of the airplane wing was found on the Reunion Island (West Indian Ocean) 5,600 km^2 from the aircraft's last Primary Surveillance Radar (PSR) communication. The second section of the right-wing flap was found between Island Mauritius and Madagascar, passing by inspection of the Australian Transport Safety Bureau (ATSB) and proved as part of the Boeing 777-200ER of the flight MH370 [8]. After three years without any conclusive location of the impact of the aircraft, on 9 March 2017, the search was suspended by Malaysian authorities, China, and Australia until further notice. At the moment I present this paper, the mystery has not been solved yet and may never be solved. Through the incident; the safety of the aviation industry becomes questionable based on radar tracking systems and exploited the need for better tracking tools.

4.3 Issue Statement

Unsuccessful research methods for Malaysian Airline Flight MH370 have been done, such as the Bayesian search method [9] that intends to assume the aircraft's constant altitude and speed to create a probability density map that efficiently associates with localization of the missing aircraft using many vectors inputs.

Another inconclusive research according to the missed plane was done in [8] that estimates the drifting trajectory and time scales of the debris based on the drifting buoys and objects drift prediction mode. After seven years of the MH370 disappearance, the search has produced no conclusion. To increase the accuracy, the Federal Aviation Administration has decided to make the transition replacement from radar towards ADS-B to ensure the security of the air navigation system.

5 ADS-B vs Radar

To better explain the difference between the radar and ADS-B, we define the Automatic Dependence Surveillance broadcast- Extended Squitter; which is a series of data that are broadcast and periodically transmit Mode S transponder, helping Air Traffic Control to track airplanes without interrogation [11]. To simplify the word; Squitter is how frequently an airplane transmits data to the controllers, and posteriorly to other airplanes. The Extender Squitter uses a 1090 MHz frequency, which provides a data source to ADS-B based on Mode S transponder.

To compare the parameters of ADS-B vs Radar, data fusion is a method to analyze the basis of the modern intelligent transportation system. The concept is used at multiple stages of data processing, [12] provides a description based on the fusion of ADS-B and radar data to prove that this approach can upgrade the accuracy of tracking in practice. Another important method is also described in the same paper, describing a hybrid estimation algorithm to combine multi-sensors with different surveillance capabilities such as Radar, Multilateration, ADS-B, and flight plan data, not only for the security aim but also for general anomalies detection. Make data fusion is very easy since most of the necessary components are available and accepted for many industries that deal with safety and security.

5.1 MSTP (Multi-sensor Tracking Processing)

Multi-Sensor Tracking Processing is a method relatively similar to MRTS and MSTS. The system Fuse multiples sensors from radar, MLAT and ADS-B to generate the most accurate surveillance image. The state equation is not changing as is using in MRTS (state vector, transition matrix and state noise covariance matrix remain the same).

- **State Vector Equation**
  Both sensors are used as follow:

$$X_k = \begin{bmatrix} x\ y\ z\ \dot{x}\ \dot{y}\ \dot{z} \end{bmatrix}^T \tag{4}$$

The matrix transition is as follow:

$$\Phi_k = \begin{bmatrix} 1 & 0 & 0 & \Delta t_k & 0 & 0 \\ 0 & 1 & 0 & 0 & \Delta t_k & 0 \\ 0 & 0 & 1 & 0 & 0 & \Delta t_k \\ 0 & 0 & 0 & 1 & 0 & 0 \\ 0 & 0 & 0 & 0 & 1 & 0 \\ 0 & 0 & 0 & 0 & 0 & 1 \end{bmatrix} \tag{5}$$

Δt_k Denotes delta time between k and k-1.

- **Kalman Adaptation:**
  Kalman filter adaptation is made with an adjustment of the state noise covariance matrix Q_k before calculate successively the covariance matrix, gain matrix and estimated adjusted vector.

The noise variance is used as follow:

$$Q_k = \begin{bmatrix} \frac{\Delta t_k^4}{4} . q & \frac{\Delta t_k^3}{2} . q \\ \frac{\Delta t_k^3}{2} . q & \Delta t_k^2 . q \end{bmatrix} \tag{6}$$

$$q = \begin{bmatrix} \sigma_{qk_{xy}}^2 & 0 & 0 \\ 0 & \sigma_{qk_{xy}}^2 & 0 \\ 0 & 0 & \sigma_{qk_z}^2 \end{bmatrix} \tag{7}$$

$\sigma_{q\,k_{xy}}^2$ Denote the variance of ground acceleration (XY coordinate) for XY plan evolution.

$\sigma_{q\,k_z}^2$ Denote variance of vertical acceleration (z coordinate) for the vertical plan evolution.

The next equation is considered as measurement vector and observation matrix determination for radar and ADS-B sources. The vector is called observation vector, similar to $Z_k = [R\ \ Az\ \ El]^T$ in radar situation and $Z_k = [x\ y\ z]^T$ in ADS-B situation.

In radar situation this conduces to a non-linear observation matrix as follow:

$$H_k = \begin{bmatrix} \dfrac{\partial R}{\partial x} & \dfrac{\partial R}{\partial y} & \dfrac{\partial R}{\partial z} & 0 & 0 & 0 \\[2mm] \dfrac{\partial AR}{\partial x} & \dfrac{\partial Az}{\partial y} & \dfrac{\partial Az}{\partial z} & 0 & 0 & 0 \\[2mm] \dfrac{\partial El}{\partial x} & \dfrac{\partial El}{\partial y} & \dfrac{\partial El}{\partial z} & 0 & 0 & 0 \end{bmatrix} \tag{8}$$

In ADS-B situation, this conduces to a linear observation matrix as follow:

$$H_k = \begin{bmatrix} 1 & 0 & 0 & 0 & 0 & 0 \\ 0 & 1 & 0 & 0 & 0 & 0 \\ 0 & 0 & 1 & 0 & 0 & 0 \end{bmatrix} \tag{9}$$

5.2 Evaluation Features

The performance of ADS-B vs radar is analyzed as follow:

- Theoretical Evaluation (Table 2)

Table 2. Basic comparison between Radar and ADS-B

Radar	ADS-B
Aircraft location is transmitted every twelve seconds or more	Aircraft location is transmitted constantly
Range limitation is founded in some areas	The aircraft can be detected without limit restriction
Ground stations depend on human participation	Aircraft provide data without human participation
Extremely expensive to buy, install and maintain	Proved less expensive to buy, install and maintain
Less efficient in search and rescue (MH-370 main case)	More efficient in search and rescue

- Characteristic Evaluation (Table 3)

This characteristic evaluation report is derived from different software: the radar parameters are obtained from RPS United State Radars, the positional accuracy is extremely worst, for Terminal = (0.1–0.2 nm) and En-Route = (0.3–1.0 nm), while ADS-B parameters are obtained from the FAA Performance Requirements Document, the Navigation Accuracy Category for Position presents different outputs (NAC$_p$ = 9, 8, 7). Note that Navigation Accuracy for Velocity (NAC$_v$ = 1) or higher but the heading accuracy is not given [13].

Table 3. Radar and ADS-B parametric evaluation

Parameters	Radar		ADS-B	
	Terminal	En-Route	Terminal	En-Route
Update rate	≥4.9 s	≥12 s	2 s (96%)	5 s (96%)
Update timing	Radar scan		Asynchronous	
Positional accuracy	0.1–0,2 nm (600–1200) (1σ)	0.3–1.0 nm (1800–6000) (1σ)	35–100′ (95%)NACp = 9 100–300′(95%)NACp = 8 300–600′(95%)NACp = 7	
Positional bias	±1800 @ 60 nm	±1800 @ 250 nm	None –	
Velocity accuracy	Velocity accuracy	Depends on tracker	6–20 kts (96%) NACv = 1	
Heading accuracy	Depends on tracker	Depends on tracker	$\leq 5°$ @250 kts $\leq 2°$ @600 kts	

- **Positional Estimation** (Fig. 6)

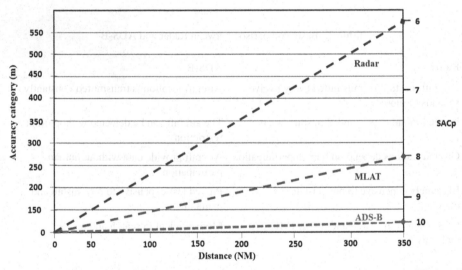

Fig. 6. Estimation of positional accuracy comparison when using radar, MLAT and ADS-B based on Surveillance Accuracy Category for Position (SACp), [12] MLAT (Multilateration) is defined as the developing reservation widely view as ADS-B. It can supply surveillance to aircraft transponders equipped with ADS-B. In Fig. 6, we can see that ADS-B and MLAT are providing the best surveillance tracking accuracy than radar over a range of 350 Nautical Miles (NM). To analyze this performance, we focus on the Surveillance Accuracy Category for Position (SACp) [12]; where the radar = 6 SACp, MLAT = 8 SACp and the most accurate position is provided by ADS-B = 10 SACp over a range of 350 nm. Those parameters are also used to clarify aircraft separation in a specific airspace.

- **Statistical Data** (Fig. 7)

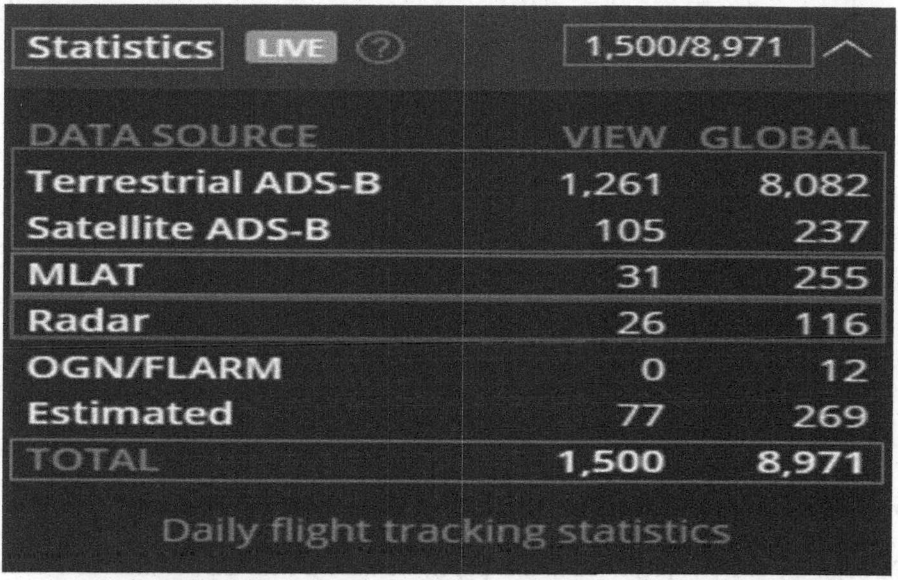

Statistics LIVE ⑦		1,500/8,971 ⌃
DATA SOURCE	**VIEW**	**GLOBAL**
Terrestrial ADS-B	1,261	8,082
Satellite ADS-B	105	237
MLAT	31	255
Radar	26	116
OGN/FLARM	0	12
Estimated	77	269
TOTAL	**1,500**	**8,971**

Daily flight tracking statistics

Fig. 7. Daily flight tracking statistic is a source from FR24. We can see that the number of airplanes tracked by radar per hour is 26 planes a day, while per hour ADS-B can track more than 1261 airplanes in real-time with supplemented information such as flight level, cruising speed, estimated time arrival, distance traveled, left distance to reach the destination, the flight path, type of aircraft, current weather on the flight path and so on. These details give more credits to ADS-B without leaving any doubt to unlike the traditional radar tracking system.

- **Multiple Sensors Coverage Area**

Through this performance, the ADS-B coverage area shows the best results and is higher than MLAT and radar, the performance also shows that ADS-B can track planes in some areas that are impossible to track by radar, and providing the best accuracy. The complement finding also proves that ADS-B can track aircraft in areas already covered by radar with high accuracy (Fig. 8).

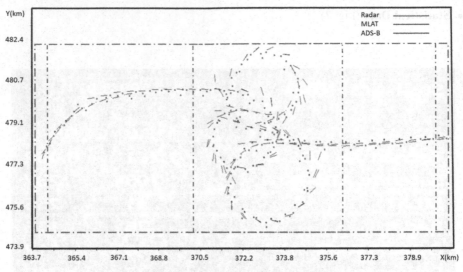

Fig. 8. Tracking accuracy comparison

6 Discussion and Recommendation Based on the Security System

Through the analysis presented in this paper, we have a clear answer that ADS-B has high accuracy on airspace surveillance and better tracking performance than radar since it provides supplemented coverage areas that cannot be covered by traditional radar. Future researches from our paper will focus on the congestion of the sky since both are combined: manned and unmanned aircraft that can cause serious collisions during the flight [14]. The vital peculiarity to keep the sky safe is providing constant localization of all planes in the sky. We know from [15] that the position data of ADS-B is provided by the global navigation satellite system, consequently will cause an impact on the safety and reliability of ADS-B performance. The ADS-B data link is vulnerable to attackers, it means that any passive enemy can easily access and analyze the unencrypted data of ADS-B [15]. The impact of malicious attackers on ADS-B can be classified as Aircraft Recognition, Ground Station Flood Denial, Ground Station Target Ghost Inject, Airplane Flood Denial, Airplane Target Ghost Inject, and Ground Station Diverse Ghost Inject. In [16] deal with Anomalies and Intrusions Detection by Sensor Clock Tracking of ADS-B, the Kalman Filter is the method proposed to detect onboard anomalies or fake messages injected by malicious attackers which affect with high consequences the future of air traffic surveillance (NextGen).

- Our finding in this paper is that we have provided analytical evidence that can help to raise the safety and reliability of the airspace to avoid any mid-air disaster. We never want to face a situation such as MH370, it is demonstrated that with the implementation of ADS-B, the security will be increased, and we expect that plane will never disappear from the sky without tracking the exact position.
- Our security recommendation is that the FAA must provide additional training and intensify investigations about the vulnerability of ADS-B to protect their encrypted

data; if a problem is presented, investigators should be able to deal with the issue and its means that education must be provided by the aviation community. With the revolution of technology, attackers are constantly looking for strategies that allow them to assault the system, we suggest that the FAA must expend their efforts and invest money to find a mechanism to implement regulations or any invention that blocks malicious attackers to get access to ADS-B data.

7 Conclusion

This research discusses the impact of the transition from radar towards ADS-B based on accuracy issues presented by traditional radar. The transformation of the Air Traffic Control is based on the implementation of Automatic Dependent Surveillance-Broadcast providing more accuracy and reliability on tracking aircraft. The impact of Malaysia Airline Flight MH370 is the greatest mystery that conducted the implementation of ADS-B. Through this disappearance, a need for better tracking tools was presented and implemented by 2020. The air traffic is constantly increasing, Automatic Dependent Surveillance-Broadcast leaves no doubt to fear, the system can track planes with high accuracy and providing constant updates of the currents flights. This method is relatively new and deals with many issues to ensure the safety of the system. Note that ADS-B is an achievement for general aviation but the FAA is concerning about the safety and vulnerability of the system. The aviation industry believes that security is the main priority of passengers, protect ADS-B data from attackers becomes a challenge of the NextGen plan, which the security is also a priority. Experts and researchers are working together looking for a mechanism to maintain aviation safe without any risk. The future of ADS-B upgrades traffic situation awareness with alert; the probability of mid air collision risk will decrease and aircrafts equipped with TCAS II will not be mandated.

Acknowledgment. This paper is completed under the guidance of Professor Liu Qingling, the teacher has made a lot of effort to supply materials for the completion of this paper. Here I would like to express my high respect and heartfelt thanks to Professor Liu Qingling for your cultivation and the great support. Finally, I would like to thanks my family for their help in my studies.

References

1. Koshy, D.G., Rao, S.N.: A study of various aircraft communication technologies. In: 2017 2nd International Conference on Communication and Electronics Systems (ICCES), vol. 2018, no. January, pp. 521–524 (2017)
2. Onoja, A.E., Oluwadamilola, A.M., Ajao, L.A.: Embedded system based Radio Detection and Ranging (RADAR) system using Arduino and ultra-sonic sensor. Am. J. Embed. Syst. Appl. 5(1), 7–12 (2017)
3. Eliseev, A.V.: Determining working area of three-position passive radar for aircraft surveillance. In: 2020 International Multi-Conference on Industrial Engineering and Modern Technologies (FarEastCon) 2020, pp. 1–6 (2020)

4. Khudov, H., Lishchenko, V., Irkha, A., Serdjuk, O.: The method of the high accuracy finding 2D coordinates in MIMO-radar based on existing surveillance radars. In: 2019 International Conference on Information and Telecommunication Technologies and Radio Electronics (UkrMiCo) 2019 - Proceedings, pp. 2019–2022 (2019)
5. McCallie, D., Butts, J., Mills, R.: Security analysis of the ADS-B implementation in the next generation air transportation system. Int. J. Crit. Infrastruct. Prot. **4**(2), 78–87 (2011)
6. Tabassum, A., Allen, N., Semke, W.: ADS-B message contents evaluation and breakdown of anomalies. In: 2017 IEEE/AIAA 36th Digital Avionics Systems Conference (DASC), pp. 1–8 (2017)
7. Gao, J., et al.: Drifting trajectory analysis of debris from MH370 in the southern Indian Ocean. In: Ocean. 2016 - Shanghai, pp. 1–4 (2016)
8. Skaddan, R., Alhashemi, N., Zaini, M., Khuraishi, M.: Design of an improved decision search system for missing aircrafts: MH370 case study the deconstruction of Houdini's greatest act. In: 2017 Systems and Information Engineering Design Symposium (SIEDS) 2017, pp. 73–78 (2017)
9. Holland, I.D.: MH370 burst frequency offset analysis and implications on descent rate at end of flight. IEEE Aerosp. Electron. Syst. Mag. **33**(2), 24–33 (2018)
10. Campbell, S.D., Grappel, R.D., Flavin, J.M.: Multi-sensor processing for aircraft surveillance in mixed radar/ADS-B environments. In: 2008 Tyrrhenian International Workshop on Digital Communications-Enhanced Surveillance of Aircraft and Vehicles TIWDC/ESAV 2008, no. October (2008)
11. Yeste-Ojeda, O., Landry, R.: ADS-B authentication compliant with mode-S extended squitter using PSK modulation. In: 2015 IEEE 18th International Conference on Intelligent Transportation Systems Proceedings, ITSC, vol. 2015, no. October, pp. 1773–1778 (2015)
12. Strohmeier, M., Lenders, V., Martinovic, I.: On the security of the automatic dependent surveillance-broadcast protocol. IEEE Commun. Surv. Tutorials **17**(2), 1066–1087 (2015)
13. Baud, O., Honore, N., Taupin, O.: Radar/ADS-B data fusion architecture for experimentation purpose. In: 2006 9th International Conference on Information Fusion, FUSION (2006)
14. Ji, H., Yao, P., Wang, H., Wu, J.: Simulation of unmanned aircraft system performing surveillance mission based on advanced distributed architecture. In: 2018 IEEE CSAA Guidance, Navigation and Control Conference (CGNCC) 2018 (2018)
15. Strohmeier, M., Schäfer, M., Lenders, V., Martinovic, I.: Realities and challenges of nextgen air traffic management: the case of ADS-B. IEEE Commun. Mag. **52**(5), 111–118 (2014)
16. Leonardi, M.: ADS-B anomalies and intrusions detection by sensor clocks tracking. IEEE Trans. Aerosp. Electron. Syst. **55**(5), 2370–2381 (2019)

A New Contingency Axiomatic System for Rough Sets

Sujie Guan⬤, Shaobo Deng(✉)⬤, Hui Wang(✉)⬤, and Min Li⬤

School of Information Engineering, NanChang Institute of Technology,
Nanchang 330099, China
huiwang@whu.edu.cn

Abstract. Contingency logic is well-known to study the principles of reasoning involving necessity, possibility, contingency and non-contingency. However, there are some defects in existing contingency axiomatic systems. For instances, (NCR)$_i$ is an infinite inference rule. The definition of accessibility relations and the corresponding axiom schema are very complex. To tackle these issues, a new contingency axiomatic system is proposed in this paper. Firstly, a new concise accessibility relation is defined for the axiomatic system; Then, two simpler axiom schemas of the axiomatic system are designed to replace the axiom schema K. This is helpful to prove the soundness and completeness theorems for the axiomatic system. Finally, rough sets can be perfectly formalized by our proposed axiomatic system. Theoretical analysis proves that a complete formal system is achieved. In addition, the concepts of *"precise"* or *"rough"* of rough sets can be described without the help of semantics functions of metalanguage.

Keywords: Rough sets · Intelligent computing · Contingency logic · Axiomatic system

1 Introduction

The contingency logic is a kind of modal logic, which is well-known to study the principles of reasoning involving necessity [1], possibility [2,3], contingency [4,5], non-contingency [6–8] and related notions. A logic having the operator $\triangle^1$ with the intended reading of $\triangle\phi$ being "it is non-contingent whether ϕ" is called a contingency logic. Thus for any formula ϕ, $\triangle\phi \equiv \square^2\phi \vee \square\neg\phi$, where $\square$ may be the modality for **K**, **D**, **T**, **4**, **S4** or **S5** [1,9–11].

If $\square$ is the modality of **K** [2], **D** [2], or **4** [8], then $\square$ cannot be defined in terms of $\triangle$. A general account of the logic of non-contingency has not emerged so quickly. The non-contingency or contingency logic based version of **K** was proposed by Humberstone [2], and the logic system contained the inference rule (NCR)$_i$, which played the same role as the axiom schema K; Nevertheless,

---

[1] "$\triangle$" is a logical symbol.
[2] "$\square$" is a logical symbol.

© Springer Nature Singapore Pte Ltd. 2021
Y. Tan et al. (Eds.): DMBD 2021, CCIS 1454, pp. 375–386, 2021.
https://doi.org/10.1007/978-981-16-7502-7_36

(NCR)$_i$ is an infinite rule and Humberstone suggested that a simpler inference rule or an axiom schema(axiom schemas) should be proposed.

If $\Box$ is the modality of **T**, **S4** or **S5**, then $\Box$ can be defined in terms of $\triangle$ [8,12,13]. The problem of defining necessity in terms of non-contingency or contingency has been solved in an axiomatic system of non-contingency logic which is at least as strong as $(\mathbf{KT})_\triangle$ [7,12,14]. Recently, Fan [15] proposed a novel method and axiomatized contingency logic over various frames based on "almost-definability" schema. An accessibility relation R is defined to prove the completeness theorem for the logic system. Then, a corresponding axiom schema is designed to play the same role with the axiom schema K. However, the definition of R and the corresponding axiom schema are relatively complex. So, we shall give a concise definition of an accessibility relation and simpler axiom schemas or inference rules.

From the above discussions, there are some defects in existing contingency logic systems. So, it is worthy to construct a new contingency axiomatic system. Firstly, an appropriate and concise definition of an accessibility relation is proposed in this paper. Then, two simpler axiom schemas of the axiomatic system are designed to replace the axiom schema K. Finally, rough sets can be perfectly formalized by our proposed axiomatic system.

The main contributions of this paper include two aspects: 1) a new logic system for the contingency logic (namely **S5**$_\triangle$) is designed and a new concise accessibility relation is defined to prove the completeness theorem for **S5**$_\triangle$; and 2) the concepts of "*precise*" or "*rough*" of rough sets can be perfectly described.

The rest of the paper is organized as follows. In Sect. 2, a new contingency axiomatic system **S5**$_\triangle$ is proposed. Section 3 describes an application instance which can be perfectly formalized by **S5**$_\triangle$ without the help of semantics functions of metalanguage. Finally, the work is concluded and summarized in Sect. 4.

2   The System S5$_\triangle$

Our base language is that of classical propositional logic with $\neg$ and $\rightarrow$ as primitive connectives. We add two connectives, $\triangle$ and ∇, for non-contingency and contingency, respectively. We take contingency as primitive and define non-contingency by the condition:$\nabla\phi = \neg\triangle\neg\phi$.

A Kripke model for **S5**$_\triangle$ is a structure $\langle W, R, I \rangle$, where W is a non-empty set of possible worlds, and $R \subseteq W^2$ is an equivalence relation defined over the members of W, and I is an interpretation such that for any propositional variable p $I(p) \subseteq W$ and for any $w \in I(p)$ p is true in the possible world w.

The notion ϕ is true in M at w (written $M, w \vDash \phi$) is defined in the standard way. As usual, ϕ is false in M at w (written $M, w \nvDash \phi$) iff it is not true in M at w. The clause for $\triangle$ is defined as:

$$M, w \vDash \phi \text{ iff for all } w' \in W \text{ if } wRw' \text{ then } M, w' \vDash \phi \text{ or}$$
$$\text{for all } w' \in W \text{ if } wRw' \text{ then } M, w' \nvDash \phi$$

The notion that formula is true in a model, a frame and all the members of some class of frames is defined as the standard way (Hughes [1]).

Now we give the following axiom schemas and inference rules of $S5_\triangle$.

Axiom schemas:

$$\textbf{L1 } \phi \to (\psi \to \phi)$$
$$\textbf{L2 } (\phi \to (\psi \to \mu)) \to ((\phi \to \psi) \to (\phi \to \mu))$$
$$\textbf{L3 } (\neg\psi \to \neg\phi) \to (\phi \to \psi)$$
$$\textbf{L4 } (\triangle\phi \wedge \triangle\psi) \to \triangle(\phi \wedge \psi)$$
$$\textbf{L5 } \triangle\nabla\phi$$
$$\textbf{L6 } \triangle\phi \wedge \nabla\neg\psi \to \nabla(\triangle\phi \wedge \neg\psi)$$
$$\textbf{L7 } \nabla\phi \wedge \nabla\neg\psi \to \nabla(\nabla\phi \wedge \neg\psi)$$
$$\textbf{L8 } \triangle\phi \to \triangle\neg\phi$$

Inference rules:

$$(MP) \ \frac{\phi, \phi \to \psi}{\psi}$$

$$(N) \ \frac{\phi}{\triangle\phi}$$

$$(RE) \ \frac{\phi \leftrightarrow \psi}{\triangle\phi \leftrightarrow \triangle\psi}$$

By these axiom schemas and inference rules, we can obtain:

(1) $L5'$ $\triangle\triangle\phi$.
(2) $L6'$ $\triangle((\triangle\phi_1 \wedge ... \wedge \triangle\phi_n) \to \psi) \to ((\triangle\phi_1 \wedge ... \wedge \triangle\phi_n) \to \triangle\psi)$.
(3) $L8'$ $\triangle((\nabla\phi_1 \wedge ... \wedge \nabla\phi_n) \to \psi) \to ((\nabla\phi_1 \wedge ... \wedge \nabla\phi_n) \to \triangle\psi)$.
(4) $L8''$ $\triangle((\triangle\phi_1 \wedge ... \wedge \triangle\phi_k \wedge \nabla\psi_{k+1} \wedge ... \wedge \nabla\psi_n) \to \psi) \to ((\triangle\phi_1 \wedge ... \wedge \triangle\phi_k \wedge \nabla\phi_{k+1} \wedge ... \wedge \nabla\phi_n) \to \triangle\psi)$.

Theorem 1. (The Soundness Theorem): *For any set of formulas Γ and any formula ϕ, if $\Gamma \vdash \phi$, then $\Gamma \vDash \phi$.*

Proof. For any set of formulas Γ and any formula ϕ, since $\Gamma \vdash \phi$, ϕ is the last member of a sequence which is a deduction from Γ. So we can use induction on the number of the sequence to prove this theorem.

The completeness theorem for $S5_\triangle$ will be proved in this section. We need to define a new concise accessibility relation based on the set of all sets of maximal consistent sets of formulas. The proof method has some difference from the classical canonical model method [1].

Theorem 2. *[1]: Suppose that Σ is a consistent set of formulas. Then there is a maximal consistent set of formulas Σ^* such that $\Sigma \subseteq \Sigma^*$.*

In constructing a canonical model in which the possible worlds are maximal consistent sets of formulas we will have to specify when one world is accessible from another. Therefore, the accessibility relation R, in the canonical model for this paper, is defined as follows:

Definition 1. *For any two maximal consistent sets Σ_1^*, Σ_2^*, we shall say that $\Sigma_1^* R \Sigma_2^*$ iff Σ_1^* and Σ_2^* satisfy the condition that: for any formula ϕ,*

(1) if $\triangle\phi \in \Sigma_1^*$ and $\phi \in \Sigma_1^*$ then $\phi \in \Sigma_2^*$, written: $\triangle_1^-(\Sigma_1^*) = \{\phi : \triangle\phi \in \Sigma_1^*$ and $\phi \in \Sigma_1^*\}$; and

(2) if $\triangle\phi \in \Sigma_1^*$ and $\neg\phi \in \Sigma_1^*$ then $\neg\phi \in \Sigma_2^*$, written: $\triangle_2^-(\Sigma_1^*) = \{\neg\phi : \triangle\phi \in \Sigma_1^*$ and $\neg\phi \in \Sigma_1^*\}$.

Therefore, we can say that $\Sigma_1^* R \Sigma_2^*$ iff $\triangle_1^-(\Sigma_1^*) \cup \triangle_2^-(\Sigma_1^*) \subseteq \Sigma_2^*$.

Obviously, the above definition of R is more concise than that of others [2, 7, 12, 14, 15]. The corresponding axiom schemas($L6, L7$) are more simpler than others axiom schemas [2, 7, 12, 14, 15].

Theorem 3. *Let Γ^* be the set of all maximal consistent sets. For any $\Sigma_1^*, \Sigma_2^* \in \Gamma^*$, we define $\Sigma_1^* R \Sigma_2^*$ iff $\triangle_1^-(\Sigma_1^*) \cup \triangle_2^-(\Sigma_1^*) \subseteq \Sigma_2^*$, then the relation R is an equivalence relation on Γ^*.*

Proof. In order to prove that R is an equivalence relation, we shall prove the following three conditions:

1) For any $\Sigma^* \in \Gamma^*$, $\Sigma^* R \Sigma^*$.
2) For any $\Sigma_1^*, \Sigma_2^* \in \Gamma^*$, if $\Sigma_1^* R \Sigma_2^*$ then $\Sigma_2^* R \Sigma_1^*$.
3) For any $\Sigma_1^*, \Sigma_2^*, \Sigma_3^* \in \Gamma^*$, if $\Sigma_1^* R \Sigma_2^*$ and $\Sigma_2^* R \Sigma_3^*$ then $\Sigma_1^* R \Sigma_3^*$.

We only prove Item 2), which is shown as follows:

The proof of 2). We shall prove that if $\Sigma_1^* R \Sigma_2^*$, then $\Sigma_2^* R \Sigma_1^*$, i.e., if $\triangle_1^-(\Sigma_1^*) \cup \triangle_2^-(\Sigma_1^*) \subseteq \Sigma_2^*$ then $\triangle_1^-(\Sigma_2^*) \cup \triangle_2^-(\Sigma_2^*) \subseteq \Sigma_1^*$.

The proof procedure is shown as the following four steps:

Step 1. We shall prove that for any formula α, $\alpha \in \Sigma_2^*$ or $\neg\alpha \in \Sigma_2^*$, which is shown as follows:

Since Σ_2^* is a maximal consistent set of formulas, for any formula α, $\alpha \in \Sigma_2^*$ or $\neg\alpha \in \Sigma_2^*$.

Step 2. We shall prove that for any formula α if $\triangle\alpha \in \Sigma_2^*$ then $\triangle\alpha \in \Sigma_1^*$ and ($\alpha \in \Sigma_1^*$ or $\neg\alpha \in \Sigma_1^*$). The proof is shown as follows:

Since $\vdash \triangle\triangle\alpha$, $\triangle\triangle\alpha \in \Sigma_1^*$.

By Step 1, it follows that $\triangle\alpha \in \Sigma_1^*$ or $\neg\triangle\alpha \in \Sigma_1^*$.

Suppose $\neg\triangle\alpha \in \Sigma_1^*$. Since $\triangle\triangle\alpha \in \Sigma_1^*$, by the definition of the relation R it follows that $\neg\triangle\alpha \in \Sigma_2^*$. Therefore, $\neg\triangle\alpha \in \Sigma_2^*$ and $\triangle\alpha \in \Sigma_2^*$. It follows that Σ_2^* is inconsistent, which contradicts the hypothesis of this theorem. Therefore, it follows that $\triangle\alpha \in \Sigma_1^*$, then by Step 1 we have $\alpha \in \Sigma_1^*$ or $\neg\alpha \in \Sigma_1^*$.

Step 3. We shall prove that:

(i) For any formula α, if $\triangle\alpha \in \Sigma_2^*$ and $\alpha \in \Sigma_2^*$ then $\alpha \in \Sigma_1^*$; or
(ii) For any formula α, if $\triangle\alpha \in \Sigma_2^*$ and $\neg\alpha \in \Sigma_2^*$ then $\neg\alpha \in \Sigma_1^*$.

We prove them with reductio ad absurdum, respectively, as follows:

As for (i), suppose $\alpha \notin \Sigma_1^*$, then $\neg\alpha \in \Sigma_1^*$.

Since $\triangle\alpha \in \Sigma_2^*$, $\triangle\alpha \in \Sigma_1^*$ by Step 2.

As for $\triangle\alpha \in \Sigma_1^*$ and $\neg\alpha \in \Sigma_1^*$, by the definition of R it follows that $\neg\alpha \in \Sigma_2^*$. Therefore, $\neg\alpha \in \Sigma_2^*$ and $\alpha \in \Sigma_2^*$. It follows that Σ_2^* is not consistent, which is a contradiction to the hypothesis of this theorem. Therefore, for any formula α, if $\triangle\alpha \in \Sigma_2^*$ and $\alpha \in \Sigma_2^*$ then $\alpha \in \Sigma_1^*$.

As for (ii), suppose $\neg\alpha \notin \Sigma_1^*$, then $\alpha \in \Sigma_1^*$.

Since $\triangle\alpha \in \Sigma_2^*$, $\triangle\alpha \in \Sigma_1^*$ by Step 2.

As for $\triangle\alpha \in \Sigma_1^*$ and $\alpha \in \Sigma_1^*$, by the definition of R it follows that $\alpha \in \Sigma_2^*$. Therefore, $\neg\alpha \in \Sigma_2^*$ and $\alpha \in \Sigma_2^*$. Then it follows that Σ_2^* is not consistent, which contradicts the hypothesis of this theorem. So for any formula α, if $\triangle\alpha \in \Sigma_2^*$ and $\neg\alpha \in \Sigma_2^*$ then $\neg\alpha \in \Sigma_1^*$.

Step 4. Now we prove $\triangle_1^-(\Sigma_2^*) \cup \triangle_2^-(\Sigma_2^*) \subseteq \Sigma_1^*$, which is shown as follows:

By the definition of $\triangle_1^-(\Sigma_2^*)$, for any formula α, if $\alpha \in \triangle_1^-(\Sigma_2^*)$, then it follows that $\triangle\alpha \in \Sigma_2^*$ and $\alpha \in \Sigma_2^*$. By Step 3, for any formula α, if $\triangle\alpha \in \Sigma_2^*$ and $\alpha \in \Sigma_2^*$ then $\alpha \in \Sigma_1^*$. Therefore, for any formula α if $\alpha \in \triangle_1^-(\Sigma_2^*)$ then $\alpha \in \Sigma_1^*$, i.e., $\triangle_1^-(\Sigma_2^*) \subseteq \Sigma_1^*$.

By the definition of $\triangle_2^-(\Sigma_2^*)$, for any formula α, if $\neg\alpha \in \triangle_1^-(\Sigma_2^*)$, then it follows that $\triangle\alpha \in \Sigma_2^*$ and $\neg\alpha \in \Sigma_2^*$. By Step 3, for any formula α, if $\triangle\alpha \in \Sigma_2^*$ and $\neg\alpha \in \Sigma_2^*$ then $\neg\alpha \in \Sigma_1^*$. Therefore, for any formula α if $\neg\alpha \in \wedge_2^-(\Sigma_2^*)$ then $\neg\alpha \in \Sigma_1^*$, that is to say, $\triangle_2^-(\Sigma_2^*) \subseteq \Sigma_1^*$.

Since $\triangle_1^-(\Sigma_2^*) \subseteq \Sigma_1^*$ and $\triangle_2^-(\Sigma_2^*) \subseteq \Sigma_1^*$, it follows that $\triangle_1^-(\Sigma_2^*) \cup \triangle_2^-(\Sigma_2^*) \subseteq \Sigma_1^*$.

$\square$

Proposition 1. *Let Γ be any maximal consistent set of formulas, then we have*

(1) for any formula ϕ, if $\triangle\phi \in \Gamma$ then $\triangle\phi \in \triangle_1^-(\Gamma) \cup \triangle_2^-(\Gamma)$.

(2) for any formula ϕ, if $\nabla\phi \in \Gamma$ then $\nabla\phi \in \triangle_1^-(\Gamma) \cup \triangle_2^-(\Gamma)$.

Theorem 4. *Let Γ be any maximal consistent set of formulas containing $\neg\triangle\psi$, then both $\triangle_1^-(\Gamma) \cup \triangle_2^-(\Gamma) \cup \{\neg\psi\}$ and $\triangle_1^-(\Gamma) \cup \triangle_2^-(\Gamma) \cup \{\psi\}$ are consistent, where $\triangle_1^-(\Gamma) = \{\phi : \triangle\phi \in \Gamma$ and $\phi \in \Gamma\}$ and $\triangle_2^-(\Gamma) = \{\neg\phi : \triangle\phi \in \Gamma$ and $\neg\phi \in \Gamma\}$.*

Proof. Since Γ is a maximal consistent set and $\vdash \triangle\triangle\psi$, it follows that: for any formula ϕ, $\triangle\triangle\phi \in \Gamma$ and $\triangle\phi \in \Gamma$ or $\neg\triangle\phi \in \Gamma$. Then it follows that Γ must contain formulas of the form $\triangle\alpha$ or formulas of the form $\nabla\beta$. By Proposition 1 $\triangle_1^-(\Gamma) \cup \triangle_2^-(\Gamma)$ contains the same formulas of the form $\triangle\alpha$ or $\nabla\beta$ as Γ. Now we prove that $\triangle_1^-(\Gamma) \cup \triangle_2^-(\Gamma) \cup \{\neg\psi\}$ and $\triangle_1^-(\Gamma) \cup \triangle_2^-(\Gamma) \cup \{\psi\}$ are consistent, respectively, as follows:

(1) First, we shall prove $\triangle_1^-(\Gamma) \cup \triangle_2^-(\Gamma) \cup \{\neg\psi\}$ is consistent.

Assume that $\triangle_1^-(\Gamma) \cup \triangle_2^-(\Gamma) \cup \{\neg\psi\}$ is not consistent. This means that there is a finite subset $\{\triangle\phi_1, ..., \triangle\phi_k, \nabla\phi_{k+1}, ..., \nabla\phi_n, \neg\psi\} \subseteq \triangle_1^-(\Gamma) \cup \triangle_2^-(\Gamma) \cup \{\neg\psi\}$ such that:

$$\vdash \neg(\triangle\phi_1 \wedge ... \wedge \triangle\phi_k \wedge \nabla\phi_{k+1} \wedge ... \wedge \nabla\phi_n \wedge \neg\psi)^3,$$

where $\{\triangle\phi_1, ..., \triangle\phi_k, \nabla\phi_{k+1}, ..., \nabla\phi_n\} \subseteq \Gamma$ and $n > k \geq 1$.

Then

$$\vdash \neg(\triangle\phi_1 \wedge ... \wedge \triangle\phi_k \wedge \nabla\phi_{k+1} \wedge ... \wedge \nabla\phi_n \wedge \neg\psi)$$

$\text{iff} \vdash (\triangle\phi_1 \wedge ... \wedge \triangle\phi_k \wedge \nabla\phi_{k+1} \wedge ... \wedge \nabla\phi_n) \to \psi$

$\text{iff} \vdash \triangle((\triangle\phi_1 \wedge ... \wedge \triangle\phi_k \wedge \nabla\phi_{k+1} \wedge ... \wedge \nabla\phi_n) \to \psi)$ (by N)

$\text{iff} \vdash \triangle((\triangle\phi_1 \wedge ... \wedge \triangle\phi_k \wedge \nabla\phi_{k+1} \wedge ... \wedge \nabla\phi_n) \to \psi) \to$

$\quad (\triangle\phi_1 \wedge ... \wedge \triangle\phi_k \wedge \nabla\phi_{k+1} \wedge ... \wedge \nabla\phi_n \to \triangle\psi)$ (by $L8''$)

$\text{iff} \vdash \triangle\phi_1 \wedge ... \wedge \triangle\phi_k \wedge \nabla\phi_{k+1} \wedge ... \wedge \nabla\phi_n \to \triangle\psi$ (by MP)

$\text{iff} \vdash \neg(\triangle\phi_1 \wedge ... \wedge \triangle\phi_k \wedge \nabla\phi_{k+1} \wedge ... \wedge \nabla\phi_n \wedge \neg\triangle\psi)$

So it follows that $\{\triangle\phi_1, ..., \triangle\phi_k, \nabla\phi_{k+1}, ..., \nabla\phi_n, \neg\triangle\psi\}$ is not consistent. Since $\{\triangle\phi_1, ..., \triangle\phi_k, \nabla\phi_{k+1}, ..., \nabla\phi_n, \neg\triangle\psi\}$ is a subset of Γ, Γ is also not consistent, which is a contradiction to the hypothesis of this theorem.

(2) Then, we shall prove $\triangle_1^-(\Gamma) \cup \triangle_2^-(\Gamma) \cup \{\psi\}$ is consistent.

The proof is similar to (1).
However, we need consider the following special case:

(3) $\triangle_1^-(\Gamma) \cup \triangle_2^-(\Gamma)$ does not contain any formula of the form $\triangle\alpha$ and $\nabla\beta$.

By Step 1, we know that for any formula ϕ, if $\triangle\phi \notin \triangle_1^-(\Gamma) \cup \triangle_2^-(\Gamma)$, then $\triangle\phi \notin \Gamma$; or for any formula ϕ, if $\nabla\phi \notin \triangle_1^-(\Gamma) \cup \triangle_2^-(\Gamma)$, then $\nabla\phi \notin \Gamma$.

Since $\triangle_1^-(\Gamma) \cup \triangle_2^-(\Gamma)$ contains no formulas of the form $\triangle\alpha$ and contains no formulas of the form $\nabla\beta$, it follows that $\triangle_1^-(\Gamma) \cup \triangle_2^-(\Gamma) = \emptyset$ by the definition of $\triangle_1^-(\Gamma) \cup \triangle_2^-(\Gamma)$. Then we give the following proof:

(3.1) Firstly, we shall prove that $\{\neg\psi\}$ is consistent.

Assume that $\{\neg\psi\}$ is not consistent.
Since $\{\neg\psi\}$ is not consistent, $\vdash \psi$. By the reference rule N it follows that $\vdash \triangle\psi$.
For $\vdash \triangle\psi$, $\triangle\psi \in \Gamma$.
Since $\triangle\psi \in \Gamma$ and $\neg\triangle\psi \in \Gamma$, it follows that Γ is not consistent in this case, which is a contradiction to the hypothesis of this theorem.

(3.2) Then, we shall prove that $\{\psi\}$ is consistent.

Assume that $\{\psi\}$ is not consistent.
Since $\{\psi\}$ is not consistent, $\vdash \neg\psi$, by the reference rule N it follows that $\vdash \triangle\neg\psi$.
For $\triangle\psi \leftrightarrow \triangle\neg\psi$, it follows that $\vdash \triangle\psi$. Thereby $\triangle\psi \in \Gamma$.
For $\triangle\psi \in \Gamma$ and $\neg\triangle\psi \in \Gamma$, it follows that Γ is not consistent in this case, which is a contradiction to the hypothesis of this theorem.

---

[3] Λ is S-inconsistent iff there are $\alpha_1,...,\alpha_n \in \Lambda$ such that $\vdash_S \neg(\alpha_1 \wedge ... \wedge \alpha_n)$. The idea is that in S you can prove that a contradiction arises from the members of Λ, where S may be the systems $K,D,T,S4$ and $S5$, and so on [1].

The canonical model for $\mathbf{S5}_\triangle$, M, is like any other model, a triple $\langle W, R, I \rangle$. W is the set of all sets of maximal consistent sets of formulas. I.e. $w \in W$ iff w is a maximal consistent set of formulas. If w and w' are both in W, then wRw' iff $\triangle_1^-(w) \cup \triangle_2^-(w) \subseteq w'$. In the case of any propositional variable p $I(p) \subseteq W$ and for any $w \in I(p)$ p is true at w iff $p \in w$. In the case of other formula this has to be proved as follows:

Theorem 5. *Let $M = \langle W, R, I \rangle$ be the canonical model for $\mathbf{S5}_\triangle$. Then for any formula ϕ and any world w, $M, w \models \phi$ iff $\phi \in w$.*

Proof. We use induction on the structures of formulas to prove the following cases:

Case a: $\phi := p$: By definition, this theorem holds.

Case b: $\phi := \neg\alpha$:
$M, w \models \neg\alpha$
iff $M, w \nvDash \alpha$
iff $\alpha \notin w$
iff $\neg\alpha \in w$

Case c: $\phi := \alpha \to \beta$:
$\alpha \to \beta \notin w$
iff $\neg(\alpha \to \beta) \in w$
iff $\alpha \in w$ and $\neg\beta \in w$
iff $M, w \models \alpha$ and $M, w \nvDash \beta$
iff $M, w \nvDash \alpha \to \beta$

Case d: $\phi := \triangle\alpha$:

$\triangle\alpha \notin w$, then $\neg\triangle\alpha \in w$. By Theorem 4 , both $\triangle_1^-(w) \cup \triangle_2^-(w) \cup \{\neg\alpha\}$ and $\triangle_1^-(w) \cup \triangle_2^-(w) \cup \{\alpha\}$ are consistent.

By Theorem 2, we can enlarge $\triangle_1^-(w) \cup \triangle_2^-(w) \cup \{\neg\alpha\}$ and $\triangle_1^-(w) \cup \triangle_2^-(w) \cup \{\alpha\}$ into maximal consistent sets of formulas w_1 and w_2, respectively, that is to say, there exist w_1, w_2 such that $\triangle_1^-(w) \cup \triangle_2^-(w) \cup \{\neg\alpha\} \subseteq w_1$ and $\triangle_1^-(w) \cup \triangle_2^-(w) \cup \{\alpha\} \subseteq w_2$.

Since $\triangle_1^-(w) \cup \triangle_2^-(w) \subseteq w_1$ and $\triangle_1^-(w) \cup \triangle_2^-(w) \subseteq w_2$, it follows that wRw_1 and wRw_2 by the definition of R.

For $\neg\alpha \in w_1$ and $\alpha \in w_2$, it follows that $M, w_1 \models \neg\alpha$ and $M, w_2 \models \alpha$ by induction hypothesis, that is to say, there exist w_1, w_2 such that wRw_1 and wRw_2 and $M, w_1 \models \neg\alpha$ and $M, w_2 \models \alpha$. So it follows that $M, w \nvDash \triangle\alpha$. $\square$

Theorem 6. *(The Completeness Theorem) For any set of formulas Γ and any formula ϕ, if $\Gamma \models \phi$, then $\Gamma \vdash \phi$.*

Proof. Suppose that $\Gamma \nvdash \phi$, then $\Gamma \cup \{\neg\phi\}$ is consistent. So there is a maximal consistent set of formulas w_0 such that $\Gamma \cup \{\neg\phi\} \subseteq w_0$ by Theorem 2. Then by Theorems 2, 3, 4, 5 and Definitions 1 we can prove this theorem.

3   Formalization of Rough Sets

We simply introduce rough set theory, then formulating rough sets by $S5_\triangle$ is to
be described in Sect. 3.2.

3.1   Rough Sets

Rough set theory, proposed by Z. Pawlak in 1982, is a new mathematical
tool to deal with quantitative uncertainty, vagueness and imprecision information [16,17]. It also has the ability of deduction [18], reduction [19] and common
sense reasoning [20,21]. In the past decades, rough set theory has been widely
applied in the fields of machine learning [22], knowledge acquisition, decision
analysis, knowledge discovery in databases, expert system [23] and pattern recognition [24].

Suppose we are given a finite set $U \neq \emptyset$ of objets we are interested in, and
the relation R is an equivalence relation on the set U. $[x] = \{y \in U : xRy\}$ is
called equivalence class of R [16,17].

Let $M = (U, R)$ be an approximate space, where R is an equivalence relation on U, and then by the properties of partition U/R we can define lower
approximation and upper approximation for any subset X of U as follows:

$$R_*(X) = \cup\{Y \in U/R : Y \subseteq X\}$$
$$R^*(X) = \cup\{Y \in U/R : Y \cap X \neq \emptyset\}$$

The lower approximation of X is the collection of those objects which can be
classified with full certainty as members of the set X.

The upper approximation of X consists of objects with which we can not
exclude the possibility that those objects may belong to X. Then:

1) X is precise(not rough) with respect to R iff $R_*(X) = R^*(X)$
2) X is rough with respect to R iff $R_*(X) \neq R^*(X)$.

Directly from the definition approximations we can get some properties of
the lower and the upper approximations. Please refer to [16].

3.2   Formalization of Rough Sets

We can formalize rough sets without the help of semantics functions of metalanguage, while existing methods can formalize rough sets only from the semantic
level by a certain semantics function of metalanguage [16,25–28].

For any approximate space (U, R) let (U, R) be a frame $\langle W, R \rangle$, that is to say,
we do not make any change on the language ,the syntax and the semantics of
$\mathbf{S5}_\triangle$. What we need to do is that let $U = W$ and the equivalence relation R be an
accessibility relation on W. So it follows that the formal system for rough sets,
which is obtained by formalizing rough sets with $\mathbf{S5}_\triangle$, is sound and complete
with respect to all of equivalence frames. So we can perfectly formalize rough
sets, compared with other formal system obtained by other logics [16,25–29].

Now, we need to explain why $\triangle$ can correspond to two kinds of equivalence
classes by the following proposition:

Proposition 2. $\triangle$ *can correspond to two kinds of equivalence classes.*

Proof. Given any model M, any possible world $w \in W$ and any formula ϕ, $M, w \vDash \triangle\phi$ iff

(1) for any $w' \in W$ if wRw' then $M, w' \vDash \phi$; or
(2) for any $w' \in W$ if wRw' then $M, w' \nvDash \phi$.

So it follows that $M, w \vDash \triangle\phi$ iff

(3) for any $w' \in [w]$, $M, w' \vDash \phi$; or
(4) for any $w' \in [w]$, $M, w' \nvDash \phi$,

where $[w] = \{w' : wRw'\}$ and $[w] \in W/R$.

We know that an equivalence class means that each member of the equivalence class has a common property. So from (3) and (4) it follows that $\triangle$ corresponds to two kinds of equivalence classes, i.e., one is that all its members satisfy some property, while the other is that all its members do not satisfy that property. □

Then, we shall prove that the logic system can describe the concepts of *"precise"* or *"rough"* of rough sets without the help of semantics functions of metalanguage by the following propositions:

Proposition 3. *Given any model M and any formula ϕ, $M \vdash \triangle\phi$ iff $\{w : M, w \vDash \phi\}$ is not rough(or precise).*

Proof. ($\Rightarrow$)
Since R is an equivalence relation on W, we can obtain W/R. Let $X = \{w : M, w \vDash \phi\}$. Since $M \vDash \triangle\phi$, for any $w \in W$ $M, w \vDash \triangle\phi$. Therefore, $M, w \vDash \triangle\psi$. Hence, we have:

(1) For any $w' \in W$ if wRw' then $M, w' \vDash \phi$; or
(2) For any $w' \in W$ if wRw' then $M, w' \nvDash \phi$

For (1), we have:

(3) For any $w' \in [w]$, $M, w' \vDash \phi$;

For (2), we have:

(4) For any $w' \in [w]$, $M, w' \nvDash \phi$;

From (3), it follows that $[w] \subseteq X$.
From (4), it follows that $[w] \cap X = \emptyset$.
Therefore, for any $w \in W$, it follows that $[w] \subseteq X$ or $[w] \cap X = \emptyset$. By Definition 7 and Proposition 2, $R_*(X) = R^*(X)$. Therefore, $\{w : M, w \vDash \phi\}$ is not rough.

($\Leftarrow$)
Since R is an equivalence relation on W, we can obtain W/R. Let $X = \{w : M, w \vDash \phi\}$.
Since X is not rough, $R_*(X) = R^*(X)$. By Definition 7, it follows that for any $w \in W$, we have

(1) $[w] \subseteq X$; or
(2) $[w] \cap X = \emptyset$.

From (1), it follows that

(3) for any $w' \in [w]$, $M, w' \vDash \phi$, that is to say, for any $w' \in W$ if wRw' then $M, w' \vDash \phi$.

From (2), it follows that

(4) for any $w' \in [w]$, $M, w' \nvDash \phi$, that is to say, for any $w' \in W$ if wRw' then $M, w' \nvDash \phi$.

From (3) and (4), $M, w \vDash \triangle\phi$.
Since for any $w \in W$ $M, w \vDash \triangle\phi$, it follows that $M \vDash \triangle\phi$.

$\square$

Proposition 4. *Given any model M and any formula ϕ, $\{w : M, w \vDash \phi\}$ is rough iff there exists $w \in W$ such that $M, w \vDash \nabla\phi$.*

3.3 Comparison with Other Works

Rough sets at present can be formalized by propositional logic, predicate logic(first order logic), modal logic and the logic system of this paper. The comparison with other works are shown as follows:

(1) When rough sets was formalized by propositional logic or predicate logic, an incomplete formal system could be obtained and a semantics function of metalanguage m was defined in order to describe the upper and lower approximation operators [16, 25–28]. But we can not describe the concepts of *"precise"* or *"rough"* of rough sets by the incomplete formal system.
(2) When rough sets was formalized by modal propositional logic, the modality $\square$ corresponded to the lower approximation operator [29]. However, we can not describe the concepts of *"precise"* or *"rough"* of rough sets.
(3) When formalizing rough sets by $\mathbf{S5}_\triangle$ in this paper, for any approximate space (U, R), let the approximate space (U, R) be a frame $\langle W, R \rangle$, that is to say, we do not make any change on the language, the syntax and the semantics of $\mathbf{S5}_\triangle$. What we need to do is that let $U = W$ and the equivalence relation R be an accessibility relation on W. So the formal system for rough sets, which is obtained by formalizing rough sets with $\mathbf{S5}_\triangle$, is sound and complete with respect to the class of all equivalence frames. The modality $\triangle$ corresponds to two kinds of equivalence classes (Proposition 3). Then we can describe the concepts of *"precise"* or *"rough"* of rough sets without the help of semantics functions of metalanguage (Proposition 4 and Proposition 5).

4   Conclusion

In this paper, we redefine a new accessibility relation and give corresponding axiom schemas($\mathbf{L6, L7}$) to show a contingency logic. Then we successfully give an example of the application of this contingency system in the field of computer science. How to formalize other theories of computer science will be investigated in the future work.

Acknowledgment. This work is partially supported by the Science and Technology Project of Jiangxi Provincial Education Department (Nos. GJJ161109, GJJ201917 and GJJ190941), and the National Science Foundation of China (Nos. 61763032 and 61562061).

References

1. Hughes, G.E., Cresswell, M.J., Cresswell, M.M.: A New Introduction to Modal Logic, Psychology Press, East Sussex (1996)
2. Humberstone, L.: The logic of non-contingency. Notre Dame J. Formal Log. **36**(2), 214–229 (1995)
3. Cresswell, M.J.: Necessity and contingency. Studia Log. **47**(2), 145–149 (1988)
4. Pizzi, C.: Bimodal fragments of contingency logics. Log. Anal. **224**, 425–438 (2013)
5. Pizzi, C.: Relative contingency and bimodality. Log. Univ. **7**(1), 113–123 (2013)
6. Humberstone, L.: Zolin and pizzi: defining necessity from noncontingency. Erkenntnis **78**(6), 1275–1302 (2013)
7. Montgomery, H., Routley, R.: Contingency and non-contingency bases for normal modal logics. Log. Anal. **9**(35/36), 318–328 (1966)
8. Steven, T.K.: Minimal non-contingency logic. Notre Dame J. Formal Log. **36**(2), 230–234 (1995)
9. Rosalie, I.: Uniform interpolation and sequent calculi in modal logic. Arch. Math. Log. **58**(1-2), 155–181 (2019)
10. Manisha, J., Alexandre, M., Martins, M.A.: A fuzzy modal logic for fuzzy transition systems. Electron. Notes Theor. Comput. Sci. **348**, 85–103 (2020)
11. Anantha, P., Ramanujam, R.: The monodic fragment of propositional term modal logic. Studia Log. **107**(3), 533–557 (2019)
12. Montgomery, H., Routley, R.: Non-contingency axioms for s4 and s5. Log. Anal. **11**(43), 422–424 (1968)
13. Montgomery, H., Routley, R.: Modalities in a sequence of normal noncontingency modal systems. Log. Anal. **12**(47), 225–227 (1969)
14. Pizzi, C.: Necessity and relative contingency. Studia Log. **85**(3), 395–410 (2007)
15. Fan, J., Wang, Y., Van Ditmarsch, H.: Contingency and knowing whether. Rev. Symb. Log. **8**(1), 75–107 (2015)
16. Pawlak, Z.: Rough logic. Bull. Polish Acad. Sci. Tech. Sci. **35**, 253–258 (1987)
17. Zdzisław, P.: Rough sets: Theoretical aspects of reasoning about data. Springer Science & Business Media (2012)
18. Salem, S.B., Naouali, S., Chtourou, Z.: A rough set based algorithm for updating the modes in categorical clustering. Int. J. Mach. Learn. Cybern. **12**(7), 2069–2090 (2021). https://doi.org/10.1007/s13042-021-01293-w

19. Hamed, A., Sobhy, A., Nassar, H.: Distributed approach for computing rough set approximations of big incomplete information systems. Inform. Sci. **547**, 427–449 (2021)
20. Wang, C., Shi, Y., Fan, X., Shao, M.: Attribute reduction based on k-nearest neighborhood rough sets. Int. J. Approximate Reason. **106**, 18–31 (2019)
21. Jihong, W., Hongmei, C., Zhong, Y., Tianrui, L., Xiaoling, Y., BinBin, S.: A novel hybrid feature selection method considering feature interaction in neighborhood rough set. Knowledge-Based Systems, p. 107167 (2021)
22. Wang, H., Wang, W., Xiao, S., Cui, Z., Minyang, X., Zhou, X.: Improving artificial bee colony algorithm using a new neighborhood selection mechanism. Inform. Sci. **527**, 227–240 (2020)
23. Wang, H., et al.: Artificial bee colony algorithm based on knowledge fusion. Complex Intell. Syst. **7**(3), 1139–1152 (2020). https://doi.org/10.1007/s40747-020-00171-2
24. Yao, Y.: Three-way granular computing, rough sets, and formal concept analysis. Int. J. Approximate Reason. **116**, 106–125 (2020)
25. Orlowska, E.: A logic of indiscernibility relations. Symposium on Computation Theory, pp. 177–186. Berlin, Heidelberg (1984)
26. Helena, R., Andrzej, S.: Rough concepts logic. Symposium on Computation Theory, p. 288–297. Berlin, Heidelberg (1985)
27. Qing, L., Lan, L.: Rough logic and its reasoning. Transactions on Computational Science II, pp. 84–99. Berlin, Heidelberg (2008)
28. Düntsch, I.: A logic for rough sets. Theor. Comput. Sci. **179**(1–2), 427–436 (1997)
29. Yao, Y.Y., Tsau, Y.L.: Generalization of rough sets using modal logics. Intell. Autom. Soft Comput. **2**(2), 103–119 (1996)

Health Index Construction and Remaining Useful Life Prediction of Mechanical Axis Based on Action Cycle Similarity

Hanlin Zeng[1], Hong Xiao[1], Yubin Zhou[1], Wenchao Jiang[1(✉)], and Dongjun Ning[2]

[1] School of Computer Science and Technology, Guangdong University of Technology, Guangzhou 510006, China
jiangwenchao@gdut.edu.cn

[2] Taotall Technology Development Co., Ltd, Guangzhou 510635, China

Abstract. Aiming at the low efficiency of manual detection in the axis health management of the industrial robot, a health index (HI) construction method based on action cycle similarity measurement is proposed. Furthermore, the remaining useful life prediction is carried out by Long Short-Term Memory (LSTM) network. Firstly, MPdist is used to calculate the comparison distance, and then the health index is constructed. Secondly, the long short-term memory network model is trained by the health index set. Finally, the MPdist-LSTM model is used to calculate the remaining useful life (RUL) automatically. The experimental results show that the monotonicity and trend of HI constructed by the MPdist algorithm improve by 0.07 and 0.13 compared with Dynamic Time Warping (DTW), Euclidean Distance (ED), and Time Domain Eigenvalue (TDE). The R-square of RUL prediction based on the MPdist-LSTM model reaches 0.96, which is higher than MPdist-RNN, DTW-LSTM, and TDE LSTM model.

Keywords: MPdist · Long short-term memory · Similarity measure · Health index construction · Remaining useful life

1 Introduction

Industrial robots are widely used in the processing of large and complex parts [1]. In particular, six-axis industrial robots play a vital role in the automatic production system [2]. At the same time, the accuracy degradation and failure problems of six-axis industrial robots are also severe, which brings enormous production risks and economic losses to enterprises [3]. The mechanical axis is the core component of industrial robot motion. Tracking the health states of the mechanical axis and predicting its potential failure is very important for robot health management. The mechanical axis failure does not occur suddenly. It goes through a degradation process from normal operation state to failure state. To manage the health of the mechanical axis of industrial robots, it is necessary to build a reasonable health index for the mechanical axis. Then extract feature information from the historical monitoring data to identify and quantify the degradation level of the mechanical axis and predict its remaining useful life.

© Springer Nature Singapore Pte Ltd. 2021
Y. Tan et al. (Eds.): DMBD 2021, CCIS 1454, pp. 387–401, 2021.
https://doi.org/10.1007/978-981-16-7502-7_37

Currently, there have been many studies on the construction of the health index and the prediction of remaining useful life for industrial equipment. It is mainly divided into model-based methods and data-driven methods. However, it is tough to model and analyze complex equipment mechanisms in most real industrial production environments, ensuring the model's accuracy. Therefore, in the context of big data of sensor detection, data-driven evaluation and prediction methods have become the mainstream. Data-driven prediction methods can be divided into direct prediction and indirect prediction [4]. Direct prediction is RUL prediction based on equipment degradation characteristics. Indirect prediction is to construct Health Index (HI) based on equipment degradation characteristics and then make RUL prediction based on HI. In general, indirect forecasting is more accurate, so it becomes the mainstream method. Kumar et al. used three different statistical methods to obtain the vibration signals of rolling bearings and construct their health index [5]. In order to comprehensively assess the system health status, Peng et al. proposed an unsupervised health index construction method based on deep belief networks (DBN) [6]. They implemented historical data feature extraction by DBN and then used reconstruction error to construct the health index. Guo et al. used Deep Convolutional Neural Networks (DCNN) to learn in-depth features of bearings and mapped the learned features to health index by nonlinear transformation, which was used for bearing health management [7]. Later they further proposed the HI construction method based on a trend burr convolutional neural network [8] for bearing health management. Chen et al. used CNN to extract the local temporal information in signal data and combined it with RNN for information connection to achieve bearing health index construction [9]. Mao W et al. proposed a structural adversarial neural network (SDANN) [10], a method based on deep transfer learning to achieve bearing fault diagnosis under multiple operating conditions.

However, the above research mainly focuses on the health index of specific components in specific fields such as bearings and gearboxes, and the methods are not universal. In addition, there are little researches on health prediction and state management of the six-axis industrial robot mechanical axis. Unlike ordinary simple rotating machinery, the instantaneous transformation of mechanical axis geometric shape is more complex. Moreover, its mechanical structure is complex, so it is not easy to establish an accurate mathematical model. Therefore, the method based on statistical and machine learning has become the mainstream choice of robot health monitoring [11, 16]. These methods include principal component analysis (PCA) [12, 12], linear discriminant analysis (FDA) [12], singular spectrum analysis (SSA) [13], Hilbert Transform (HT) [13] and wavelet analysis [14, 15], etc.

In actual production, the mechanical axis performs a series of actions periodically. If we ignore the action periodicity and only analyze the degradation based on data, the accuracy of the robot degradation analysis will be affected by the different data at different periods of the action cycle. Therefore, this paper proposes a health index construction and remaining useful life prediction method for six-axis industrial robots based on action cycle similarity measurement. Firstly, MPdist is used to focus on the similarity of sub-cycle sequences between different action cycles. The comparison distance between normal cycle data and degenerate cycle data is calculated, and then the health index is constructed. Secondly, the long short-term memory network model is trained by the health index set, and the mapping relationship between health index and remaining useful life is established. Finally, the MPdist-LSTM model is used to automatically calculate the remaining useful life and give an early warning in time. The experimental results show that: compared with other methods, the monotonicity and trend of the proposed method are 0.07 and 0.13 higher than other methods, and the RUL prediction accuracy is higher, and the error interval is smaller, which proves the effectiveness of the proposed method.

2 Construction of Health Index

The MPdist method is a new distance measurement method [17, 18]. It can compare time series of different lengths and has strong robustness to spikes, omissions, baseline wandering, and other problems. MPdist method believes that two time series are similar if they share many similar subsequences and are independent of the matching order of the subsequences [19, 20]. At the same time, MPdist can tolerate the displacement of two subsequence data points.

In actual working scenarios, the mechanical axis of the industrial robot performs specific actions periodically, and there may be irregular pauses before different action cycles. As a result, there may be some pause or translation between periodic data. As shown in Fig. 1, compare two sequences with 50 sample points translation, where T2 is the sequence formed by 50 sample points backward translation of sequence T1. The comparison distances calculated by the three methods before translation is all 0, and the comparison results after translation are shown in Table 1. It can be seen from Table 1 that MP distance is more suitable than DTW distance and Euclidean distance to evaluate the degradation of industrial robots with cyclic action.

Table 1. Comparison of the misaligned distance of action cycle in different methods

Method	Distance
MPdist	0
DTW	10709
Euclidean	43559

2.1 Similarity Measures Based on MPdist

The input of MPdist algorithm are two time series T_1 and T_2 to be compared, and the length L of the compared subsequence. The output is the comparison distance, which is called MP distance. The MP distance calculation steps are as follows:

Firstly, subsequences with length L of time series T_1 and T_2 are extracted by the sliding window of size L, and subsequence sets Sub_{T_1} and Sub_{T_2} are constructed. Where $3 \leq L \leq minlength(T_1, T_2)$.

Secondly, the $1NN - join$ function is used to find each other's closest neighbors in the subsequence set Sub_{T_1} and Sub_{T_2}, they are saved in the similar connection set $J_{T1,2}$ and $J_{T2,1}$ respectively. Meanwhile, the Euclidean distance of each pair of nearest neighbor subsequences in $J_{T1,2}$ and $J_{T2,1}$ is saved in the array $P_{(T1,T2)}$ [19].

Finally, calculate the MP distance, as shown in formula (1).

$$MPdist = \begin{cases} k^{th} \text{ of sorted } P_{(T1,T2)}, & |P_{(T1,T2)}| > k \\ max(P_{(T1,T2)}), & |P_{(T1,T2)}| \leq k \end{cases} \tag{1}$$

The $1NN - join$ function represents two subsequences $Sub_{T_1}(i, L)$ and $Sub_{T_2}(j, L)$ are the nearest neighbors. If they have the smallest Euclidean distance, then the $1NN - join$ function returns $true$. $Sub_{T_1}(i, L)$ represents the subsequence of length L starting from the position i of time series T_1. sorted $P_{(T1,T2)}$ represents $P_{(T1,T2)}$ after ascending sort. $|P_{(T1,T2)}|$ represents the number of elements in the similarity connection set, and k is five percent of the sum of the lengths of T_1 and T_2.

2.2 Health Index Construction Based on MPdist

As the robot runs longer and longer, the mechanical axis degrades gradually, and the distance of similar subperiods shared in the two sequences of different degradation cycles increases gradually. The MPdist algorithm is used to compare the similarity of the data. According to the time sequence of data collection, the data files are named $t_1–t_n$. Taking the data at t_1 as standard data, the data at time t_2 to t_n are compared with standard data by similarity, and the comparison distance is obtained, that is, a time-based MP distance curve. The comparison process is shown in Fig. 1. MP distance is negatively correlated with mechanical axis health, the greater the MP distance is, the more serious the degradation is.

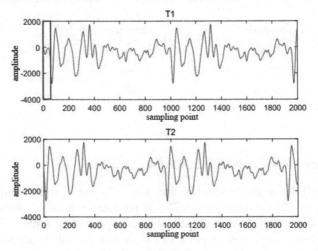

Fig. 1. Scheme of similarity comparison

The monotonicity, robustness, and trend of the health index are chosen as evaluation indicators. The calculation of monotony, robustness, and trend [21] are shown in formulas (2), (3), and (4) respectively.

$$Mon(HI) = \frac{1}{n-1} |Num_+ - Num_-| \tag{2}$$

$$Rob(HI) = \frac{1}{n} \sum_{t=1}^{n} \exp\left(-\left|\frac{HI_t - HI_t}{HI_t}\right|\right) \tag{3}$$

$$Tre(HI) = \frac{\left|n \sum_{t=1}^{n} HI_t \times t - \sum_{t=1}^{n} HI_t \sum_{t=1}^{n} t\right|}{\sqrt{\left[n \sum_{t=1}^{n} HI_t^2 - \left(\sum_{t=1}^{n} t\right)^2\right]\left[n \sum_{t=1}^{n} t^2 - \left(\sum_{t=1}^{n} t\right)^2\right]}} \tag{4}$$

Where $Mon(HI)$ is the monotonicity, Num_+ is the number of $HI_t > HI_{t-1}$. In the same way, Num_- is the number of $HI_t < HI_{t-1}$. And the n is the number of HI. $Rob(HI)$ is robustness indicator, HI_t represents the HI at time t, and HI_t represents the value of HI after differential smoothing. $Tre(HI)$ is trend indicator, t represents the t moment.

3   Remaining Useful Life Prediction

The mechanical axis degradation of industrial robots is a gradual aging process, and the historical operation of the robot will affect the operation of the mechanical axis in the future. The long short-term memory network can deeply mine the time series characteristics, hysteresis, and randomness of robot operation data. The network structure of LSTM consists of three "gates" and a memory cell. The three "gates" are the input gate, forget gate, and output gate. The input gate is used to control the input information of the neural unit at the current moment, the forget gate is used to retain the historical state information stored in the neural unit at the previous moment, and the output gate is used to control the output information of the neural unit at the current moment.

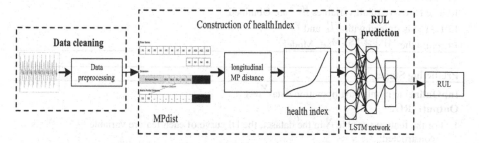

Fig. 2. Remaining useful life prediction framework based on MPdist-LSTM

The traditional remaining useful life prediction method based on LSTM usually trains the model with operation data and then predicts the remaining useful life. This paper proposes a remaining useful life prediction method based on MPdist-LSTM. The specific framework is shown in Fig. 2. The MPdist-LSTM model is divided into two layers. They are the training layer based on the historical aging data set and the prediction layer based on online monitoring data. The residual life prediction method proposed in this paper can be divided into two stages. They are the training stage and predicting stage.

Three kinds of statistics are chosen as the performance evaluation metrics of the prediction model [14]. They are mean absolute error (MAE), root mean square error (RMSE) and determination coefficient (R-Square, R^2). The smaller the MAE and RMSE are, the smaller the prediction error is and the higher the prediction accuracy is. R^2 represents the effect of measuring the model to predict unknown samples. The closer the R^2 value is to 1, the better the model fitting effect is and the higher the prediction accuracy is.

Training Stage

Input: Aging data set X and true RUL label Y

Output: $MPdist\text{-}LSTM_{best}$ Model

1. Data preprocessing
2. The first 5% data is divided into normal data X_{normal}, and the last 95% data is divided into degradation process data X_{fault}^T
3. For the feature variable N in the dataset, the HI curve of each feature variable $n(n \in N)$ is constructed:
4. for n in N:
5.   for t in T:
6.   MPdist algorithm is used to calculate the MP distance f_t between X_{normal} and X_{fault}^t
7.   The MP distance curve $f_T = \{f_1, f_2, \ldots, f_t\}$ is Obtained
8.   The last 5% of f_T is divided into failure data f_{fault}
9.   for t in T:
10.   Calculate the HI value,
$$HI_t = \left\{ \sqrt{(f_t - f_{fault})^2} \mid t = 1, 2, \ldots, T \right\}$$
11. The HI curve is Obtained
12. The HI curve of all variables HI_t^n are Obtained
13. LSTM is trained with HI_t^n and Y
14. return the $MPdist\text{-}LSTM_{best}$ Model

Predicting Stage

InpOnlineine monitoring operation data X_{test}

Output: RUL

1. For the feature variable N in the dataset, the HI curve of each feature variable $n(n \in N)$ is constructed:
2. for n in N:
3.   MPdist algorithm is used to calculate the MP distance f between X_{normal} and X_{test}
4.   Calculate the HI value,
$$HI_t = \left\{ \sqrt{(f_t - f_{fault})^2} \mid t = 1, 2, \ldots, T \right\}$$
5. The HI curve of all variables HI^n are Obtained
6. The RUL is predicted by $MPdist\text{-}LSTM_{best}$ Model
7. return RUL

In addition, in order to evaluate the prediction effect of state transition better, this paper uses relative accuracy (RA), error range (ER), early prediction (EP), and late prediction (LP) as evaluation metrics to further evaluate the prediction results of state transition. The definitions of early prediction and late prediction are shown in Fig. 3. The prediction error is shown in Eq. (3). When $STT_{error} > 0$, it is denoted as late prediction, and when $STT_{error} < 0$, it is denoted as the early prediction.

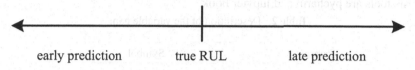

early prediction   true RUL   late prediction

Fig. 3. Schematic diagram of early prediction and late prediction

In actual application scenarios, the impact of early prediction and late prediction is different. Early prediction could give early warning and reduce losses, while late prediction may lead to certain losses. Therefore, the evaluation system of the model is more friendly to the early prediction than to the late prediction.

$$STT_{error} = STT_{predict} - ST \tag{5}$$

4 Experiments and Analysis

4.1 Data Collection

According to the design of the industrial robot, the driver will provide current and voltage signals, which are closely related to the output torque and speed of the motor. At the same time, some drivers also provide encoder signal, which is often used for robot position feedback. When the robot fault occurs, such as gear fracture, connection device falling off, and abnormal feedback device, it will be reflected in the driver current, voltage, and encoder signal.

Fig. 4. Six-axis industrial robot of a company

As shown in Fig. 4, the accelerated aging experiment was carried out with the six-axis industrial robots, and then the aging dataset was constructed. The robot executed the aging program and ran continuously for one month. The data of multiple operation variables of the robot were collected. Moreover, the symbol definitions of all data variables are shown in the Table 2. The data contains more than 5 million pieces of data for each robot, about 900 action cycles, and the sampling frequency is 4 ms, including nine variables. The symbol definitions of all data variables are shown in Table 2. Data analysis tools are pycharm and jupyter book.

Table 2. Description of the variable name

Parameter	Symbol
Command position	pcmd
Feedback position	pfb
Command torque	tcmd
Feedback torque	tfb
Command acceleration	acmd
Feedback acceleration	afb
Command speed	vcmd
Feedback speed	vfb
Position error	pe

4.2   Health Index Construction

At first, we analyzed the collected data of 9 variables. According to the expert experience and statistical analysis, we screened out three variables with periodic invariance. Then, the PCA method was used to reduce the dimension of the feature and combined with Pearson correlation coefficient, the feedback torque (TFB), feedback speed (VFB), and position error (PE) which can reflect the aging trend, were selected as the characteristic aging variables.

According to the periodic operation characteristics of the mechanical axis, the time series T_1 and T_2 set as the sampling data of multiple cycles of the mechanical axis operation, and the comparison sub series L length of one or more cycles. In order to explore the optimal length relationship between time series T_1, T_2 and L, taking the feedback torque of 2-axis of NO.1 robot as an example, the monotonicity, robustness and trend of MP distance are calculated by comparing T_1, T_2 and L as different ratios. The results are shown in Table 3. As can be seen from Table 3, when the ratio of T_1 and T_2 to L is 5:1, the monotony and robustness of MP distance curve are the best, and as the ratio increases, the algorithm complexity becomes higher, while the monotony and robustness of MP distance curve do not significantly improve. Therefore, as shown in Fig. 5, we chose the data of 5 cycles with different movements of the mechanical axis as T_1 and T_2, and the length of the subsequence L is 1 cycle, which was used as the input of the algorithm. We input the normal data and the degraded data in turn into the MPdist algorithm to calculate the MP distance.

Table 3. Comparison of evaluation results of MP distance curves with different ratios

The ratio of T1 or T2 to L	Mon	Rub	Tre
2:1	0.2370	0.8350	0.6784
3:1	0.4682	0.9615	0.8674
4:1	0.5376	0.9665	0.8870
5:1	**0.5607**	**0.9684**	**0.9065**
6:1	0.5460	0.9679	0.8952
7:1	0.5607	0.9679	0.9065
8:1	0.5517	0.9665	0.8806

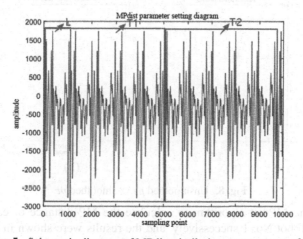

Fig. 5. Schematic diagram of MPdist similarity measurement of tfb

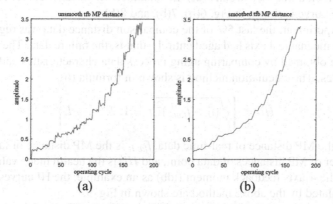

Fig. 6. Unsmoothed *tfb* vs smoothed *tfb*

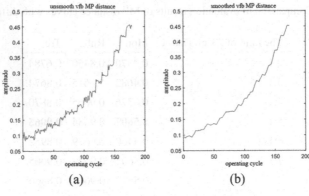

Fig. 7. Unsmoothed *vfb* vs smoothed *vfb*

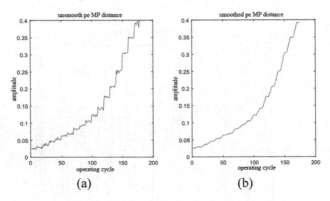

Fig. 8. Unsmoothed *pe* vs smoothed *pe*

We used the MPdist algorithm to calculate the MP distance of each variable of the 4-axis of Robot No. 1 successively, and the results were shown in Fig. 6(a), 7(a), and 8(a). Where the abscissa represents the running cycle, and the ordinate represents the MP distance. To reduce the impact of random volatility on the data, the difference smoothing method was used to construct the smoothed MP distance curve. The smoothed MP distance curve is shown in Fig. 6(b), 7(b), and 8(b).

In the experiment, the last 5% of the comparison distance data was regarded as the data that the mechanical axis had aged entirely, that is, the failure data. The health index value can be obtained by comparing aging process data characteristics and failure data characteristics. The calculation method is shown in formula (6).

$$HI_t = \left\{ \sqrt{\left(f_t - f_{fault}\right)^2} \middle| t = 1, 2, 3 \ldots L \right\} \tag{6}$$

Where f_t is the MP distance of real-time data, f_{fault} is the MP distance of failure data, L is the number of MP distances of data point, and HI_t is the health index value of point t.

Taking the 4-axis feedback moment (tdb) as an example, the HI curves of the three robots calculated by the above method are shown in Fig. 9.

It can be seen from Fig. 9 that there are obvious differences in the degradation trend of the three robots. The HI curve of the 4-axis of No. 1 robot drops fastest, which indicates

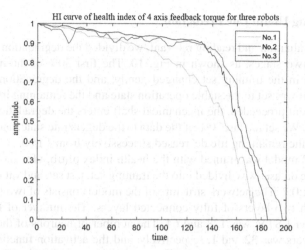

Fig. 9. HI curve of four axis's tfb for three robots

that the 4-axis of robot No. 1 degenerates faster than robot No. 2 and robot No. 3. The experimental results are consistent with the actual situation, proving that the health index constructed in this paper can better reflect the real degradation trend of the mechanical axis.

To further prove the effectiveness of the constructed health index, monotony, robustness, and trend were used as an evaluation metric, and the commonly used time series similarity comparison methods were compared with the method based on the MPdist method. The results are shown in Table 4. As shown from Table 4, the health index constructed based on MPdist, DTW, ED, and time-domain feature has little difference in robustness, but HI constructed based on the MPdist method has the best monotony and trend.

The operation of the mechanical axis has a certain action cycle. The operation time of each action cycle is different, and there are pauses between different cycles. This data feature is more consistent with the feature that the MPdist method shares more similar subsequences, and the evaluation effect of health indicators based on the MPdist method is better. The MPdist method is more suitable for such data characteristics, and the evaluation of health index based on the MPdist method is more effective.

Table 4. Health index evaluation table

Method	Mon	Rub	Tre
MPdist	**0.5607**	0.9684	**0.9065**
DTW	0.4913	**0.9696**	0.7706
ED	0.0580	0.9502	0.2037
TDE	0.1329	0.9524	0.3106

4.3 Remaining Useful Life Prediction

After expert evaluation and reading relevant, we divided the degradation of the mechanical axis into two stages, as shown in Fig. 10. The first 30% of the mechanical axis operation data in the training set changed gently, and the degradation trend was not noticeable, so it was set to the stable operation state and the remaining life was 1. As the aging experiment proceeded, the mechanical shaft enters the degradation stage, gradually degrading. We set the last 70% of the data to the degenerate state, and as the running time went on, the remaining life decreased successively from 1 to 0.

The LSTM model was trained with the health index of tfb, vfb, and pe constructed by MPdist. The dataset was divided into the training set, test set, and validation set in the ratio of 0.6:0.2:0.2. The network structure of the model consists of two layers of LSTM combined with two layers of fully connected layers. The number of hidden neurons of the two-layer LSTM was 128 and 64. The number of neurons of the two-layer full connection layers was 32 and 1, respectively, and the activation function is Relu. The input and output structure of the neural network layer was shown in Fig. 11.

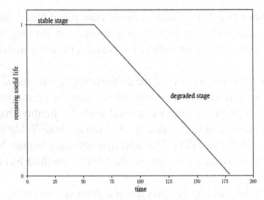

Fig. 10. Schematic diagram of remaining useful life marking

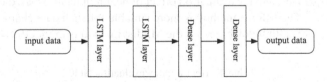

Fig. 11. Structure diagram of input and output of the neural network

The adjustment of the LSTM time step is shown in Table 5. From 3 to 6, the prediction effect becomes better. From 6 to 20, the prediction effect gradually becomes worse. Therefore, the best time step is 6. To verify the effectiveness of constructing the health index based on MP distance, 34 test samples were input into the trained model for remaining useful life prediction. The prediction result is shown in Fig. 12. Then, the prediction effects of MP distance, DTW distance combination, time-domain eigenvalues

Table 5. Evaluation table of LSTM network time step adjustment

LSTM model	MAE	RMSE	R^2
Time_step = 3	0.0366	0.0652	0.9575
Time_step = 6	0.0289	0.0569	0.9669
Time_step = 10	0.0366	0.0705	0.9472
Time_step = 20	0.0324	0.0763	0.9285

combined with LSTM network, MPdist combined with RNN, and LSTM were compared. The results were shown in Table 6.

It can be seen from Table 6 that the MAE, RMSE and R^2 of the remaining useful life prediction model based on MP distance health index are 0.0289, 0.0569, and 0.9669 respectively, the error interval is $[-8, 12]$, the number of the early prediction is 19, and the number of the late prediction is 13, which are better than other methods.

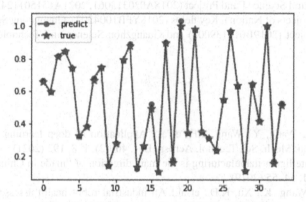

Fig. 12. Prediction results of MPdist-LSTM

Table 6. Evaluation table of remaining useful life prediction

Method	MAE	RMSE	R_2	ER	EP	LP
MPdist-LSTM	**0.0289**	**0.0569**	**0.9669**	**$[-8, 12]$**	**19**	**13**
MPdist-RNN	0.0305	0.0671	0.9437	$[-16, 15]$	15	18
DTW-LSTM	0.0338	0.0721	0.9358	$[-48, 20]$	14	20
TDE-LSTM	0.1047	0.1346	0.7818	$[-32, 48]$	16	18
LSTM	0.1064	0.2104	0.5019	$[-60, 60]$	15	19

5 Conclusion

To solve the problem of inefficiency and low accuracy in mechanical axis health management of industrial robots, this paper proposes a method of mechanical axis health index construction. The MPdist algorithm is used to calculate the deviation degree between action cycles in different degradation periods to measure the degradation level and then constructed the health index. The experiments were conducted in the accelerated aging dataset of the six-axis industrial robot. The experimental results show that the monotonicity and trend of the HI constructed by MPdist are improved by 0.07 and 0.13 compared with DTW, ED, and TDE respectively.

The health HI construction method and RUL prediction model proposed in this paper are mainly based on the single scenario of the mechanical axis, without considering the changes of the mechanical axis in different application scenarios. In the future, we will explore the degradation of the mechanical axis in combination with different scenarios.

Acknowledgement. This paper is supported by the Key Technology Project of Foshan City in 2019 (1920001001367), National Natural Science and Guangdong Joint Fund Project (U2001201), Guangdong Natural Science Fund Project (2018A030313061, 2021A1515011243), Research and Development Projects of National Key fields (2018YFB1004202), Guangdong Science and Technology Plan Project (2019B010139001) and Guangzhou Science and Technology Plan Project (201902020016).

References

1. Wang, T.Z., Wang, Y., Wang, Y.F., et al.: Application of deep learning in robot chatter identification. Mech. Sci. Technol. Aerosp. Eng. **40**(02), 188–192 (2021)
2. Zhou, J.: Intelligent manufacturing is the main direction of "made in China 2025." Enterp. Observer **11**, 54–55 (2019)
3. Zhao, W., Wang, K., Xu, K.D., et al.: An industrial robot health assessment method for intelligent manufacturing. Robot **42**(04), 460–468 (2020)
4. Peng, Y., Liu, D.T.: Data-driven prognostics and health management: a review of recent advances. Chin. J. Sci. Instr. **35**(03), 481–495 (2014)
5. Kumar, H.S., Pai, S.P., Sriram, N.S., et al.: Rolling element bearing fault diagnostics: development of health index. Proc. Inst. Mech. Eng. C J. Mech. Eng. Sci. **231**(21), 3923–3939 (2017)
6. Peng, K.X., Pi, Y.T., Jiao, R.H., et al.: Health indicator construction and remaining useful life prediction for aircraft engine. Control Theory Appl. **37**(04), 713–720 (2020)
7. Guo, L., Lei, Y., Li, N., et al.: Deep convolution feature learning for health indicator construction of bearings. In: Prognostics and System Health Management Conference (PHM-Harbin), Piscataway, NJ, pp. 1–6. IEEE (2017)
8. Guo, L., Lei, Y., Li, N., et al.: Machinery health indicator construction based on convolutional neural networks considering trend burr. Neurocomputing **292**, 142–150 (2018)
9. Chen, L., Xu, G., Zhang, S., et al.: Health indicator construction of machinery based on end-to-end trainable convolution recurrent neural networks. J. Manuf. Syst. **54**, 1–11 (2020)
10. Mao, W., Liu, Y., Ding, L., et al.: A new structured domain adversarial neural network for transfer fault diagnosis of rolling bearings under different working conditions. IEEE Trans. Instrum. Meas. **2020**(70), 1–13 (2020)

11. Jaber, A.A., Bicker, R.: Development of a condition monitoring algorithm for industrial robots based on artificial intelligence and signal processing techniques. Int. J. Electr. Comput. Eng. **8**(2), 996 (2018)
12. Chen, Y., Wang, H., Zhang, J., et al.: Automated recognition of robotic manipulation failures in high-throughput biodosimetry tool. Expert Syst. Appl. **39**(10), 9602–9611 (2012)
13. Algburi, R.N.A., Gao, H.: Health assessment and fault detection system for an industrial robot using the rotary encoder signal. Energies **12**(14), 2816 (2019)
14. Zhao, H.M.: The fault diagnostic studies of industrial robot based on signal analysis. Shenyang Jianzhu University, Shenyang, pp. 1–27 (2014)
15. Jaber, A.A., Bicker, R.: Fault diagnosis of industrial robot gears based on discrete wavelet transform and artificial neural network. Insight-Non-Destr. Test. Condition Monit. **58**(4), 179–186 (2016)
16. Fink, O., Wang, Q., Svensen, M., et al.: Potential, challenges and future directions for deep learning in prognostics and health management applications. Eng. Appl. Artif. Intell. **92**, 103678 (2020)
17. Gharghabi, S., Imani, S., Bagnall, A., et al.: Matrix Profile XII: MPdist: a novel time series distance measure to allow data mining in more challenging scenarios. In: ICDM 2018: 2018 IEEE International Conference on Data Mining, pp. 965–970. IEEE (2018)
18. Yeh, C.C.M., Zhu, Y., Ulanova, L., et al.: Matrix profile I: all pairs similarity joins for time series: a unifying view that includes motifs, discords and shapelets. In: ICDM 2016: 2016 IEEE 16th International Conference on Data Mining, pp. 1317–1322. Piscataway, NJ. IEEE (2016)
19. Senin, P.: Dynamic time warping algorithm review. Inf. Comput. Sci. Dept. Univ. Hawaii Manoa Honolulu USA **855**(1–23), 40 (2008)
20. Jeong, Y.S., Jeong, M.K., Omitaomu, O.A.: Weighted dynamic time warping for time series classification. Pattern Recogn. **44**(9), 2231–2240 (2011)
21. Zhang, B., Zhang, L., Xu, J.: Degradation feature selection for remaining useful life prediction of rolling element bearings. Qual. Reliab. Eng. Int. **32**(2), 547–554 (2016)

Approximation Relation for Rough Sets

Shaobo Deng[(✉)] [iD], Huihui Lu [iD], Sujie Guan [iD], Min Li [iD], and Hui Wang [iD]

School of Information Engineering, NanChang Institute Of Technology,
Nanchang 330099, China
huiwang@whu.edu.cn

Abstract. Rough set theory has the ability of deduction, reduction and common sense reasoning. First, this paper proposes the definition of the approximation relation; then, a kind of measurement method based on the approximation relation is proposed to judge whether any two sets are approximate with each other and then we can mine all of the sets that are approximate with a certain set by the measurement method in any approximation space; finally, this paper discusses algebraic properties for the measurement method, furthermore, we give its algebraic structure, which is proved a new standard boolean algebra for Rough sets.

Keywords: Rough sets · The lower approximation · The upper approximation · Boolean algebra · Approximation classes

1 Introduction

Rough sets was introduced by Pawlak [1] and can be used to describe vague information. Rough sets has numerous practical application, such as development of decision table [2], data mining [3] and knowledge discovery [4] and so on. Attribute reduction in rough set theory serves as a fundamental topic for information processing [5–9]. Meanwhile, algebraic structures are parts of the foundation of rough sets [10–15]. Rough sets has been generalized into various models for meeting practical challenges from approximation spaces to multigranulation spaces [16–20], such as the variable precision rough set, decision-theoretic rough set, game-theoretic rough set and the theory of three-way decision and so on [21–24].

Given any approximation space (U, R), where the relation R is an equivalence relation on the universe U. For any $A \in P(U)$ we can use the upper approximation set $\overline{A}$ and the lower approximation $\underline{A}$ to approximate A. If A is precise with respect to R, then $\underline{A} = \overline{A}$; otherwise, A is rough. Nevertheless, we are not content to know these. If A is rough, how do we measure that a certain set B is "approximate" with A in the approximate space? Obviously, we can use the lower and upper approximation sets to do this, i.e., for any two set $A, B \in P(U)$, if $\underline{A} = \underline{B}$ and $\overline{A} = \overline{B}$ then we think that A and B are approximate with each other (which shall be defined in Sect. 2), because we in the approximation space (U, R) have no better method to distinguish A from B when using lower approximation sets and upper approximation sets to approximate A and B. So we are

Y. Tan et al. (Eds.): DMBD 2021, CCIS 1454, pp. 402–417, 2021.
https://doi.org/10.1007/978-981-16-7502-7_38

more interested in how to give a kind of measurement method that is used to judge whether two sets are approximate with each other in any approximate space, and how can we find out all of sets which are approximate with A by this measurement method. In fact, that two sets are approximate in an approximation space is very common, nevertheless, relatively few studies have been done.

So in this paper we give a kind of measurement method. By the definition of measurement method we can judge whether two set are approximate with each other or not. Furthermore, we present a kind of algebraic structure $\langle P(U)/ \simeq, +, \times, -, 0, 1\rangle$ for approximation relations based on Rough sets and prove that $\langle P(U)/ \simeq, +, \times, -, 0, 1\rangle$ is a standard boolean algebra ($P(U)/ \simeq = \{(A) : A \in P(U)$ and $A \subseteq U\}$ shall be defined in Sect. 3), which is different from the stone algebraic structure or other algebraic structures for Rough sets [10–15, 25].

This paper is organized as follows: in Sect. 2, we briefly introduce Rough sets. Section 3 gives the definition of approximation relation and discuss some properties of the approximation relation. Section 4 gives approximation class and a new standard boolean algebra for approximation class based on Rough sets. The last section concludes the whole paper.

2   Rough Sets

Rough sets, proposed by Z. Pawlak in 1982, is a new mathematical tool to deal with quantitative uncertainty, vagueness and imprecision information, and has the ability of deduction, reduction and common sense reasoning. So this theory has been widely applied in the fields of machine learning [26], knowledge acquisition, decision analysis, knowledge discovery in databases, expert system and pattern recognition [27], and so on.

Suppose that we are given a finite set $U \neq \emptyset$ of objets we are interested in. Then the relation R on the set U is an equivalence relation iff it is reflexive, symmetric and transitive [1].

Let $M = (U, R)$ be an approximation space, where R is an equivalence relation on U, then by the properties of partition U/R, we can define lower approximation and upper approximation for any subset X of U as follows:

Definition 1. *[1] Let $M = (U, R)$ be an approximation space, for any set $X \subseteq U$, the lower approximation and upper approximation of X on M are defined respectively as follows:*

$$\underline{X} = \cup\{Y \in U/R : Y \subseteq X\}$$
$$\overline{X} = \cup\{Y \in U/R : Y \cap X \neq \emptyset\}$$

The lower approximation of X is the collection of those objects which can be classified with full certainty as members of the set X.

The upper approximation of X consists of objects with which we can not exclude the possibility that those objects may belong to X.

The following properties are obvious:

Proposition 1. *[1]*

1) X is precise with respect to R iff $\underline{X} = \overline{X}$
2) X is rough with respect to R iff $\underline{X} \neq \overline{X}$.

Directly from Definition 1 we can get the following properties of the lower and the upper approximations:

Proposition 2. *[1]*

1) $\underline{A} \subseteq A \subseteq \overline{A}$
2) $\underline{\emptyset} = \overline{\emptyset} = \emptyset, \underline{U} = \overline{U} = U$
3) $\overline{A \cup B} = \overline{A} \cup \overline{B}$
4) $\underline{A \cap B} = \underline{A} \cap \underline{B}$
5) $A \subseteq B \Rightarrow \underline{A} \subseteq \underline{B}$
6) $A \subseteq B \Rightarrow \overline{A} \subseteq \overline{B}$
7) $\underline{A \cup B} \supseteq \underline{A} \cup \underline{B}$
8) $\overline{A \cap B} \subseteq \overline{A} \cap \overline{B}$
9) $\underline{\sim A} = \sim \overline{A}$
10) $\overline{\sim A} = \sim \underline{A}$
11) $\underline{(\underline{A})} = \overline{(\underline{A})} = \underline{A}$
12) $\overline{(\overline{A})} = \underline{(\overline{A})} = \overline{A}$

Proof. In the what following, we mainly apply the item 9)–12). So we only prove the items 9)–12). For others the proof procedures are omitted. Please refer to some literatures.

9) $x \in \underline{\sim A}$ iff $[x] \subseteq \sim A$ iff $[x] \cap A = \emptyset$ iff $x \notin \overline{A}$ iff $x \in \sim \overline{A}$, then $\underline{\sim A} = \sim \overline{A}$.

10) By substitution $\sim A$ for A in 9) we get $\overline{\sim A} = \sim \underline{A}$.

11a) From 1) $\underline{(\underline{A})} \subseteq \underline{A}$, thus we have to show that $\underline{A} \subseteq \underline{(\underline{A})}$. If $x \in \underline{A}$ then $[x] \subseteq A$, hence $\overline{[x]} \subseteq \underline{A}$, but $\underline{[x]} = [x]$, thus $[x] \subseteq \underline{A}$ and $x \in \underline{A}$, that is $\underline{A} \subseteq \underline{(\underline{A})}$.

11b) From 1) $\overline{A} \subseteq \overline{(\underline{A})}$, thus we only need to show $\overline{(\underline{A})} \subseteq \underline{A}$. If $x \in \overline{(\underline{A})}$, then $[x] \cap \underline{A} \neq \emptyset$, i.e. there exists $y \in [x]$ such that $y \in \underline{A}$, hence $[y] \subseteq A$ but $[x] = [y]$, so $[x] \subseteq A$ and $x \in \underline{A}$, that is to say, $\overline{(\underline{A})} \subseteq \underline{A}$.

12) The proof procedure is similar to 11).

3   Approximation Relation for Rough Sets

Given any approximation space $M = (U, R)$ and any set $A \subseteq U$, we are more used to judging whether A is precise or rough with respect to the approximation space. Nevertheless, if A is rough with respect to R, i.e. $\underline{A} \neq \overline{A}$, there may exist a certain set B such that $\underline{A} = \underline{B}$ and $\overline{A} = \overline{B}$. It is obvious that A and B are approximate with respect to this approximation space, because in the approximation space we have no better method to distinguish A from B when using lower approximation sets and upper approximation sets to approximate A and B. We observe that two sets are approximate with each other is very common in any approximation space. Nevertheless , relatively few studies have been done. For any $A \in P(U)$ we are more interested in how to measure whether a certain set is approximate with A. So we give the following definition:

Definition 2. *Let $M = (U, R)$ be an approximation space, where U is a domain and R is an equivalence relation on U. Then we define the approximation relation $\simeq_R$ as follows:*

for any set $A, X \in P(U)$, $X \simeq_R A$ iff $\underline{X} = \underline{A}$ and $\overline{X} = \overline{A}$.

In the what following, we often omit the subscript R of $X \simeq_R A$, written $X \simeq A$ if there is no confusion.

Definition 2 is proposed to judge whether any two sets are approximate with each other. Obviously, for $A \in P(U)$, $A \simeq A$.

For any $A, B \in P(U)$, we can show $A \simeq B$ in Fig. 1, where $BND_R(A) = \overline{A} - \underline{A}$.

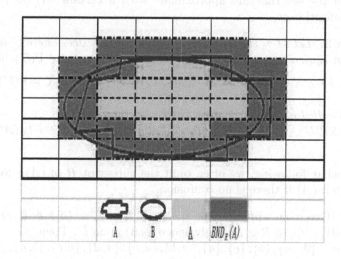

Fig. 1. $A \simeq B$.

Proposition 3. *For any approximation space $M = (U, R)$, $\simeq$ is an equivalence relation on $P(U)$.*

(1) For any $A \in P(U)$, $A \simeq A$.
(2) For any $A, B \in P(U)$, if $A \simeq B$ then $B \simeq A$.
(3) For any $A, B, C \in P(U)$, if $A \simeq B$ and $B \simeq C$ then $A \simeq C$.

Proposition 4. *For any approximation space $M = (U, R)$ and any $A, B \in P(U)$, if $A \simeq B$, then we have:*

(1) $\underline{A} \subseteq A \cap B \subseteq \overline{A}$, or $\underline{B} \subseteq A \cap B \subseteq \overline{B}$
(2) $\overline{A} - \underline{A} = \overline{B} - \underline{B}$

Proof. (1) Since $A \simeq B$, $\underline{A} = \underline{B}$ and $\overline{A} = \overline{B}$. Since $\underline{A} \subseteq A \subseteq \overline{A}$ and $\underline{B} \subseteq B \subseteq \overline{B}$, we have $\underline{A} \subseteq A \cap B \subseteq \overline{A}$ or $\underline{B} \subseteq A \cap B \subseteq \overline{B}$.

(2) Since $A \simeq B$, we have $\underline{A} = \underline{B}$ and $\overline{A} = \overline{B}$. We know that $A = (A - \underline{A}) \cup \underline{A}$ and $B = (B - \underline{B}) \cup \underline{B}$, where $(A - \underline{A}) \cap \underline{A} = \emptyset$ and $(B - \underline{B}) \cap \underline{B} = \emptyset$. By Proposition 2.2, we have $\overline{A} = \overline{(A - \underline{A})} \cup \overline{(\underline{A})}$ and $\overline{B} = \overline{(B - \underline{B})} \cup \overline{(\underline{B})}$. Then we have $\overline{(\underline{A})} = \underline{A} = \underline{B} = \overline{(\underline{B})}$. Since $(A - \underline{A}) \cap \underline{A} = \emptyset$ and $(B - \underline{B}) \cap \underline{B} = \emptyset$, $\overline{(A - \underline{A})} \cap \overline{(\underline{A})} = \emptyset$ and $\overline{(B - \underline{B})} \cap \overline{(\underline{B})} = \emptyset$. So $\overline{A - \underline{A}} = \overline{B - \underline{B}}$.

4 Approximation Class and Its Algebraic Structure

4.1 Approximation Class

By Definition 2, we can judge which set is approximate with a certain set. Then we mine all the set that are approximate with a certain set. So we give the following definition.

Definition 3. *Let $M = (U, R)$ be an approximation space, where U is a domain and R is an equivalence relation on U. Then for any set $A \in P(U)$, define*

$(A)_R = \{X : X \in P(U) \text{ and } X \simeq A\}$, *i.e.* $(A)_R = \{X : X \in P(U) \text{ and } \underline{X} = \underline{A} \text{ and } \overline{X} = \overline{A}\}$

$(A)_R$ *is called an approximation class with respect to R.*

Then let $P(U)/ \simeq$ be the collection of all distinct relative sets $(A)_R$ for $A \in \mathcal{P}(U)$.

In the what following, we often omit the subscript R of $(A)_R$ for any $A \in P(U)$, written (A) if there is no confusion.

Example 1. Given an approximate space (U, R), $U = \{a, b, c, d\}$ and $U/R = \{\{a, b\}, \{c, d\}\}$, where R is an equivalence relation on U. Then
$$P(U) = \{\emptyset, \{a\}, \{b\}, \{c\}, \{d\}, \{a, b\}, \{a, c\}, \{a, d\}, \{b, c\}, \{b, d\}, \{c, d\}, \{a, b, c\}, \{a, b, d\}, \{a, c, d\}, \{b, c, d\}, \{a, b, c, d\}\}.$$
By Definition 2, we have
$\{a, c\} \simeq \{a, d\}, \{a\} \simeq \{b\}$.
By Definition 3, we have
$(\{a\}) = \{\{a\}, \{b\}\}$,
$(\{a, c\}) = (\{a, d\}) = (\{b, c\}) = (\{b, d\}) = \{\{a, c\}, \{a, d\}, \{b, c\}, \{b, d\}\}$.
$(\{a, b\}) = \{\{a, b\}\}$

For any approximation class, we obtain the following proposition:

Proposition 5. *(1) $A \in (A)_R$*
(2) If $A \in (B)_R$, then $(A)_R = (B)_R$
(3) $(\underline{A})_R = \{\underline{A}\}$
(4) $(\overline{A})_R = \{\overline{A}\}$
(5) $(A)_R \cup (B)_R \subseteq (A \cup B)_R$
(6) $(A \cap B)_R \subseteq (A)_R \cap (B)_R$
(7) $(\emptyset) = \{\emptyset\}, (U) = \{U\}$
(8) $\bigcup_{A \subseteq U} (A)_R = P(U)$

Proof. (3): Since $(\underline{A}) = \overline{(A)} = A$, A is precise, and then $(\underline{A})_R = \{\underline{A}\}$.

(4): just as the item (3), it is easy to prove $(\overline{A})_R = \{\overline{A}\}$.

(5) and (6): By Definition 2 and Proposition 4, we can obtain this proposition.

Proposition 6. *(i) if $\overline{A} = \underline{A}$ then*

$$|(A)| = 1$$

(i) if $\overline{A} \neq \underline{A}$ then

$$|(A)| = \prod_{Y \subseteq (\overline{A} - \underline{A}) \ and \ Y \in U/R} (2^{|Y|} - 2)$$

Proof. (i) Obviously, if $\underline{A} = \overline{A}$, A is precise with respect to R and $(A) = \{A\}$, and then $|(A)| = 1$.

(ii) If $\underline{A} \neq \overline{A}$, A is rough with respect to R. For any $B \in (A)$, $\underline{A} \subseteq B \subseteq \overline{A}$. Then we have

$$B = \underline{A} \cup \left(\bigcup_{Y' \subset Y \subseteq (\overline{A} \ \underline{A})} Y' \right)$$

where $Y \in U/R$ and $Y' \subset Y$ and $Y' \neq \emptyset$. Obviously, for each such Y, $Y' \in (Y) - \{\emptyset\} - \{Y\}$. Then there are $2^{|Y|} - 2$ such subsets of Y. So $|(A)| = \prod_{Y \subseteq (\overline{A} - \underline{A})} (2^{|Y|} - 2)$.

Theorem 1. *Let $M = (U, R)$ be an approximation space. Then $\mathrm{P}(U)/ \simeq$ is a partition of $\mathrm{P}(U)$.*

Proof. By Proposition 3, $\simeq$ is an equivalence relation on $P(U)$, then we obtain the theorem.

5   Algebraic Structure for Approximation Class

5.1   A Boolean Algebra

Here, we give a brief introduction for a boolean algebra as follows:

A boolean algebra [28] is a 6-tuple $\langle U, \vee, \wedge, -, 0, 1 \rangle$. For any $a, b \in U$ there exist $a \vee b \in U$ and $a \wedge b \in U$ satisfying the following conditions:

i) commutative laws: $a \vee b = b \vee a$, $a \wedge b = b \wedge a$;
ii) associative laws: $a \vee (b \vee c) = (a \vee b) \vee c$, $a \wedge (b \wedge c) = (a \wedge b) \wedge c$;
iii) distribute laws: $a \vee (b \wedge c) = (a \vee b) \wedge (a \vee c)$, $a \wedge (b \vee c) = (a \wedge b) \vee (a \wedge c)$;
iv) $a \wedge 1 = a$, $a \vee 0 = a$;
v) for any $a \in U$, there exists $-a$ such that $a \vee -a = 1$ and $a \wedge -a = 0$,

where

- U is the space of the Boolean algebra $\langle U, \vee, \wedge, -, 0, 1 \rangle$;
- $\vee$ is the union operation of the algebra;
- $\wedge$ is the intersection operation of the algebra;
- $-$ is the negation operation of the algebra;
- 0 is the zero element of the algebra;
- 1 is the unity element of the algebra.

Example 2. Let U be a finite non-empty set, then $\langle P(U), \cup, \cap, \sim, \emptyset, U \rangle$ is a boolean algebra, where

- $P(U)$ is the power set of U;
- $\cup$ is the union operation for subsets;
- $\cap$ is the intersection operation for subsets;
- $\sim$ is the complement operation of certain set;
- $\emptyset$ is the zero element of the algebra;
- U is the biggest element of the algebra.

Given an universe $U = \{a, b, c, d\}$, the Hasse diagram of the boolean algebra $< P(U), \cup, \cap, \sim, \emptyset, U >$ is shown as the following figure:

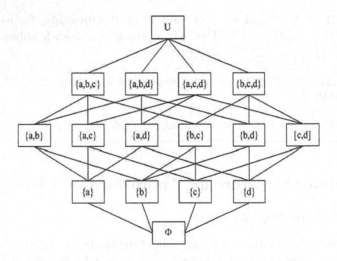

Fig. 2. The Hasse diagram of $< P(U), \cap, \cup, \sim, \emptyset, U >$

5.2   The Boolean Algebra for Approximation Class

This paper shall give a kind of new algebraic structure base on approximation class for Rough sets, which shall be proved a standard boolean algebra for Rough sets and is completely different from the current algebraic structures for Rough sets.

Definition 4. *For any* $(A), (B) \in P(U)/ \simeq$, *define a relation* $\leq$ *on* $P(U)/ \simeq$ *as follows:*

$(A) \leq (B)$ *iff* $\underline{A} \subseteq \underline{B}$ *and* $\overline{A} \subseteq \overline{B}$.

It is easy to prove that the relation $\leq$ is a partial order. So we have:

Proposition 7. $\langle P(U)/ \simeq, \leq \rangle$ *is a lattice.*

Definition 5. *Given any* $(A), (B) \in P(U)/ \simeq$, *define operations* $+$, $\times$ *and* $-$ *on* $P(U)/ \simeq$ *as follows:*

$$(A) + (B) = \{X : X \in P(U) \text{ and } \underline{X} = \underline{A} \cup \underline{B} \text{ and } \overline{X} = \overline{A} \cup \overline{B}\}$$

$$(A) \times (B) = \{X : X \in P(U) \text{ and } \underline{X} = \underline{A} \cap \underline{B} \text{ and } \overline{X} = \overline{A} \cap \overline{B}\}$$

$$-(A) = \{X : X \in P(U) \text{ and } \overline{X} = \sim \underline{A} \text{ and } \underline{X} = \overline{\sim A}\}$$

where $\sim A = U - A$.

Obviously, these operations have the characteristics of Rough sets, and then we obtain the following proposition.

Proposition 8. *For any* $A, B \in P(U)$,

i) $(\underline{A \cup B}) = (\underline{A}) + (\underline{B})$, $(\overline{A \cup B}) = (\overline{A}) + (\overline{B})$
ii) $(\underline{A \cap B}) = (\underline{A}) \times (\underline{B})$, $(\overline{A \cap B}) = (\overline{A}) \times (\overline{B})$
iii) $(\underline{A \cup \overline{B}}) = (\underline{A}) + (\overline{B})$, $(\overline{A \cap \underline{B}}) = (\overline{A}) \times (\underline{B})$

Proof. When proving the items i) and ii), we would pay attention to $\underline{A}$ and $\overline{A}$ that are precise with respect to R.

The items iii)-v) can be proved by Definition 2.   □

Proposition 8 describes the relationship between the operations on Sets and these operations on approximation classes. For any $A' \in (A)$ and any $B' \in (B)$, we have the following theorem:

Theorem 2. *For any* $A' \in (A)$ *and any* $B' \in (B)$,

i). $(A') + (B') = (A) + (B)$
ii). $(A') \times (B') = (A) \times (B)$
iii). $-(A') = -(A)$

Proof. For any $A' \in (A)$, $\overline{A'} = \overline{A}$ and $\underline{A'} = \underline{A}$. By Definition 3.1 and 3.2, $(A') = \{X : X \in P(U)$ and $\overline{X} = \overline{A'}$ and $\underline{X} = \underline{A'}\}$. It follows that $(A') = \{X : X \in P(U)$ and $\overline{X} = \overline{A}$ and $\underline{X} = \underline{A}\}$. Then $(A') = (A)$. Similarly, $(B') = (B)$. So $(A') + (B') = (A) + (B)$, $(A') \times (B') = (A) \times (B)$ and $-(A') = -(A)$.

Now, we discuss several important laws for the operations $+$ and $\times$ as follows:

Theorem 3. *(Commutative Laws) For any* $A, B \in P(U)$

i). $(A) + (B) = (B) + (A)$
ii). $(A) \times (B) = (B) \times (A)$.

Proof. i) By Definition 5, $(A) + (B) = (B) + (A)$.
   ii). The proof procedure is similar to i).   □

Theorem 4. *(Associative Laws) For any* $A, B, C \in P(U)$

i). $(A) + ((B) + (C)) = ((A) + (B)) + (C)$
ii). $(A) \times ((B) \times (C)) = ((A) \times (B)) \times (C)$

Proof. i). $(B) + (C) = \{X : X \in P(U)$ and $\underline{X} = \underline{B} \cup \underline{C}$ and $\overline{X} = \overline{B} \cup \overline{C}\}$.
   So $(A) + ((B) + (C)) = \{X : X \in P(U)$ and $\underline{X} = \underline{A} \cap \underline{B} \cap \underline{C}$ and $\overline{X} = \overline{A} \cup \overline{B} \cup \overline{C}\}$.
   While $((A) + (B)) = \{X : X \in P(U)$ and $\underline{X} = \underline{A} \cap \underline{B}$ and $\overline{X} = \overline{A} \cup \overline{B}\}$.
   Then $((A) + (B)) + (C) = \{X : X \in P(U)$ and $\underline{X} = \underline{A} \cap \underline{B} \cap \underline{C}$ and $\overline{X} = \overline{A} \cup \overline{B} \cup \overline{C}\}$. So $(A) + ((B) + (C)) = ((A) + (B)) + (C)$.
ii). The proof procedure is similar to i).

Theorem 5. *(Distributive Laws) For any* $A, B, C \in P(U)$

i). $(A) + ((B) \times (C)) = ((A) + (B)) \times ((A) + (C))$
ii). $(A) \times ((B) + (C)) = ((A) \times (B)) + ((A) \times (C))$

Proof. i). $(B) \times (C) = \{X : X \in P(U)$ and $\underline{X} = \underline{B} \cap \underline{C}$ and $\overline{X} = \overline{B} \cap \overline{C}\}$.
   So $(A) + ((B) \times (C)) = \{X : X \in P(U)$ and $\underline{X} = \underline{A} \cup (\underline{B} \cap \underline{C})$ and $\overline{X} = \overline{A} \cup (\overline{B} \cap \overline{C})\}$.
   While $(A) + (B) = \{X : X \in P(U)$ and $\underline{X} = \underline{A} \cup \underline{B}$ and $\overline{X} = \overline{A} \cup \overline{B}\}$.
   $(A) + (C) = \{X : X \in P(U)$ and $\underline{X} = \underline{A} \cup \underline{C}$ and $\overline{X} = \overline{A} \cup \overline{C}\}$.
   So $((A) + (B)) \times ((A) + (C)) = \{X : X \in P(U)$ and $\underline{X} = (\underline{A} \cup \underline{B}) \cap (\underline{A} \cup \underline{C})$ and $\overline{X} = (\overline{A} \cup \overline{B}) \cap (\overline{A} \cup \overline{B})\}$.
   $((A) + (B)) \times ((A) + (C)) = \{X : X \in P(U)$ and $\underline{X} = \underline{A} \cup (\underline{B} \cap \underline{C})$ and $\overline{X} = \overline{A} \cup (\overline{B} \cap \overline{C})\}$. So $(A) + (B) \times (C) = ((A) + (B)) \times ((A) + (C))$.
ii). The proof procedure is similar to i).

Theorem 6. *(The de Morgan laws:) For any* $A, B \in P(U)$

$i)$ $-((A) + (B)) = -(A) \times -(B)$
$ii)$ $-((A) \times (B)) = -(A) + -(B)$.

Proof. i) Let $(C) = (A) + (B)$, then $\underline{C} = \underline{A} \cup \underline{B}$ and $\overline{C} = \overline{A} \cup \overline{B}$

$$- ((A) + (B))$$
$$= -(C)$$
$$= \{X : X \in P(U) \text{ and } \underline{X} = \overline{\sim C} \text{ and } \overline{X} = \underline{\sim C}\}$$
$$= \{X : X \in P(U) \text{ and } \underline{X} =\sim \underline{C} \text{ and } \overline{X} =\sim \overline{C}\}$$
$$= \{X : X \in P(U) \text{ and } \underline{X} =\sim (\underline{A} \cup \underline{B}) \text{ and } \overline{X} =\sim (\overline{A} \cup \overline{B})\}$$
$$= \{X : X \in P(U) \text{ and } \underline{X} =\sim \underline{A} \cap \sim \underline{B} \text{ and } \overline{X} =\sim \overline{A} \cap \sim \overline{B})\}$$

By Definition 2, we have:

$$- (A) = \{X : X \in P(U) \text{ and } \underline{X} = \overline{\sim A} \text{ and } \overline{X} = \underline{\sim A}\}$$
$$= \{X : X \in P(U) \text{ and } \underline{X} =\sim \underline{A} \text{ and } \overline{X} =\sim \overline{A}\}$$
$$- (B) = \{X : X \in P(U) \text{ and } \underline{X} = \overline{\sim B} \text{ and } \overline{X} = \underline{\sim B}\}$$
$$= \{X : X \in P(U) \text{ and } \underline{X} =\sim \underline{B} \text{ and } \overline{X} =\sim \overline{B}\}$$

Then by Definition 5, we have
$-(A) \times -(B) = \{X : X \in P(U) \text{ and } \underline{X} =\sim \underline{A} \cap \sim \underline{B} \text{ and } \overline{X} =\sim \overline{A} \cap \sim \overline{B})\}$
So $-((A) + (B)) = -(A) \times -(B)$.
ii) Let $(C) = (A) \times (B)$, then $\underline{C} = \underline{A} \cap \underline{B}$ and $\overline{C} = \overline{A} \cap \overline{B}$

$- ((A) \times (B))$
$= -(C)$
$= \{X : X \in P(U) \text{ and } \underline{X} = \overline{\sim C} \text{ and } \overline{X} = \underline{\sim C}\}$
$= \{X : X \in P(U) \text{ and } \underline{X} =\sim \underline{C} \text{ and } \overline{X} =\sim \overline{C}\}$
$= \{X : X \in P(U) \text{ and } \underline{X} =\sim (\underline{A} \cap \underline{B}) \text{ and } \overline{X} =\sim (\overline{A} \cap \overline{B})\}$
$= \{X : X \in P(U) \text{ and } \underline{X} =\sim \underline{A} \cup \sim \underline{B} \text{ and } \overline{X} =\sim \overline{A} \cup \sim \overline{B})\}$
$- (A) + -(B)$
$= \{X : X \in P(U) \text{ and } \underline{X} = \overline{\sim A} \cup \overline{\sim B} \text{ and } \overline{X} = \underline{\sim A} \cup \underline{\sim B}\}$
$= \{X : X \in P(U) \text{ and } \underline{X} =\sim \underline{A} \cup \sim \underline{B} \text{ and } \overline{X} =\sim \overline{A} \cup \sim \overline{B})\}$ So $- ((A) \times (B)) = -(A) + -(B)$.

Definition 6. *Let*
$0 = (\emptyset)$
$1 = (U)$

Theorem 7. $< P(U)/ \simeq, +, \times, -, 0, 1 >$ *is a standard boolean algebra.*

Proof. It is easy to follow that $P(U)/ \simeq$ is closed under the operations $+, \times, -$. For any $(A), (B)$ and $C) \in P(U)$, We need to prove the following laws:

(i): commutative laws:

$$(A) + (B) = (B) + (A)$$
$$(A) \times (B) = (B) \times (A).$$

(ii): associative laws:

$$(A) + ((B) + (C)) = ((A) + (B)) + (C)$$
$$(A) \times ((B) \times (C)) = ((A) \times (B)) \times (C)$$

(iii): distributive laws:

$$(A) + (B) \times (C) = ((A) + (B)) \times ((A) + (C))$$
$$(A) \times (B) + (C) = ((A) \times (B)) + ((A) \times (C))$$

(iv): $(A) + (\emptyset) = (A)$ and $(A) \times (U) = (A)$
(v): there exists $-(A) \in P(U)/\simeq$ such that $(A) + (-(A)) = (U)$ and $(A) \times (-(A)) = (\emptyset)$.

As for (i)–(iii), we have proved them in the proofs of Theorems 3–5, respectively.

As for (iv), by Definitions 2, Definition 5 and $\overline{\emptyset} = \underline{\emptyset} = \emptyset$, it follows that

$(A) + (\emptyset)$
$\quad = \{X : X \in P(U) \text{ and } \overline{X} = \overline{A} \cup \overline{\emptyset} \text{ and } \overline{X} = \underline{A} \cup \underline{\emptyset}\}$
$\quad = \{X : X \in P(U) \text{ and } \overline{X} = \overline{A} \text{ and } \overline{X} = \underline{A}\} \qquad (\text{ by } \underline{\emptyset} = \overline{\emptyset} = \emptyset)$
$\quad = (A).$

And for $\overline{U} = \underline{U} = U$, then

$(A) \times (U)$
$\quad = \{X : X \in P(U) \text{ and } \overline{X} = \overline{A} \cap \overline{U} \text{ and } \overline{X} = \underline{A} \cap \underline{U}\}$
$\quad = \{X : X \in P(U) \text{ and } \overline{X} = \overline{A} \text{ and } \overline{X} = \underline{A}\} \qquad (\text{ by } \underline{U} = \overline{U} = U)$
$\quad = (A).$

As for (v), by Definition 2, we have
$-(A) = \{X : X \in P(U) \text{ and } \overline{X} = -\overline{A} \text{ and } \underline{A} \cap \underline{X} = \emptyset\},$
and
$(A) = \{X : X \in P(U) \text{ and } \overline{X} = \overline{A} \text{ and } \underline{A} = \underline{X}\}.$
Then,

$(A) + (-(A))$
$\quad = \{X : X \in P(U) \text{ and } \overline{X} = \overline{A} \cup \sim \underline{A} \text{ and } \underline{X} = \underline{A} \cup \overline{\sim A}\}$
$\quad = \{X : X \in P(U) \text{ and } \overline{X} = \overline{A} \cup (U - \overline{A}) \text{ and } \underline{X} = \underline{A} \cup (U - \underline{A})\}$
$\quad = \{X : X \in P(U) \text{ and } \underline{X} = U \text{ and } \overline{X} = U\}$
$\quad = (U).$

So $(A) + (-(A)) = 1$.
Then,

$$(A) \times (-(A))$$
$$= \{X : X \in P(U) \text{ and } \overline{X} = \overline{A} \cap \sim A \text{ and } \underline{X} = \underline{A} \cap \overline{\sim A}\}$$
$$= \{X : X \in P(U) \text{ and } \overline{X} = \overline{A} \cap (U - \overline{A}) \text{ and } \underline{X} = \underline{A} \cap (U - \underline{A})\}$$
$$= \{X : X \in P(U) \text{ and } \underline{X} = \emptyset \text{ and } \overline{X} = \emptyset\}$$
$$= (\emptyset).$$

So $(A) \times (-(A)) = 0$.

Let $S = \{X : \underline{X} = \overline{X} \text{ and } X \in P(U)\}$, that is to say, S is a set of all precise sets with respect to R. Then we have the following theorem:

Theorem 8. *A boolean algebra $<S, \cap, \cup, \sim, \emptyset, U>$ is homomorphism to $<P(U)/ \simeq, +, \times, -, 0, 1>$.*

Proof. Construct a mapping from S to $P(U)/ \simeq$, i.e., $f : S \to P(U)/ \simeq$ as follows:
For any $X \in S$, $f(X) = (X)$.
Then, for any $A, B \in S$, we need to prove the following three items:

i) $f(A \cup B) = f(A) + f(B)$
ii) $f(A \cap B) = f(A) \times f(B)$
iii) $f(\sim A) = -f(A)$

The proofs are shown as follows:

i):

$$f(A \cup B)$$
$$= (A \cup B)$$
$$= \{X : X \in P(U) \text{ and } \underline{X} = \underline{A \cup B} \text{ and } \overline{X} = \overline{A \cup B}\}$$
$$= \{X : X \in P(U) \text{ and } \underline{X} = \underline{A} \cup \underline{B} \text{ and } \overline{X} = \overline{A} \cup \overline{B}\} \text{ (A and B are precise)}$$
$$= (A) + (B)$$
$$= f(A) + f(B).$$

ii):

$$f(A \cap B)$$
$$= (A \cap B)$$
$$= \{X : X \in P(U) \text{ and } \underline{X} = \underline{A \cap B} \text{ and } \overline{X} = \overline{A \cap B}\}$$
$$= \{X : X \in P(U) \text{ and } \underline{X} = \underline{A} \cap \underline{B} \text{ and } \overline{X} = \overline{A} \cap \overline{B}\} \text{ (A and B are precise)}$$
$$= (A) \times (B)$$
$$= f(A) \times f(B).$$

iii):

$$f(\sim A)$$
$$= (\sim A)$$
$$= \{X : X \in P(U) \text{ and } \overline{X} = \overline{\sim A} \text{ and } \underline{X} = \underline{\sim A}\}$$
$$= \{X : X \in P(U) \text{ and } \overline{X} =\sim \underline{A} \text{ and } \underline{X} =\sim \overline{A}\} \text{ (by 9), 10) of Proposition 2)}$$
$$= \{X : X \in P(U) \text{ and } \overline{X} =\sim \overline{A} \text{ and } \underline{X} =\sim \overline{A}\} \qquad \text{(A is precise)}$$
$$= \{X : X \in P(U) \text{ and } \overline{X} = \underline{\sim A} \text{ and } \underline{X} = \overline{\sim A}\}$$
$$= -(A)$$
$$= -f(A).$$

Example 3. . Given an approximate space (U, R), $U = \{a, b, c, d\}$ and $U/R = \{\{a, b\}, \{c, d\}\}$, where R is an equivalence relation on U. Then:

$$P(U) = \{\emptyset, \{a\}, \{b\}, \{c\}, \{d\}, \{a, b\}, \{a, c\}, \{a, d\}, \{b, c\}, \{b, d\}, \{c, d\}, \{a, b, c\},$$
$$\{a, b, d\}, \quad \{a, c, d\}, \{b, c, d\}, \{a, b, c, d\}\}.$$

So

$$(\emptyset) = \{\emptyset\}$$
$$(\{a\}) = (\{b\}) = \{\{a\}, \{b\}\}$$
$$(\{c\}) = (\{d\}) = \{\{c\}, \{d\}\}$$
$$(\{a, b\}) = \{\{a, b\}\}$$
$$(\{a, c\}) = (\{a, d\}) = (\{b, c\}) = (\{b, d\}) = \{\{a, c\}, \{a, d\}, \{b, c\}, \{b, d\}\}$$
$$(\{c, d\}) = \{\{c, d\}\}$$
$$(\{a, b, c\}) = (\{a, b, d\}) = \{\{a, b, c\}, \{a, b, d\}\}$$
$$(\{a, c, d\}) = (\{b, c, d\}) = \{\{a, c, d\}, \{b, c, d\}\}$$
$$(\{a, b, c, d\}) = \{\{a, b, c, d\}\}$$

Then

$$P(U)/ \simeq = \{(\emptyset), (\{a\}), (\{c\}), (\{a, b\}), (\{a, c\}), (\{c, d\}), (\{a, b, c\}), (\{a, c, d\}), (\{a, b, c, d\})\}.$$

The Hasse diagram of the boolean algebra $<P(U)/ \simeq, +, \times, -, 0, 1>$ is shown as the following figure:

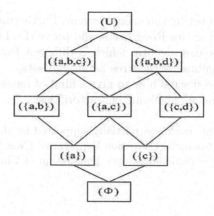

Fig. 3. The hasse diagram of $<P(U)/\simeq, +, \times, -, 0, 1>$

Theorem 9. *For any* $(A), (B) \in P(U)/\simeq,$
$(A) \leq (B)$ *iff* $(A) + (B) = (B)$ *iff* $(A) \times (B) = (A)$

5.3 Comparison with Other Works

To date, the algebraic structures based on equivalence classes for Rough sets [10–15, 25] are often defined as follows:

- $\langle P(U)/\approx, \preceq, \sqcap, \sqcup, \neg, L, 0, 1 \rangle$, where $P(U)/\approx = \{\langle A, B \rangle : A \subseteq B \text{ and } A, B \subseteq U\}$, and L was the lower approximation operator, or
- $\langle A, \preceq, \sqcap, \sqcup, \neg, L, 0, 1 \rangle$, where $A = \{\langle a, b \rangle : a \preceq b \text{ and } a, b \in A\}$, and L was the lower approximation operator.

Obviously, the exiting algebraic structures for Rough sets contain the lower approximation operator, and it intuitively reflects the characteristics for Rough sets.

In this paper, we analyze the characteristics for approximation class, and define a new standard boolean algebra based on approximation class for Rough sets, $<P(U)/\simeq, +, \times, -, 0, 1>$. The operations $+, \times$ and $-$ of the boolean algebra in this paper have the characteristics of Rough sets. The domain and the operators of the boolean algebra are completely different from that of the current algebraic structures [10–12, 14, 15, 25]. Clearly, the algebraic structure of this paper is a kind of new structure for Rough sets and proved a standard boolean algebra.

6 Conclusions

For any approximation space, we define a kind of measurement for judging whether a certain set is "approximate" with the other or not. Even if two sets may be completely unequal, we can also judge. Then we can mine which sets are approximate with that set by this measurement. Furthermore, we present a kind of new algebraic structure for Rough sets, and prove this kind of algebraic structure is a standard boolean algebra, which is different from the stone algebraic structure or others algebraic structures for Rough sets.

Our next work is to discuss how to give a kind of measurement for imprecise information system and its algebraic characteristics.

Acknowledgment. This work was partially supported by the Science and Technology Project of Jiangxi Provincial Education Department (Nos. GJJ201917, GJJ161109 and GJJ190941), and the National Science Foundation of China (Nos. 61763032 and 61562061).

References

1. Pawlak, Z.: Rough sets. Int. J. Comput. Inform. Sci. **11**(5), 341–356 (1982)
2. Pawlak, Z.: Rough set approach to knowledge-based decision support. Eur. J. Oper. Res. **99**(1), 48–57 (1997)
3. Yufeng, Y.: A novel data mining algorithm based on rough set. In: Software Engineering and Knowledge Engineering: Theory and Practice, pp. 1115–1121. Springer (2012). https://doi.org/10.1007/978-3-642-03718-4_136
4. Nguyen, S.H., Nguyen, H.S.: A rough set approach to knowledge discovery by relation approximation. In: Greco, S., Bouchon-Meunier, B., Coletti, G., Fedrizzi, M., Matarazzo, B., Yager, R.R. (eds.) IPMU 2012. CCIS, vol. 297, pp. 331–340. Springer, Heidelberg (2012). https://doi.org/10.1007/978-3-642-31709-5_34
5. Wen, S.D., Bao, Q.H.: Attribute reduction in ordered decision tables via evidence theory. Inform. Sci. **364**, 91–110 (2016)
6. Bingjiao, F., Tsang, E.C.C., Weihua, X., Jianhang, Y.: Double-quantitative rough fuzzy set based decisions: A logical operations method. Information Sciences (2016)
7. Qinghua, H., Yu, D., Zongxia, X., Jinfu, L.: Fuzzy probabilistic approximation spaces and their information measures. IEEE Trans. Fuzzy Syst. **14**(2), 191–201 (2006)
8. Duo, Q.M., Yan, Z., Yi, Y., Li, H.X., Xu, F.F.: Relative reducts in consistent and inconsistent decision tables of the pawlak rough set model. Inform. Sci. **179**(24), 4140–4150 (2009)
9. Ma, X.A., Wang, G., Hong, Yu., Li, T.: Decision region distribution preservation reduction in decision-theoretic rough set model. Inform. Sci. **278**, 614–640 (2014)
10. Zbigniew, B.: Algebraic structures of rough sets. In: Rough Sets, Fuzzy Sets and Knowledge Discovery, pp. 242–247. Springer (1994). https://doi.org/10.1007/978-1-4471-3238-7_29
11. Cattaneo, G., Ciucci, D.: Algebraic structures for rough sets. In: Peters, J.F., Skowron, A., Dubois, D., Grzymała-Busse, J.W., Inuiguchi, M., Polkowski, L. (eds.) Transactions on Rough Sets II. LNCS, vol. 3135, pp. 208–252. Springer, Heidelberg (2004). https://doi.org/10.1007/978-3-540-27778-1_12
12. Qi, G., Liu, W.: Rough operations on boolean algebras. Inform. Sci. **173**(1), 49–63 (2005)
13. Liu, G.-L.: Rough sets over the boolean algebras. In: International Workshop on Rough Sets, Fuzzy Sets, Data Mining, and Granular- Soft Computing. LNCS (LNAI), vol. 3641, pp. 124–131. Springer, Heidelberg (2005). https://doi.org/10.1007/11548669_13

14. Liu, G., Zhu, W.: The algebraic structures of generalized rough set theory. Inform. Sci. **178**(21), 4105–4113 (2008)
15. Mohua, B., Chakraborty, M.K.: Rough sets through algebraic logic. Fundam. Inform. **28**(3), 211–221 (1996)
16. Yiyu, Y., Yanhong, S.: Rough set models in multigranulation spaces. Elsevier Science Inc. (2016)
17. Xibei, Y., Xiaoning, S., Huili, D., Jingyu, Y.: Multi-granulation rough set: from crisp to fuzzy case. Ann. Fuzzy Math. Inform. **1**(1), 55–70 (2011)
18. Minlun, Y.: Multigranulations rough set method of attribute reduction in information systems based on evidence theory. J. Appl. Math. **2014**(4), 1–9 (2014)
19. Anhui, T., Weizhi, W., Jinjin, L., Guoping, L.: Evidence-theory-based numerical characterization of multigranulation rough sets in incomplete information systems. Fuzzy Sets Syst. **294**(C), 18–35 (2015)
20. She, Y., He, X., Shi, H., Qian, Y.: A multiple-valued logic approach for multigranulation rough set model. Int. J. Approximate Reason. **82**, 270–284 (2017)
21. Yao, Y.: Three-way granular computing, rough sets, and formal concept analysis. Int. J. Approximate Reason. **116**, 106–125 (2020)
22. Hameda, H.N.A., Sobhy, A.: Distributed approach for computing rough set approximations of big incomplete information systems - sciencedirect. Inform. Sci. **547**, 427–449 (2021)
23. Yang, X., Chen, H., Li, T., Wan, J., Sang, B.: Neighborhood rough sets with distance metric learning for feature selection. Knowl.-Based Syst. **224**, 107076 (2021)
24. Zied, C., Semeh, B.S., Sami, N.: A rough set based algorithm for updating the modes in categorical clustering. Int. J. Mach. Learn. Cybern. **12**, 2069–2090 (2021)
25. Jacek, P., Pomykala, J.M.: The stone algebra of rough sets. Bull. Polish Acad. Sci. Math. **36**(7–8), 495–508 (1988)
26. Wang, H., Wang, W., Xiao, S., Cui, Z., Minyang, X., Zhou, X.: Improving artificial bee colony algorithm using a new neighborhood selection mechanism. Inform. Sci. **527**, 227–240 (2020)
27. Wang, H., et al.: Artificial bee colony algorithm based on knowledge fusion. Complex Intell. Syst. **7**(3), 1139–1152 (2020). https://doi.org/10.1007/s40747-020-00171-2
28. Whitesitt, J.E.: Boolean Algebra and its applications. Courier Dover Publications (1995)

The Effect of Organizational Learning Ability on Innovative Behavior of Scientific Research Personnel in Universities

Tian Meng[✉]

Shandong University of Finance and Economics, Ji'nan, Shandong, China
tiantian81630@sina.com

Abstract. The literature research has found that the knowledge innovation transformation mechanism of university researchers from the perspective of resource conservation theory (COR) in dynamic environment is a hot topic in the field of academic research. In this paper, the 6 universities of Shandong Province, 472 scientific research teachers as the research object, using the method of Bootstrapping test found: (1) organizational learning ability has an important influence on Teachers' scientific research innovation behavior, the effect of internal and external interaction is better than participation in decision-making; (2) the environment dynamic learning ability and innovation behavior in Inter Organizational play a positive regulatory role, and in the uncertain environment, making more obvious effect than the external interaction. The research conclusion provides a theoretical basis for promoting innovative behavior of scientific research personnel in universities, and has theoretical and practical significance.

Keywords: Organizational learning ability · Environmental dynamics · Employee innovation behavior

1 Introduction

Colleges and universities are the main organizational form that transforms knowledge resources into innovative intellectual resources, and scientific research teachers are the carriers of resource transformation. The Resource Conservation Theory (COR) believes that in the process of transforming knowledge and skills into innovative intellectual resources, different contingency factors such as the environment will show a differentiated transformation mechanism [1]. However, recent studies have pointed out that in many universities, the innovative behavior of researchers is not motivated or promoted, but is hindered and restricted [2], among them are the issue of hardware resources in universities and the issue of soft environmental governance. Innovation of scientific researchers is a social interaction process such as cognition, communication, and participation [3]. The process of obtaining innovative intellectual resources not only shows the process of internal knowledge acquisition, optimization, and integration, but also the process of collecting, exchanging, and sharing external information. Therefore, it

© Springer Nature Singapore Pte Ltd. 2021
Y. Tan et al. (Eds.): DMBD 2021, CCIS 1454, pp. 418–429, 2021.
https://doi.org/10.1007/978-981-16-7502-7_39

is extremely urgent to explore how to stimulate the innovative behavior of university researchers with soft environment management elements.

Resource dependence theory believes that all resource activities in an organization must depend on the contingent influence of the environment. Environmental characteristics directly affect the transformation process of knowledge resources. Li Dehuang [4] believes that future research should focus on expanding its boundary conditions and clarify the mechanism of scientific research resource transformation from a broader boundary. For a long time, research on how to transform knowledge resources into innovative intellectual resources has mainly focused on organizational forms such as enterprises [5], while ignoring the individual innovation of university researchers. Judging from the few research results of universities, they mainly focus on the conventional level of innovation intelligence research, such as industry-university-research [6], ecosystem [7], and government support [8], but rarely pay attention to the softness of knowledge and environment. Innovative research on resource dimensions. To this end, this article focuses on 472 scientific research teachers in 6 universities in Shandong Province, putting internal and external knowledge learning capabilities, environmental dynamics, and innovative behavior under the same theoretical framework, and then constructs an adjustment model. The research conclusions provide a useful reference for the practice of scientific research innovation management in colleges and universities.

2 Research Hypothesis

2.1 The Effect of Organizational Learning Ability on Innovation Behavior

Organizational learning is an important behavioral variable that affects employee behavior and performance. The organization itself does not have the ability to learn, but relies on the members of the organization to share knowledge with each other, communicate with other organizations, customers, research institutes, and suppliers to learn [9, 10], that is, the acquisition of organizational learning resources comes from the internal and external channels of the organization. Forbes [11] and Chipika [12] once proposed that the acquisition of internal resources for organizational learning mainly depends on the participation of employees in organizational decision-making, and the acquisition of external resources mainly comes from the collection, analysis, and sharing of information with external organizations. Therefore, this article chooses decision participation variables as the essential reflection of the organization's internal learning, and uses external interaction variables as the core characteristics of the organization's external learning. Decision-making participation in organizational learning is mainly manifested in the importance of opinions, that is, managers are willing to listen to the opinions of employees in major organizational decisions, and the opinions can affect organizational decision-making, and employees can feel the importance of their own opinions. External interaction in organizational learning is mainly manifested as content, procedural and interactive, that is, collecting external information is one of the work content of employees, the organization has special organizational procedures to collect, analyze and share external information, and the organization encourages employees to interact with external organizations Contact and interaction [13]. Resource-based theory regards the knowledge of organizational learning as an important organizational resource, which can be transformed into other forms of resources through organizational practice and the participation of scientific researchers. Universities are typical knowledge-based organizations, and the conversion efficiency of their knowledge resources directly determines their scientific research performance. Bishop [14] believes that an important pre-influencing factor for team performance improvement is resource saturation, which includes knowledge resources, human resources, financial resources and other forms, and knowledge resources are the core element of scientific research team performance improvement. Szulanski [15] found that lack of resources is the main factor that weakens the individual innovation ability of scientific researchers, while Krimsky [16] and Wan Fengfeng [17] believe that the key to the performance effect of scientific research teams lies in the protection of knowledge resources. Only when knowledge resources are effectively allocated and transformed can scientific research goals be achieved and scientific innovation capabilities enhanced.

Many previous studies have shown that organizational learning in an enterprise has an important impact on employee innovation [12], but few studies have clarified the relationship between organizational learning ability and employee innovation behavior by using university researchers as the research object. The Resource Conservation Theory (COR) believes that knowledge is an important resource, and researchers can transform it into other forms of resources. Real [18] believes that the process of organizational learning and the assets formed by organizational learning are accompanied by the process of resource transformation, which will help researchers to form unique competitive capabilities. Among them, the meta-learning system (learning how to learn) will promote scientific researchers to be more creative and gain a competitive advantage. Scholars such as Argyris [19] believe that under the same organizational conditions, organizational learning can increase the organization's innovative capabilities in the future. Stata [20] found that organizational learning can lead to innovation, especially in a knowledge-intensive industry, the learning of individuals and organizations to guide innovation can become the only source of sustainable competitive advantage in the organization. Scholars such as Mabey [21] believe that organizational learning is the main factor for the organization to maintain innovation, and Glynn [22] also believes that organizational learning capabilities will not only affect the initial stage of innovation, but also the execution stage of innovation. The ability to organize learning is a vital ability for research personnel to maintain a competitive advantage, and it is the source of lasting competitive advantage for universities. Zhou Ronghu [23] believes that learning universities are a soft environment for R&D personnel to carry out scientific research and innovation. In the process of transforming knowledge resources into innovative resources, the knowledge acquisition of organizational learning ability is the source of the entire resource chain. Based on this, the author believes that the internal and external knowledge resources obtained by the scientific research personnel of universities will be transformed into the innovative intellectual resources of the scientific researchers to a certain extent, and the positive transformation of internal and external knowledge resources is different. For this reason, the following hypotheses are proposed:

H1: Organizational learning ability has a significant positive impact on the innovative behavior of researchers.

H1a: External interaction has a significant positive impact on the innovation behavior of researchers.

H1b: Participation in decision-making has a significant positive impact on the innovation behavior of researchers.

2.2 The Regulating Effect of Environmental Dynamics

Resource dependence theory believes that an organization is a series of resource aggregates, and all its resource activities depend on the contingent factors of the external environment. Some scholars believe that environmental contingency factors are mainly manifested in environmental dynamics or uncertainty [24]. Environmental dynamics refers to the uncertainty of the environment and the speed of environmental changes, which are mainly manifested in the supply of raw materials, product demand, customer demand, technological changes, etc. [25]. Specifically, scientific researchers are the main body of resource transformation activities. If in a highly dynamic environment, scientific researchers will be resource threatening, and they will try their best to use all resources in the process of transforming knowledge and skill resources into innovative intellectual resources to deal with this environmental uncertainty; If in a stable environment, researchers will reserve their own resources to deal with the uncertainty of the scientific research environment in the future, and use part of their own resources for the transformation of innovative intellectual resources. Many previous studies have confirmed the above conclusions. For example, Shu Yiming [26] found that in a highly dynamic environment, it is beneficial for employees to conduct informal communication more effectively and create a communication atmosphere, but it will significantly reduce the frequency of communication; He Xia [27] demonstrated from the perspective of organizational learning that environmental dynamics play a positive regulatory role in the transformation of knowledge resources. However, the research results of some scholars are inconsistent. For example, Yu Shaozhong [28] found that in the transformation of a series of resources such as relational resources, economic resources, and human resources, environmental dynamics played a negative regulatory effect; Feng Junzheng [29] empirical research based on a sample of 204 companies shows that technological dynamics promote the transformation of innovative intellectual resources, while market dynamics have no influence. Other empirical evidence, such as Chen Shou [30] also found that environmental dynamics can weaken the efficiency of resource transformation. Chen Shou [31] believes that the reason for the difference in the above research is probably due to the complementary and substitution effects of different forms of resources, and the complementary and substitution effects of the environment are differentiated in different organizational forms. Based on previous studies on the inconsistency of the role of environmental dynamics in the process of resource transformation, this article believes that the highly dynamic research environment will bring external threats to the transformation of knowledge resources for researchers, prompting researchers to use all surrounding knowledge resources to deal with environmental problems. Certainty to increase the stability of resource transformation and the accuracy of scientific research strategies (Fig. 1). For this reason, the following hypotheses are proposed:

H2: Environmental dynamics play a positive role in regulating the relationship between organizational learning ability and innovative behavior.

H2a: Environmental dynamics play a positive role in regulating the relationship between external interaction and innovative behavior.

H2b: Environmental dynamics play a positive role in the relationship between participation in decision-making and innovative behavior.

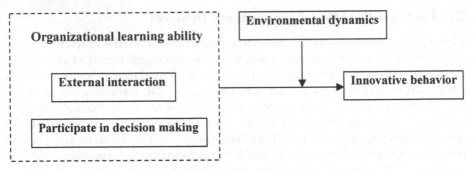

Fig. 1. Theoretical model

3   Research Design

3.1   Sample Survey

The subjects of this study are scientific research teachers from 6 universities in Shandong Province. In order to avoid homology variance, we issued questionnaires at the beginning of 2016 and the end of 2016 respectively. Among them, organizational learning ability, environmental dynamics, and employee innovation behavior data are all collected from teachers who are actually engaged in scientific research in colleges and universities. All questionnaire survey personnel adhere to the principle of voluntariness. The questionnaires were distributed and collected by paper courier and e-mail. A total of 600 copies were distributed, and 503 questionnaires were collected. After excluding too many missed answers and unqualified questionnaires that were obviously not taken seriously. There were 472 valid questionnaires, and the overall response rate of the questionnaires in this study was 83.8%, of which the effective sample recovery rate was 93.8%. Among the teachers surveyed, males accounted for 34.1% and females accounted for 65.9%; 57% are under 35 years old, 30.6% are 35–45 years old, 12.4% are 45–60 years old; working years accounted for 25%, 3–5 years accounted for 36.9%, 6–10. The annual proportion is 22.9%, and the proportion for more than 10 years is 15.3%; the title of professor accounts for 2.1%, the title of associate professor accounts for 39.8%, and the title of lecturer accounts for 58.1%.

3.2   Variable Measurement

The research questionnaire uses a Likert 5-point scale (1 = completely agree; 5 = completely disagree), and they are all existing maturity scales in foreign countries. The specific measurements are as follows:

(1) Organizational learning ability. Using Alegre [13] and other revised organizational learning ability scale, a total of 7 items, mainly including two dimensions of external interaction (EI) and participation in decision-making (DI), example items include "organization encourages employees to actively communicate" and so on. The factor loading is between 0.763–0.957, the external interaction Cronbachα coefficient is 0.858, and the participating decision-making Cronbachα coefficient is 0.759, showing high reliability.

(2) Environmental dynamics (ED). Using the environmental characteristic scale developed by Jansen [32], there are a total of 4 items, example items are "the market environment faced by the company often changes drastically", etc. The factor loadings are all between 0.663–0.922, and the Cronbach alpha coefficient is 0.803, which shows good reliability.

(3) Employee Innovation Behavior (IB). Using a single-dimensional scale developed by Scott [33], there are 6 items in total, and the example items are "At work, I will actively seek to apply new technologies, new procedures or new methods", etc. The factor loadings are all between 0.793–0.892, and the Cronbach alpha coefficient is 0.911, which shows good reliability.

(4) Control variables. This paper draws on the research of Wang Ting [34] and others, setting gender, age, working years, and job title as control variables.

4 Data Analysis Results

4.1 Confirmatory Factor Analysis

In this study, Harman's single factor method was used to test homology variance, and SPSS23.0 was used to perform principal component analysis on all data, explaining 72.98% of the total variance, which was greater than 60%. And the first factor explains 25.51% of the total variation, which is less than 50%, indicating that the homology variance of the data is within an acceptable range. The overall KMO value is 0.868, and the statistics of Barlett's test are significantat the level of less than 0.001%, indicating that it is suitable for factor analysis. On this basis, the Lisrel8.7 structural equation was further used to test the discriminative validity of the four factors involved in this study. The analysis results are shown in Table 1. The comparison shows that among the four models, the basic model has the best fit, SRMR is 0.037, which is less than 0.8, GFI, NFI and other fitting indicators are all greater than 0.8, χ^2/df is slightly higher than the standard value, indicating that the four. The variables have good discriminating validity. According to the above test, it is found that the load of each factor is greater than 0.6, indicating that each factor has good convergence validity.

Table 1. Discrimination validity test of research conception.

	χ^2	SRMR	RMSEA	GFI	AGFI	NFI	NNFI	RFI	IFI	CFI	χ^2/df
Basic model[a]	544.21	0.037	0.14	0.84	0.73	0.92	0.90	0.89	0.93	0.93	8.78
Alternative model 1	1004.88	0.037	0.16	0.68	0.73	0.89	0.86	0.85	0.90	0.90	14.77
Alternative model 2	1637.28	0.081	0.22	0.69	0.53	0.70	0.75	0.60	0.71	0.71	24.44
Alternative model 3	2610.03	0.080	0.26	0.56	0.40	0.52	0.73	0.44	0.53	0.53	33.90

[a] Basic model: external interaction, participation in decision-making, environmental dynamics, and employee innovation behavior;
Alternative model 1: external interaction + participation in decision-making, environmental dynamics, and employee innovative behavior;
Alternative model 2: external interaction + participation in decision-making + environmental dynamics, employee innovation behavior;
Alternative model 3: external interaction + participation in decision-making + environmental dynamics + employee innovation behavior.

4.2 Descriptive Statistical Analysis

Table 2 shows the mean, standard deviation and correlation coefficient of each variable.

Participation in decision-making is significantly positively correlated with innovation behavior (r = 0.476, p < 0.01), and external interaction is significantly positively correlated with innovation behavior (r = 0.476, p < 0.01). The correlation between environmental dynamics and participation in decision-making, external interaction, and innovative behavior is not strong (r = 0.140, p < 0.1; r = 0.027, p < 0.1), which lays the foundation for further hypothesis testing.

Table 2. Descriptive statistics, correlation coefficients and reliability of research variables.

Variable name	Mean	Standard deviation	1	2	3	4
1 Participate in decision making	3.03	1.02	(0.759)			
2 External interaction	3.42	0.84	0.333**	(0.858)		
3 Environmental dynamics	3.44	0.65	0.140*	0.027	(0.803)	
4 Innovative behavior	3.33	0.78	0.476**	0.452**	0.185*	(0.911)

4.3 Overall Hypothesis Test

Hypothesis 1 proposes that the organizational learning ability (participation in decision-making, external interaction) of colleges and universities has a significant positive impact on the innovative behavior of scientific researchers. This paper uses SPSS23.0 to test the direct effects of DI and EI on IB. As shown in Table 3, using employee innovation behavior (IB) as the dependent variable, and on the basis of controlling the latent variables such as gender, age, working years, and title, we introduce Participate in decision-making (DI) and external interaction (EI). The results showed that the effect of DI/EI on IB was $\beta = 0.373/\beta = 0.439$ (p < 0.01), the variation explanation degree was 13.8% and 19.1%, and the F value was 76.097 and 112.027, respectively. The T values are 8.138 and 10.584 respectively, which are both greater than the standard value of 2.238. It shows that the regression model has passed F test and T test, that is, participation in decision-making and external interaction have a positive effect on employee innovation behavior. Hypothesis 1 has been verified.

Table 3. Regression analysis of EI and DI to IB.

Independent variable	Dependent variable	standard β	T	Adjustment R^2	F
Participate in decision making (DI)	Innovative behavior	0.373	8.723	0.138	76.097
External interaction (EI)		0.439	10.584	0.191	112.027
Standard regression equation	Innovative behavior = 0.373 Participation in decision-making; innovative behavior = 0.439 external interaction				

Hypothesis 2 proposes that environmental dynamics play a positive role in the relationship between organizational learning ability (participation in decision-making, external interaction) and innovative behavior. This paper uses Bootstrapping (samples = 5000, 95% confidence interval) test method to analyze the moderating effect of environmental dynamics (ED) on organizational learning ability (OL) and innovative behavior (IB), as shown in Table 4. The results show that when ED is at a low level, the effect of ED on the relationship between EI and IB is $\beta = 1.262/\beta = 1.137$, and the 95% confidence interval is [1.111,1.412]/[0.999,1.276], not including Zero, the standard errors are 0.077/0.071, both are less than 0.1; When ED is at a high level, the effect of ED on the relationship between EI and IB is $\beta = 0.865/\beta = 0.923$, and the 95% confidence interval is [0.744,0.986]/[0.810,1.036] excluding zero. The standard errors were 0.062/0.057, all of which were less than 0.1. That is to say, ED plays a positive regulatory role among EI, DI and IB. Assumption 2 is verified.

According to the data test results, the schematic diagrams of the regulating effect of ED in the relationship between DI, EI and IB are shown in Fig. 2 and Fig. 3. Taking plus or minus one standard deviation as the grouping standard, the organizational learning ability and environmental dynamics are divided into two groups: high and low. It can be seen from the figure that under the same conditions of organizational learning ability,

Table 4. Bootstrapping test of the moderating effect of ED between EI, DI and IB

Result variable	Moderating effect				
	Adjusted variable (ED)[a]	Effect	Standard error	95% Confidence interval	
				Lower limit	Upper limit
IB	Low/low	1.262/1.137	0.077/0.071	1.111/0.999	1.412/1.276
	High/high	0.865/0.923	0.062/0.057	0.744/0.810	0.986/1.036

[a] Low/low respectively represent the influence of the low value of ED on the reltionship between EI, DI and IB.

high-level environmental dynamics will bring higher levels of innovative behavior, and low-level organizational learning ability has a smaller effect on innovation behavior. Comparing Fig. 2 and Fig. 3, we can see that the absolute value of the slope of environmental dynamics in Fig. 2 is greater than that in Fig. 3. This also confirms that under the same environment, participation in decision-making has a stronger explanatory power for employees' innovative behavior than external interaction.

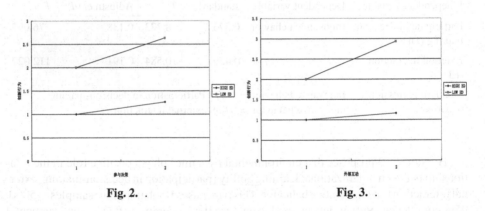

Fig. 2. .   Fig. 3. .

5   Conclusions, Management Implications and Limitations

In recent years, organizational behavior, human resource management and psychology are important progress in college scientific research personnel knowledge – innovative resource conversion path research [5], but there are still two limitations: First, the research perspective is too traditional. It is mainly focused on the perspective of learning process, and only reflects the external dynamic changes of learning knowledge and innovation, and does not reflect its internal resource change process; Second, the research content is too simple, organizing learning ability is an ability to organize absorption, integration, optimization, upgrade and transformation knowledge, and its knowledge source path may have differences in transformation efficiency. To this end, existing research urgently needs to refine its intrinsic mechanisms and expand its transformation boundary conditions. In view of this, this paper mainly solves two problems based on the COR perspective: First, whether the internal and external knowledge of internal and external knowledge is different from the impact of researchers' innovation behavior, which is more exclusive; The second is whether the dynamic changes of the scientific research environment have promoted or hindered. In response to the above two aspects, this paper passed the theoretical deduction and the use of 472 scientific research teacher sample data, and the following two aspects:

(1) Organizational learning ability has a significant positive impact on the innovation behavior of college scientific research personnel, in which the decision-making interpretation of innovation behavior is 19.1%, and external interaction interpretation innovation behavior is 13.8%. This is probably because college scientific researchers need to participate in the important decisions in colleges and universities. Compared to the matter, teachers are more enthusiastic about team scientific research, and there is fresh information exchange. Resource preservation Theory believes that knowledge is an important organizational resource, under certain conditions, it can achieve resource conversion. In the past, many also indirectly confirmed the influence of knowledge absorption capabilities of college scientific researchers on their innovation performance, such as Zhang Tree [35] believed that knowledge transfer was a core element of innovation, and the emergence of researchers' innovative consciousness relied on specific knowledge activities. This research conclusion expands and deepens the previous research results, and the organizational learning activities are subdivided into external interactions and internal participation. And this paper compares the contribution of external and internal learning on researchers' innovation behavior, which provides a useful reference for research management and scientific research performance in colleges and universities.

(2) Environmental Dynamics extends forward adjustment between organizational learning capabilities and innovation behavior. College researchers in high uncertain environments can call all its own resources and external resources to promote knowledge resources into innovative intellectual resources. And in a dynamic environment, participation decisions are more capable of promoting innovation than external interactions. This is an inherent consistency with the research conclusions of Li Dehuang [4]. In high-dynamic environments, researchers' knowledge integration is more beneficial to improve research performance. The open environment creates a multivariate and faulty research atmosphere for researchers, promoting internal learning and external exchanges of researchers.

This study concludes that there is an important revelation of the management practice of college scientific research personnel. First, it warnizes the importance of college managers to enhance the organizational's soft environment uncertain atmosphere. It is recommended that colleges and universities pay more attention to teachers' research decision-making, while environmental factors can strengthen the above organizational resource conversion effect. Collectors should listen to the views of scientific research teachers in organizing major decisions, and this opinion can affect the organization's decision-making, making research teachers to feel the importance of their own opinions. Second, while colleges and universities pay attention to research decisions, it is also necessary to increase the information exchange of scientific research staff and external scientific research teams, pay attention to training for research teachers in collecting external information. Colleges and universities must organize special organizational procedures collection, analysis, and share external information, and organize teachers to communicate and interact with external universities. However, if the resource resources in colleges and universities are given priority to consider the decision-making participation of researchers. In this study, there are two constitutive limits. First, the research sample is limited to 6 universities in Shandong Province, follow-up research can expand to national colleges and universities; Second, research data is only from colleges and universities, and there is no enterprise. The impact of external information interaction and decision-making participation on innovation behavior does not further confirm the same differential effect in the enterprise.

References

1. Hobfoll, S.E.: Conservation of resource caravans and engaged settings. J. Occup. Organ. Psychol. **84**(1), 116–122 (2011)
2. Haiyan, F.: Research on performance evaluation and management of innovative ability of scientific research teams in universities. Sci. Res. Manage. **36**(1), 32–34 (2015). (in Chinese)
3. Higgins, C., Duxbury, L., Johnson, K.L.: The impact of intrinsic and extrinsic motivation on job choice in generation Y. In: 4th Annual Siena College Student Conference in Business. New York (2009)
4. Li, D., Jin, L.: Organizational support, knowledge integration and scientific research team innovation performance-based on the organizational environment and innovation atmosphere. Technol. Econ. Manag. Res. **4**(7), 41–45 (2014). (in Chinese)
5. Chen, Y.: Research on the coupling of organizational learning, knowledge management and organizational innovation. Lib. Inf. Work **54**(2), 140–143 (2010). (in Chinese)
6. Yan, J.: Research on the classification and implementation paths of collaborative innovation models of industry, university and research in universities. Technol. Prog. Countermeas. **18**, 27–31 (2014). (in Chinese)
7. Wang, M., Li, Y., Zhang, Y.: Function construction of knowledge ecosystem of university library. Library J. **8**, 45–48 (2016). (in Chinese)
8. Yuan, C., Wang, R., Li, Y., et al.: An empirical analysis of the impact of government support on university knowledge innovation. Sci. Sci. Sci. Technol. Manage. **2**, 124–133 (2014). (in Chinese)
9. Li, Z., Wang, X.: Research on the relationship between organizational learning and customer knowledge management ability-the adjustment of relationship embeddedness. Sci. Sci. Sci. Technol. Manage. **36**(3), 152–162 (2015). (in Chinese)
10. Bångens, L., Araujo, L.: The structures and processes of learning. A case study. J. Bus. Res. **55**(7), 571–581 (2002)
11. Forbes, N., Wield, D.: From Followers to Leaders: Managing Innovation and Technology. Routledge, London (2002)
12. Chipika, S., Wilson, G.: Enabling technological learning among light engineering SMEs in Zimbabwe through networking. Technovation **26**(8), 969–979 (2006)
13. Alegre, J., Chiva, R.: Assessing the impact of organizational learning capability on product innovation performance: an empirical test. Technovation **28**(6), 315–326 (2008)
14. Bishop, S.K.: Cross-functional project teams in functionally aligned organizations. Project Manage. J. **30**(3), 6–12 (1999)

15. Szulanski, G.: Exploring internal stickiness: impediments to the transfer of best practice within the firm. Strateg. Manag. J. **17**(S2), 27–43 (2015)
16. Krimsky, S., Ennis, J.G., Weissman, R.: Academic-corporate ties in biotechnology: a quantitative study. Sci. Technol. Hum. Values **16**(3), 275–87 (1991)
17. Wang, F., Lv, W.: Research on the paradigm of resource allocation of science and technology innovation teams in universities. Chin. Univ. Sci. Technol. **8**, 68–71 (2009). (in Chinese)
18. Real, J.C.: Determinants of organisational learning in the generation of technological distinctive competencies. Int. J. Technol. Manage. **35**(1), 284–307 (2006)
19. Argyris, C., Schon, D.: Organizational Learning: A Theory of Action Perspective. Addison-Wesley, Reading Mass (1978)
20. Stata, R.: Organizational learning – the key to management innovation. MIT Sloan Manage. Rev. **30**(3), 63–74 (1989)
21. Mabey, C., Salaman, G.: Strategic Human Resource Management. Blackwell, Oxford (1995)
22. Glynn, M.A.: Innovative genius: a framework for relating individual and organizational intelligences to innovation. Acad. Manage. Rev. **21**(4), 1081–1111 (1996)
23. Zhou, R., Yu, Y.: On the construction of university learning organization. Sci. Technol. Inf. Dev. Econ. **17**(25), 242–244 (2007). (in Chinese)
24. Liu, D., Chen, X.P., Yao, X.: From autonomy to creativity: a multilevel investigation of the mediating role of harmonious passion. J. Appl. Psychol. **96**(2), 294–309 (2011)
25. Liang, X., Picken, J.C.: Top management team communication networks, environmental uncertainty, and organizational performance: a contingency view. J. Managerial Issues **22**(4), 436–455 (2010)
26. Shu, Y., Hao, Z.: The impact of senior management team communication on decision-making performance: the moderating effect of environmental dynamics. Sci. Sci. Sci. Technol. Manage. **36**(4), 170–180 (2015). (in Chinese)
27. He, X., Su, X.: Research on the legitimacy of strategic alliances and organizations of new ventures—based on the perspective of organizational learning. Sci. Res. Manag. **37**(2), 90–97 (2016). (in Chinese)
28. Yu, S.: Research on the Impact mechanism of entrepreneurial resources on entrepreneurship performance—based on the moderating effect of environmental dynamics. Sci. Sci. Sci. Technol. Manage. **34**(6), 131–139 (2013). (in Chinese)
29. Feng, J.: Research on the driving factors of breakthrough innovation and disruptive innovation in enterprises—the perspective of environmental dynamics and hostility. Sci. Res. **31**(9), 1422–1432 (2013). (in Chinese)
30. Chen, S., Zhang, H., Li, C. et al.: The impact of resource efficiency on enterprise performance: based on the analysis of environmental dynamics regulation. Manage. Rev. **25**(12), (2013) (in Chinese)
31. Chen, S., Shi, X., Wu, S.: The impact of the synergy of complementary resources and innovation resources on corporate performance—the moderating effect of environmental dynamics. Syst. Eng. **1**, 61–67 (2015). (in Chinese)
32. Jansen, J.J.P., Bosch, F.A.J.V.D., Volberda, H.W.: Exploratory innovation, exploitative innovation, and performance: effects of organizational antecedents and environmental moderators. Erim Rep. **52**(11), 1661–1674 (2006)
33. Scott, S.G., Bruce, R.A.: Determinants of innovation behavior: a path model of individual innovation in the workplace. Acad. Manage. J. **3**, 580–607 (1994)
34. Wang, T., Xu, P., Zhu, H.: Research on the relationship between work-family balance of scientific researchers and organizational performance. Sci. Res. **29**(1), 121–126 (2011). (in Chinese)
35. Zhang, S.: Research on the mechanism of tacit knowledge transfer in the process of knowledge innovation. Lib. Inf. Work **57**(4), 54–59 (2013). (in Chinese)

ABAC: Anonymous Bilateral Access Control Protocol with Traceability for Fog-Assisted Mobile Crowdsensing

Biwen Chen[1,3], Zhongming Wang[1], Tao Xiang[1(✉)], Lei Yang[1], Hongyang Yan[2], and Jin Li[2]

[1] College of Computer Science, Chongqing University, 400044 Chongqing, China
txiang@cqu.edu.cn
[2] Institute of Artificial Intelligence and Blockchain, Guangzhou University, Guangzhou, China
[3] Guangxi Key Laboratory of Trusted Software, Guilin University of Electronic Technology, Guilin, China

Abstract. Fog-assisted mobile crowdsensing (MCS) has been applied to various applications to improve the quality of big data services. As two indispensable services of fog-assisted MCS, privacy protection and flexible access control have attracted widespread attention. Although there are already some cryptographic solutions to address the above concerns, they still have some limitations in the development of mobile crowdsensing, such as lacking anonymous protection and only providing unilateral access control (i.g., who can read). Thus, we propose an anonymous bilateral access control protocol (ABAC) with traceability for secure big data transmission in fog-assisted MCS. By combining the designed access control encryption scheme and an efficient group signature, ABAC not only protects the identity privacy of participants but also achieves access control in terms of reading and writing simultaneously. Security analysis and experimental evaluations demonstrate that ABAC fits the requirements of fog-assisted MCS.

Keywords: Mobile crowdsensing · Big data · Access control · Group signature · Traceability

1 Introduction

Mobile crowdsensing (MCS) [3,5,11] is a noticeable sensing paradigm that is suitable for various new types of context-aware services and applications. In MCS, a large amount of data generated by different sources are shared and processed to extract something of common interest. Thanks to the rapid promotion of computing and communication capabilities of smart devices, MCS has been greatly used to perform more complex big data tasks, such as air pollution monitoring and analysis [12] and energy saving [17]. However, as the scale of the MCS system becomes larger, the efficiency and security issues need to be

© Springer Nature Singapore Pte Ltd. 2021
Y. Tan et al. (Eds.): DMBD 2021, CCIS 1454, pp. 430–444, 2021.
https://doi.org/10.1007/978-981-16-7502-7_40

addressed more urgently. Due to the advantages of fog computing, fog-assisted MCS has been designed to improve the quality of the big data service of MCS. Fog-assisted MCS system exists two key characteristics: 1) fog nodes are scattered and switchable; 2) fog-assisted MCS system can save the bandwidth by letting fog nodes process sensing data. Fog-assisted MCS system can provide more flexible and better service through collaborating with each other [15].

1.1 Motivation

Although the fog-assisted MCS is widely used, there exist several security concerns to be addressed urgently in the big data scenario. 1) The confidentiality of data should be protected. Due to the openness of fog-assisted mobile crowd-sensing, a malicious adversary can obtain sensitive information by eavesdropping on the channels if the data is transmitted in plaintext forms. 2) The bilateral access control mechanism should be made available to fog-assisted MCS. A few existing cryptographic schemes (e.g., IBE and ABE) achieve unilateral access control. However, these works only focus on preventing entities from *Reading* data, lacking preventing unauthorized parties from *Writing* data to others they are not allowed to communicate with. In addition, considering the difference of terminal devices, the access control policy should support the function that assigns different rights to participants equipped with different devices. For example, a participant with an HD video camera and an inferior voice recorder should have higher power for video sensing tasks than voice recording tasks. Although access control encryption (ACE) [4] is a novel cryptographic primitive that supports the bilateral access control for *Reading* and *Writing* simultaneously, most existing ACE schemes are hardly adapted to fog-assisted MCS because of their high computation and communication overhead.

Furthermore, privacy protection has become a must-have security feature in practical applications, especially identity information protection. For example, the entities may wish to perform sensitive tasks while hiding their identities, and thus there needs to be an anonymous data transmitting mechanism. However, the anonymity may incur that some malicious entities will engage in illegal activities. To prevent that, tracing technology should be also needed to be provided to reveal the real identity of malicious entities.

To solve the above concerns, we first construct an efficient variant ACE scheme by compressing the size of ciphertexts and reducing computational overhead, and our scheme supports bilateral access control policy. Then, by combining our ACE scheme and a secure group signature, we propose an efficient anonymous bilateral access control protocol (ABAC) with traceability. ABAC inherits the advantages of group signature, protecting the identity privacy of each group member while providing the capabilities of tracking user identity. The main contributions of this paper are as follows:

- We propose a variant access control encryption scheme with formal security proofs. The proposed scheme supports not only the bilateral access control policy but also has a constant ciphertext length.

- We build an efficient anonymous bilateral access control protocol for fog-assisted MCS. The protocol can support data confidence, user anonymity, traceability, and fine-grained bilateral access control at the same time.
- We analyze the security of our protocol and evaluate its performance. The analysis and experimental results show that our protocol will enhance the adoption of fog-assisted MCS because of its effectiveness and security.

1.2   Organization

The rest of this paper is organized as follows. Section 2 gives the related work. Section 3 introduces some preliminaries required by this paper. Section 4 introduces the system model and design goal. Section 5 presents the detail of our proposed protocol. Section 6 and 7 provide the security analysis and the performance, respectively. Finally, Sect. 8 concludes this paper.

2   Related Work

Privacy protection is one of the hot research topics. Miao et al. [13] proposed the first privacy-preserving truth discovery framework (PPTD). Their PPTD performs the weighted aggregation on the encrypted data of users using a homomorphic cryptosystem. However, it has considerable computation and communication costs for users. Later, Xu et al. [19] introduced a new design that achieves better performance. It takes additive homomorphic privacy protection data aggregation and super-increasing sequence technology to achieve high performance and strong privacy protection. However, it is brittle in the presence of compromised users because their design requires all users to share a secret key. Other researchers [14,22] also proposed some new protocols for efficient and privacy-preserving truth discovery. Recently, Zheng et al. [21] designed a new system architecture to address the privacy issues. To protect the location information, Liu et al. [10] proposed a homomorphic encryption based secure framework, where the *SKD-tree* is used to address the efficiency issue. Considering the privacy disclosure problems, Xiao et al. [18] provided a user recruitment protocol by leveraging the secret sharing scheme.

To provide fine-grained protection on mobile devices, Ye et al. [20] proposed an attribute-tree-based context-aware access control model to protect user's privacy and confidential information. Ni et al. [16] pointed out that the anonymity is an important security feature for the applications of MCS. They also introduced a secure and efficient data deduplication scheme to increase the accuracy of task assignments. Gisdakis et al. [6] designed a holistic solution to address the main challenges faced by MCS from the view of security, privacy, and accountability. Li et al. [9] focused on the privacy problem of auction-based participant selection used for MCS systems. They proposed a scalable participant selection scheme and guaranteed the overall truthfulness and security of participants. Jin et al. [8] proposed a new MCS system framework by integrating an incentive mechanism, a data aggregation scheme, and a data perturbation technology. In total, designing new solutions with different features is urgently needed to further enhance the practicability of the MCS system.

3 Preliminary

3.1 Notations

To facilitate reading, we give the main notations used throughout the paper. We take $[n]$ to represent the list $\{1, 2, 3, \cdots, n\}$. Assuming there are n hierarchical security labels on objects and clearances for subjects in the system. We use the set $P : [n] \times [n] \in \{0, 1\}$ to denote the access policies defined in MCS system. If $P[i, j] = 1$, it means the user in layer $i \in [n]$ is allowed to send a message to the user in layer $j \in [n]$. Let $\mathbb{G}$ represent a group with the generator g and the prime order p and l_i represent the i-th access level and ke_{l_i}, kd_{l_i} represent user's encryption key and decryption key under the l_i, respectively. Let ks represent the sanitization key of sanitizer in the ACE scheme.

3.2 Bilinear Pairing Map

Let $\mathbb{G}_1$, $\mathbb{G}_2$ and $\mathbb{G}_T$ be three cyclic groups of the same prime order p, g_1 and g_2 be two generators of $\mathbb{G}_1$ and $\mathbb{G}_2$, respectively. A bilinear pairing map e is an operation $e : \mathbb{G}_1 \times \mathbb{G}_2 \to \mathbb{G}_T$ with the following properties:

1. Bilinearity: For all $u \in \mathbb{G}_1$, $v \in \mathbb{G}_2$ and $a, b \in \mathbb{Z}_p^*$, $e(u^a, v^b) = e(u, v)^{ab}$.
2. Non-degeneracy: $e(g_1, g_2) \neq 1$.
3. Computability: Given two elements $P \in \mathbb{G}_1$ and $Q \in \mathbb{G}_2$, there exists a polynomial time algorithm to compute $e(P, Q) \in \mathbb{G}_T$.

3.3 Group Signature

Group signature (GS) is a cryptographic primitive, which allows a group member to anonymously sign a message on behalf of the group. GS provides properties such as anonymity and traceability. Although various GS schemes have been proposed, an efficient GS is more suitable for fog-assisted MCS, such as the scheme presented by Ho et al. [7]. Here, we give a simple description as follows.

- GS.Setup(λ). Once receiving a security parameter λ as input, the manager firstly chooses a secure hash function H and three cyclic groups $\mathbb{G}_1, \mathbb{G}_2, \mathbb{G}_T$ with the same prime order p and the bilinear pairing map $e : \mathbb{G}_1 \times \mathbb{G}_2 \to \mathbb{G}_T$. Then, it determines that (g_1, g_2) are the generators of $\mathbb{G}_1$ and $\mathbb{G}_2$, respectively. It randomly picks three elements $(r, s, t) \in Z_p^*$ as the main secret key and computes $(R = g_1^r, S = g_2^s, T = g_1^t)$ as the group public key. Finally, it outputs the public parameters $pp = (\mathbb{G}_1, \mathbb{G}_2, \mathbb{G}_T, e, g_1, g_2, p, H, R, S, T)$ and keeps the managing key $sk = (r, s)$ and the opening key $ok = t$ secretly.

- GS.Enroll(pp, i, sk). For each group member i, the manager picks a random number $x_i \in Z_p^*$ and computes $z_i = (r - x_i)(sx_i)^{-1} \in Z_p^*$ and $Z_i = g_1^{z_i} \in \mathbb{G}_1$. Then, it sends $gsk[i] = (x_i, Z_i)$ to the group member i as his signature key. It computes $tag_i = H(x_i \cdot Z_i)$ and maintains tag_i in a member list $L = (ID_i, tag_i)$, where ID_i denotes the real identity of the group member i.
- GS.GSig($pp, gpk, gsk[i], m$). It randomly picks an element $k \in Z_p^*$ and outputs a signature $\sigma = (c_1, c_2, c, \omega)$, where $c_1 = g_1^k, c_2 = Z_i^{x_i} + T^k, Q = e(T, S)^k$, $c = H(m, c_1, c_2, Q)$, and $\omega = (kc + x_i)$.
- GS.GVerify(pp, gpk, m, σ). It takes the group public key $gpk = (R, S, T)$, a message m, and the group signature $\sigma = (c_1, c_2, c, \omega)$ as input, and computes $Q' = \frac{e(c_2, S)e(g_1, g_2)^\omega}{e(c_1^c + R, g_2)}$. The verifier accepts the signature σ if the equation $c = H(m, c_1, c_2, Q')$ holds, otherwise, rejects it.
- GS.Open(pp, ok, m, σ). It takes the opening key $ok = t$, a message m and a signature $\sigma = (c_1, c_2, c, \omega)$ as input, and outputs a real identity or $\perp$. The manager first verifies the validity of the signature σ by executing the GS.GVerify algorithm. If the signature is valid, the manager continues to the following steps, otherwise, it terminates the algorithm. Then, it computes a tag $tag_i = H(x_i \cdot Z_i) = H(c_2 - tc_1)$ and retrieves the true identity ID from the list L by the values of tag_i.

4   Models and Goals

4.1   System Model

As shown in Fig. 1, there are five entities in the ABAC, including participants, data requesters, fog nodes, cloud-server, and trusted authority(TA). The tasks of each entity are described as follows.

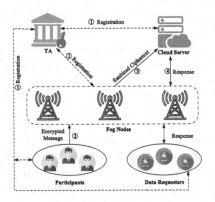

Fig. 1. System model.

- **Trusted Authority**. The trusted authority is responsible for initializing the entire system, generating secret keys for all registered entities, revoking the privilege of entities, and tracking the identity of the malicious user.
- **Participants**. A participant first registers his identity with TA to obtain the privilege of his level. Then, it collects the data and encrypts them with his encryption key. Finally, it uploads the ciphertexts to the cloud server.
- **Data Requesters**. A data requester first registers his identity with TA to obtain the privilege of his level. Then, it sends a request to a nearby fog node and receives a response (contains the corresponding ciphertexts) from the fog node. Finally, it decrypts ciphertexts to obtain the data sent by participants.
- **Fog Nodes**. The fog node is located at the network edge and works as a relay point between participants/requesters and the cloud server. Specifically, it mixes the data reports before they arrive at the cloud server and returns responses to requesters.
- **Cloud Server**. The cloud server is a centralized service provider. It takes charge of storing data and responding to the requests from the node fogs.

Our model achieves the hierarchy access control policy, where different levels have different rights and the levels are in a superior-subordinate relationship.

4.2 Threat Model

We assume that both the participants and data requesters may be malicious, which means a malicious participant tries to send a message beyond his level and a malicious requester tries to decrypt a ciphertext with a higher level. Meanwhile, we assume that both the fog nodes and the cloud server are semi-honest, that is, they are curious about inferring the private information but honestly following our protocol. The participants submit encrypted sensing data to the fog node, and the requesters only receive sanitized ciphertexts from the cloud server. That is, the requesters cannot directly obtain the ciphertexts that are sanitized.

4.3 Design Goals

Based on existing literature, an anonymous bilateral access control protocol with traceability should satisfy the following requirements.

1. **Confidentiality**. It is a basic requirement that external adversaries cannot recover any meaningful information from the intercepted ciphertexts. Only the intended receiver can obtain the content of the message(sensing data).
2. **Anonymity**. It guarantees that the adversary cannot determine the real identity of entities via simple analysises of ciphertexts or messages. It is even impossible for an attacker to identify whether two sensing messages are generated by the same participant.
3. **Traceability**. It ensures that the TA is capable of tracking the identity of a malicious entity that deviates from the pre-defined protocol.

4. **Fine-Grained Bilateral Access Control**. It allows to control not only what users are allowed to read, but also what users are allowed to write. Specifically, the participanta are required to bind the corresponding privilege level based on their identities, and they can only send/decrypt the ciphertexts corresponding to their privilege level.

5 Our Design

We construct a variant ACE scheme with security proofs and propose an anonymous bilateral access control protocol with traceability, named ABAC.

5.1 Variant ACE Scheme

We propose a lightweight construction of ACE under its security definition [4], which consists of a tuple ACE = (Setup, KeyGen, Enc, San, Dec) and three types of entities (*participant, sanitizer, requester*).

- $(pp, msk) \leftarrow \mathsf{Setup}(1^\lambda, P)$. The algorithm takes as input a security parameter λ and a access control policy P with size of $[n] \times [n]$, and outputs the public parameter pp and the master secret key msk. It first chooses the parameters $(\mathbb{G}, p, g)$ and randomly picks n pairs $(\alpha_i, x_i)_{i \in [n]} \in Z_p^*$. Then, it computes $h_i = g^{x_i}$, outputs the public parameter $pp = (\mathbb{G}, p, g, h_i)_{i \in [n]}$ and the master secret key $msk = (\alpha_i, x_i)_{i \in [n]}$.
- $(ke_i, kd_i, ks_i) \leftarrow \mathsf{KeyGen}(pp, msk, P, i, t)$. The algorithm takes as input the public parameter pp, msk, P, i, and $t \in \{participant, sanitizer, requester\}$, and outputs the corresponding secret keys (ke_i, kd_i, ks_i). The detailed processes are as follows:
  - If $t = participant$, it computes $ke_i = \mathsf{KeyGen}(msk, i, par) = g^{\alpha_i}$.
  - If $t = requester$, for each level $j \in P$, it computes $kd_{ij} = \mathsf{KeyGen}(msk, i, j, req) = dk_{ij}$, where $dk_{ij} = -x_i$ if $P(i, j) = 1$; otherwise, dk_{ij} is set to random bits.
  - If $t = sanitizer$, it computes $ks_i = \mathsf{KeyGen}(msk, i, san) = g^{-\alpha_i}$.
- $(C_i) \leftarrow \mathsf{Enc}(pp, m, ke_i, i)$. The algorithm takes as input the public parameter pp, a message m and an encryption key ke_i with level i, and outputs a ciphertext C_i. It chooses random numbers $r_1, r_2 \in Z_p^*$ and computes the ciphertext: $C_i = (c_0, c_1, c_2, c_3, c_4) = (g^{r_1}, ke_i h_i^{r_1}, g^{r_2}, mh_i^{r_2}, i)$.
- $(C_i') \leftarrow \mathsf{San}(pp, C, ks_i, i)$. The algorithm takes as input the public parameter pp, a ciphertext $C_i = (c_0, c_1, c_2, c_3, c_4)$ and a sanitizer key ks_i, and outputs a sanitized ciphertext C_i'. It chooses random numbers $s_1, s_2 \in Z_p^*$ and computes the sanitized ciphertext: $C_i' = (c_0', c_1', c_2') = (c_2 c_0^{s_1} g^{s_2}, c_3(ks_i c_1)^{s_1} h_i^{s_2}, i)$.
- $(m' \ or \ \bot) \leftarrow \mathsf{Dec}(pp, C_i', kd_{ij})$. The algorithm takes as input the public parameter pp, a sanitized ciphertext $C_i' = (c_0', c_1', c_2')$ and a decryption key kd_{ij}, and outputs a message: $m' = c_1'(c_0')^{kd_{ij}}$.

Security. The following theorems prove that our proposed ACE construction satisfies the fundamental security requirements: **No-Read** and **No-Write**.

Theorem 1. *Our ACE scheme satisfies the security definition of no-read rule assuming that the DDH assumption holds in $\mathbb{G}$.*

Proof. Assume that there exist an adversary $\mathcal{A}$ that breaks the ACE no-read rule with non-negligible advantage ϵ, then we can construct a simulator $\mathcal{A}'$ that wins the DDH problem with non-negligible advantage.

Assuming that the following PPT algorithm $\mathcal{A}'$ attempts to address the DDH problem. $\mathcal{A}'$ receives an instance $(\mathbb{G}, p, g, h_1, h_2, h_3)$ of DDH, where $h_1 = g^x$, $h_2 = g^y$ and h_3 is either g^{xy} or g^z (for uniform x, y, z). The goal of $\mathcal{A}'$ is to determine the real case. Given a problem instance (g, g^a, g^b, Z) over the group $(\mathbb{G}, p, g)$ as input, $\mathcal{A}'$ submits $i^* \in [n]$ to be challenged and runs $\mathcal{A}$ as a subroutine and works as follows.

- **Setup.** $\mathcal{A}'$ randomly picks n pairs $(\alpha_i, x_i)_{i \in [n]}$ from Z_p^*, computes $h_i = g^{x_i}$ for $i \in [n]$ and $i \neq i^*$. Then, it sets $pp = (\mathbb{G}, p, g, h_i)_{i \in [n]}$, where $h_{i^*} = g^a$, which implies $x_{i^*} = a$.
- **Query Phase 1.**
  1) **KeyGen Query.** $\mathcal{A}$ can query $\mathcal{O}_G$ in this phase. $\mathcal{A}$ submits queries (i, t) and $\mathcal{A}'$ outputs the corresponding keys according to the elements it has picked. If $q = (i, participant)$, $\mathcal{A}'$ outputs α_i; if $q = (i, sanitizer)$, $\mathcal{A}'$ outputs $-\alpha_i$; if $q = (j, requester)$, $\mathcal{A}'$ outputs $\{-x_i\}_{i \in [n]}$.
  2) **Encryption Query.** $\mathcal{A}$ can query $\mathcal{O}_E$ in this phase. $\mathcal{A}$ submits a query (i, m) and $\mathcal{A}'$ responds $C_m = \mathsf{ACE.Enc}(ke_i, m)$ using ke_i as encryption key.
- **Challenge.** $\mathcal{A}$ outputs messages m_0, m_1 to be challenge. $\mathcal{A}'$ chooses a random bit $c \in \{0, 1\}$ and constructs the response ciphertext CT^* as $CT^* = (g^{r_1}, h_{i^*}{}^{r_1}, g^b, Z \cdot m_c, i^*)$, where g^b and Z are from (g, g^a, g^b, Z). Let $r_2 = b$, if $Z = g^{ab}$, then $CT^* = (g^{r_1}, h_{i^*}{}^{r_1}, g^{r_2}, h_{i^*}{}^{r_2} \cdot m_c, i^*)$. Therefore, CT^* is a correct encrypted ciphertext of m_c.
- **Query Phase 2.** $\mathcal{A}$ can query $\mathcal{O}_G$ and $\mathcal{O}_E$, like in the Query Phase 1.
- **Guess.** $\mathcal{A}$ returns a bit c'. $\mathcal{A}'$ returns true if $c' = c$. Otherwise, false.

This completes the simulation process. We now analyze the probability of A' solving the DDH problem. We divide the analysis into following two cases: Case 1: $Z = g^{ab}$. Then $\mathcal{A}$ maintains his advantage ϵ, and guesses b' correctly with probability $1/2 + \epsilon$. Case 2: $Z \neq g^{ab}$. Then Z is random in $\mathbb{G}$, thus CT^* is uniform in C because m_c is encrypted using Z, which cannot be obtained by calculating the parameters owned by $\mathcal{A}$. Hence, $\mathcal{A}$ has no advantage over random guessing, i.e. he has probability $1/2$ of guessing correctly.

Therefore, the advantage of solving the DDH problem is $Adv_{\mathcal{A}'}^{No-Read}(\lambda) = [(1/2 + \epsilon) - (1/2)] = \epsilon/2$. This completes the proof.

Theorem 2. *Our ACE scheme satisfies the security definition of no-write rule assuming that the DDH assumption holds in $\mathbb{G}$.*

Proof. Assume that there exist an adversary $\mathcal{A}$ that breaks the ACE no-write rule with non-negligible advantage ϵ, then we can construct a simulator $\mathcal{A}'$ that wins the DDH problem with non-negligible advantage. A PPT adversary $\mathcal{A}'$

attempts to solve the DDH problem. $\mathcal{A}'$ receives $(\mathbb{G}, q, g, h_1, h_2, h_3)$ where $h_1 = g^x$, $h_2 = g^y$, and h_3 is either g^{xy} or g^z (for uniform x, y, z); the goal of $\mathcal{A}'$ is to select the real case. Given (g, g^a, g^b, Z) over the group $(\mathbb{G}, p, g)$ as input, $\mathcal{A}'$ runs $\mathcal{A}$ as a subroutine and works as follows.

- **Initial** and **Setup**. The queries are the same as Theorem 1.
- **Query Phase 1**.
  1) **Key Query**. $\mathcal{A}$ makes key queries for $\mathcal{O}_S$ in this phase. $\mathcal{A}$ submits a query $q = (i, participant)$, $\mathcal{A}'$ outputs α_i.
  2) **San Query**. $\mathcal{A}$ makes sanitized ciphertext queries for $\mathcal{O}_E$ in this phase. $\mathcal{A}$ submits (i, m) and simulator $\mathcal{A}'$ responds the sanitized ciphertext $C' = $ ACE.San$(ks_i, $ ACE.Enc$(ke_i, m))$using key ke_i and key ks_i.
- **Challenge**. $\mathcal{A}$ outputs c to be challenge. $\mathcal{A}'$ chooses a random bit $\tau \in \{0, 1\}$ and constructs the response sanitized ciphertext CT^* as $CT_\tau^* = (c_2 c_0^{s_1} g^b, c_3((g^a)^{-1} c_1)^{s_1} Z, i^*)$, where g^b and Z are from (g, g^a, g^b, Z). Let $s_2 = b$, if $Z = g^{ab}$, then $CT_\tau^* = (c_2 c_0^{s_1} g^{s_2}, c_3(ks_{i^*} c_1)^{s_1} h_{i^*}^{s_2}, i^*)$. Therefore, CT^* is correct sanitized ciphertext when given the inputs (c, i^*).
- **Query Phase 2**.
  1) **Key query**. $\mathcal{A}$ makes key queries for $\mathcal{O}_R$ in this phase. $\mathcal{A}$ submits a query $q = (j, requester)$, $\mathcal{A}'$ outputs $\{-x_i\}_{i \in S}$.
  2) **San Query**. $\mathcal{A}$ makes sanitized ciphertext queries for $\mathcal{O}_E$ in this phase. $\mathcal{A}$ submits (i, m) and simulator $\mathcal{A}'$ responds the sanitized ciphertext $C' = $ ACE.San$(ks_i, $ ACE.Enc$(ke_i, m))$ using key ke_i and key ks_i.
- **Guess**. $\mathcal{A}$ returns a bit τ'. $\mathcal{A}'$ returns true if $\tau' = \tau$. Otherwise, false.

The analysis is similar to the previous proof. Therefore, if $\mathcal{A}$ breaks the no-write game with advantage ϵ, then $\mathcal{A}'$ can solve DDH problem with advantage of $\frac{\epsilon}{2}$(non-negligible). This completes the proof.

5.2   ABAC Protocol

Our protocol consists of six phases: **Initialization**, **Registration**, **Encryption**, **Sanitization**, **Decryption**, and **Open**. Meanwhile, let ACE.X, GS.X denote the algorithm X of the ACE scheme and group signature, respectively.

Initialization. The TA initializes system parameters and distributes the corresponding keys as follows: **ACE parameters**. The TA takes a security parameter λ and access control policy P as input, runs the ACE.Setup(λ, P) algorithm to get the public parameter and master secret key (PP_{ACE}, msk). **GS parameters**. The TA takes a security parameter λ as input, runs the GS.Setup(λ) algorithm to generate parameters $(PP_{GS}, gpk_{l_i}, gsk_{l_i}, ok_{l_i})_{l_i \in [n]}$ for each level l_i. **Release parameters**. The TA publishes the public keys $\{gpk_{l_i}\}_{l_i \in [n]}$ to all fog nodes and broadcasts public parameters (PP_{ACE}, PP_{GSi}) to all entities.

Registration. We present the registration processes of a task participant with identity id_s, a requester with identity id_r and a fog node, respectively. For the participant id_s, the TA first verifies his identity and determines the level l_i of access control policy. Then, TA executes the ACE.KeyGen(PP_{ACE}, $msk, l_i, participant$) and the GS.Enroll(id_s, gsk_{l_i}) to generate the corresponding encryption key ke_{l_i} and a signature key gsk_{id_s}. Finally, the TA sends the secret keys (ke_{l_i}, gsk_{id_s}) to the participant. For the requester id_r, the TA first verifies his identity and determines the level l_j of access control policy. Then, the TA runs the ACE.KeyGen($PP_{ACE}, msk, l_j, requester$) algorithm to generate a decryption key kd_{l_j}. Finally, the TA sends kd_{l_j} to the requester. Note that if $P(l_i, l_j) \neq 1$ holds, kd_{l_j} is a random element in Z_p^*. For the fog node, the TA executes the ACE.KeyGen($PP_{ACE}, msk, l_j, sanitizer$) algorithm to generate a sanitized key ks_{l_j}.

Encryption. When a participant id_s with level l_i tries to send a message m to a requester id_r in an anonymous way. The participant takes its encryption key ke_{l_i} and m as input, and executes the algorithm ACE.Enc($PP_{ACE}, m, ke_{l_i}, l_i$) to get the ciphertext C_{l_i}. Then, it runs the GS.GSig($gpk_{l_i}, gsk_{id_s}, C_{l_i}$) to a signature σ_{l_i} and sends the encrypted message $C = (C_{l_i}, \sigma_{l_i}, l_i)$ to a fog node.

Sanitization. In this phase, the fog node takes charge of processing the ciphertexts from the participants and sending the newly sanitized ciphertexts to the cloud server. Once receiving the ciphertext C from a participant with level l_i, the fog node first runs GS.Verify(gpk, σ_{l_i}, c) to check whether the signature σ is valid. The fog node executes the following steps if the signature σ_{l_i} is valid, otherwise he refuses the illegal transmission and terminates the sanitization process. The fog node picks ks_i as input, and executes algorithm ACE.San($PP_{ACE}, C_{l_i}, ks_{l_i}, l_i$) to generate the sanitized ciphertext CT_{l_i}. The fog node sends the sanitized ciphertext (CT_{l_i}, l_j) to the cloud server.

Decryption. In this phase, the requester with level l_j can ask for data from the cloud server through the fog node. The requester with level l_j first downloads the ciphertexts with level l_j from the cloud server through the fog node. Then it takes a ciphertext CT_{l_i} its decryption key kd_{l_j} as input, runs the algorithm ACE.Dec(CT_{l_i}, kd_{l_j}) to obtain the message. Only when the requester is a legitimate party according to the policy P, in other words, $P[l_i, l_j] = 1$, then it can get the original message m successfully; otherwise, it gets nothing about m.

Open. If there is a malicious participant in the above processes, the TA needs to reveal his real identity. The TA first recovers a tag tag_{l_i} of a signature σ_{l_i} from the malicious participant by executing the GS.Open($ok, C_{l_i}, \sigma_{l_i}$) algorithm, where ok is an opening key and C_{l_i} acts as a message of signature. The TA retrieves the real identity by tag_{l_i} from the $list = (ID_s, tag_{l_i})$.

6 Security Analysis

- **Confidentiality.** To guarantee the confidentiality of messages, each participant needs to encrypt m_i under his encryption key $ke_i = g^{\alpha_i}$. The encrypted message is re-encrypted by the fog node. Therefore, the confidentiality of m_i directly depends on the security of the proposed ACE scheme, We have proved that our proposed ACE construction satisfies the security definitions.

- **Anonymity**. The anonymity requires that the signatures do not reveal the identity of the signer. The anonymity is defined via an anonymit game, where the adversary's goal is to identify the index that is used to create the signature. In this game, the adversary $\mathcal{A}$ is allowed to collect all communication messages. However, $\mathcal{A}$ can never know the identity of the users but only know that which level do they belong to, since the anonymity of the group signature.
- **Traceability**. The traceability ensures that the adversary $\mathcal{A}$ cannot produce a signature such that it is unable to identify the origin of the signature. In the traceability game, $\mathcal{A}$ is allowed to corrupt any user, but it is not allowed to corrupt the group manager since he can produce dummy users. He wins if he can create a signature, whose signer cannot be identified or signer when creating a legal signature. Our ABAC protocol is clear traceable for the group signature.
- **Fine-Grained Bilateral Access Control**. As we use the ACE scheme to generate and distribute encryption keys, decryption keys, and sanitizer keys, we can make all data access satisfy our predetermined legal access policy P. The policy ensures that only the legal user can read or write as they own the correct keys, and no one can disrupt the access control policy P as our scheme satisfied the "no-read" rule and "no-write" rule.

7   Performance Evaluation

We implement our proposed ABAC protocol and evaluate its performance based on the PBC library (version 0.5.14) [2] and the GMP library (version 6.1.2) [1]. We use a Raspberry Pi (Quad-Core ARM Cortex A72, 1.5GHz, 2GB RAM, Raspberry Pi OS) to simulate an end smart device and use a PC (Intel Xeon(R) E5-1650 V4, 3.60GHz, 64GB RAM, Ubuntu 20.04) to act as a server. All the experimental results are the average of 100 runs for each test (Fig. 1).

Table 1. Statistical operations during the implementation process of ABAC

Phase	Cryptographic algorithms	Main cryptographic operations
Initialization	ACE.Setup + GS.Setup	$(n + 3) \cdot Exp$
Registration	ACE.KeyGen + GS.Enroll	$2 \cdot Exp$ or $3 \cdot Exp$
Encryption	ACE.Enc + GS.GSig	$3 \cdot Exp + 1 \cdot BP$
Sanitization	ACE.San + GS.Verify	$4 \cdot Exp + 3 \cdot BP$
Decryption	ACE.Dec	$1 \cdot Exp$
Open	GS.Open	$1 \cdot Exp$

Based on the statistical results, we can obtain a preliminary theoretical evaluation of the performance of ABAC. Exp denotes the exponent operation in group $\mathbb{G}_1$, BP denotes the bilinear pairing operation, and n denotes the number of levels in access control policy P. The main time costs of the above operations are 4.853 ms, 6.312 ms, 11.546 ms in the Raspberry, while they are 1.607 ms, 1.209 ms, 3.610 ms in the server. In addition, there are two situations at the registration state because the roles of the registered entity are different. If the entity is a participant or requester, the main operations are $2 \cdot Exp$, while the main operations are $3 \cdot Exp$ if the entity is a sanitizer.

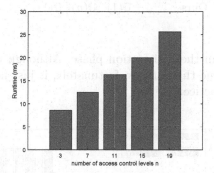

Fig. 2. Time costs of initialization phase under different n.

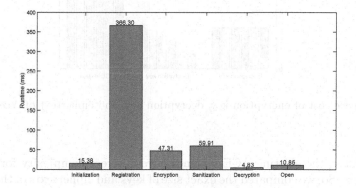

Fig. 3. Time cost of each phase of ABAC.

Then, to accurately evaluate the performance, we test the running time of our scheme both on PC and on Raspberry Pi. In our protocol, the initialization phase is related to the number of access control levels n. Figure 2 indicates that the time overhead of the initialization phase increases linearly with n. The time costs of the registration phase are related to the number of participants. Both the Enc algorithm and Dec algorithm are executed on Raspberry Pi. We initialize the system with 100 participants and the number of access control levels $n = 10$.

Figure 3 gives the running time of our protocol. From Fig. 3, it is obvious that the decryption process costs the minimum time, and the registration phase costs the maximum time. The main reason is that the TA needs to generate all

Table 2. Space cost of different ACE schemes

Scheme	ke	kd	C
Damgård [4]	$\mathbb{O}(n)$	$\mathbb{O}(1)$	$\mathbb{O}(n)$
Kim et al.	$\mathbb{O}(1)$	$\mathbb{O}(1)$	$poly(logN)$
Tan et al.	$\mathbb{O}(n)$	$\mathbb{O}(1)$	$\mathbb{O}(n)$
Ours	$\mathbb{O}(1)$	$\mathbb{O}(n)$	$\mathbb{O}(1)$

keys for each entity in the registration phase. Although the registration phase costs a little more time than others, fortunately, it just needs to run only once in our protocol in practice.

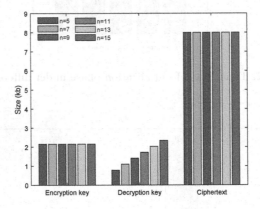

Fig. 4. Space cost of encryption key, decryption key, and ciphertext of ABAC with n growth.

Moreover, the existing ACE schemes have different complexity for keys and ciphertexts. So, we compared the exact size of keys and ciphertexts of the schemes used for experimental evaluation between some ACE schemes and ours. We have compared the items for size of encryption key ke, decryption key kd, and ciphertext C on Table 2. Figure 4 shows the effect of the parameter n on the encryption key ke, decryption key kd, and ciphertext C space costs in our scheme, where the parameters are set to $5, 7, \cdots, 15$. As shown in Fig. 4, the size of the decryption key has a linear relationship with the length of the parameter n, the size of the encryption key and ciphertext are not affected by the change of the parameter n. This is consistent with our theoretical analysis.

8   Conclusion

In this paper, considering the security and privacy problems of data access control in fog-assisted mobile crowdsensing, we first design an efficient access control encryption scheme with compact ciphertext size. Then, based on the proposed ACE and in combination with a constant-size group signature, we build an anonymous bilateral access control protocol with traceability for fog-assisted mobile crowdsensing. The security analysis and experimental evaluation show that the proposed protocol achieves the intended goals and meets the needs of fog-assisted mobile crowdsensing.

Acknowledgment. This work was supported by the National Natural Science Foundation of China (Nos. U20A20176 and 62072062), the Natural Science Foundation of Chongqing, China (No. cstc2019jcyjjqX0026), and the Guangxi Key Laboratory of Trusted Software (No. KX202043).

References

1. The GNU multiple precision arithmetic library. https://gmplib.org/
2. The pairing-based cryptography library. https://crypto.stanford.edu/pbc/
3. Capponi, A., Fiandrino, C., Kantarci, B., Foschini, L., Kliazovich, D., Bouvry, P.: A survey on mobile crowdsensing systems: challenges, solutions, and opportunities. IEEE Commun. Surv. Tutor. **21**(3), 2419–2465 (2019). https://doi.org/10.1109/COMST.2019.2914030
4. Damgård, I., Haagh, H., Orlandi, C.: Access control encryption: enforcing information flow with cryptography. In: Hirt, M., Smith, A. (eds.) TCC 2016. LNCS, vol. 9986, pp. 547–576. Springer, Heidelberg (2016). https://doi.org/10.1007/978-3-662-53644-5_21
5. Ganti, R.K., Ye, F., Lei, H.: Mobile crowdsensing: current state and future challenges. IEEE Commun. Mag. **49**(11), 32–39 (2011). https://doi.org/10.1109/MCOM.2011.6069707
6. Gisdakis, S., Giannetsos, T., Papadimitratos, P.: Security, privacy, and incentive provision for mobile crowd sensing systems. IEEE Internet Things J. **3**(5), 839–853 (2016). https://doi.org/10.1109/JIOT.2016.2560768
7. Ho, T.H., Yen, L.H., Tseng, C.C.: Simple-yet-efficient construction and revocation of group signatures. Int. J. Found. Comput. Sci. **26**(5), 611–624 (2015). https://doi.org/10.1142/S0129054115500343
8. Jin, H., Su, L., Xiao, H., Nahrstedt, K.: Inception: incentivizing privacy-preserving data aggregation for mobile crowd sensing systems. In: Proceedings of ACM International Symposium on Mobile Ad Hoc Networking and Computing (MobiHoc), pp. 341–350 (2016). https://doi.org/10.1145/2942358.2942375
9. Li, T., Jung, T., Qiu, Z., Li, H., Cao, L., Wang, Y.: Scalable privacy-preserving participant selection for mobile crowdsensing systems: participant grouping and secure group bidding. IEEE Trans. Netw. Sci. Eng. **7**(2), 855–868 (2018). https://doi.org/10.1109/TNSE.2018.2791948
10. Liu, B., Chen, L., Zhu, X., Zhang, Y., Zhang, C., Qiu, W.: Protecting location privacy in spatial crowdsourcing using encrypted data. In: Proceedings of International Conference on Extending Database Technology (EDBT) (2017). https://doi.org/10.5441/002/edbt.2017.49
11. Liu, J., Shen, H., Narman, H.S., Chung, W., Lin, Z.: A survey of mobile crowdsensing techniques: a critical component for the internet of things. ACM Trans. Cyber-Physical Syst. **2**(3), 1–26 (2018). https://doi.org/10.1145/3185504

12. Marjanović, M., Grubeša, S., Žarko, I.P.: Air and noise pollution monitoring in the city of Zagreb by using mobile crowdsensing. In: Proceedings of International Conference on Software, Telecommunications and Computer Networks (SoftCOM), pp. 1–5 (2017). https://doi.org/10.23919/SOFTCOM.2017.8115502

13. Miao, C., et al.: Cloud-enabled privacy-preserving truth discovery in crowd sensing systems. In: Proceedings of ACM Conference on Embedded Networked Sensor Systems (SenSys), pp. 183–196 (2015). https://doi.org/10.1145/2809695.2809719

14. Miao, C., Su, L., Jiang, W., Li, Y., Tian, M.: A lightweight privacy-preserving truth discovery framework for mobile crowd sensing systems. In: Proceedings of IEEE Conference on Computer Communications (INFOCOM) (2017). https://doi.org/10.1109/INFOCOM.2017.8057114

15. Ni, J., Zhang, A., Lin, X., Shen, X.S.: Security, privacy, and fairness in fog-based vehicular crowdsensing. IEEE Commun. Mag. **55**(6), 146–152 (2017). https://doi.org/10.1109/MCOM.2017.1600679

16. Ni, J., Zhang, K., Yu, Y., Lin, X., Shen, X.S.: Providing task allocation and secure deduplication for mobile crowdsensing via fog computing. IEEE Trans. Dependable Secure Comput. **17**(3), 581–594 (2018). https://doi.org/10.1109/TDSC.2018.2791432

17. Wang, J., Wang, Y., Zhang, D., Helal, S.: Energy saving techniques in mobile crowd sensing: current state and future opportunities. IEEE Commun. Mag. **56**(5), 164–169 (2018). https://doi.org/10.1109/MCOM.2018.1700644

18. Xiao, M., Wu, J., Zhang, S., Yu, J.: Secret-sharing-based secure user recruitment protocol for mobile crowdsensing. In: Proceedings of IEEE Conference on Computer Communications (INFOCOM) (2017). https://doi.org/10.1109/INFOCOM.2017.8057032

19. Xu, G., Li, H., Tan, C., Liu, D., Dai, Y., Yang, K.: Achieving efficient and privacy-preserving truth discovery in crowd sensing systems. Comput. Secur. **69**, 114–126 (2017). https://doi.org/10.1016/j.cose.2016.11.014

20. Ye, D., Mei, Y., Shang, Y., Zhu, J., Ouyang, K.: Mobile crowd-sensing context aware based fine-grained access control mode. Multimedia Tools Appl. **75**(21), 13977–13993 (2015). https://doi.org/10.1007/s11042-015-2693-3

21. Zheng, Y., Duan, H., Wang, C.: Learning the truth privately and confidently: encrypted confidence-aware truth discovery in mobile crowdsensing. IEEE Trans. Inf. Forensics Secur. **13**(10), 2475–2489 (2018). https://doi.org/10.1109/TIFS.2018.2819134

22. Zheng, Y., Duan, H., Yuan, X., Wang, C.: Privacy-aware and efficient mobile crowdsensing with truth discovery. IEEE Trans. Dependable Secure Comput. **17**(1), 121–133 (2017). https://doi.org/10.1109/TDSC.2017.2753245

Sector Error-Oriented Durability-Aware Fast Repair in Erasure-Coded Cloud Storage Systems

Yifei Xiao[1] , Shijie Zhou[1(✉)] , Linpeng Zhong[1] , and Zhao Zhang[2]

[1] School of Information and Software Engineering, University of Electronic Science and Technology of China, Chengdu, China
sjzhou@uestc.edu.cn
[2] School of Public Affairs and Administration, University of Electronic Science and Technology of China, Chengdu, China

Abstract. There is a variety of erasure-coded data placement schemes that make a great contribution to data repair. To repair data, the operator should replace the failed node with a new node first. However, almost all these schemes assume the node replacement process (NRP) is done quickly, which is not true. Generally, NRP includes failure detection and failure repair, which may take hours or even days. Long delay of replacement may cause the recovered data lost again due to the lack of durability. To improve data durability, we propose a novel scheme called Sector Error-Oriented Durability-Aware Fast Repair (SEDRepair), which carefully couples data migration and data reconstruction in parallel for data repair. We conduct mathematical analysis and compute the optimal repair in our model. The results show that, compared to the traditional erasure coding methods, SEDRepair saves the repair time by up to 60% in most cases and improves data durability while keeping minimal storage.

Keywords: Data repair · Node replacement · Sector error · Data durability · Erasure coding

1 Introduction

As failures are the norm in cloud storage systems, improving data reliability while maintaining the system performance during data repair is one of the most important challenges in the literature [12]. To guarantee data reliability in the face of failures, erasure coding techniques are gaining popularity due to their comparable fault tolerance with reduced storage overhead compared to simple replication.

A variety of data placement schemes based on erasure coding make a great contribution for data reliability [1,3,6,8,15]. To recover data, the operator should replace the failed node with a new node first. However, almost all these schemes assume the node replacement process (NRP) is done quickly, which is not true. Figure 1 shows an abstract model to characterize gray failure [9], which means

© Springer Nature Singapore Pte Ltd. 2021
Y. Tan et al. (Eds.): DMBD 2021, CCIS 1454, pp. 445–459, 2021.
https://doi.org/10.1007/978-981-16-7502-7_41

the external app observes a failure but the internal observer does not. While the model also reveals the general process of NRP, which is used to handle simple crash and fail-stop (CFS) failures. In general, as shown in Fig. 1, the process of NRP includes 2 steps: ❶ failure detection, in which the observer detect a CFS failure based on the external app's report or its own probing. If both the app and the observer agree that the system is experiencing a failure, a CFS failure can be confirmed, ❷ failure repair, in which the node replacement should be done and the reactor will do some repair work, such as rebooting or reconstruction.

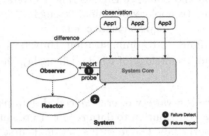

Fig. 1. The abstract model of a data center, in which there are 2 logical entities: a system, which provides a service, and an app, which uses system. Examples of a system include a distributed storage service, a data center network, a web search service, and an IaaS platform. An app could be a web application, a user, or an operator. The observer can check a failure either from the app's reports or its own probes, and this process is called **failure detection**. Once a failure is confirmed, the observer can inform reactor to handle it, such as rebooting or reconstruction, and this process is called **failure repair**.

NRP is not easy because every part of the process can be time-consuming. In failure detection, the observer asks the error detector to run at a certain period. The interval of detection can not be too short to degrade the performance of the system, or be too long to pick up the failure too late. Besides, nodes can become unavailable for a large number of reasons (e.g., a storage node is overloaded, a node binary may crash, a machine may experience a hardware error [5]). Fortunately, the vast majority of such unavailability events are transient and do not result in permanent data loss, but it still needs 15 min to filter most transient failures since less than 10% of events had node unavailability with a duration under 15 min [5]. Besides, waiting for the app's observation is also time-consuming, because users may not report or report soon even when they are afflicted by failures. In failure repair, the reboot scheme will take some time and NRP is also time-consuming since the system is online 24/7 while those operators are not. Therefore, NRP cannot be done immediately, the delay can be hours or even days.

The longer the delay NRP takes, the higher the risk of losing recovered data. To the best of our knowledge, there are only memories or caches can be used to save recovered data before NRP. Memory overflow, server malfunction or power outage could take place at any time, thus the updates of recovered data may be lost permanently due to the lack of durability (updates are very common, more than 90% of write requests are updates [18]).

It has long been recognized that encoding data into its erasure-coded form will incur a much heavier computation load than simple replication [20], thus there have been extensive studies on improving the repair performance of erasure coding, such as proposing theoretically proven erasure codes that minimize the repair traffic or I/Os [8,18] or proposing methods based on XOR operations to reduce the computation load [16], or to accelerate the computation by better utilizing the resources in modern CPUs [23]. **However, simple replication can offer continuous data durability in the face of failures, which is overlooked in the literature.** Against the above backdrop, we restrict our attention to data repair based on continuous data durability where it is required that any storage nodes can not impede data durability even during data repairing. To this end, we seek to answer the following questions: 1) How to guarantee data durability before NRP? Can we provide continuous data durability without adding extra storage (e.g., store data in other healthy nodes)? 2) Based on 1), how to repair lost blocks quickly after NRP?

To answer the above questions, we did a lot of research and proposed an effective scheme called Sector Error-Oriented Durability-Aware Fast Repair (SEDRepair) to speed up data repair.

- We first start to issue the problem of continuous data durability, and we mathematically analyze the optimal repair and its conditions to be met.
- We propose Sector Error-Oriented Durability-Aware Fast Repair (SEDRepair) to provide fast repair based on data durability when the sector error occurs.
- Our work is generic, i.e., it can combine with other erasure codes and tackle multi-failure cases.
- We conduct extensive test results and show that SEDRepair can effectively reduce the total repair time while maintaining continuous data durability.

The rest of the paper is organized as follows. In Sect. 2, we introduce background and our motivation. In Sect. 3, we conduct mathematical analysis of our model. In Sect. 4, we present the implementation of SEDRepair. We evaluate SEDRepair in Sect. 5 and introduce the related work in Sect. 6. Finally, the conclusion of our work is in Sect. 7.

2 Background and Motivation

2.1 Erasure Codes and RS Codes

A leading technique to achieve strong fault-tolerance in cloud storage systems is to utilize erasure codes. Erasure codes are usually specified by two parameters: the number of data symbols k to be encoded, and the number of coded symbols n to be produced [22]. The data symbols and the coded symbols are usually assumed to be in finite field $GF(2^w)$ in computer systems. A (n, k) erasure codes storage system composed of n nodes dedicates k nodes to data, and the remaining $(n - k)$ nodes are dedicated to coding.

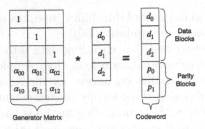

Fig. 2. The encoding process of RS(5, 3). The leftmost matrix is called *generator matrix*, which encodes data blocks (d_0, d_1, d_2) into codeword $(d_0, d_1, d_2, p_0, p_1)$.

RS codes [17] are a well-known erasure code construction and have been widely deployed in production [7,14,15,17,21]. RS(n, k) encodes k uncoded equal-size blocks into a stripe with n coded equal-size blocks via linear combinations based on $GF(2^w)$. Figure 2 shows the typical encoding process of RS(5, 3), where the leftmost matrix is called *generator matrix*, which can be generated from Vandermonde matrix [17] or Cauchy matrix [2]. The top k rows of the generator matrix compose a $k \times k$ *identity matrix* (here $k = 3$). The remaining m rows are called *coding matrix* [15] (here $m = n - k = 2$). The generator matrix encodes the data blocks (denoted by d_0, d_1, d_2) into a *codeword* $(d_0, d_1, d_2, p_0, p_1)$. Each block can refer to one symbol in the codeword. After encoding, data blocks (d_0, d_1, d_2) will be sent to the corresponding data nodes and the parity blocks (p_0, p_1) will be sent to the corresponding parity nodes. From Fig. 2 we can infer that, in a (n, k) RS-based cloud storage system, each parity block could be represented by the linear combination of the k data blocks with the following equation,

$$p_i = \sum_{j=0}^{k-1} \alpha_{i,j} d_j, i \in [0, m-1] \tag{1}$$

In this paper, we also use RS codes to generate the parity blocks.

2.2   Motivation

As mentioned in Sect. 1, NRP can be time-consuming, which may lead a lack of data durability for a long time. However, most of data repair schemes overlooked this problem, which increases the risk of losing data. In this paper, we seek to fill this gap in the literature.

Besides, there is a large body of work that overlooked the accessibility of the failed node with sector error, thus we utilize it to accelerate the process of data repair as well as improving data durability.

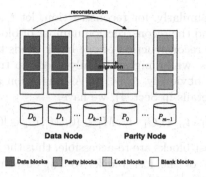

Fig. 3. The repair model for BN. (Color figure online)

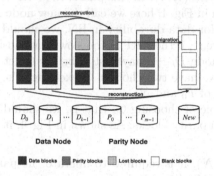

Fig. 4. The repair model for AN (the new node is as a data node).

3   Mathmatical Analysis

We conduct simple mathematical analysis to provide preliminary insights into the performance gain of the theoretical optimal repair over the conventional repair in a cloud storage system. For ease of presentation, we assume there is only one failed node.

In our model, we employ RS(n, k), thus we have k data nodes and $n - k$ parity nodes. We label the data nodes as $D_i, i \in [0, k-1]$ and the parity nodes as $P_j, j \in [0, m-1], m = n - k$. Generally, every node has identical number of blocks, and we denote it as U. Furthermore, as we only consider the failed node with sector error, i.e., we can use parts of the failed node. Let M denote the accessible number of blocks, thus the number of lost blocks is $U - M$. As shown in Fig. 3, the failed node D_{k-1} has $U - M$ lost blocks colored gray and M good blocks colored yellow.

As mentioned above, according to whether the NRP is done, we divided data repair into 2 phases: ① BN (before NRP), ② AN (after NRP).

For the First Phase (BN): As mentioned earlier, in BN, we can couple migration and reconstruction. For migration, let t_m, M_1 denote the time to migrate a block from one node to another node and the migration number of blocks in BN, respectively. Similarly, for reconstruction, let t_r, C_1 denote the time to reconstruct a block and the reconstruction number of blocks in BN, respectively. As Eq. (1) shows, the reconstruction of one block needs to receive k blocks from other k healthy nodes, while migration only needs to transmit one block from one node to another, obviously, $t_m < t_r$. As migration and reconstruction can run in parallel (see details in Sect. 4), we have,

$$T_1 = M_1 \cdot t_m = C_1 \cdot t_r, M_1 \in (0, M], C_1 \in [0, U - M] \tag{2}$$

Now, $(C_1 + M_1)$ lost blocks are re-accessible, thus the meta info server should change the addresses of the lost blocks to P_0, ensuring smooth connections between users and these lost blocks.

For the Second Phase (AN): In this phase, the NRP is done, i.e., a new node is available (as shown in Fig. 4, here we call the new node N). As P_0 stores some data blocks of D_{k-1} for data durability in BN, we should decide the roles of P_0 and N in this phase (e.g., if the NRP is too slow that most blocks of P_0 are data blocks of the failed node D_{k-1}, maybe it is better to let P_0 replace D_{k-1} as a new data node). So we have two choices: ① exchange the roles of P_0 and N, or ② maintain the roles of P_0 and N.

Taking the example of choosing ①, that is, we should fully fill P_0 with data blocks and fill N with parity blocks. As shown in Fig. 4, it is required to do three things:

1. Migration ($P_0 \rightarrow N$), it is required to migrate the parity blocks from P_0 to N, as P_0 receives M_1 data blocks from migration and C_1 data blocks from reconstruction in BN, there are $U - M_1 - C_1$ parity blocks colored green left which can be migrated to N (as $t_m < t_r$, we prefer to employ migration).
2. Reconstruction for N ($ER \rightarrow N$, ER means erasure coding), there are $M_1 + C_1$ blank blocks of N demanding to be filled by reconstruction.
3. Reconstruction for P_0 ($ER \rightarrow P_0$), as P_0 moves $U - M_1 - C_1$ parity blocks to N, these positions should be filled with data blocks by reconstruction.

Let T_2 and T be the repair time of AN and the total repair time, respectively. So we have,

$$\begin{aligned} T_2 = max((U - M_1 - C_1) \cdot t_m, \\ (M_1 + C_1) \cdot t_r, (U - M_1 - C_1) \cdot t_r) \\ = max((M_1 + C_1) \cdot t_r, (U - M_1 - C_1) \cdot t_r) \end{aligned} \tag{3}$$

$$T = T_1 + T_2 \tag{4}$$

From Eq. (2) to Eq. (4), we can readily show that T is minimized when $(M_1 + C_1) \cdot t_r = (U - M_1 - C_1) \cdot t_r$, so we get,

$$C_1 = \frac{t_m}{t_r} M_1 \tag{5}$$

$$C_1 + M_1 = \frac{U}{2} \tag{6}$$

If we choose ②, similarly, it is required to do three things:

1. Migration ($P_0 \rightarrow N$), as P_0 receives M_1 data blocks from migration and C_1 data blocks from reconstruction in BN, we have $M_1 + C_1$ data blocks colored yellow which can be migrated to N.
2. Reconstruction for N ($ER \rightarrow N$), N still need $U - M_1 - C_1$ data blocks which are generated by reconstruction.
3. Reconstruction for P_0 ($ER \rightarrow P_0$), as P_0 moves $M_1 + C_1$ parity blocks to N, these positions should be filled with data blocks by reconstruction.

So we have,

$$
\begin{aligned}
T_2 &= max((M_1 + C_1) \cdot t_m, \\
&\quad (U - M_1 - C_1) \cdot t_r, (M_1 + C_1) \cdot t_r) \\
&= max((M_1 + C_1) \cdot t_r, (U - M_1 - C_1) \cdot t_r)
\end{aligned}
\tag{7}
$$

The Interesting Thing is, no Matter we Choose ① or ②, T_2 is the Same. But here is the special case: if NRP is not finished(e.g., the operator notices the failed node too late) until all the migrations and reconstructions have been completed in P_0, which means, P_0 is totally a 'DataNode'. Obviously, ① is the better choice. Except for the special case, ① and ② have the same result.

In conclusion, Eq. (5) and Eq. (6) are the conditions of achieving the optimal repair, which is in accordance with the results of our simulation experiments in Sect. 5.

In this section, we only analyze the single-failure case, but if there are m failed data nodes, e.g., $D_i, i \in [0, m-1]$ is failed, we can set $(D_i, P_i), i \in [0, m-1]$ as pairs, and use the same method to repair them. Therefore, the scheme can also be used in multi-failure cases.

4   Implementation

To address data durability in data repair, we propose a novel scheme Sector Error-Oriented Durability-Aware Fast Repair (SEDRepair), which is divided into 2 parts: 1) BN, 2) AN.

Similar to [20], to simplify our analysis, we do not address disk I/O interference, which occurs in the following cases: ❶ a node reads a block for reconstruction and reads another block for reconstruction, and ❷ a node reads a block while writing another block. Meanwhile, we do not consider the computational costs of coding operations, which are negligible compared to disk I/Os and network transmission [10].

4.1   BN

First let us review the first question: 1) How to provide data durability before NRP? As mentioned earlier, updates are common in cloud storage systems.

Before NRP, we can only store the updates of the failed node in caches or memories, however, this is dangerous. To improve the data durability, we set the parity node as the temporary place for the data blocks of the failed node, since it's known that the parity node stores linear combinations of other data blocks instead of primitive data. Therefore, it's acceptable to replace parity blocks with data blocks for data durability.

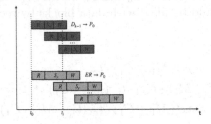

Fig. 5. The pipeline model of BN. (Color figure online)

Choosing the parity node as the temporary storage node to provide data durability is a straightforward way, but it's provably effective. Besides, it's not required to use extra storage to save data.

Feasibility for Parallel: In Sect. 3, t_m and t_r represent the time to migrate a block from one node to another node and the time to reconstruct a block of the failed node, respectively. Now we extend our general formulation to model the values of t_m and t_r in detail.

Figure 5 illuminates the reason why we can couple migration and reconstruction in parallel: for migration $(D_{k-1} \to P_0)$, t_m (the blue bars) consists of three parts:

- R, the read time of a block,
- S_m, the transmission time of a block from one node to another;
- W, the write time of a block;

For ease of presentation, we assume $R = W$. For reconstruction $(ER \to P_0)$, t_r (the green bars) also consists of three parts:

- R, the read time of a block, which occurs in k helpers,
- S_r, the total transmission time of all k helpers for sending k blocks, because $t_m < t_r$, we get $S_m < S_r$;
- W, the write time of a block;

At any moment of BN (e.g., at t_i in Fig. 5), where it is required to do three things for migration:

1. writing a block in P_0;
2. transferring a block from D_{k-1} to P_0;
3. reading a block in D_{k-1};

As mentioned above, we do not consider the disk I/O interference, thus they can run in parallel. On the other hand, we focus on the green part, where it is required to do 2 things for reconstruction: 1) transferring k blocks to P_0; 2) reading k blocks from k helpers;

Obviously, we can also perform them in parallel. Therefore, it is feasible to couple migration and reconstruction in BN.

Algorithm 1: BN Algorithm

Data:

the number of good blocks in the failed node M;

the number of blocks in a node U ;

the past time before new node is available mt;

Result:

the number of lost blocks repaired in BN C;

    // migration

1 **if** $R > S_m$ **then**

2 | $t_{max} = R; t_{min} = S_m$;

3 **else**

4 | $t_{max} = S_m; t_{min} = R$;

5 **end**

6 $mCnt = (mt - t_{min} - W)/t_{max}$;

7 $mTime = M \times t_{max} + t_{min} + W$;

8 **if** $mCnt < M$ **then**

9 | $C = mCnt$;

10 **else**

11 | $C = M$,

12 **end**

    // reconstruction

13 **if** $W > S_r$ **then**

14 | $t_{max} = W; t_{min} = S_r$;

15 **else**

16 | $t_{max} = S_r; t_{min} = W$;

17 **end**

18 $rCnt = (mt - t_{min} - R)/t_{max}$;

19 $rTime = (U - M) \times t_{max} + t_{min} + R$;

20 **if** $rCnt > (U - M)$ **then**

21 | $C = C + rCnt$;

22 **else**

23 | $C = C + (U - M)$;

24 **end**

25 $T_1 = max(mTime, rTime)$;

Algorithm Details: Algorithm 1 presents the main idea of BN. Let C denote the number of blocks in the failed node repaired in BN, and mt denote the past time before new node is available (if $T_1 < mt$, that means the repair is over but new node has not arrived). As shown in Fig. 5, we should align the blue bars based on the longest time consumer (here $R > S_m$, we align the blue bars based on R), and store it to t_{max} (lines 1–5). According to the number of good blocks M and mt, we can get the number of blocks for migration, and preserve it to C (lines 6–12).

Meanwhile, we can do reconstruction for lost blocks. Similarly, we first get the longest time consumer for pipelined work (lines 13–17), and then we can get the $rCnt$ which preserves the number of blocks for reconstruction (lines 17–24). Finally, we compute the repair time of the first phase stored in T_1 and return the number of blocks repaired C.

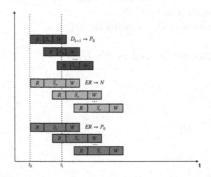

Fig. 6. The pipeline model of AN. (Color figure online)

4.2 An

Feasibility for Parallel: Similarly, Fig. 6 illuminates the reason why we can couple migration and reconstruction in parallel. At t_i, the only difference between BN and AN is that, we should read 2 blocks in every helper, but as mentioned above, we do not address the IO interference, thus we can perform them in parallel.

As the conclusion we make in Sect. 3, the AN algorithm is very easy to implement. Thus, we do not show it in this paper.

This is our answer to the second question: 2) How to fast repair lost blocks after NRP? Similar with BN, we can also couple migration and reconstruction to do the repair in parallel.

In conclusion, SEDRepair consists of two phases: BN and AN, BN is used to offer temporary data durability until the NRP is done, while AN is used to complete the conventional data repair and offer continuous data durability.

5 Performance Evaluation

Experimental Setup: To verify our model, we conduct an number of tests, which focus on the total repair time for data repair and the service time for requesting one block. All tests in this work are conducted on a workstation with an Intel Core i7 CPU (4 cores) running at 2.2 GHz, 16 GB DDR3 memory, which runs the Ubuntu 18.04 64-bit operating system and the compiler is GCC 7.3.0 which is the default compiler of the OS. Using different compilers and different compiler options may yield slightly different coding throughputs, but will not change the relative relationship among different repair methods, when the same compiler and compiler options are used across them.

In our tests, we remove all the actual operations of disk I/Os and network transmission from the prototype, and simulate the operations by computing their execution times based on the input network and disk bandwidths. We compare SEDRepair with two approaches:

1. ERT (reconstruction-only), which is the conventional method based on RS codes, ERT only use reconstruction operations;
2. ER (reconstruction-only, with durability), which is based on ERT, but ER preserves recovered data in the parity nodes in BN. That is, ER offers data durability.

We encode the blocks by RS(5, 3), RS(9, 6) (adopted by QFS [13]) and RS(14, 10) (adopted by Facebook [11]). Our implementation is based on encoding and decoding APIs from Jerasure library 2.0 [15].

We assume the following default configurations. We set the disk bandwidth as 100 MB/s and network bandwidth as 1 Gb/s. We configure both the block size and the packet size as 64 MB. The number of blocks in every node is fixed as 1000 blocks ($U = 1000$) in each experimental run for consistent test. We compare SEDRepair with ER and ERT. We plot the total repair time over ten runs.

Experiment A.1 (comparison of service time): First we consider the service time per request. As app users can directly get data from memory instead of disk, the service time only consists of read time (R in Fig. 5) and transmission time (S_m and S_r in Fig. 5). As shown in Fig. 7a, the service time of SEDRepair and ER is shorter than ERT, because ERT store recovered data in the memory of the failed node in BN, which needs k blocks from k helpers. But SEDRepair and ER first store data in the memory of the parity node in BN, which only need $k - 1$ blocks from helpers (as the parity node has a parity block for reconstruction), thus the average service time of SEDRepair and ER is 1.64 s in RS(5, 3), 3.14 s in RS(9, 6), and 5.14 s in RS(14, 10).

We next consider five possible factors for total repair time: 1) the proportion of lost blocks, 2) the parameters of n and k, 3) the first phase time T_1, 4) the block size, 5) the packet size.

Experiment A.2 (impact of lost block): Figure 7b shows the simulation results of the total repair time in different methods, in which we vary the proportion of good blocks in the failed node from 0% to 100%, among which ER is the worst, since its performance is bottlenecked by the network consumption and I/O of the failed node. ERT is better than ER in most cases, but it can not offer data durability in BN. Overall, SEDRepair reduces the repair time of both ER and ERT, for example, by 68.0% and 63.3% when P = opt, which is computed by Eq. (5) and Eq. (6).

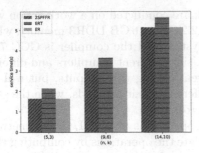

(a) The service time comparison under different (n, k).

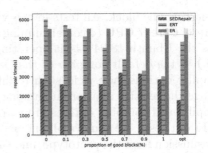

(b) The repair time comparison under different amount of good blocks.

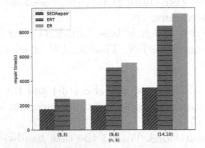

(c) The repair time comparison under different (n, k).

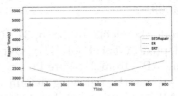

(d) The repair time comparison under different T_1.

Fig. 7. The comparison under different service time, good blocks, (n, k) and T_1.

Experiment A.2 (impact of erasure coding): We now evaluate the total repair time for different RS(n, k). Here, we focus on RS(5, 3), RS(9, 6), and RS(14, 10). We assume that $T_1 = 500$ s, the proportion of good blocks is set to 30% (i.e., $P = 300, U = 1000$). Figure 7c shows the results. The repair time of ERT and ER increases significantly in RS(9, 6) and RS(14, 10) compared to RS(5, 3), as it increases the amount of repair traffic. Overall, SEDRepair reduces the repair time of ERT and ER by 60.7% and 63.6% in RS(9, 6), 59.4% and 63.7% in RS(14, 10), and 32.1% and 33.5% in RS(5, 3), respectively.

Experiment A.3 (impact of T_1): As mentioned earlier, it may take a long time for NRP, thus we evaluate the impacts of different T_1. We keep good blocks 70% and select RS(9, 6). We range T_1 from 100 s to 900 s. As shown in Fig. 7d, the performance of ER and ERT remains unaffected by different T_1, since no matter how long it takes before the new node available, when the requests come, they can only employ reconstruction to repair data, and fill all blanks of the new node by decoding. The blue line shows the impact of T_1 for SEDRepair, where there is a minimum value near 500 s. Our analysis shows that different T_1 makes different amount of migration and computation operations, and produce different proportion of data blocks in AN. According to Eq. (5) to Eq. (6), the

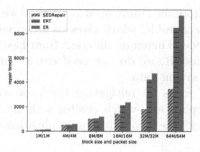

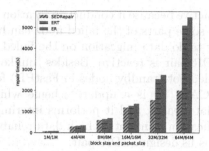

(a) The repair time under different block size and packet size in RS(14, 10).

(b) The repair time under different block size and packet size in RS(9, 6).

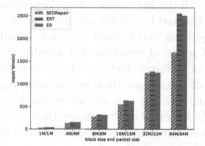

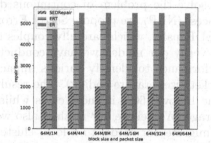

(c) The repair time under different block size and packet size in RS(5, 3).

(d) The repair time in different packet size in RS(9, 6).

Fig. 8. The repair time in different packet size.

closer $\frac{M_1}{C_1}$ is to $\frac{t_m}{t_r}$, the shorter the repair time is. Thus, it is consistent with our analysis.

Experiment A.4 (impact of block size and packet size): Figure 8 shows the repair time in the impact of different block size and packet size. We found that when the block size and packet size is small (i.e., from 1M to 8M), the difference among them is not significantly obvious in the performance of repairing data. However, if the block size > 8M, our method performs much more greater than ER and ERT, not only because of coupling migration and reconstruction, but also because the network becomes dominant. Meanwhile, we found that, as shown in Fig. 8d, the packet size has little influence on our model.

6   Related Work

We focus on the continuous data durability throughout the whole data repair. The main design of our work is mainly based on FastPR (G = 1) [20], which couples migration and reconstruction operations in parallel. But FastPR is proactive because it conducts migration before the failure occurs. From [4] we can see, some parts of the failed node can be accessible, which gives us an opportunity to do data migration on the failed node. Therefore, different from FastPR, SEDRepair is reactive. Besides, unlike FastPR, we do not need extra storage (called hot-standby nodes in FastPR) for saving data.

CAU [19] is a update scheme which focus on mitigating the rack-across update traffic, and it performs interim replication, which creates a short-lived replication to maintain high data reliability. The idea of interim replication also helps us design SEDRepair.

7   Conclusion

To solve the problem of continuous data durability before node replacement process (NRP), we propose Sector Error-Oriented Durability-Aware Fast Repair (SEDRepair), which carefully couples migration and reconstruction in parallel. To verify our model, we have conducted series of experimental studies on its performance to identify various impacts of different facts (such as block size, packet size, erasure coding). The results of tests show that we can save repair time by over 60% in most cases while maintaining fast service without extra storage. We believe our method also works in a real environment, thus we plan to migrate our model to a local cluster and Amazon EC2. Besides, the multi-failure case is also our future consideration.

Acknowledgment. We thank the anonymous reviewers for their insightful feedback. We also appreciate Jingwei Li, Zhirong Shen and Hu Xiong for their sincere help.

References

1. Blaum, M., Brady, J., Bruck, J., Menon, J.: Evenodd: an efficient scheme for tolerating double disk failures in raid architectures. IEEE Trans. Comput. **44**(2), 192–202 (1995)
2. Blömer, J., Kalfane, M., Karp, R., Karpinski, M., Luby, M., Zuckerman, D.: An XOR-based erasure-resilient coding scheme (1995)
3. Chan, J.C., Ding, Q., Lee, P.P., Chan, H.H.: Parity logging with reserved space: towards efficient updates and recovery in erasure-coded clustered storage. In: 12th {USENIX} Conference on File and Storage Technologies ({FAST} 2014), pp. 163–176 (2014)
4. Emami, T.K.: Partial disk failures and improved storage resiliency, November 2011
5. Ford, D., et al.: Availability in globally distributed storage systems (2010)
6. Huang, C., Li, J., Chen, M.: On optimizing XOR-based codes for fault-tolerant storage applications. In: 2007 IEEE Information Theory Workshop, pp. 218–223. IEEE (2007)
7. Huang, C., et al.: Erasure coding in windows azure storage, p. 2 (2012)
8. Huang, C., Xu, L.: STAR: an efficient coding scheme for correcting triple storage node failures. IEEE Trans. Comput. **57**, 889–901 (2008)

9. Huang, P., et al.: Gray failure: the achilles' heel of cloud-scale systems. In: Proceedings of the 16th Workshop on Hot Topics in Operating Systems, pp. 150–155 (2017)
10. Khan, O., Burns, R., Plank, J.S., Pierce, W., Huang, C.: Rethinking erasure codes for cloud file systems: minimizing I/O for recovery and degraded reads, p. 20 (2012)
11. Muralidhar, S., et al.: F4: Facebook's warm {BLOB} storage system. In: 11th {USENIX} Symposium on Operating Systems Design and Implementation ({OSDI} 2014), pp. 383–398 (2014)
12. Nachiappan, R., Javadi, B., Calheiros, R.N., Matawie, K.M.: Cloud storage reliability for big data applications: a state of the art survey. J. Netw. Comput. Appl. **97**, 35–47 (2017)
13. Ovsiannikov, M., Rus, S., Reeves, D., Sutter, P., Rao, S., Kelly, J.: The quantcast file system. Proc. VLDB Endow. **6**(11), 1092–1101 (2013)
14. Plank, J.S.: The raid-6 liberation code. Int. J. High Perform. Comput. Appl. **23**(3), 242–251 (2009)
15. Plank, J.S., Simmerman, S., Schuman, C.D.: Jerasure: a library in C/C++ facilitating erasure coding for storage applications-version 1.2. University of Tennessee, Technical report, CS-08-627, 23 (2008)
16. Plank, J.S., Xu, L.: Optimizing cauchy reed-solomon codes for fault-tolerant network storage applications. In: Fifth IEEE International Symposium on Network Computing and Applications (NCA 2006), pp. 173–180. IEEE (2006)
17. Reed, I.S., Solomon, G.: Polynomial codes over certain finite fields. J. Soc. Ind. Appl. Math. **8**(2), 300–304 (1960)
18. Shen, J., Zhang, K., Gu, J., Zhou, Y., Wang, X.: Efficient scheduling for multi-block updates in erasure coding based storage systems. IEEE Trans. Comput. **67**(4), 573–581 (2017)
19. Shen, Z., Lee, P.P.C.: Cross-rack-aware updates in erasure-coded data centers, p. 80 (2018)
20. Shen, Z., Li, X., Lee, P.P.C.: Fast predictive repair in erasure-coded storage, pp. 556–567 (2019)
21. Vajha, M., et al.: Clay codes: Moulding MDS codes to yield an MSR code. In: 16th USENIX Conference on File and Storage Technologies (FAST 2018), Oakland, CA, pp. 139–154. USENIX Association, February 2018
22. Wicker, S.B., Bhargava, V.K.: Reed-Solomon Codes and Their Applications. Wiley, Hoboken (1999)
23. Zhou, T., Tian, C.: Fast erasure coding for data storage: a comprehensive study of the acceleration techniques. ACM Trans. Storage (TOS) **16**(1), 1–24 (2020)

ACT: Anonymous Consensus Based on Tor

Xingyu Li[1]([✉])(iD), Ziyu Zheng[2](iD), and Pengyu Chen[1,2]

[1] Guangzhou University, No. 230, Zhonghuan West Road, Panyu District,
Guangzhou, Guangdong, China
[2] Hangzhou Dianzi University, 1158, 2nd Street, Jianggan District, Hangzhou,
Zhejiang, China

Abstract. As the core of blockchain technology, consensus mechanism
determines the security, stability and availability of the system. Most of
consensus mechanisms including Po-X, X-BFT and so on mainly focuse
on the design and improvement of the consensus layer while the privacy
of nodes is ignored. It leads to the emergence of node corruption and conspiracy attacks. In this paper, we present ACT, anonymous consensus
mechanism for consortium blockchain. ACT uses anonymous communication mechanism, based on Onion Routing Technology Tor, to protect
node privacy and prevent the corruption of consensus nodes. To reduce
the computational power consumption, ACT abandons the traditional
attempt conversion and mining mechanism while double ring threshold
signature is adopted. Besides, we design a set of identity authentication mechanism NKC for ACT based on the improved Keberos protocol,
which reduces the probability of Byzantine nodes to a certain extent.

Keywords: Blockchain · Anonymous consensus · Privacy protection ·
Internet of things

1 Introduction

Under the background of mega data era, data sharing and interconnection of all
things have become an inevitable trend. The rapid increase of IoT [1] devices
has brought many problems to network management. Privacy leaks and false
information floods the IoT [2], which greatly decreases the user experience of the
Internet of Things. In 2008, Nakamoto proposed the concept of blockchain [3].
The blockchain uses consensus mechanism to ensure multiple nodes to reach an
agreement on a certain proposal in a distributed and unreliable communication
network, which provides a new idea for solving the problem of IoT. The combination of blockchain and IoT is not only conducive to Internet of Things data
security, but also helps to reduce the cost of IoT centralization.

At present, experts and scholars have proposed their own solutions from the
perspective of the consensus mechanism in response to the challenges faced by

---

Supported by Guangzhou University.
Hangzhou Dianzi University.

the application of blockchain technology in the Internet of Things [2]. However, these still fail to consider issues such as energy consumption, communication efficiency and scalability in the IoT scenario.

In this paper, we propose ACT, a high-efficiency, consortium blockchain consensus algorithm suitable for the IoT. The approach focuses on improving the consensus efficiency and robustness of the consortium blockchain as well as protecting the privacy of the nodes in consortium blockchain. Besides, the communication network and authentication mechanism have been reconstructed. Moreover, threshold signature schemes and aggregate signatures schemes are used to replace mining to reduce computing power consumption and improve consensus efficiency.

In general, our major contributions are as follow:

- An improved network communication scheme based on tor is elaborated, which effectively improve the communication efficiency and consensus credibility.
- A complete consensus system is constructed based on the multi-channel consensus algorithm of threshold signature and the experimental results prove that the approach is feasible and compatible.

The rest of this article is structured as follows. Section 2 describes the background knowledge related to this research. Section 3 mainly introduces the anonymous consensus algorithm based on Tor. Section 4 introduces threshold signature and Sect. 5 present the experimental analysis and evaluation. Section 6 introduces the related work. Finally, we summarizes the work of the paper and prospectes the research direction of future work in Sect. 7.

2   Background

We introduce the background related to blockchain, and elaborate the advantages of DAG consensus mechanism in blockchain. Lastly, we provide the necessary knowledge of cryptography.

2.1   IoT and Tor

Cloud service devices are difficult to meet the explosive growth of management needs and data privacy protection needs due to the centralized device management scheme of the IoT.

Tor [4] based on multi-layer encryption and multi-layer proxy forwarding technology [5] can guarantee the concealment of data and identity of communicators by confusing the traffic of different users. Tor is mainly divided into four types of nodes: directory server, ordinary users, onion routing and bridge. All nodes in Tor use consistent link scheduling algorithm and data forwarding communication protocol under the coordination of directory server to ensure the smoothness of network communication. At the same time, the anonymous communication mechanism provided by tor network can improve the credibility of consensus and reduce the damage of Byzantine nodes.

In this work, we analyze the cause of the large delay in the traditional Tor. By introducing the incentive mechanism and using the link scheduling algorithm based on weighted polling scheduling to improve the network mechanism of Tor, and design an anonymous communication scheme for the consensus algorithm.

2.2 Consortium Blockchain

Blockchain is a distributed ledger storage technology [2,3]. It can be divided into public chain and license chain according to different functions. Public chain has high flexibility and scalability, but it also has many problems, such as large amount of calculation, long consensus time, privacy leakage, data fork node, Byzantine node and so on.

The Permissioned Blockchain including Private Blo-ckchain and Consortium Blockchain is a customized blockchain [6] for the privatization system, in which nodes need to be authorized to join. Private blockchain consensus cycle is short, high efficiency, and has high data privacy protection and data fork resistance ability. However, due to too strict node restrictions, it can not meet the needs of interconnection between different institutions of the Internet of things. Consortium Blockchain is a compromise between the two kinds of blockchains. It can not only reduce the number of Byzantine nodes to a certain extent, but also reduce the consumption of computing power and shorten the consensus time.

2.3 Threshold Signature

As the foundation of threshold cryptography, secret sharing scheme [7] is mainly used for secret sharing without trusted center. The biggest advantage of the algorithm is that the availability of the private key is not affected by a small number of fault participants so that it has high security and robustness. SM2 elliptic curve threshold signature algorithm [8] includes three parts: key generation, signature generation and signature verification. Before using SM2 threshold signature scheme, it is generally necessary to use secret sharing scheme to share private key d. In addition, in order to avoid the attacker to calculate the private key, we need to strictly guarantee the privacy of the random number k.

We realize consensus of nodes through introducing double ring threshold signature, which can effectively ensure the security of node data and reduce the probability of single point of failure and multi-point conspiracy. The efficient signature mechanism also greatly reduces the consumption of computing power.

3 Network Authentication Mechanism Based on Kerberos

The improved network access authentication mechanism based on Kerberos [9] adds a public key storage center and a network access view comparing the taditional Kerberos. At the same time, the original underlying cryptographic algorithm is replaced by the national standard cryptographic algorithm. The structure of the scheme is shown in Fig. 1. The detailed process of the scheme is as follows:

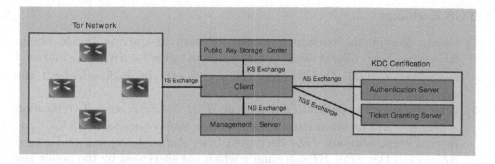

Fig. 1. Improved identity authentication scheme

KS Exchange

1) *Client* sends the access request packet containing the access request prompt *In* and ID_C to the public key storage center KS.
2) Upon receiving the request, KS will use ID_C to query the user's public key. If not, it will reply with an error message *Error* and a *DH* key negotiation parameter R_A. If the query to the reply *Client* two packets, a use *Client* public-key encryption, contains the access permission prompt *Admit*, *AS* of IP address, and As public key. The other is encrypted with the public key of *AS* and contains the user identity ID_C and IP_C.
3) If *Client* receive the packet, with the private key to decrypt and obtain IP_{AS} and $KPUB.AS$, and directly into the AS Exchange. Otherwise, *Client* reply KS a tip which contains key agreement Ck and parameter R_C packets.
4) KS takes out the R_C which is used to calculate the temporary communication key K_C and uses the $SM2$ key generation protocol to generate a set of public and private keys. At the same time, KS stores the public key and user identity information, and then replies to *Client* two packets. One is the packet encrypted with K_C contains the user's private key $KPRI.C$ and the timestamp ET_C, a random number r and so on. The other is encrypted with the public key of *AS*, and the packet contains the user ID_C, and IP_C.

After receiving the data packet, *Client* verifies whe-ther the data packet has timed out or been replayed and obtain its own private key At the same time, it also obtains the *IP* address and public key of *AS* and finally enters the *AS* Exchange.

AS Exchange

1) *Client* sends two data packets to *AS*, one packet encrypted with the public key of *AS* contains ID_C, ID_{TGS}, and r. The other is received from the previous view.
2) *AS* first decrypts the received packet with its own private key. After validation, *AS* get the public key of *Client* from KS and use it to encrypt session keys, TGT and TGS information, etc. Then *Client* enter TGS Exchange.

TGS Exchange

1) *Client* decrypt the packets from the AS with his private key to obtain $SK_{C, TGS}$. Next, *Client* takes r times $SM3$ operation for $SK'_{C, TGS}$ and send two packets to TGT. One is using $SK'_{C, TGS}$ to encrypt *Authenticator_1*, the other is TGT.

2) After receiving the packet, TGS decrypts TGT for $SK_{C, TGS}$, if verification is passed, r will be taken out and take r times $SM3$ operation for $SK'_{C, TGS}$. In next step, compare ID_C decrypted from *Authent icator_1* and return $SK_{C, NS}$, ID_C, IP_C, ET_{Ticket} and r which are encrypted by the public key of NS if they are the same. Finally reply *Client* the encrypted data with $SK'_{C, TGS}$ and encrypted *Ticket*. With $KPUB.S$.

NS Exchange

1) *Client* use $SK'_{C, TGS}$ to decrypt for $SK_{C, S}$ and *Ticket*, then r times of $SM3$ operation with $SK_{C, S}$ for $SK'_{C, S}$. At the same time, *Client* use $SK'_{C, S}$ to encrypt basic information generating *Authenticato− r_2*. Finally *Client* take *Authenticator_2* and *Ticket* together to NS.

2) NS uses $KPRI.S$ to decrypt *Ticket*, and get basic information after receiving the data, verify whether the timeout or replay if not by $SK_{C, S}$ with r times $SM3$ operation for $SK'_{C, S}$, then use it to decrypt *Authenticator_2* to obtain ID_C. Compare it with ID_C in *Ticket* and return $i + 1$ to *Client* if they are the same. Then the network management server NS communicates with *Client* by $SK'_{C, S}$. While *Client* receiving packets is represented to complete the authentication process, and goes into the TN Exchange. The network management server assigns *Client* access points and sends the public routing key at the edge of the access point to it.

TN Exchange

1) *Client* encrypts their public key $KPUB.C$ and identity information ID_C with edge router public key $KPUB.T$, and then package sent to edge routers *Client*.

The edge router uses its private key to decrypt the packets which sent from the client to obtain the client's public key. Then two sides can communicate cryptographically using the $SM2$ algorithm. The complete communication process is shown in Fig. 2.

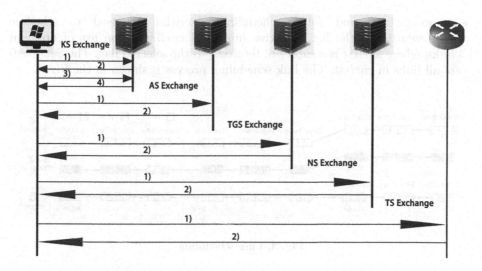

Fig. 2. Improved authentication scheme structure

4 Network Anonymous Communication Mechanism Based on Tor

In the improved network communication mechanism based on Tor, the directory server is changed into a network management server. In addition to managing routing information, the network management server also needs to receive access requests from clients and provides access parameters for users according to the network topology. The concrete implementation of the improvement scheme is as follows:

- Only members of the alliance are allowed to communicate.
- Congestion control mechanism based on Defenestrator. Each onion route maintains two credit values, namely the fixed credit value $N2$ and the variable credit value $N3$ set by the system. The algorithm flow is shown in Algorithm 1.

Algorithm 1. Congestion control mechanism

1: **while** $N_3 > 1$ **do**
2:    The routing node sends a data unit to the downlink
3:    $N_3 = N_3 - 1$
4:    $count = count + 1$
5:    **if** $count = N_2$ **then**
6:       routing node sends available queue length$(N_3 - count)$ to uplink
7:       **if** $congestion = 0$ **then**
8:          The uplink node receives data and updates it
9:       **else**
10:         $N_3 = 0$
11:      **end if**
12:   **end if**
13: **end while**

- A weighted round robin scheduling algorithm is used to schedule links.*totallist* is the list of active links and *curlist* is the list of optional links, where *curlist* is a subset of *totalist.f* is the selected flag. The Set $f = 0$ of all links in *curlist*. The link scheduling process is shown in the Fig. 3.

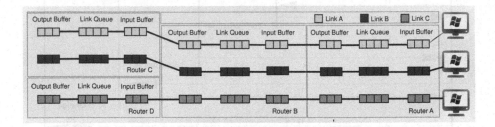

Fig. 3. Link scheduling

The implementation process of the algorithm is as follows:

  i. Select a link circularly from *curlist*, mark the selected time stamp of the link, and set $f = 1$.

  ii. If $f = 1$ of all links in the *curlist*, delete the link with the smallest weight in *curlist* and go to iii.

  iii. If the length of *curlist* is not zero, turn back to 1, otherwise turn back to iv.

  iv. The current time is used as a parameter to recalculate the weights of all active links. Add these links back to the *curlist*, set the selected flag $f = 1$, and return i.

- The maximum number of links to which the buffer can be loaded is 3. If the limit is exceeded, a new buffer will be created.
- Limit the number of proxy encryption layers to 1 at most, that is, only one encryption and decryption in a forwarding process.

5   Consensus Scheme Based on Threshold Signature

The consensus scheme based on threshold signature is the core of the algorithm. The user nodes that have passed the identity authentication and established a connection with the edge router need to agree on their transaction information through the consensus scheme. Nodes participating in the consensus communicate using the anonymous communication scheme introduced above. The consensus scheme is consisted of two modules, including node management and node consensus. The two modules will operate alternately.

5.1   Node Management

Node management is consisted of two links, including parameter update and reputation evaluation. In the parameter update link, the network management server firstly generates two sets of SM2 keys. The public keys will be sent to the distributed ledger and the inner ring node responsible for block generation in the next round. One private key will be shared to other inner ring nodes by SM2 threshold signature algorithm. The other private key will be shared to all outer ring nodes by SM2 threshold signature algorithm. All nodes needs will receive the key shares$_i$, update key share and involve to reply and verify. In this process, the network management server will strictly monitor. If some nodes do not update parameters, the network management server will deduct a certain reputation value of the nodes.

In the credibility evaluation link, the network management server will organize and count report information received within a cycle period. Then it will evaluate the reputation value of all nodes according the statistical results. The specific evaluation rules are as follows:

1) To the master nodes of the inner ring as well as outer rings, they will be regarded as honest in a verification process unless more than half of the nodes report that they are dishonesty.
2) To the remaining nodes, They will be regarded as dishonest or not involved in a verification process if the master node reports that they are dishonesty or not involved.
3) If a node is regarded as dishonest, Its reputation value will be reduced by two. If a node is regarded as honest, its reputation value will be increased by one. If a node is regarded as not involved, its reputation value will be reduced by one. All nodes have a based reputation value.
4) the calculation of reputation value is cumulative. Nodes with a high reputation value are rewarded, otherwise they are punished or even eliminated from the network. The reputation value is also recorded in the routing information for node selection.

5.2 Node Consensus

Node consensus is mainly divided into three stages, including outer loop verification, inner loop verification, and multi-channel chain crossover. We define that a consensus cycle contains the three stages and only one block will be generated in a cycle. The block contains several transactions. Figure 3 shows the abstract network of the consensus process, and Fig. 4 shows the node sequence diagram of the consensus process.

In the whole consensus process, outer loop verification mainly completes the verification of the legitimacy, effectiveness and availability of transaction information Evidence. The stage is corresponded to 1–4 of the sequence diagram in the Fig. 4 and Fig. 5. The algorithm flow at this stage is as follows: ex

1) The authenticated node submits transaction information to the direct edge router. Transaction information mainly includes the unique identification of the institution/organization, transaction time, Transaction type, transaction content, transaction hash and identity signature.

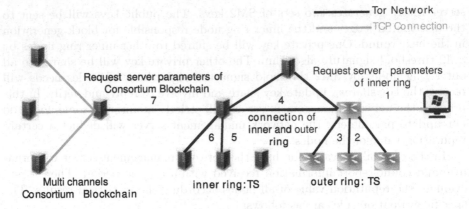

Fig. 4. Consensus process network structure

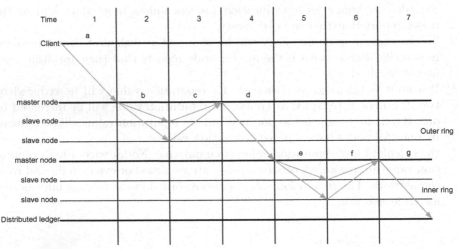

a. Submit transaction
b. Package and broadcast Transaction
c. Verify transaction and reply share
d. The threshold signature is generated and sent to the inner ring, which verifies the validity of the signature
e.When the number of transactions meets the requirements, generate and broadcast blocks
f.Verify blockand reply share
g. Submit the block to the account book and verify the signature of the account book

Fig. 5. Consensus process communication timing

2) The router listens to the transaction time and add the data to the transaction pool. During each round, a transaction will be randomly selected from the data pool. The edge router will package it and send it to all the edge routers through the tor network.

3) Other edge routers verify the legitimacy and effectiveness of the information and verify the validity after receiving the information. If the certificate passes,

the information is signed, and the signature and public key are attached to the information and fed back to the sender.

4) The sender collects all the feedback and take out the signature information. If the number of signatures exceeds 1/2 of the total number, it will use SM2 threshold signature algorithm as well as these feedback to combine the signature information, otherwise the transaction information will be discarded.

5) The sender request the network management server to obtain the communication parameters of an inner ring server and establish a communication link with it after synthesizing signature successfully.

6) The sender attaches the signature and signer's public key to the data and send to the inner ring server.

The inner loop verification is mainly used to generate block and verify the legality of block. It is the core part of the entire consensus process, corresponding to 5–7 of the sequence diagram in the Fig. 3 and Fig. 4. The algorithm flow at this stage is as follows:

1) The inner ring server verifies the correctness and validity of the signature as well as the identity of signer while receiving the information from outer ring nodes. If the verification passes, the data package will be put into the buffer. If not, it will be abandoned.

2) At the end of clock cycle, the inner ring server will package all the data in the buffer into a block. The inner ring server sends the generated blocks to all other inner ring servers through the tor network.

3) Other inner ring servers verify the legitimacy and validity of the block as well as the legitimacy of identity while receiving the block data. If the verification is passed, the block will be signed, and the signature information will be attached to the block and fed back to the sender.

4) The sender collects all feedback and takes out signature information. If the number of signatures exceeds 1/2 of the total number of inner ring servers. The sender uses the SM2 threshold signature algorithm as well as these feedback to combine the signature information, otherwise the block will be discarded.

5) The sender request the federation chain server communication parameters from the network management server and constructs a link with it after synthesizing the signature successfully.

6) The sender attaches the public key of signer at the end of the block and sent it to the federation chain server.

The cross-phase of the multi-channel chain is mainly used to achieve the sub-channel storage of blocks, which is the final stage of the consensus process. The distributed ledger takes out the block from the storage area and count the transactions in the block according to the unique identification of the company or department after verifying the validity of the identity of sender. If a company or organization has the most transactions, the block will be placed on the branch chain of the company or organization. If the bias of the new blockchain is small, it will refer to all branch blockchains with larger bias and randomly refer to one blockchain with smaller bias. The unique identifications of the bra-nches chain owner appear in the new block. The distributed ledger finally takes on the form of DAG.

6   Related Work

The Byzantine General Problem proposed by Lamport, Shostak and pease [10] studies how non fault nodes achi-eve data consistency when there may be fault nodes or malicious nodes. This problem is the focus and basis of consensus mechanism research. Castro, Liskov [11] proposes PBFT. When the number of malicious nodes do not exceed 1/3 of the total, so that honest nodes finally reach a consensus. However, once they do, the blockchain will fork.

Hyperledger proposed by Cachin [12] and improved by Androulaki [13] adopts the authorization consensus mechanism and uses Byzantine fault-tolerant consistency algorithm to realize block consensus. Dfinity proposed by Hank [21] performs hierarchical processing and node grouping on the consensus layer to complete the consensus.

The sharding consensus mechanism ELASTICO proposed by Lu [14] uses sharding technology to segment the network and transactions, which improves the consensus efficiency and avoids cross sharding communication. However, cross sharding transactions will lock up when more than 1/4 of malicious nodes. Omniledger proposed by kokoris et al. [15]. Divides blockchain into identity blockchain and transaction blockchain, and sol-ves the problem of ELASTICO by managing blockchain fragments.

In conclusion, the above consensus mechanism has improved the efficiency of consensus and the reduction of Byzantine nodes from multiple angles. However, the privacy problem of consensus process nodes is ignored. By contrast, we propose ACT to protect node privacy and reduce the joint probability of evil nodes through anonymous communication.

7   Conclusion and Future Works

The ACT algorithm designed in the research has inherited many characteristics of DAG algorithm, such as high concurrency, high expansion, easy to increase and difficult to change. Meanwhile, the algorithm achieves anonymous consensus and node privacy protection based on tor network. However, there are many problems in the design of the algorithm, such as view segmentation attack, computing power consumption, complex client configuration, single reputation evaluation mechanism and so on. In the future, this paper will continue to focus on the following directions of blockchain development trend:

1) Deep fusion and improvement of PO-X series algorithm and DAG.
2) BFT series algorithm and DAG deep fusion and improvement.
3) The fusion and improvement of hybrid consensus protocol and DAG consensus.
4) The improvement of node reputation evaluation mechanism.
5) The development and maturity of DAG based security analysis framework.

References

1. Ahmed, M.I., Kannan, G.: Secure end to end communications and data analytics in IoT integrated application using IBM Watson IoT platform. Wireless Pers. Commun. (2021). https://doi.org/10.1007/s11277-021-08439-7
2. Dorri, A., Kanhere, S.S., Jurdak, R., Gauravaram, P.: Blockchain for IoT security and privacy: the case study of a smart home. In: Proceedings of IEEE International Conference on Pervasive Computing and Communications Workshops (PerCom Workshops), pp. 618–623, March 2017
3. Nakamoto, S.: Bitcoin: a peer-to-peer electronic cash system (2008). https://bitcoin.org/bitcoin.pdf. Accessed July 2019
4. Catalano, D., Fiore, D., Gennaro, R.: A certificateless approach to onion routing. Int. J. Inf. Secur. **16**, 327–343 (2017). https://doi.org/10.1007/s10207-016-0337-x
5. Chauhan, M., Singh, A.K., Komal: Survey of onion routing approaches: advantages, limitations and future scopes. In: Pandian, A., Palanisamy, R., Ntalianis, K. (eds.) ICCBI 2019. Lecture Notes on Data Engineering and Communications Technologies, vol. 49. Springer, Cham (2020). https://doi.org/10.1007/978-3-030-43192-1_76
6. Hanke, T., Movahedi, M., Williams, D.: DFIN ITY technology overview series, consensus system (2018). https://arxiv.org/pdf/1805.04548.pdf
7. Lamport, L.: The part-time parliament. ACM Trans. Comput. Syst. (TOCS) **16**(2), 133–169 (1998)
8. Ming, S., Yuan, M., Jingqiang, L., Jiwu, J.: SM2 elliptic curve threshold cryptography algorithm. Acta Cryptologica Sinica **1**(02), 155–166 (2014)
9. Adams, C.: Kerberos authentication protocol. In: van Tilborg, H.C.A., Jajodia, S. (eds.) Encyclopedia of Cryptography and Security. Springer, Boston (2011). https://doi.org/10.1007/978-1-4419-5906-5
10. Castro, M., Liskov, B.: Practical byzantine fault tolerance. In: Proceedings of the Third USENIX Sympo sium on Operating Systems Design and Implementation (OSDI), New Orleans, LA, USA, 22–25 February 1999, pp. 173–186 (1999)
11. Cachin, C.: Architecture of the hyperledger Blockchain fabric (2016). https://pdfs.semanticscholar.org/f852/c5f3fe649f8a17ded391df0796677a59927f.pdf
12. Androulaki, E., Barger, A., Bortnikov, V., et al.: Hyperledger fabric: a distributed operating system for permissioned Blockchains. In: Proceedings of the Thirteenth EuroSys Conference (EuroSys 2018), pp. 30:1–30:15. ACM (2018)
13. Hanke, T., Movahedi, M., Williams, D.: DFINITY technology overview series, consensus system (2018). https://arxiv.org/pdf/1805.04548.pdf
14. Luu, L., Narayanan, V., Zheng, C., et al.: A secure sharding protocol for open blockchains. In: Proceedings of the 2016 ACM SIGSAC Conference on Computer and Communications Security, pp. 17–30. ACM (2016)
15. Kokoris-Kogias, E., Jovanovic, P., Gasser, L., et al.: OmniLedger: a secure, scale-out, decentralized ledger via sharding. In: Proceedings of 2018 IEEE Symposium on Security and Privacy (SP 2018), pp. 583–598. IEEE (2018)

Medical Image Fusion Based on Undecimated Dual-Tree Complex Wavelet Transform and NSCT

Nullo Majid Hamidu, Qingling Liu(✉), and Chaozhu Zhang

College of Information and Communication Engineering, Harbin Engineering University, Harbin, China
liuqingling@hrbeu.edu.cn

Abstract. Medical image fusion is one of the most effective and versatile techniques used for medical analysis and treatment. This paper describes a fusion framework that combines undecimated dual-tree complex wavelet transform (UDTCWT) and non-subsampled contourlet transform (NSCT) to cover the benefits of them both concurrently. The UDTCWT solved the dual-tree complex wavelet transform (DTCWT) by offering exact translation invariance. These properties can aid in making the system more efficient, whereby actual parent coefficients are within the fusion system. In this framework, the NSCT decomposition provides multi-scale and multi-direction scales followed by UDTCWT decomposition. Then, different fusion rules are employed to fuse the obtained coefficients, and finally, an inverse to get the combined final image. The results demonstrate that the proposed technique eventually attains accuracy and better performance than four representative fusion techniques in visual and objective evaluations.

Keywords: Multi-modal image · Image fusion · Undecimated dual-tree complex wavelet transform · Nonsubsampled contourlet transform · Averaging fusion rule

1 Introduction

For many years, discrete wavelet transform (DWT) has had many potentials in various medical image processing, including fusion. The undecimated discrete wavelet transform (UWT) is an exact shift-invariance, but it lacks directional selectivity and suffers from over-complete representation. However, it suffers from shift variance [1, 2], meaning that small shifts in the input signal will cause significantvariations in wavelet coefficients' energy distribution. Recently, DTCWT has been proposed, which offers a more compact model, a near-shift-invariance property, and an improved directional selectivity [1]. Although DTCWT improves the over-complete representation by a factor of two, it is still a compact transform due to the down-sampling at each level of transform. Hill *et al.*, in [1] proposed UDTCWT, which sums the benefits of exact translational invariance of UWT and the improved directional selectivity of DTCWT. The solution proposed in this paper comprises the combination mechanism of UDTCWT and NSCT.

© Springer Nature Singapore Pte Ltd. 2021
Y. Tan et al. (Eds.): DMBD 2021, CCIS 1454, pp. 472–484, 2021.
https://doi.org/10.1007/978-981-16-7502-7_43

2 Related Works

The wavelet transforms restricted in extracting the anatomical structures and color changes from high-frequency bands [2]. The spatial image details and spectral localization is better in DWT though it is imperfect in capturing edges. The nonsubsampled contourlet transforms (NSCTs) are shift invariants, suppressing the pseudo-Gibbs effect with accurate two-dimensional sparse representation and efficiently confined geometrical structures [3–5]. These properties resulted in acquiring the best results in terms of medical images by Liu *et al*. In addition to the limitation of existing techniques, another inadequacy reported in the literature is adopting identical strategies for processing [6]. Recent theory on UDTCWT is considered advantageous for fusion due to its outstanding intrinsic properties. The transform capably represents the frequency domain's signal to solve the limitations of both UWT and DTCWT [7]. NSCT using non-separable two-channel non-subsampled pyramids (NSPs) and non-subsampled directional filter bank (NSDFB) to extract multi-direction features. Owing to these desirable properties, we propose a dual technique using UDTCWT and NSCT for medical image fusion.

3 Theoretical

3.1 Non-subsampled Contourlet Transform

The NSCT combines the nonsubsampled pyramid (NSP) and nonsubsampled directional filter bank (NSDFB). NSDFB performs multi-scale decomposition and ensures accurate directional response, while NSP offers multi-scale property [8–10]. Shift-invariant, multi-scale and multidirectional properties of NSCT are very efficient in extracting and representing different image features [2] (Fig. 1).

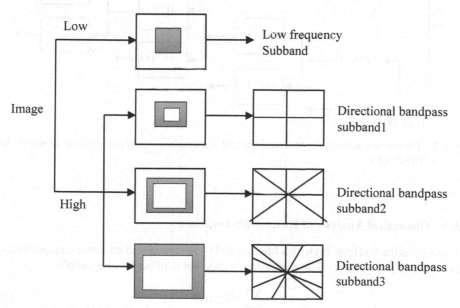

Fig. 1. Decomposition of a non-subsampled contourlet transform (Source: [11])

3.2 Undecimated Dual-Tree Complex Wavelet Transform

Aiming to solve the drawbacks caused by the DTCWT, authors in [1] have proposed an undecimated form of DTCWT, which contains no sub-sampling. Each sub-band has the exact resolution as the original image; hence, it provides a perfect shift-invariance property and improved directional selectivity. The UDTCWT combines the advantages of undecimated wavelet transform and dual-tree complex wavelet transform [11]. UWT removes shift variation and offers filter upsampling, while DTCWT provides higher directional selectivity and approximate shift-invariant [12–14]. However, DTCWT suffers from a limited number of subband coefficients related to each spatial position in the image [15]. UDTCWT overcome this problem by providing the exact resolution as the image at each subband, as shown in Fig. 2. As a result, it brings perfect shift-invariant and one-to-one relationships between subband coefficients and image pixels. As a result, UDTCWT offers the following advantages: 1) Perfect Reconstruction, 2) No aliasing, 3) directionally selective, 4) Cross-scale subband correlation and 5) Exact shift-invariant.

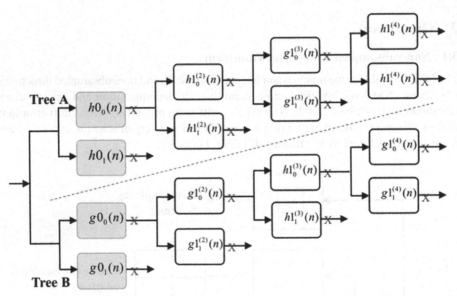

Fig. 2. The crosses indicate the positions where downsampling would generally occur within the DTCWT (Source:)

3.3 Theoretical Analysis of Exact Shift-Invariant

Taking g as the first level high pass filter $y_{\Re}$ and $y_{\Im}$ being real and imaginary, respectively, as defined by (1) and (2). The same filter is used but is offset by one sample

$$y_{\Re} = \sum_{k} g[k].x[2n - k] \tag{1}$$

$$y_\Im = \sum_k g[k].x[2n - k + 1] \tag{2}$$

$$|y[n]|^2 = |y_\Re[n] + iy_\Im[n]|^2 = (y_\Re[n])^2 + (y_\Im[n])^2 \tag{3}$$

$$y_{d\Re}[n] = \sum_k g[k].x[2n - k + 1] = y_\Im[n] \tag{4}$$

$$y_{d\Im}[n] = \sum_k g[k].x[2n - k + 2] = y_\Re[n] \tag{5}$$

$$|y_d[n]|^2 = |y_{d\Re}[n] + iy_\Im[n]|^2 = (y_\Im[n])^2 + (y_\Re[n])^2 \tag{6}$$

$$E = \sum_n |y[n]|^2 = \sum_n \left((y_\Re[n])^2 + (y_\Im[n])^2\right) \tag{7}$$

$$E_d = \sum_n |y_d[n]|^2 = \sum_n \left((y_\Re[n])^2 + (y_\Im[n + 1])^2\right) \tag{8}$$

4 Proposed Fusion Algorithm

In this section, the proposed multi-modal image fusion algorithm is presented in detail. The framework of the proposed algorithm is shown in Fig. 3. The technique combines two algorithms NSCT and UDTCWT, with a Maximum fusion rule to get superior performance.

4.1 Grayscale and Color Image Fusion

For This section extends the proposed method to fuse a grayscale image and a color image. To attain the grayscale and color image in the fusion process, we applied YUV color. It converts a color image into one luminance and two chrominance components, namely Y, U, and V. The RGB color image is converted into YUV color space to obtain the Y, U, and V channels. Then, the grayscale image and the Y channel are fused using the proposed fusion scheme. Finally, the fused color image performs inverse YUV conversion (YUV to RGB) over the Y channel, the original U channel, and the original V channel (Fig. 4).

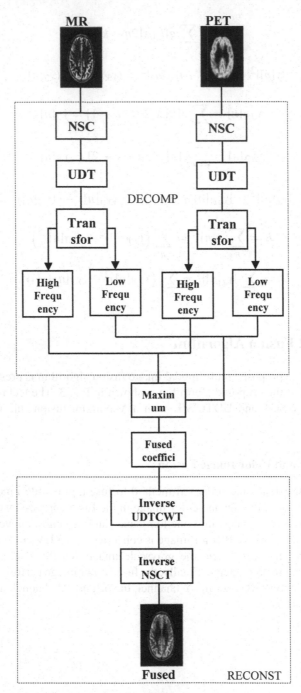

Fig. 3. Framework of the proposed algorithm

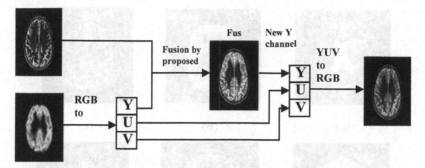

Fig. 4. Schematic of the grayscale and color image fusion method (Color figure online)

4.2 Fusion Rule

We fused the wavelet coefficients using the following rules in the proposed multi-modal medical image fusion method. $I_1(x, y)$ And $I_2(x, y)$ are the two medical images to be combined, and their coefficients are $W_1(m, n)$ and $W_2(m, n)$ respectively. Average fusion rule:

$$W(m, n) = \frac{\{W_1(m, n) + W_2(m, n)\}}{2} \tag{9}$$

Algorithm Proposed Medical Image fusion.

Step 1: Input images
Step 2: Resize aligned and registered images into 256×256
Step 3: Obtain high and low-frequency subband coefficients of input images by NSCT
Step 4: Perform NSPFB and NSDFB decomposition.
Step 5: Apply UDTCWT decomposition process into sets of complex coefficients and compute thresholds at each decomposition level.
Step 6: Calculate the absolute differences of all coefficients
Step 7: Compare the fundamental differences of corresponding coefficients, and those having a more significant value in both sources are selected.
Step 8: Combine the selected low-frequency part and high-frequency part coefficients using the maximum fusion rule.
Step 9: Perform the inverse of UDTCWT and NSCT on combined coefficients to reconstruct the image
Step 10: Final fused image

5 Experiment

The proposed method tested against various popular fusion methods. The four representative methods are NSCT-DTCWT method, NSCT method, UDWT [16], and DTCWT [17]. Test images obtained from the Harvard database. The size of all images is calibrated to 256×56 and perfectly registered. In our experiment, we utilize three pairs of authentic medical dataset shown in Fig. 5.

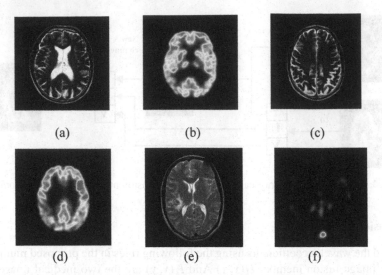

(a)   (b)   (c)

(d)   (e)   (f)

Fig. 5. Input image pairs: (a, b) image set-1; (c, d) image set-2, (e, f) image set-30

6 Objective Evaluation Metrics

Entropy (EN): Entropy calculates the level of authentic information available in the input and fused images. enormous entropy value indicates rich fused image

$$S = -\sum_{i=0}^{L-1} P_i \log(P_i) \tag{10}$$

L shows the gray level of an image and P_i is the probability of pixel gray level.

Average Gradient (AG.): describes comparison details of the fused image [18]. The larger the average density, the more precise image.

Defined by:

$$AG = \frac{1}{M \times N} \sum_{u=1}^{M} \sum_{v=1}^{N} \sqrt{\frac{(\partial f/\partial x)^2 + (\partial f/\partial x)^2}{2}} \tag{11}$$

Standard Deviation (SD): is a metric that describes the image contast [19]. Significant contrast related to high standard deviation. Given (i, j) the pixel value at the position (i, j) and μ is the mean.

Its formula:

$$SD = \sqrt{\frac{1}{M \times N} \sum_{i=1}^{M} \sum_{j=1}^{N} (F(i, j) - \mu)^2} \tag{12}$$

Cross-Entropy (CE): The low value of cross-entropy indicates a considerable similarity between the sources and fused images [20].

$$CE(I_A, I_F) = \sum_{i=0}^{L-1} P_{A_i} \log \frac{P_{A_i}}{P_{F_i}} \text{ and}$$

$$CE(I_B, I_F) = \sum_{i=0}^{L-1} P_{B_i} \log \frac{P_{B_i}}{P_{F_i}}$$

$$CE(I_A, I_B, I_F) = \frac{CE(I_A, I_F) + CE(I_B, I_F)}{2} \tag{13}$$

Mean Value (MV): This is the average brightness of the image. Given (i, j) is the pixel value at the position (i, j).

$$\mu = \frac{1}{M \times N} \sum_{i=1}^{M} \sum_{j=1}^{N} F(i, j) \tag{14}$$

Edge Intensity (EI): describes the amplitude point. The larger the value of EI, the richer the edge information of the image [21].

$$EI(u, v) = \sqrt{\nabla x F(u, v)^2 + \nabla y F(u, v)^2}$$

Where $\nabla x F(u, v)$ and $\nabla y F(u, v)$ are the first differences of image F in the x and y directions of row and column

$$\begin{cases} \nabla x F(u, v) = F(u, v) - F(u - 1, v) \\ \nabla y F(u, v) = F(u, v) - F(u, v - 1) \end{cases} \tag{15}$$

7 Experiment Results and Analysis

This section shows the results of our fusion method and the comparison experiments from Figs. 6, 7, 8. The results demonstrate better performance by our proposed fusion method. Figure 6(a) and (b) consists of Dataset-1 images. Figure 6(c)–(g) indicate the fusion output of various methods: NSCT, UDWT, DTCWT, NSCT-DTCWT, and the proposed fusion technique. Figure 7 contains Dataset-2. The final output of the proposed technique shows a better performance than the rest methods. In Fig. 8, The DTCWT, NSCT, UDWT, and NSCT-DTCWT output has fewer detailed information. Our fusion method improves the contrast and contains more explicit structure contents.

In Table 1 result, the metrics, SD, EN, AG, and EI, commonly reflect the quality of the result. The better-achieved results are indicated by the higher value of the above metrics. In addition, when evaluating fusion methods in terms of running time, we make a comparison as shown in Table 4. the running time of the proposed method is shorter. Therefore, our approach is superior to traditional methods in terms of time effectiveness and, at the same time, improves the fusion effect. The comparative performance analysis of different medical images results are shown in Figs. 9, 10, and 11 (Tables 2 and 3).

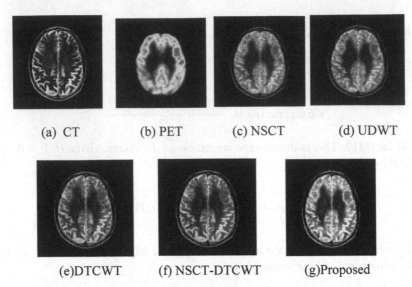

(a) CT   (b) PET   (c) NSCT   (d) UDWT

(e)DTCWT   (f) NSCT-DTCWT   (g)Proposed

Fig. 6. Fusion outcomes of different techniques in "image set 1".

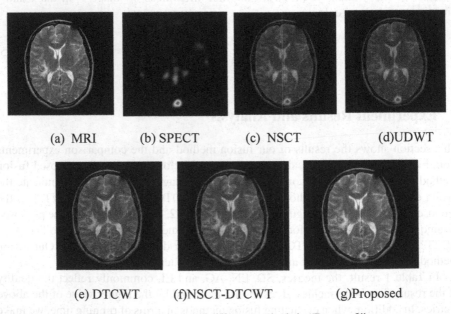

(a) MRI   (b) SPECT   (c) NSCT   (d)UDWT

(e) DTCWT   (f)NSCT-DTCWT   (g)Proposed

Fig. 7. Fusion results of different methods in "Dataset-2".

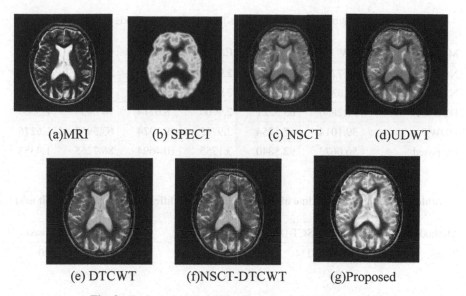

(a)MRI   (b) SPECT   (c) NSCT   (d)UDWT

(e) DTCWT   (f)NSCT-DTCWT   (g)Proposed

Fig. 8. Fusion results of different methods in "Dataset-3"

Table 1. Fusion performance values from different methods "Dataset-1"

Method	MV	SD	EN	AG	EI	CE
NSCT	24.6472	27.7105	2.7676	3.2785	32.3062	2.0112
NSCT-DTCWT	34.1815	39.8792	2.8734	4.9704	44.6340	1.7096
DTCWT	34.1690	39.8504	2.8684	4.7977	44.6015	1.6890
UDWT	24.7464	28.0596	2.8056	4.3816	35.7523	1.9796
Proposed	43.7738	52.9201	2.9469	6.3346	56.7604	1.5443

Table 2. Fusion performance values from different methods "Dataset-2"

Method	MV	SD	EN	AG	EI	CE
NSCT	32.6513	62.5717	2.8279	5.6498	54.0773	1.3867
NSCT-DTCWT	30.7616	57.5906	2.8330	7.5837	64.7331	1.3603
DTCWT	30.7394	57.5532	2.8353	7.2715	64.7725	1.3662
UDWT	32.8197	62.7725	2.8056	7.5673	57.4588	2.2195
Proposed	42.5982	77.7076	3.0048	8.9006	78.7278	1.3448

Table 3. Fusion performance values from different methods "Dataset-3"

Method	MV	SD	EN	AG	EI	CE
NSCT	38.7785	67.2473	2.9600	6.7960	58.7432	1.6484
NSCT-DTCWT	37.3314	63.5927	2.9874	9.1195	70.0720	1.5547
DTCWT	37.2880	63.5221	2.9900	8.6714	70.0459	1.5660
UDWT	39.1014	67.5754	2.9712	9.1974	63.3957	1.6276
Proposed	56.6673	92.5840	3.1755	10.4694	86.7255	1.4353

Table 4. Average running time of all source images by different fusion methods (Time/s)

Method	NSCT	NSCT-DTCWT	UDWT	DTCWT	Proposed
Time	5.2681	2.234	4.7921	3.5079	1.7020

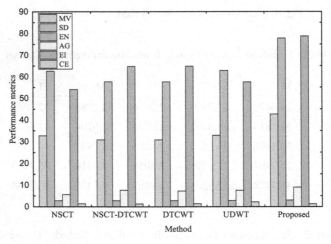

Fig. 9. Performance comparative analysis for Dataset-1

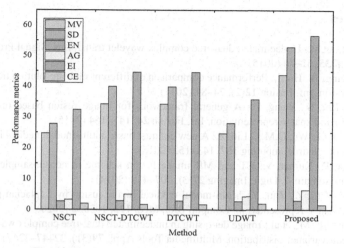

Fig. 10. Performance comparative analysis for Dataset-2

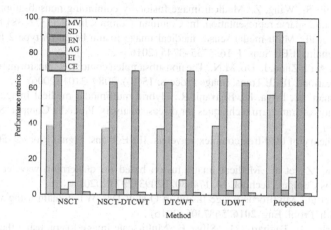

Fig. 11. Performance comparative analysis for Dataset-3

8 Conclusion

We propose a dual fusion structure using NSCT and UDTCWT. The fusion scheme exploits both techniques to overcome the existing fusion limitations listed in the literature. The proposed method involves dual decomposition, and unlike conventional multi-scale transform-based methods, our algorithms remove subsampling of DTCWT before the fusion process. The findings are validated using different metrics and notably outperform existing fusion methods.

Data Availability. The data used to support the findings of this study is available at http://www.med.harvard.edu/AANLIB/.

References

1. Hill, P.R., et al.: Undecimated dual-tree complex wavelet transforms. Signal Process. Image Commun. **35**, 61–70 (2015)
2. Li, S., Yang, B., Hu, J.: Performance comparison of different multi-resolution transforms for image fusion. Inf. Fusion **12**(2), 74–84 (2011)
3. Liu, Y., Liu, S., Wang, Z.: A general framework for image fusion based on multi-scale transform and sparse representation. Inf. Fusion **24**, 147–164 (2015)
4. Bhatnagar, G., Wu, Q.M.J., Liu, Z.: A new contrast based multi-modal medical image fusion framework. Neurocomputing **157**, 143–152 (2015)
5. Ganasala, P., Kumar, V.: CT and MR image fusion scheme in nonsubsampled contourlet transform domain. J. Digit. Imaging **27**(3), 407–418 (2014)
6. Wang, Z., Cui, Z., Zhu, Y.: Multi-modal medical image fusion by Laplacian pyramid and adaptive sparse representation. Comput. Biol. Med. **123**, 103823 (2020)
7. Saeedzarandi, M., et al.: Image denoising in undecimated dual-tree complex wavelet domain using multivariate t-distribution. Multimedia Tools Appl. **79**(31), 22447–22471 (2020)
8. Bhatnagar, G., Wu, Q.M.J., Liu, Z.: Directive contrast based multi-modal medical image fusion in NSCT domain. IEEE Trans. Multimedia **15**(5), 1014–1024 (2013)
9. Liu, Y., Liu, S., Wang, Z.: Medical image fusion by combining nonsubsampled contourlet transform and sparse representation. In: Commun. Comput. Inf. Sci. 372–381 (2014)
10. Yang, Y., et al.: Multi-modal sensor medical image fusion based on type-2 fuzzy logic in NSCT domain. IEEE Sens. J. **16**, 3735–3745 (2016)
11. da Cunha, A.L., Zhou, J., Do, M.N.: The nonsubsampled contourlet transform: theory, design, and applications. IEEE Trans. Image Process. **15**(10), 3089–3101 (2006)
12. Balakrishnan, R., Priya, R., Bhavani, R.: Hybrid multimodal medical image fusion using combination of transform techniques for disease analysis. Procedia Comput. Sci. **152**, 150–157 (2019)
13. Yu, R.: Theory of dual-tree complex wavelets. IEEE Trans. Signal Process. **56**, 4263–4273 (2008)
14. Zhancheng, Z., et al.: Medical image fusion based on quaternion wavelet transform. J. Algorithms Comput. Technol. **14**, 1748302620931297 (2020)
15. Tian, Y., et al.: Multifocus image fusion in Q-shift DTCWT domain using various fusion rules. Math. Probl. Eng. **2016**, 5637306 (2016)
16. Ellmauthaler, A., Pagliari, C.L., Silva, E.: Multi-scale image fusion using the undecimated wavelet transform with spectral factorization and nonorthogonal filter banks. IEEE Trans. Image Process. **22**(3), 1005–1017 (2013)
17. Kushwaha, A., et al.: 3D medical image fusion using dual-tree complex wavelet transform. In: 2015 International Conference on Control, Automation and Information Sciences (ICCAIS) (2015)
18. Aishwarya, N., Bennila Thangammal, C.: A novel multi-modal medical image fusion using sparse representation and modified spatial frequency. Int. J. Imaging Syst. Technol. **28**(3), 175–185 (2018)
19. Chang, L., et al.: An image decomposition fusion method for medical images. Math. Probl. Eng. **2020**, 4513183 (2020)
20. Yin, M., et al.: A novel image fusion algorithm based on nonsubsampled shearlet transform. Optik **125**(10), 2274–2282 (2014)
21. Sreeja, G., Saraniya, O.: Image fusion through deep convolutional neural network. In: Deep Learning and Parallel Computing Environment for Bioengineering Systems, pp. 37–52. Elsevier (2019). https://doi.org/10.1016/B978-0-12-816718-2.00010-5

A Multi-branch Ensemble Agent Network
for Multi-agent Reinforcement Learning

Renlong Chen[1,2] and Ying Tan[1,2(✉)]

[1] Nanjing Kangbo Intelligent Health Academy, Nanjing 211100, China
[2] Key Laboratory of Machine Perception (Ministry of Education), Peking University,
Beijing 100871, China
{reo,ytan}@pku.edu.cn

Abstract. Multi-agent Reinforcement Learning (MARL) has drawn wide attention in recent years as a bunch of real-world complex scenes can be abstracted as multi-agent systems (MAS). Partially observable cooperative multi-agent setting, in which agents have to learn to coordinate with allies by actions conditioning on their own partial observation and share a single global reward each time-step, is the most concerned MAS by existing MARL algorithms with centralized training and decentralized executing. One key challenge is how to make effective oriented exploration. In this work, we propose a new agent network called Multi-branch Ensemble Agent Network (MEAN) to encourage the oriented exploration. We evaluate our MEAN with existing Q-learning based MARL algorithms on Star-Craft II micro-management challenges. Extensive evaluations show that algorithms equipped with MEAN achieve much better performance on both homogeneous and heterogeneous scenarios compared with the initial algorithms.

Keywords: Multi-agent reinforcement learning · Multi-branch ensemble · Multi-agent systems · Swarm intelligence

1 Introduction

Over the past decades, multi-agent reinforcement learning (MRAL) has been studied extensively and developed a lot, which plays an important role in addressing many real-world problems, such as autonomous car designing, game strategy, robot swarm coordination, complex control tasks, etc. In a multi-agent system (MAS), agents are required to obtain a policy which can coordinate with other agents to gain maximized accumulated global rewards.

While there are many challenges for optimizing a policy of MRAL. Firstly, the size of joint action space expands exponentially as the number of agents grows [4, 10]. Secondly, the learning process is unstable and non-markovian because the agent not only interacts with environment but also interacts with other agents with changing policies [6, 7]. Furthermore, the credit assignment is also one of the biggest challenges in fully cooperative scenarios. Those challenges make it extremely difficult to train agents individually in MAS. The paradigm of centralized training with decentralized execution (CTDE) [9] has drawn more attention recently for alleviating the above constraints.

© Springer Nature Singapore Pte Ltd. 2021
Y. Tan et al. (Eds.): DMBD 2021, CCIS 1454, pp. 485–498, 2021.
https://doi.org/10.1007/978-981-16-7502-7_44

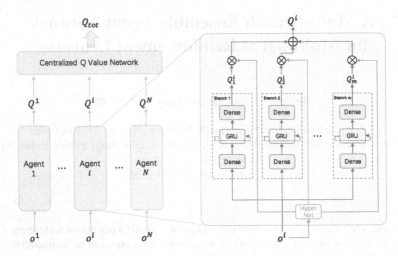

Fig. 1. The MEAN Framework. The left block is the overall architecture consisting of individual value function networks for N agents and a centralized value function network to assign credit. The right block is MEAN, including m branches. Each branch is a basic DRQN composed of a fully-connected layer and a GRU layer, followed by a fully-connected layer with dimension of number of actions.

In CTDE, each agent can only select its action conditioning on the local observation. To coordinate all agents, a centralized Q value function shared by all agents is usually needed during centralized training. The centralized Q value function builds a connection between the global reward and individual value function of each agent. However, it is often impractical to learn a centralized value function directly due to the curse of dimensionality, quite apart from connecting the individual value functions. Many algorithms tend to put forward some structural hypothesis. For example, VDN [14] assumes that the centralized value is the sum of individual values from all agents, QMIX [10] assumes that the centralized value function is a monotonic function of individual value functions. QTRAN [13] further relaxes those restrictions to a more general assumption that optimal joint action derived from centralized value is equivalent to optimal action chosen from agents' individual Q value functions.

Those algorithms under CTDE structure are usually based on Q learning. Despite Q learning has achieved great success in single agent environment tasks, where the environment has dense rewards that are easy to find by taking random sequences of actions. However, it tends to fail when the rewards are sparse and hard to find. Poor exploration is an inherent defect of Q learning [3] as it follows the bellman optimal equation to iterate value function. ε-greedy is one of the most extensively used techniques to encourage exploration in Q learning. ε-greedy generates random actions instead of action which makes Q value optimal by a decay probability. ε-greedy can only provide random exploration in practice. Unfortunately, random exploration usually does not work in multi-agent systems because coordinated actions are rarely searched by random exploration. Oriented exploration is needed in multi-agent tasks.

To tackle down this problem, we propose a novel agent architecture called Multi-branch Ensemble Agent Network (MEAN). MEAN improves oriented exploration by introducing multi-branch ensemble in individual Q value function which makes the final individual value as a sample from a distribution. The pseudo distribution contains the information learned from the past training episode transition data, meanwhile the structure makes sure that the ensembled Q value is an unbiased estimation of original individual Q value. The knowledge distillation furthermore helps each branch to learn from ensembled individual Q value.

We evaluate MEAN with VDN, QMIX and QTRAN which are most representative Q-learning based CTDE algorithms on a range of StarCraft II micro-management tasks. Experiments show that our MEAN achieves significant improvement comparing to original algorithms and helps to explore winning states in very early episodes. Ablation experiments show how knowledge distillation and exploration loss improve oriented exploration.

The remains of this paper are as follow, we first introduce some background knowledge for multi-agent reinforcement learning and multi-branch ensemble. Then we describe Multi-branch Ensemble Agent Network Architecture. Next, evaluation of the proposed method in StarCraft Multi-Agent Challenge are provided. Conclusion of this paper is given in the last section.

2 Background

2.1 Dec-POMDP

A multi-agent task could be formulated as a decentralized partially observable Markov decision process (Dec-POMDP) [2]. It's formally defined as a tuple

$$G = \langle N, s, \vec{A}, T, \vec{r}, \vec{O}, Z, \gamma \rangle \tag{1}$$

where N is the number of agents. s denotes the state of the environment to which agents have no access during interaction with the environment. $\vec{A} = (A_1, A_2, \ldots, A_N)$ denotes the set of joint action where A_i is the local actions set agent i can take at each time-step which controlled by its own policy $\pi_i : O_i \times A_i \rightarrow [0, 1]$. State transition function is $T(s'|s, \vec{a}) : S \times \vec{A} \times S \rightarrow [0, 1]$. The joint reward function $\vec{r} = (r_1, r_2, \ldots, r_N) :$ $S \times \vec{A} \rightarrow \vec{N}$ consists of individual reward r_i. $\vec{O} = (O_1, O_2, \ldots, O_N)$ denotes the set of joint observation controlled by the observation function $Z : S \times \vec{A} \rightarrow \vec{O}$. The scenario discount factor is $\gamma \in [0, 1]$.

There are generally two types of multi-agent tasks according to whether there are competitive goals among allies or not. We focus on fully cooperative tasks. In those settings, agents will share an identical reward $r = r_1 = r_2 = \cdots = r_N$. The multi-agent system aims at learning a policy $\pi_i(a_i|o_i)$ which maximizes the expectation of discounted accumulated return $\mathbb{E}(G)$ where $G = \sum_{t=0}^{T} \gamma^t r^t$, T is the accumulated horizon.

Algorithm 1. Training Procedure for MEAN

1: Initialize individual Q network and target network with parameters θ and θ^- respectively, centralized Q network with parameters θ^c, replay buffer $\mathcal{D}$ with capacity $N_{\mathcal{D}}$, training batch size N_b and other hyper-parameters
2: **for** each training step **do**
3:     **for** each episode **do**
4:         **for** $t = 1$ to $max\ time - step$ **do**
5:             Obtain global state s_t
6:             **for** $i = 1$ to $Number\ of\ agents$ **do**
7:                 Obtain observation o_i^t for each agent i
8:                 Compute weights g according to partial observation o_i^t
9:                 Compute individual Q value Q^i according to outputs of each branch and weights g
10:             **end for**
11:             Execute joint action a_t in environment
12:             Obtain the global reward r_t
13:         **end for**
14:         Store episode transitions in $\mathcal{D}$, replacing the oldest episode if $|\mathcal{D}| \geq N_{\mathcal{D}}$
15:     **end for**
16:     Sample a batch of N_b episodes from $\mathcal{D}$
17:     Calculate TD-loss $\mathcal{L}_e$ according to Eq. 6 and $\mathcal{L}_b$ for each branch if needed
18:     Calculate knowledge distillation loss $\mathcal{L}_{kd}$ according to Eq. 7
19:     Calculate exploration loss according to Eq. 11
20:     Update θ by minimizing $\mathcal{L} = \mathcal{L}_{TD} + \alpha\mathcal{L}_{kd} + \beta\mathcal{L}_e$
21:     Update target network parameters $\theta \to \theta^-$ every C training steps
22: **end for**

2.2   Reinforcement Learning

Reinforcement Learning [15] has been widely investigated to solve the single agent POMDP problems. Q-learning uses value iteration to update an action-value function $Q(s, a) = \mathbb{E}[G|S = s, A = a]$ by $a^* = \arg\max_a Q(s, a)$. However, when using Q-learning to solve some complex problems, it encounters the problem of high dimensional curse on both state and action spaces since traditional Q-learning uses table or parameterized function to represent the Q function. Deep Q Network (DQN) [8] tackles down this problem by using a deep neural network to represent Q function. There have been several techniques applied to stabilize the training process of DQN, such as target network and experience replay. The original DQN updates parameters θ by minimizing the following TD loss

$$L(\theta) = \mathbb{E}_{(s,a,r,s')}[(r + \gamma \max_{a'} Q(s', a'; \theta^-) - Q(s, a; \theta))^2] \tag{2}$$

where $Q(s', a'; \theta^-)$ is the target network whose parameters θ^- synchronizes with the main network parameters θ.

2.3 Multi-branch Ensemble Knowledge Distillation

There have been a lot of existing methods for knowledge distillation. A typical distillation process starts with a larger network with high-capacity parameters or architecture as a teacher model, followed by training a smaller student network targeting predicting the teacher network's outputs or some high-level feature representations [1,5,11]. [5] improved a small network by distilling knowledge from a larger teacher network. The rationale behind knowledge distillation is that a larger network's prediction provides extra supervision than conventional supervised learning with objective function using training data labels. However, conventional knowledge distillation methods require a two-stage training process or rely on a pre-trained powerful teacher model. [18] proposed a multi-branch ensemble strategy for one-stage online distillation.

3 Methods

3.1 Hypothesis Constraints for Centralized Value Function

The joint action space of all agents in a multi-agent system surges exponentially with respect to the increase of the number of agents, which makes it impractical to learn a single value function for all agents in some scenarios, implying that utilizing an individual value function conditioning on local observation for each agent is one of the feasible ways. Meanwhile, to coordinate allies' behaviors, we have to train a centralized value function for all agents. To learn a stable and trainable centralized value function, we have to incorporate a hypothesis constraint for centralized value function. One practical hypothesis constraint is as follow

$$
\arg\max_{a} Q_{tot}(o, a) = \begin{pmatrix} \arg\max_{a^1} Q^1(o^1, a^1) \\ \vdots \\ \arg\max_{a^N} Q^N(o^N, a^N) \end{pmatrix} \tag{3}
$$

Equation 3 establishes a structural constraint linkage between individual value functions and the centralized value function, therefore, this hypothesis constraint could be regarded as a form of credit assignment. However, it is impractical to use Eq. 3 directly in training phase because it lacks a formulaic factorization to compute.

The following non-negative linear assumption is a sufficient condition for Eq. 3

$$
Q_{tot}(o, a) = \sum_{i=1}^{N} \alpha^i Q^i(o^i, a^i) \tag{4}
$$

$$
\alpha^i \geq 0
$$

where Q_{tot} denotes the centralized Q value function and Q^i is the individual Q value function for agent i. VDN simply sets all combination coefficients $\alpha^i, i \in \{1, \cdots, N\}$ to 1, which is a quite strong constraint. QMIX relaxes the constraint to a general additive value factorization by enforcing $\partial Q_{tot}/\partial Q^i \geq 0, i \in \{1, \cdots, N\}$. Therefore, VDN can be regarded as a special case of the QMIX algorithm. QTRAN relaxes the constraint even further and exploration in a larger hypothesis space structured by a sufficient and necessary condition of Eq. 3. To this end, QTRAN has to optimize the joint value function in the full joint action space, so that QTRAN suffers from computational challenge and the scalability. Applicable range of QTRAN are therefore limited.

Table 1. The features of all scenarios in experiments

Map name	Allies	Enemies
3m	3 Marines	3 Marines
8m	8 Marines	8 Marines
2s3z	2 Stalkers & 3 Zealots	2 Stalkers & 3 Zealots
3s5z	3 Stalkers & 5 Zealots	3 Stalkers & 5 Zealots
1c3s5z	1 Colossi, 5 Stalkers & 5 Zealots	1 Colossi, 5 Stalkers & 5 Zealots
3s_vs_3z	3 Stalkers	3 Zealots

3.2   Multi-branch Ensemble Agent Network

Here we describe our Multi-branch Ensemble Agent Network and Fig. 1 depicts the overview of MEAN architecture. For description convenience, we take vanilla VDN [14] as a backend mixer example. It is straightforward to apply MEAN to algorithms with other Q value mixers, such as QMIX [10] and QTRAN [13]. To this end, we assume that VDN has a mixer network as well, which simply sums all individual Q value to get Q_{tot}.

During the execution phase, at time-step t, agent i takes as input the agent's observation o_t^i, each branch with parameters θ_j computes individual value function $Q_j^i(o_t^i, a^i; \theta_j)$ based on those inputs. The Hyper network produces the weight coefficient $g(o_t^i)$. We therefore ensemble outputs of m branches by the hyper network to the individual value function we use in execution as

$$Q^i(o_t^i, a^i; \theta) = \sum_{j=0}^{m} g_j \cdot Q_j^i(o_t^i, a^i; \theta_j) \qquad (5)$$

During the training phase, the centralized Q value is produced by $Q_{tot}(o, a, s; \theta) = \sum_{i=1}^{N} Q^i(o^i, a^i)$. The vanilla algorithm trains the network by TD loss defined as

$$\mathcal{L}_e(\theta) = \sum_{i=1}^{b} [y_{tot}^i - Q_{tot}(o, a, s; \theta))]^2 \qquad (6)$$

where b is the batch size of sampled transitions per training iteration, $y_{tot} = r + \gamma \max_{a'} Q_{tot}(o', a', s'; \theta^-)$ and θ^- denotes the parameters of the target network.

In algorithms which satisfy the hypothesis of Eq. 4, we can similarly get the Q_{tot}^i composed of the Q_j^i by each branch. We can enhance the learning process of each branch by minimizing the TD loss w.r.t Q_{tot}^i defined as $\mathcal{L}_b(\theta) = \sum_{i=1}^{b} \sum_{j=1}^{m} [y_{tot}^i - Q_{tot}^j(o, a, s; \theta))^2]$, where m denotes the number of branches, $Q_{tot}^j = \sum_{i=1}^{N} \alpha^i Q_j^i(o^i, a^i)$. In those setups, the final TD loss is $\mathcal{L}_{TD} = \mathcal{L}_e + \mathcal{L}_b$, otherwise, the final TD loss $\mathcal{L}_{TD}$ is identical with $\mathcal{L}_e$.

Knowledge Distillation. Besides the TD loss w.r.t Q_j^i, we can enhance each branch by distilling knowledge from ensembled teacher back into branches. To quantify the alignment between branches and the ensembled teacher, we use

$$\mathcal{L}_{kd} = \sum_{i=1}^{N} \sum_{j=1}^{m} \|Q_j^i - Q^i\|_2^2 \tag{7}$$

where $\| \cdot \|_2^2$ is the squared L_2-norm. For algorithms with Actor-Critic architecture, we use Kullback Leibler Divergence

$$\mathcal{L}_{kd} = \sum_{i=1}^{N} \sum_{j=1}^{m} p_e(a|o; \theta_e) \log \frac{p_e(a|o; \theta_e)}{p_j(a|o; \theta_j)} \tag{8}$$

where $|A|$ represents the number of action dimension, p_e and p_j represent the softmax predictions of actions of the ensembled teacher and branch respectively, θ_e and θ_j are for the parameters of the ensembled teacher and branch respectively.

Table 2. Mean performance of the test win percentage

Map	IQL	COMA	VDN		QMIX		QTRAN	
			Original	MEAN	Original	MEAN	Original	MEAN
3m	**100**	91	97	**100**	95	96	86	66
8m	91	94	75	**99**	91	98	93	86
2s3z	39	66	80	91	86	**99**	32	95
3s5z	0	0	30	91	78	**95**	0	20
1c3s5z	7	30	90	99	**100**	**100**	42	90
3s_vs_3z	0	0	56	98	14	**100**	0	21

Oriented Exploration. A large number of works apply ε-greedy action selector to implement exploration in Q learning. The basic idea of ε-greedy is choosing random actions for agents with a decay probability. However, ε-greedy exploration is a random strategy which provides none oriented exploration. Despite the action selection in Q learning does not require a softmax probability, softmax function is monotonically increasing, which indicates $\arg\max_a Q(o, a) = \arg\max_a \sigma(Q(o, a))$, we can consider an action selection probability w.r.t the Q value instead in the following discussion.

Different from the policy gradient based methods, we cannot sample actions by the probability. Nevertheless, in multi-branch ensemble architecture, the final probability is composed of probabilities from each branch. Therefore, in multi-branch ensemble setup, the probability is no longer deterministic. Meanwhile, since each branch is trained under the same objective function, the probability from each branch can be considered as a sample from a distribution. Consider a m-branch agent with binary actions, assume that $P(a = 1) = \theta_i$ of branch i is sampled from a normal distribution with mean value μ and variance σ^2. The overall mean value and variance of final probability $\theta = \sum_{i=1}^{m} g_i \theta_i$ are as follow

$$
\begin{aligned}
\mathbb{E}(\theta) = \mathbb{E}(\sum_{i=1}^{m} g_i \theta_i) = \mu \sum_{i=1}^{m} g_i = \mu \\
\mathbb{D}(\theta) = \mathbb{D}(\sum_{i=1}^{m} g_i \theta_i) = \sigma^2 \cdot \sum_{i=1}^{m} \sum_{j=1}^{m} g_i g_j = \sigma^2
\end{aligned}
\tag{9}
$$

In order to encourage exploration, a larger variance σ^2 is needed. To satisfy this requirement, we can penalize the normalized cosine similarity of outputs from each branch by squared Frobenius norm. Let $\mathbf{H}^i$ be the normalized matrix of branch outputs of agent i, the exploration loss encourages orthogonality between branches

$$
\mathcal{L}_e = \sum_{i=1}^{N} \|\mathbf{H}^{i^\top} \mathbf{H}^i\|_F^2
\tag{10}
$$

where $\|\cdot\|_F^2$ denotes squared Frobenius norm. However, using Eq. 10 to encourage exploration will hurt the Q value training process because squared Frobenius norm would cause the mean value of weighted Q value converged to $\mathbf{0}$. We propose a revised version of exploration loss defined as:

$$
\mathcal{L}_e = \sum_{i=1}^{N} \|(\mathbf{H}^i - \overline{\mathbf{H}}^i)^\top (\mathbf{H}^i - \overline{\mathbf{H}}^i)\|_F^2
\tag{11}
$$

We experiment with those two kinds of exploration losses, which we will discuss in detail.

Here we describe the overall goal of training as minimizing the following loss:

$$
\mathcal{L} = \mathcal{L}_{TD} + \alpha \mathcal{L}_{kd} + \beta \mathcal{L}_e
\tag{12}
$$

where α, β are hyper-parameters to control the interaction of the loss terms. The general training procedure for MEAN is provided in Algorithm 1.

4   Experiments and Results

4.1   Experimental Setup

In this section, we describe our experimental setup. We test our method in the StarCraft Multi-Agent Challenge (SMAC) environment [12]. In this environment, each agent controls an individual unit. There is a built-in multi-level AI strategy controlling the enemy units by handcrafted heuristics. In our experiments, we set the difficulty level of built-in AI to level 7, which means "very difficult". The final goal is to defeat the enemy by eliminating all opponent units. Efficacious micro-managements of units are supposed

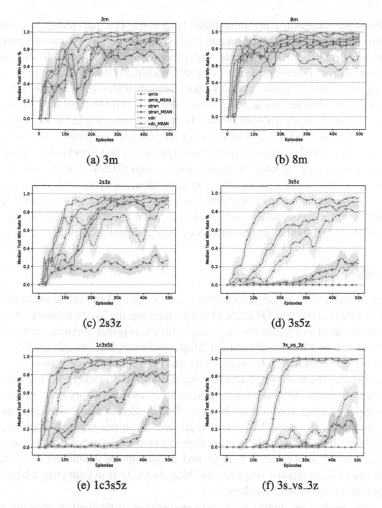

Fig. 2. Median test win rate of VDN, QMIX, QTRAN and revised algorithms with our MEAN architecture in six different scenarios. Revised algorithms and original algorithms are shown in solid lines and dashed lines of the same color respectively. 25–75% percentiles are plotted shaded. All plots share the same legend in (a).

to cause damage on enemies to the full while minimize damage received. It's a challenging task to learn an efficacious cooperative strategy in such a POMDP environment, therefore SMAC became a widely used benchmark for evaluating MARL methods.

4.2 Training Configurations

The architecture of agent's Q network used in both compared algorithms and single branch network in our method is a DRQN, which contains an embedding layer and a GRU layer followed by a fully connected layer with $|A|$ outputs. The hidden state's dimension of the embedding layer and GRU layer is 64. The individual Q network takes as input the agent's local observation and the last chosen action. In our experiments, we share the parameters across all agents' individual Q networks. To yield diverse strategies, we concatenate a one-hot vector of agent's number to the original input. The architectures of our method's mixer networks are identical with their original architectures. All hidden states' dimensions are 64 as well. We set γ at 0.99. Replay buffer size is set to 5000 episodes. In each training phase, 32 episodes are sampled from replay buffer. All Target networks used are updated after every 200 training phases. We use ε-greedy action selector in which ε anneals from 1. to 0.05 at the first 50000 steps to encourage exploration in the earliest training phase and remains 0.05 to ensure a minimal randomness during the whole training. We test all methods at every 50 training interactive episodes on 20 evaluation episodes with ε set to 0. Considering the balance of performance and training speed, we use 4 branches for each agent with MEAN and take one branch which generates the biggest mean coefficient in test rounds.

4.3 Results

Our method can easily be applied to the existing state-of-the-art algorithms such as VDN [14], QMIX [10] and QTRAN [13] by changing the agent network. To evaluate the improvement of our method comparing with the original version, we test them on several StarCraft II Micro-management Maps, including 3m, 8m, 2s3z, 3s5z, 1c3s5z, 3s_vs_3z, which contain both homogeneous and heterogeneous scenarios.

Table 1 shows the features of all maps we considered. All maps have different number or types of agents. The map name indicates the scenario setup. m, s, z and c denote different types of agents, which are Marine, Stalker, Zealot and Colossus respectively. In Map 3m, both sides have 3 Marines, there are 8 Marines on both sides in Map 8m similarly. Map 2s3z, 3s5z and 1c3s5z are heterogeneous & symmetric, there are 2 Stalkers & 3 Zealots, 3 Stalkers & 5 Zealots and 1 Colossus & 2 Stalkers & 3 Zealots on both sides of those scenarios respectively. Map 3s_vs_3z is asymmetric where ally has 3 Stalker while enemy has 3 Zealots.

The main evaluation metric is the win percentage of evaluation episodes over the course of training. The resulting plots include the median performance as well as the 25–75% percentiles to avoid outliers' effect. The learning curves of comparing algorithms on all scenarios are shown in Fig. 2. Quantitative comparisons of all algorithms after training for 50,000 episodes are provided in Table 2. The performance of IQL [16] and COMA [4] are also provided in Table 2 for reference.

Overall, we could see that our MEAN architecture improves all comparing algorithms in maps 2s3z, 3s5z, 1c3s5z, 3s_vs_3z. In homogeneous and symmetric scenarios such as 3m and 8m, MEAN improves the performance of VDN and QMIX. Even though both VDN and QMIX achieve over 95% mean win rate in Map 3m, MEAN improves the performance of these two algorithms. In Map 8m, MEAN helps VDN to win almost all test runs. However, MEAN fails to improve the performance of QTRAN on these two maps. The rationale behind is that symmetric scenarios with small group scale brings more uncertainties, which means random exploration is enough to search winning states. Meanwhile QTRAN has been suffered from the unstable training process. The oriented exploration strategy of MEAN worsens the effects of instability which preponderates over the benefit of oriented exploration. When it comes to harder scenarios where random exploration is no longer capable to search winning state like heterogeneous & symmetric scenarios, such as 2s3z, 3s5z, 1c3s5z, MEAN improves QTRAN significantly. In those scenarios, VDN and QMIX with MEAN achieve over 90% mean win rate. In Map 3s_vs_3z, only VDN and QMIX with MEAN have learned an effective policy to ensure success. As depicted in Fig. 2, algorithms with MEAN start to win battles earlier than their original versions, especially in Map 3s5z, 1c3s5z and 3s_vs_3z where random exploration cannot provide effective exploration.

We also compare our MEAN with SMIX (λ) [17]. SMIX (λ) alleviates the sparse experiences and unstable nature of MAS by enhancing the quality of centralized value function. SMIX (λ) is beneficial to other CTDE methods as well by replacing their centralized value function estimator. We apply our MEAN on SMIX (λ) and compare all three modifications with VDN and QMIX in Map 3s5z and 3s_vs_3z. Experiments show that algorithms with MEAN achieve the best performance. To be specific, vdn_MEAN and smix_MEAN_vdn outperform vdn and smix_vdn. MEAN helps algorithms to explore winning states in the very early episodes. All four compared QMIX algorithms have learned effective policy in Map 3s5z and only the original QMIX failed in Map 3s_vs_3z. There are significant gaps between the learning curves of qmix_MEAN and smix_MEAN_qmix in both scenarios which indicate that MEAN architecture improves complex centralized value function less than simple centralized value function (Fig. 3).

4.4   Ablation

We also perform ablation experiments to investigate the influences of knowledge distillation loss and exploration loss. We take VDN as an example back-end for comparison in Map 3s5z as this map is both difficult and heterogeneous.

Amount of Parameters. Despite only one branch is used in tests, we also test the original VDN with hidden size of 256 to show that simply scaling up the amount of parameters cannot perform adequate exploration in difficult tasks. Meanwhile, we scale down the amount of parameters trained in each branch to 16 hidden unit per layer, and use all 4 branches in tests marked as vdn_MEAN_16. Experiment results in Fig. 4a show that both VDNs with MEAN outperform original VDNs in Map 3s5z which indicates that the improvement brought by MEAN does not benefit from the large amount of parameters during training. We will furthermore discuss the influences of knowledge distillation loss and exploration loss.

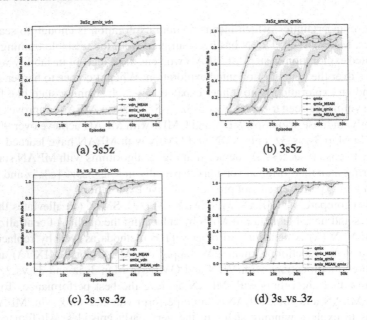

Fig. 3. Median test win rate of VDN, QMIX and revised algorithms with SMIX and our MEAN architecture in 3s5z and 3s_vs_3z.

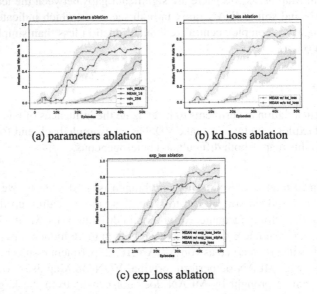

Fig. 4. Median test win rate of ablation experiments in 3s5z.

Knowledge Distillation Loss. To investigate the influence of knowledge distillation loss (kd_loss), we compare MEAN with and without kd_loss. As shown in Fig. 4b, the learning curve of MEAN without kd loss is more flat which means the learning of individual value function is slower than that of with kd_loss. The experiment results conform to the anticipated benefit of knowledge distillation.

Exploration Loss. To investigate the influence of exploration loss (exp_loss), we first compare exp loss with Eq. 10 and Eq. 11 abbreviated as exp_loss_α and exp_loss_β respectively. Figure 4c shows that MEAN with exp_loss_β achieves more stable training process and higher performance. The result has verified the discussion above. Next, we evaluate MEAN with and without exploration loss. As depicted in Fig. 4c, the oriented exploration that exp_loss brought works well which reveals the necessity of exploration loss and oriented exploration.

5   Conclusion

In this paper, Multi-branch Ensemble Agent Network is proposed to solve the oriented exploration problem in Dec-POMDP multi-agent systems. A new norm function is introduced to encourage oriented exploration besides random exploration provided by ε-greedy. It is shown that MEAN architecture has explored winning state in the very early episodes and significantly improves performance of varied comparing algorithms with DRQN agents and the revised algorithms achieve state-of-the-art performance on various scenarios of StarCraft II micro-management tasks.

Acknowledgement. This work is supported by the Swarm Intelligence Project of Nanjing Kangbo Intelligent Health Academy, and partially supported by Science and Technology Innovation 2030 - "New Generation Artificial Intelligence" Major Project (Grant Nos.: 2018AAA0102301 and 2018AAA0100302) and by the National Natural Science Foundation of China (Grant No. 62076010).

References

1. Ba, J., Caruana, R.: Do deep nets really need to be deep? In: Advances in Neural Information Processing Systems, pp. 2654–2662 (2014)
2. Bernstein, D.S., Givan, R., Immerman, N., Zilberstein, S.: The complexity of decentralized control of Markov decision processes. Math. Oper. Res. **27**(4), 819–840 (2002)
3. Burda, Y., Edwards, H., Storkey, A., Klimov, O.: Exploration by random network distillation. arXiv preprint arXiv:1810.12894 (2018)
4. Foerster, J., Farquhar, G., Afouras, T., Nardelli, N., Whiteson, S.: Counterfactual multi-agent policy gradients. arXiv preprint arXiv:1705.08926 (2017)
5. Hinton, G., Vinyals, O., Dean, J.: Distilling the knowledge in a neural network. arXiv preprint arXiv:1503.02531 (2015)
6. Laurent, G.J., Matignon, L., Fort-Piat, L., et al.: The world of independent learners is not Markovian. Int. J. Knowl. Based Intell. Eng. Syst. **15**(1), 55–64 (2011)
7. Lowe, R., Wu, Y.I., Tamar, A., Harb, J., Abbeel, O.P., Mordatch, I.: Multi-agent actor-critic for mixed cooperative-competitive environments. In: Advances in Neural Information Processing Systems, pp. 6379–6390 (2017)
8. Mnih, V., et al.: Human-level control through deep reinforcement learning. Nature **518**(7540), 529–533 (2015)

9. Oliehoek, F.A., Spaan, M.T., Vlassis, N.: Optimal and approximate Q-value functions for decentralized POMDPs. J. Artif. Intell. Res. **32**, 289–353 (2008)
10. Rashid, T., Samvelyan, M., De Witt, C.S., Farquhar, G., Foerster, J., Whiteson, S.: QMIX: monotonic value function factorisation for deep multi-agent reinforcement learning. arXiv preprint arXiv:1803.11485 (2018)
11. Romero, A., et al.: FitNets: hints for thin deep nets. arXiv preprint arXiv:1412.6550 (2014)
12. Samvelyan, M., et al.: The StarCraft multi-agent challenge. CoRR abs/1902.04043 (2019)
13. Son, K., Kim, D., Kang, W.J., Hostallero, D.E., Yi, Y.: QTRAN: learning to factorize with transformation for cooperative multi-agent reinforcement learning. arXiv preprint arXiv:1905.05408 (2019)
14. Sunehag, P., et al.: Value-decomposition networks for cooperative multi-agent learning based on team reward. In: AAMAS, pp. 2085–2087 (2018)
15. Sutton, R.S., Barto, A.G., et al.: Introduction to Reinforcement Learning, vol. 135. MIT Press Cambridge (1998)
16. Tan, M.: Multi-agent reinforcement learning: independent vs. cooperative agents. In: Proceedings of the Tenth International Conference on Machine Learning, pp. 330–337 (1993)
17. Wen, C., Yao, X., Wang, Y., Tan, X.: SMIX (λ): enhancing centralized value functions for cooperative multi-agent reinforcement learning. In: AAAI, pp. 7301–7308 (2020)
18. Zhu, X., Gong, S., et al.: Knowledge distillation by on-the-fly native ensemble. In: Advances in Neural Information Processing Systems, pp. 7517–7527 (2018)

Author Index

Printed in the United States
by Baker & Taylor Publisher Services

Printed in the United States
by Baker & Taylor Publisher Services